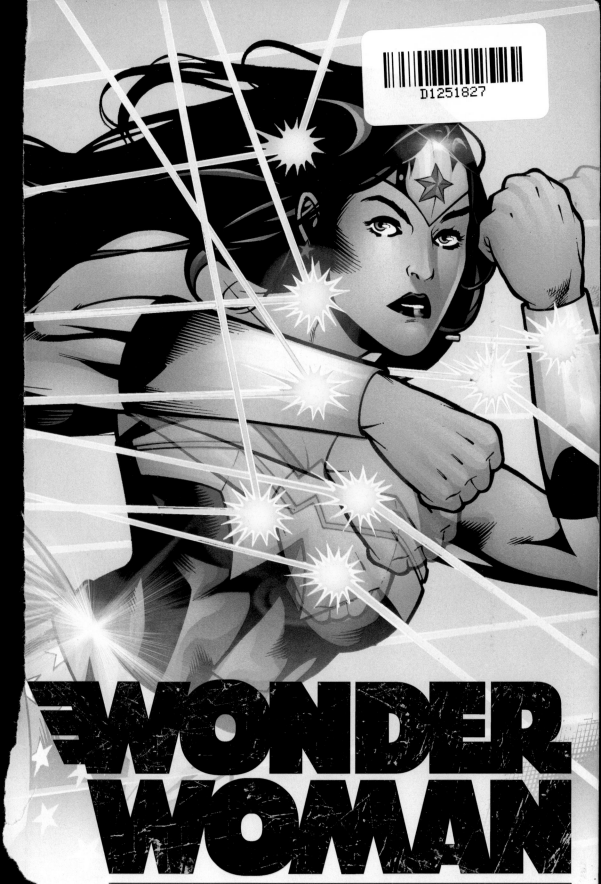

WONDER WOMAN

BY GREG RUCKA

VOLUME 1

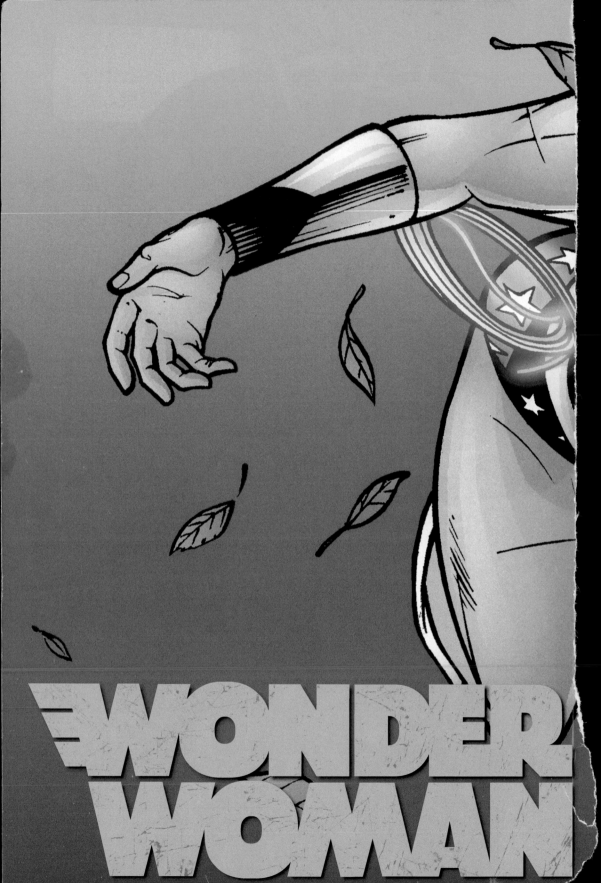

WONDER WOMAN

BY GREG RUCKA

VOLUME

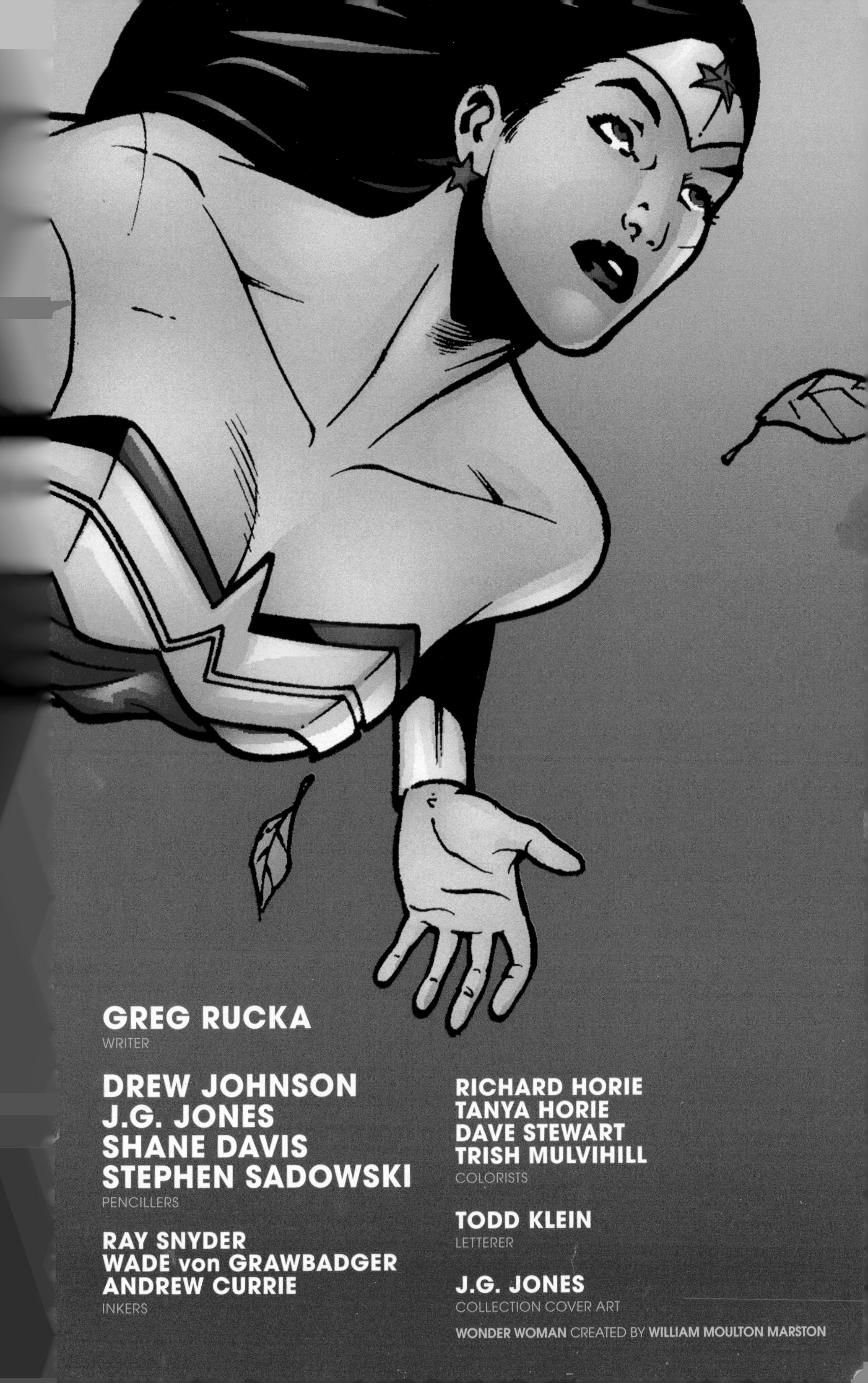

GREG RUCKA
WRITER

DREW JOHNSON
J.G. JONES
SHANE DAVIS
STEPHEN SADOWSKI
PENCILLERS

RAY SNYDER
WADE von GRAWBADGER
ANDREW CURRIE
INKERS

RICHARD HORIE
TANYA HORIE
DAVE STEWART
TRISH MULVIHILL
COLORISTS

TODD KLEIN
LETTERER

J.G. JONES
COLLECTION COVER ART

WONDER WOMAN CREATED BY **WILLIAM MOULTON MARSTON**

WONDER WOMAN BY GREG RUCKA VOLUME 1

Published by DC Comics.
Compilation Copyright © 2016 DC Comics. All Rights Reserved.

Originally published in single magazine form as WONDER WOMAN
195-205 and WONDER WOMAN: THE HIKETEIA © 2002-2004
DC Comics. All Rights Reserved. All characters, their distinctive
likenesses and related elements featured in this publication are
trademarks of DC Comics. The stories, characters and incidents
featured in this publication are entirely fictional. DC Comics does not
read or accept unsolicited ideas, stories or artwork.

DC Comics, 2900 West Alameda Avenue, Burbank, CA 91505
Printed by RR Donnelley, Owensville, MO, USA. 06/10/16. First printing.
ISBN: 978-1-4012-6332-4

Library of Congress Cataloging-in-Publication Data

Names: Rucka, Greg, author. I Jones, J. G., illustrator. I Johnson, Drew,
   illustrator.
Title: Wonder Woman by Greg Rucka. Volume 1 / Greg Rucka, J. G. Jones, Drew
   Johnson.
Description: Burbank, CA : DC Comics, [2016]
Identifiers: LCCN 2016018383 I ISBN 9781401263324 (paperback)
Subjects: LCSH: Comic books, strips, etc. I BISAC: COMICS & GRAPHIC NOVELS /
   Superheroes.
Classification: LCC PN6728.W6 R785 2016 I DDC 741.5/973—dc23
LC record available at https://lccn.loc.gov/2016018383

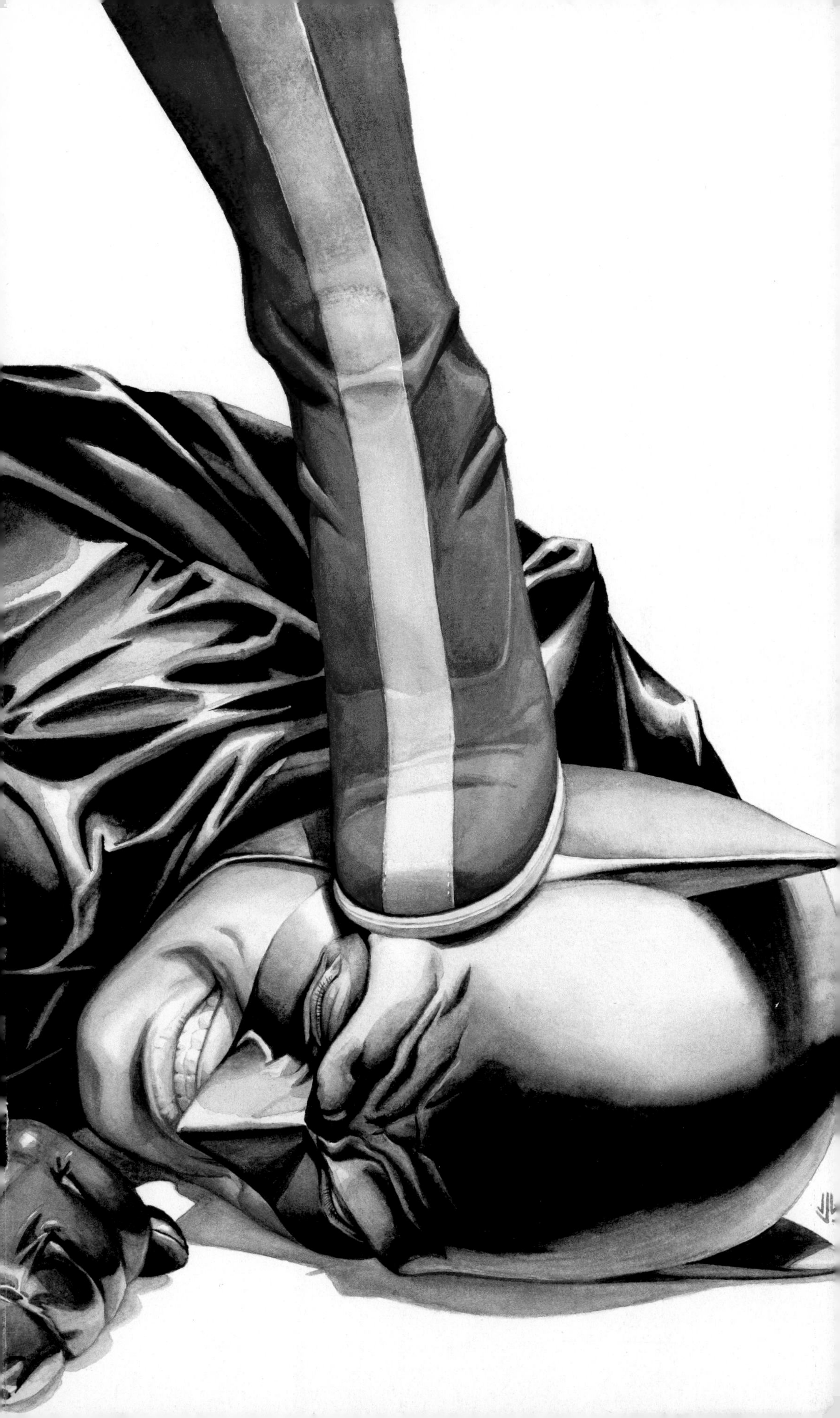

“THE HIKETEIA”

J.G. Jones – *pencils*
Wade von Grawbadger – *inks*
Dave Stewart - *colors*
J.G. Jones – *cover art*

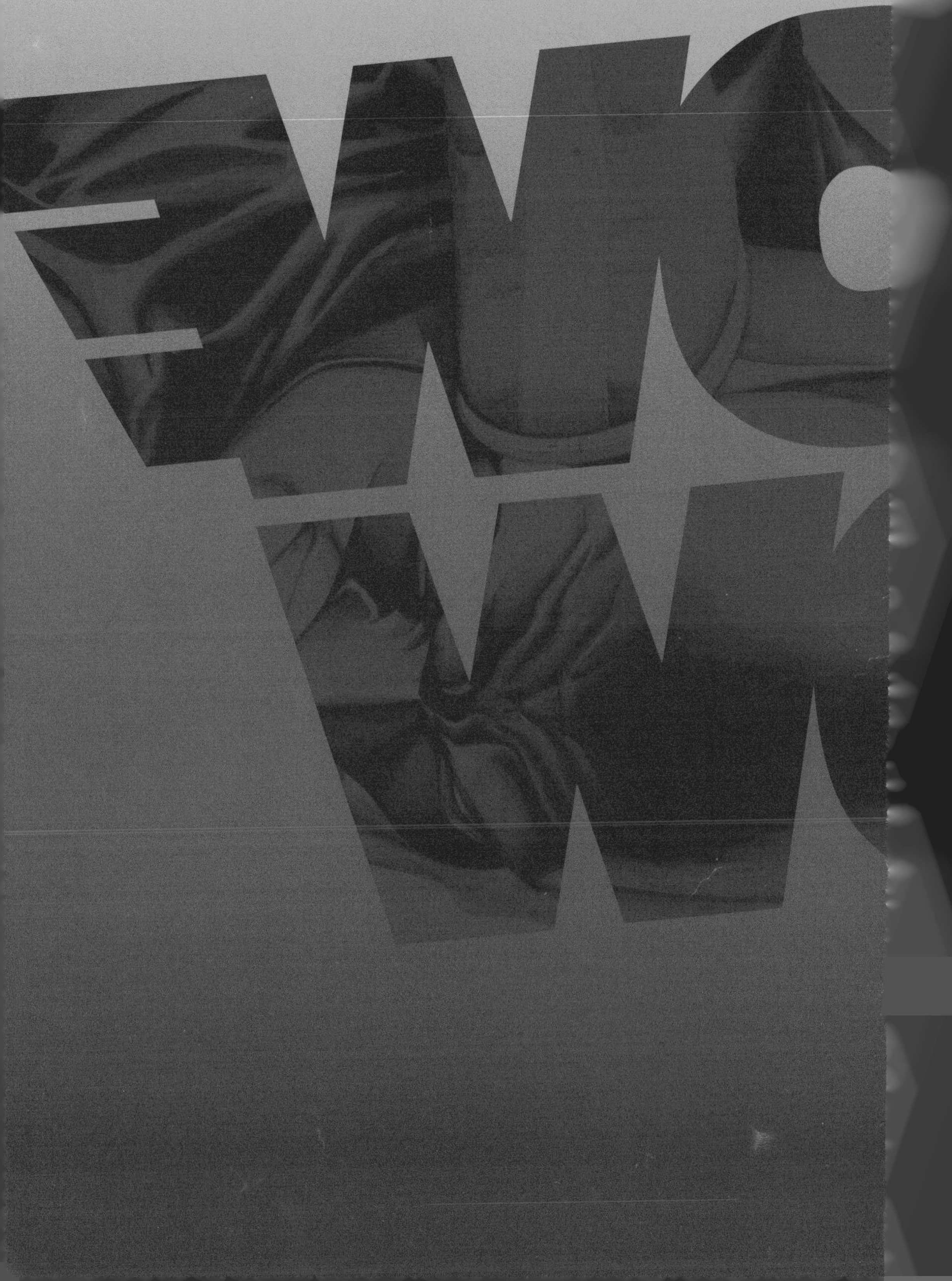

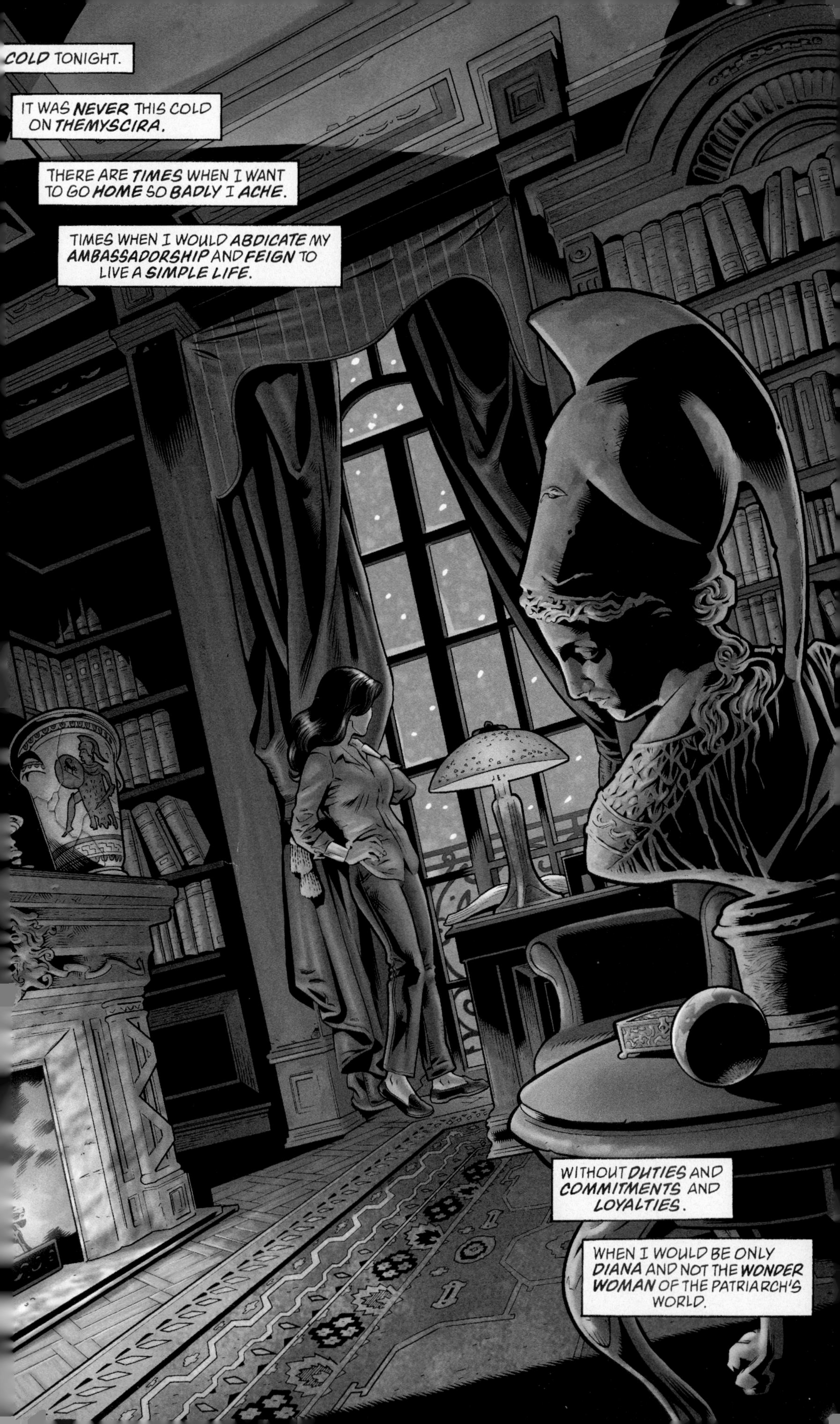
COLD TONIGHT.
IT WAS NEVER THIS COLD ON THEMYSCIRA.
THERE ARE TIMES WHEN I WANT TO GO HOME SO BADLY I ACHE.
TIMES WHEN I WOULD ABDICATE MY AMBASSADORSHIP AND FEIGN TO LIVE A SIMPLE LIFE.
WITHOUT DUTIES AND COMMITMENTS AND LOYALTIES.
WHEN I WOULD BE ONLY DIANA AND NOT THE WONDER WOMAN OF THE PATRIARCH'S WORLD.

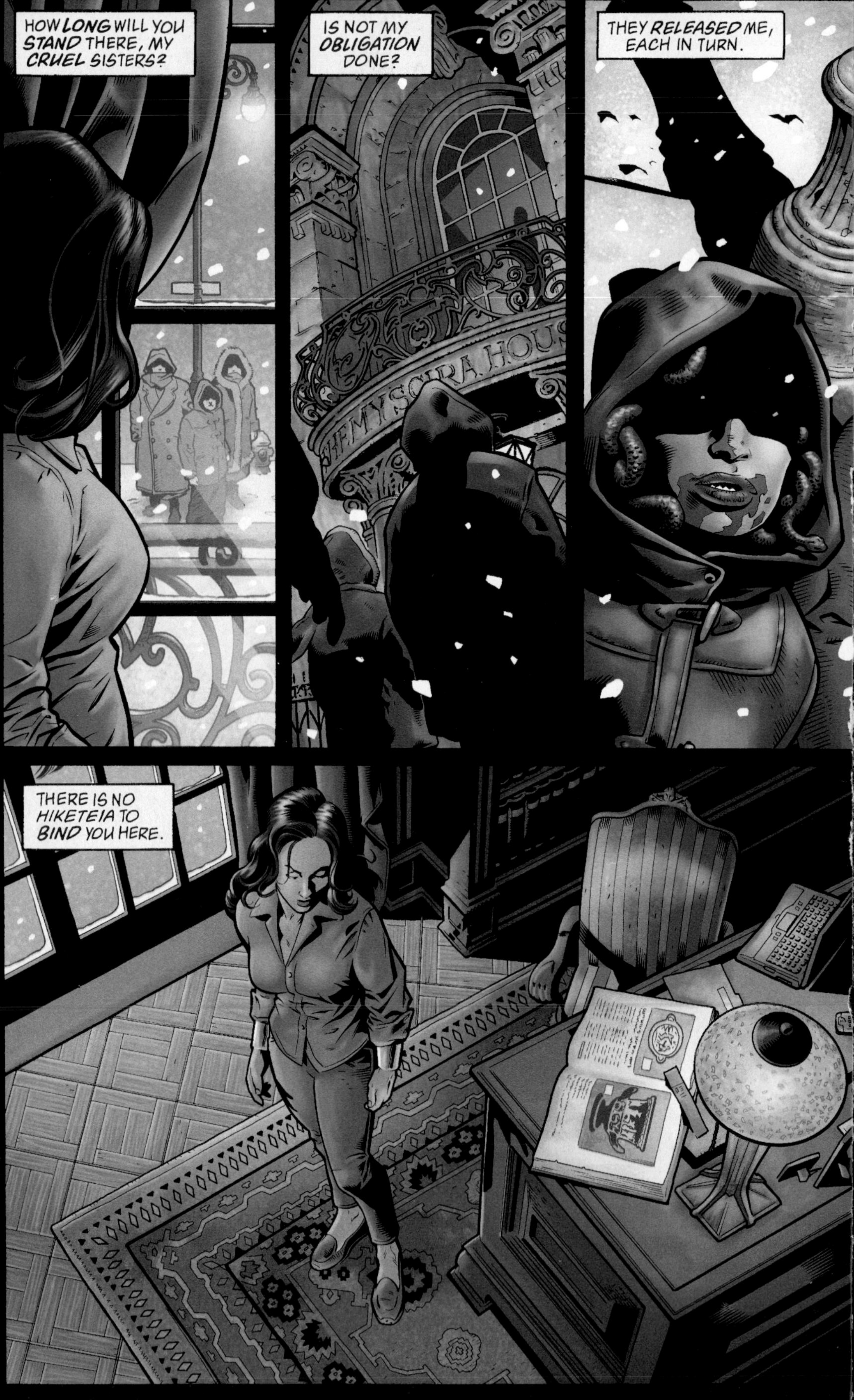
HOW LONG WILL YOU STAND THERE, MY CRUEL SISTERS?
IS NOT MY OBLIGATION DONE?
THEY RELEASED ME, EACH IN TURN.
THEMYSCIRA HOUS
THERE IS NO HIKETEIA TO BIND YOU HERE.

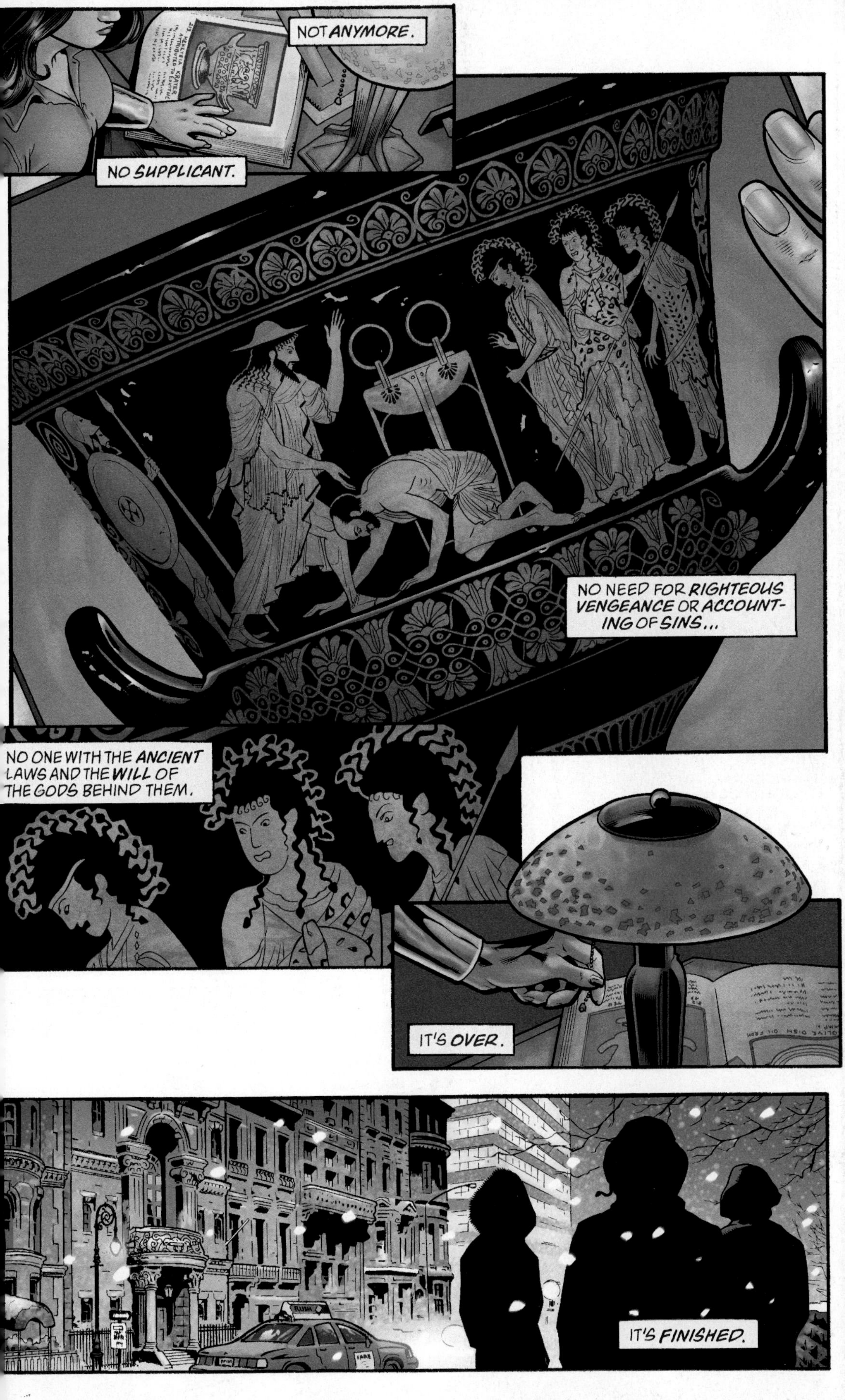
NOT ANYMORE.
NO SUPPLICANT.
NO NEED FOR RIGHTEOUS VENGEANCE OR ACCOUNTING OF SINS...
NO ONE WITH THE ANCIENT LAWS AND THE WILL OF THE GODS BEHIND THEM.
IT'S OVER.
IT'S FINISHED.

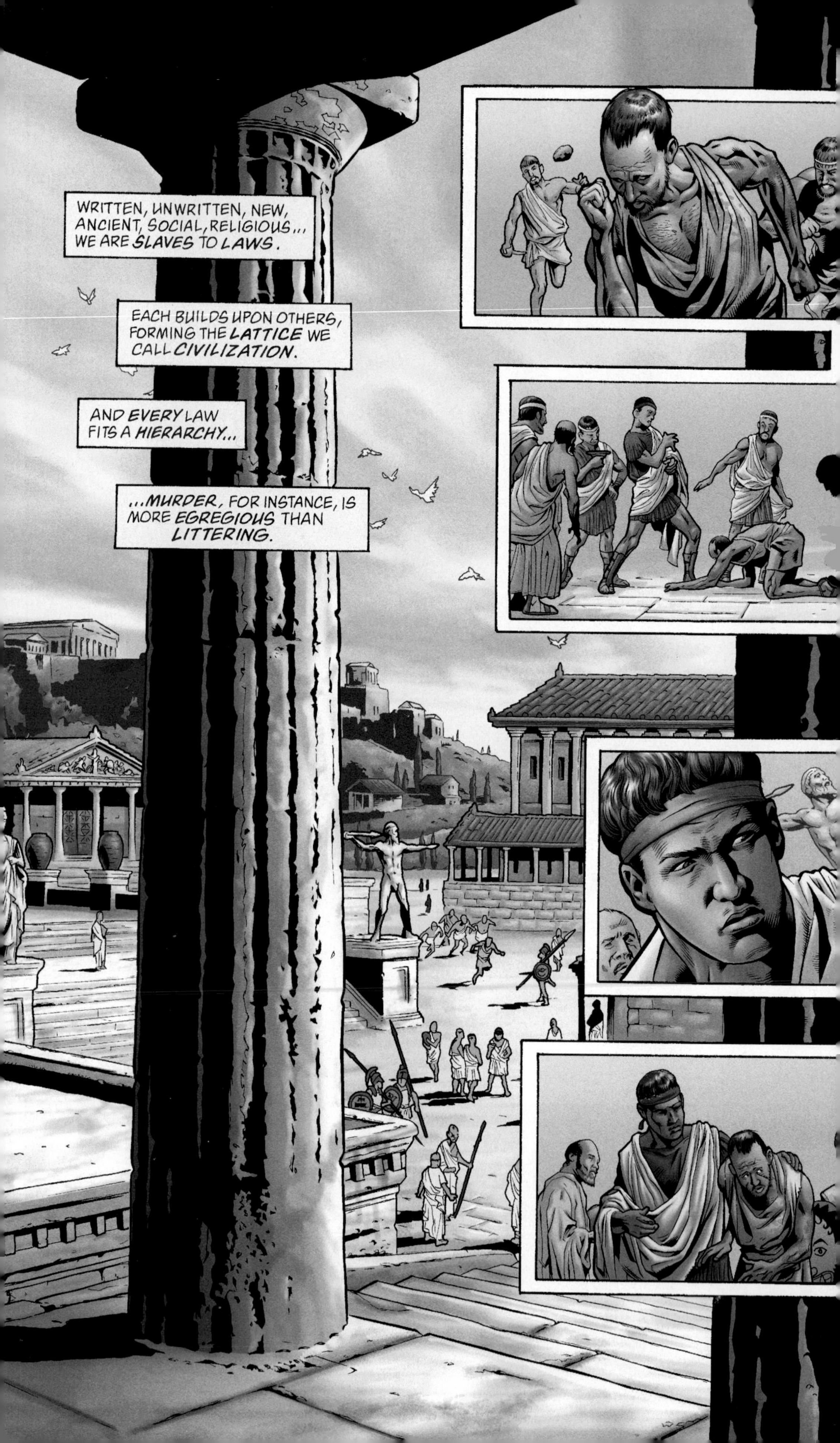
WRITTEN, UNWRITTEN, NEW, ANCIENT, SOCIAL, RELIGIOUS... WE ARE SLAVES TO LAWS.
EACH BUILDS UPON OTHERS, FORMING THE LATTICE WE CALL CIVILIZATION.
AND EVERY LAW FITS A HIERARCHY...
...MURDER, FOR INSTANCE, IS MORE EGREGIOUS THAN LITTERING.

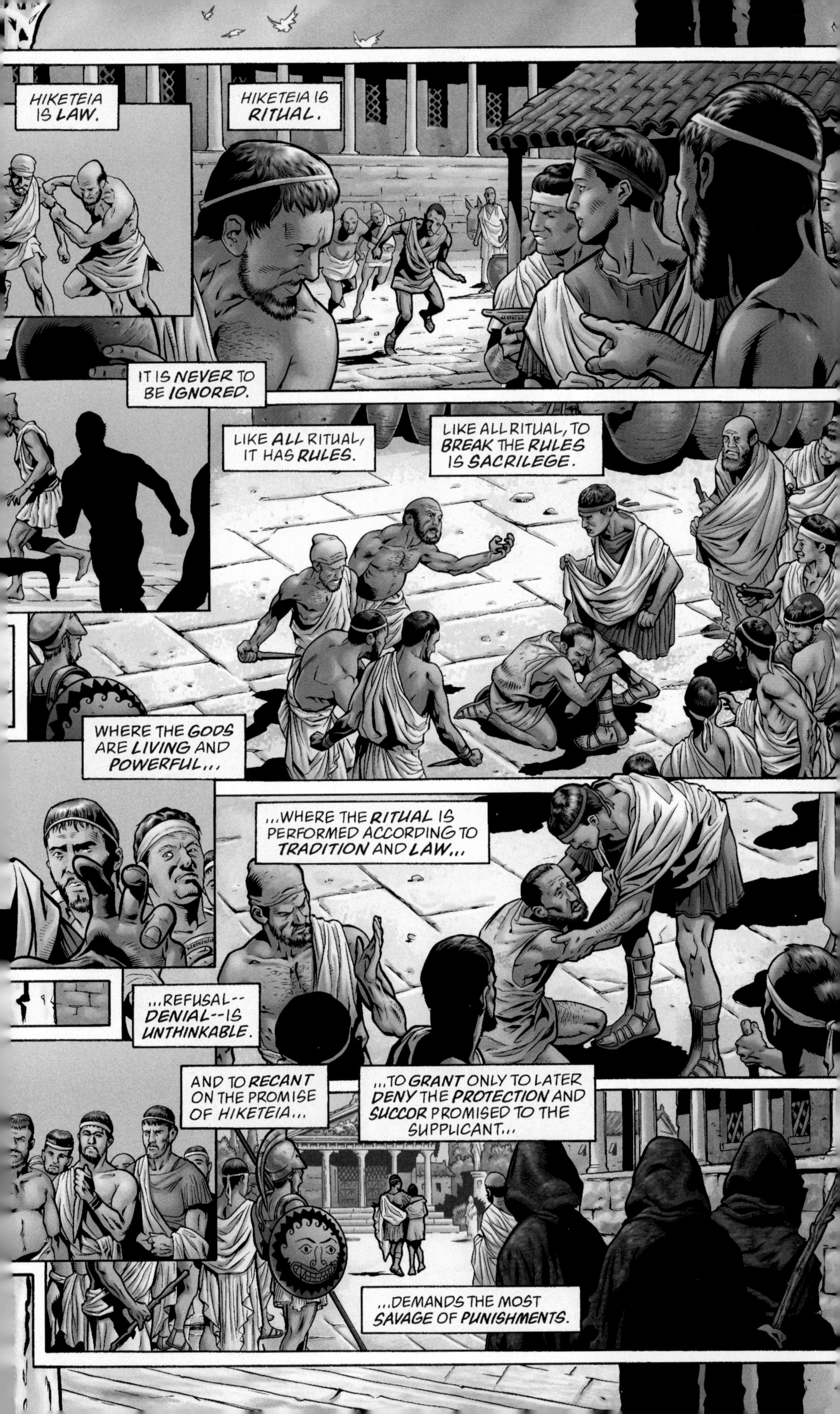
HIKETEIA IS LAW.
HIKETEIA IS RITUAL.
IT IS NEVER TO BE IGNORED.
LIKE ALL RITUAL, IT HAS RULES.
LIKE ALL RITUAL, TO BREAK THE RULES IS SACRILEGE.
WHERE THE GODS ARE LIVING AND POWERFUL...
...WHERE THE RITUAL IS PERFORMED ACCORDING TO TRADITION AND LAW...
...REFUSAL--DENIAL--IS UNTHINKABLE.
AND TO RECANT ON THE PROMISE OF HIKETEIA...
...TO GRANT ONLY TO LATER DENY THE PROTECTION AND SUCCOR PROMISED TO THE SUPPLICANT...
...DEMANDS THE MOST SAVAGE OF PUNISHMENTS.

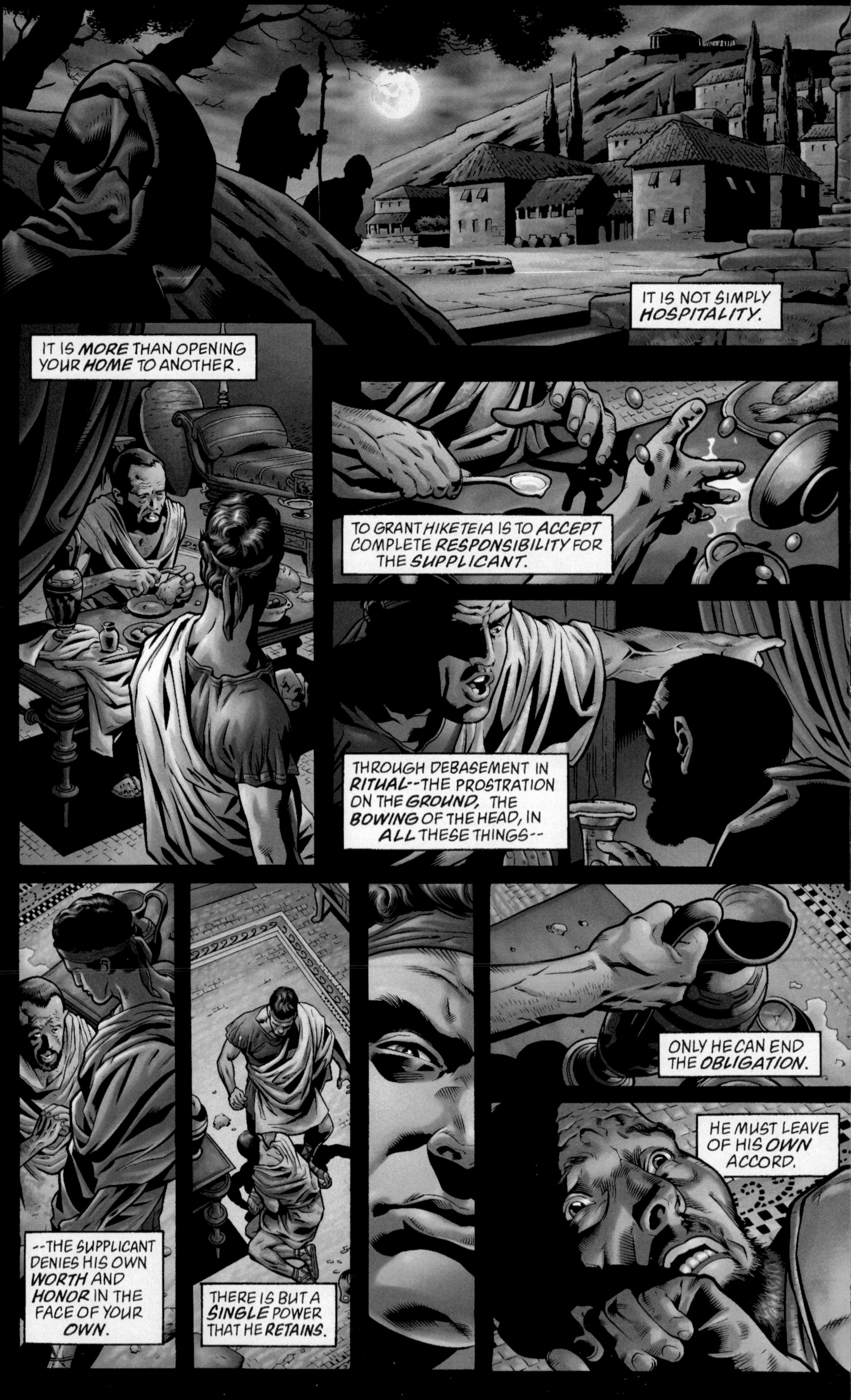
IT IS NOT SIMPLY HOSPITALITY.
IT IS MORE THAN OPENING YOUR HOME TO ANOTHER.
TO GRANT HIKETEIA IS TO ACCEPT COMPLETE RESPONSIBILITY FOR THE SUPPLICANT.
THROUGH DEBASEMENT IN RITUAL--THE PROSTRATION ON THE GROUND, THE BOWING OF THE HEAD, IN ALL THESE THINGS--
--THE SUPPLICANT DENIES HIS OWN WORTH AND HONOR IN THE FACE OF YOUR OWN.
THERE IS BUT A SINGLE POWER THAT HE RETAINS.
ONLY HE CAN END THE OBLIGATION.
HE MUST LEAVE OF HIS OWN ACCORD.

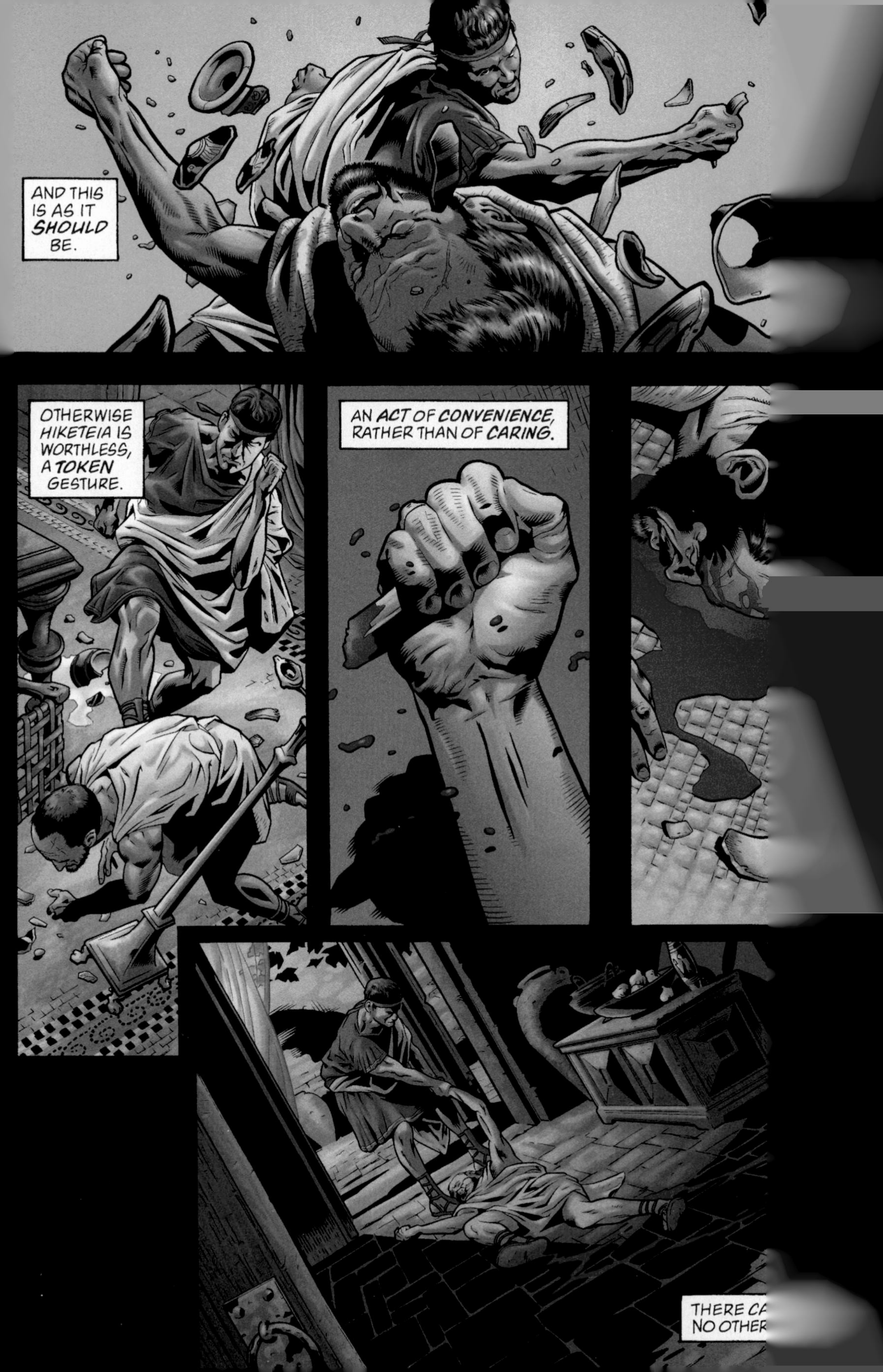
AND THIS IS AS IT SHOULD BE.
OTHERWISE HIKETEIA IS WORTHLESS, A TOKEN GESTURE.
AN ACT OF CONVENIENCE, RATHER THAN OF CARING.
THERE CA
NO OTHER

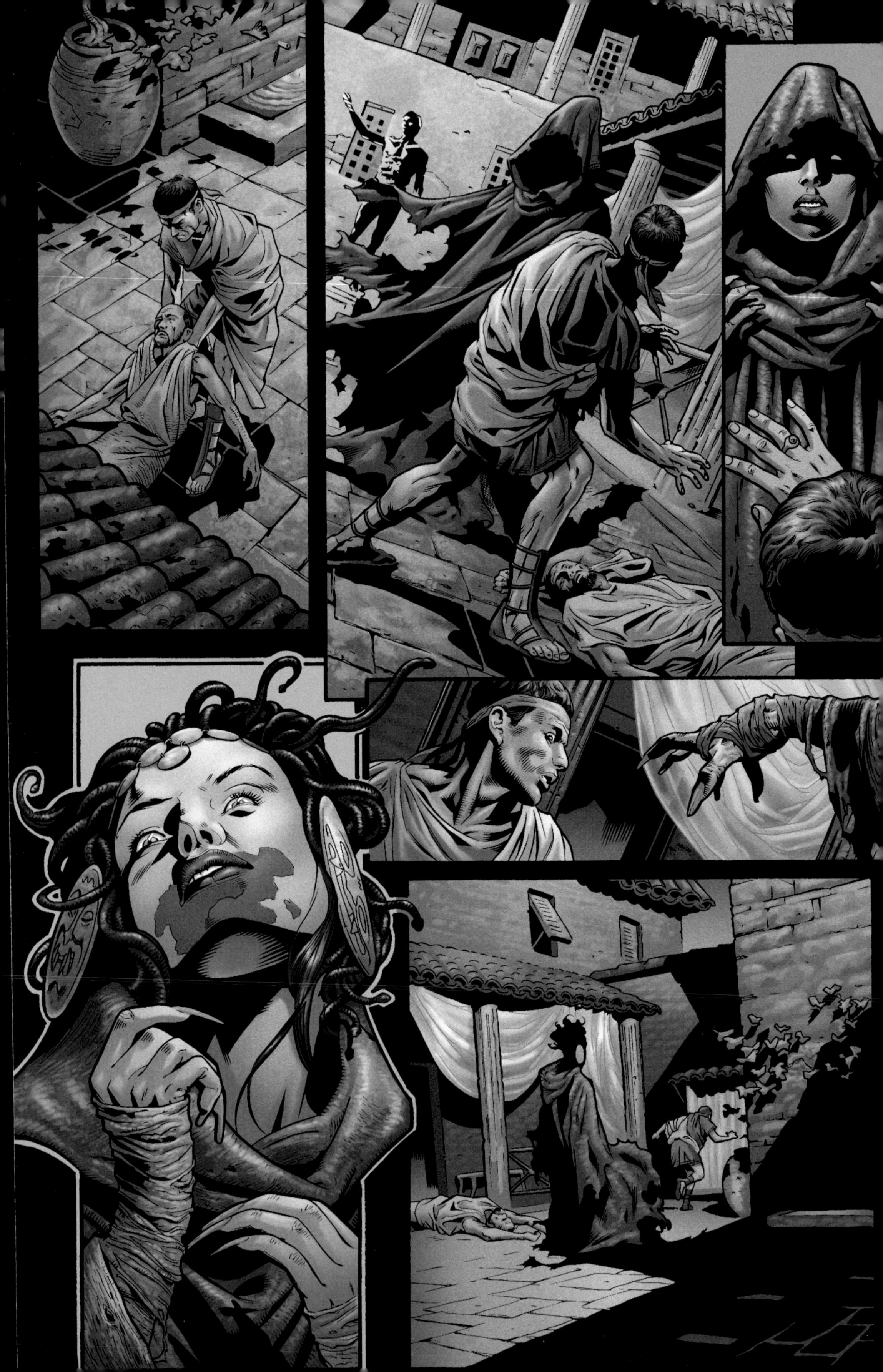

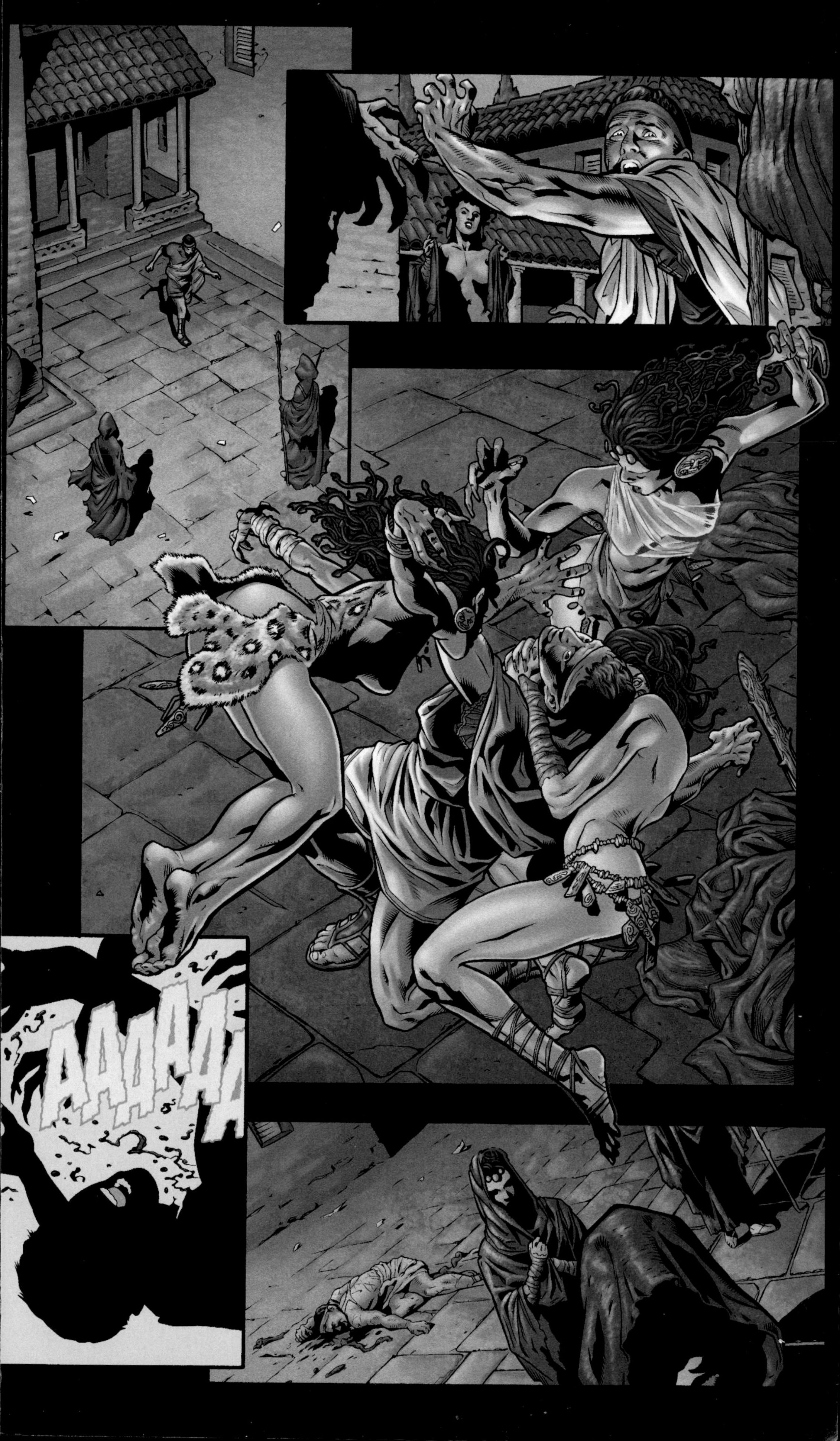
AAAAA

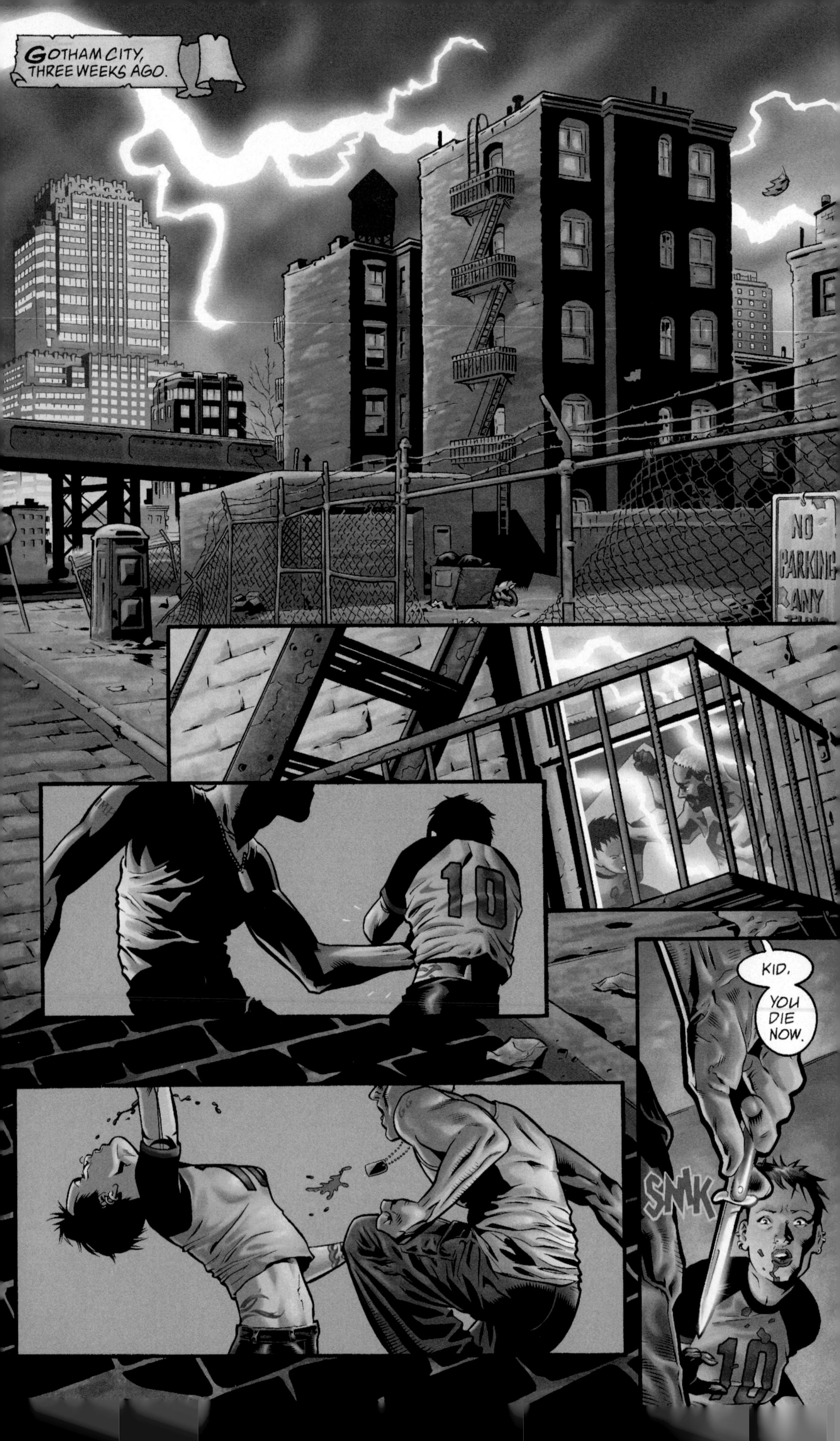
GOTHAM CITY, THREE WEEKS AGO.
NO PARKING ANY
KID.
YOU DIE NOW.
SNIK

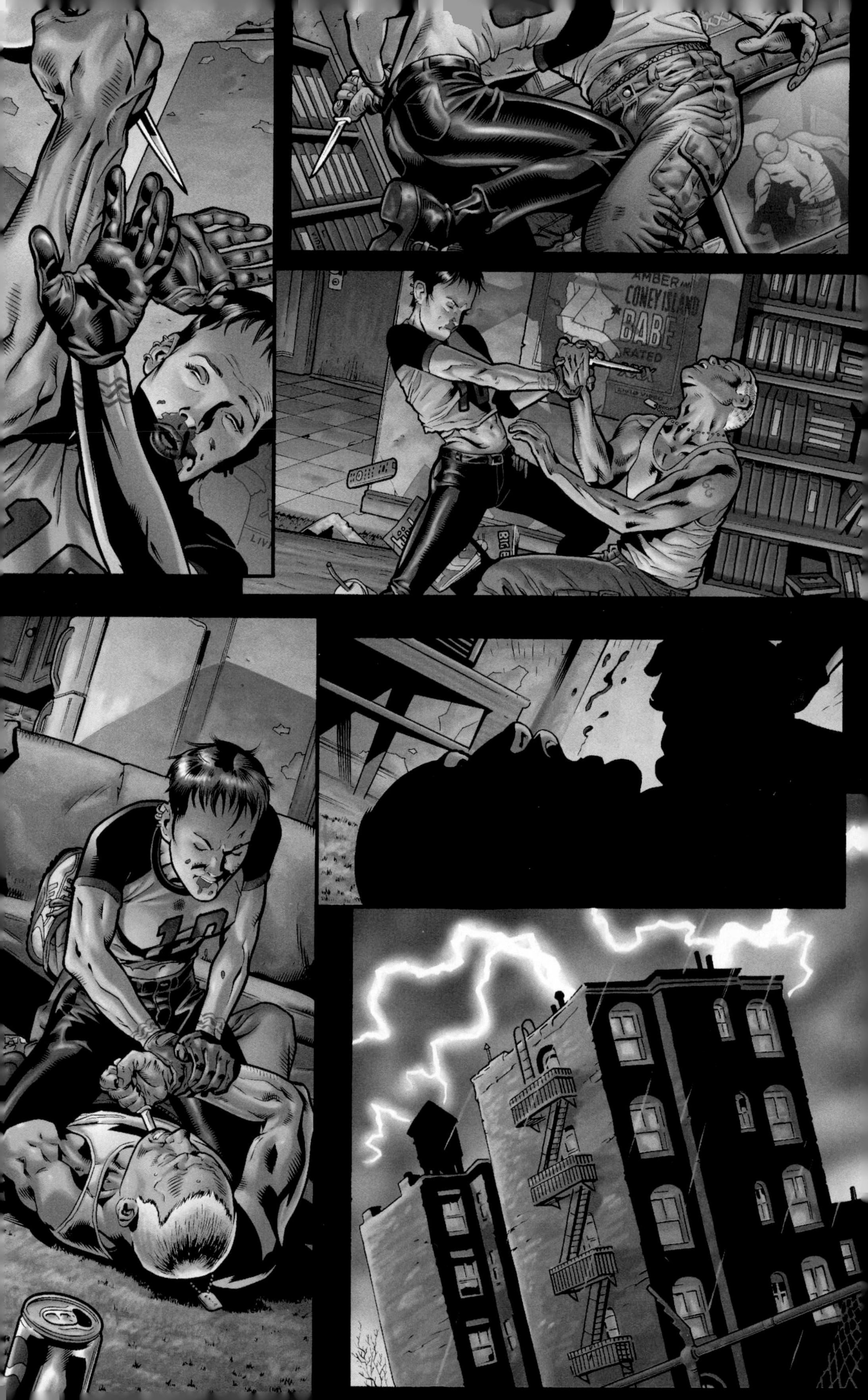
AMBER
CONEY ISLAND
BABE
RATED

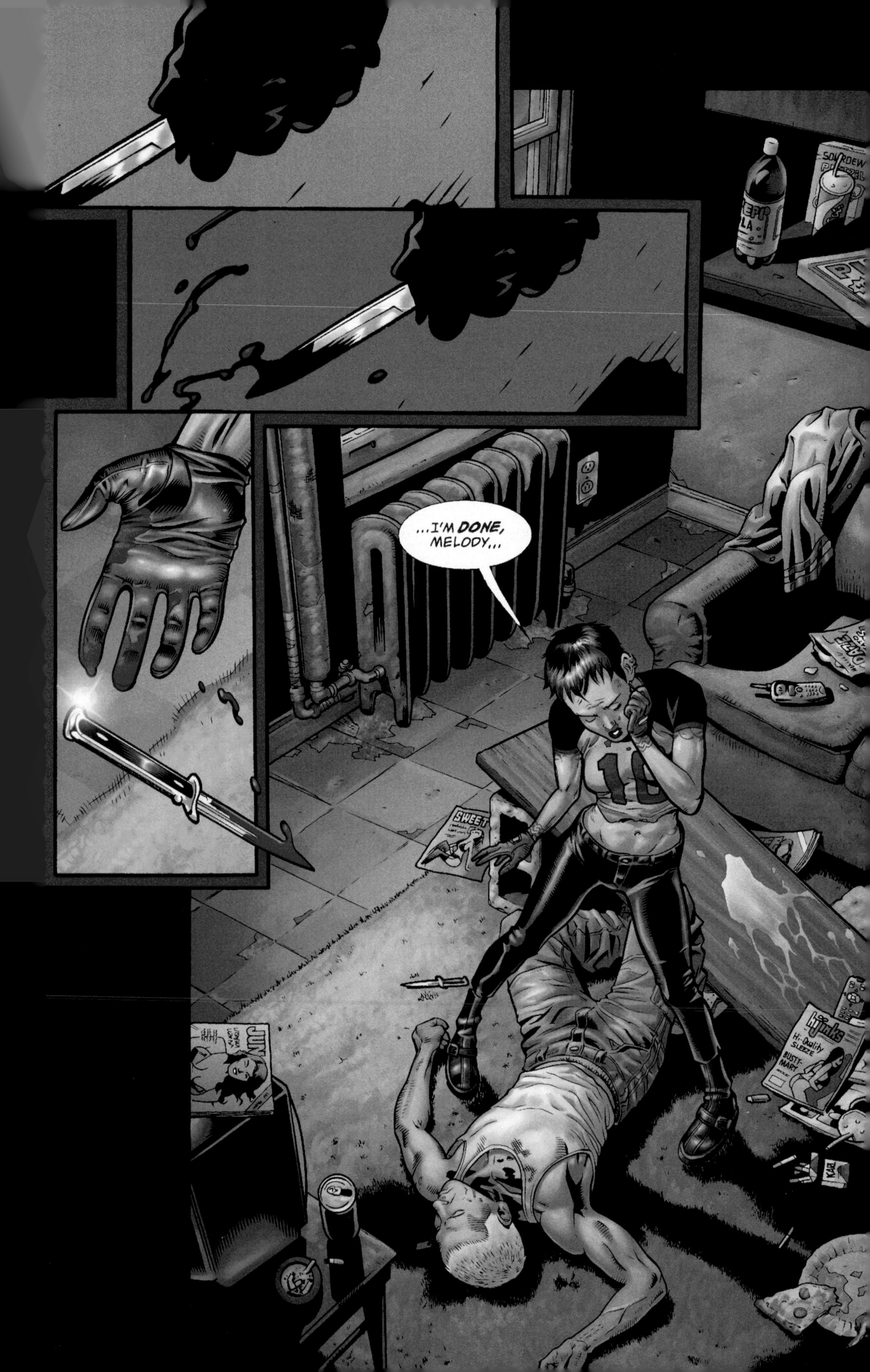
...I'M DONE, MELODY...

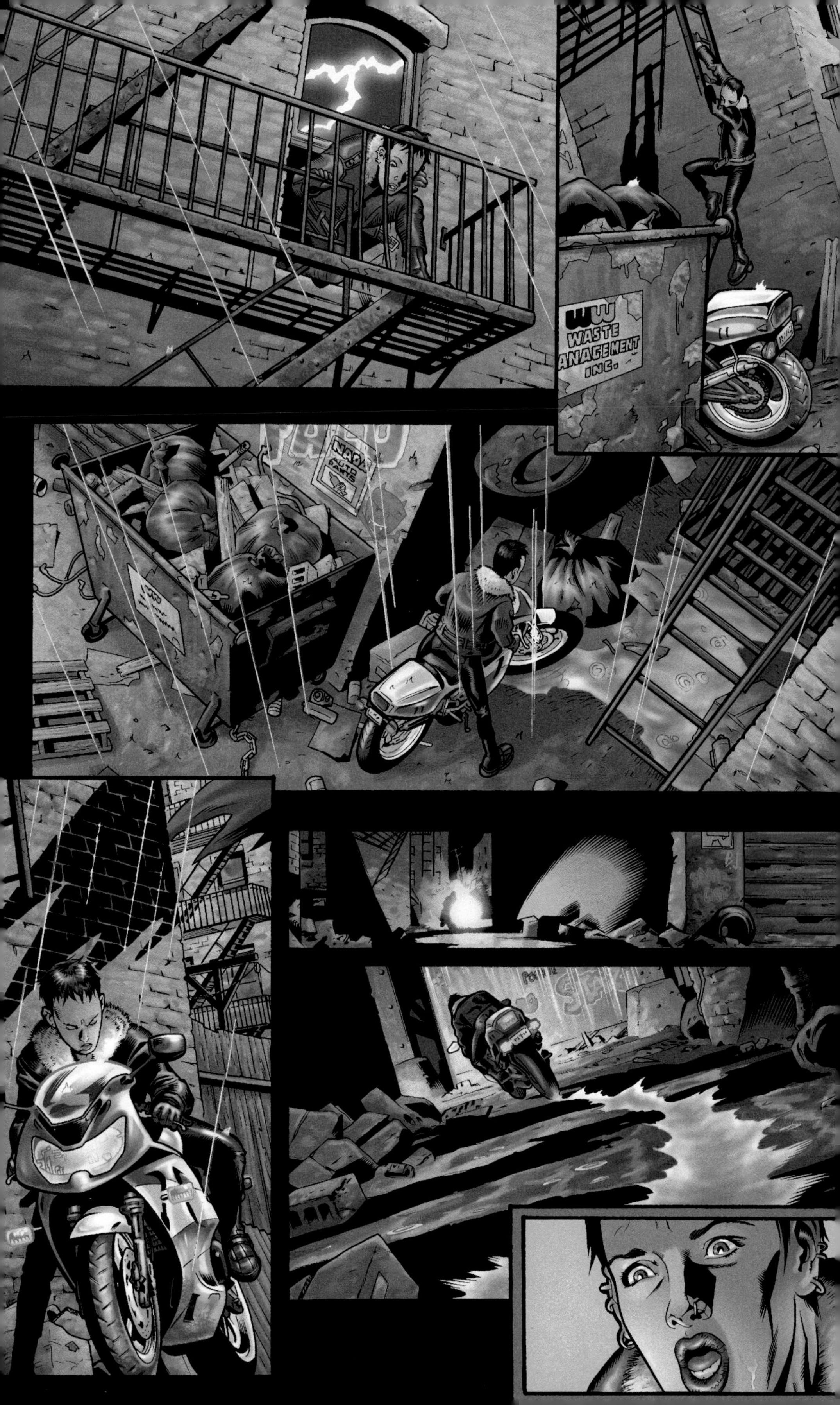
WW WASTE
ANAGEMENT
INC.
NADA AUTO PARTS

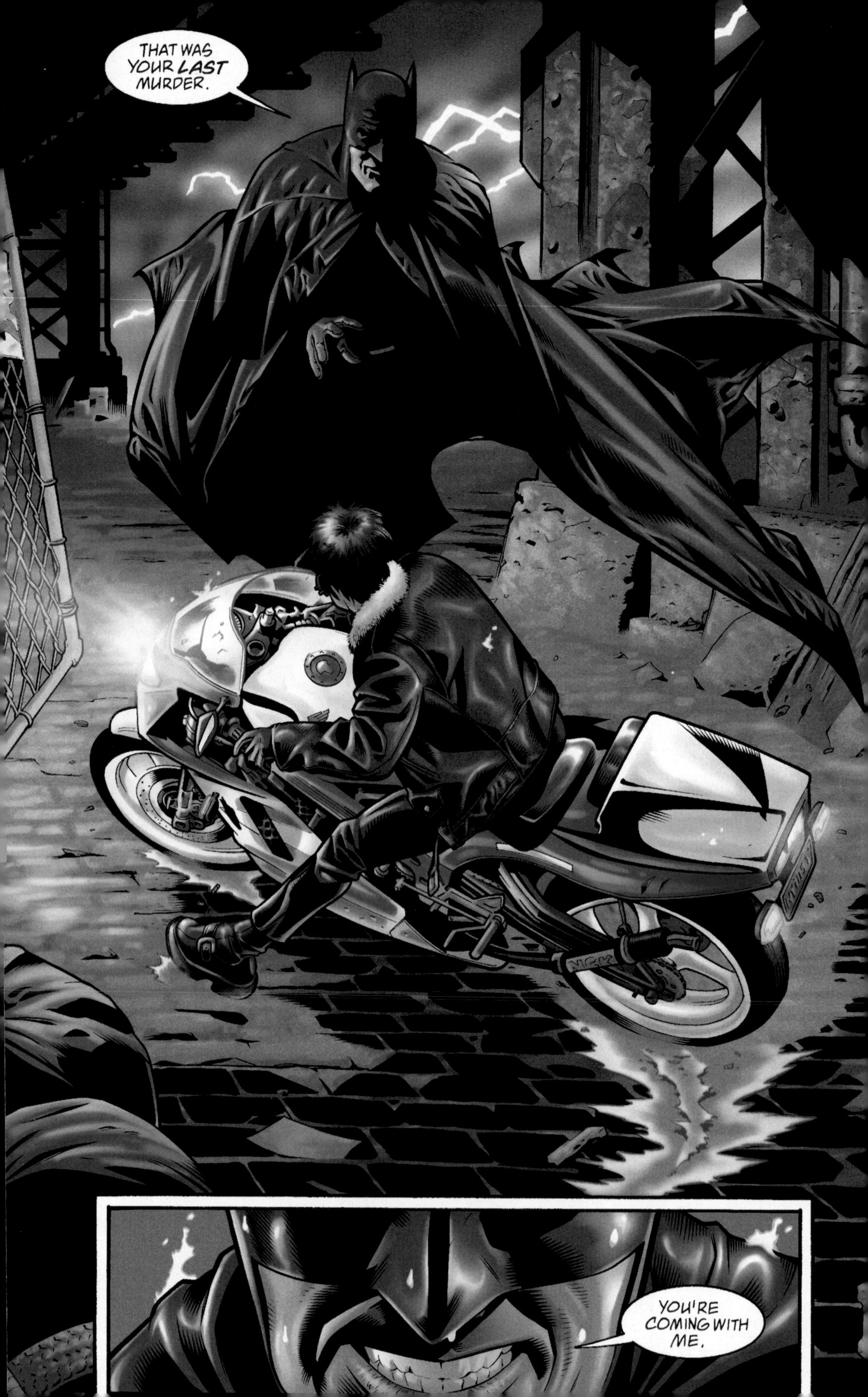
THAT WAS YOUR LAST MURDER.
YOU'RE COMING WITH ME.

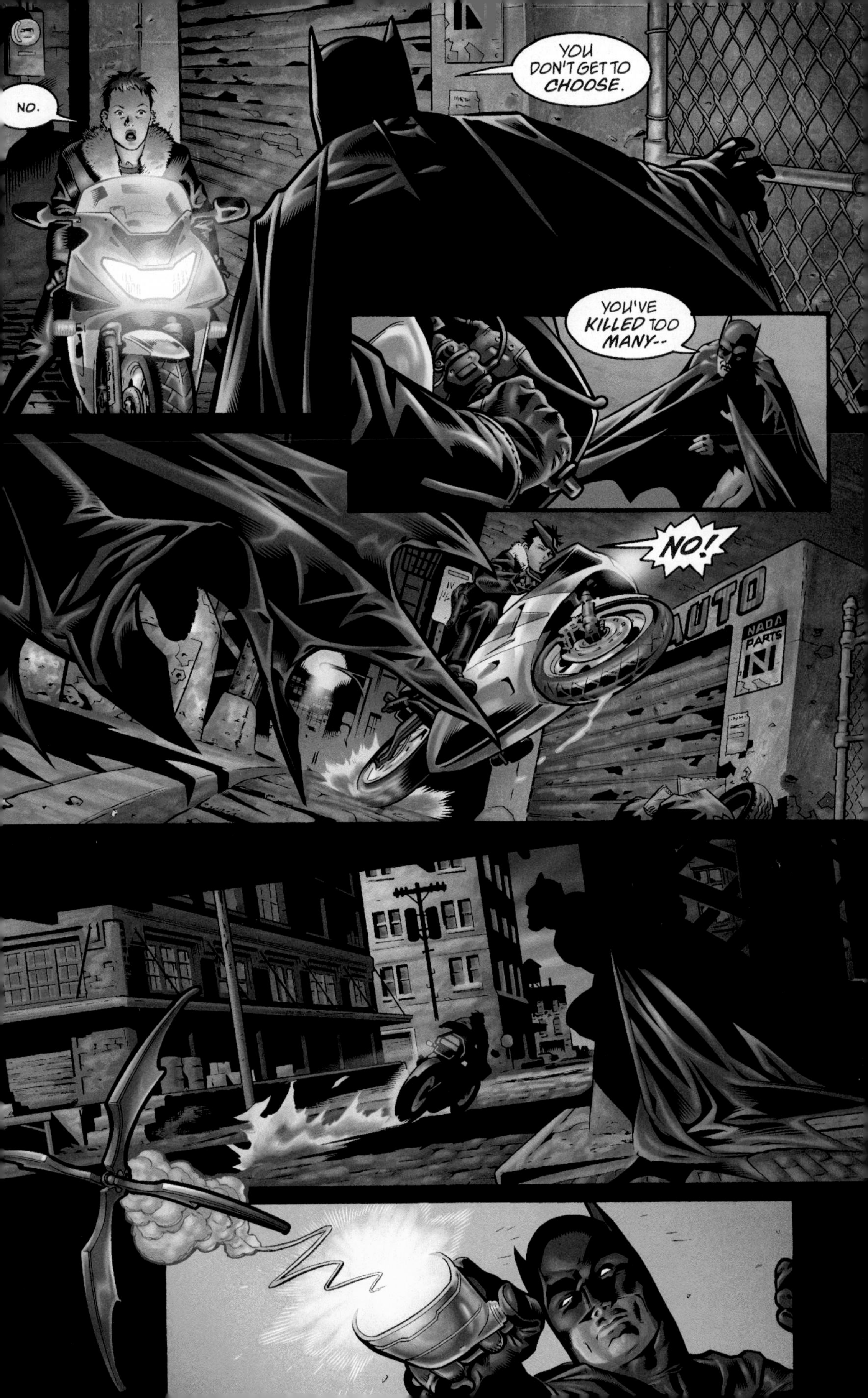
NO.
YOU DON'T GET TO CHOOSE.
YOU'VE KILLED TOO MANY--
NO!
AUTO
NADA PARTS
N

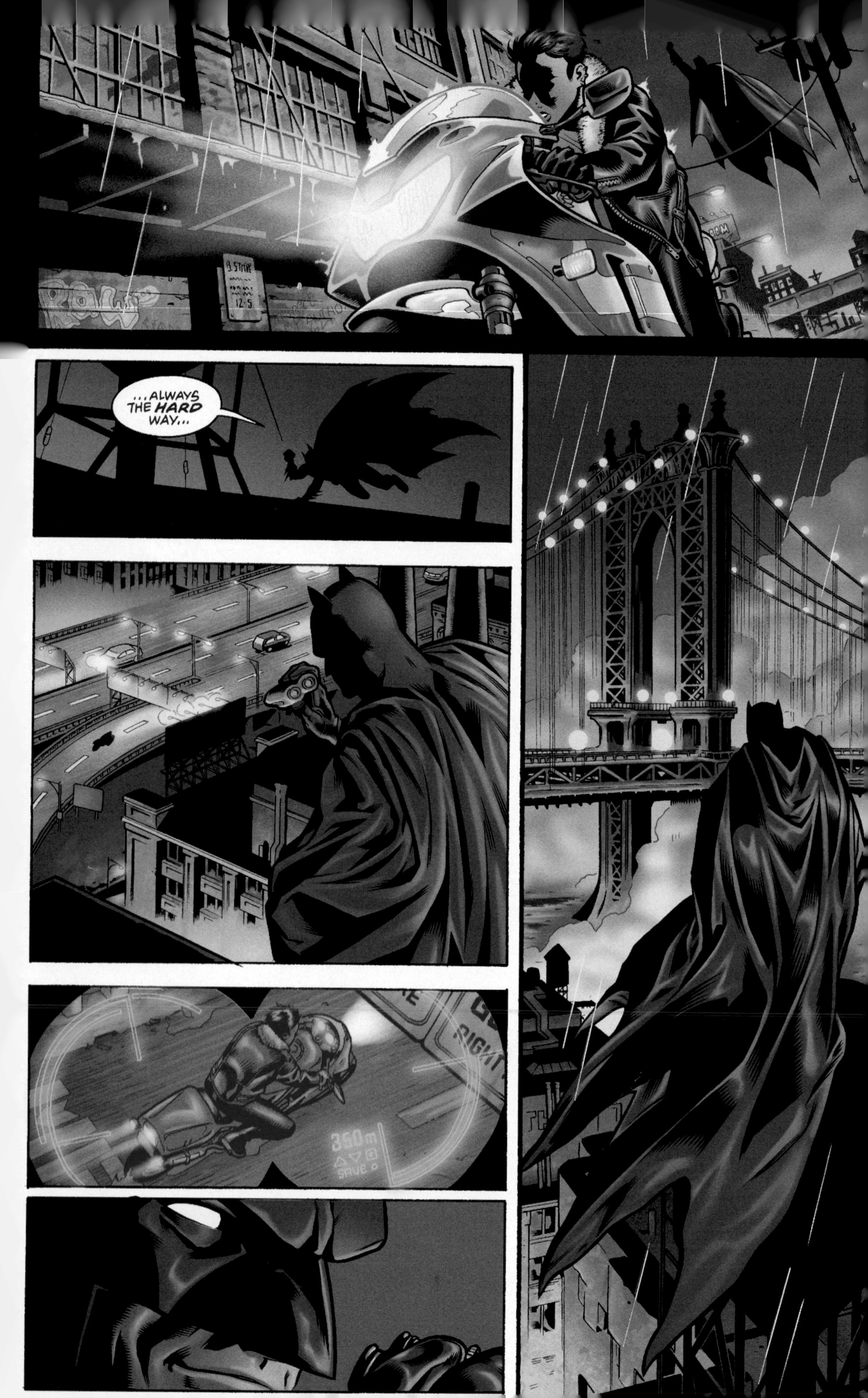
...ALWAYS THE HARD WAY...
360m

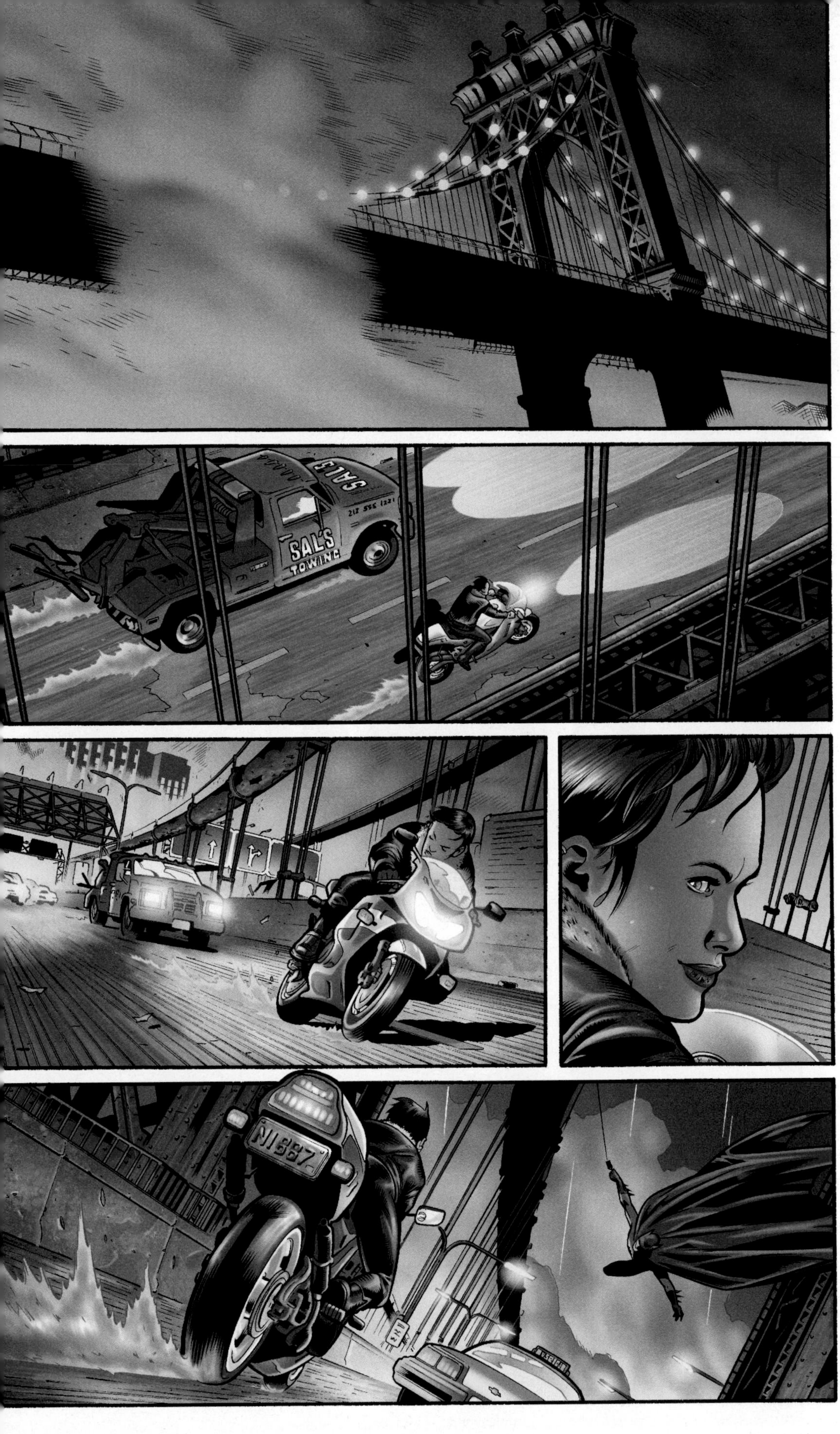
SAL'S
212 555 1221
SAL'S
TOWING
NI667

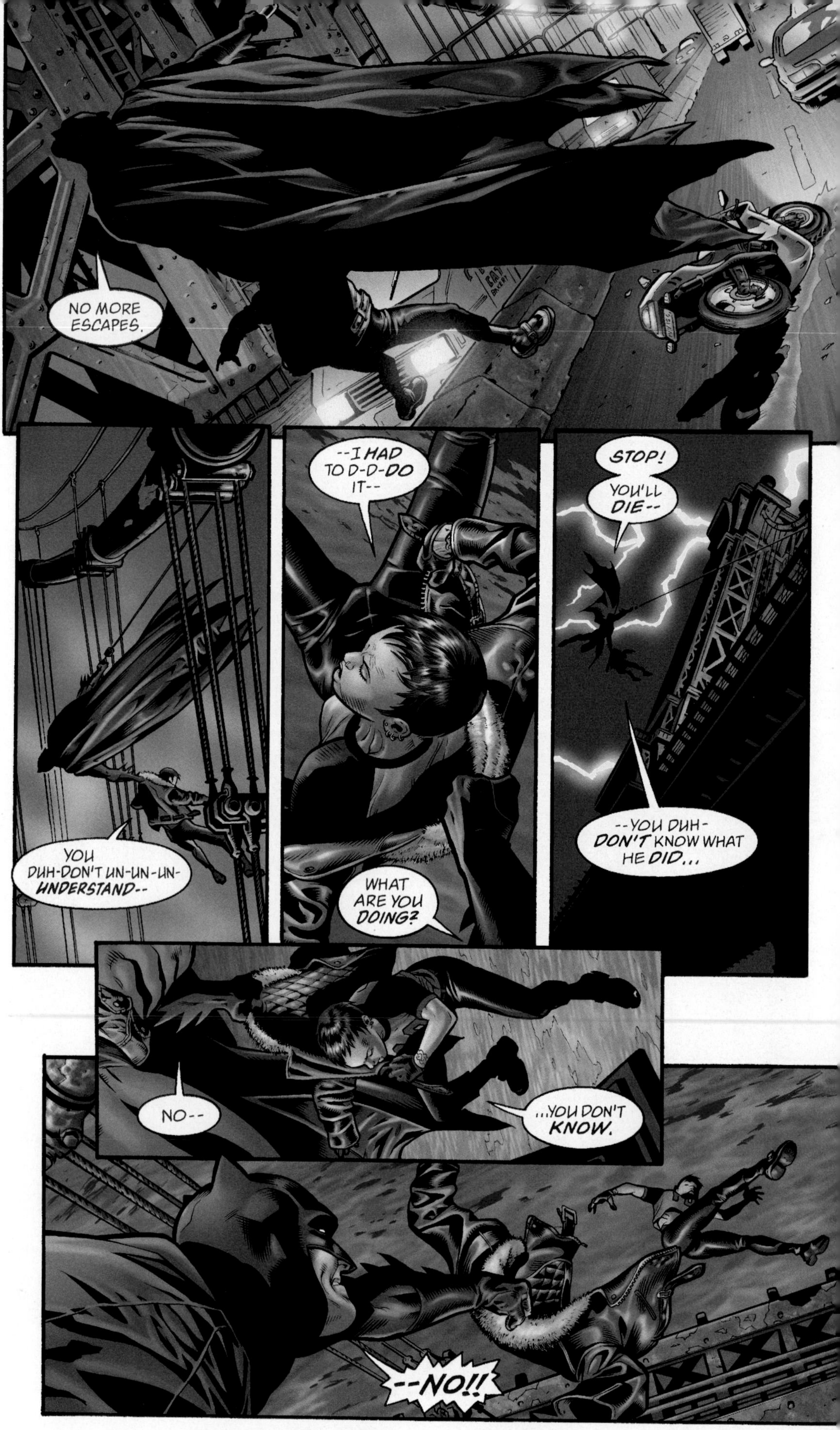
NO MORE ESCAPES.
YOU DUH-DON'T UN-UN-UN-UNDERSTAND--
--I HAD TO D-D-DO IT--
WHAT ARE YOU DOING?
STOP! YOU'LL DIE--
--YOU DUH-DON'T KNOW WHAT HE DID...
NO--
...YOU DON'T KNOW.
--NO!!

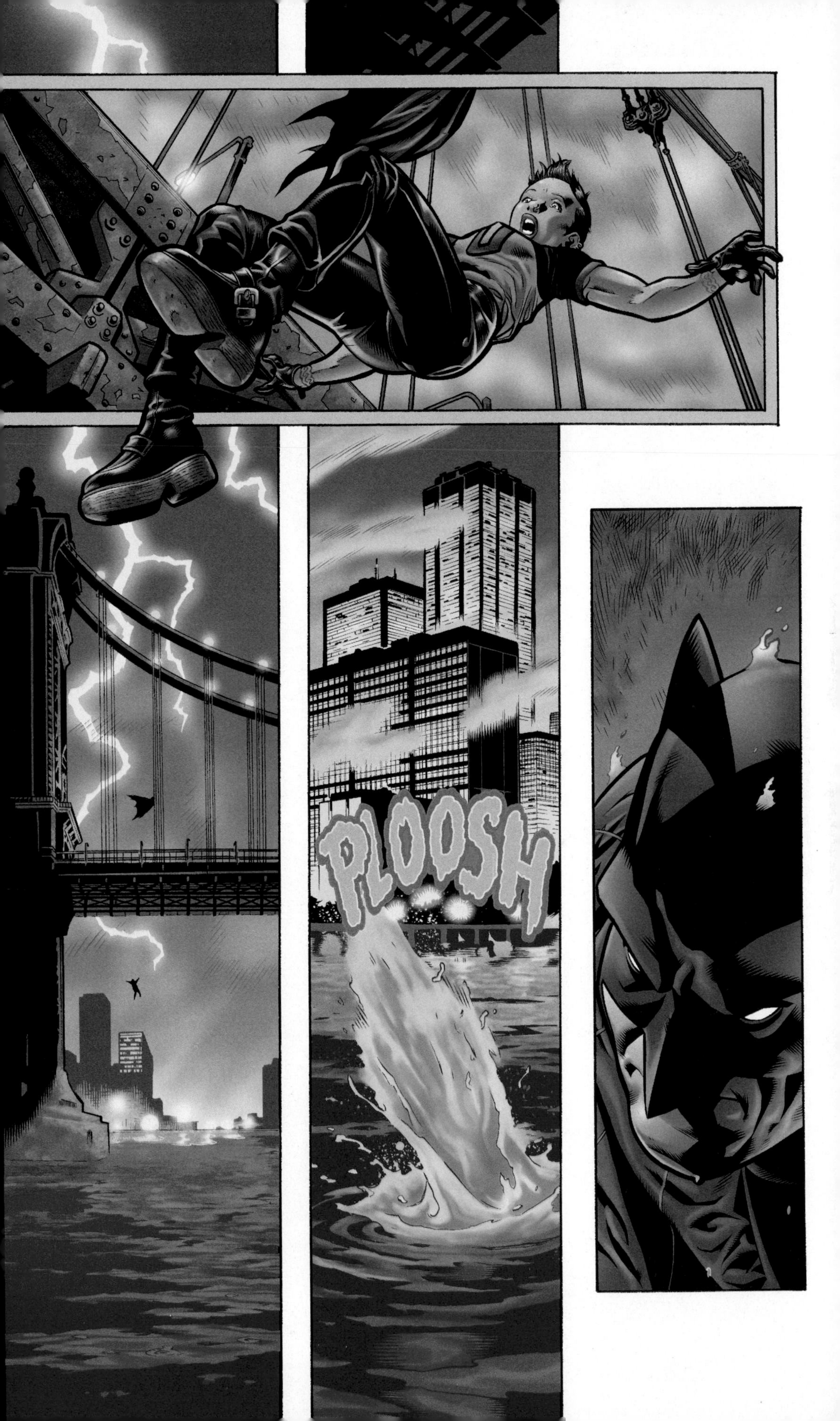
PLOOSH

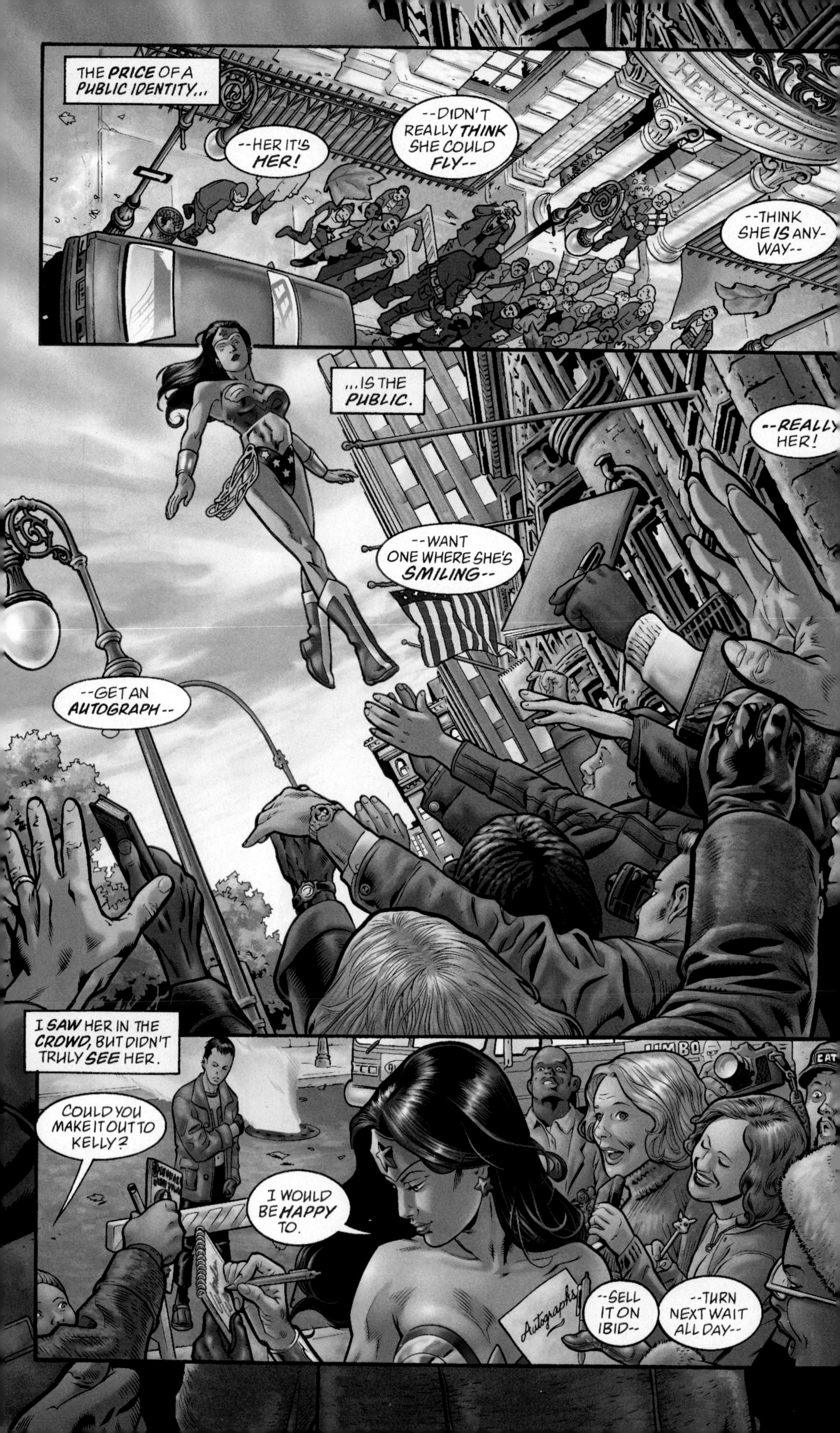
THE PRICE OF A PUBLIC IDENTITY...
--HER IT'S HER!
--DIDN'T REALLY THINK SHE COULD FLY--
--THINK SHE IS ANY-WAY--
...IS THE PUBLIC.
--REALLY HER!
--WANT ONE WHERE SHE'S SMILING--
--GET AN AUTOGRAPH--
I SAW HER IN THE CROWD, BUT DIDN'T TRULY SEE HER.
COULD YOU MAKE IT OUT TO KELLY?
I WOULD BE HAPPY TO.
--SELL IT ON IBID--
--TURN NEXT WAIT ALL DAY--

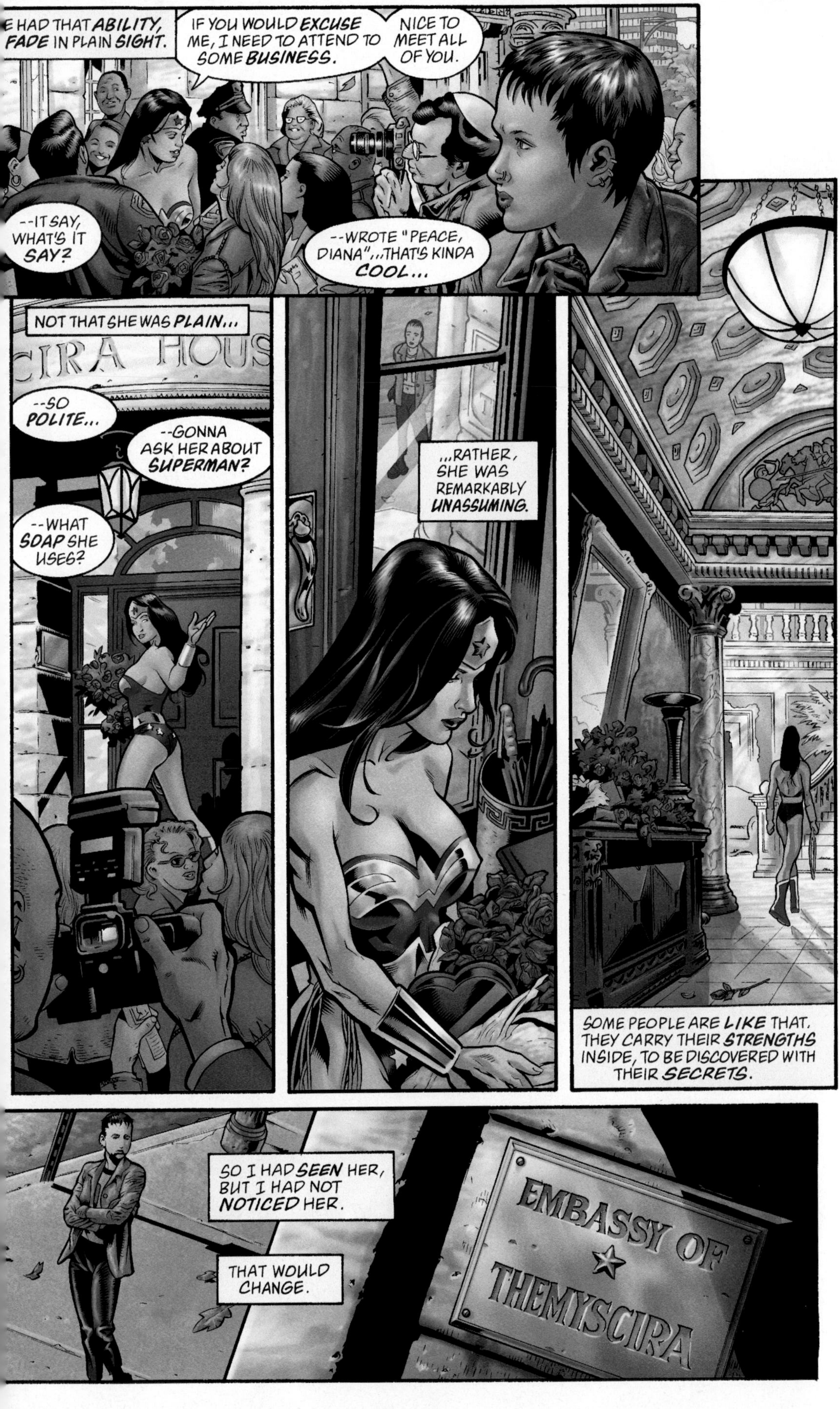
E HAD THAT ABILITY, FADE IN PLAIN SIGHT.
IF YOU WOULD EXCUSE ME, I NEED TO ATTEND TO SOME BUSINESS.
NICE TO MEET ALL OF YOU.
--IT SAY, WHAT'S IT SAY?
--WROTE "PEACE, DIANA"...THAT'S KINDA COOL...
NOT THAT SHE WAS PLAIN...
CIRA HOUS
--SO POLITE...
--GONNA ASK HER ABOUT SUPERMAN?
--WHAT SOAP SHE USES?
...RATHER, SHE WAS REMARKABLY UNASSUMING.
SOME PEOPLE ARE LIKE THAT. THEY CARRY THEIR STRENGTHS INSIDE, TO BE DISCOVERED WITH THEIR SECRETS.
SO I HAD SEEN HER, BUT I HAD NOT NOTICED HER.
THAT WOULD CHANGE.
EMBASSY OF THEMYSCIRA

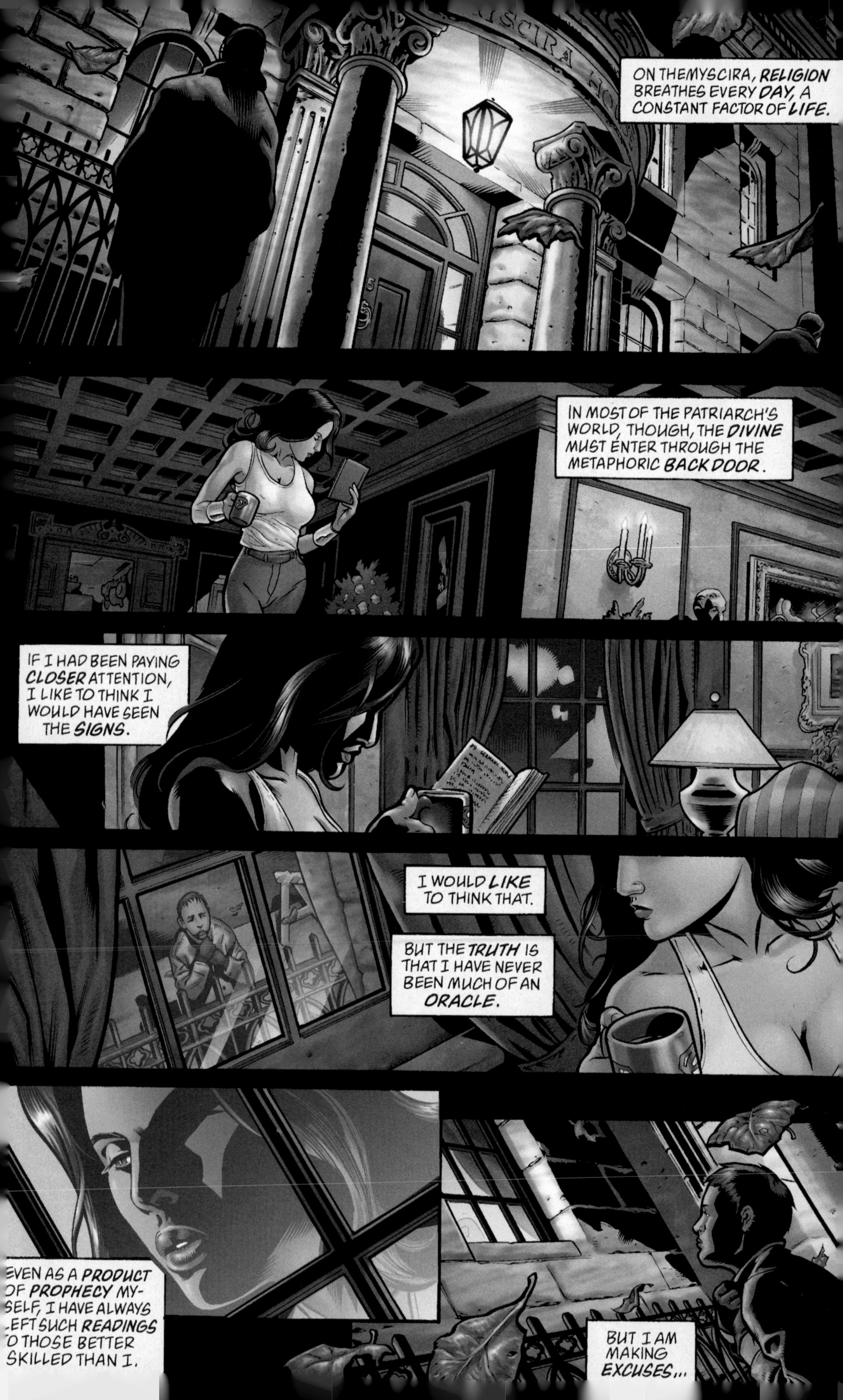
ON THEMYSCIRA, RELIGION BREATHES EVERY DAY, A CONSTANT FACTOR OF LIFE.
IN MOST OF THE PATRIARCH'S WORLD, THOUGH, THE DIVINE MUST ENTER THROUGH THE METAPHORIC BACK DOOR.
IF I HAD BEEN PAYING CLOSER ATTENTION, I LIKE TO THINK I WOULD HAVE SEEN THE SIGNS.
I WOULD LIKE TO THINK THAT.
BUT THE TRUTH IS THAT I HAVE NEVER BEEN MUCH OF AN ORACLE.
EVEN AS A PRODUCT OF PROPHECY MY-SELF, I HAVE ALWAYS LEFT SUCH READINGS TO THOSE BETTER SKILLED THAN I.
BUT I AM MAKING EXCUSES...

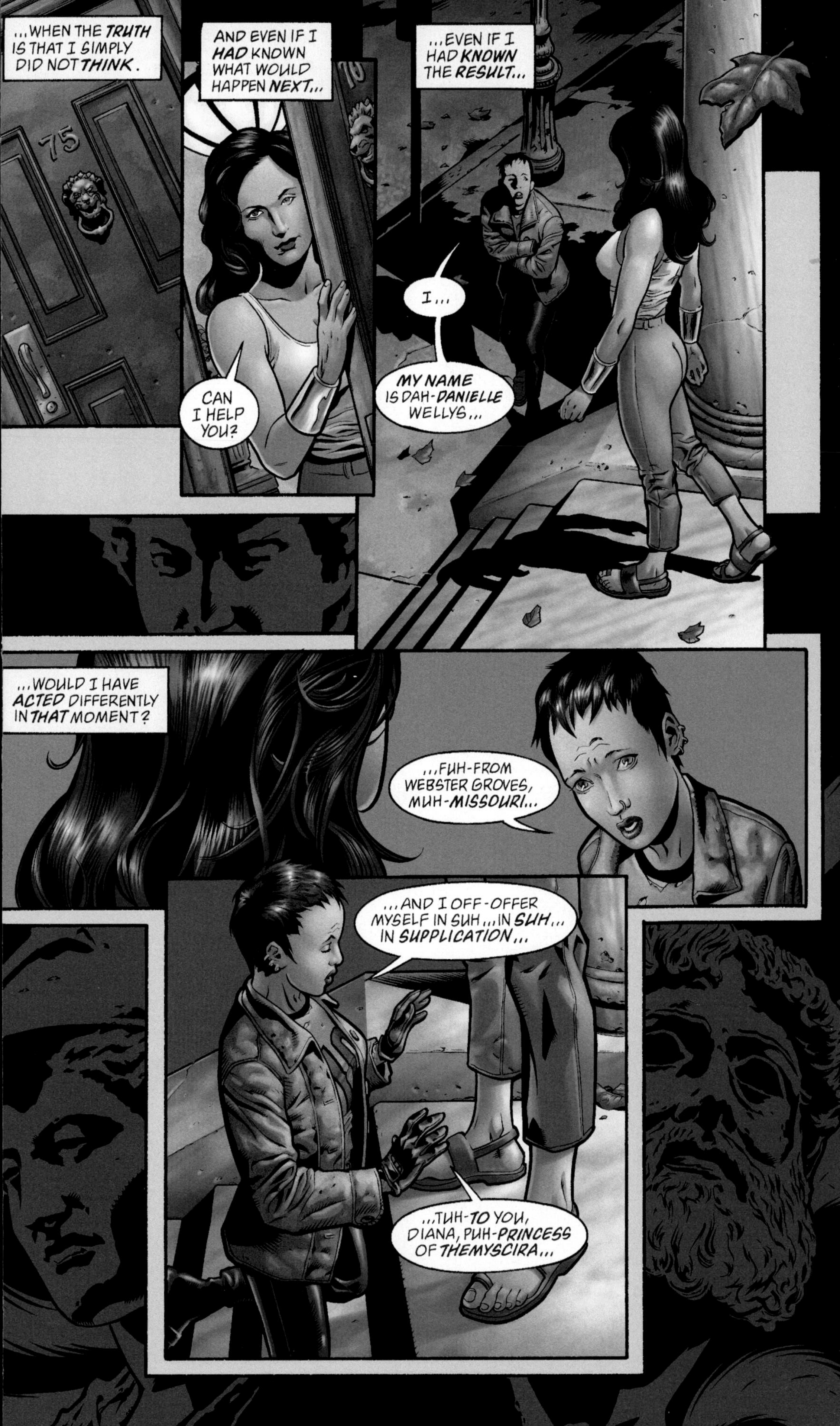
...WHEN THE TRUTH IS THAT I SIMPLY DID NOT THINK.
AND EVEN IF I HAD KNOWN WHAT WOULD HAPPEN NEXT...
CAN I HELP YOU?
...EVEN IF I HAD KNOWN THE RESULT...
I...
MY NAME IS DAH-DANIELLE WELLYS...
...WOULD I HAVE ACTED DIFFERENTLY IN THAT MOMENT?
...FUH-FROM WEBSTER GROVES, MUH-MISSOURI...
...AND I OFF-OFFER MYSELF IN SUH... IN SUH... IN SUPPLICATION...
...TUH-TO YOU, DIANA, PUH-PRINCESS OF THEMYSCIRA...

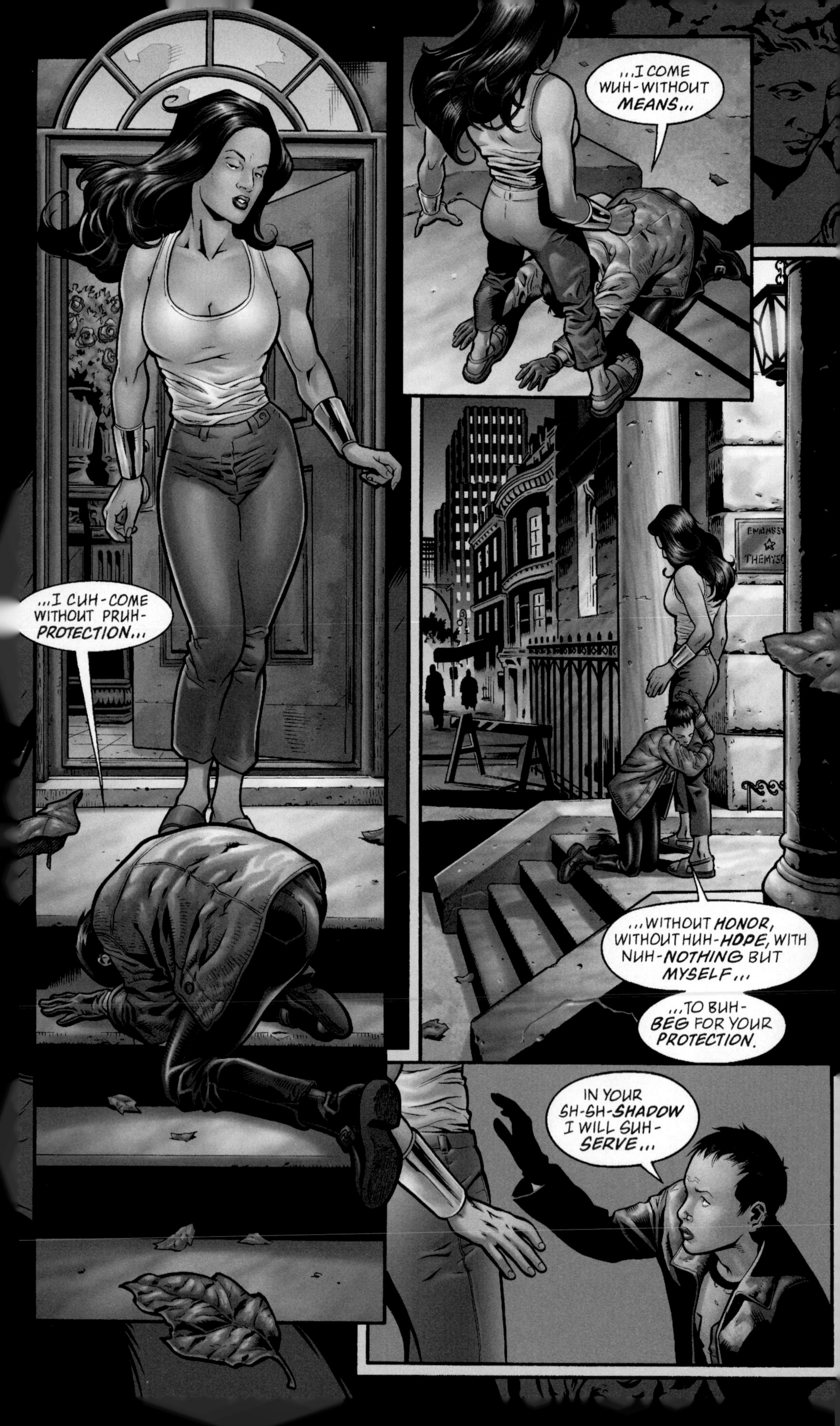
...I CUH-COME WITHOUT PRUH-PROTECTION...
...I COME WUH-WITHOUT MEANS...
EMBASSY THEMYSC
...WITHOUT HONOR, WITHOUT HUH-HOPE, WITH NUH-NOTHING BUT MYSELF...
...TO BUH-BEG FOR YOUR PROTECTION.
IN YOUR SH-SH-SHADOW I WILL SUH-SERVE...

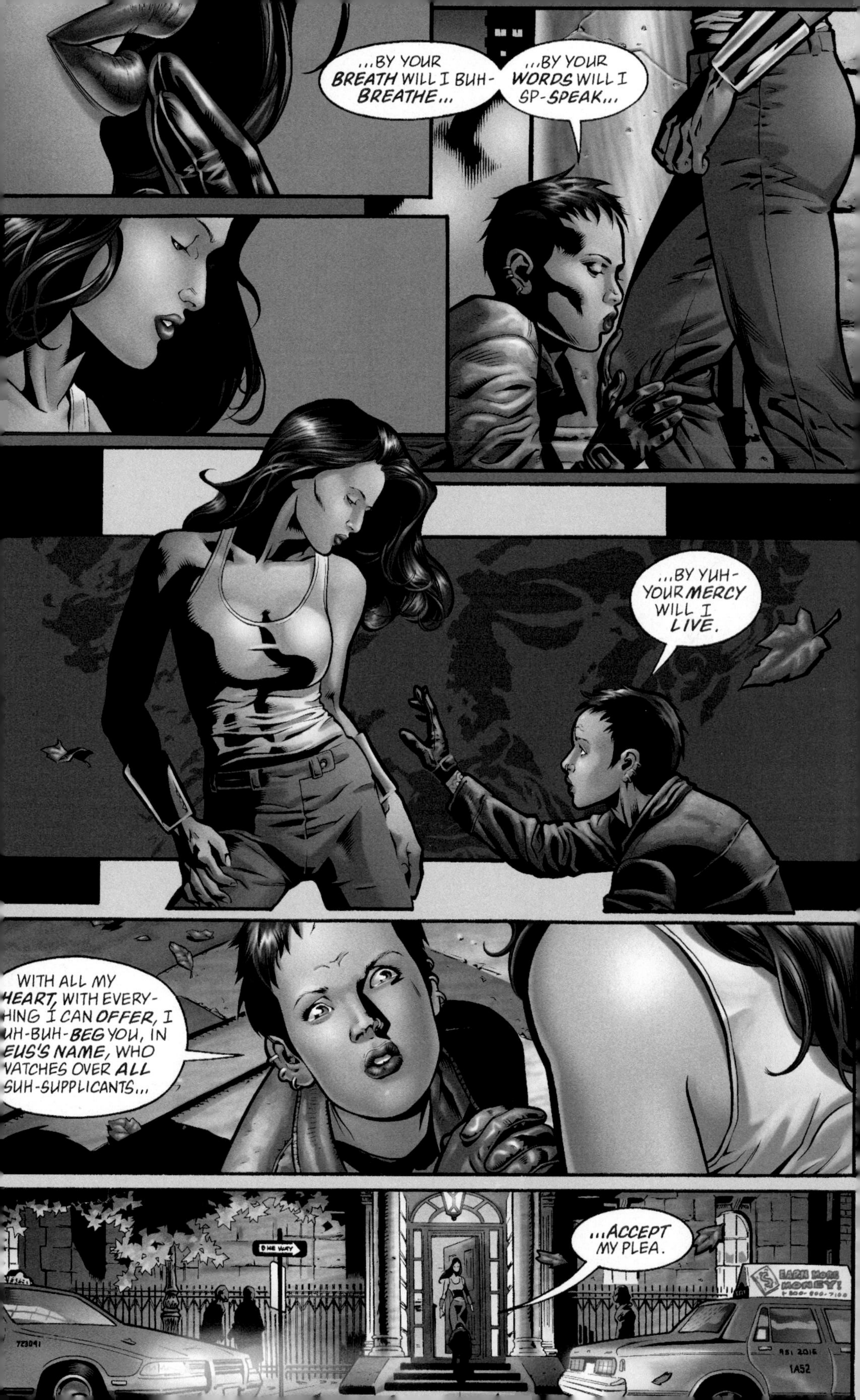
...BY YOUR BREATH WILL I BUH-BREATHE...
...BY YOUR WORDS WILL I SP-SPEAK...
...BY YUH-YOUR MERCY WILL I LIVE.
WITH ALL MY HEART, WITH EVERY-HING I CAN OFFER, I UH-BUH-BEG YOU, IN EUS'S NAME, WHO VATCHES OVER ALL SUH-SUPPLICANTS...
...ACCEPT MY PLEA.

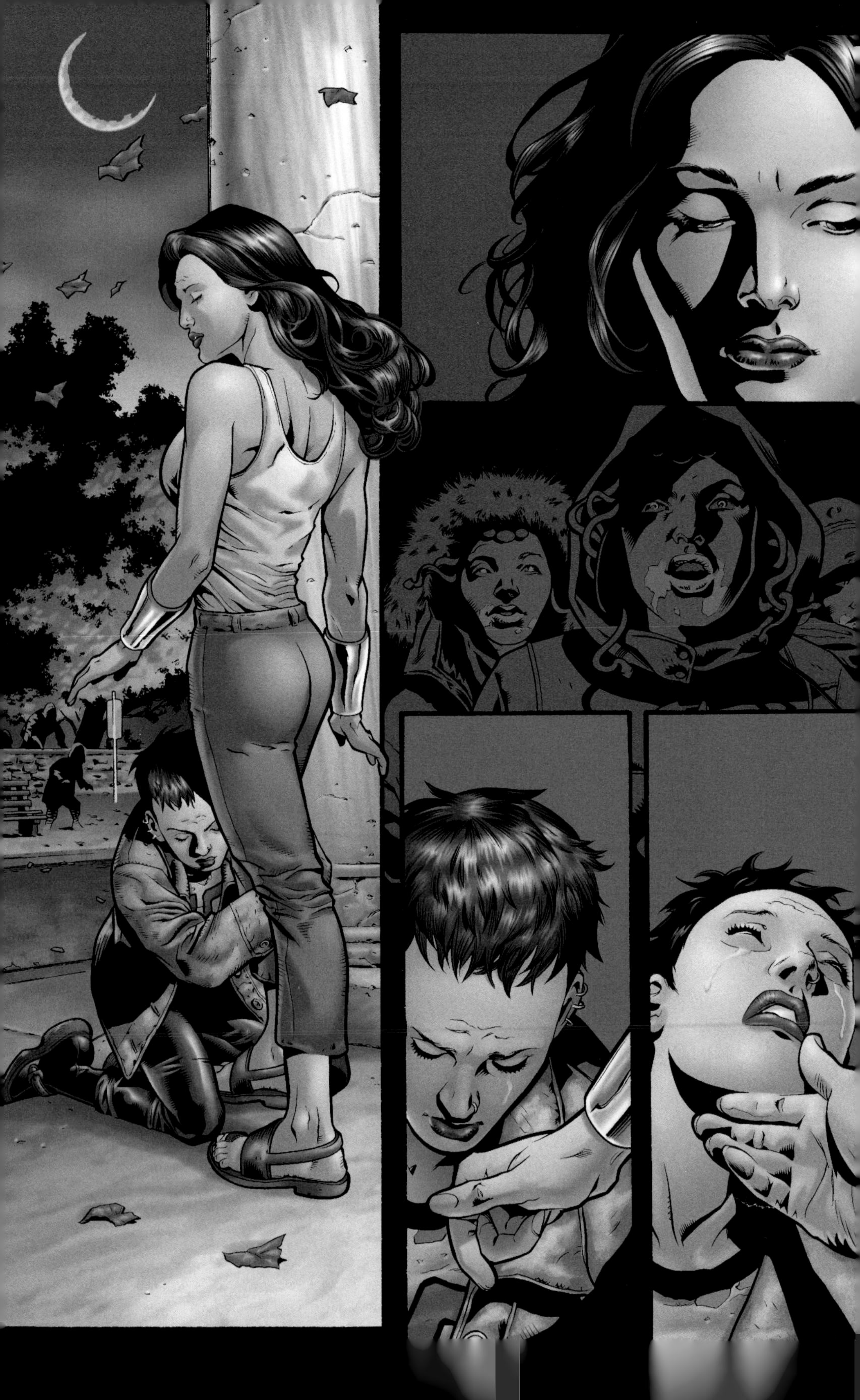

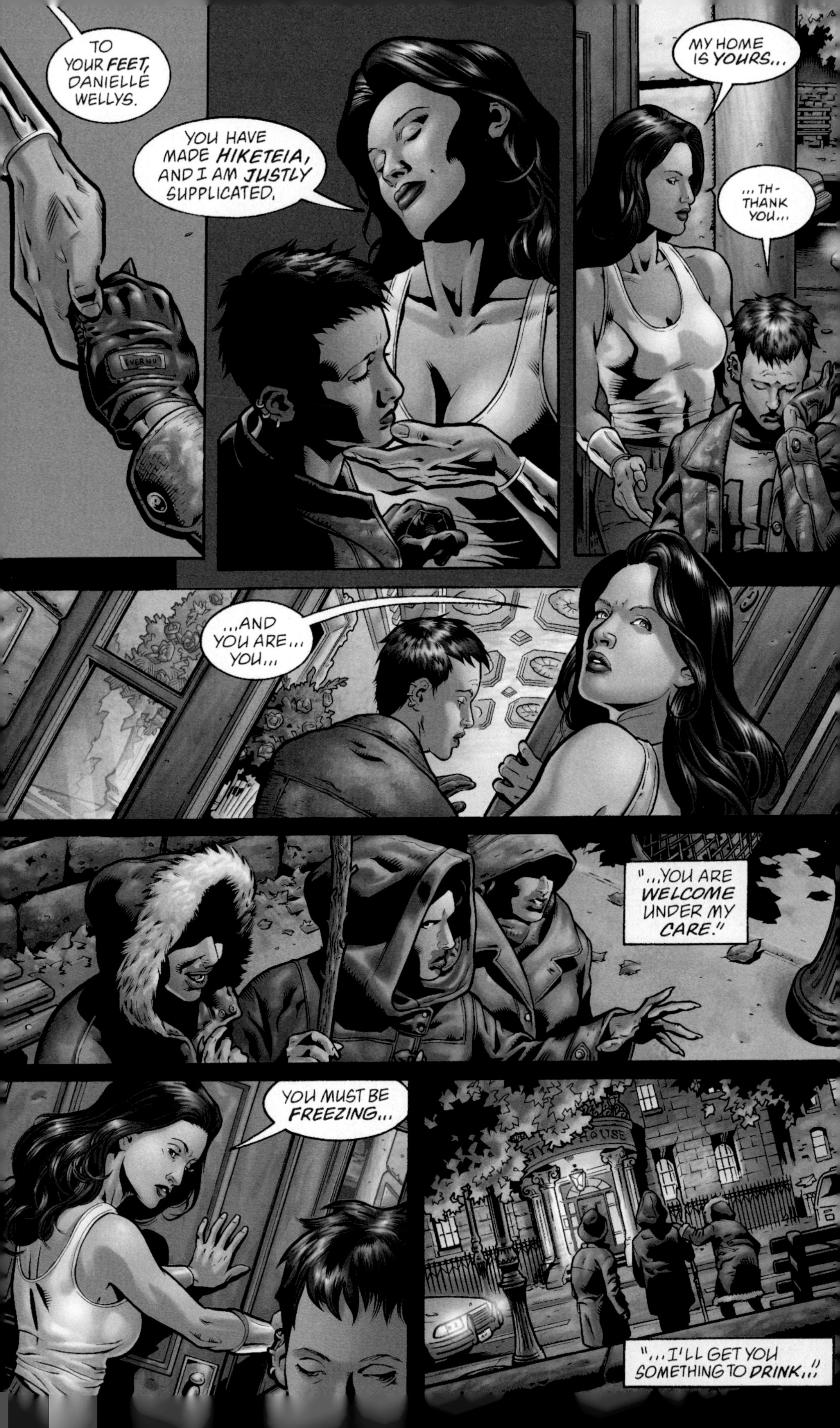

TO YOUR FEET, DANIELLE WELLYS.
YOU HAVE MADE HIKETEIA, AND I AM JUSTLY SUPPLICATED.
MY HOME IS YOURS...
...TH- THANK YOU...
...AND YOU ARE... YOU...
"...YOU ARE WELCOME UNDER MY CARE."
YOU MUST BE FREEZING...
"...I'LL GET YOU SOMETHING TO DRINK..."

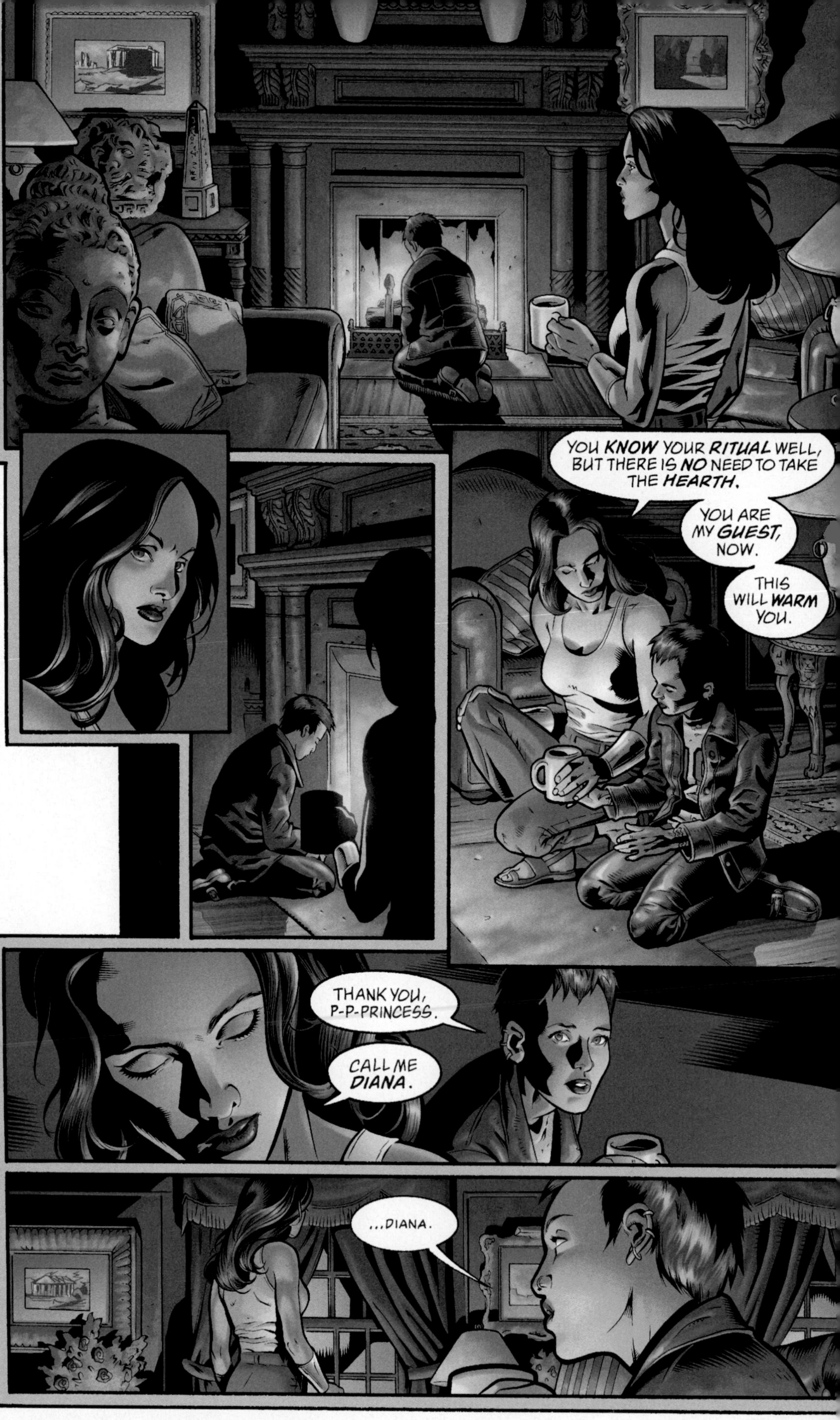
YOU KNOW YOUR RITUAL WELL, BUT THERE IS NO NEED TO TAKE THE HEARTH.
YOU ARE MY GUEST, NOW.
THIS WILL WARM YOU.
THANK YOU, P-P-PRINCESS.
CALL ME DIANA.
...DIANA.

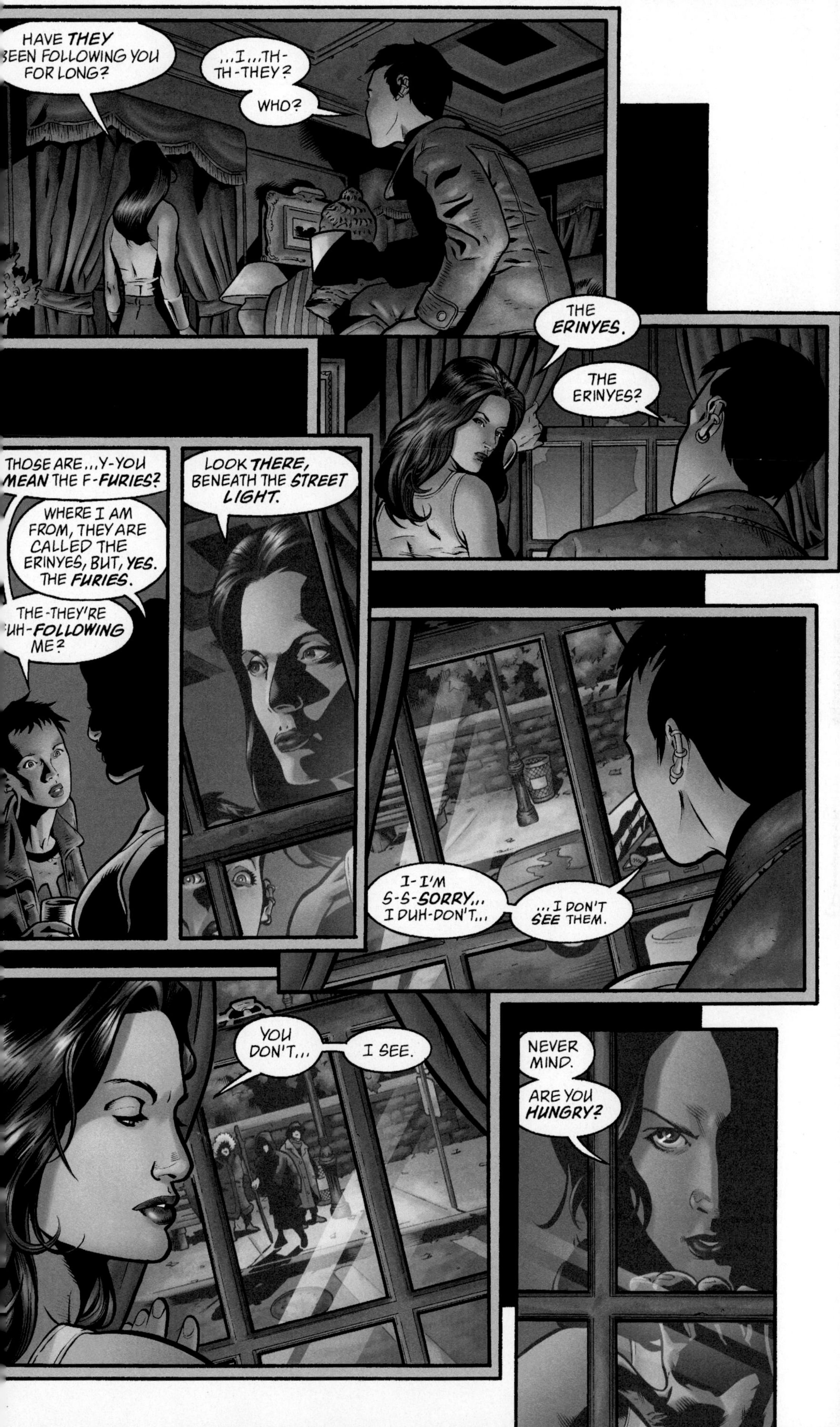
HAVE THEY BEEN FOLLOWING YOU FOR LONG?
...I...TH-TH-THEY?
WHO?
THE ERINYES.
THE ERINYES?
THOSE ARE...Y-YOU MEAN THE F-FURIES?
WHERE I AM FROM, THEY ARE CALLED THE ERINYES, BUT, YES. THE FURIES.
THE-THEY'RE FUH-FOLLOWING ME?
LOOK THERE, BENEATH THE STREET LIGHT.
I-I'M S-S-SORRY... I DUH-DON'T...
...I DON'T SEE THEM.
YOU DON'T...
I SEE.
NEVER MIND.
ARE YOU HUNGRY?

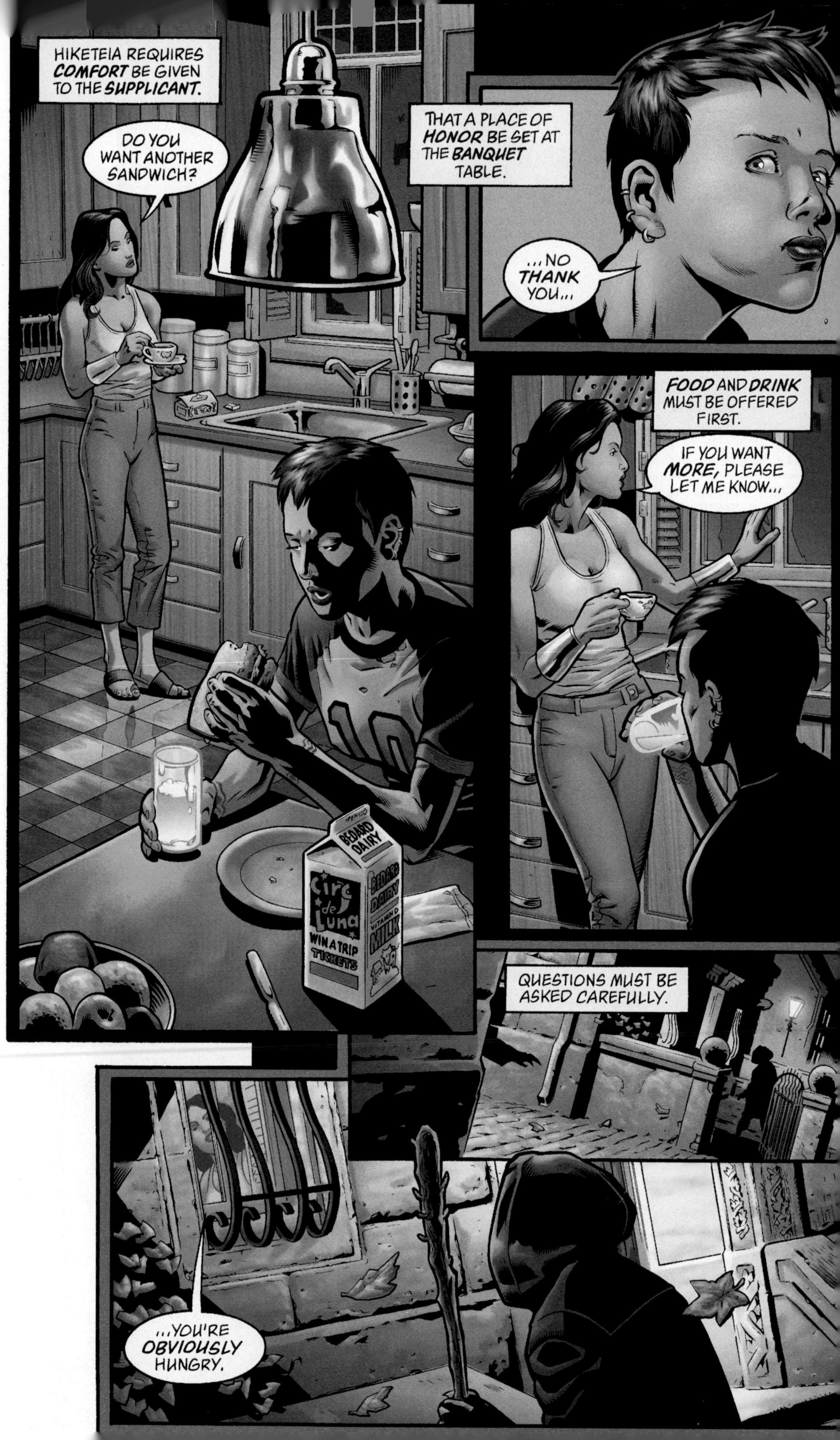
HIKETEIA REQUIRES COMFORT BE GIVEN TO THE SUPPLICANT.
DO YOU WANT ANOTHER SANDWICH?
THAT A PLACE OF HONOR BE SET AT THE BANQUET TABLE.
...NO THANK YOU...
FOOD AND DRINK MUST BE OFFERED FIRST.
IF YOU WANT MORE, PLEASE LET ME KNOW...
QUESTIONS MUST BE ASKED CAREFULLY.
...YOU'RE OBVIOUSLY HUNGRY.
BEDARD DAIRY
Cirque de Luna
WIN A TRIP
TICKETS
VITAMIN D
MILK

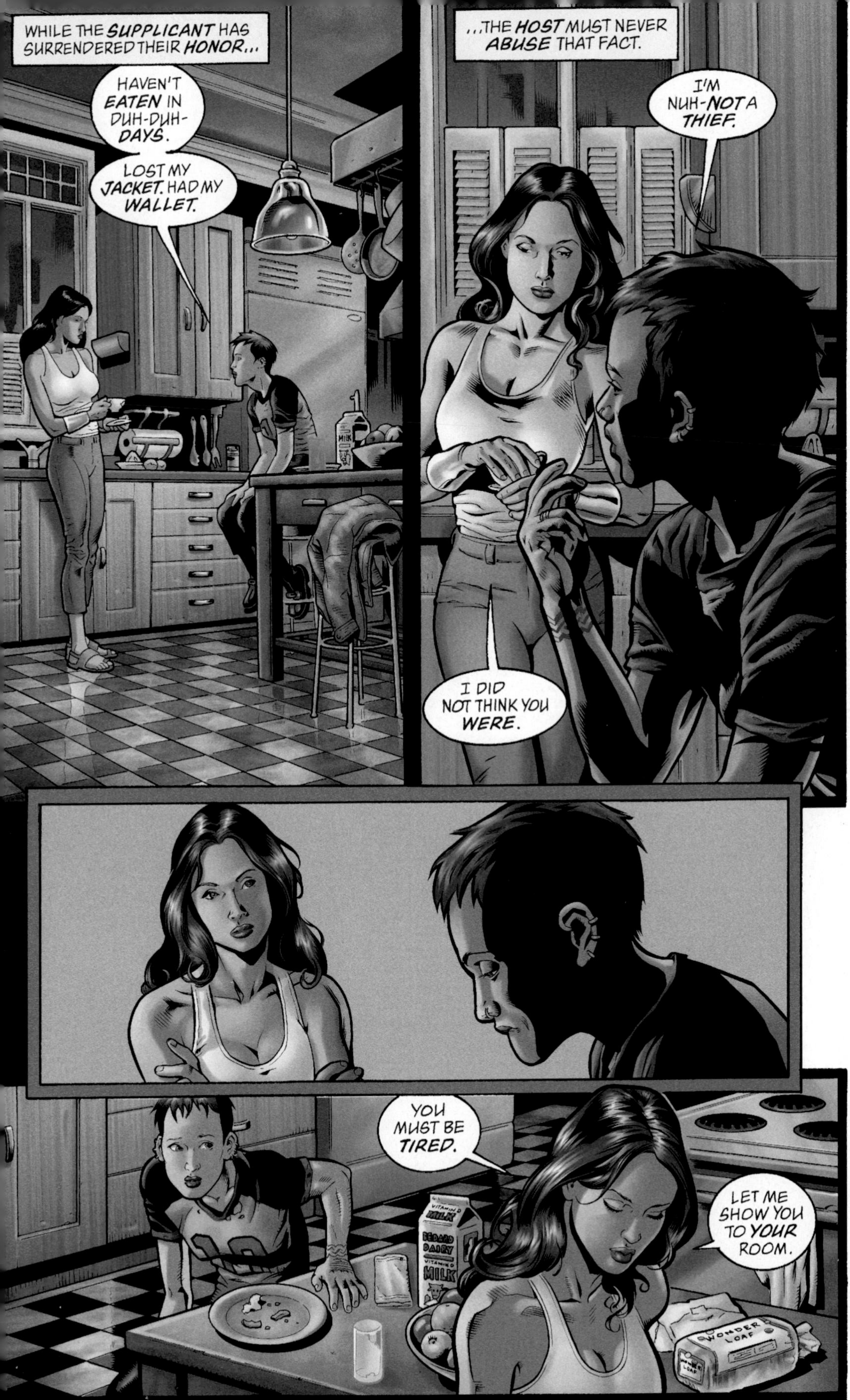
WHILE THE SUPPLICANT HAS SURRENDERED THEIR HONOR...
HAVEN'T EATEN IN DUH-DUH-DAYS.
LOST MY JACKET. HAD MY WALLET.
...THE HOST MUST NEVER ABUSE THAT FACT.
I'M NUH-NOT A THIEF.
I DID NOT THINK YOU WERE.
YOU MUST BE TIRED.
LET ME SHOW YOU TO YOUR ROOM.

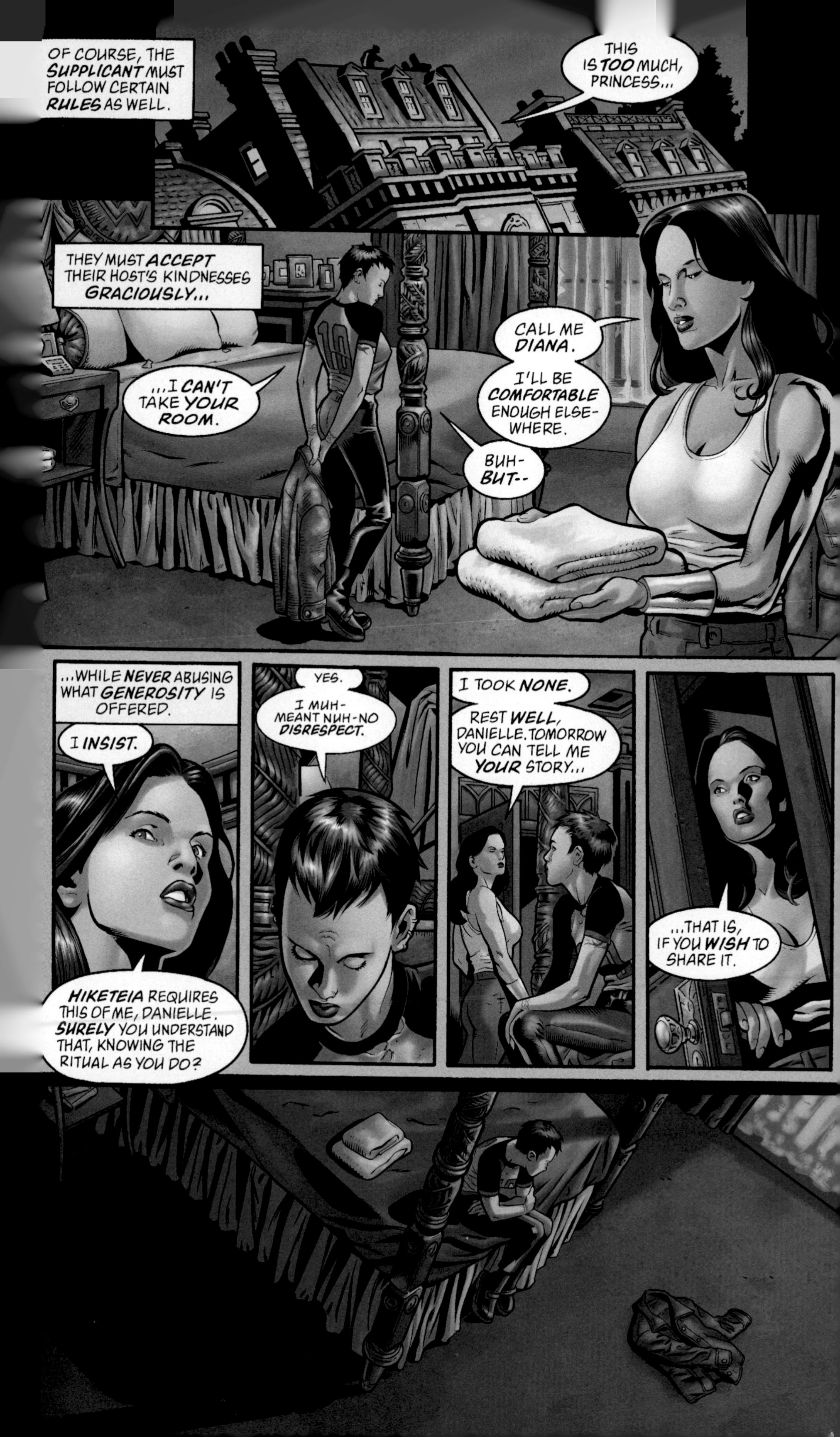
OF COURSE, THE SUPPLICANT MUST FOLLOW CERTAIN RULES AS WELL.
THIS IS TOO MUCH, PRINCESS...
THEY MUST ACCEPT THEIR HOST'S KINDNESSES GRACIOUSLY...
...I CAN'T TAKE YOUR ROOM.
CALL ME DIANA.
I'LL BE COMFORTABLE ENOUGH ELSE-WHERE.
BUH-BUT--
...WHILE NEVER ABUSING WHAT GENEROSITY IS OFFERED.
I INSIST.
HIKETEIA REQUIRES THIS OF ME, DANIELLE. SURELY YOU UNDERSTAND THAT, KNOWING THE RITUAL AS YOU DO?
YES.
I MUH-MEANT NUH-NO DISRESPECT.
I TOOK NONE.
REST WELL, DANIELLE. TOMORROW YOU CAN TELL ME YOUR STORY...
...THAT IS, IF YOU WISH TO SHARE IT.

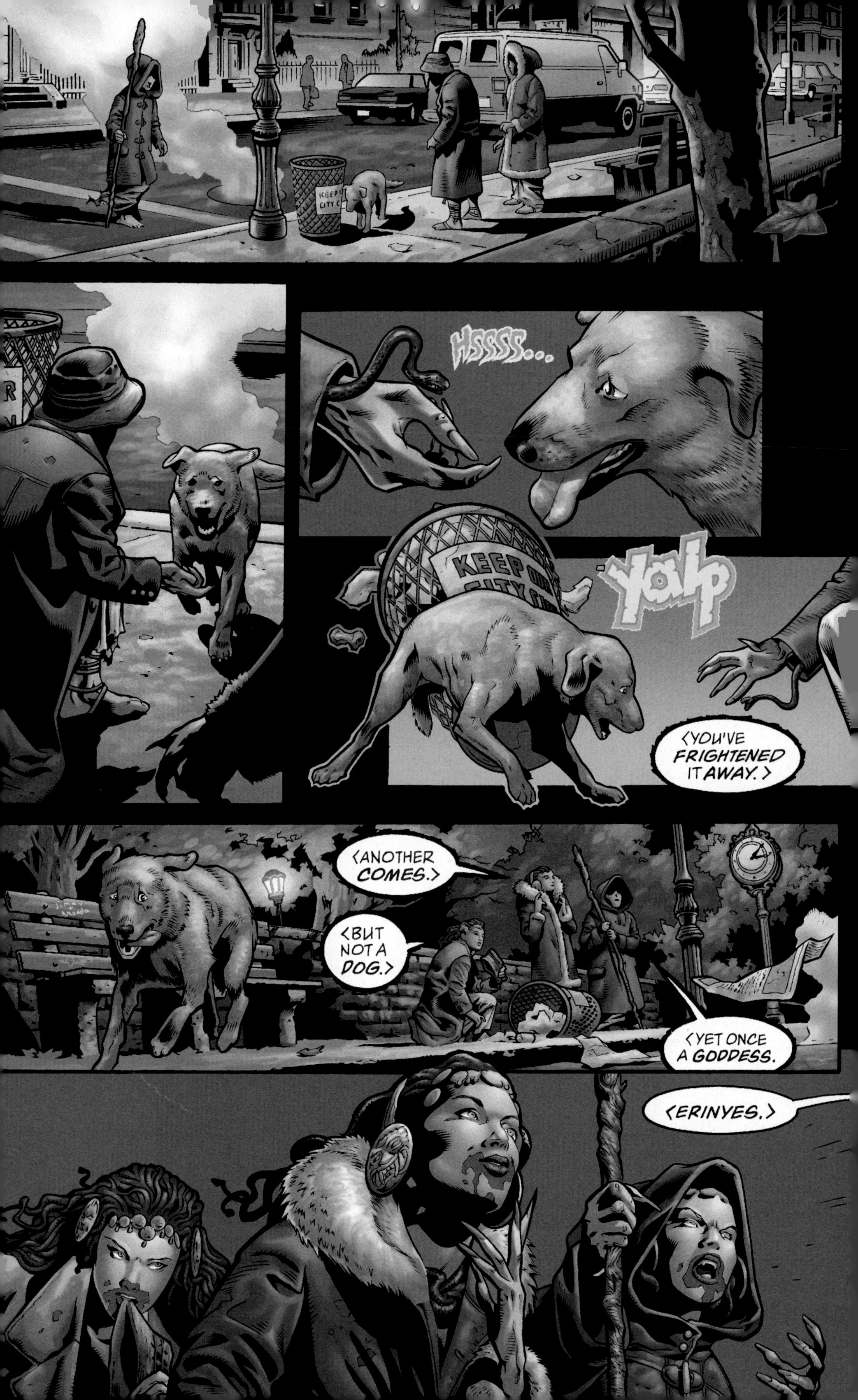
KEEP CITY C
HSSSS...
KEEP
YAIP
<YOU'VE FRIGHTENED IT AWAY.>
<ANOTHER COMES.>
<BUT NOT A DOG.>
<YET ONCE A GODDESS.
<ERINYES.>

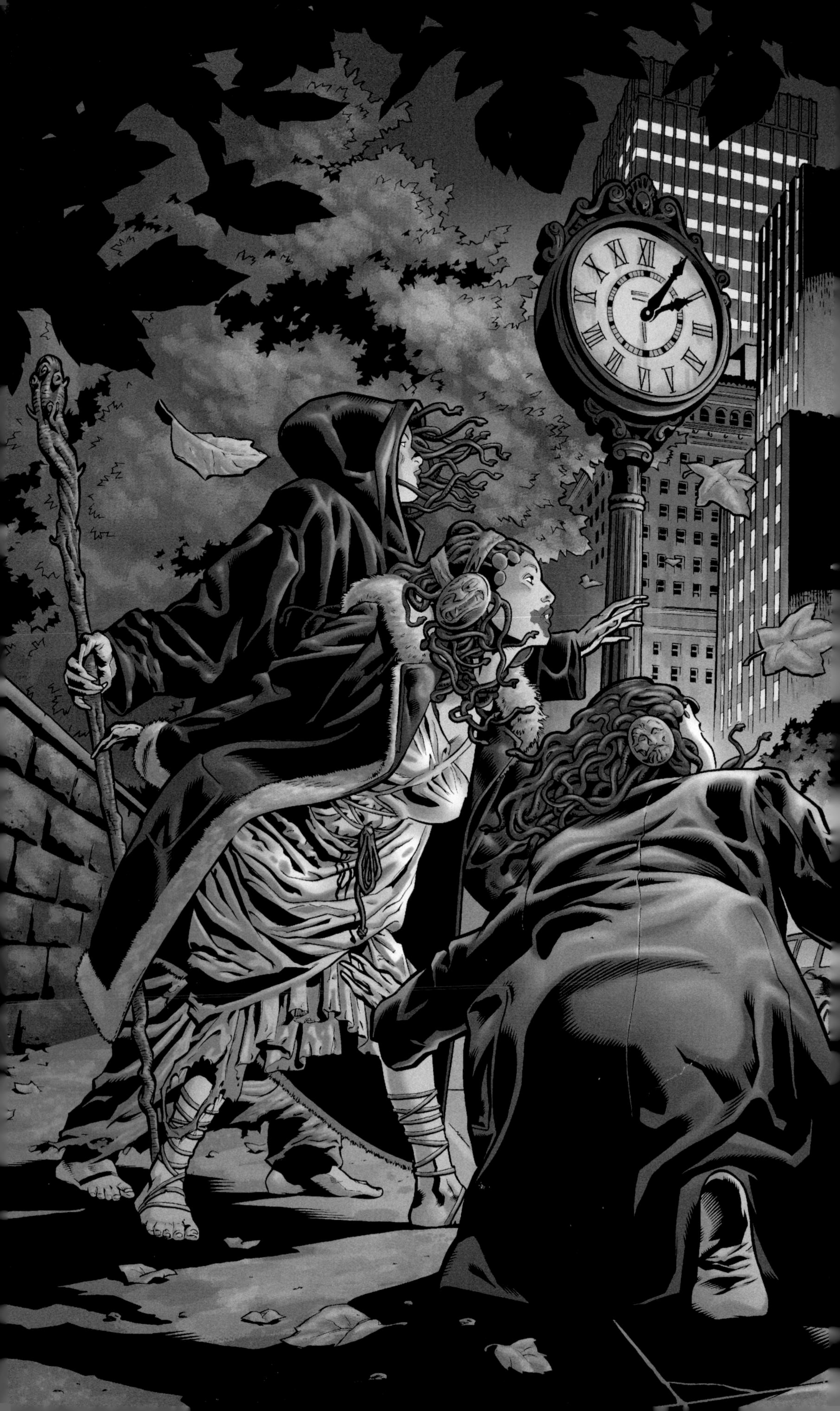

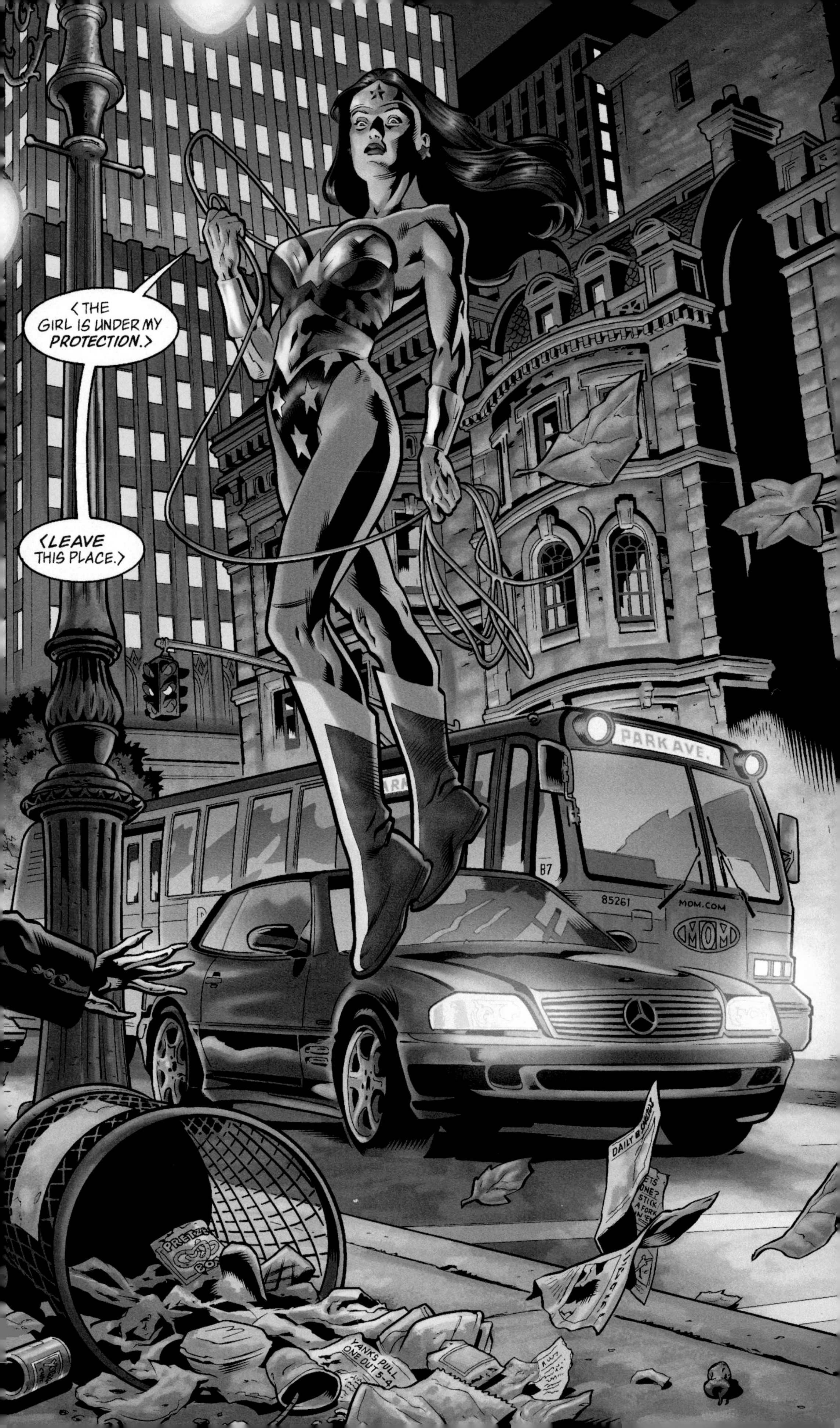
<THE GIRL IS UNDER MY PROTECTION.>
<LEAVE THIS PLACE.>
PARK AVE.
B7
85261
MOM.COM
MOM
YANKS PULL ONE OUT 5-4

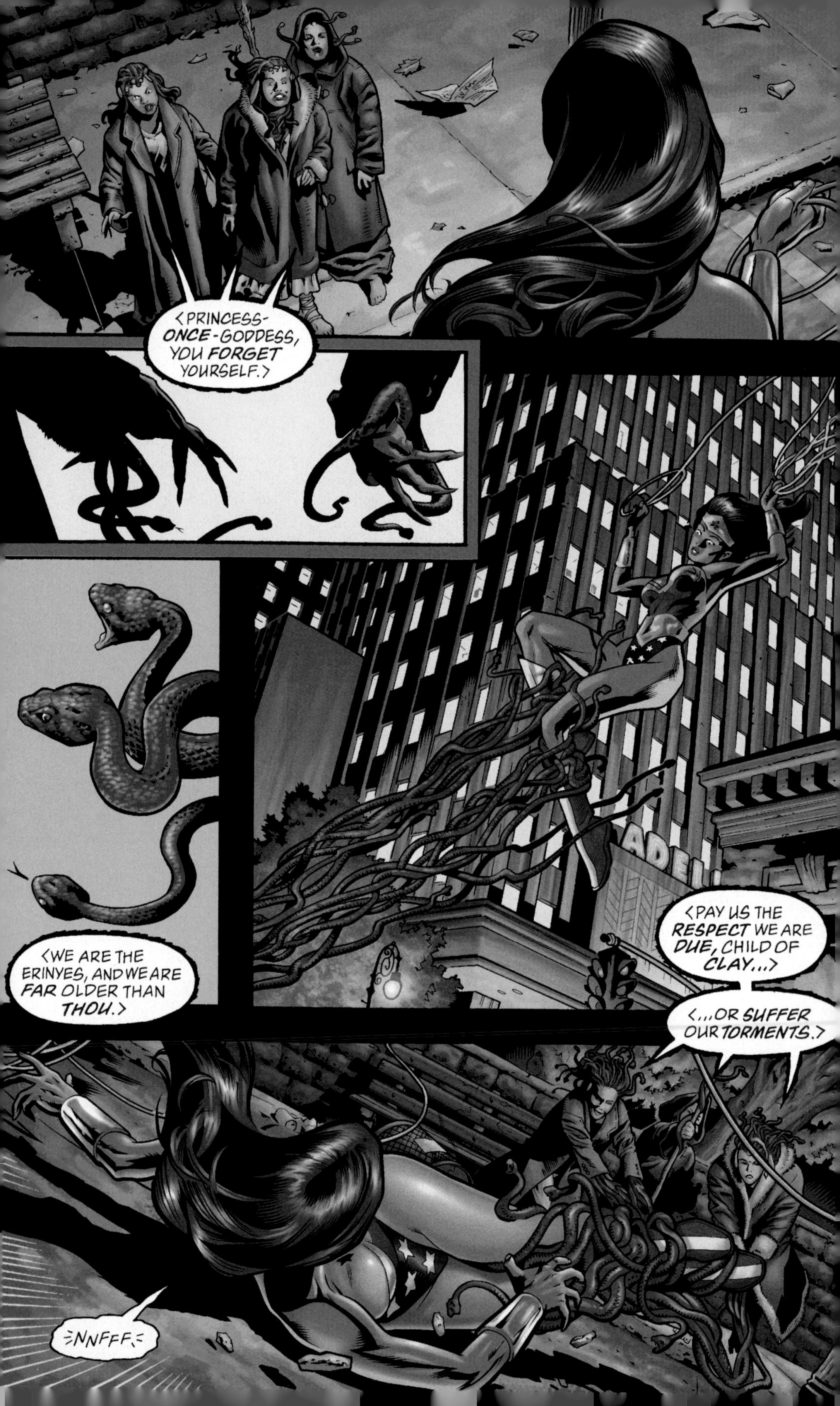

<PRINCESS-ONCE-GODDESS, YOU FORGET YOURSELF.>
<WE ARE THE ERINYES, AND WE ARE FAR OLDER THAN THOU.>
<PAY US THE RESPECT WE ARE DUE, CHILD OF CLAY...>
<...OR SUFFER OUR TORMENTS.>
=NNFFF=

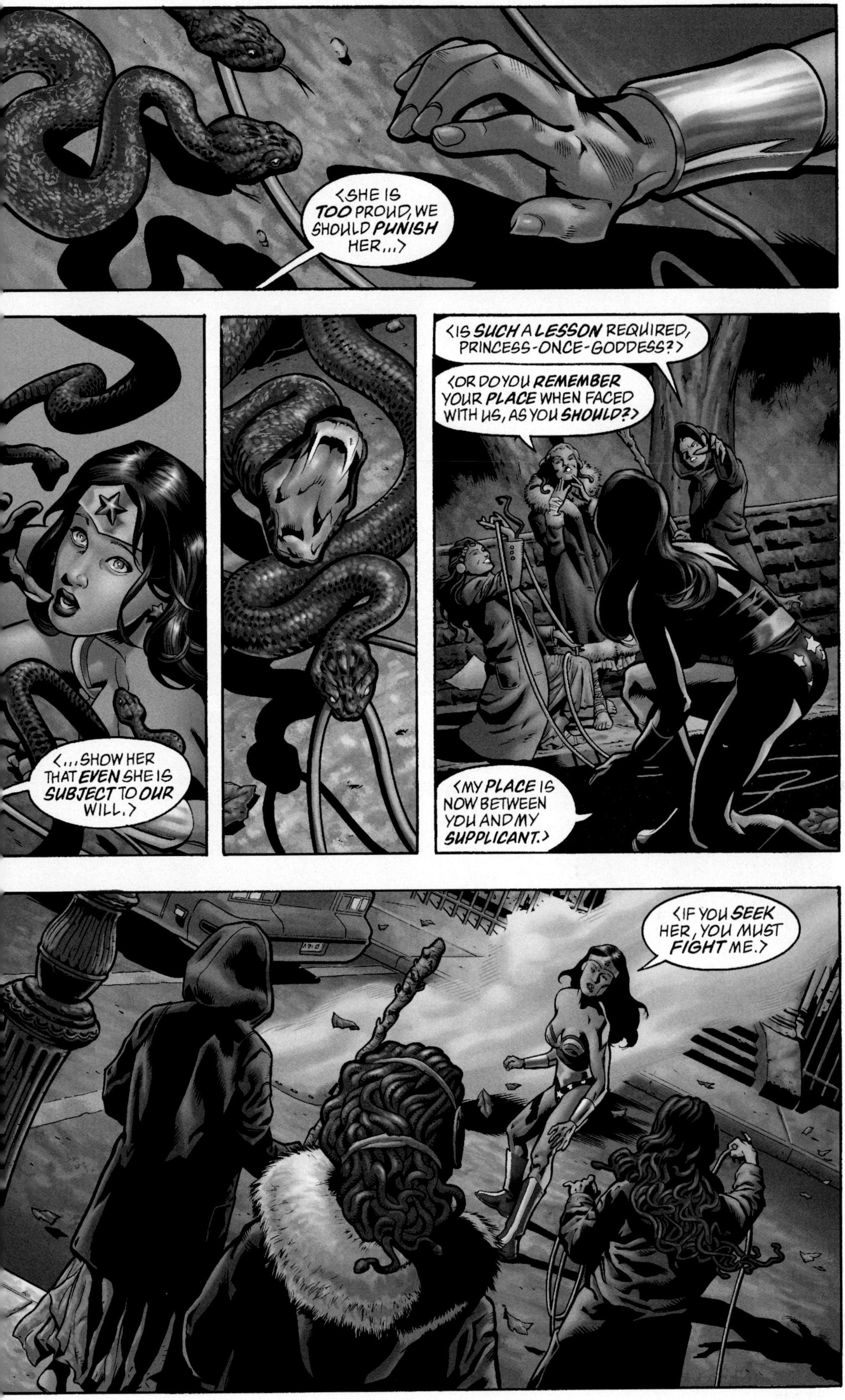

<SHE IS TOO PROUD, WE SHOULD PUNISH HER...>
<...SHOW HER THAT EVEN SHE IS SUBJECT TO OUR WILL.>
<IS SUCH A LESSON REQUIRED, PRINCESS-ONCE-GODDESS?>
<OR DO YOU REMEMBER YOUR PLACE WHEN FACED WITH US, AS YOU SHOULD?>
<MY PLACE IS NOW BETWEEN YOU AND MY SUPPLICANT.>
<IF YOU SEEK HER, YOU MUST FIGHT ME.>

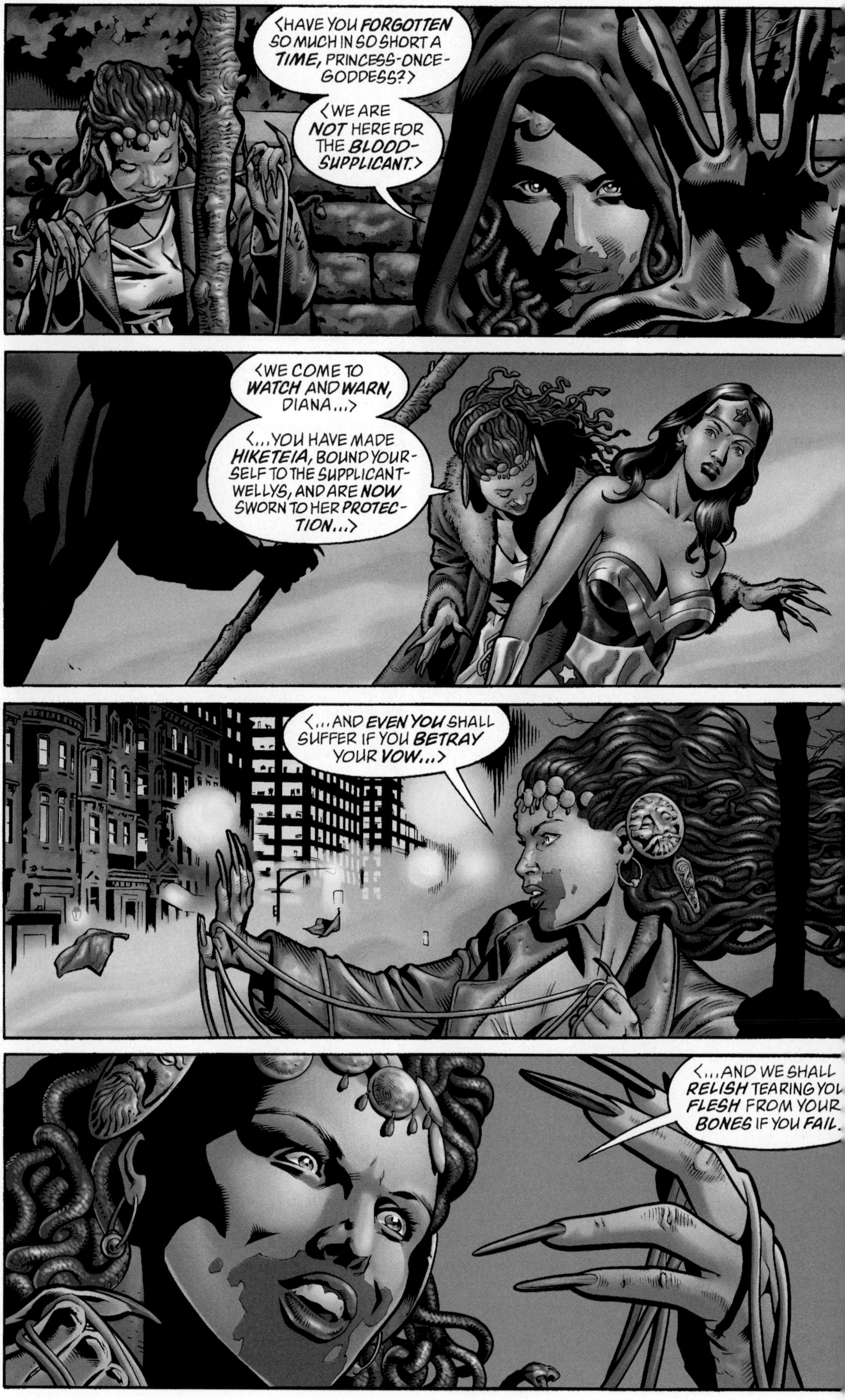
<HAVE YOU FORGOTTEN SO MUCH IN SO SHORT A TIME, PRINCESS-ONCE-GODDESS?>
<WE ARE NOT HERE FOR THE BLOOD-SUPPLICANT.>
<WE COME TO WATCH AND WARN, DIANA...>
<...YOU HAVE MADE HIKETEIA, BOUND YOURSELF TO THE SUPPLICANT-WELLYS, AND ARE NOW SWORN TO HER PROTECTION...>
<...AND EVEN YOU SHALL SUFFER IF YOU BETRAY YOUR VOW...>
<...AND WE SHALL RELISH TEARING YOU FLESH FROM YOUR BONES IF YOU FAIL.

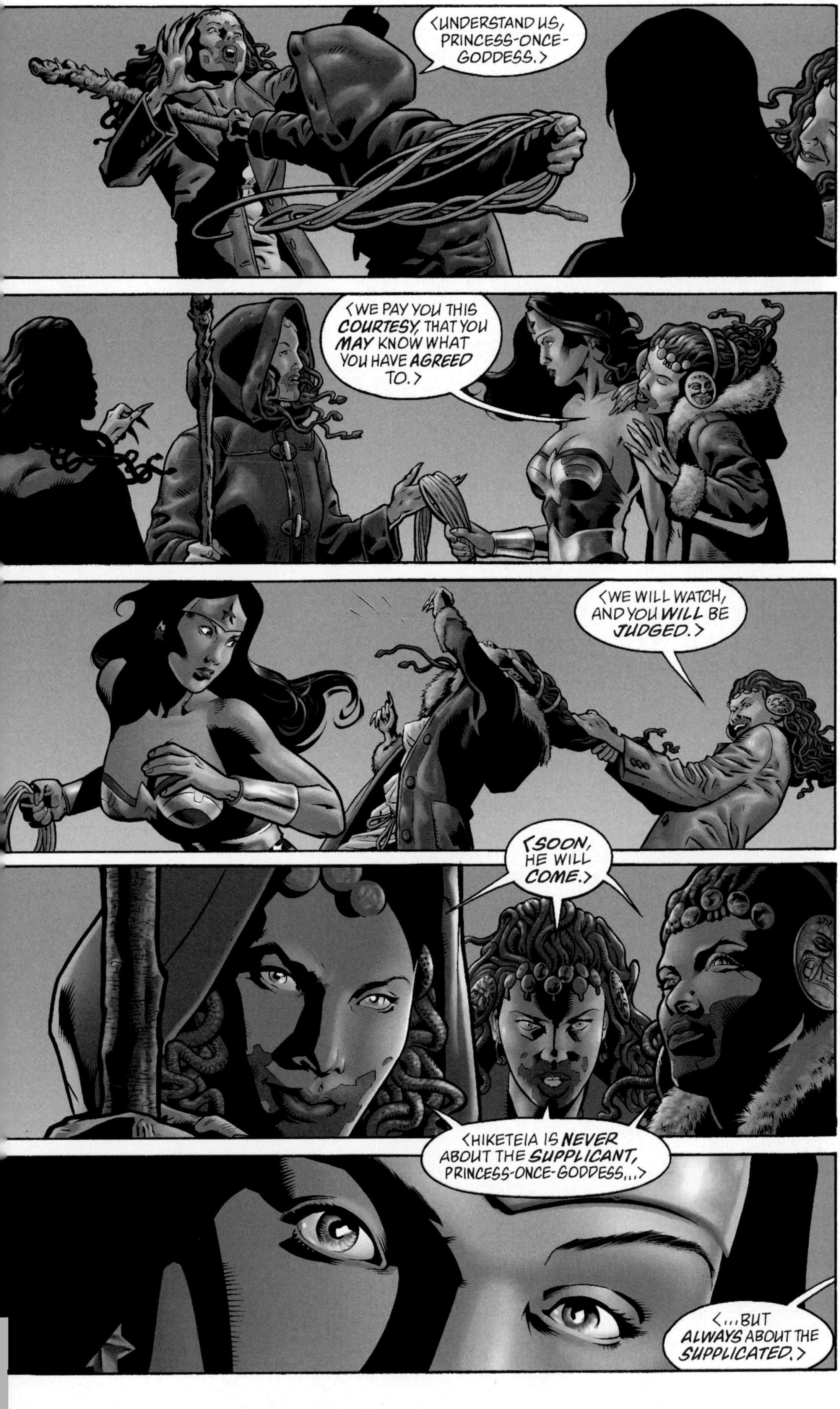

<UNDERSTAND US, PRINCESS-ONCE-GODDESS.>
<WE PAY YOU THIS COURTESY, THAT YOU MAY KNOW WHAT YOU HAVE AGREED TO.>
<WE WILL WATCH, AND YOU WILL BE JUDGED.>
<SOON, HE WILL COME.>
<HIKETEIA IS NEVER ABOUT THE SUPPLICANT, PRINCESS-ONCE-GODDESS...>
<...BUT ALWAYS ABOUT THE SUPPLICATED.>

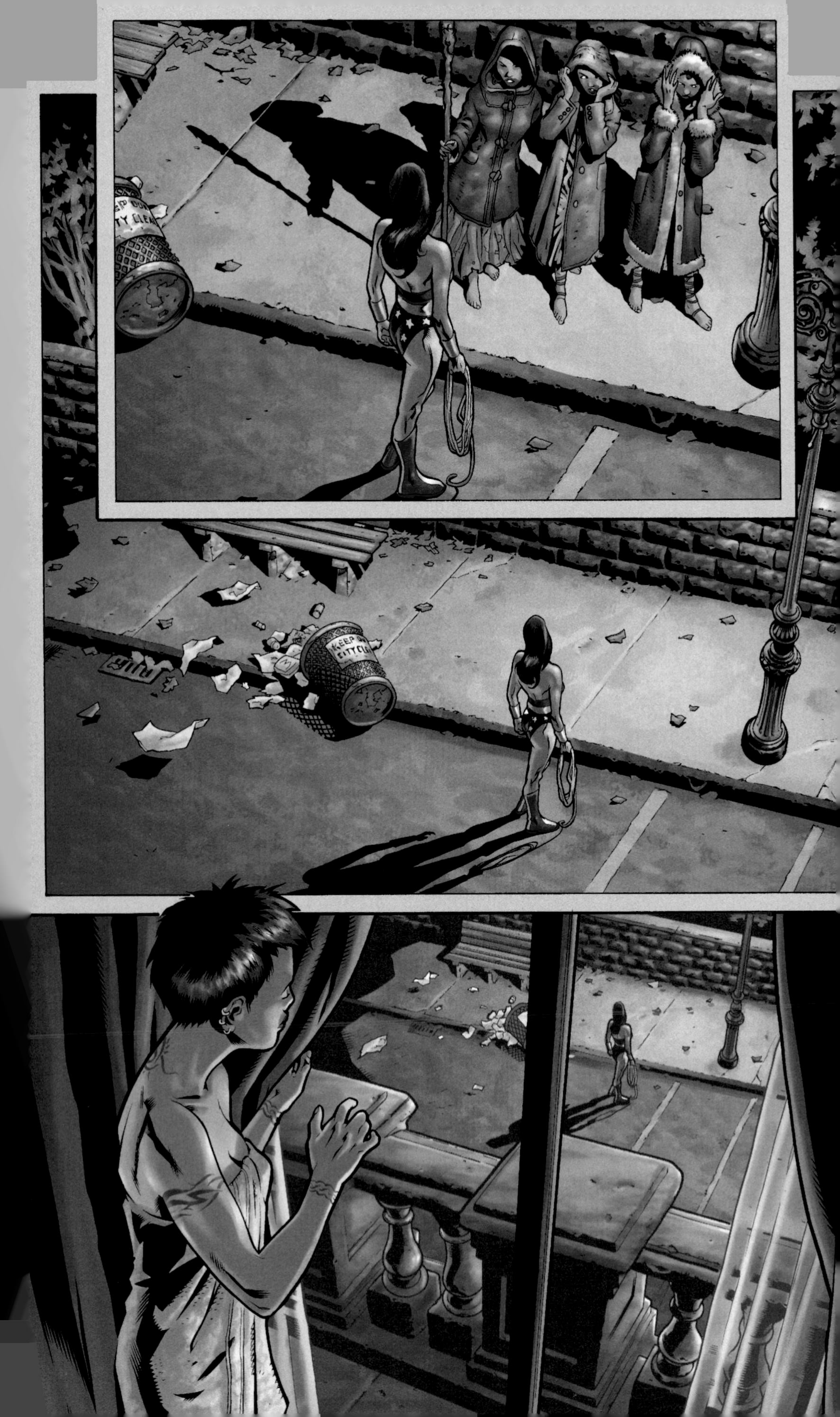

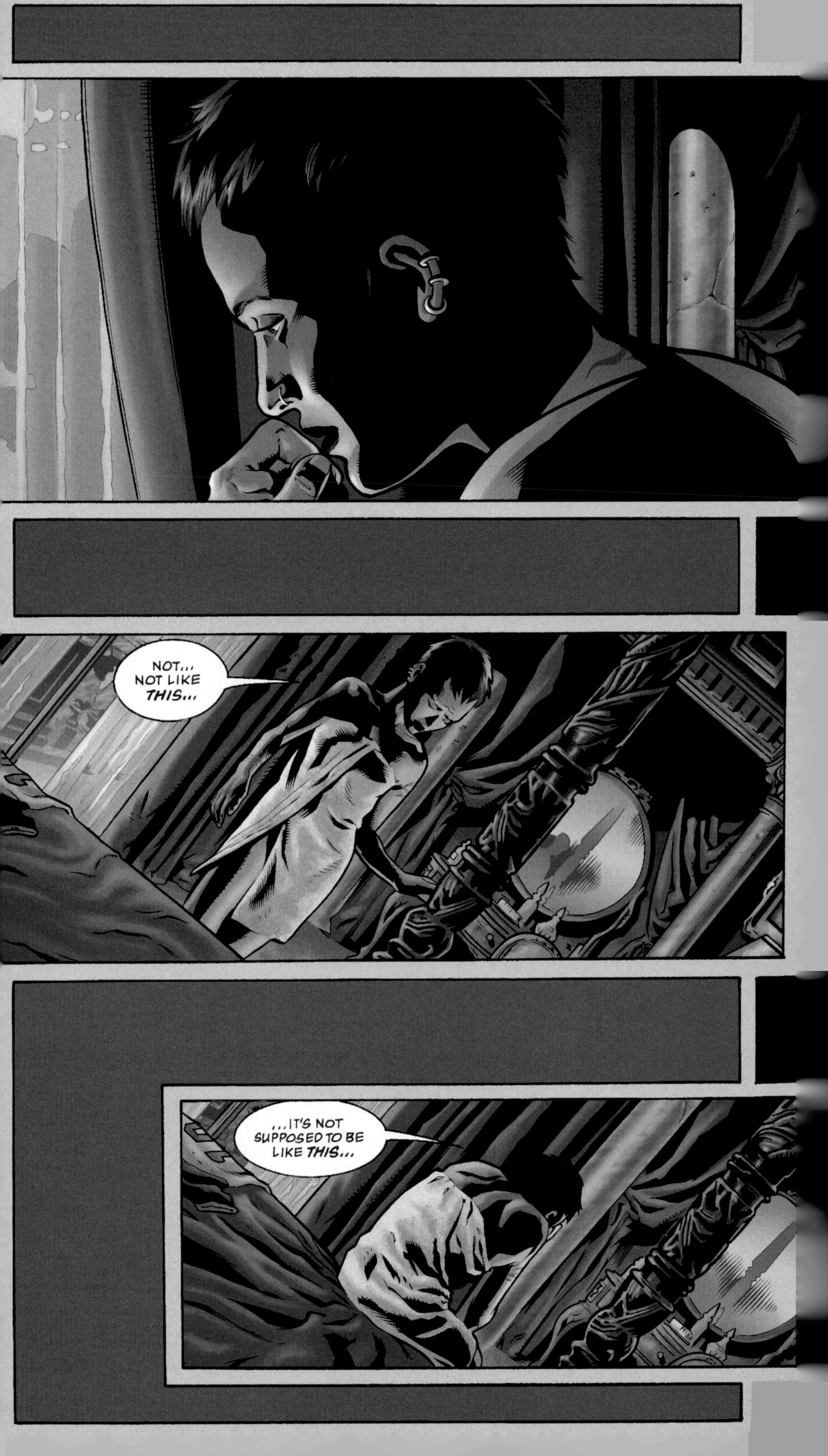
NOT...
NOT LIKE
THIS...
...IT'S NOT
SUPPOSED TO BE
LIKE *THIS*...

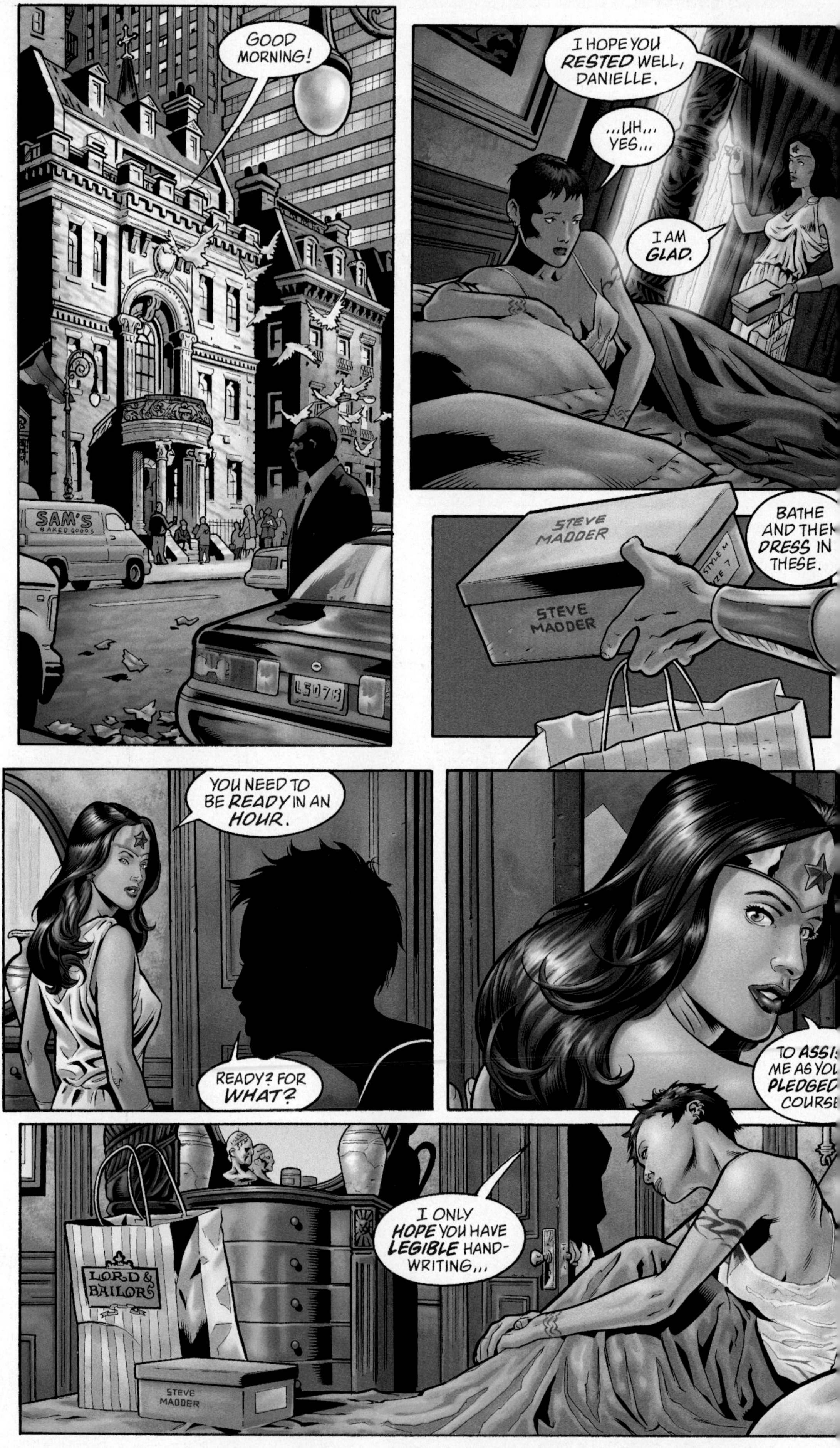
GOOD MORNING!
SAM'S BAKED GOODS
I HOPE YOU RESTED WELL, DANIELLE.
...UH... YES...
I AM GLAD.
STEVE MADDER
STEVE MADDER
BATHE AND THEN DRESS IN THESE.
YOU NEED TO BE READY IN AN HOUR.
READY? FOR WHAT?
TO ASSIS ME AS YOU PLEDGED COURSE
LORD & BAILOR
STEVE MADDER
I ONLY HOPE YOU HAVE LEGIBLE HAND-WRITING...

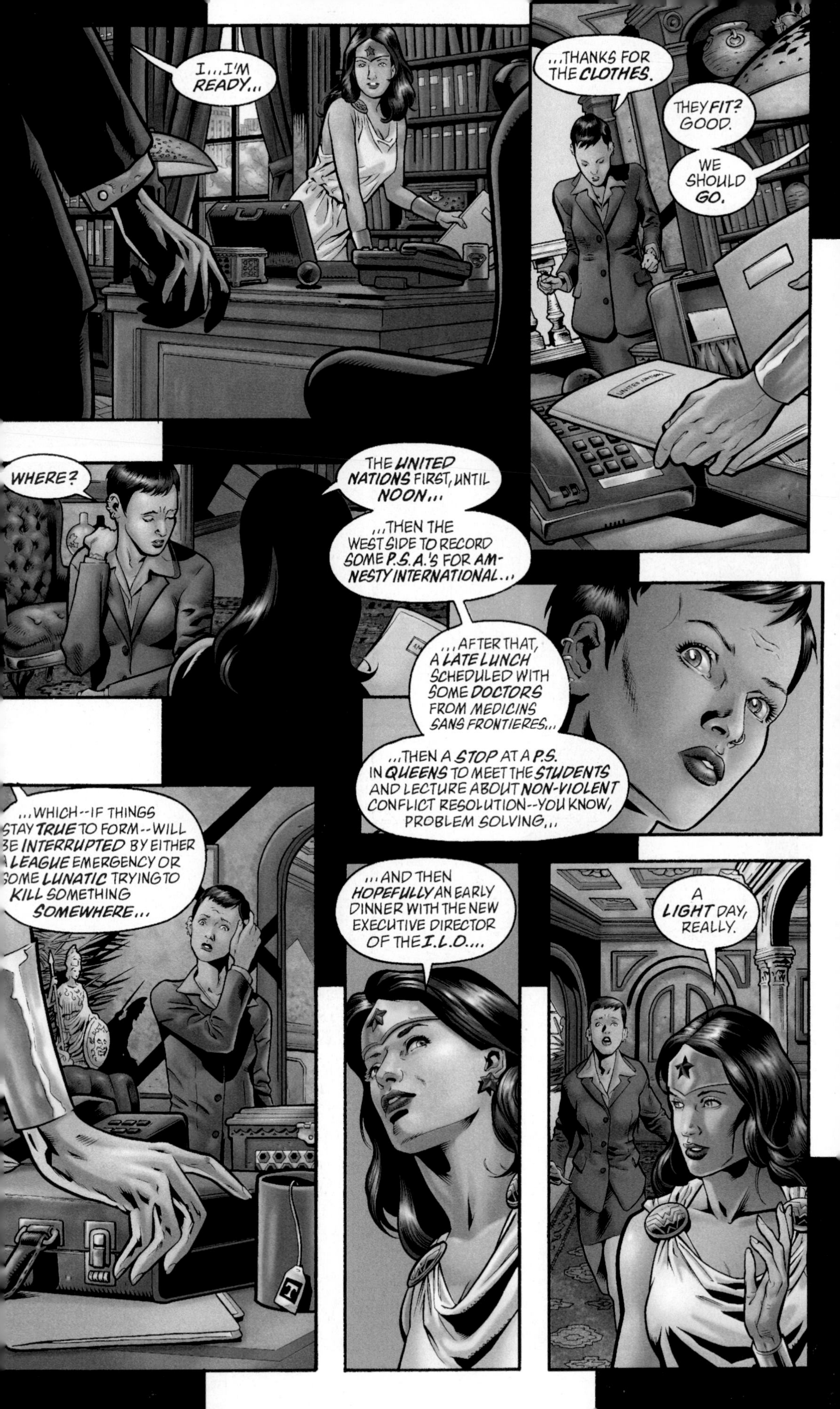
I...I'M READY...
...THANKS FOR THE CLOTHES.
THEY FIT? GOOD.
WE SHOULD GO.
WHERE?
THE UNITED NATIONS FIRST, UNTIL NOON...
...THEN THE WEST SIDE TO RECORD SOME P.S.A.'S FOR AMNESTY INTERNATIONAL...
...AFTER THAT, A LATE LUNCH SCHEDULED WITH SOME DOCTORS FROM MEDICINS SANS FRONTIERES...
...THEN A STOP AT A P.S. IN QUEENS TO MEET THE STUDENTS AND LECTURE ABOUT NON-VIOLENT CONFLICT RESOLUTION--YOU KNOW, PROBLEM SOLVING...
...WHICH--IF THINGS STAY TRUE TO FORM--WILL BE INTERRUPTED BY EITHER A LEAGUE EMERGENCY OR SOME LUNATIC TRYING TO KILL SOMETHING SOMEWHERE...
...AND THEN HOPEFULLY AN EARLY DINNER WITH THE NEW EXECUTIVE DIRECTOR OF THE I.L.O....
A LIGHT DAY, REALLY.

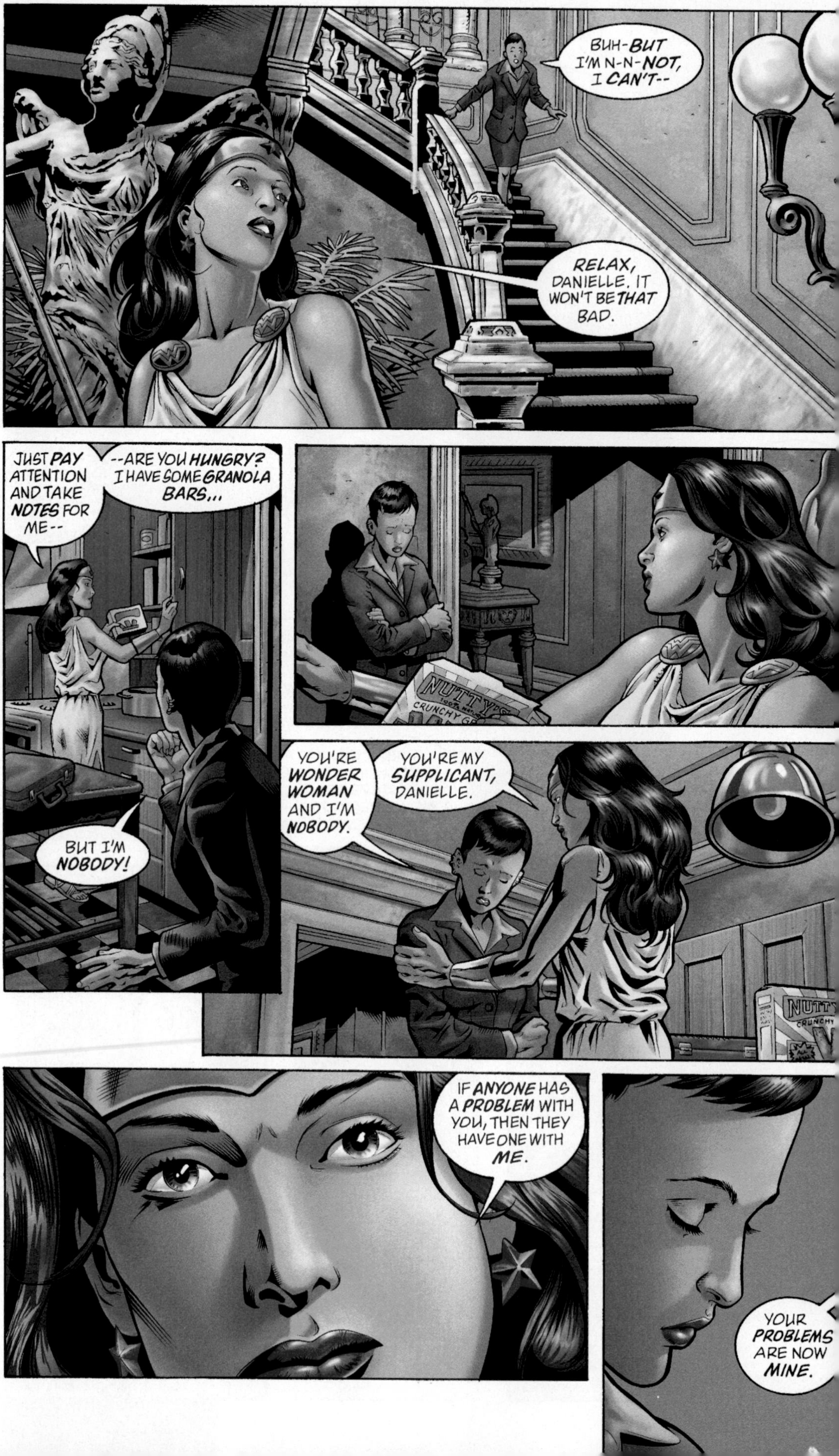
BUH-BUT I'M N-N-NOT, I CAN'T--
RELAX, DANIELLE. IT WON'T BE THAT BAD.
JUST PAY ATTENTION AND TAKE NOTES FOR ME--
--ARE YOU HUNGRY? I HAVE SOME GRANOLA BARS...
BUT I'M NOBODY!
NUTTY'S CRUNCHY
YOU'RE WONDER WOMAN AND I'M NOBODY.
YOU'RE MY SUPPLICANT, DANIELLE.
IF ANYONE HAS A PROBLEM WITH YOU, THEN THEY HAVE ONE WITH ME.
YOUR PROBLEMS ARE NOW MINE.

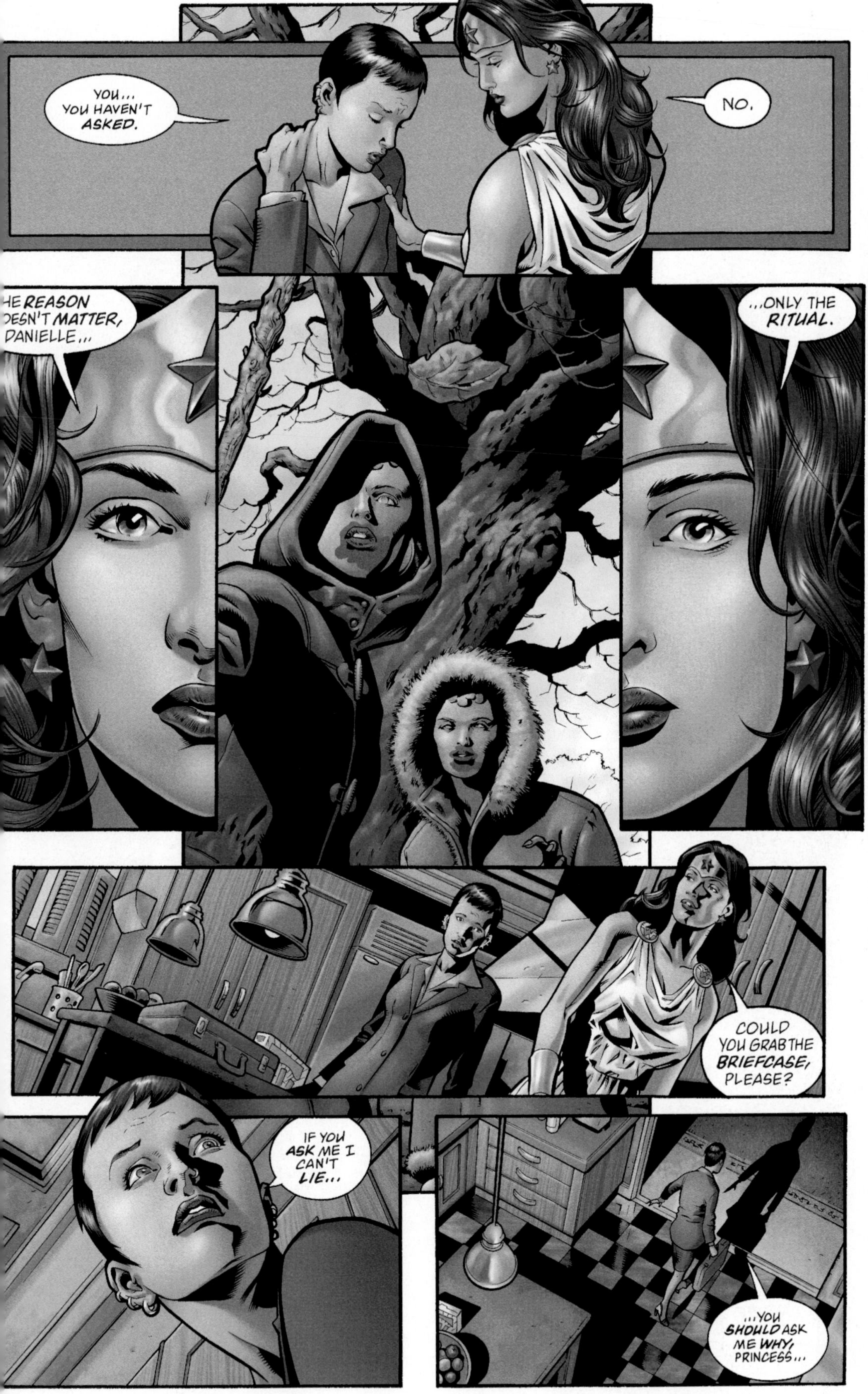
YOU...
YOU HAVEN'T
ASKED.
NO.
HE REASON
DESN'T MATTER,
DANIELLE...
...ONLY THE
RITUAL.
COULD
YOU GRAB THE
BRIEFCASE,
PLEASE?
IF YOU
ASK ME I
CAN'T
LIE...
...YOU
SHOULD ASK
ME WHY,
PRINCESS...

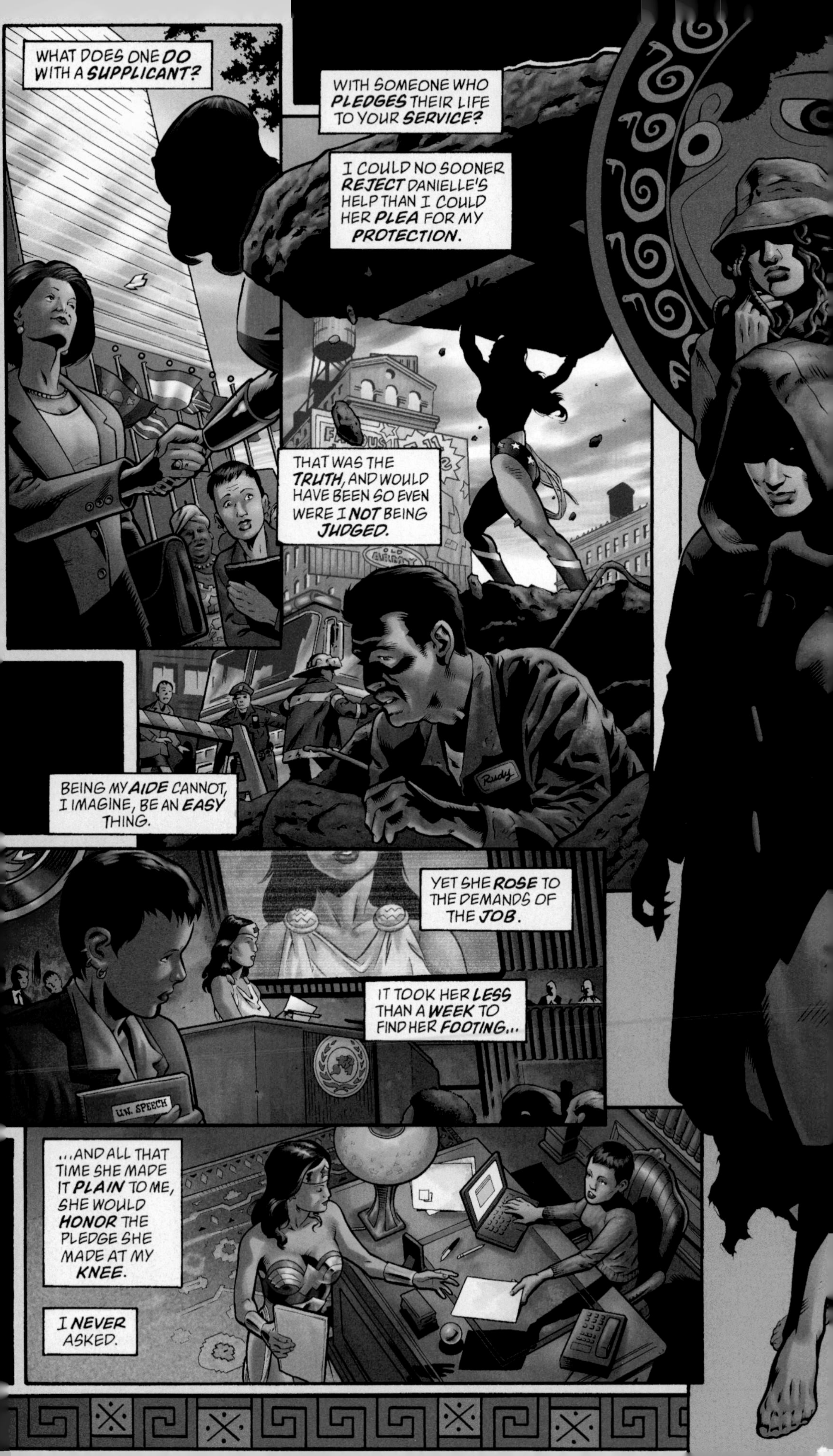
WHAT DOES ONE DO WITH A SUPPLICANT?
WITH SOMEONE WHO PLEDGES THEIR LIFE TO YOUR SERVICE?
I COULD NO SOONER REJECT DANIELLE'S HELP THAN I COULD HER PLEA FOR MY PROTECTION.
THAT WAS THE TRUTH, AND WOULD HAVE BEEN SO EVEN WERE I NOT BEING JUDGED.
Rudy
BEING MY AIDE CANNOT, I IMAGINE, BE AN EASY THING.
YET SHE ROSE TO THE DEMANDS OF THE JOB.
IT TOOK HER LESS THAN A WEEK TO FIND HER FOOTING...
U.N. SPEECH
...AND ALL THAT TIME SHE MADE IT PLAIN TO ME, SHE WOULD HONOR THE PLEDGE SHE MADE AT MY KNEE.
I NEVER ASKED.

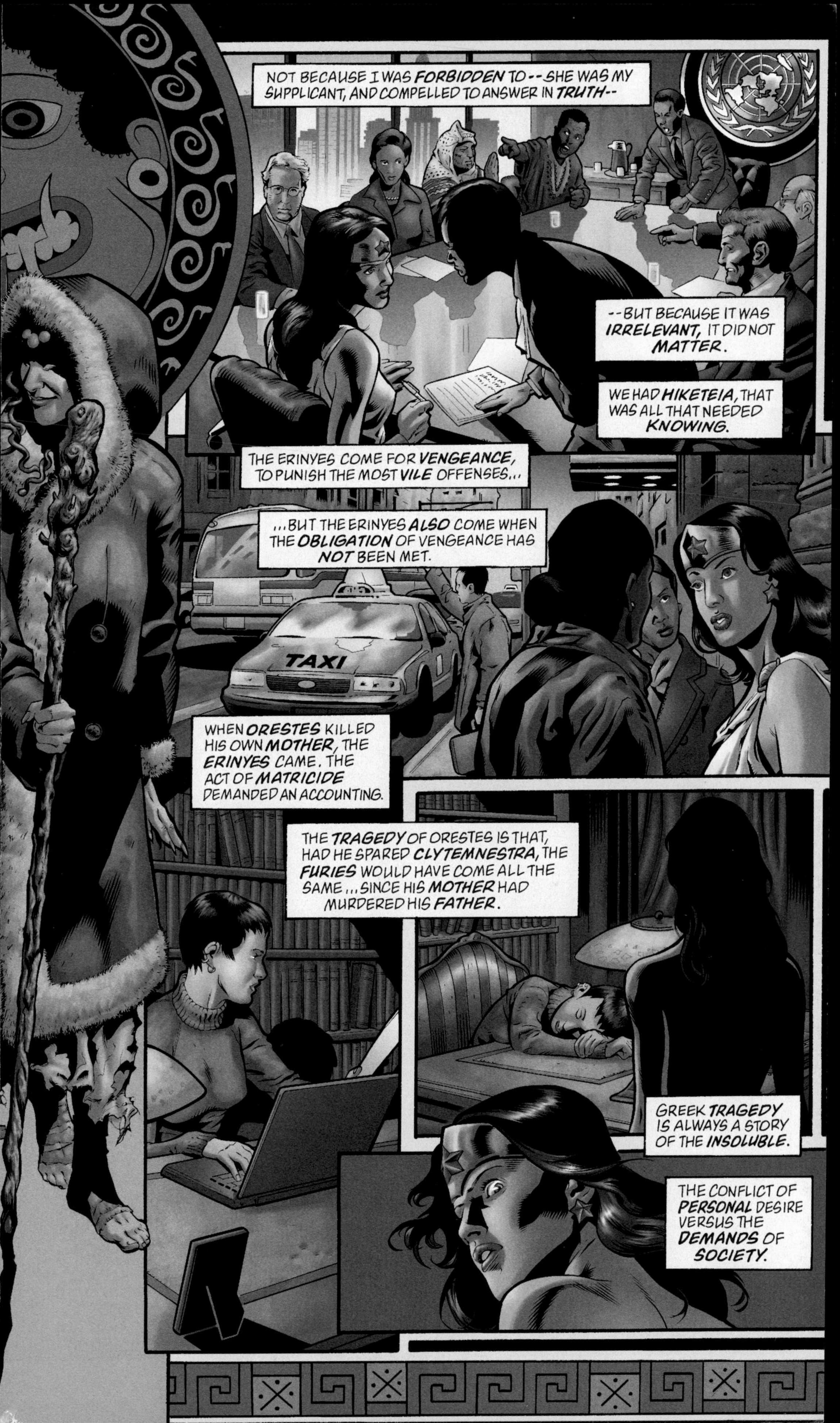
NOT BECAUSE I WAS FORBIDDEN TO -- SHE WAS MY SUPPLICANT, AND COMPELLED TO ANSWER IN TRUTH--
--BUT BECAUSE IT WAS IRRELEVANT, IT DID NOT MATTER.
WE HAD HIKETEIA, THAT WAS ALL THAT NEEDED KNOWING.
THE ERINYES COME FOR VENGEANCE, TO PUNISH THE MOST VILE OFFENSES...
...BUT THE ERINYES ALSO COME WHEN THE OBLIGATION OF VENGEANCE HAS NOT BEEN MET.
TAXI
WHEN ORESTES KILLED HIS OWN MOTHER, THE ERINYES CAME. THE ACT OF MATRICIDE DEMANDED AN ACCOUNTING.
THE TRAGEDY OF ORESTES IS THAT, HAD HE SPARED CLYTEMNESTRA, THE FURIES WOULD HAVE COME ALL THE SAME... SINCE HIS MOTHER HAD MURDERED HIS FATHER.
GREEK TRAGEDY IS ALWAYS A STORY OF THE INSOLUBLE.
THE CONFLICT OF PERSONAL DESIRE VERSUS THE DEMANDS OF SOCIETY.

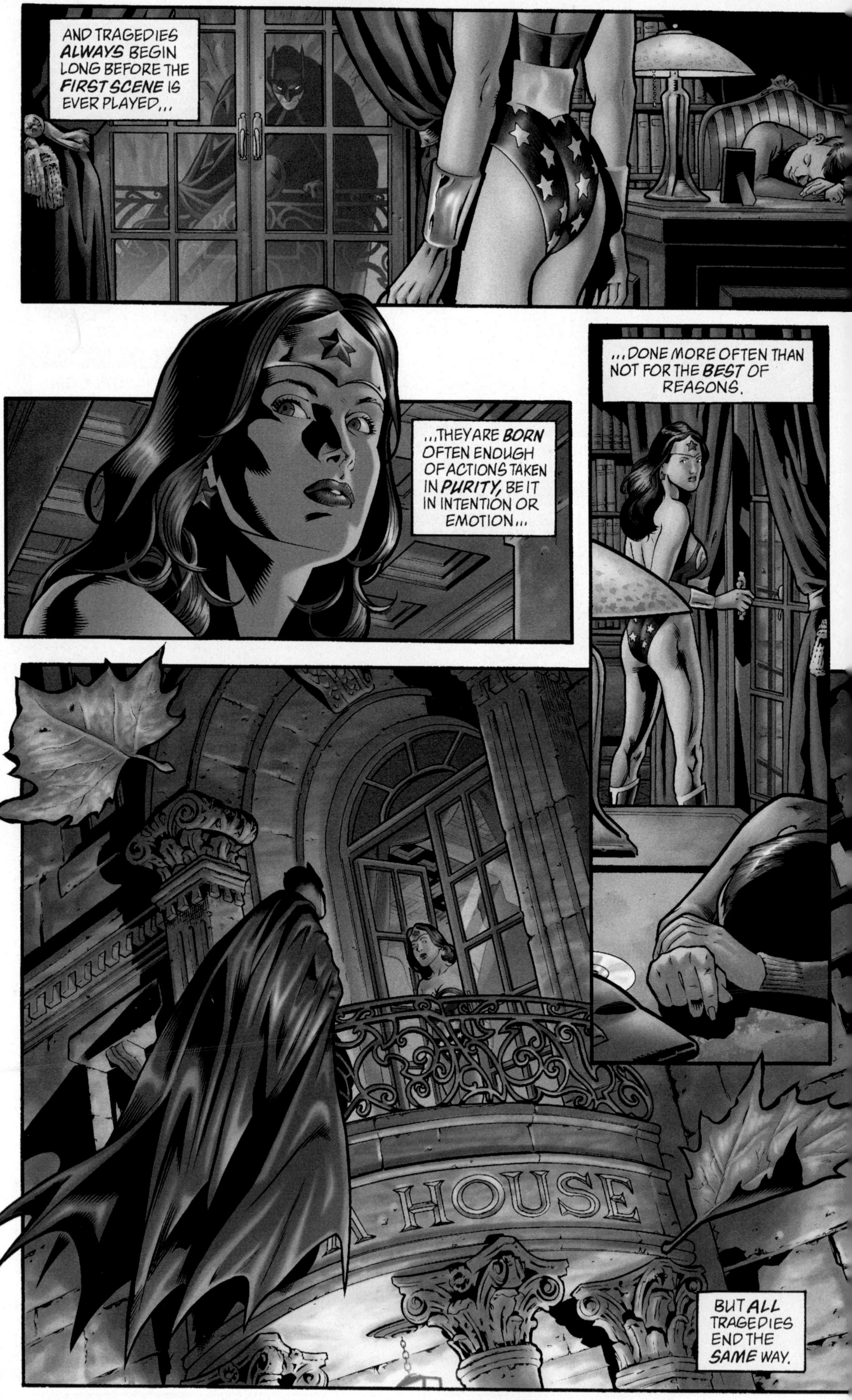

AND TRAGEDIES ALWAYS BEGIN LONG BEFORE THE FIRST SCENE IS EVER PLAYED...
...THEY ARE BORN OFTEN ENOUGH OF ACTIONS TAKEN IN PURITY, BE IT IN INTENTION OR EMOTION...
...DONE MORE OFTEN THAN NOT FOR THE BEST OF REASONS.
HOUSE
BUT ALL TRAGEDIES END THE SAME WAY.

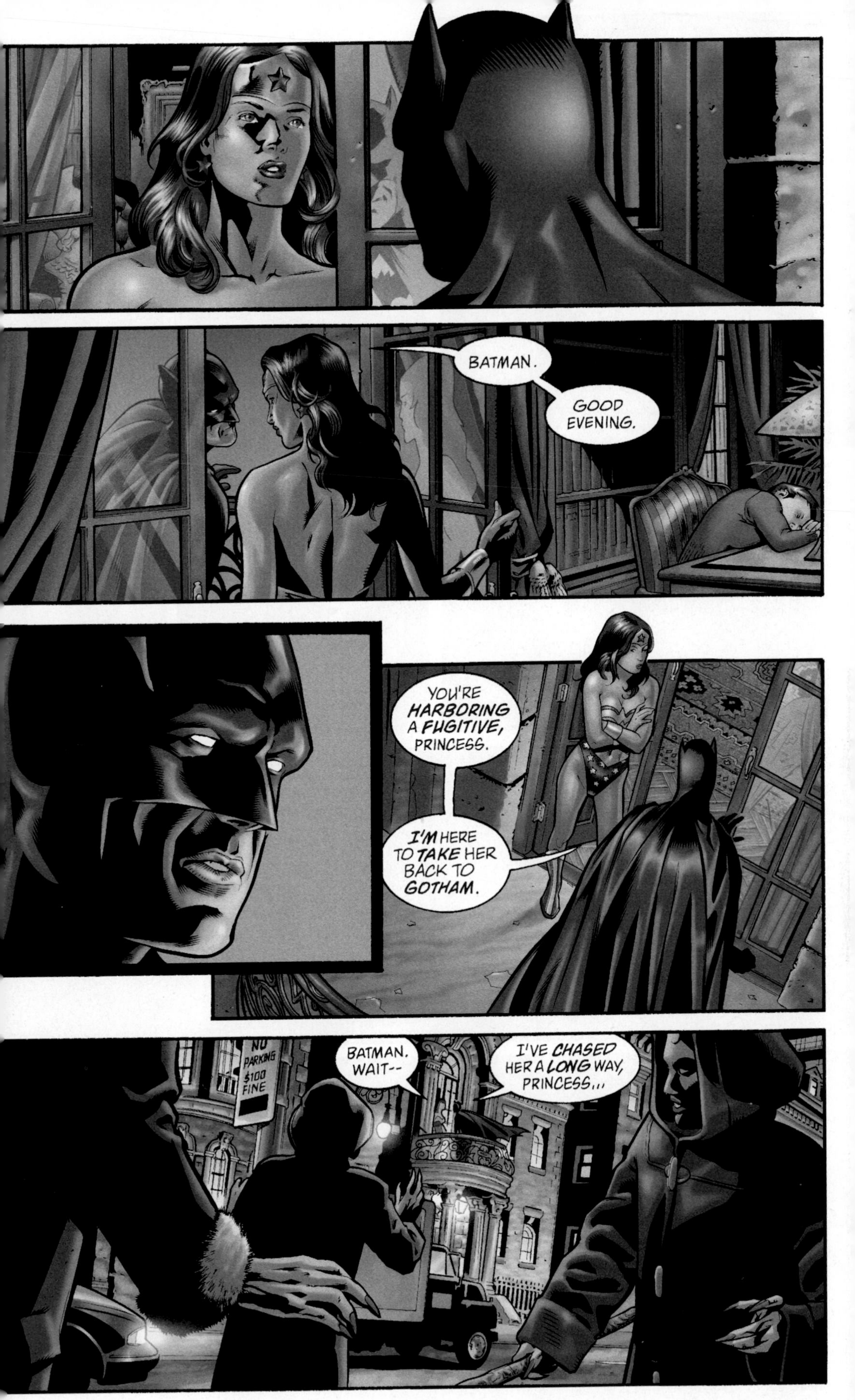
BATMAN.
GOOD EVENING.
YOU'RE HARBORING A FUGITIVE, PRINCESS.
I'M HERE TO TAKE HER BACK TO GOTHAM.
NO PARKING $100 FINE
BATMAN. WAIT--
I'VE CHASED HER A LONG WAY, PRINCESS...

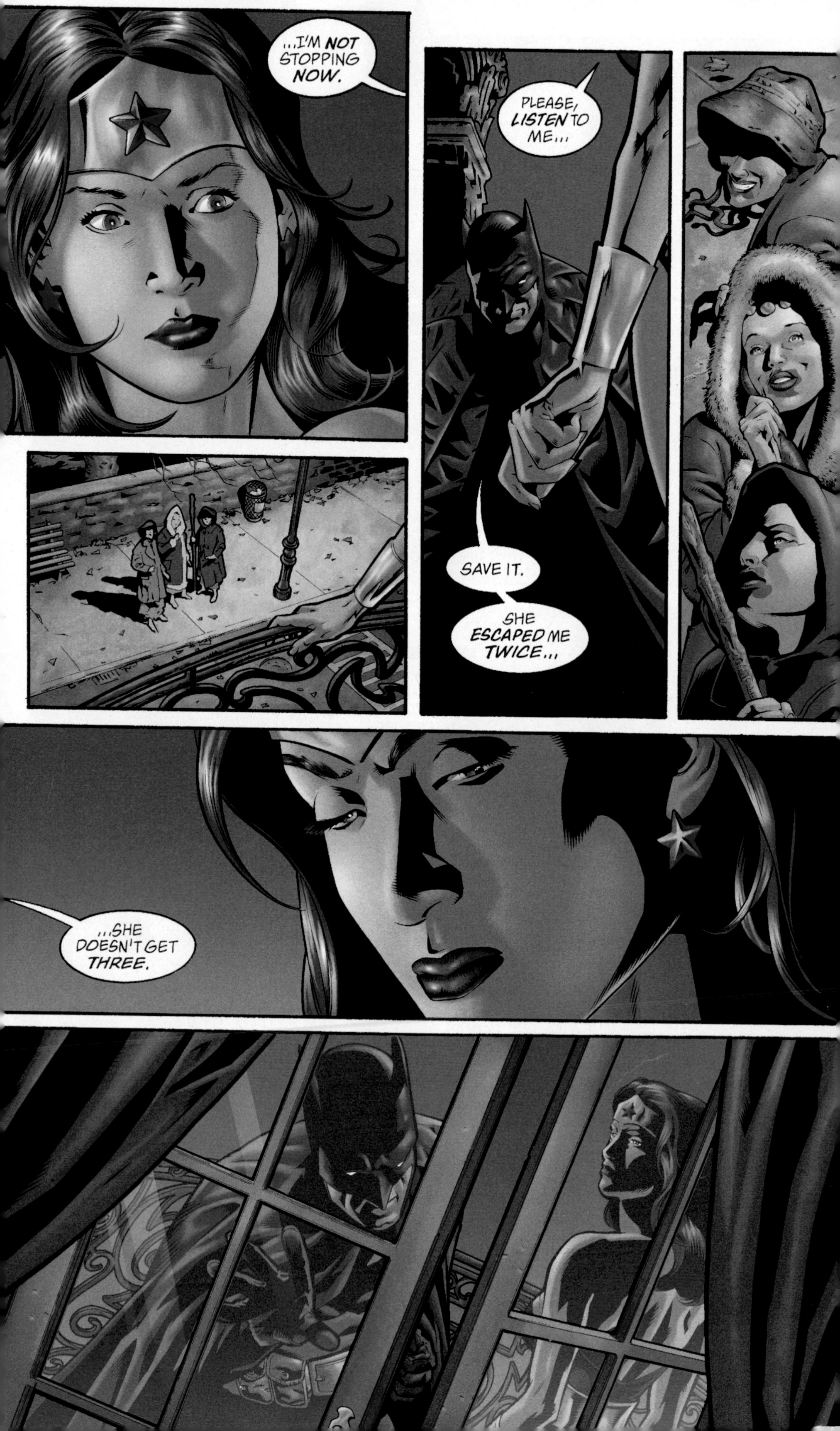
...I'M NOT STOPPING NOW.
PLEASE, LISTEN TO ME...
SAVE IT.
SHE ESCAPED ME TWICE...
...SHE DOESN'T GET THREE.

NO.

I CAN-NOT ALLOW IT.

SHE'S A KILLER, PRINCESS.

IT DOESN'T MATTER.

IT SHOULD.

TO ME, IT CERTAINLY DOES.

NOW IF YOU'LL EXCUSE--

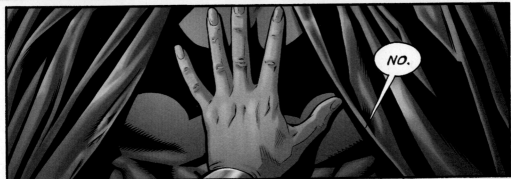

NO.

I CANNOT ALLOW THIS.

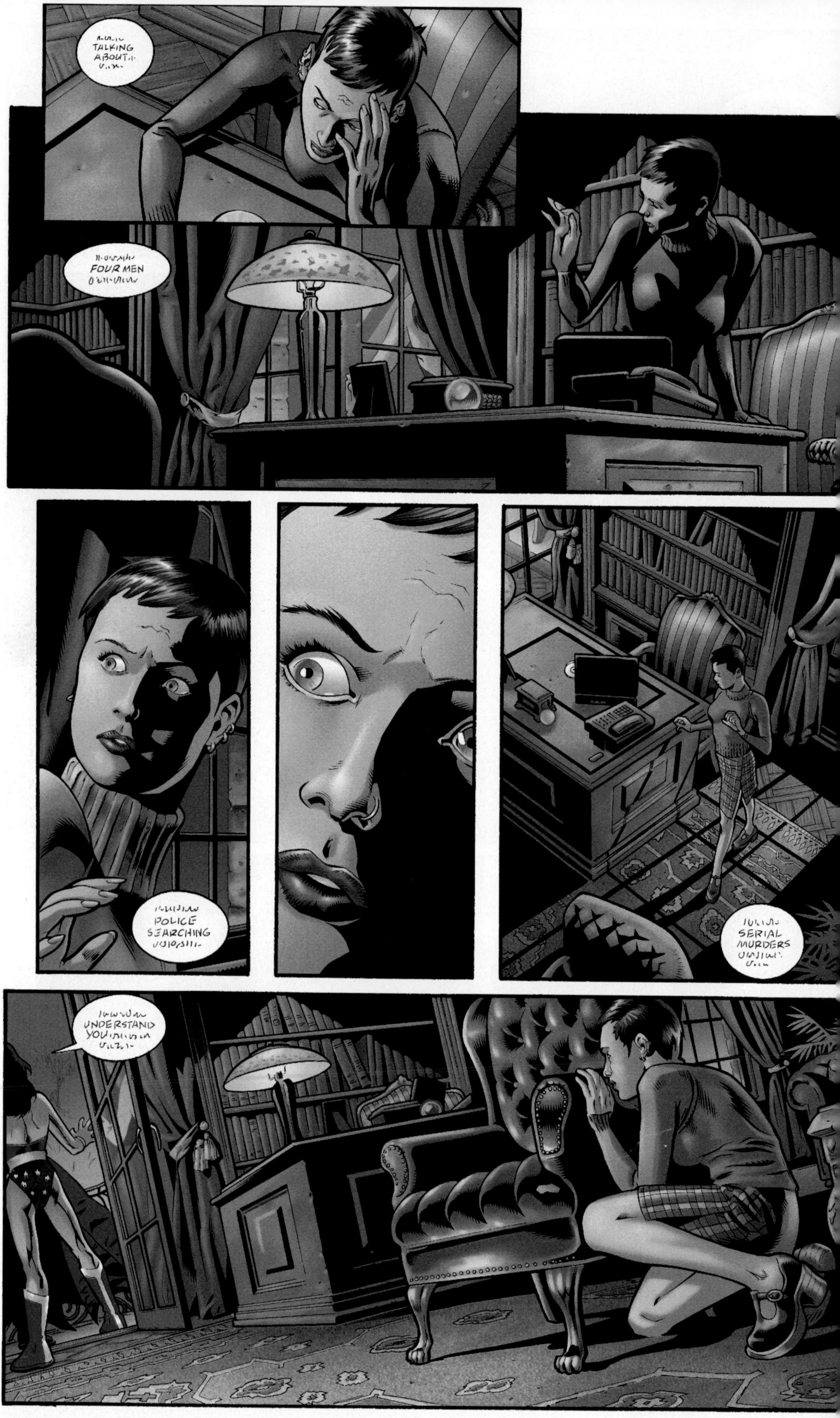
TALKING ABOUT
FOUR MEN
POLICE SEARCHING
SERIAL MURDERS
UNDERSTAND YOU

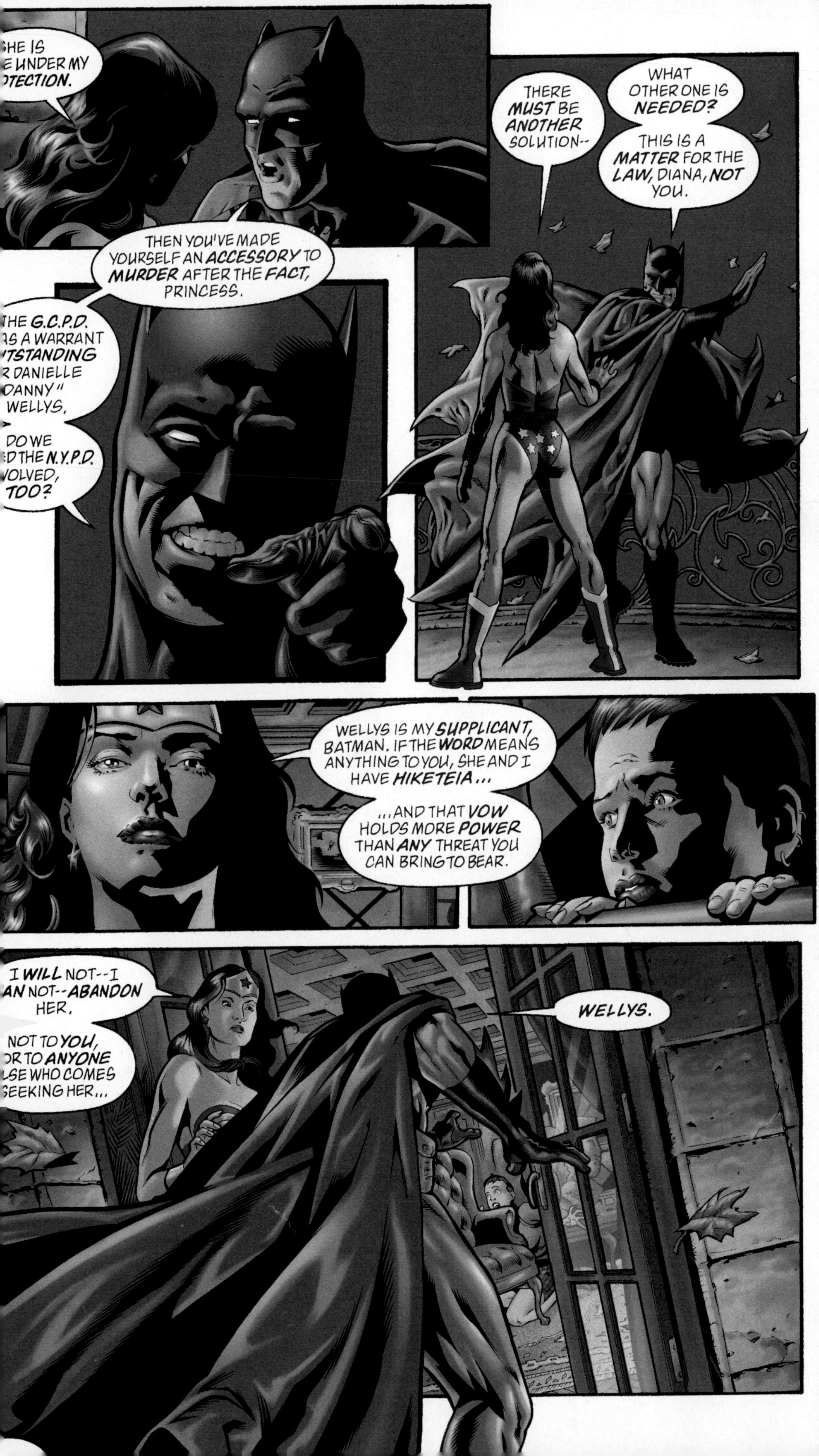
HE IS E UNDER MY OTECTION.
THEN YOU'VE MADE YOURSELF AN ACCESSORY TO MURDER AFTER THE FACT, PRINCESS.
HE G.C.P.D. AS A WARRANT TSTANDING R DANIELLE DANNY" WELLYS.
DO WE ED THE N.Y.P.D. VOLVED, TOO?
THERE MUST BE ANOTHER SOLUTION--
WHAT OTHER ONE IS NEEDED?
THIS IS A MATTER FOR THE LAW, DIANA, NOT YOU.
WELLYS IS MY SUPPLICANT, BATMAN. IF THE WORD MEANS ANYTHING TO YOU, SHE AND I HAVE HIKETEIA...
...AND THAT VOW HOLDS MORE POWER THAN ANY THREAT YOU CAN BRING TO BEAR.
I WILL NOT--I AN NOT--ABANDON HER.
NOT TO YOU, R TO ANYONE SE WHO COMES EEKING HER...
WELLYS.

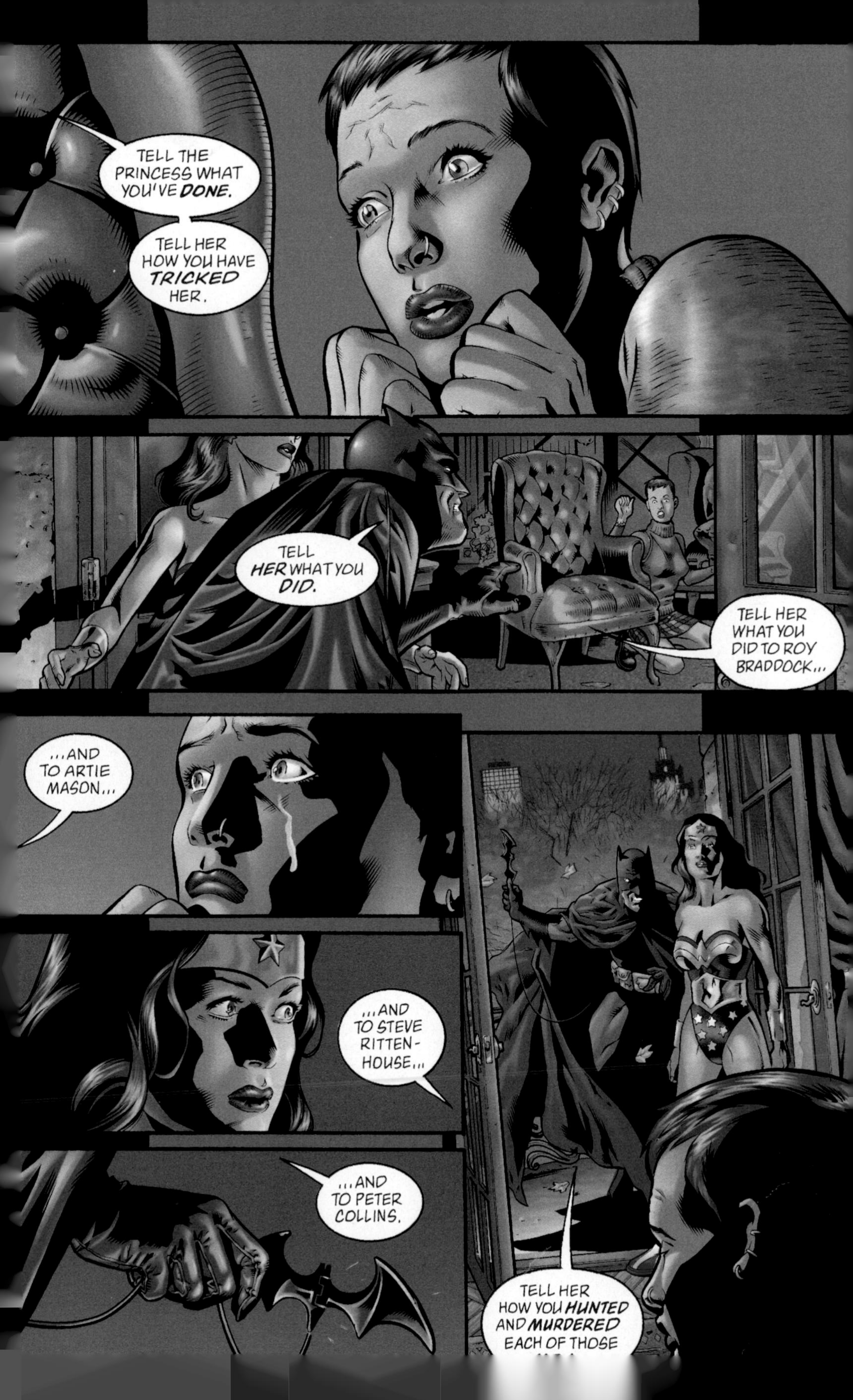
TELL THE PRINCESS WHAT YOU'VE DONE.
TELL HER HOW YOU HAVE TRICKED HER.
TELL HER WHAT YOU DID.
TELL HER WHAT YOU DID TO ROY BRADDOCK...
...AND TO ARTIE MASON...
...AND TO STEVE RITTEN-HOUSE...
...AND TO PETER COLLINS.
TELL HER HOW YOU HUNTED AND MURDERED EACH OF THOSE

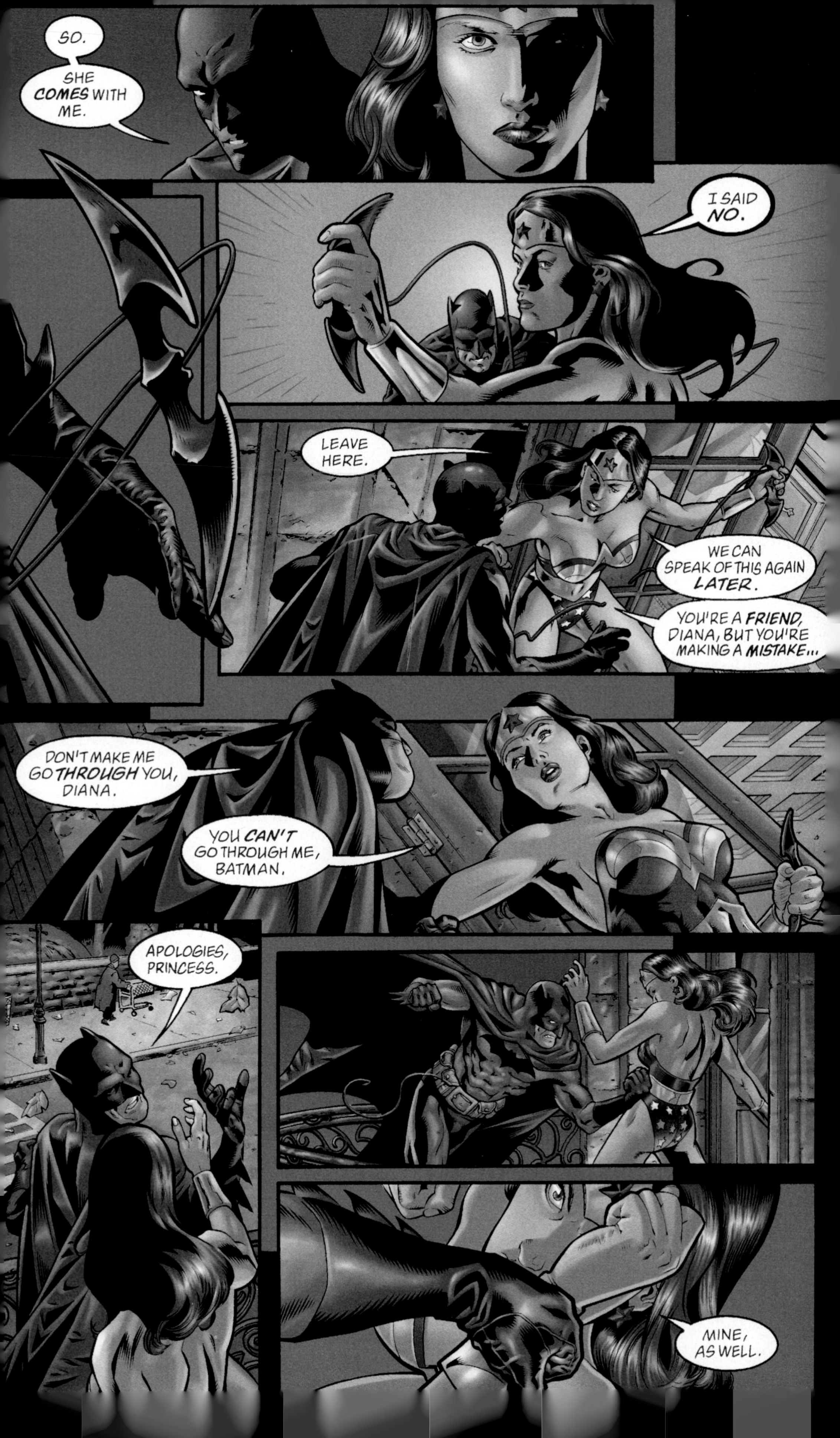
SO.
SHE COMES WITH ME.
I SAID NO.
LEAVE HERE.
WE CAN SPEAK OF THIS AGAIN LATER.
YOU'RE A FRIEND, DIANA, BUT YOU'RE MAKING A MISTAKE...
DON'T MAKE ME GO THROUGH YOU, DIANA.
YOU CAN'T GO THROUGH ME, BATMAN.
APOLOGIES, PRINCESS.
MINE, AS WELL.

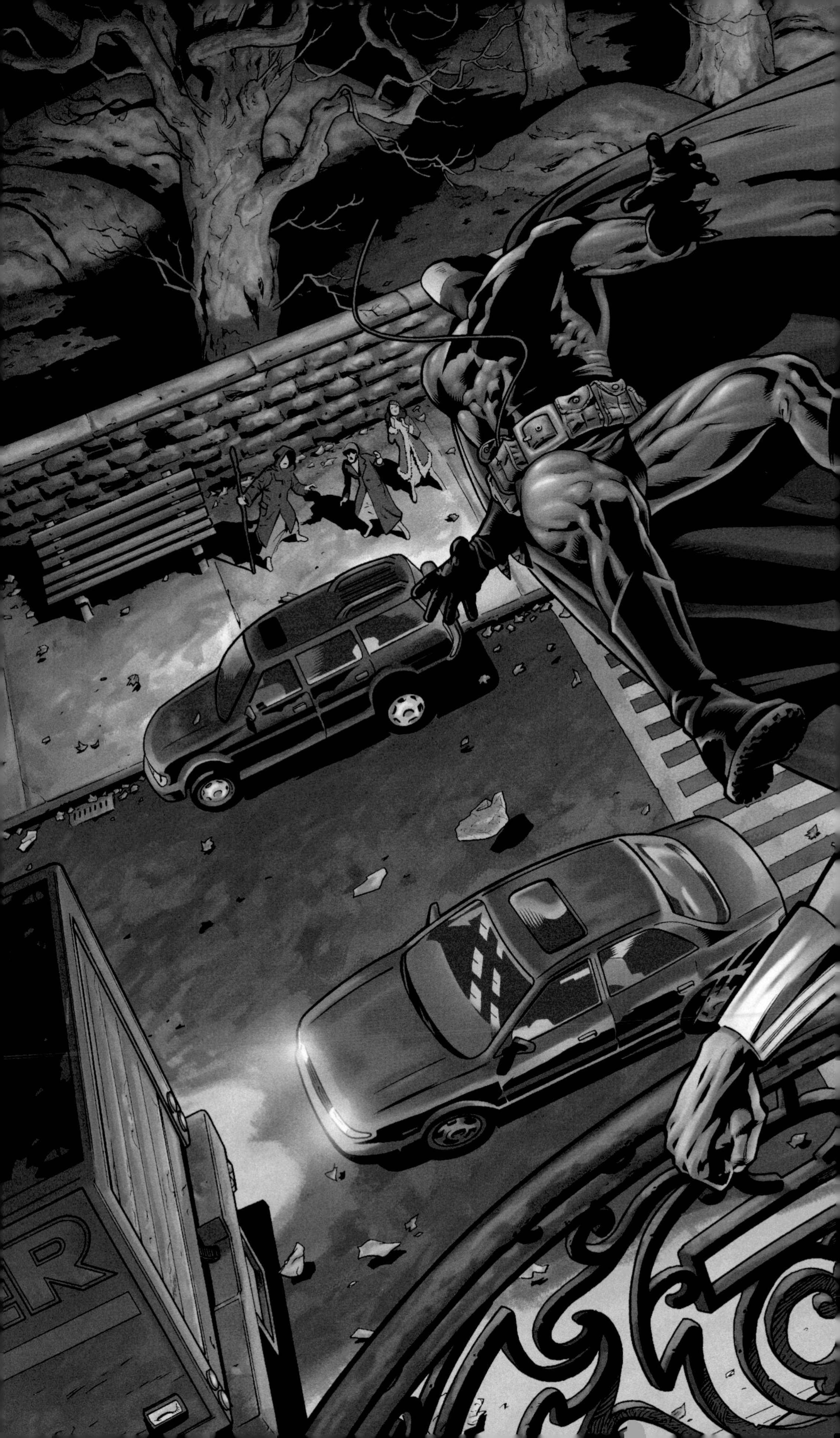

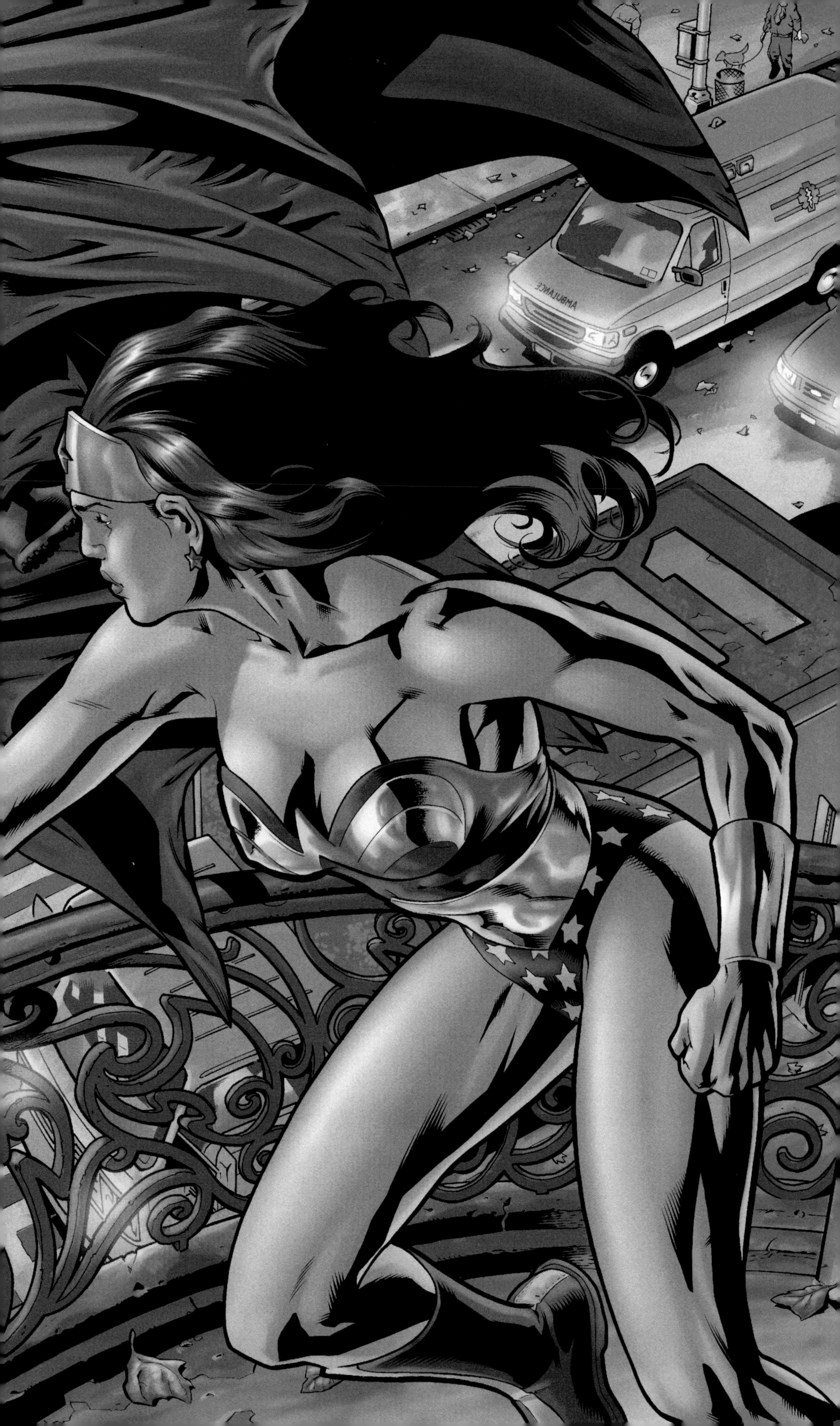

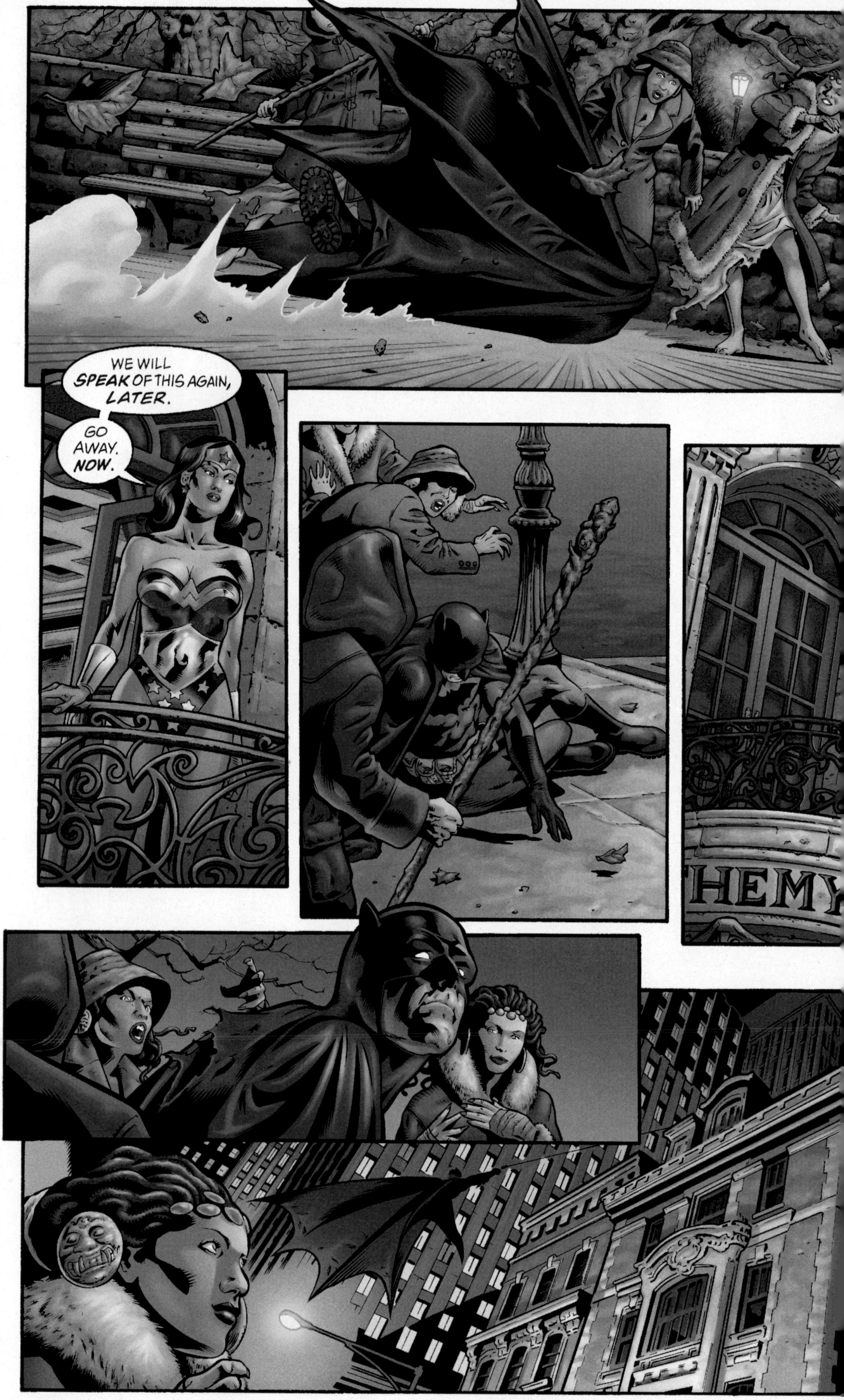
WE WILL SPEAK OF THIS AGAIN, LATER.
GO AWAY. NOW.
HEMY

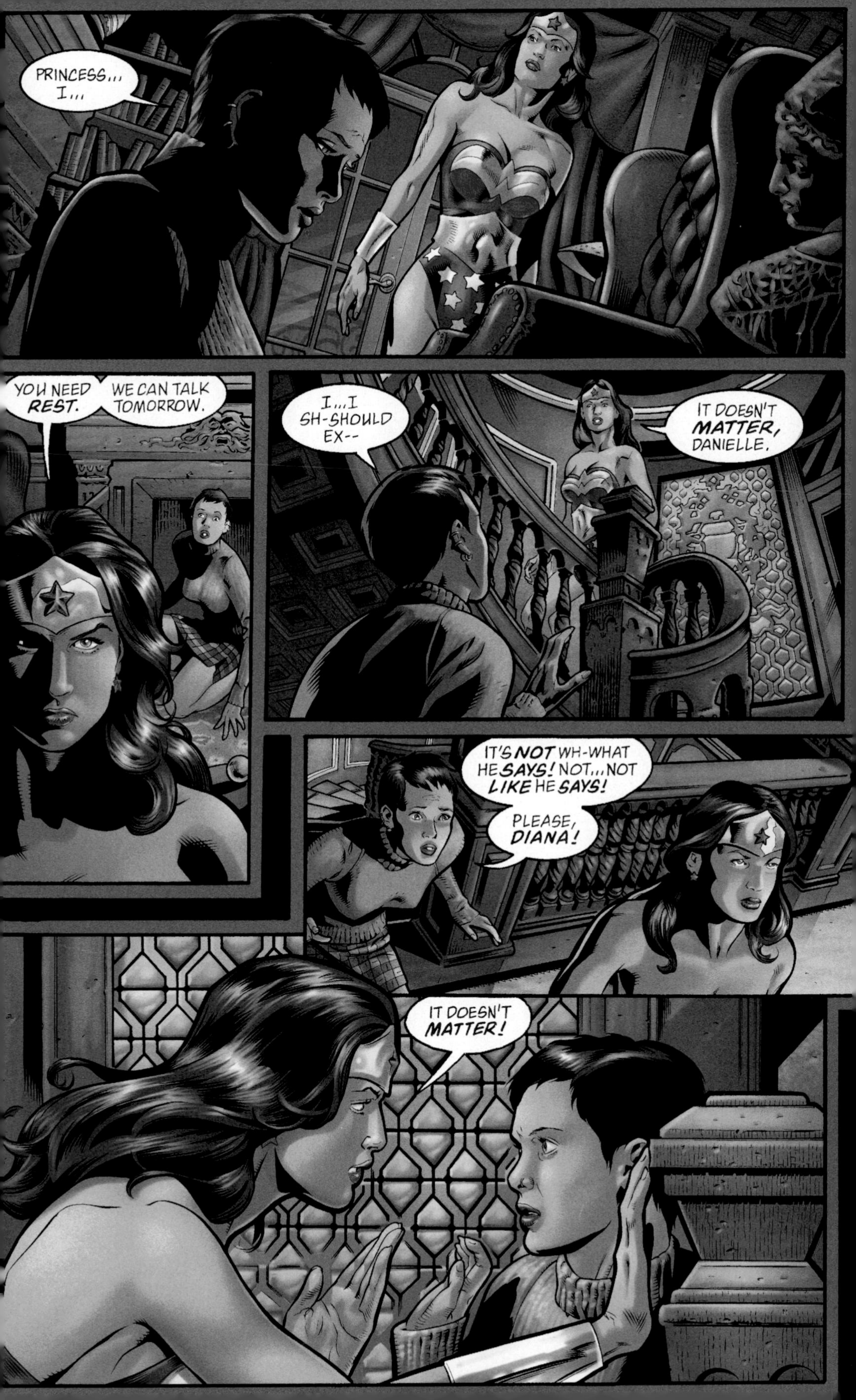
PRINCESS... I...
YOU NEED REST.
WE CAN TALK TOMORROW.
I...I SH-SHOULD EX--
IT DOESN'T MATTER, DANIELLE.
IT'S NOT WH-WHAT HE SAYS! NOT...NOT LIKE HE SAYS!
PLEASE, DIANA!
IT DOESN'T MATTER!

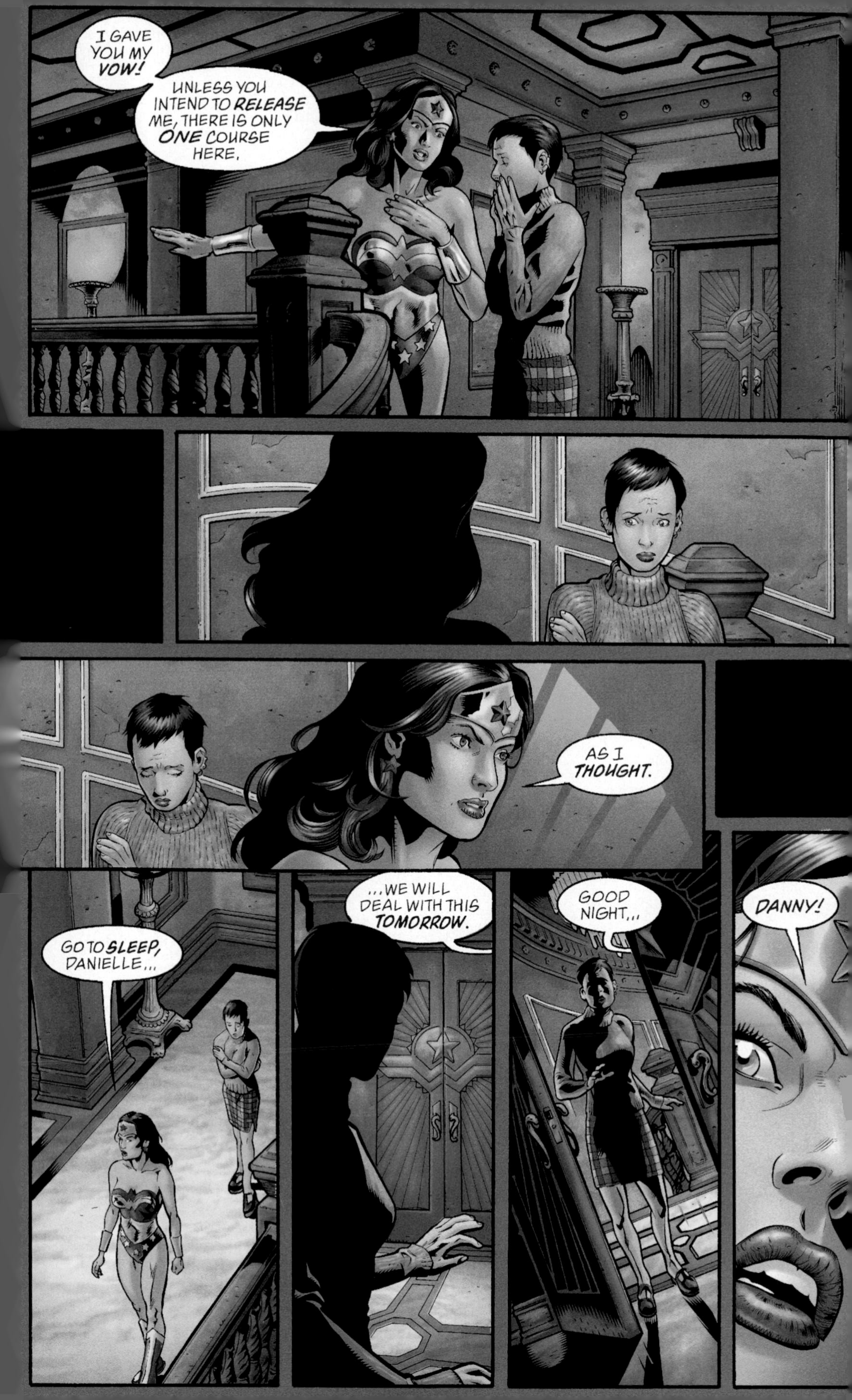
I GAVE YOU MY VOW!
UNLESS YOU INTEND TO RELEASE ME, THERE IS ONLY ONE COURSE HERE.
AS I THOUGHT.
GO TO SLEEP, DANIELLE...
...WE WILL DEAL WITH THIS TOMORROW.
GOOD NIGHT...
DANNY!

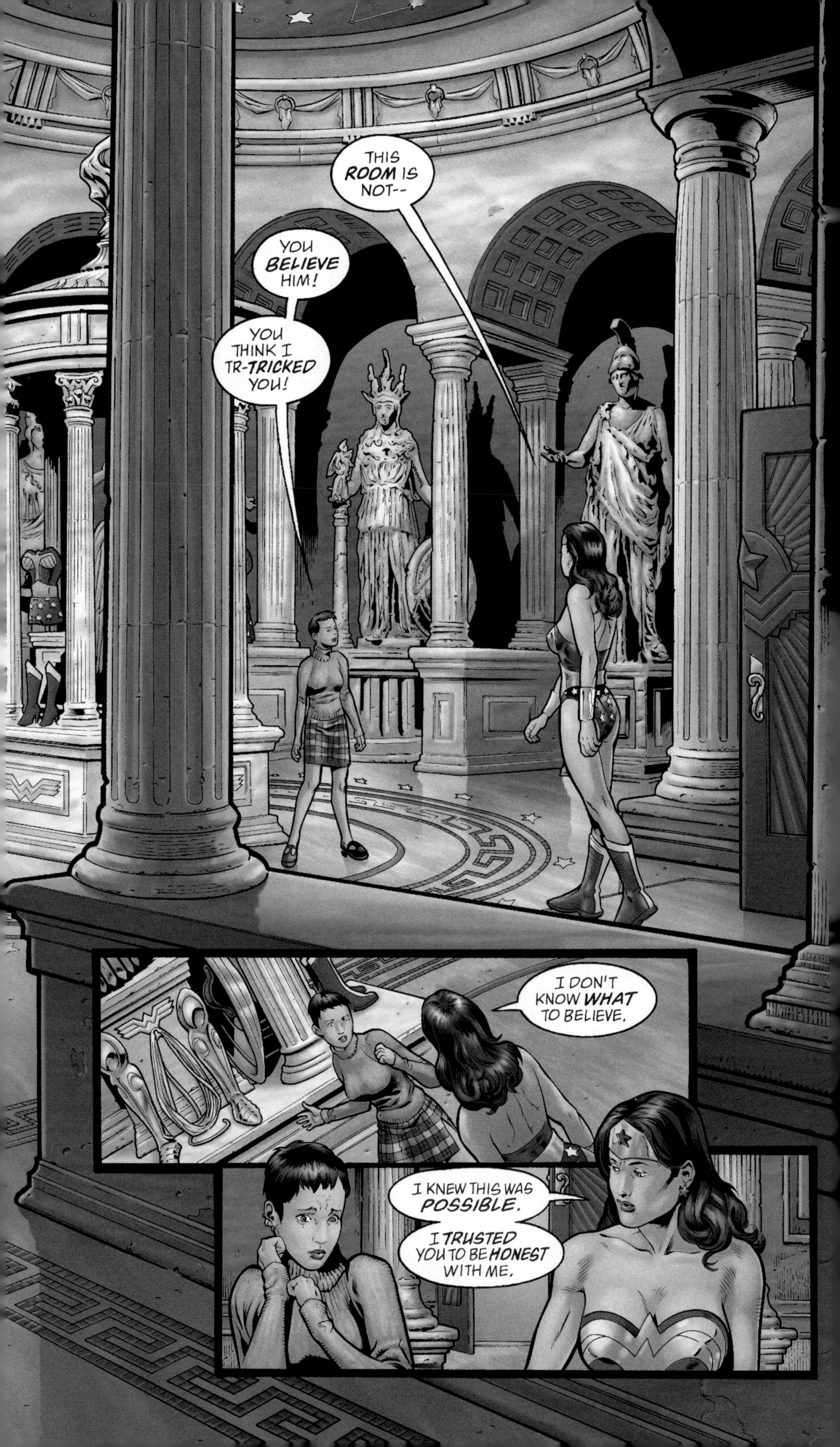
THIS ROOM IS NOT--
YOU BELIEVE HIM!
YOU THINK I TR-TRICKED YOU!
I DON'T KNOW WHAT TO BELIEVE.
I KNEW THIS WAS POSSIBLE.
I TRUSTED YOU TO BE HONEST WITH ME.

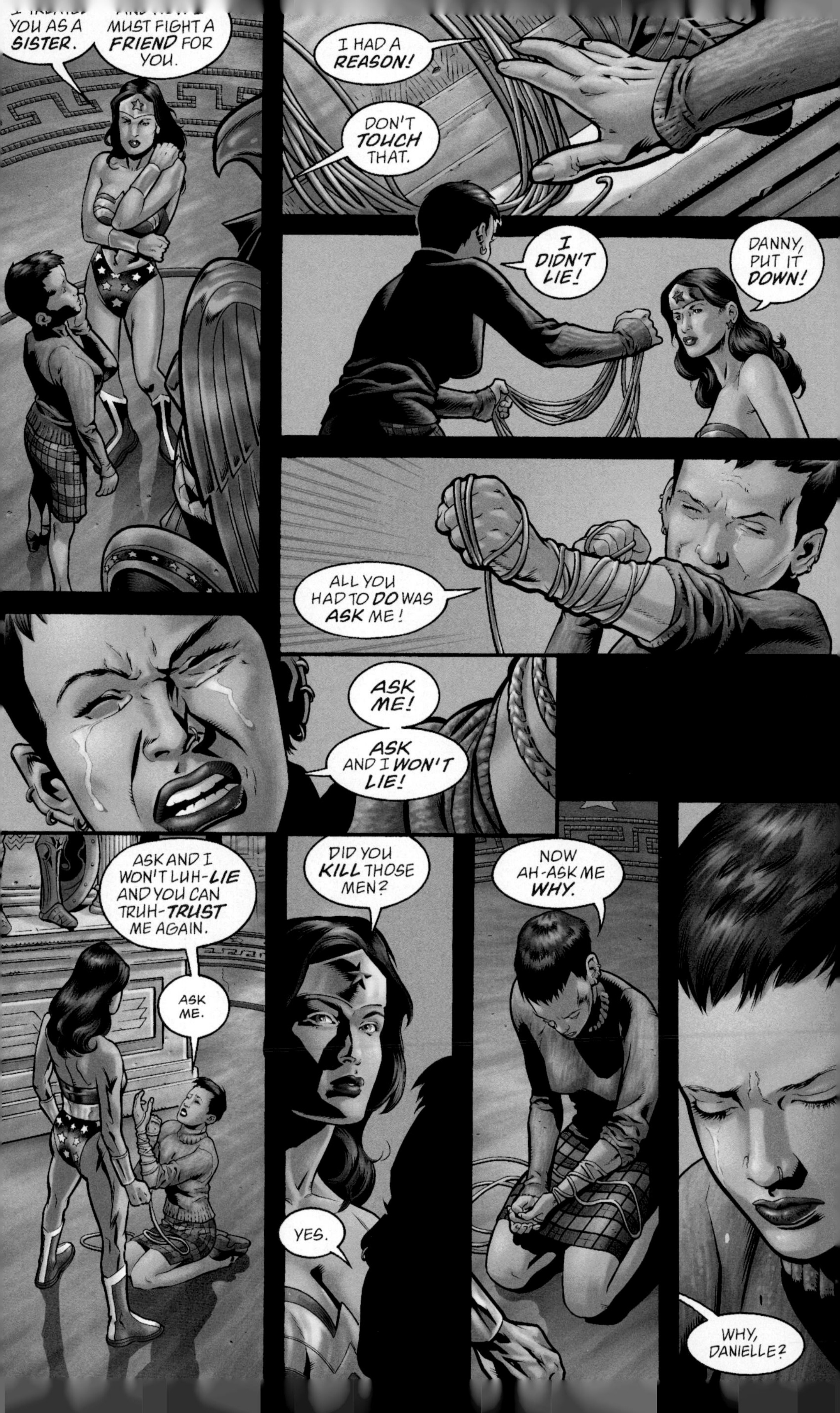
YOU AS A SISTER.
MUST FIGHT A FRIEND FOR YOU.
I HAD A REASON!
DON'T TOUCH THAT.
I DIDN'T LIE!
DANNY, PUT IT DOWN!
ALL YOU HAD TO DO WAS ASK ME!
ASK ME!
ASK AND I WON'T LIE!
ASK AND I WON'T LUH-LIE AND YOU CAN TRUH-TRUST ME AGAIN.
ASK ME.
DID YOU KILL THOSE MEN?
YES.
NOW AH-ASK ME WHY.
WHY, DANIELLE?

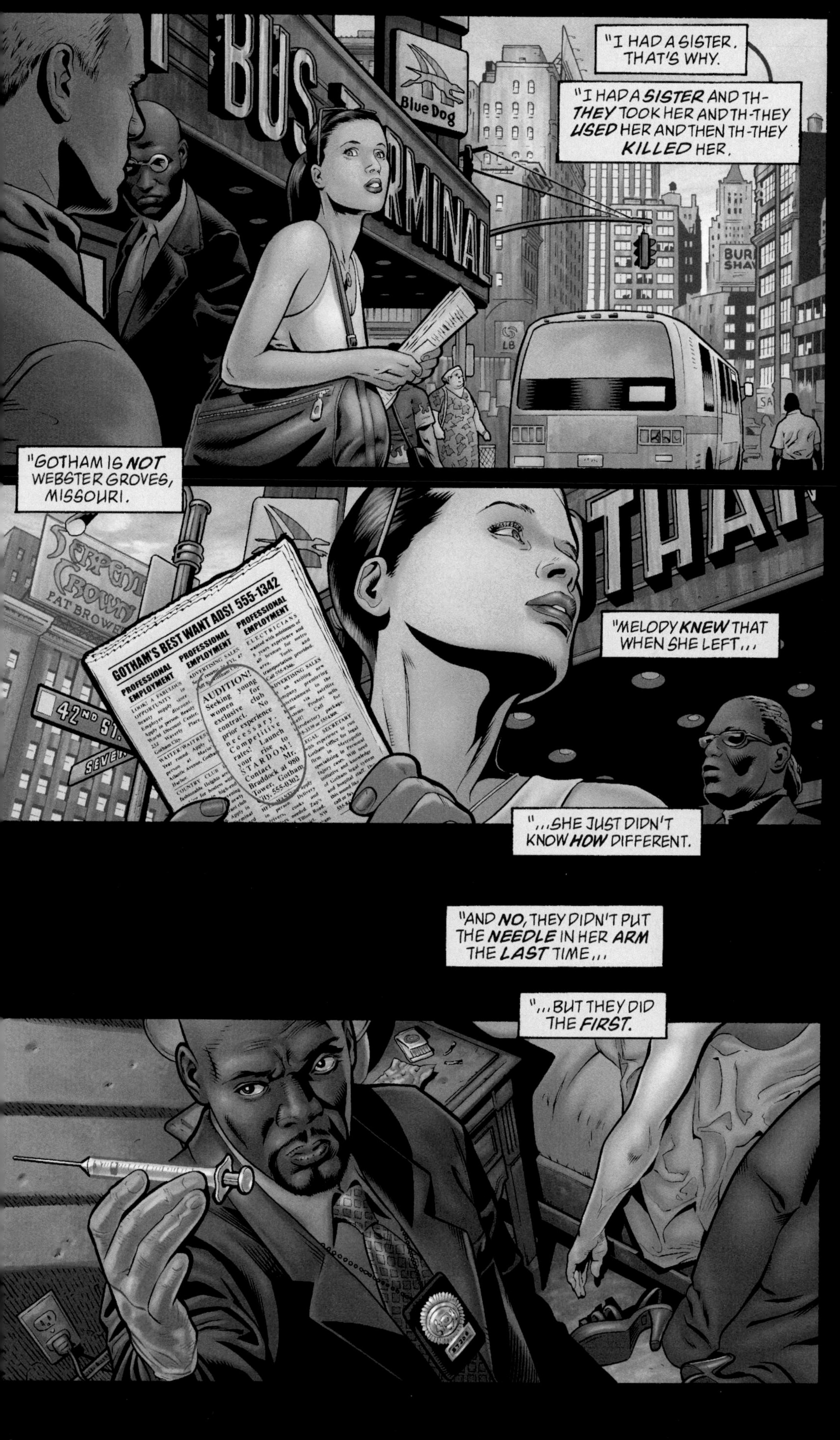
"I HAD A SISTER. THAT'S WHY.
"I HAD A SISTER AND TH-THEY TOOK HER AND TH-THEY USED HER AND THEN TH-THEY KILLED HER.
Blue Dog
"GOTHAM IS NOT WEBSTER GROVES, MISSOURI.
GOTHAM'S BEST WANT ADS! 555-1342
PROFESSIONAL EMPLOYMENT
42ND ST.
"MELODY KNEW THAT WHEN SHE LEFT...
"...SHE JUST DIDN'T KNOW HOW DIFFERENT.
"AND NO, THEY DIDN'T PUT THE NEEDLE IN HER ARM THE LAST TIME...
"...BUT THEY DID THE FIRST.

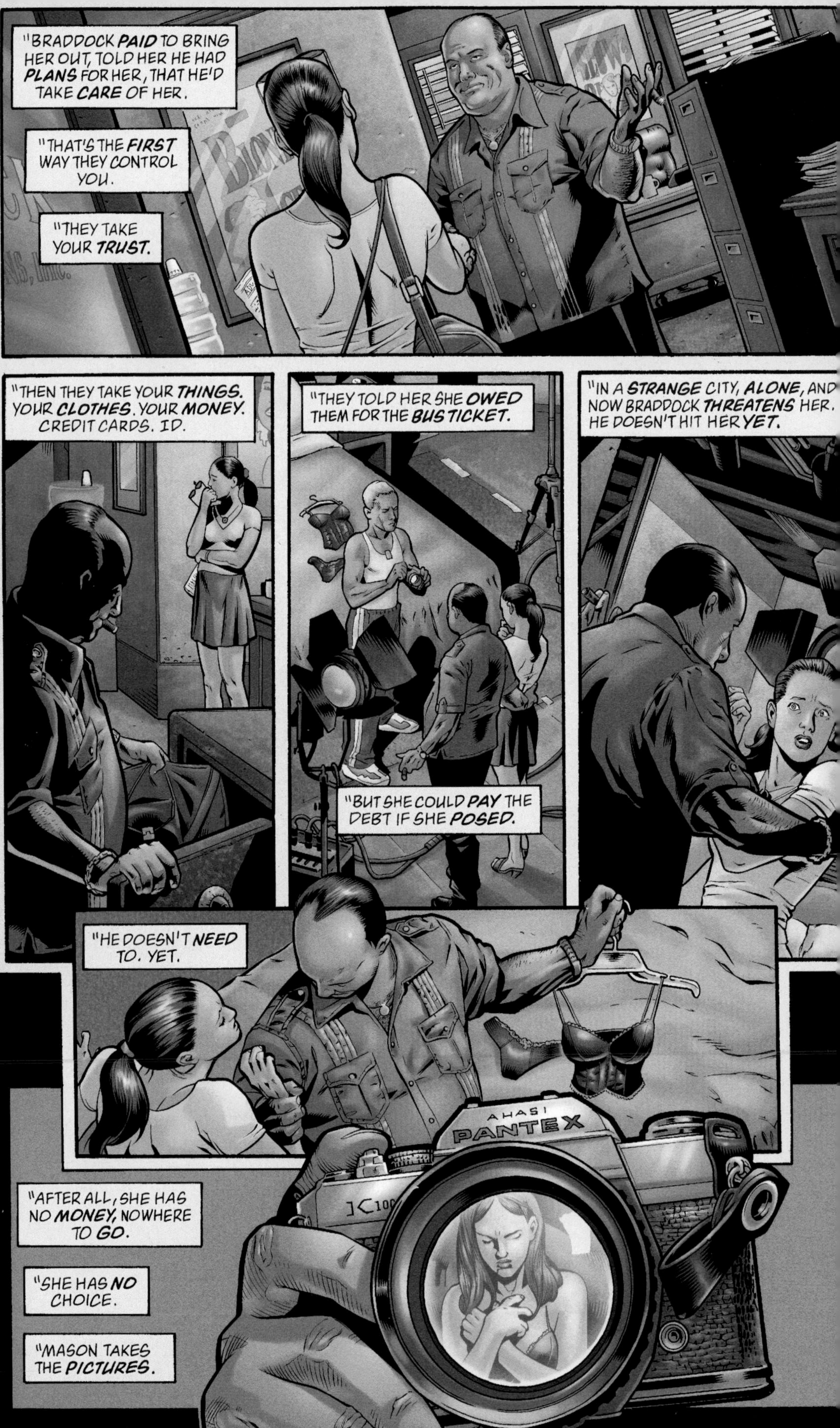
"BRADDOCK PAID TO BRING HER OUT, TOLD HER HE HAD PLANS FOR HER, THAT HE'D TAKE CARE OF HER.
"THAT'S THE FIRST WAY THEY CONTROL YOU.
"THEY TAKE YOUR TRUST.
"THEN THEY TAKE YOUR THINGS. YOUR CLOTHES. YOUR MONEY. CREDIT CARDS. ID.
"THEY TOLD HER SHE OWED THEM FOR THE BUS TICKET.
"BUT SHE COULD PAY THE DEBT IF SHE POSED.
"IN A STRANGE CITY, ALONE, AND NOW BRADDOCK THREATENS HER. HE DOESN'T HIT HER YET.
"HE DOESN'T NEED TO. YET.
AHASI
PANTEX
"AFTER ALL, SHE HAS NO MONEY, NOWHERE TO GO.
"SHE HAS NO CHOICE.
"MASON TAKES THE PICTURES.

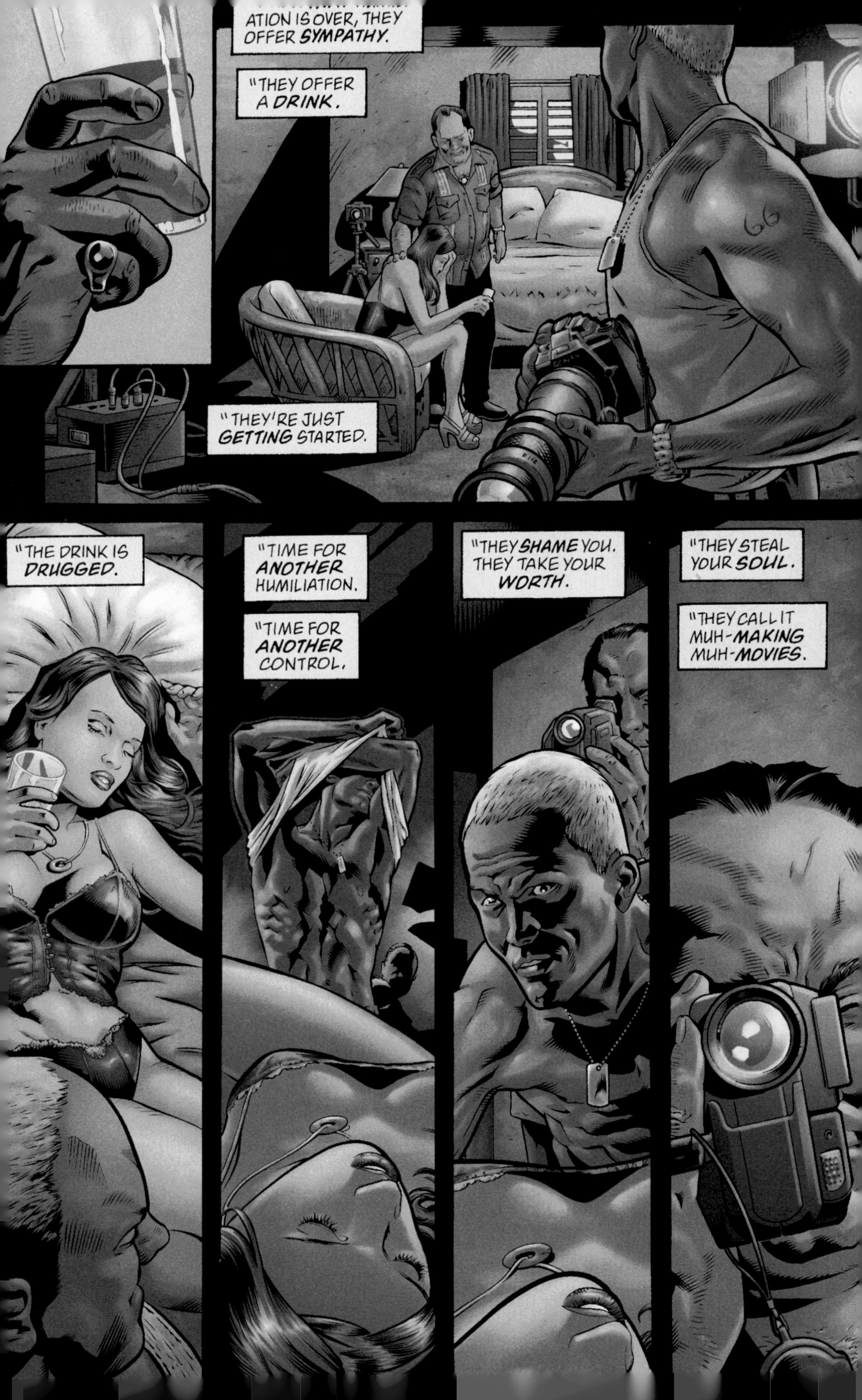
ATION IS OVER, THEY OFFER SYMPATHY.
"THEY OFFER A DRINK.
"THEY'RE JUST GETTING STARTED.
"THE DRINK IS DRUGGED.
"TIME FOR ANOTHER HUMILIATION.
"TIME FOR ANOTHER CONTROL.
"THEY SHAME YOU. THEY TAKE YOUR WORTH.
"THEY STEAL YOUR SOUL.
"THEY CALL IT MUH-MAKING MUH-MOVIES.

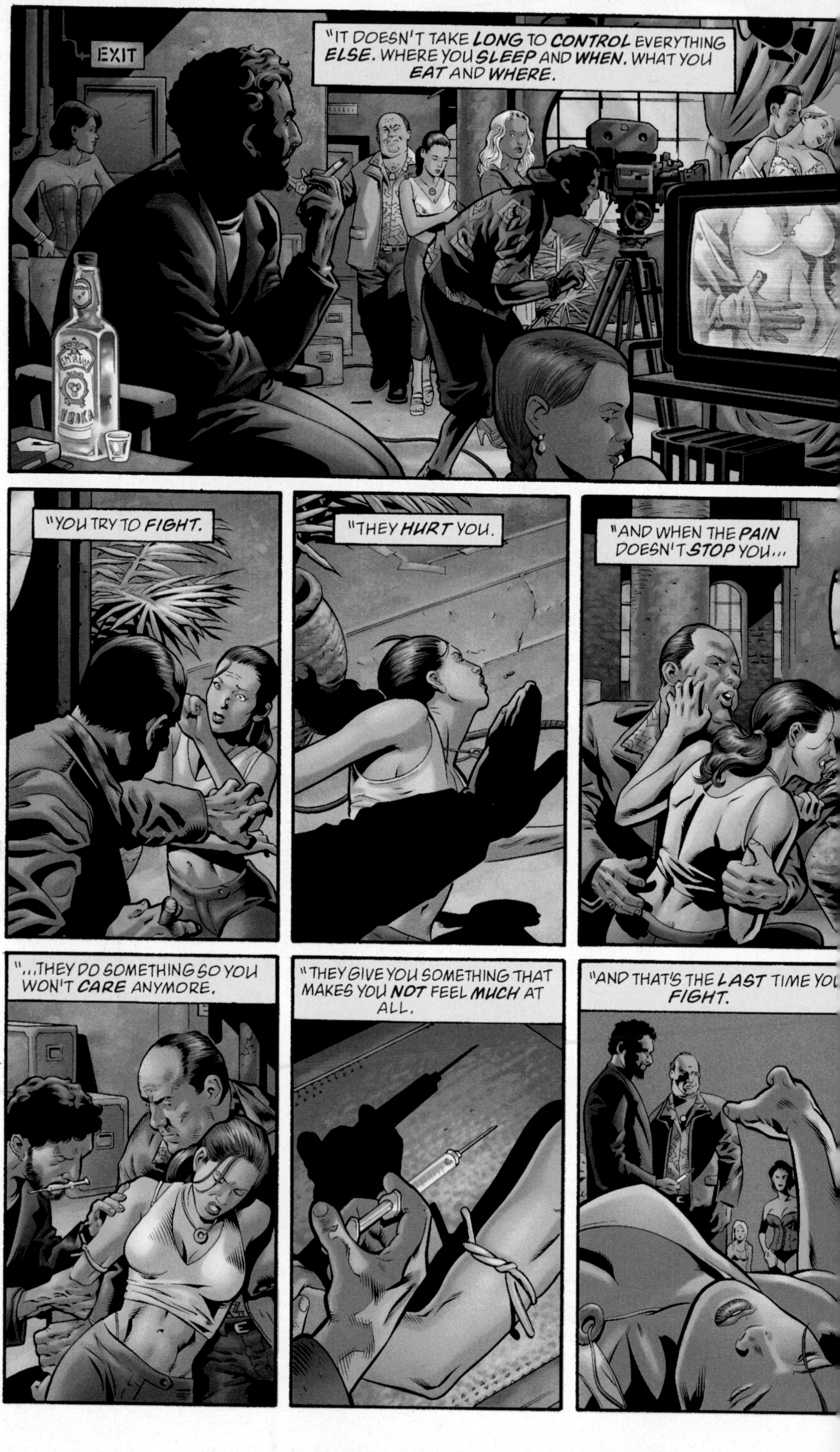
"IT DOESN'T TAKE LONG TO CONTROL EVERYTHING ELSE. WHERE YOU SLEEP AND WHEN. WHAT YOU EAT AND WHERE.
EXIT
SMIRNOFF VODKA
"YOU TRY TO FIGHT.
"THEY HURT YOU.
"AND WHEN THE PAIN DOESN'T STOP YOU...
"...THEY DO SOMETHING SO YOU WON'T CARE ANYMORE.
"THEY GIVE YOU SOMETHING THAT MAKES YOU NOT FEEL MUCH AT ALL.
"AND THAT'S THE LAST TIME YOU FIGHT.

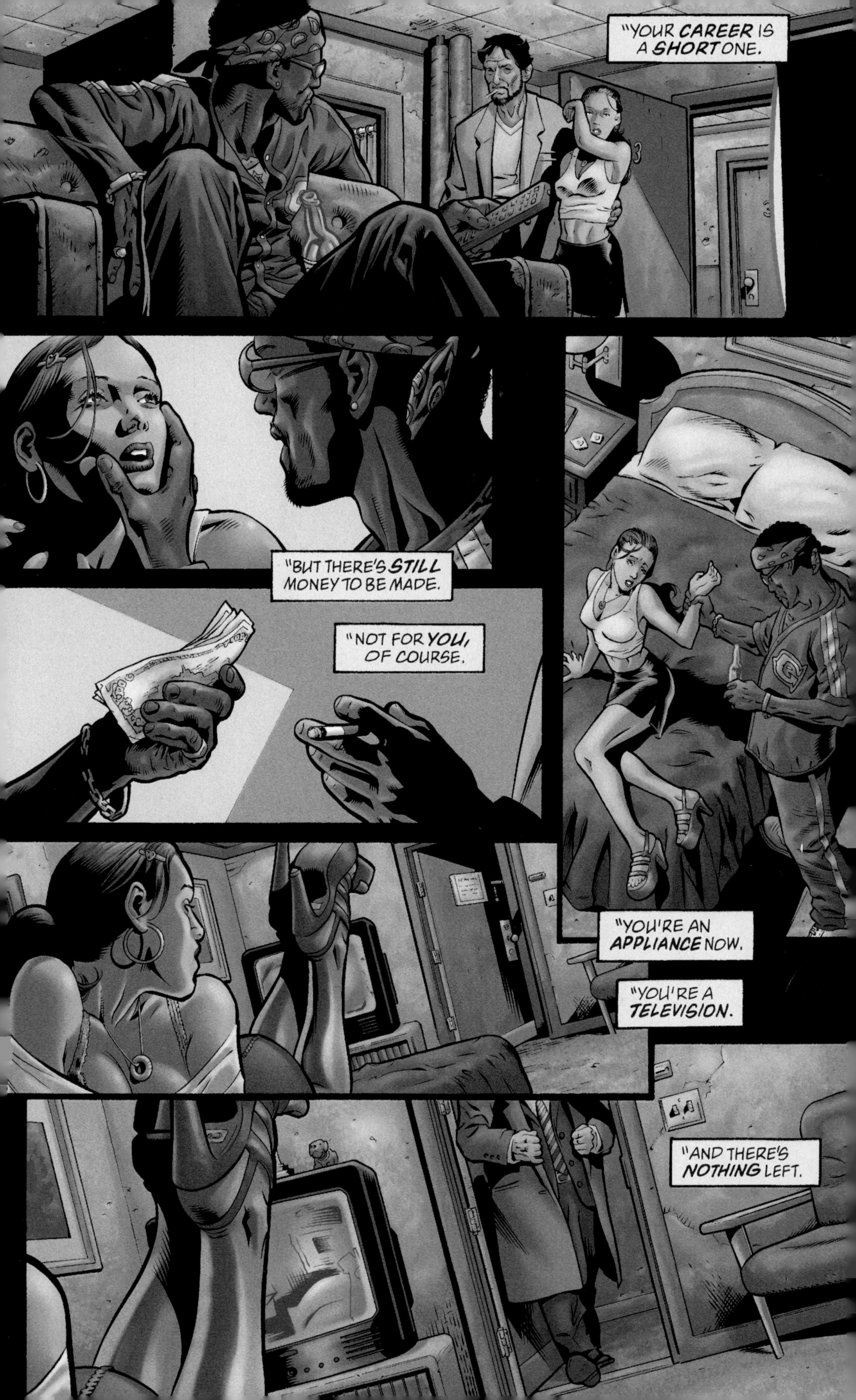

"YOUR CAREER IS A SHORT ONE.
"BUT THERE'S STILL MONEY TO BE MADE.
"NOT FOR YOU, OF COURSE.
"YOU'RE AN APPLIANCE NOW.
"YOU'RE A TELEVISION.
"AND THERE'S NOTHING LEFT.

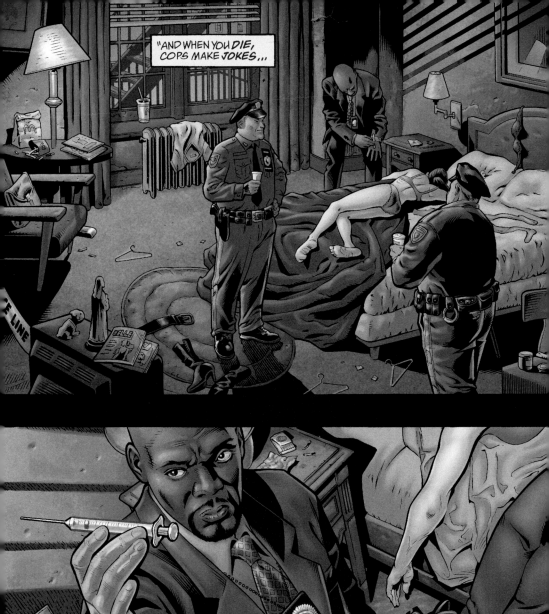

"AND WHEN YOU *DIE*, COPS MAKE *JOKES*...

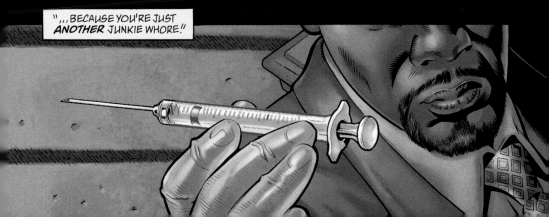

"...BECAUSE YOU'RE JUST *ANOTHER* JUNKIE WHORE!"

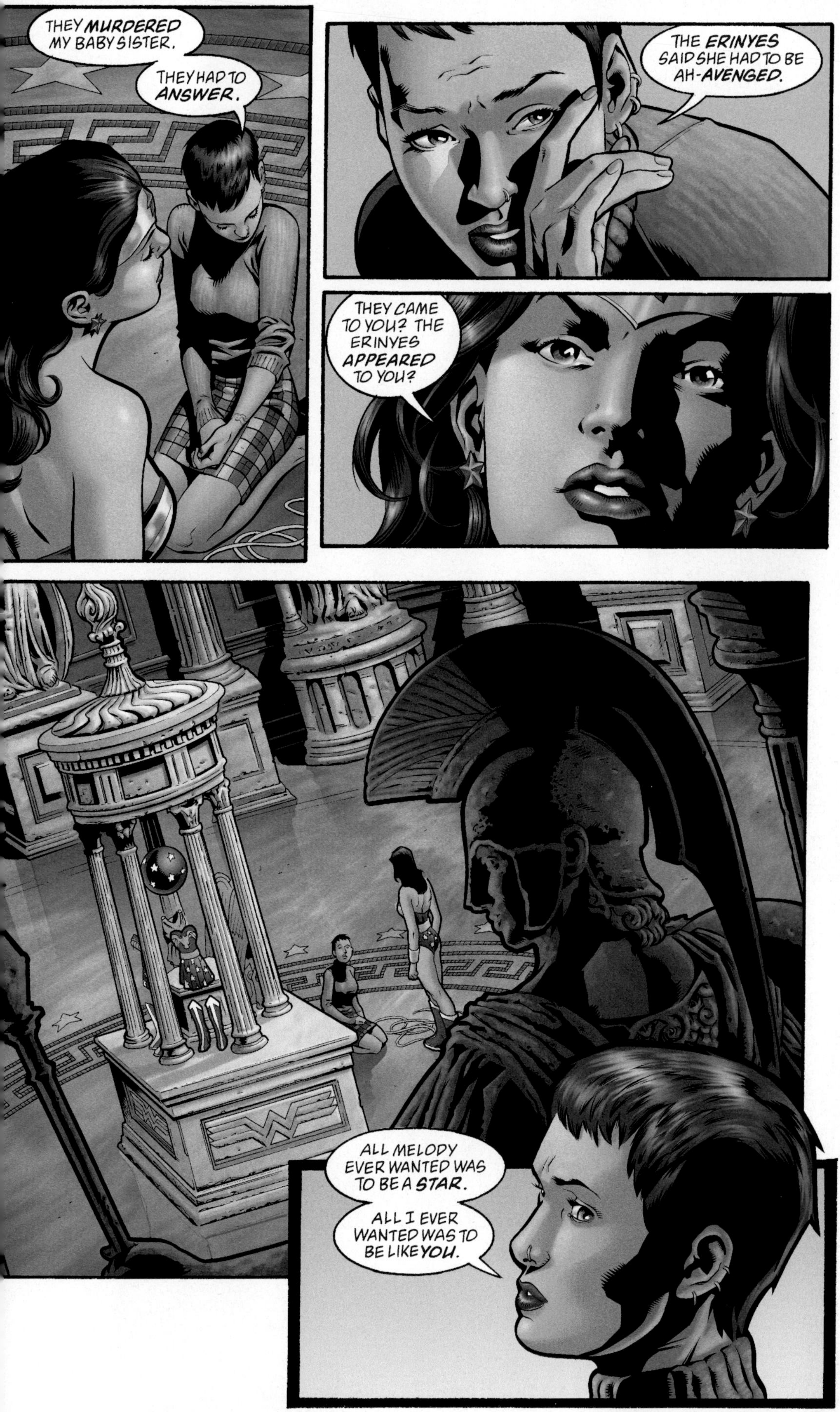
THEY MURDERED MY BABY SISTER.
THEY HAD TO ANSWER.
THE ERINYES SAID SHE HAD TO BE AH-AVENGED.
THEY CAME TO YOU? THE ERINYES APPEARED TO YOU?
ALL MELODY EVER WANTED WAS TO BE A STAR.
ALL I EVER WANTED WAS TO BE LIKE YOU.

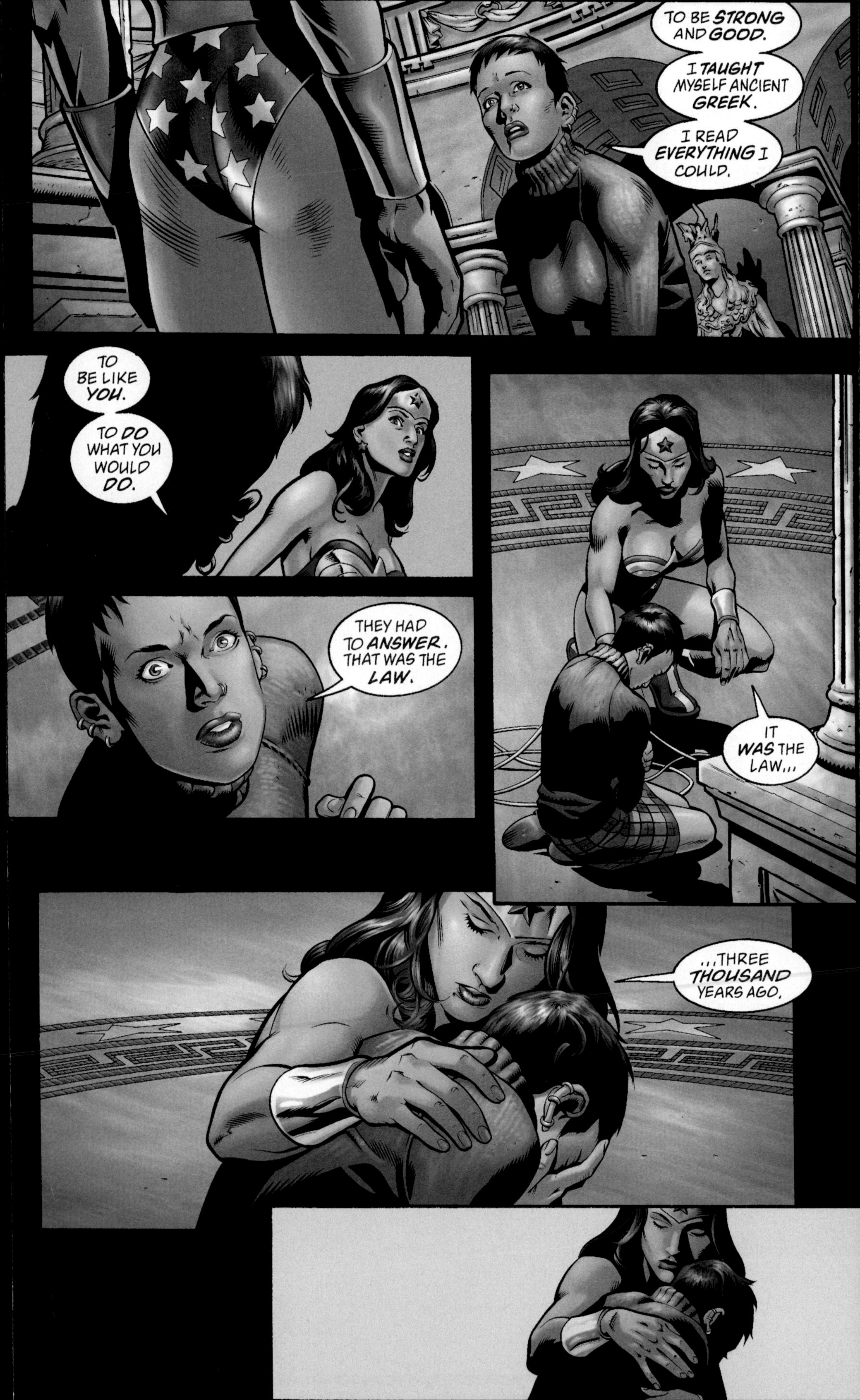
TO BE STRONG AND GOOD.
I TAUGHT MYSELF ANCIENT GREEK.
I READ EVERYTHING I COULD.
TO BE LIKE YOU.
TO DO WHAT YOU WOULD DO.
THEY HAD TO ANSWER. THAT WAS THE LAW.
IT WAS THE LAW...
...THREE THOUSAND YEARS AGO.

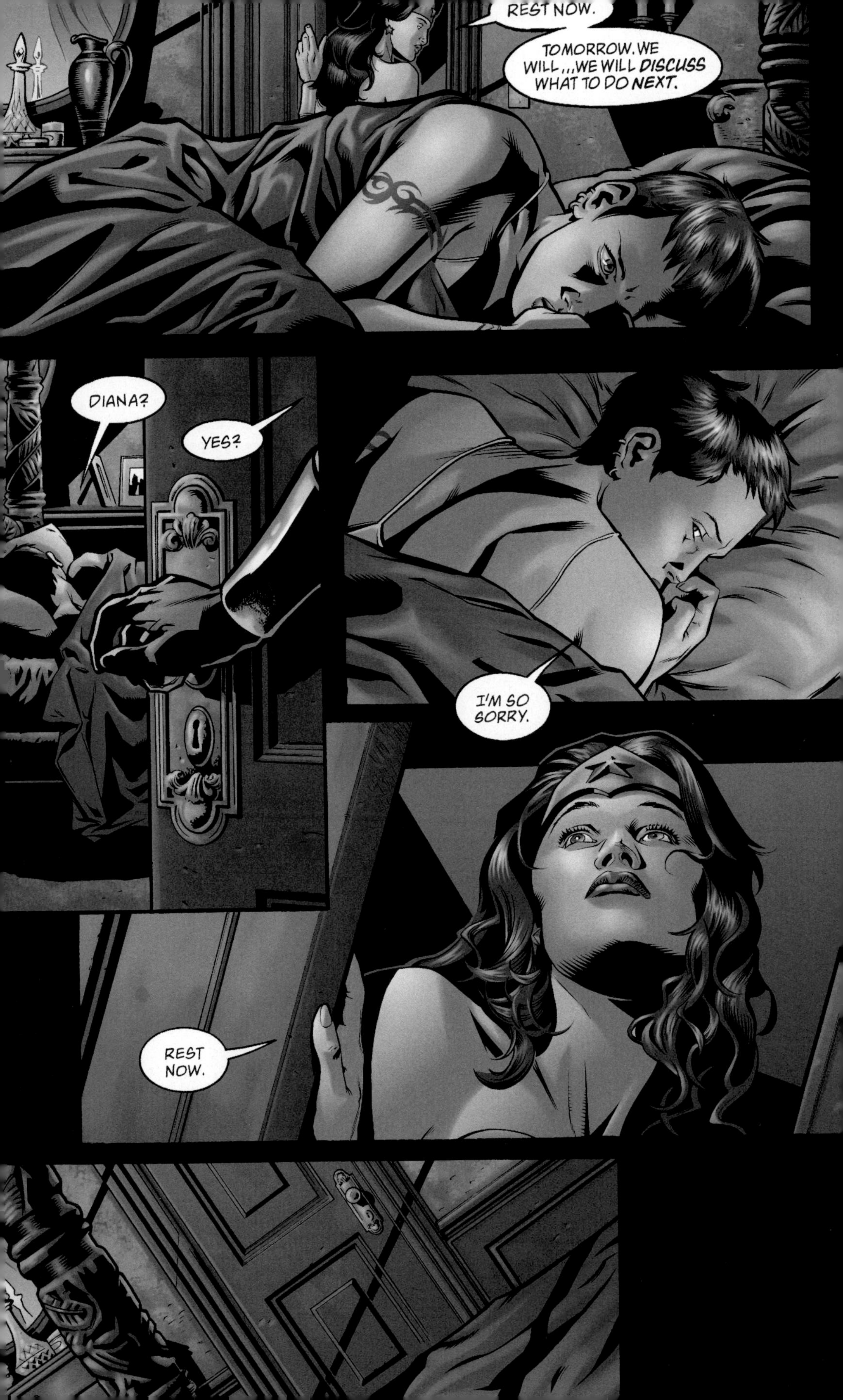
REST NOW.
TOMORROW. WE WILL ... WE WILL DISCUSS WHAT TO DO NEXT.
DIANA?
YES?
I'M SO SORRY.
REST NOW.

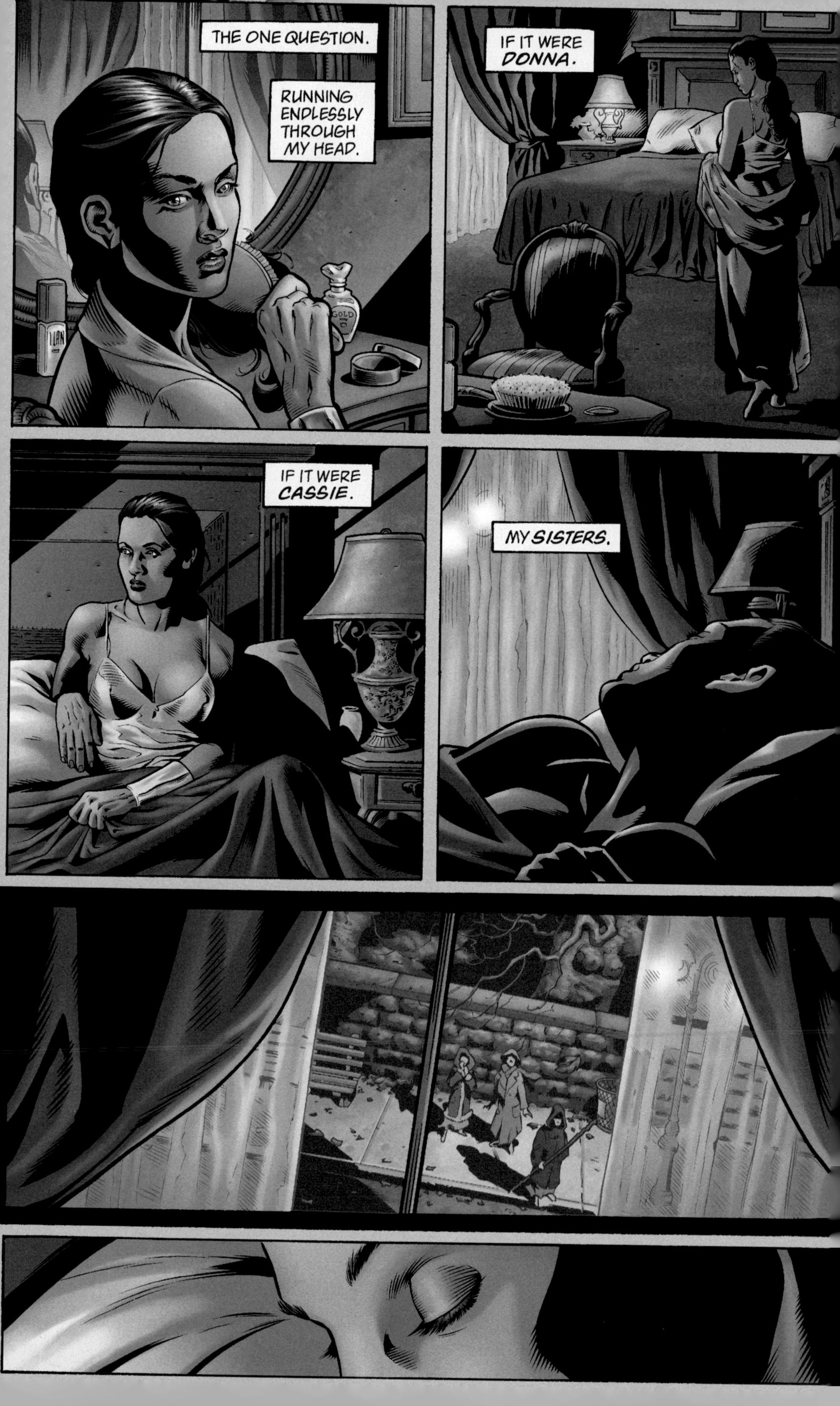
THE ONE QUESTION.
RUNNING ENDLESSLY THROUGH MY HEAD.
IF IT WERE DONNA.
IF IT WERE CASSIE.
MY SISTERS.

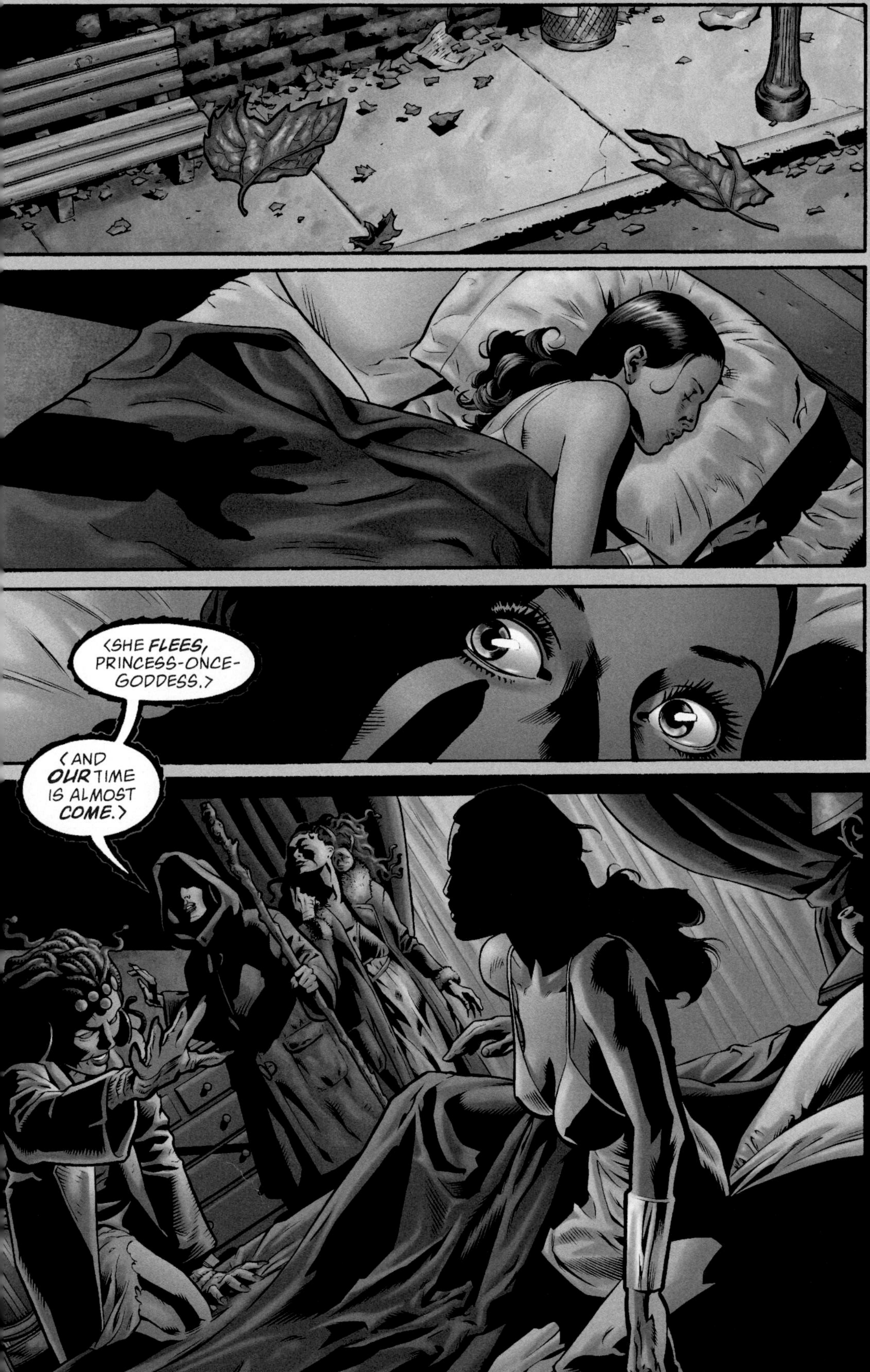
<SHE **FLEES**, PRINCESS-ONCE-GODDESS.>
<AND **OUR** TIME IS ALMOST **COME**.>

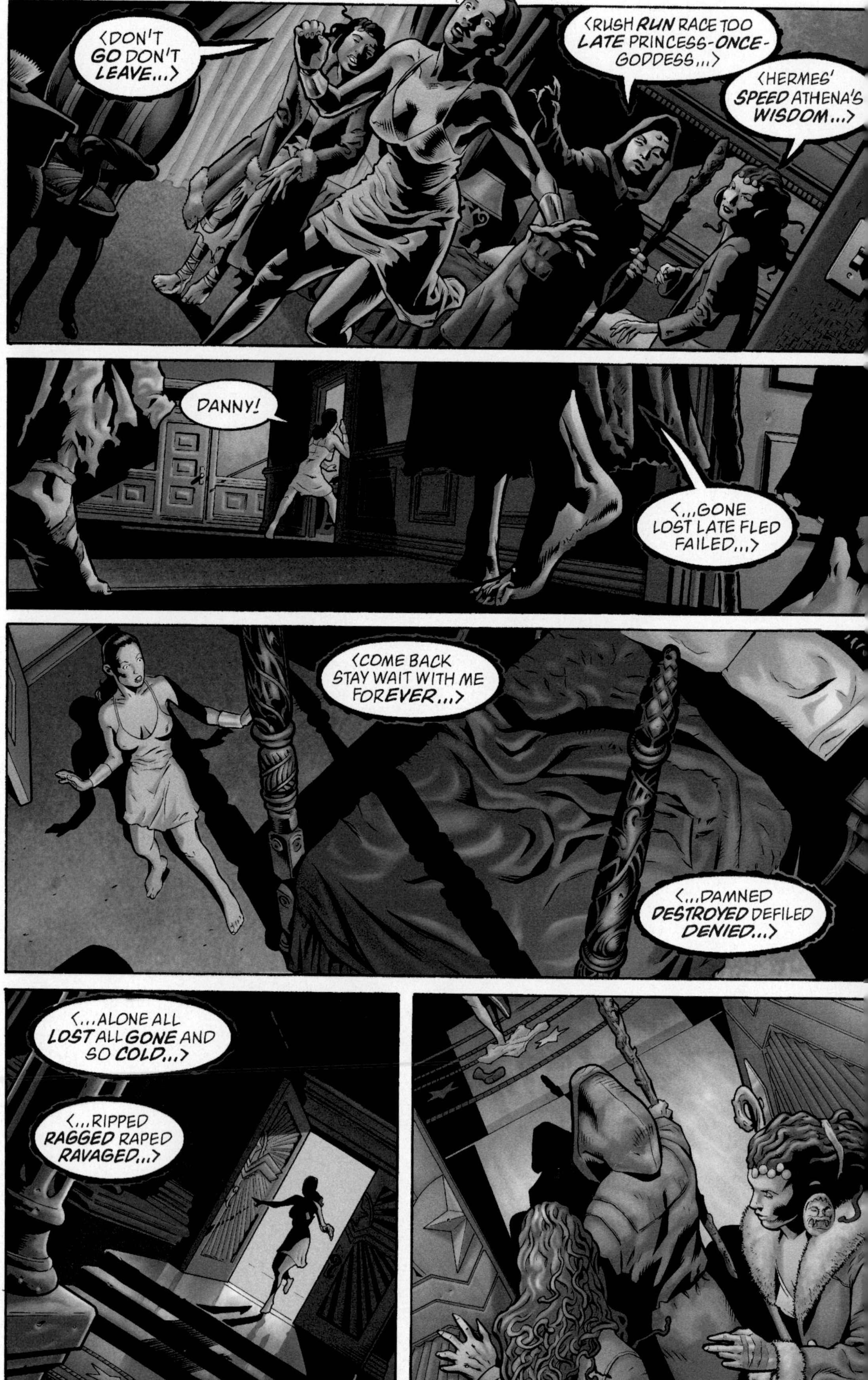
<DON'T GO DON'T LEAVE...>
<RUSH RUN RACE TOO LATE PRINCESS-ONCE-GODDESS...>
<HERMES' SPEED ATHENA'S WISDOM...>
DANNY!
<...GONE LOST LATE FLED FAILED...>
<COME BACK STAY WAIT WITH ME FOREVER...>
<...DAMNED DESTROYED DEFILED DENIED...>
<...ALONE ALL LOST ALL GONE AND SO COLD...>
<...RIPPED RAGGED RAPED RAVAGED...>

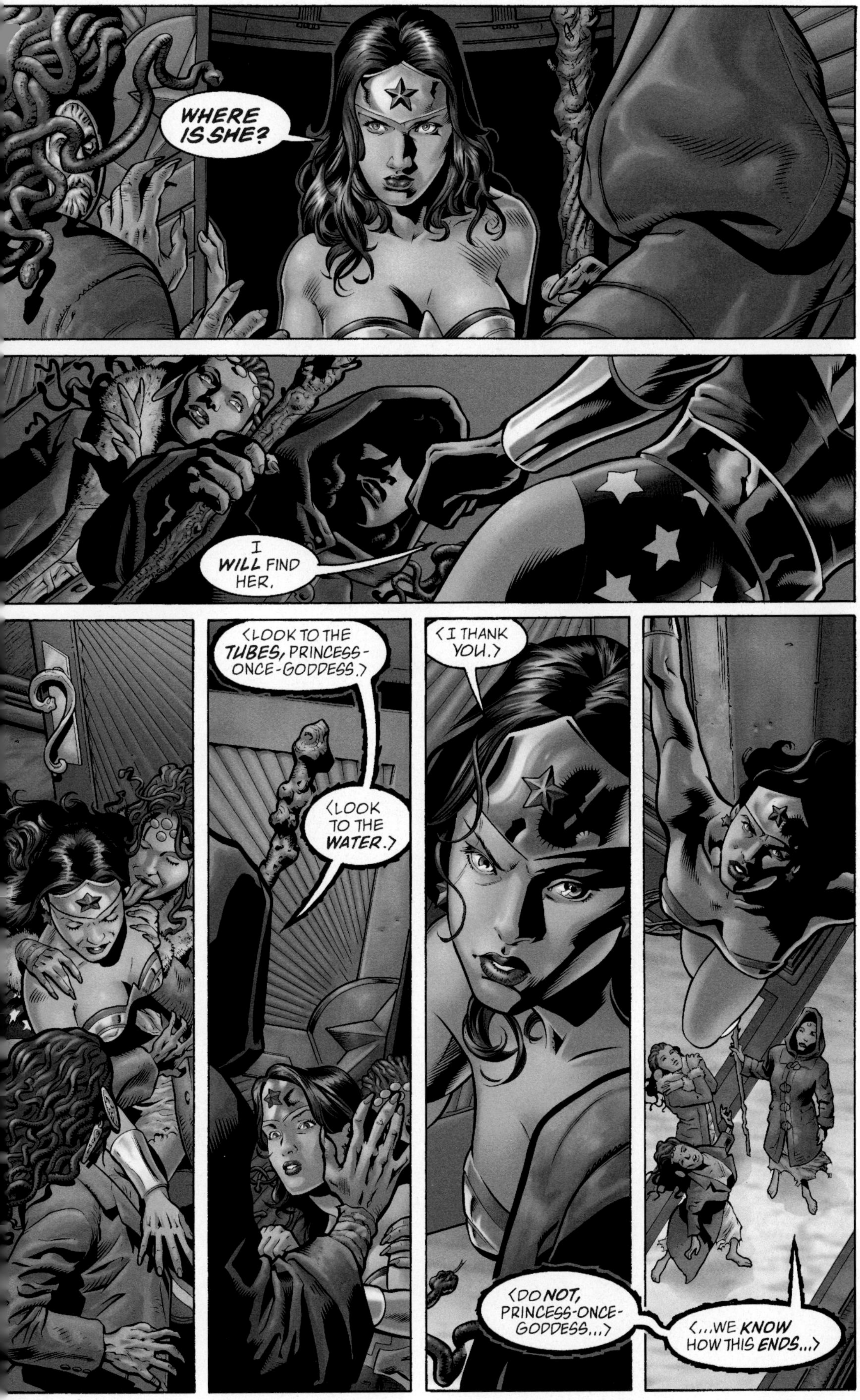

WHERE IS SHE?
I WILL FIND HER.
<LOOK TO THE TUBES, PRINCESS-ONCE-GODDESS.>
<LOOK TO THE WATER.>
<I THANK YOU.>
<DO NOT, PRINCESS-ONCE-GODDESS...>
<...WE KNOW HOW THIS ENDS...>

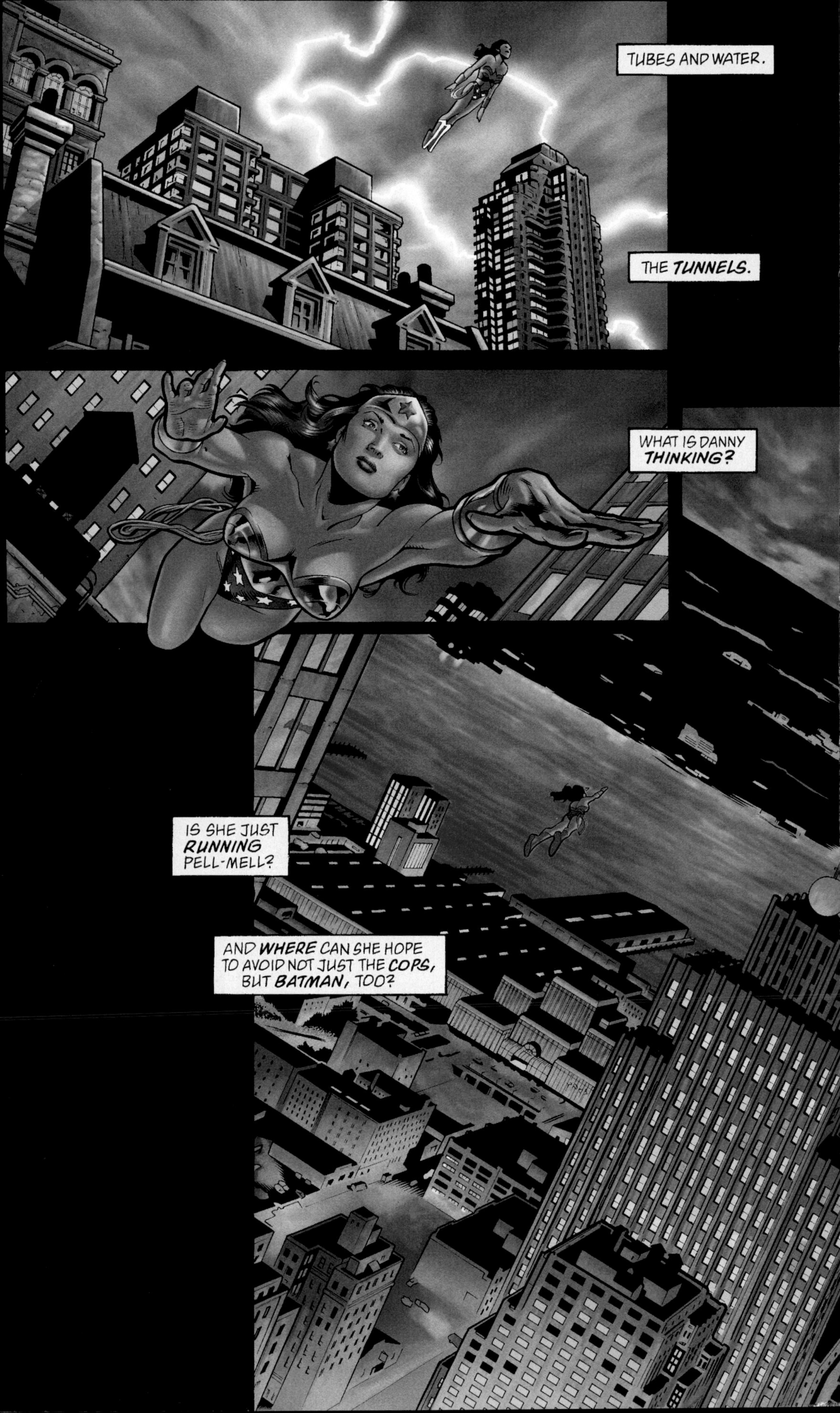

TUBES AND WATER.
THE TUNNELS.
WHAT IS DANNY THINKING?
IS SHE JUST RUNNING PELL-MELL?
AND WHERE CAN SHE HOPE TO AVOID NOT JUST THE COPS, BUT BATMAN, TOO?

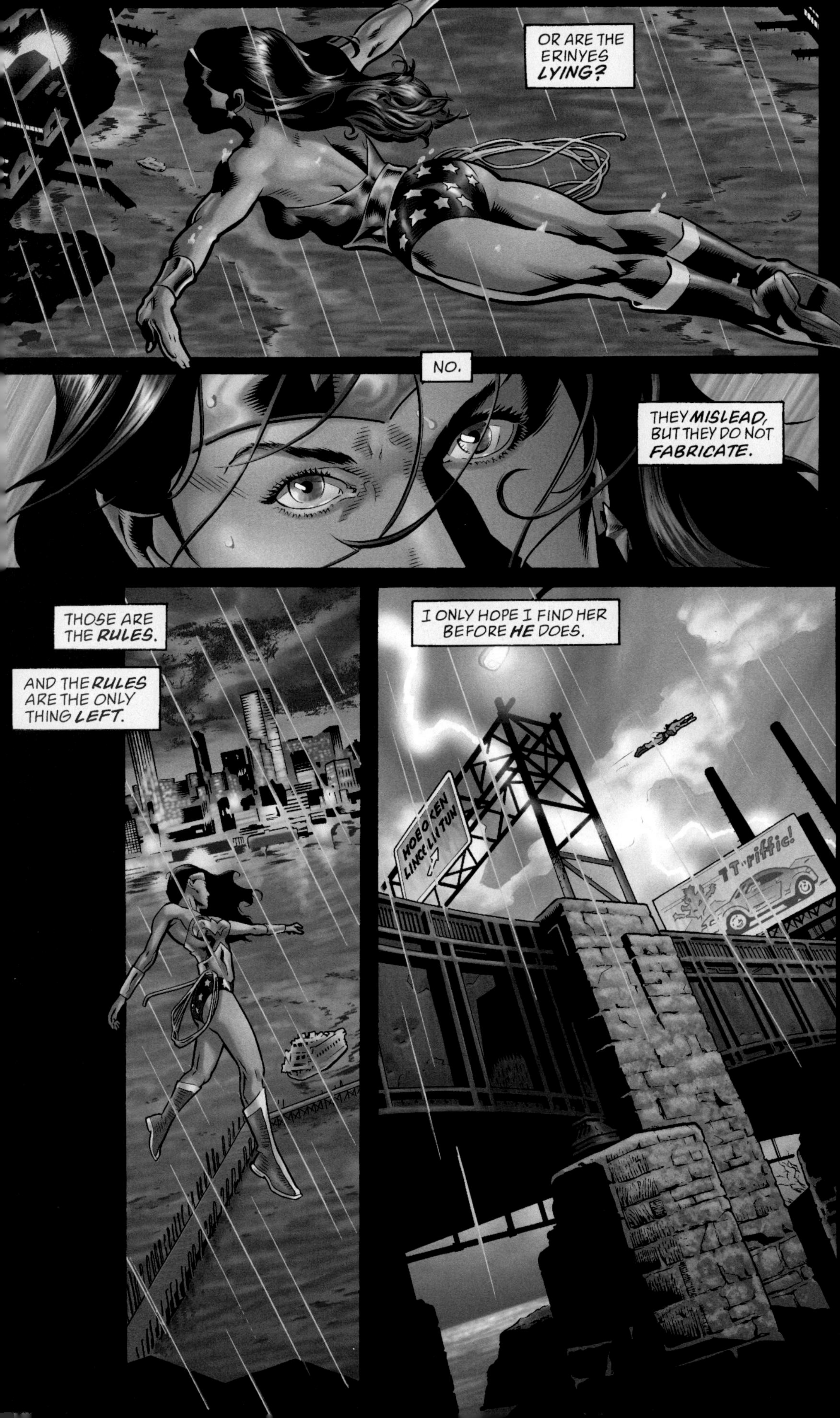
OR ARE THE ERINYES LYING?
NO.
THEY MISLEAD, BUT THEY DO NOT FABRICATE.
THOSE ARE THE RULES.
AND THE RULES ARE THE ONLY THING LEFT.
I ONLY HOPE I FIND HER BEFORE HE DOES.
T-riffic!

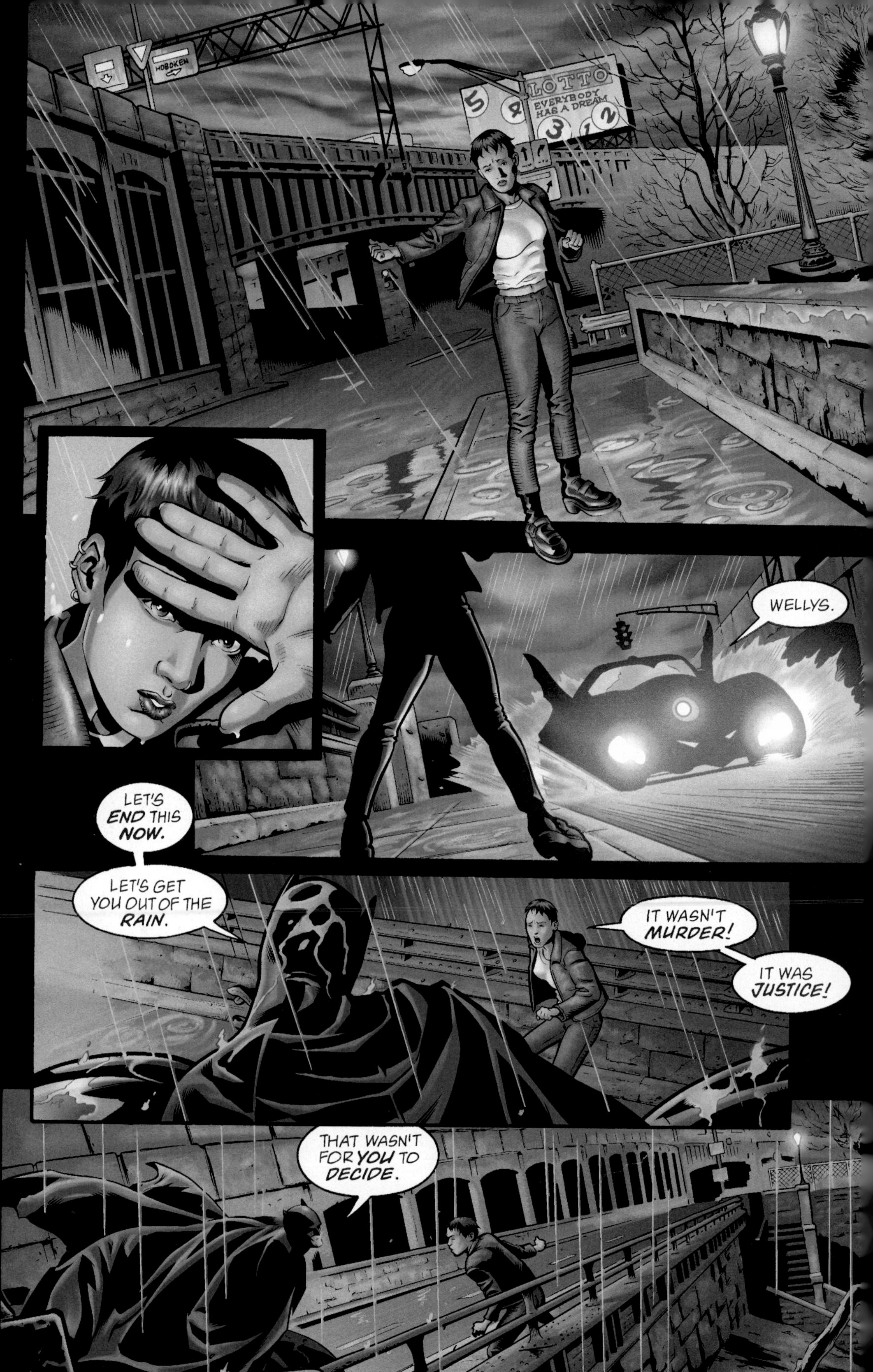
HOBOKEN
LOTTO
EVERYBODY HAS A DREAM
5 4 3 1 2
WELLYS.
LET'S END THIS NOW.
LET'S GET YOU OUT OF THE RAIN.
IT WASN'T MURDER!
IT WAS JUSTICE!
THAT WASN'T FOR YOU TO DECIDE.

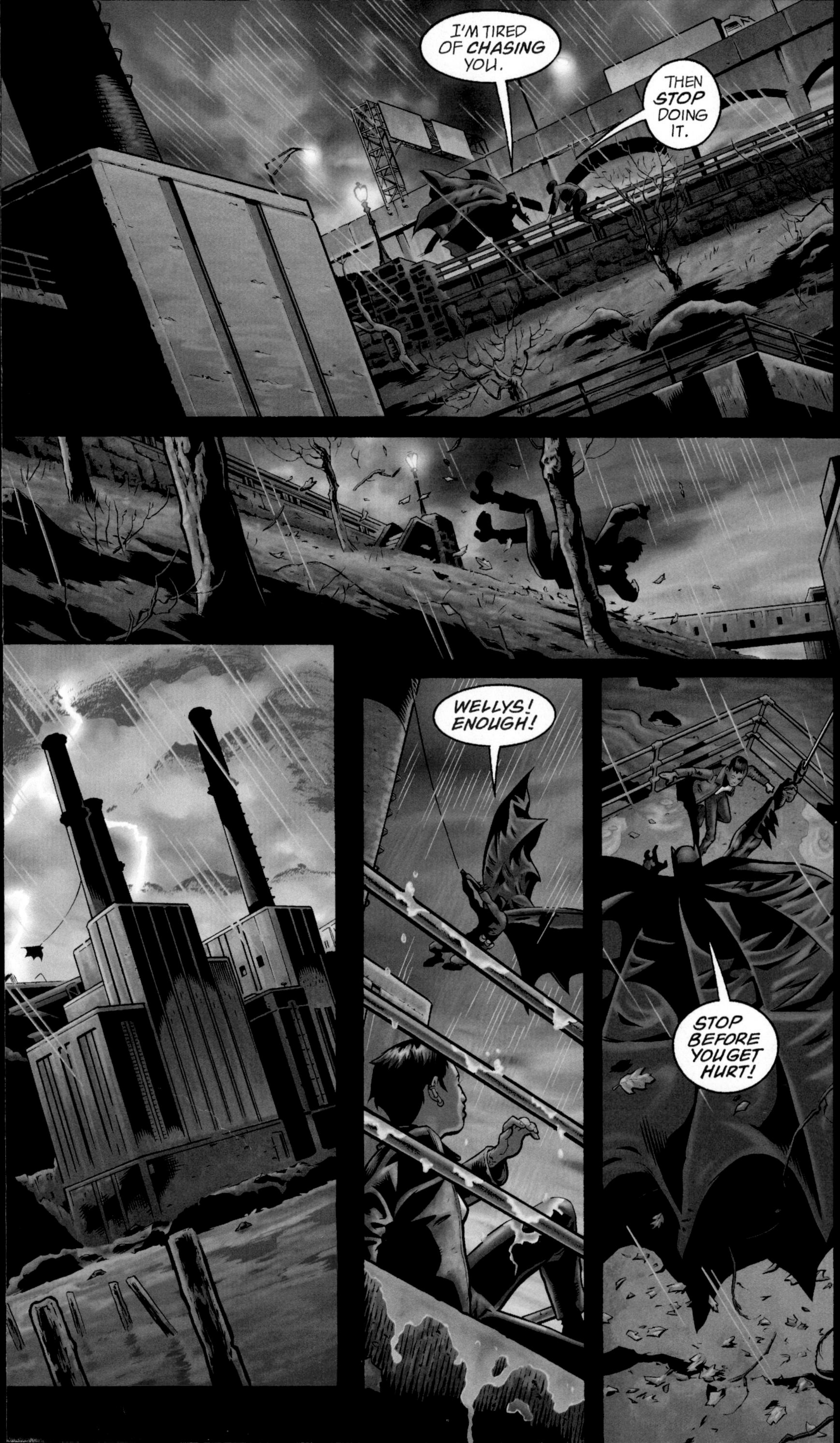
I'M TIRED OF CHASING YOU.
THEN STOP DOING IT.
WELLYS! ENOUGH!
STOP BEFORE YOU GET HURT!

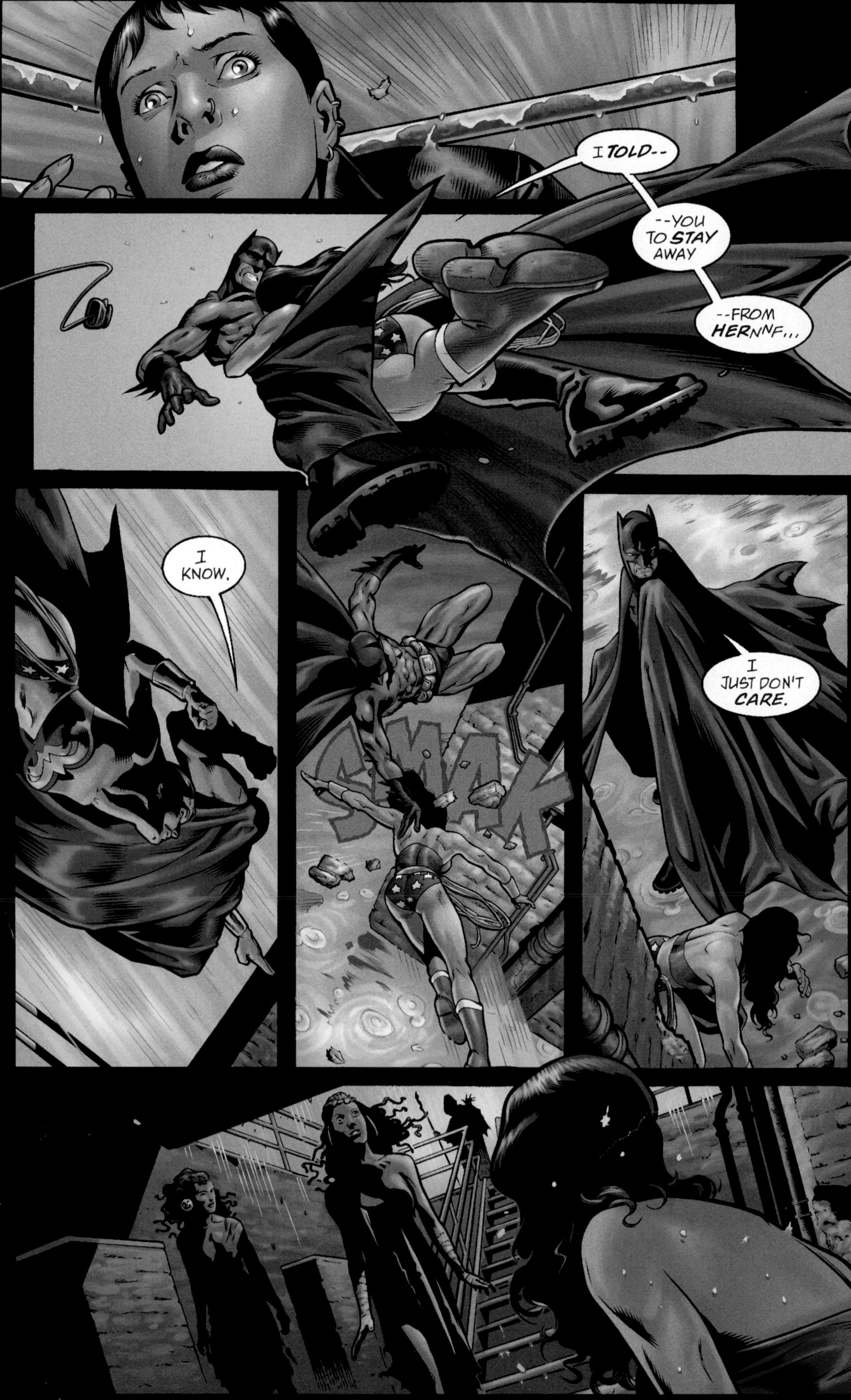
I TOLD--
--YOU TO STAY AWAY
--FROM HERNNF...
I KNOW.
SMAK
I JUST DON'T CARE.

DAMN YOU, *NO*--

--DON'T YOU *UNDERSTAND*--

--I DON'T HAVE A *CHOICE!*

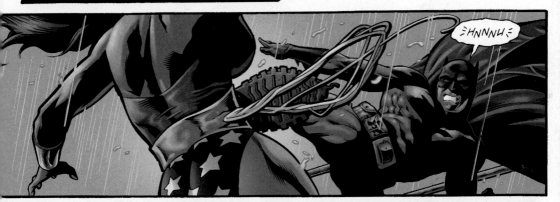

≈HNNNH≈

BRUCE...

...DON'T MAKE ME STOP YOU.

YOU *DON'T HAVE* A *CHOICE...*

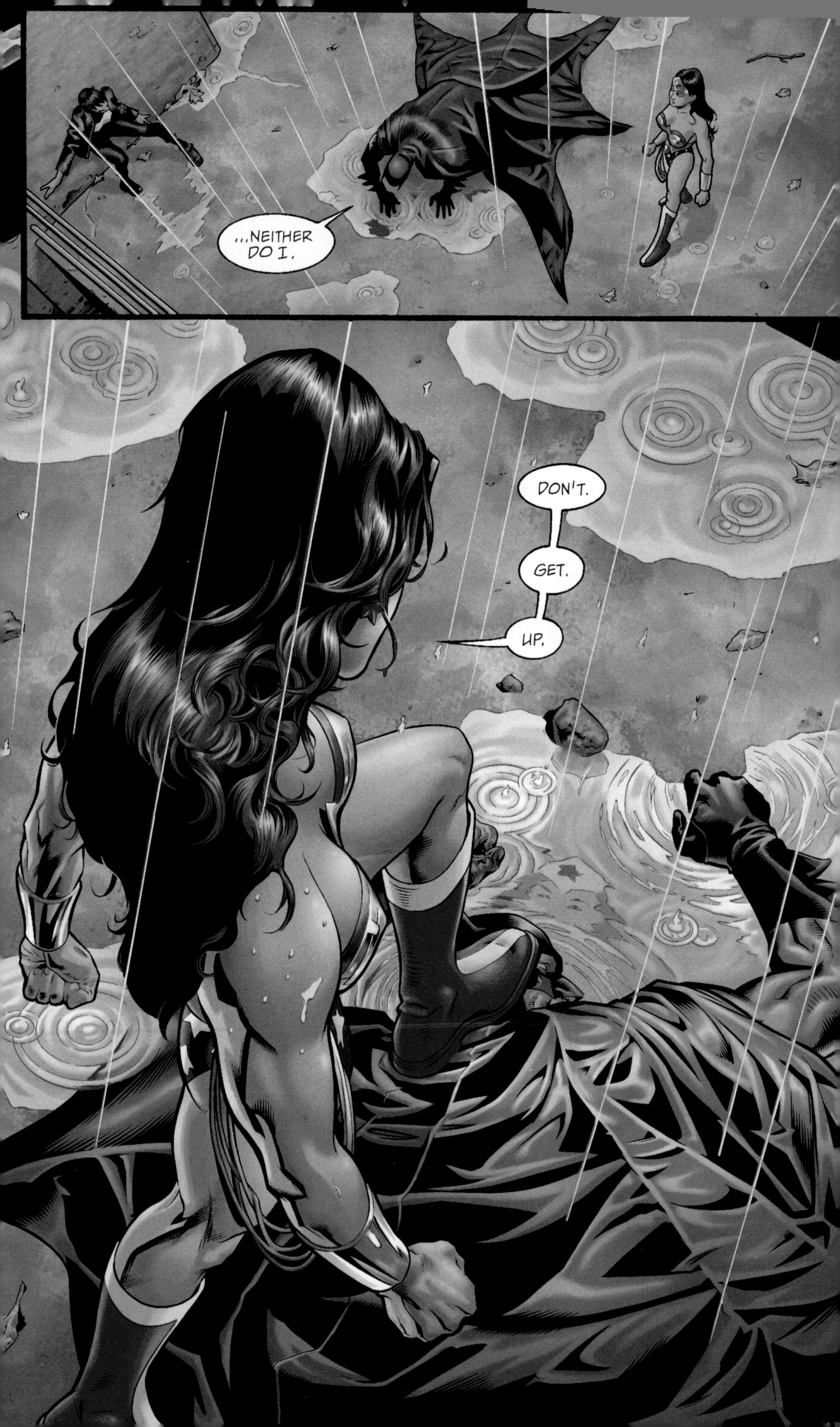
...NEITHER DO I.
DON'T.
GET.
UP.

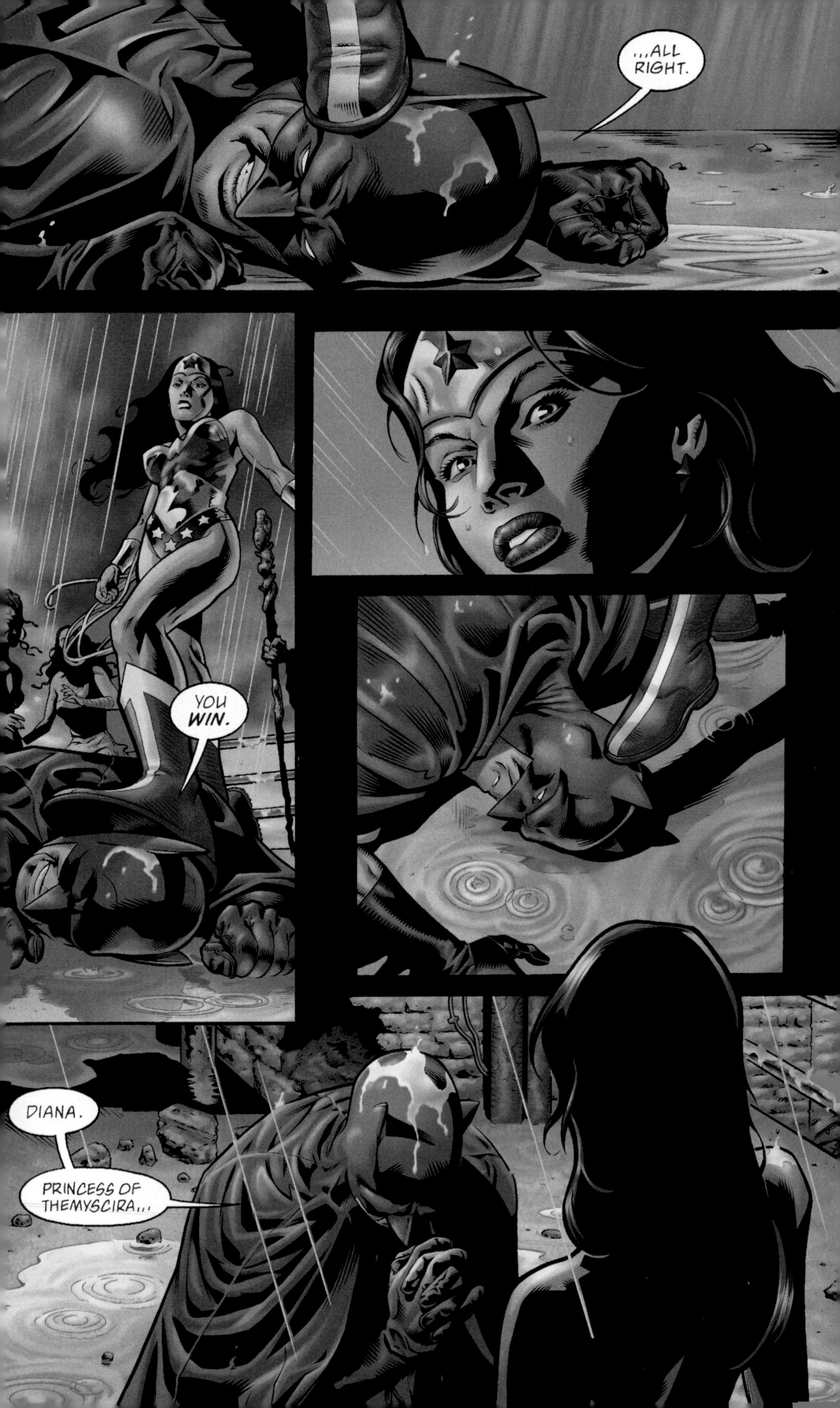
...ALL RIGHT.
YOU WIN.
DIANA.
PRINCESS OF THEMYSCIRA...

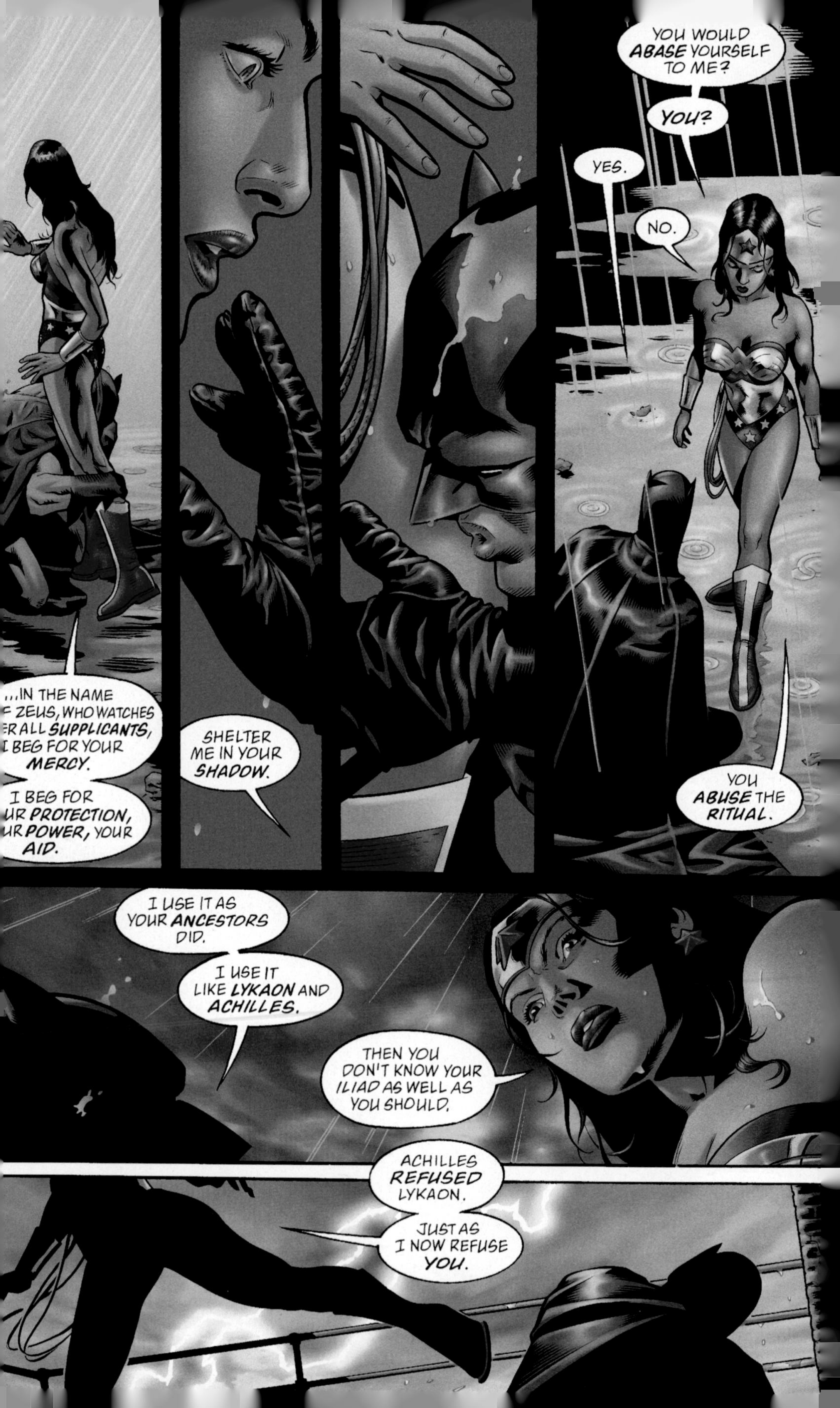
...IN THE NAME
F ZEUS, WHO WATCHES
ER ALL SUPPLICANTS,
I BEG FOR YOUR
MERCY.
I BEG FOR
UR PROTECTION,
UR POWER, YOUR
AID.
SHELTER ME IN YOUR SHADOW.
YOU WOULD ABASE YOURSELF TO ME?
YOU?
YES.
NO.
YOU ABUSE THE RITUAL.
I USE IT AS YOUR ANCESTORS DID.
I USE IT LIKE LYKAON AND ACHILLES.
THEN YOU DON'T KNOW YOUR ILIAD AS WELL AS YOU SHOULD.
ACHILLES REFUSED LYKAON.
JUST AS I NOW REFUSE YOU.

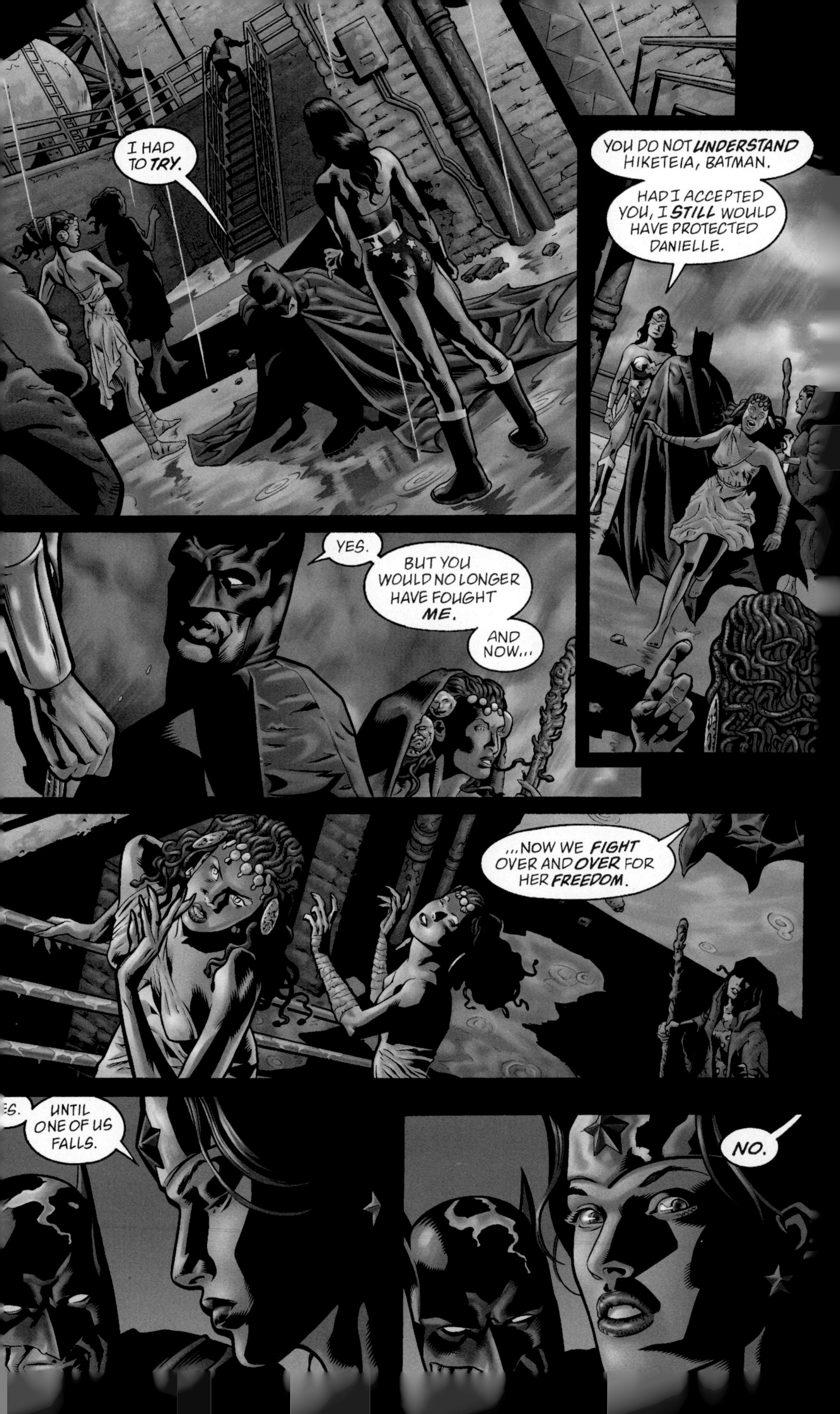
I HAD TO TRY.
YOU DO NOT UNDERSTAND HIKETEIA, BATMAN.
HAD I ACCEPTED YOU, I STILL WOULD HAVE PROTECTED DANIELLE.
YES.
BUT YOU WOULD NO LONGER HAVE FOUGHT ME.
AND NOW...
...NOW WE FIGHT OVER AND OVER FOR HER FREEDOM.
UNTIL ONE OF US FALLS.
NO.

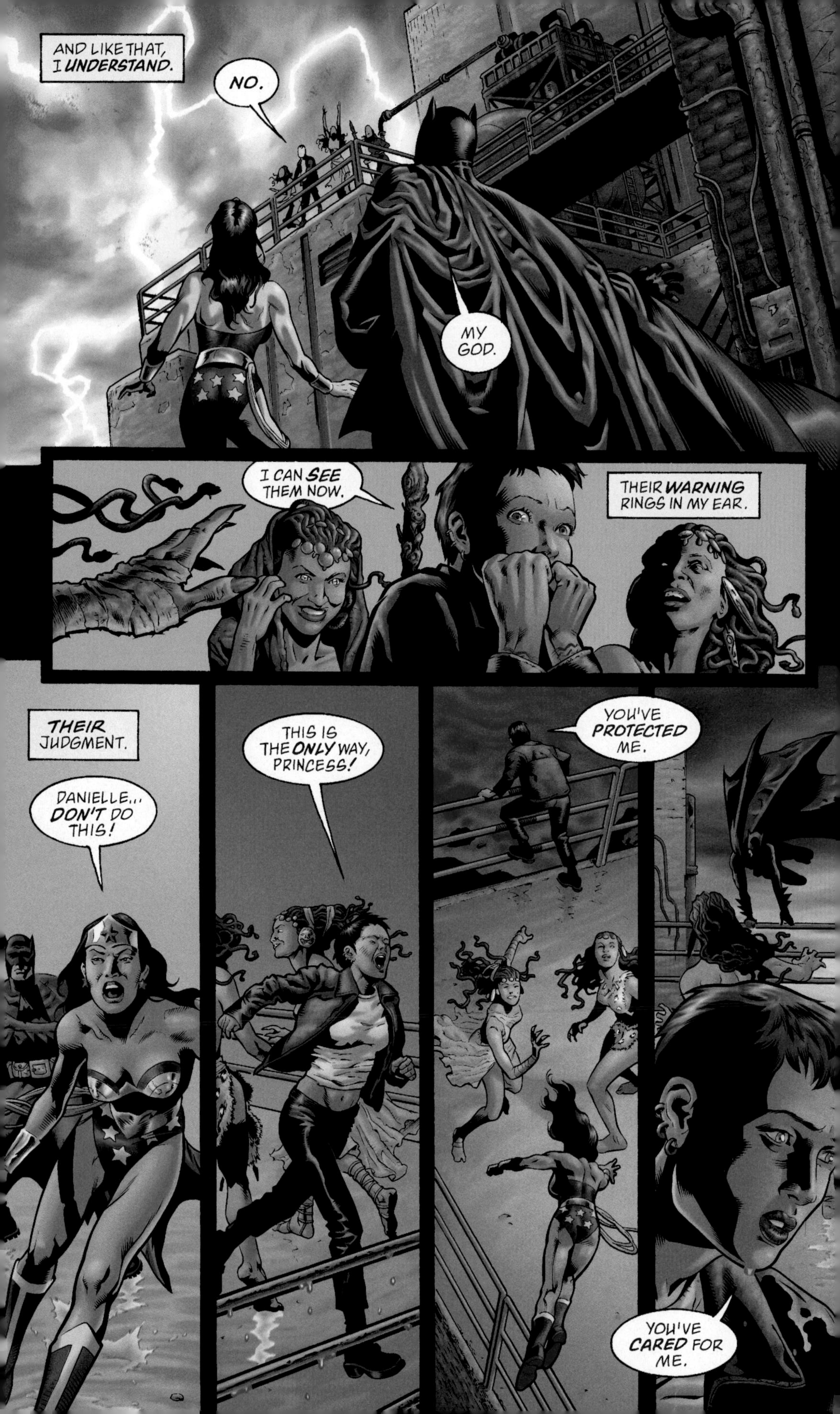
AND LIKE THAT, I **UNDERSTAND**.
NO.
MY GOD.
I CAN **SEE** THEM NOW.
THEIR **WARNING** RINGS IN MY EAR.
THEIR JUDGMENT.
DANIELLE... **DON'T** DO THIS!
THIS IS THE **ONLY** WAY, PRINCESS!
YOU'VE **PROTECTED** ME.
YOU'VE **CARED** FOR ME.

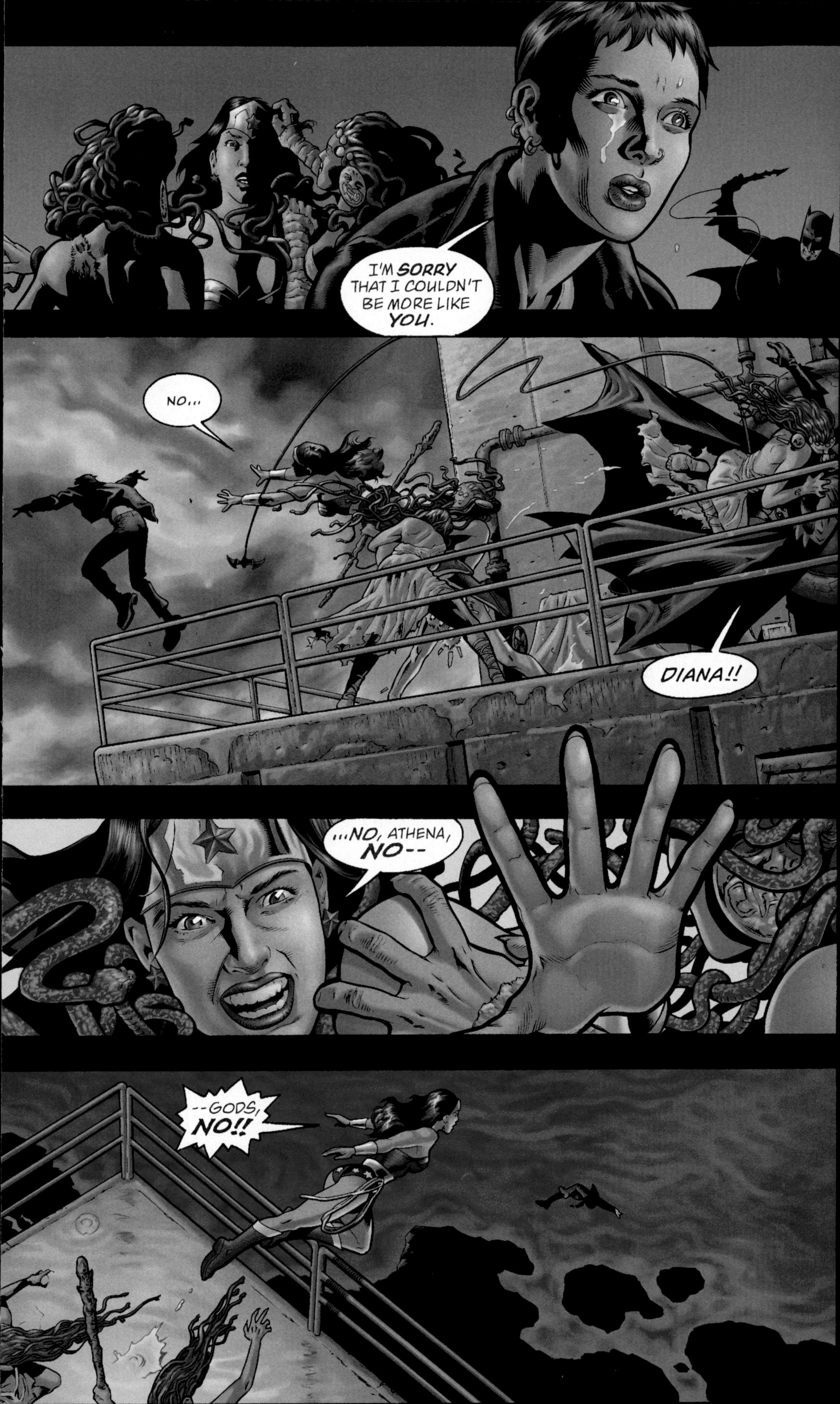
I'M SORRY THAT I COULDN'T BE MORE LIKE YOU.
NO...
DIANA!!
...NO, ATHENA, NO--
--GODS, NO!!

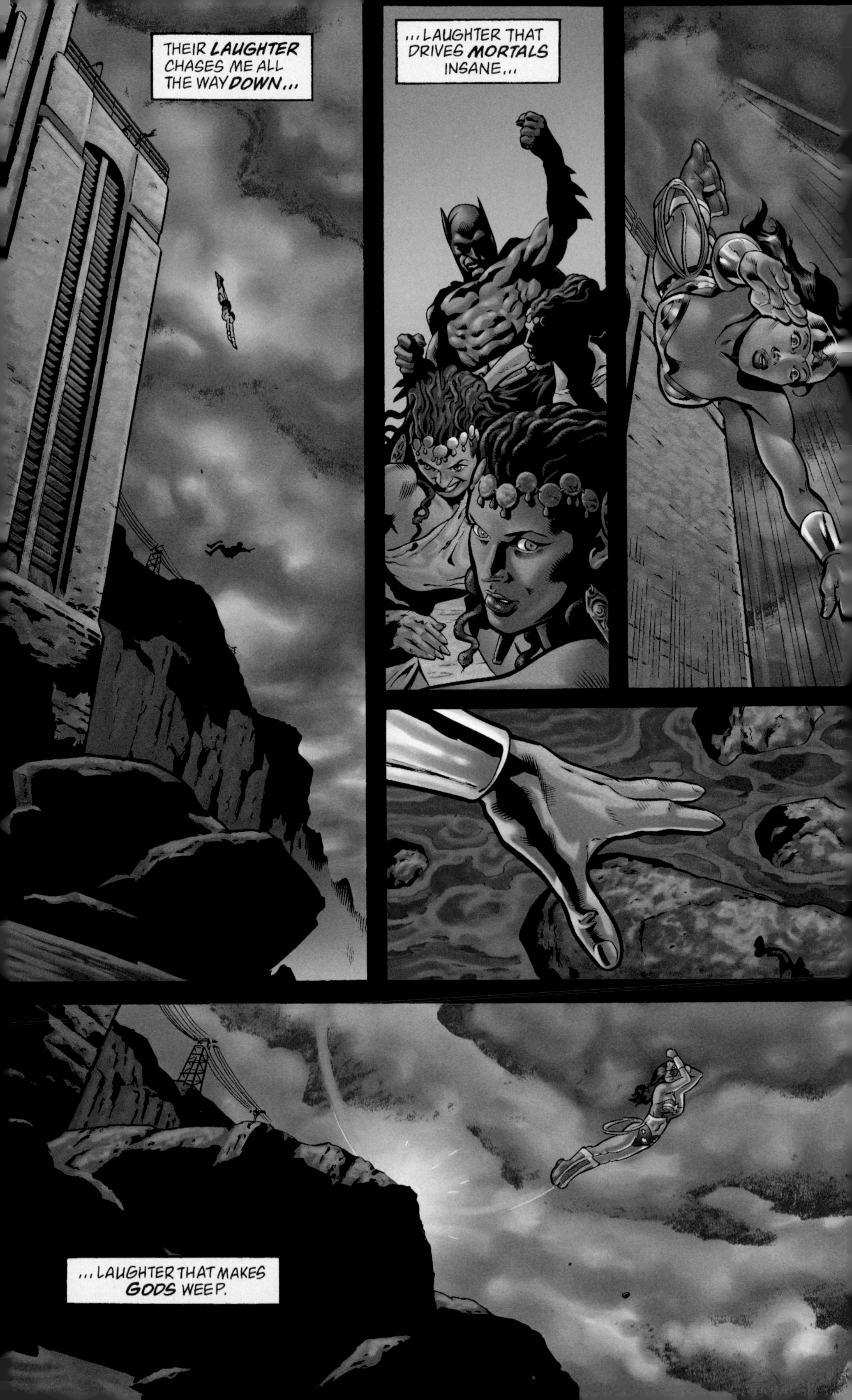
THEIR LAUGHTER CHASES ME ALL THE WAY DOWN...
...LAUGHTER THAT DRIVES MORTALS INSANE...
...LAUGHTER THAT MAKES GODS WEEP.

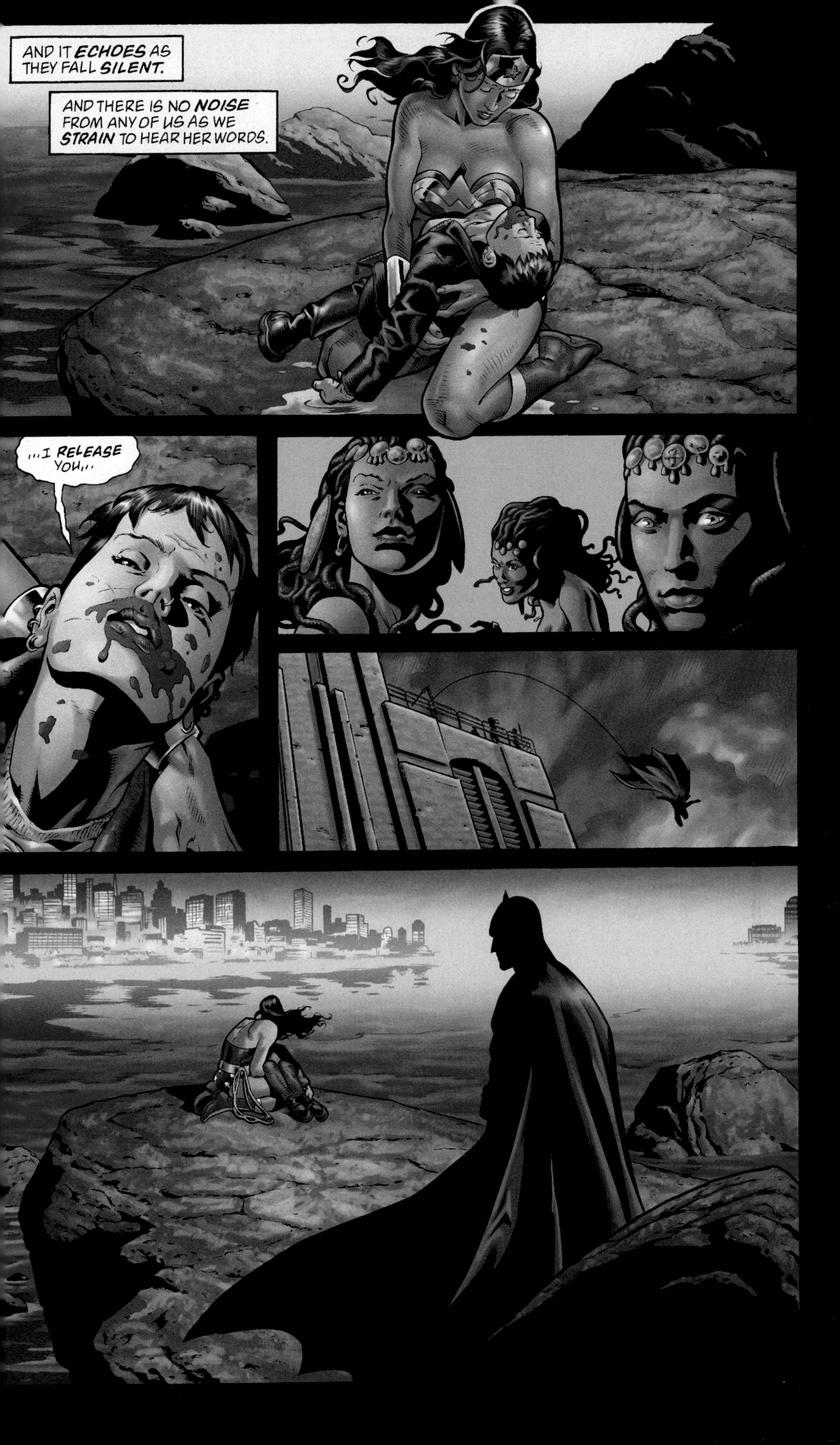
AND IT ECHOES AS THEY FALL SILENT.
AND THERE IS NO NOISE FROM ANY OF US AS WE STRAIN TO HEAR HER WORDS.
...I RELEASE YOU...

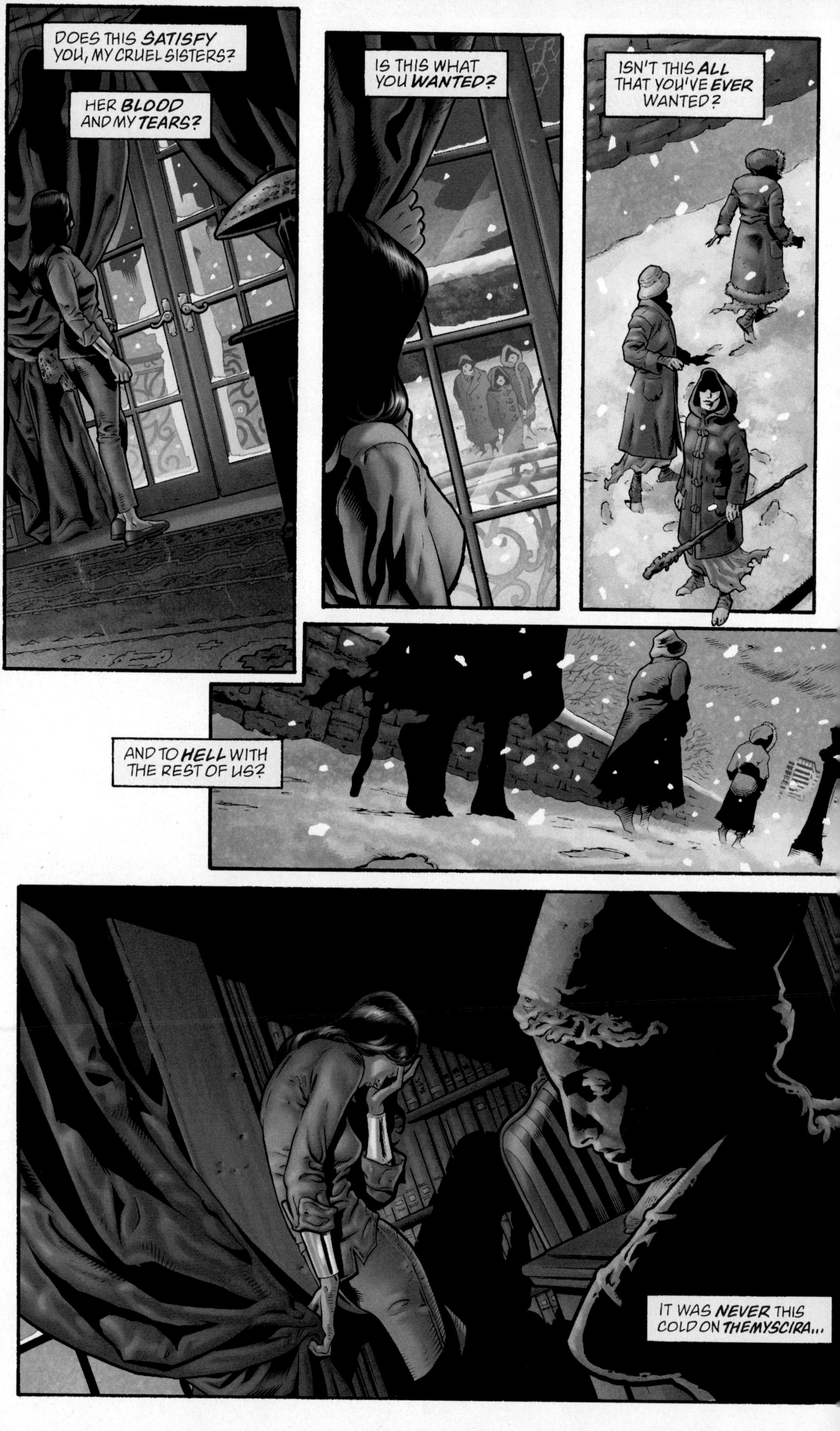
DOES THIS SATISFY YOU, MY CRUEL SISTERS?
HER BLOOD AND MY TEARS?
IS THIS WHAT YOU WANTED?
ISN'T THIS ALL THAT YOU'VE EVER WANTED?
AND TO HELL WITH THE REST OF US?
IT WAS NEVER THIS COLD ON THEMYSCIRA...

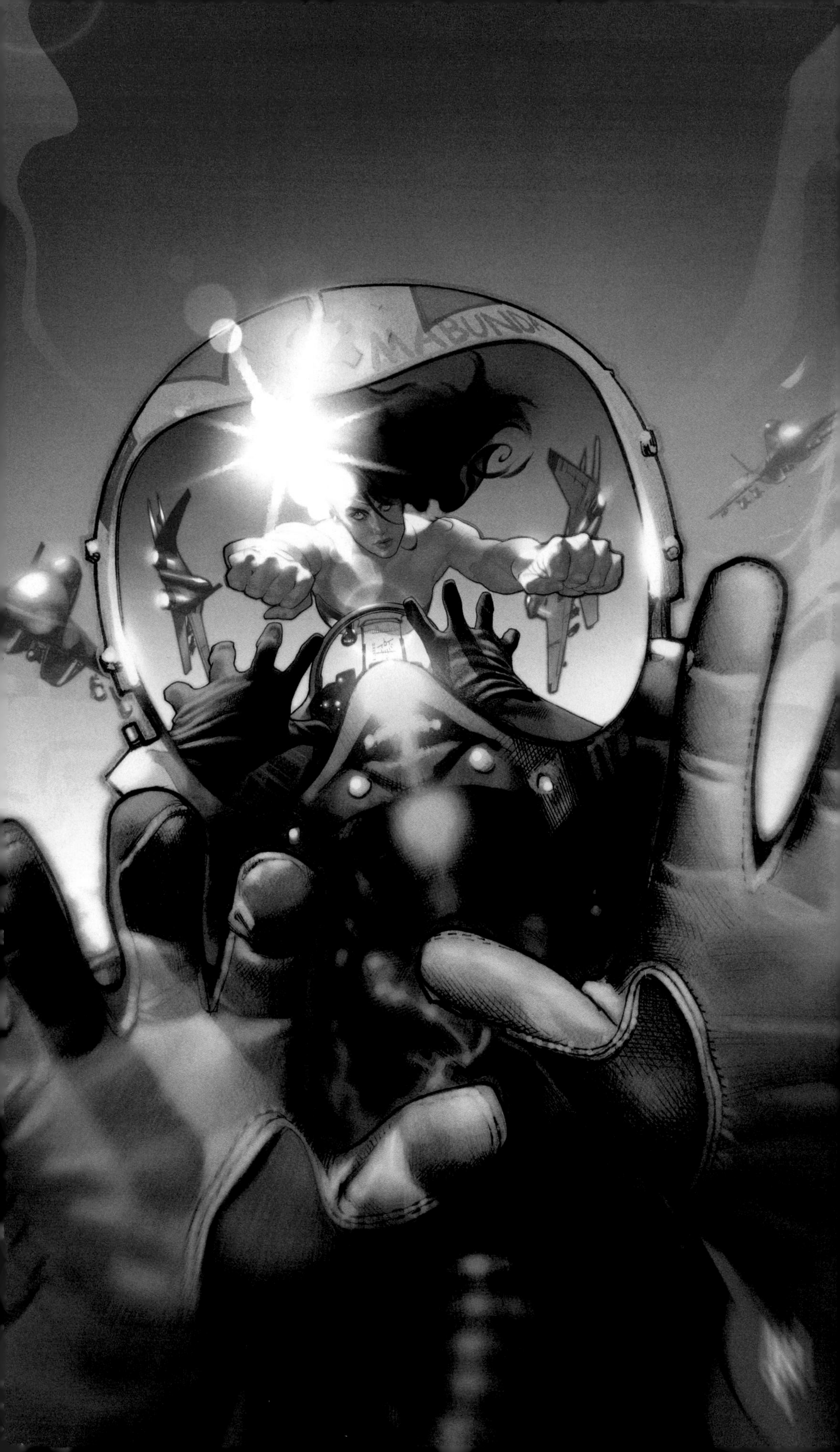
MABUNDA

"THE MISSION"

Drew Johnson – *pencils*
Ray Snyder – *inks*
Trish Mulvihill - *colors*
Adam Hughes – *cover art*

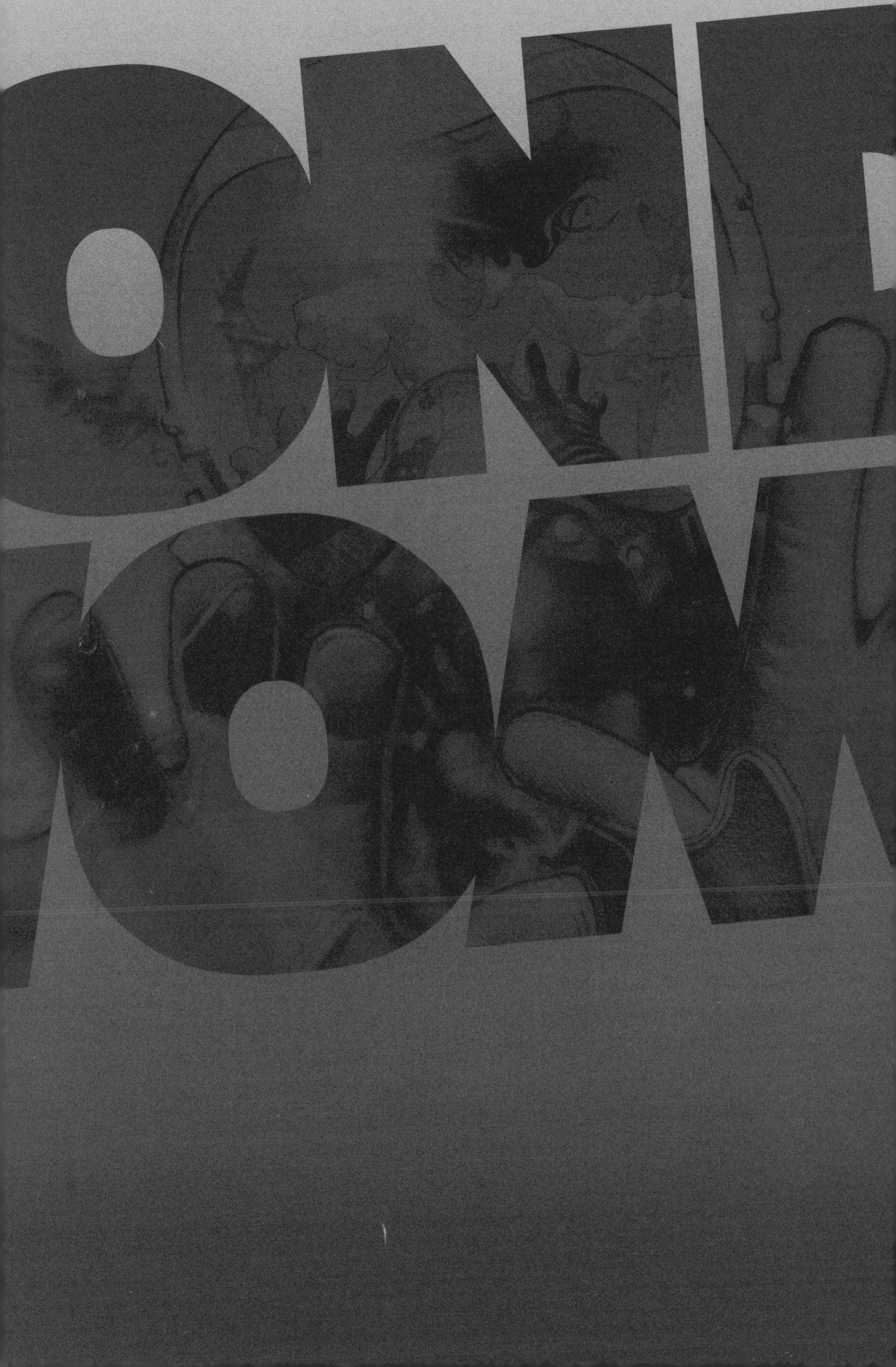

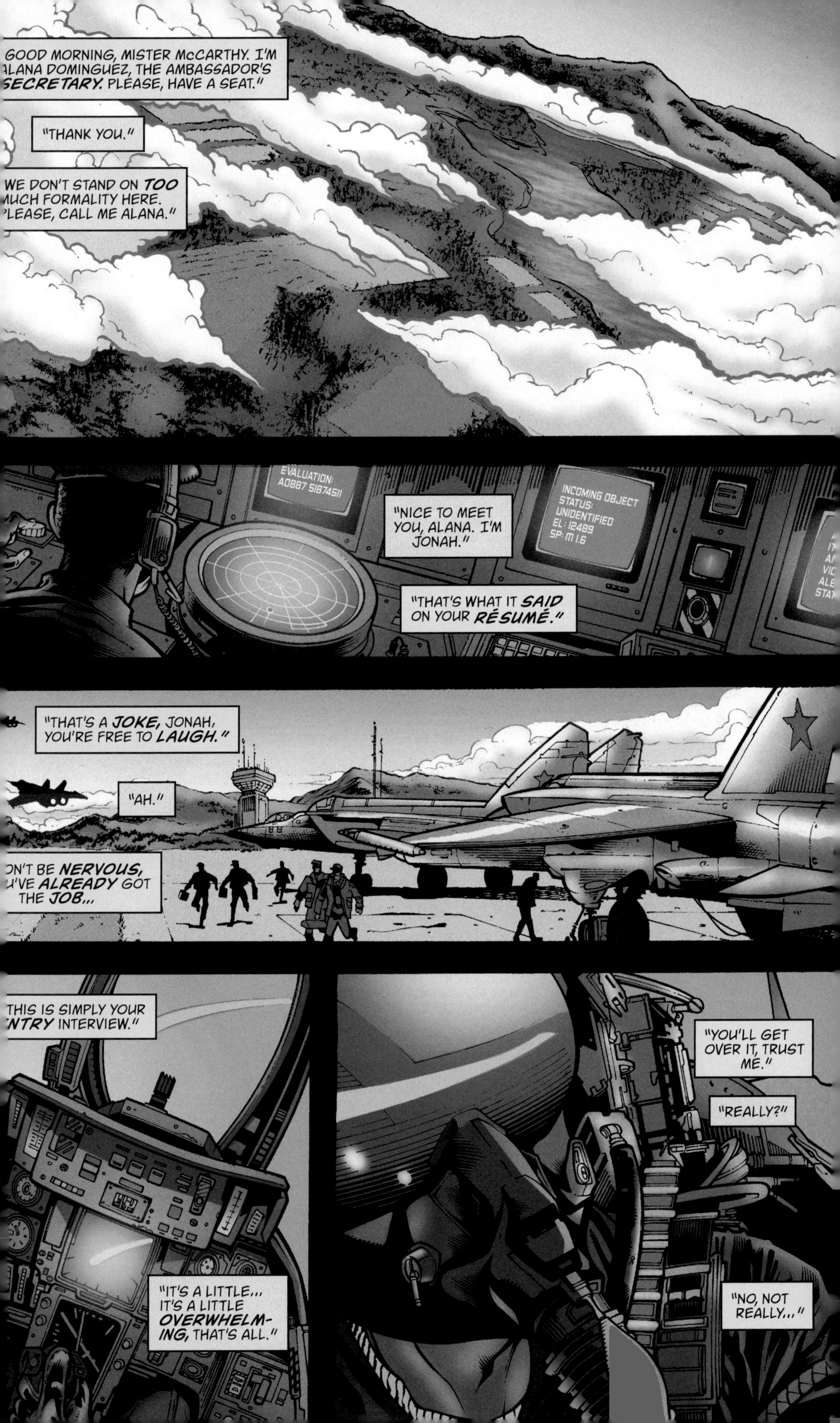

GOOD MORNING, MISTER McCARTHY. I'M ALANA DOMINGUEZ, THE AMBASSADOR'S SECRETARY. PLEASE, HAVE A SEAT."
"THANK YOU."
WE DON'T STAND ON TOO MUCH FORMALITY HERE. 'LEASE, CALL ME ALANA."
EVALUATION: A0887 5187451I
"NICE TO MEET YOU, ALANA. I'M JONAH."
INCOMING OBJECT STATUS: UNIDENTIFIED EL: 12489 SP: M 1.6
"THAT'S WHAT IT SAID ON YOUR RÉSUMÉ."
"THAT'S A JOKE, JONAH, YOU'RE FREE TO LAUGH."
"AH."
ON'T BE NERVOUS, U'VE ALREADY GOT THE JOB...
THIS IS SIMPLY YOUR NTRY INTERVIEW."
"IT'S A LITTLE... IT'S A LITTLE OVERWHELMING, THAT'S ALL."
"YOU'LL GET OVER IT, TRUST ME."
"REALLY?"
"NO, NOT REALLY..."

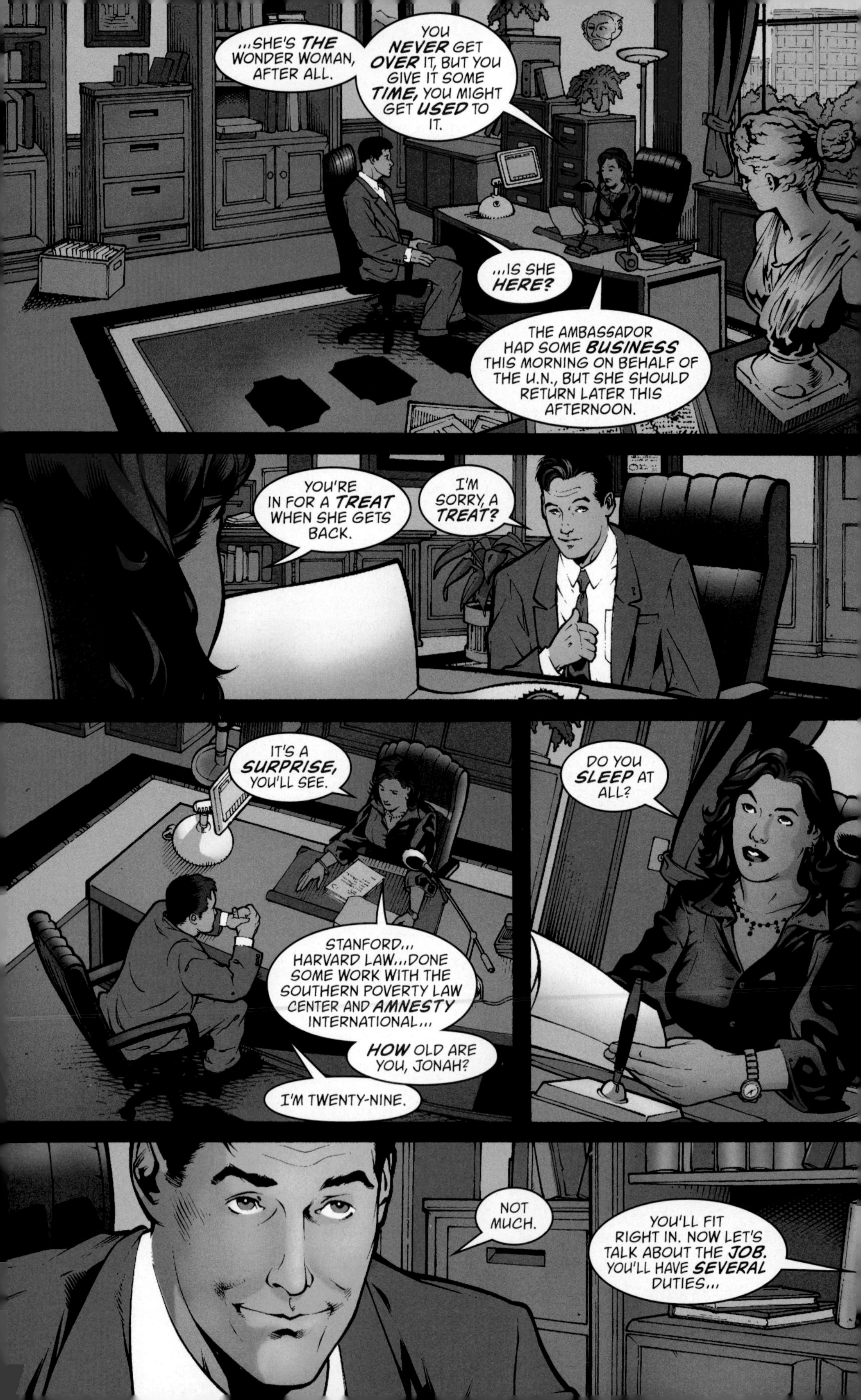
...SHE'S THE WONDER WOMAN, AFTER ALL.
YOU NEVER GET OVER IT, BUT YOU GIVE IT SOME TIME, YOU MIGHT GET USED TO IT.
...IS SHE HERE?
THE AMBASSADOR HAD SOME BUSINESS THIS MORNING ON BEHALF OF THE U.N., BUT SHE SHOULD RETURN LATER THIS AFTERNOON.
YOU'RE IN FOR A TREAT WHEN SHE GETS BACK.
I'M SORRY, A TREAT?
IT'S A SURPRISE, YOU'LL SEE.
STANFORD... HARVARD LAW...DONE SOME WORK WITH THE SOUTHERN POVERTY LAW CENTER AND AMNESTY INTERNATIONAL...
HOW OLD ARE YOU, JONAH?
I'M TWENTY-NINE.
DO YOU SLEEP AT ALL?
NOT MUCH.
YOU'LL FIT RIGHT IN. NOW LET'S TALK ABOUT THE JOB. YOU'LL HAVE SEVERAL DUTIES...

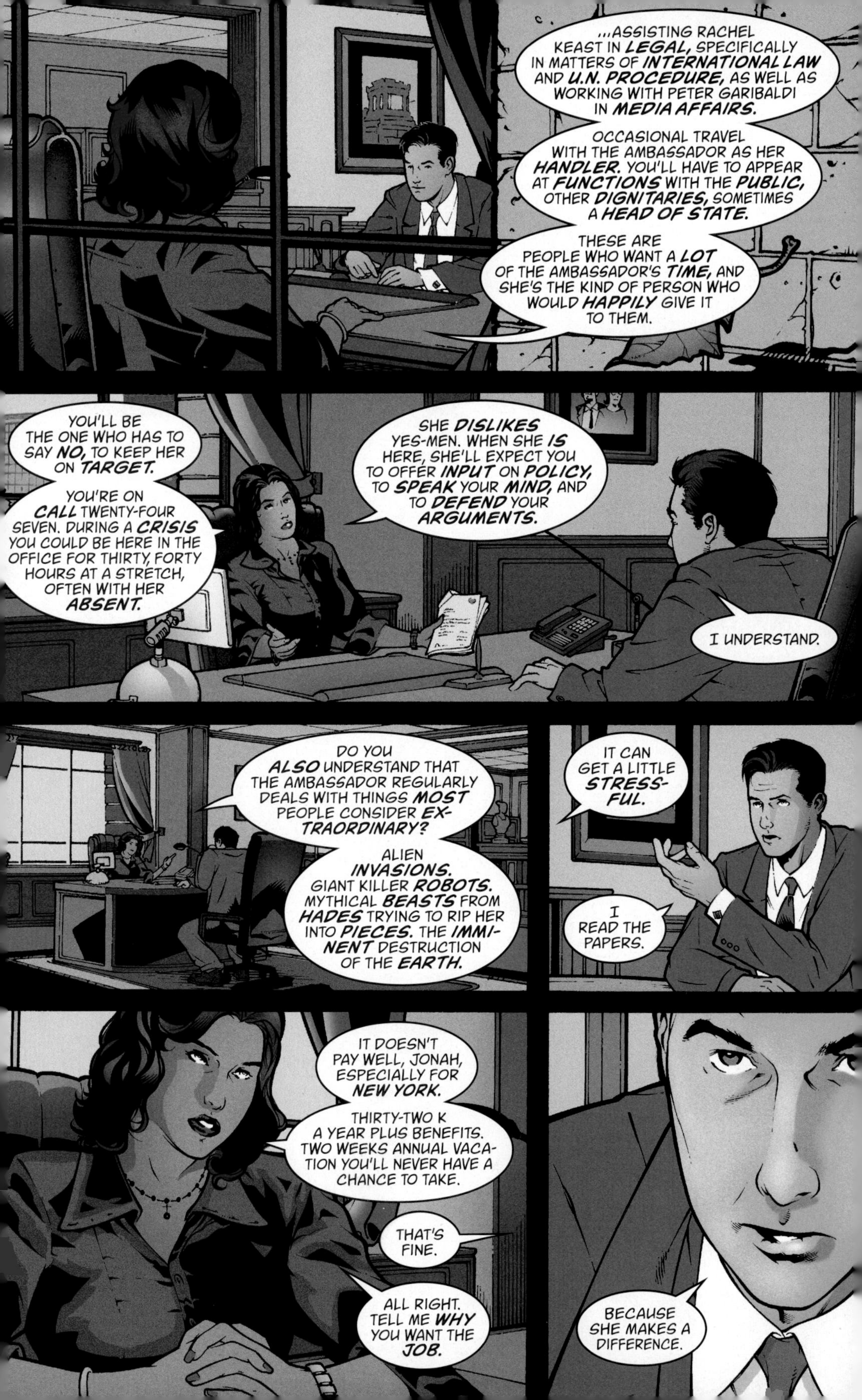
...ASSISTING RACHEL KEAST IN LEGAL, SPECIFICALLY IN MATTERS OF INTERNATIONAL LAW AND U.N. PROCEDURE, AS WELL AS WORKING WITH PETER GARIBALDI IN MEDIA AFFAIRS.
OCCASIONAL TRAVEL WITH THE AMBASSADOR AS HER HANDLER. YOU'LL HAVE TO APPEAR AT FUNCTIONS WITH THE PUBLIC, OTHER DIGNITARIES, SOMETIMES A HEAD OF STATE.
THESE ARE PEOPLE WHO WANT A LOT OF THE AMBASSADOR'S TIME, AND SHE'S THE KIND OF PERSON WHO WOULD HAPPILY GIVE IT TO THEM.
YOU'LL BE THE ONE WHO HAS TO SAY NO, TO KEEP HER ON TARGET.
YOU'RE ON CALL TWENTY-FOUR SEVEN. DURING A CRISIS YOU COULD BE HERE IN THE OFFICE FOR THIRTY, FORTY HOURS AT A STRETCH, OFTEN WITH HER ABSENT.
SHE DISLIKES YES-MEN. WHEN SHE IS HERE, SHE'LL EXPECT YOU TO OFFER INPUT ON POLICY, TO SPEAK YOUR MIND, AND TO DEFEND YOUR ARGUMENTS.
I UNDERSTAND.
DO YOU ALSO UNDERSTAND THAT THE AMBASSADOR REGULARLY DEALS WITH THINGS MOST PEOPLE CONSIDER EX-TRAORDINARY?
ALIEN INVASIONS. GIANT KILLER ROBOTS. MYTHICAL BEASTS FROM HADES TRYING TO RIP HER INTO PIECES. THE IMMI-NENT DESTRUCTION OF THE EARTH.
IT CAN GET A LITTLE STRESS-FUL.
I READ THE PAPERS.
IT DOESN'T PAY WELL, JONAH, ESPECIALLY FOR NEW YORK.
THIRTY-TWO K A YEAR PLUS BENEFITS. TWO WEEKS ANNUAL VACA-TION YOU'LL NEVER HAVE A CHANCE TO TAKE.
THAT'S FINE.
ALL RIGHT. TELL ME WHY YOU WANT THE JOB.
BECAUSE SHE MAKES A DIFFERENCE.

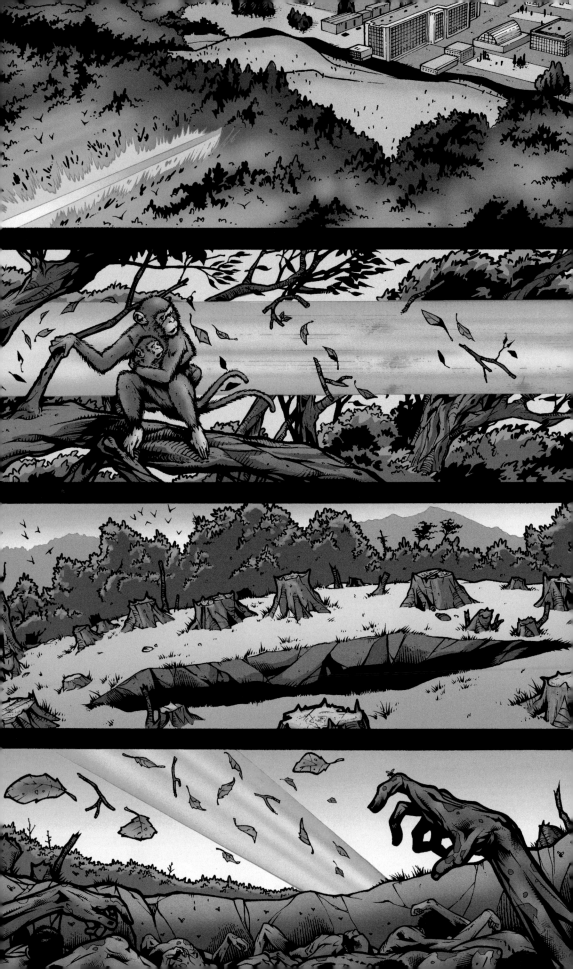

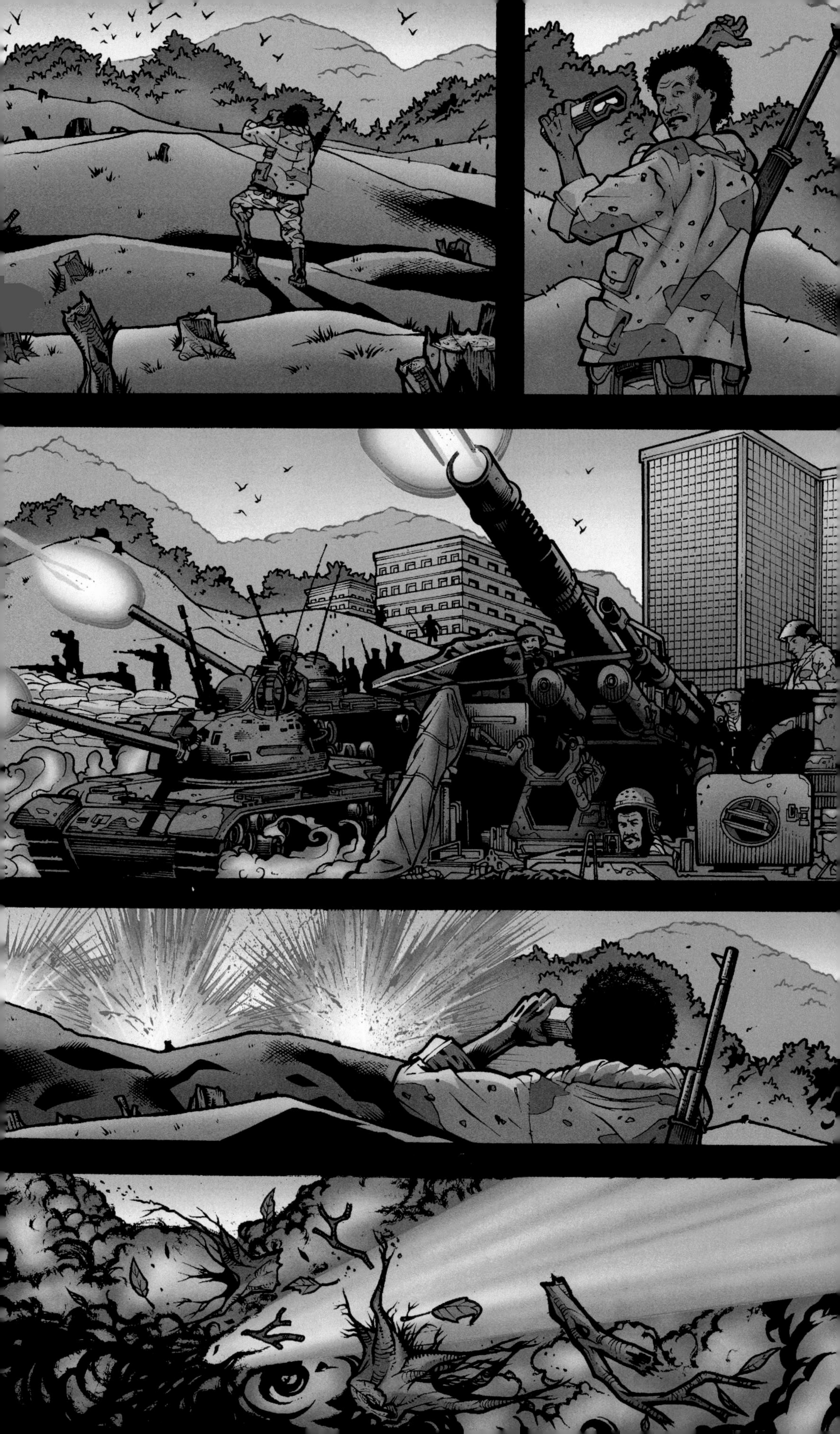

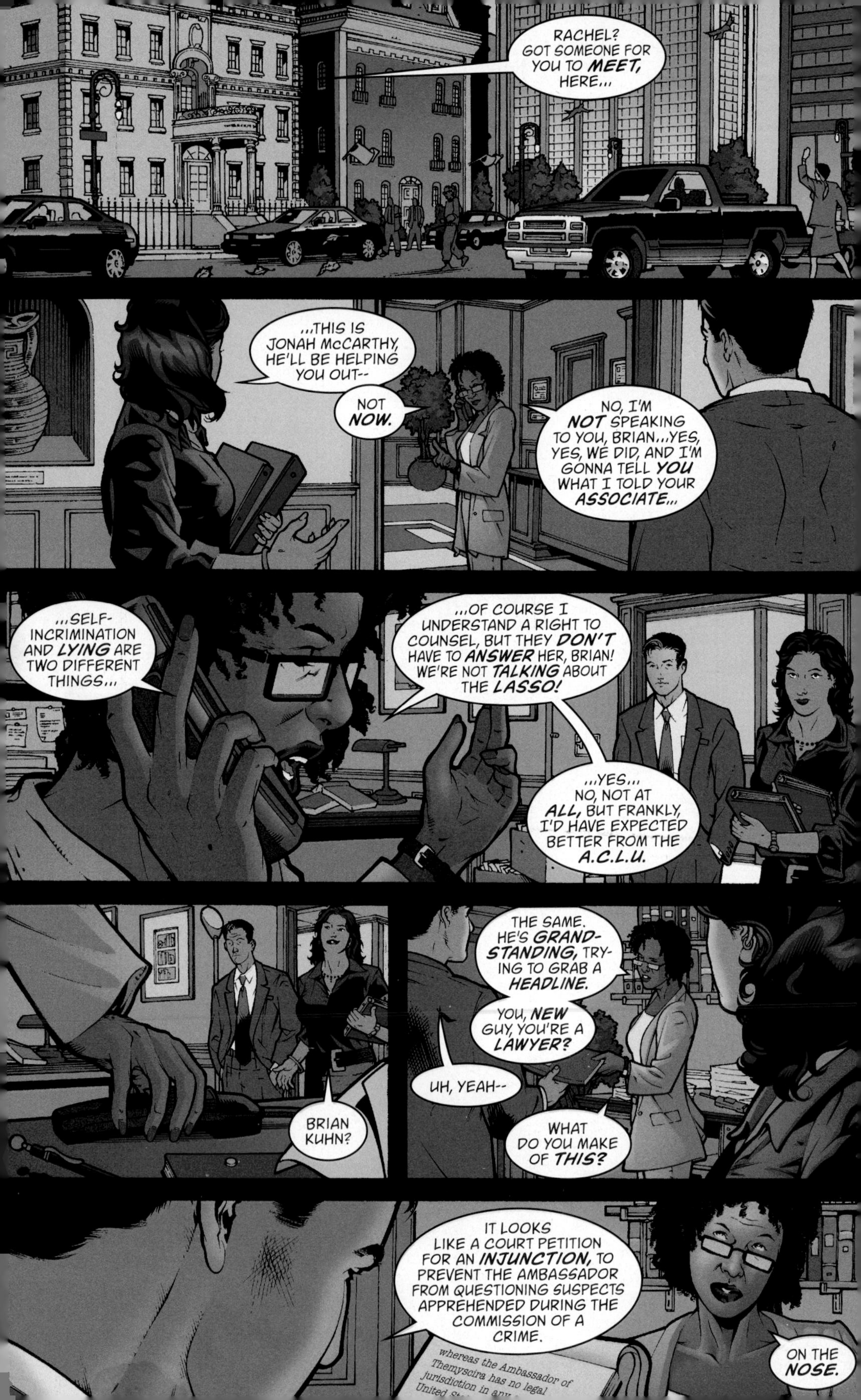
RACHEL? GOT SOMEONE FOR YOU TO MEET, HERE...
...THIS IS JONAH McCARTHY, HE'LL BE HELPING YOU OUT--
NOT NOW.
NO, I'M NOT SPEAKING TO YOU, BRIAN...YES, YES, WE DID, AND I'M GONNA TELL YOU WHAT I TOLD YOUR ASSOCIATE...
...SELF-INCRIMINATION AND LYING ARE TWO DIFFERENT THINGS...
...OF COURSE I UNDERSTAND A RIGHT TO COUNSEL, BUT THEY DON'T HAVE TO ANSWER HER, BRIAN! WE'RE NOT TALKING ABOUT THE LASSO!
...YES... NO, NOT AT ALL, BUT FRANKLY, I'D HAVE EXPECTED BETTER FROM THE A.C.L.U.
BRIAN KUHN?
THE SAME. HE'S GRAND-STANDING, TRYING TO GRAB A HEADLINE.
YOU, NEW GUY, YOU'RE A LAWYER?
UH, YEAH--
WHAT DO YOU MAKE OF THIS?
IT LOOKS LIKE A COURT PETITION FOR AN INJUNCTION, TO PREVENT THE AMBASSADOR FROM QUESTIONING SUSPECTS APPREHENDED DURING THE COMMISSION OF A CRIME.
whereas the Ambassador of
Themyscira has no legal
ON THE NOSE.

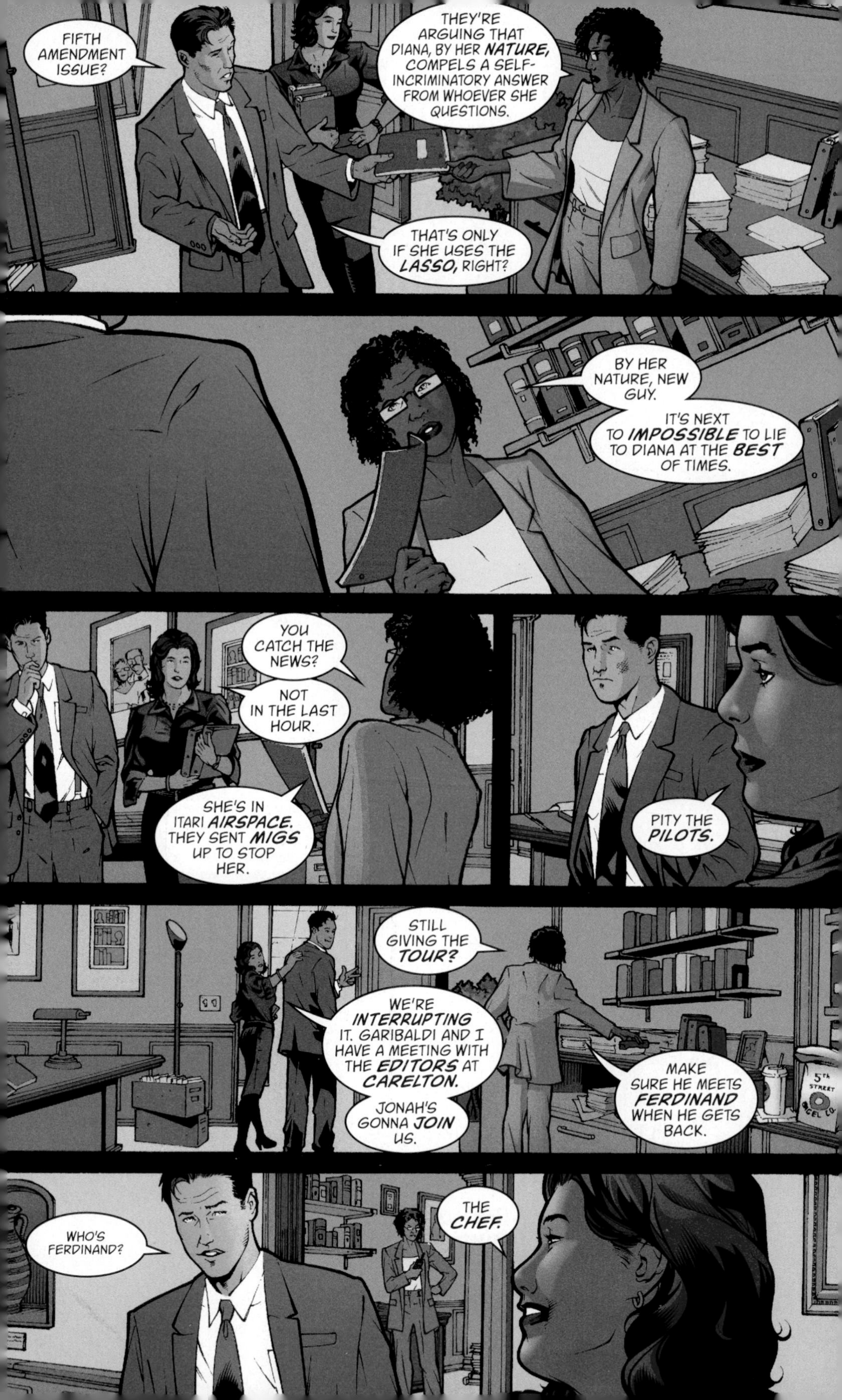

FIFTH AMENDMENT ISSUE?
THEY'RE ARGUING THAT DIANA, BY HER NATURE, COMPELS A SELF-INCRIMINATORY ANSWER FROM WHOEVER SHE QUESTIONS.
THAT'S ONLY IF SHE USES THE LASSO, RIGHT?
BY HER NATURE, NEW GUY.
IT'S NEXT TO IMPOSSIBLE TO LIE TO DIANA AT THE BEST OF TIMES.
YOU CATCH THE NEWS?
NOT IN THE LAST HOUR.
SHE'S IN ITARI AIRSPACE. THEY SENT MIGS UP TO STOP HER.
PITY THE PILOTS.
STILL GIVING THE TOUR?
WE'RE INTERRUPTING IT. GARIBALDI AND I HAVE A MEETING WITH THE EDITORS AT CARELTON.
JONAH'S GONNA JOIN US.
MAKE SURE HE MEETS FERDINAND WHEN HE GETS BACK.
WHO'S FERDINAND?
THE CHEF.

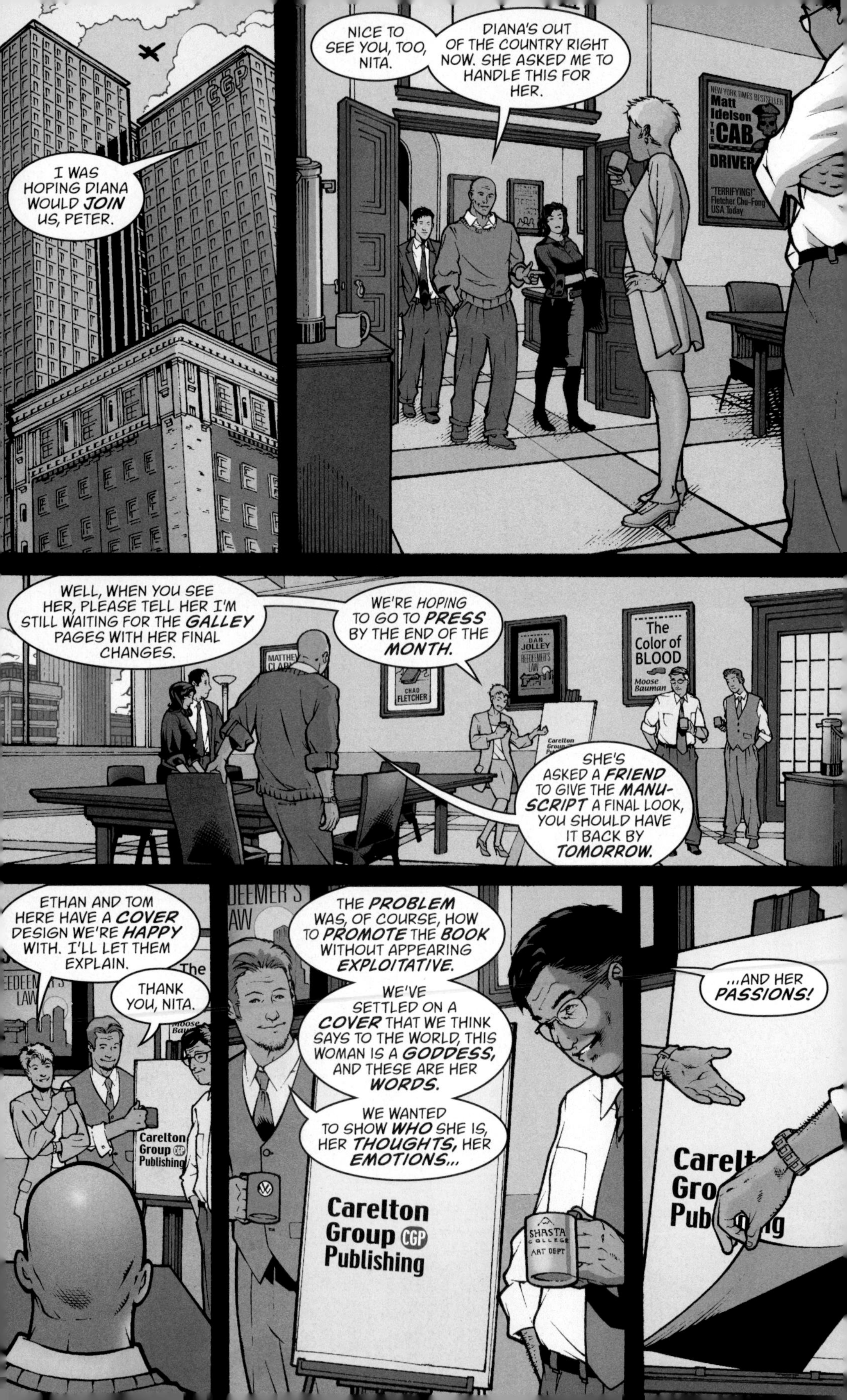
CGP
I WAS HOPING DIANA WOULD JOIN US, PETER.
NICE TO SEE YOU, TOO, NITA.
DIANA'S OUT OF THE COUNTRY RIGHT NOW. SHE ASKED ME TO HANDLE THIS FOR HER.
NEW YORK TIMES BESTSELLER Matt Idelson THE CAB DRIVER "TERRIFYING!" Fletcher Chu-Fong USA Today
WELL, WHEN YOU SEE HER, PLEASE TELL HER I'M STILL WAITING FOR THE GALLEY PAGES WITH HER FINAL CHANGES.
WE'RE HOPING TO GO TO PRESS BY THE END OF THE MONTH.
CHAD FLETCHER
DAN JOLLEY REDEEMER'S LAW
The Color of BLOOD Moose Bauman
SHE'S ASKED A FRIEND TO GIVE THE MANUSCRIPT A FINAL LOOK, YOU SHOULD HAVE IT BACK BY TOMORROW.
ETHAN AND TOM HERE HAVE A COVER DESIGN WE'RE HAPPY WITH. I'LL LET THEM EXPLAIN.
THANK YOU, NITA.
Carelton Group CGP Publishing
THE PROBLEM WAS, OF COURSE, HOW TO PROMOTE THE BOOK WITHOUT APPEARING EXPLOITATIVE.
WE'VE SETTLED ON A COVER THAT WE THINK SAYS TO THE WORLD, THIS WOMAN IS A GODDESS, AND THESE ARE HER WORDS.
WE WANTED TO SHOW WHO SHE IS, HER THOUGHTS, HER EMOTIONS...
Carelton Group CGP Publishing
SHASTA COLLEGE ART DEPT
...AND HER PASSIONS!

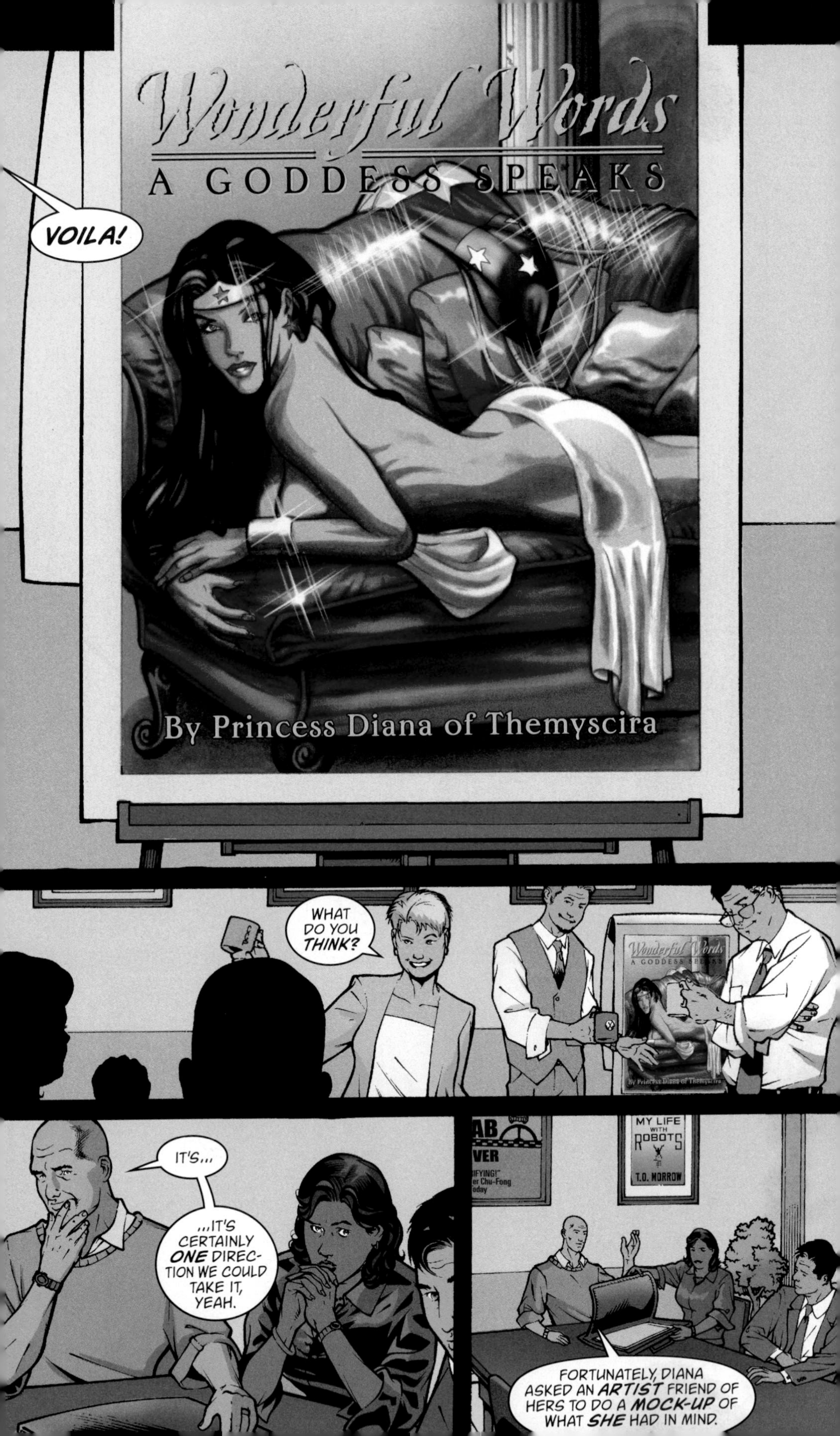
Wonderful Words
A GODDESS SPEAKS
By Princess Diana of Themyscira
VOILA!
WHAT DO YOU THINK?
IT'S...
...IT'S CERTAINLY ONE DIRECTION WE COULD TAKE IT, YEAH.
MY LIFE WITH ROBOTS
T.O. MORROW
FORTUNATELY, DIANA ASKED AN ARTIST FRIEND OF HERS TO DO A MOCK-UP OF WHAT SHE HAD IN MIND.

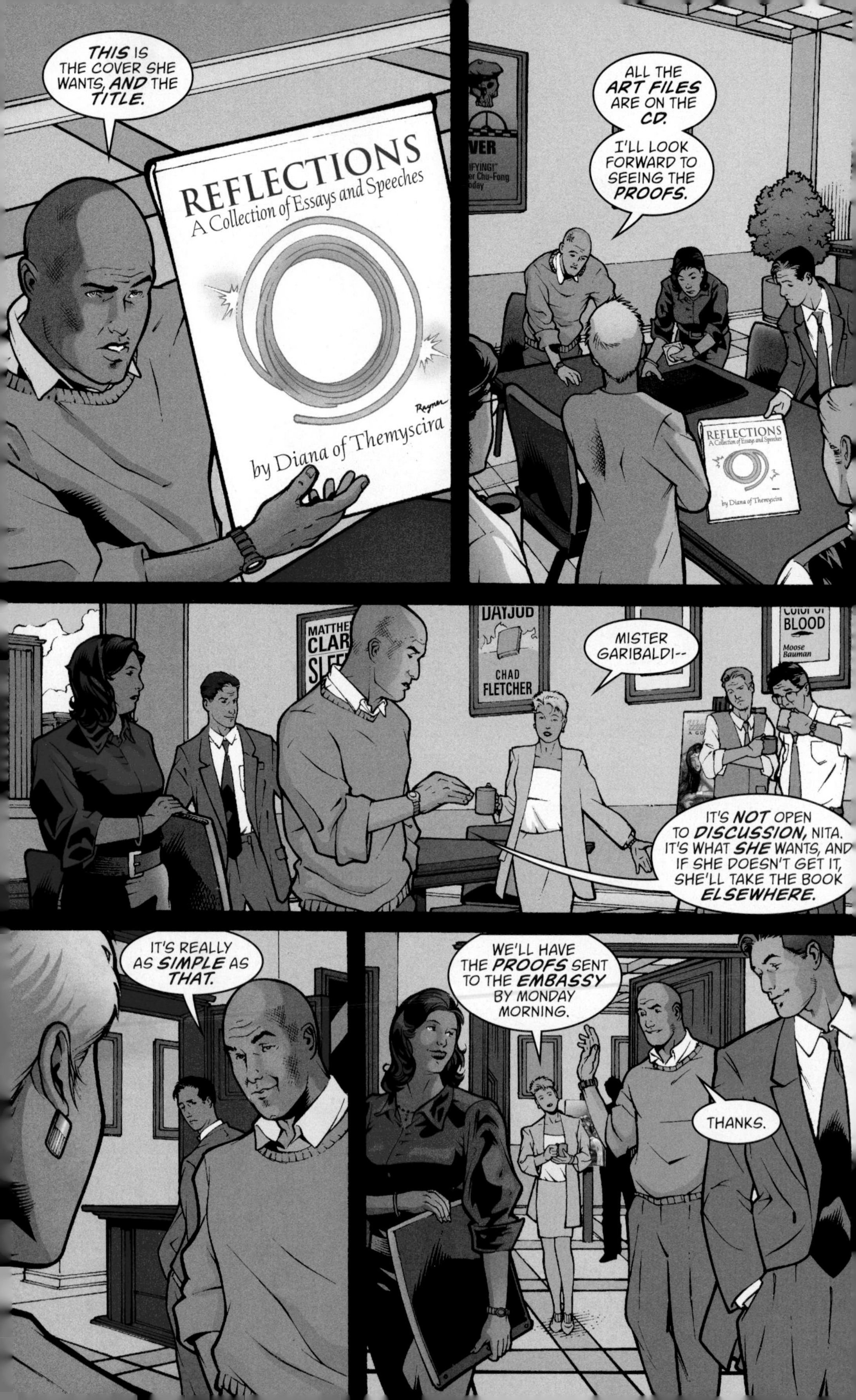
THIS IS THE COVER SHE WANTS, AND THE TITLE.
REFLECTIONS
A Collection of Essays and Speeches
by Diana of Themyscira
ALL THE ART FILES ARE ON THE CD.
I'LL LOOK FORWARD TO SEEING THE PROOFS.
CHAD FLETCHER
BLOOD
Moose Bauman
MISTER GARIBALDI--
IT'S NOT OPEN TO DISCUSSION, NITA. IT'S WHAT SHE WANTS, AND IF SHE DOESN'T GET IT, SHE'LL TAKE THE BOOK ELSEWHERE.
IT'S REALLY AS SIMPLE AS THAT.
WE'LL HAVE THE PROOFS SENT TO THE EMBASSY BY MONDAY MORNING.
THANKS.

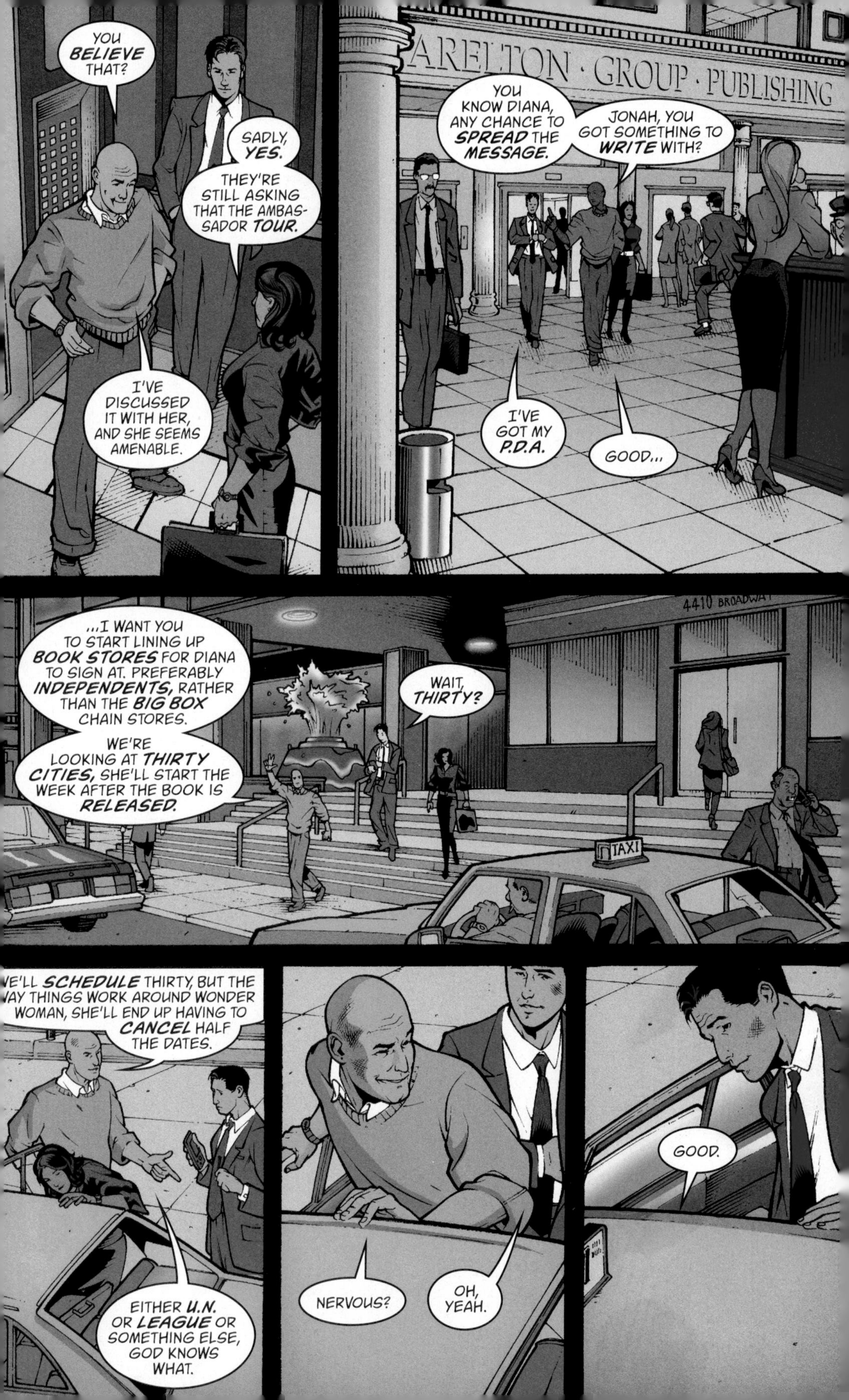
YOU BELIEVE THAT?
SADLY, YES.
THEY'RE STILL ASKING THAT THE AMBAS-SADOR TOUR.
I'VE DISCUSSED IT WITH HER, AND SHE SEEMS AMENABLE.
ARELTON · GROUP · PUBLISHING
YOU KNOW DIANA, ANY CHANCE TO SPREAD THE MESSAGE.
JONAH, YOU GOT SOMETHING TO WRITE WITH?
I'VE GOT MY P.D.A.
GOOD...
4410 BROADWAY
...I WANT YOU TO START LINING UP BOOK STORES FOR DIANA TO SIGN AT. PREFERABLY INDEPENDENTS, RATHER THAN THE BIG BOX CHAIN STORES.
WE'RE LOOKING AT THIRTY CITIES, SHE'LL START THE WEEK AFTER THE BOOK IS RELEASED.
WAIT, THIRTY?
TAXI
WE'LL SCHEDULE THIRTY, BUT THE WAY THINGS WORK AROUND WONDER WOMAN, SHE'LL END UP HAVING TO CANCEL HALF THE DATES.
EITHER U.N. OR LEAGUE OR SOMETHING ELSE, GOD KNOWS WHAT.
NERVOUS?
OH, YEAH.
GOOD.

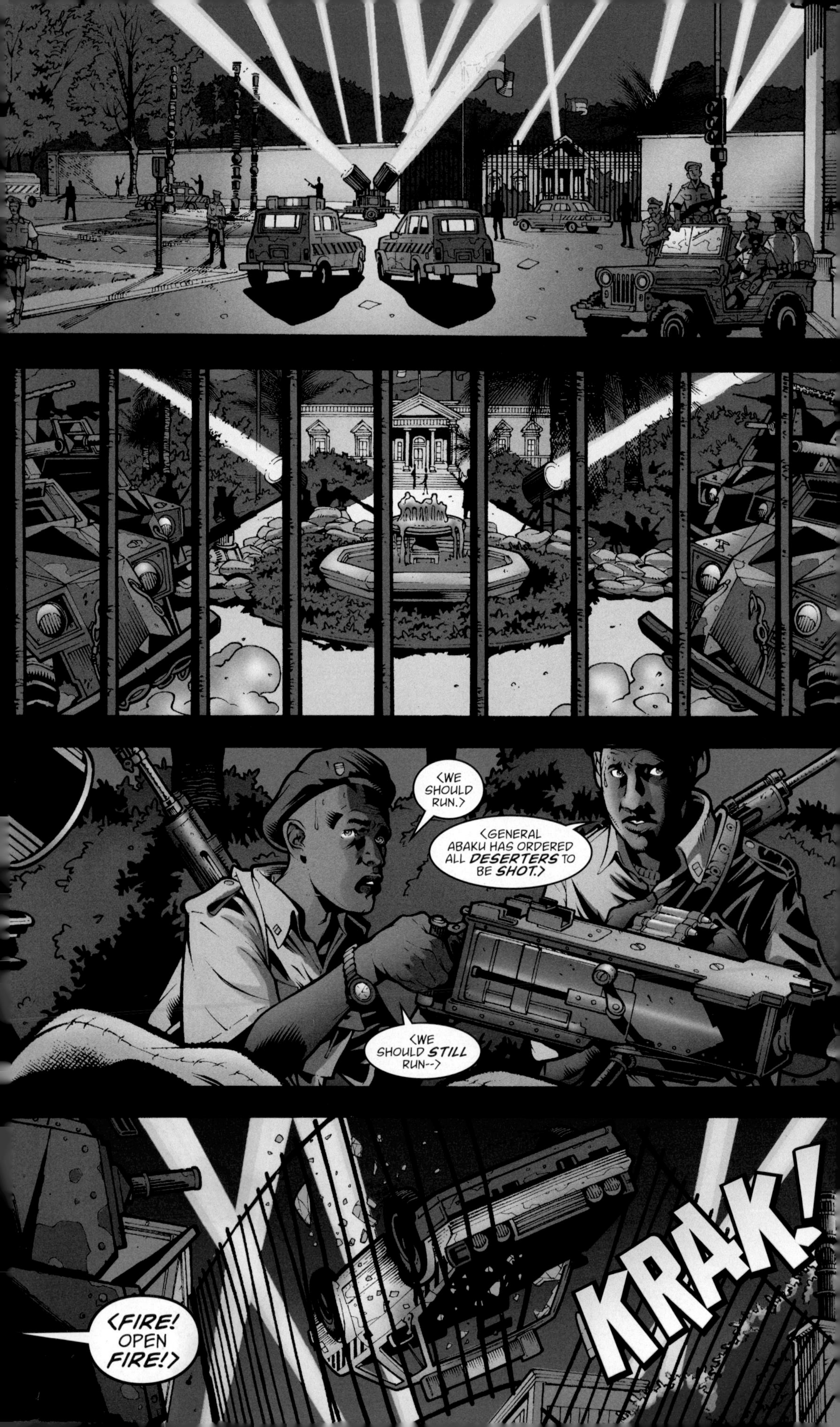
<WE SHOULD RUN.>
<GENERAL ABAKU HAS ORDERED ALL DESERTERS TO BE SHOT.>
<WE SHOULD STILL RUN-->
<FIRE! OPEN FIRE!>
KRAK!

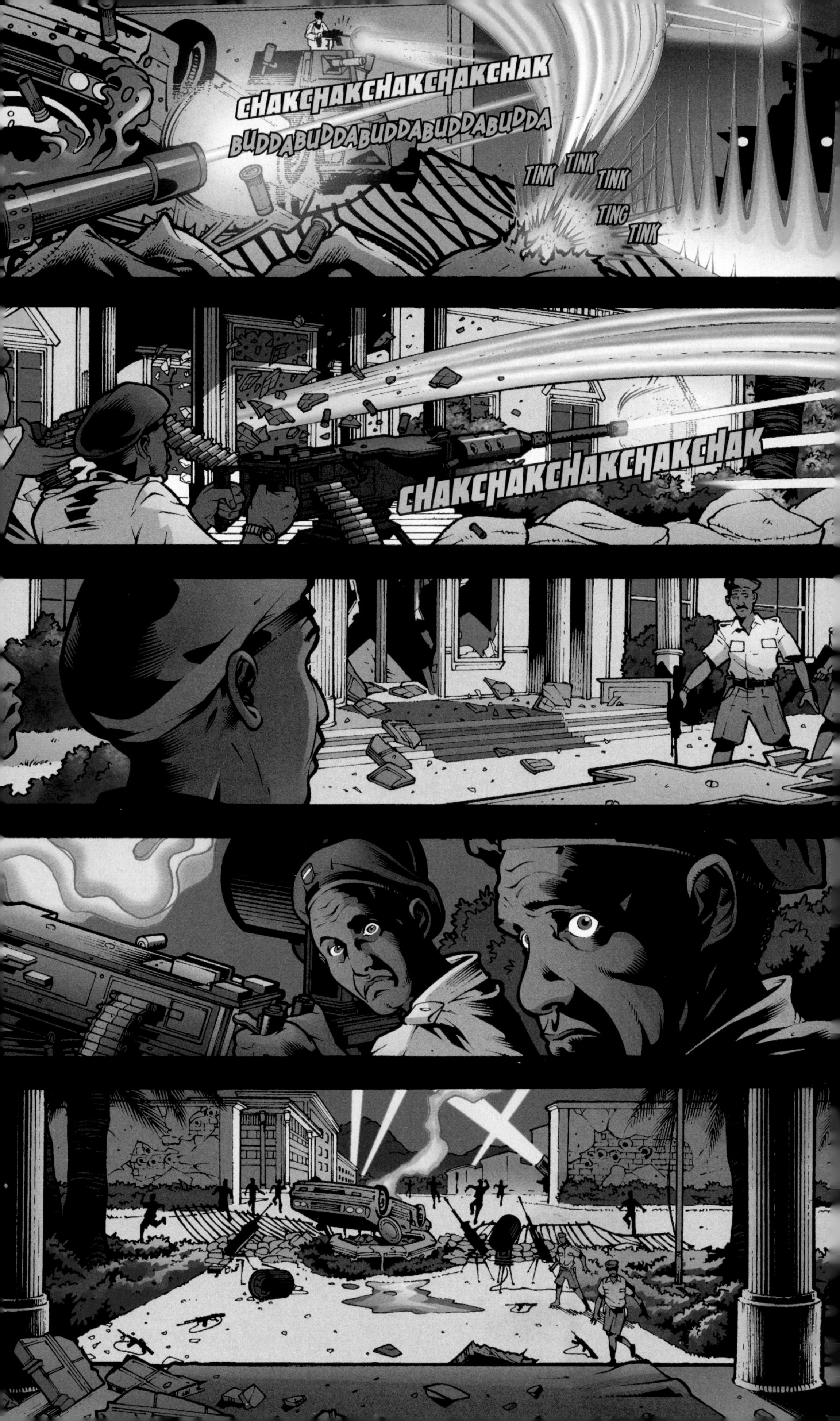
CHAKCHAKCHAKCHAKCHAK
BUDDABUDDABUDDABUDDABUDDA
TINK
TINK
TINK
TING
TINK
CHAKCHAKCHAKCHAKCHAK

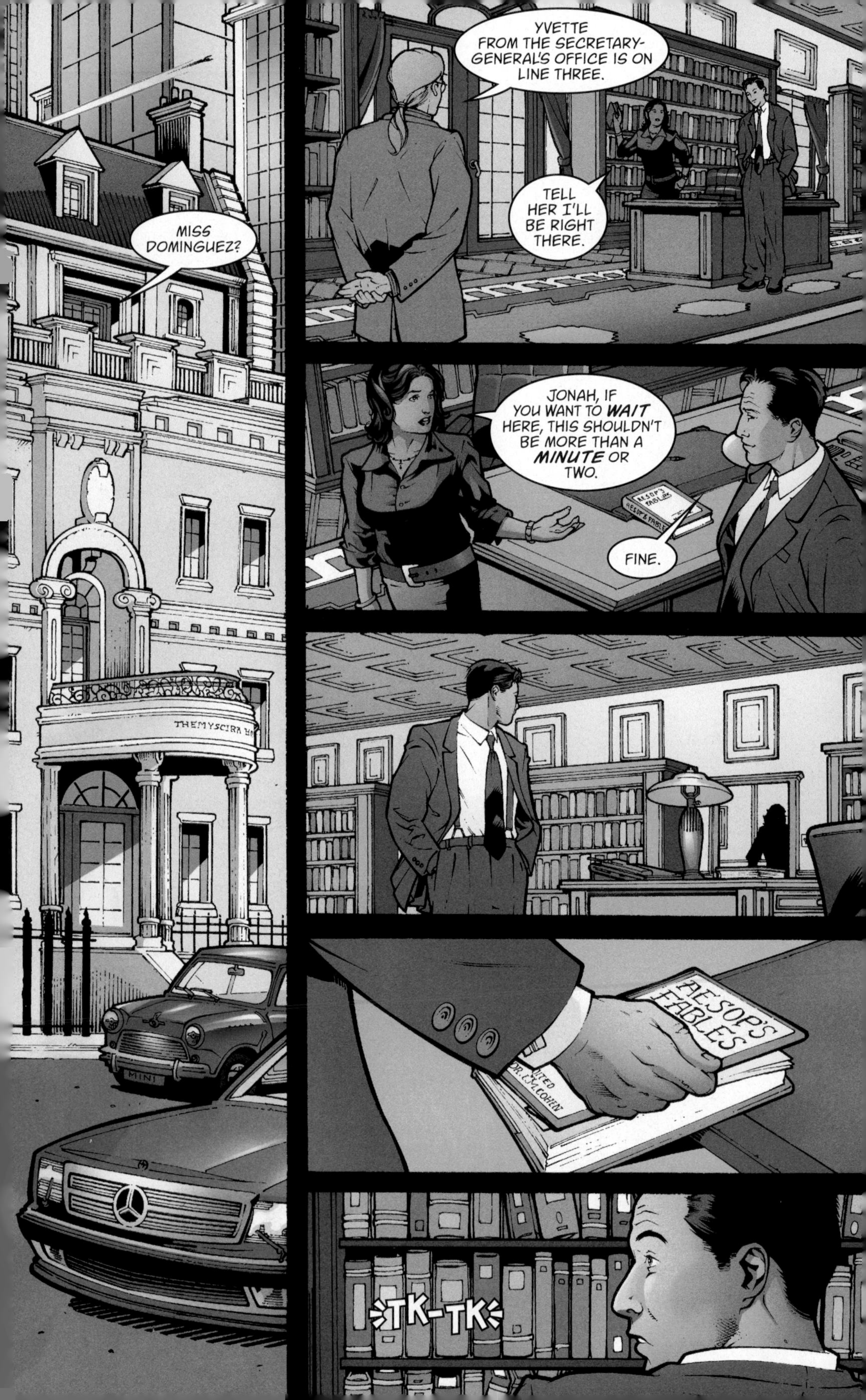

MISS DOMINGUEZ?
THEMYSCIRA
YVETTE FROM THE SECRETARY-GENERAL'S OFFICE IS ON LINE THREE.
TELL HER I'LL BE RIGHT THERE.
JONAH, IF YOU WANT TO WAIT HERE, THIS SHOULDN'T BE MORE THAN A MINUTE OR TWO.
FINE.
AESOP'S FABLES
MINI
AESOP'S FABLES
TK-TK

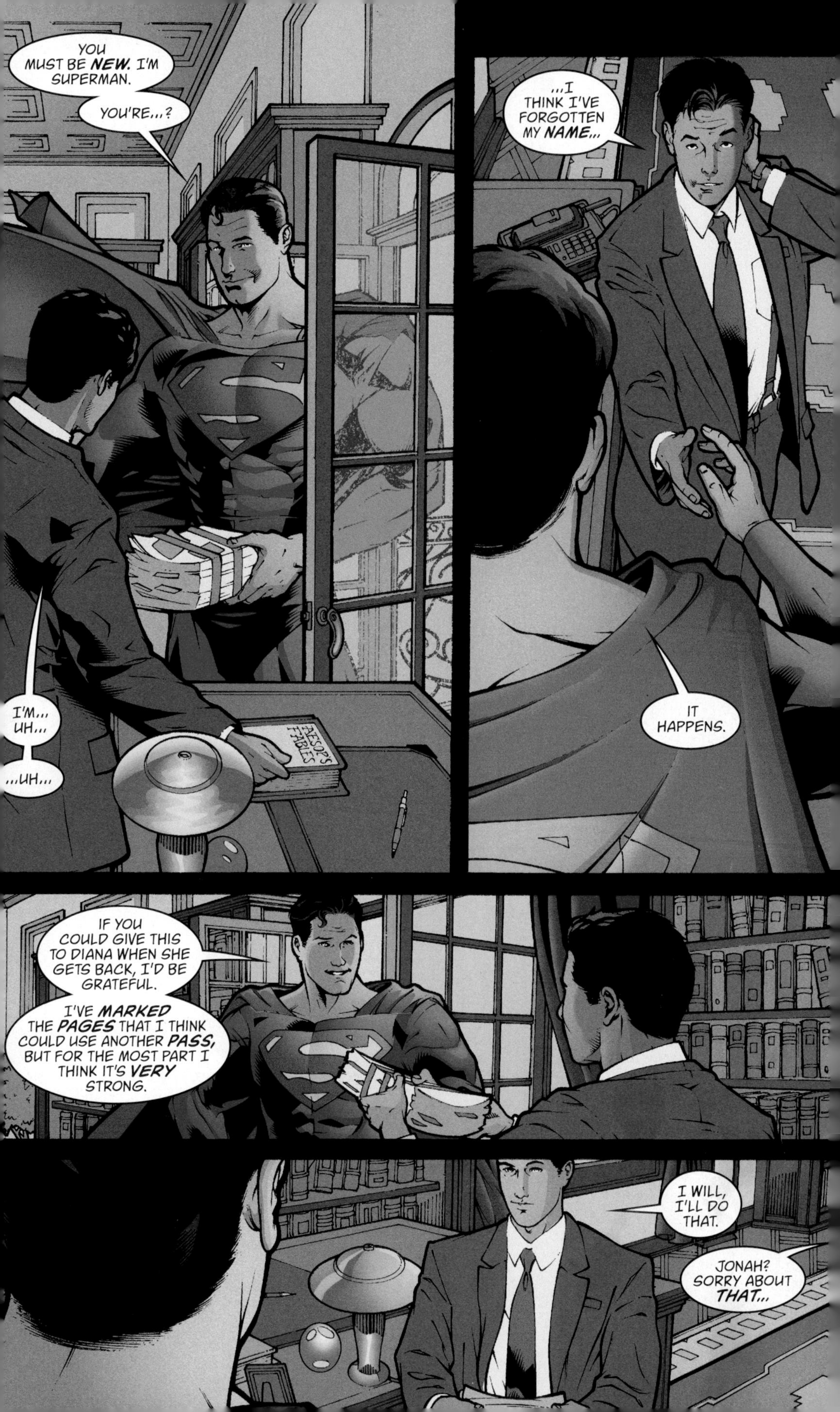
YOU MUST BE NEW. I'M SUPERMAN.
YOU'RE...?
I'M... UH...
...UH...
AESOP'S FABLES
...I THINK I'VE FORGOTTEN MY NAME...
IT HAPPENS.
IF YOU COULD GIVE THIS TO DIANA WHEN SHE GETS BACK, I'D BE GRATEFUL.
I'VE MARKED THE PAGES THAT I THINK COULD USE ANOTHER PASS, BUT FOR THE MOST PART I THINK IT'S VERY STRONG.
I WILL, I'LL DO THAT.
JONAH? SORRY ABOUT THAT...

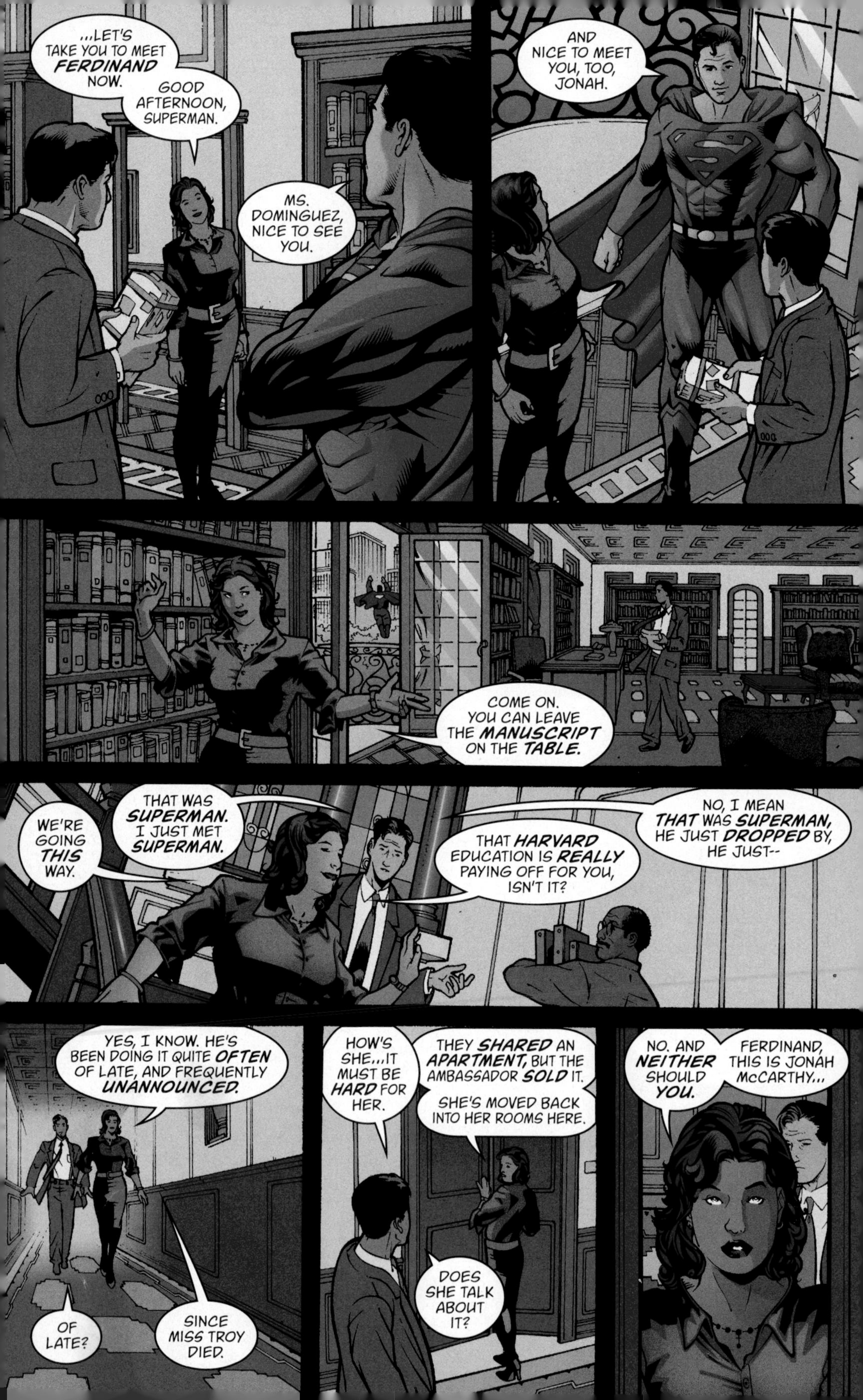
...LET'S TAKE YOU TO MEET FERDINAND NOW.
GOOD AFTERNOON, SUPERMAN.
MS. DOMINGUEZ, NICE TO SEE YOU.
AND NICE TO MEET YOU, TOO, JONAH.
COME ON. YOU CAN LEAVE THE MANUSCRIPT ON THE TABLE.
WE'RE GOING THIS WAY.
THAT WAS SUPERMAN. I JUST MET SUPERMAN.
THAT HARVARD EDUCATION IS REALLY PAYING OFF FOR YOU, ISN'T IT?
NO, I MEAN THAT WAS SUPERMAN, HE JUST DROPPED BY, HE JUST--
YES, I KNOW. HE'S BEEN DOING IT QUITE OFTEN OF LATE, AND FREQUENTLY UNANNOUNCED.
OF LATE?
SINCE MISS TROY DIED.
HOW'S SHE...IT MUST BE HARD FOR HER.
THEY SHARED AN APARTMENT, BUT THE AMBASSADOR SOLD IT.
SHE'S MOVED BACK INTO HER ROOMS HERE.
DOES SHE TALK ABOUT IT?
NO. AND NEITHER SHOULD YOU.
FERDINAND, THIS IS JONAH McCARTHY...

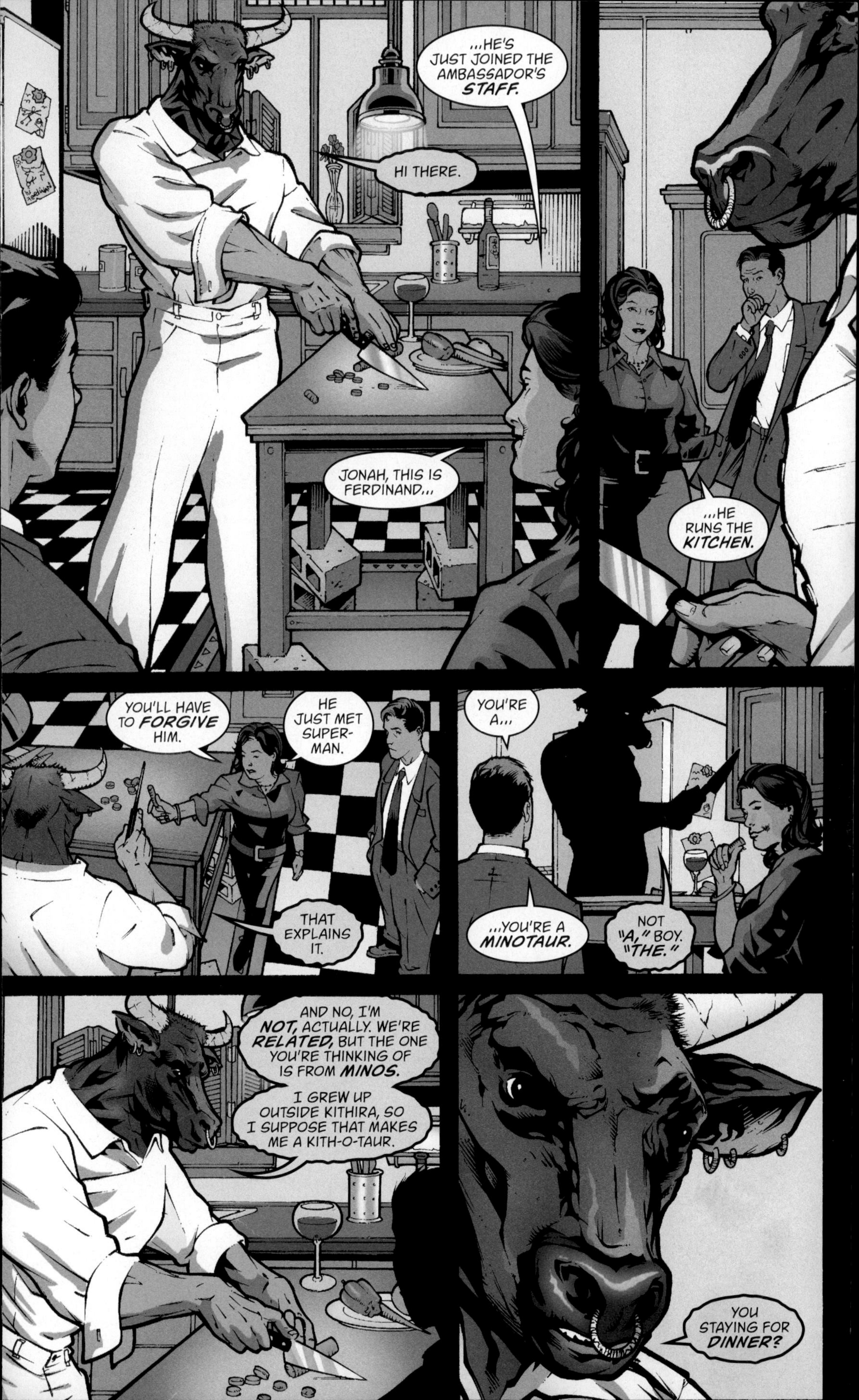
HI THERE.
...HE'S JUST JOINED THE AMBASSADOR'S STAFF.
JONAH, THIS IS FERDINAND...
...HE RUNS THE KITCHEN.
YOU'LL HAVE TO FORGIVE HIM.
HE JUST MET SUPER-MAN.
THAT EXPLAINS IT.
YOU'RE A...
...YOU'RE A MINOTAUR.
NOT "A," BOY. "THE."
AND NO, I'M NOT, ACTUALLY. WE'RE RELATED, BUT THE ONE YOU'RE THINKING OF IS FROM MINOS.
I GREW UP OUTSIDE KITHIRA, SO I SUPPOSE THAT MAKES ME A KITH-O-TAUR.
YOU STAYING FOR DINNER?

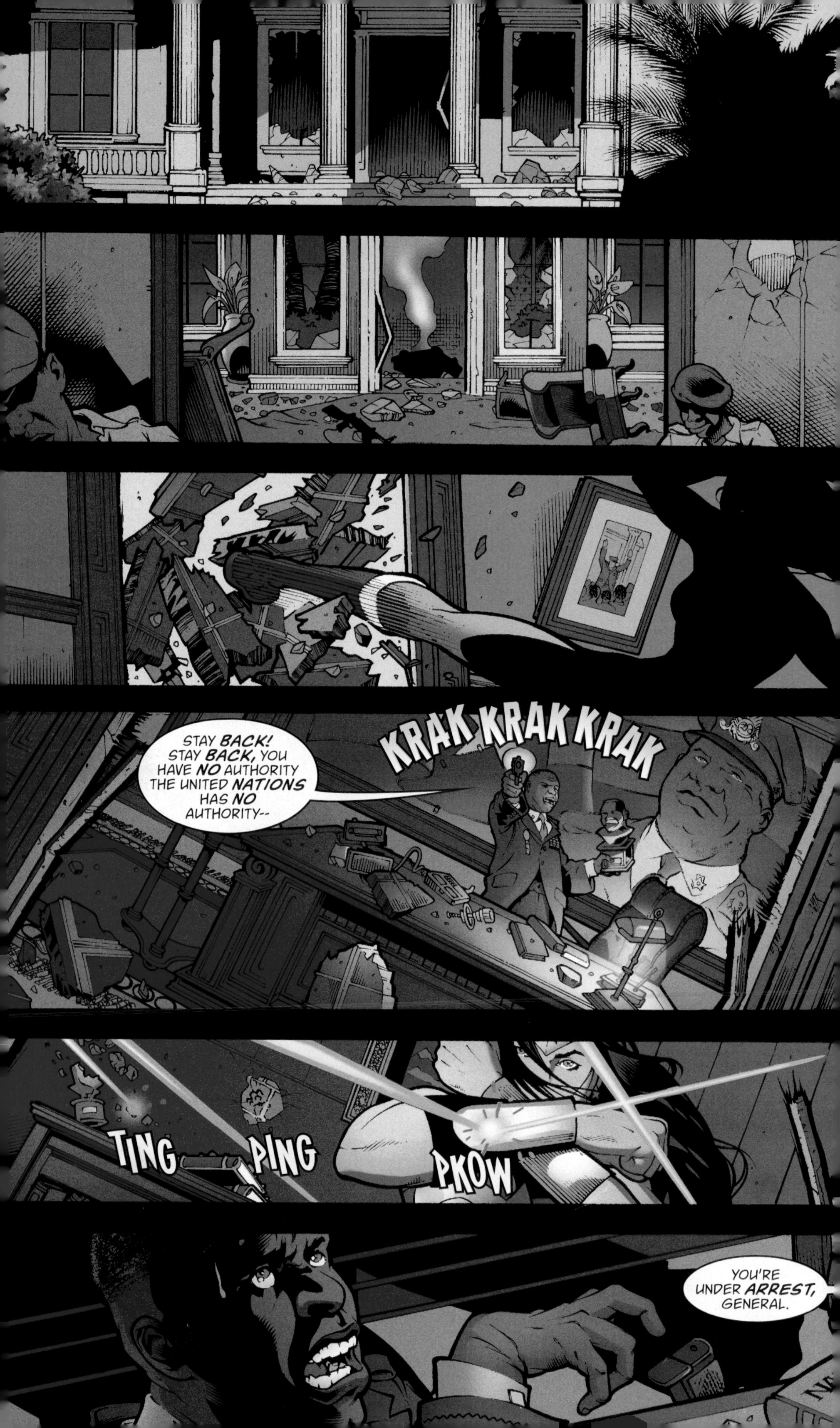
STAY BACK! STAY BACK, YOU HAVE NO AUTHORITY THE UNITED NATIONS HAS NO AUTHORITY--
KRAK KRAK KRAK
TING
PING
PKOW
YOU'RE UNDER ARREST, GENERAL.

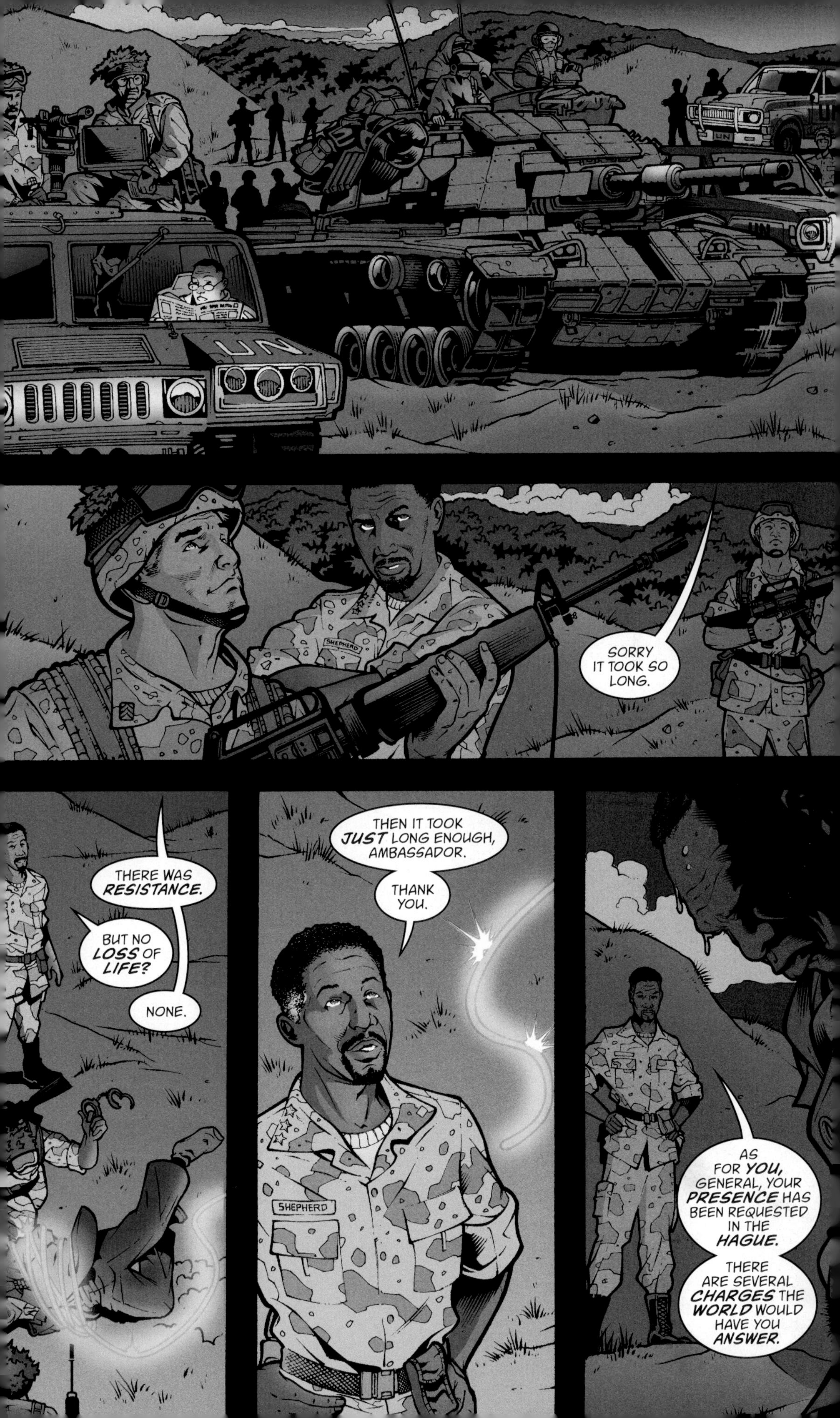
UN
SORRY IT TOOK SO LONG.
SHEPHERD
THERE WAS RESISTANCE.
BUT NO LOSS OF LIFE?
NONE.
THEN IT TOOK JUST LONG ENOUGH, AMBASSADOR.
THANK YOU.
SHEPHERD
AS FOR YOU, GENERAL, YOUR PRESENCE HAS BEEN REQUESTED IN THE HAGUE.
THERE ARE SEVERAL CHARGES THE WORLD WOULD HAVE YOU ANSWER.

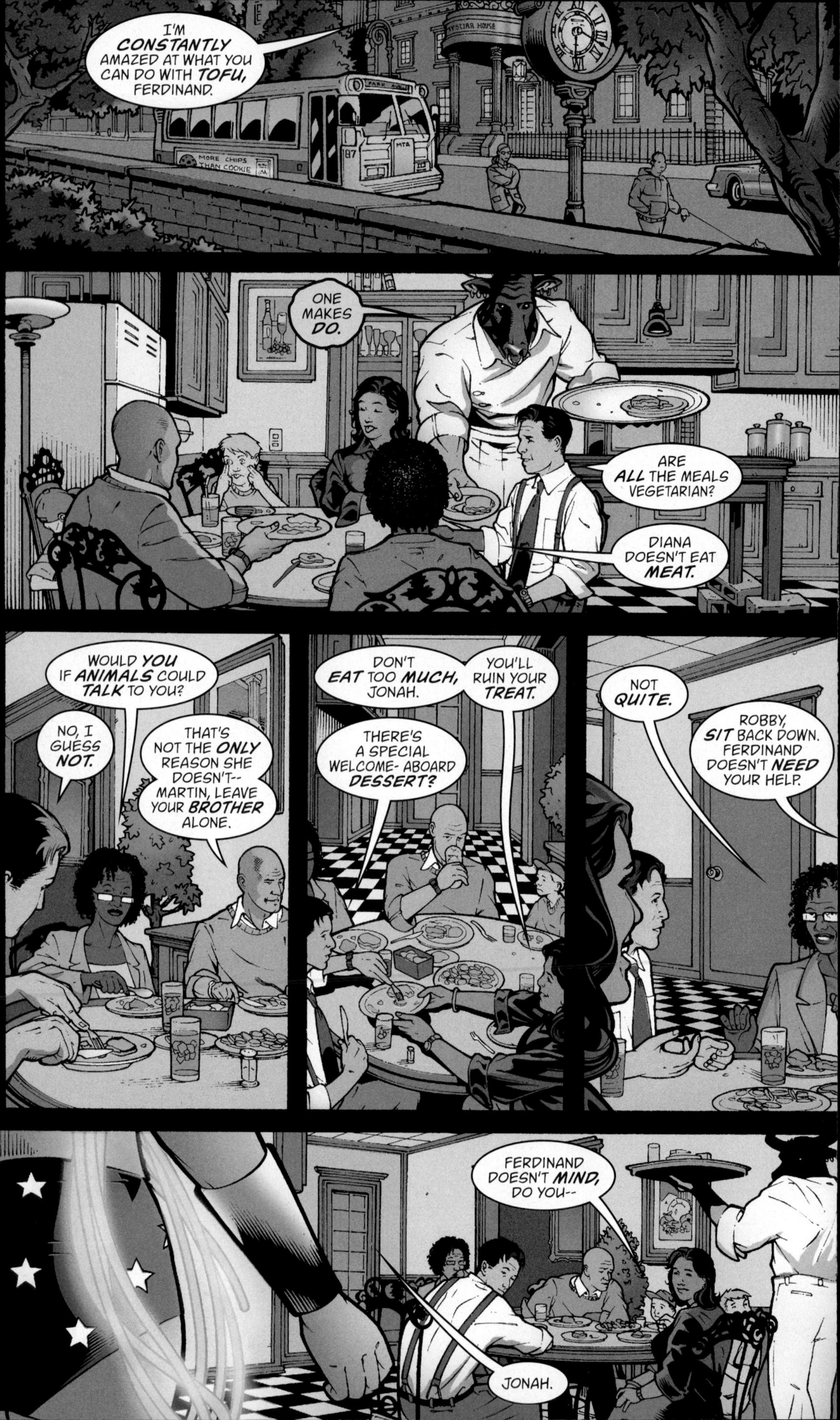

MYSTIAR HOUSE
PARK AVE
MORE CHIPS THAN COOKIE
I'M CONSTANTLY AMAZED AT WHAT YOU CAN DO WITH TOFU, FERDINAND.
ONE MAKES DO.
ARE ALL THE MEALS VEGETARIAN?
DIANA DOESN'T EAT MEAT.
WOULD YOU IF ANIMALS COULD TALK TO YOU?
NO, I GUESS NOT.
THAT'S NOT THE ONLY REASON SHE DOESN'T-- MARTIN, LEAVE YOUR BROTHER ALONE.
DON'T EAT TOO MUCH, JONAH.
YOU'LL RUIN YOUR TREAT.
THERE'S A SPECIAL WELCOME- ABOARD DESSERT?
NOT QUITE.
ROBBY, SIT BACK DOWN. FERDINAND DOESN'T NEED YOUR HELP.
FERDINAND DOESN'T MIND, DO YOU--
JONAH.

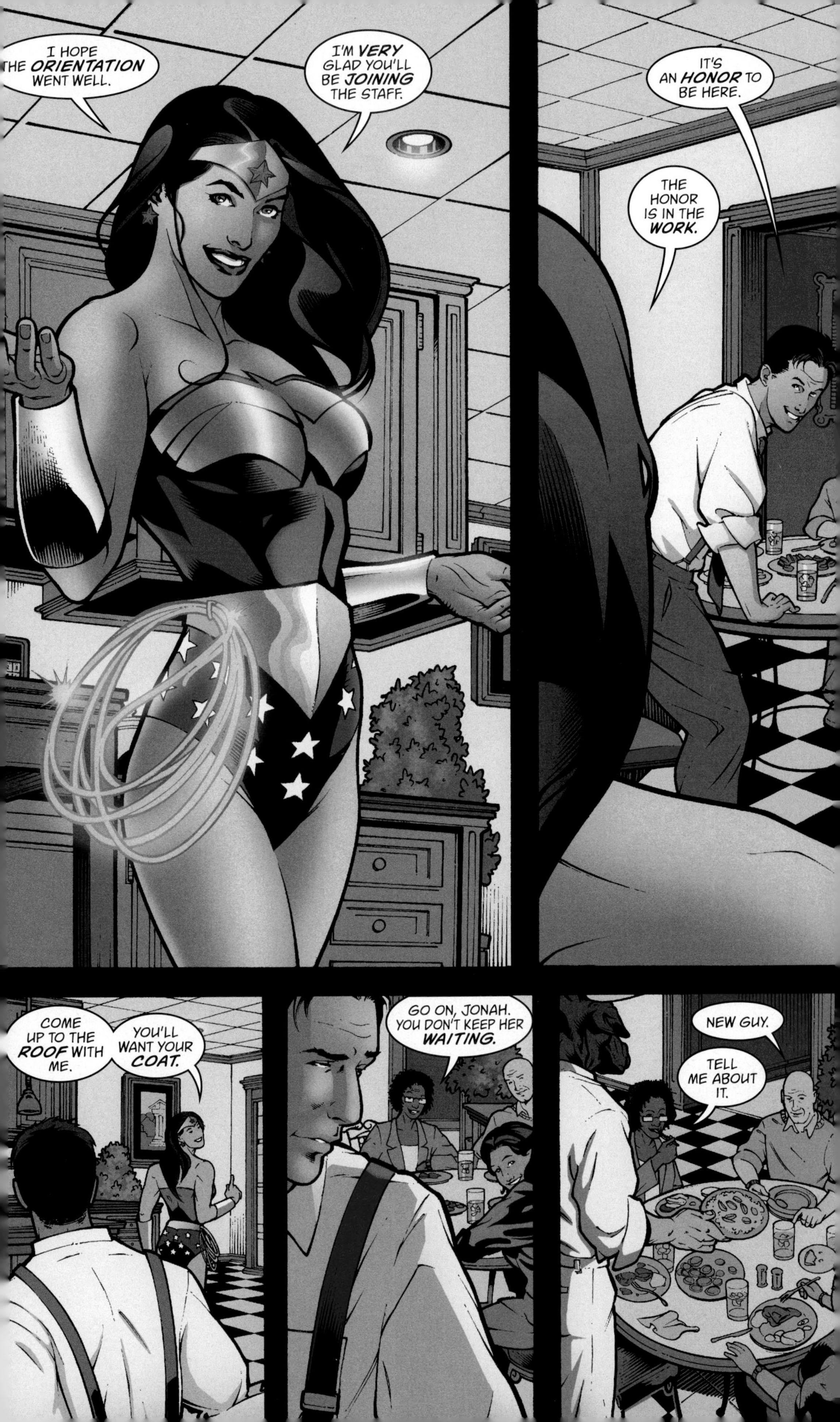

I HOPE THE ORIENTATION WENT WELL.
I'M VERY GLAD YOU'LL BE JOINING THE STAFF.
IT'S AN HONOR TO BE HERE.
THE HONOR IS IN THE WORK.
COME UP TO THE ROOF WITH ME.
YOU'LL WANT YOUR COAT.
GO ON, JONAH. YOU DON'T KEEP HER WAITING.
NEW GUY.
TELL ME ABOUT IT.

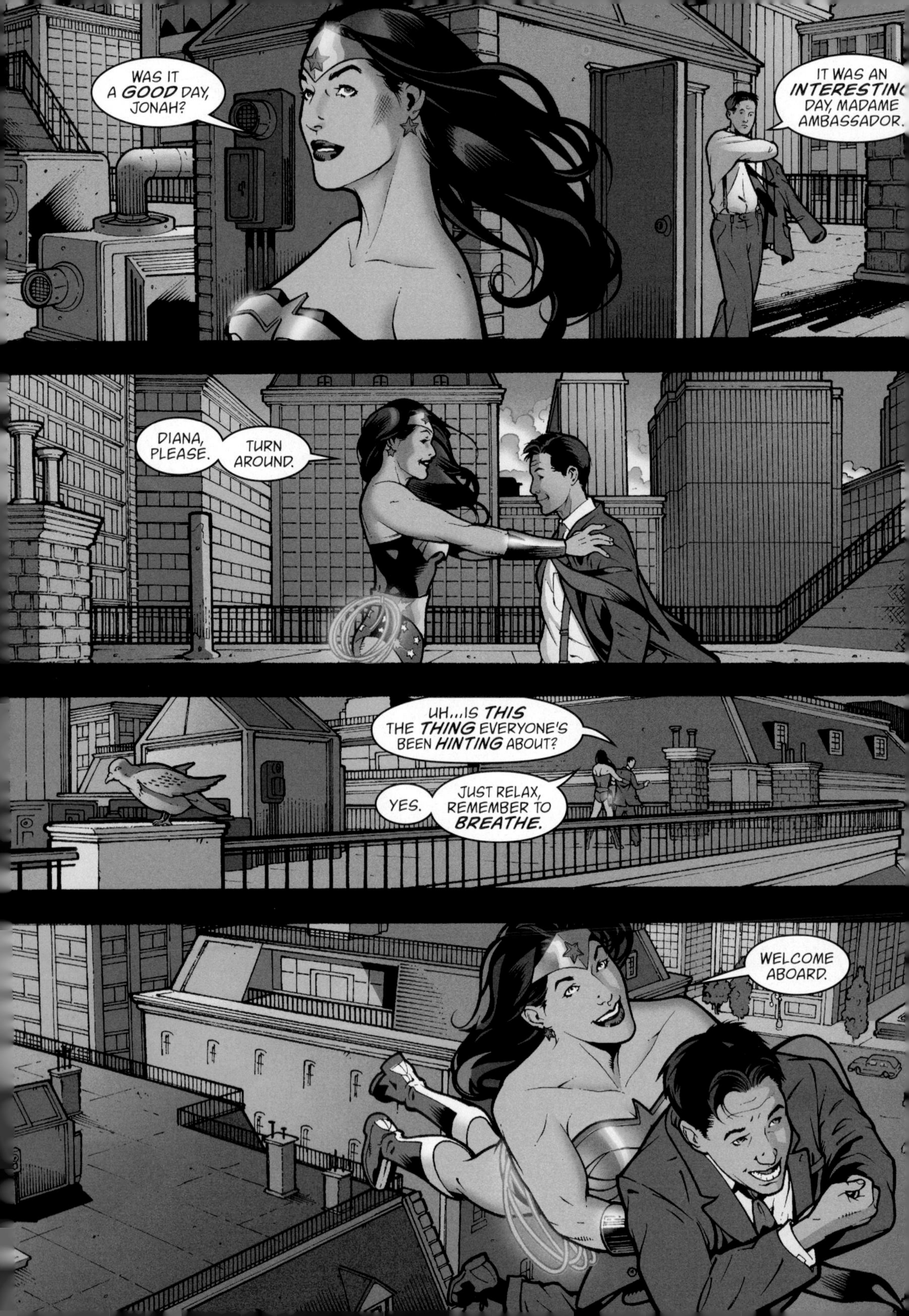
WAS IT A GOOD DAY, JONAH?
IT WAS AN INTERESTING DAY, MADAME AMBASSADOR.
DIANA, PLEASE.
TURN AROUND.
UH...IS THIS THE THING EVERYONE'S BEEN HINTING ABOUT?
YES.
JUST RELAX, REMEMBER TO BREATHE.
WELCOME ABOARD.

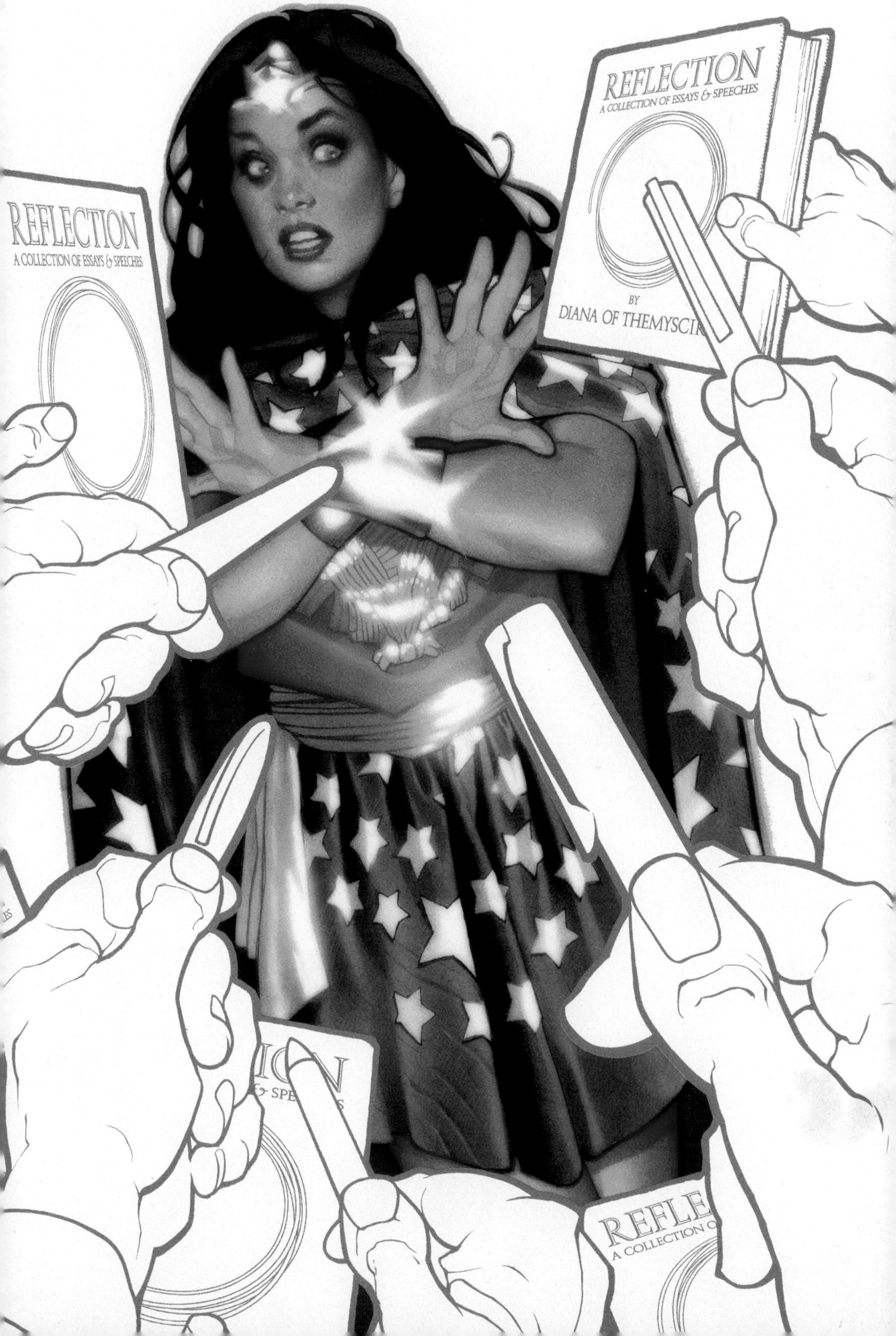
REFLECTION
A COLLECTION OF ESSAYS & SPEECHES
BY
DIANA OF THEMYSCIR
REFLECTION
A COLLECTION OF ESSAYS & SPEECHES
REFLE
A COLLECTION O

"DOWN TO EARTH: PART ONE"

Drew Johnson – *pencils*
Ray Snyder – *inks*
Trish Mulvihill - *colors*
Adam Hughes – *cover art*

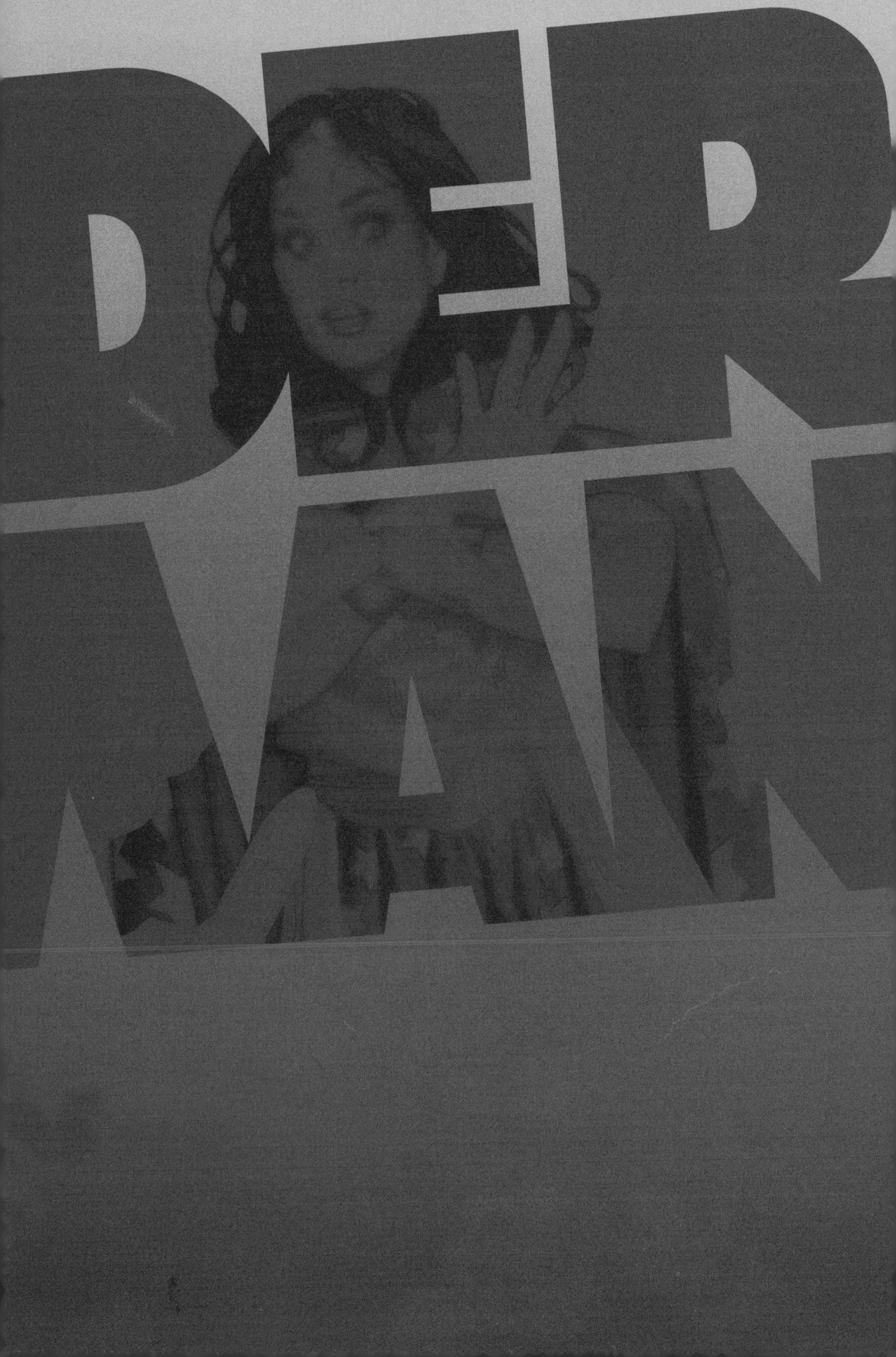

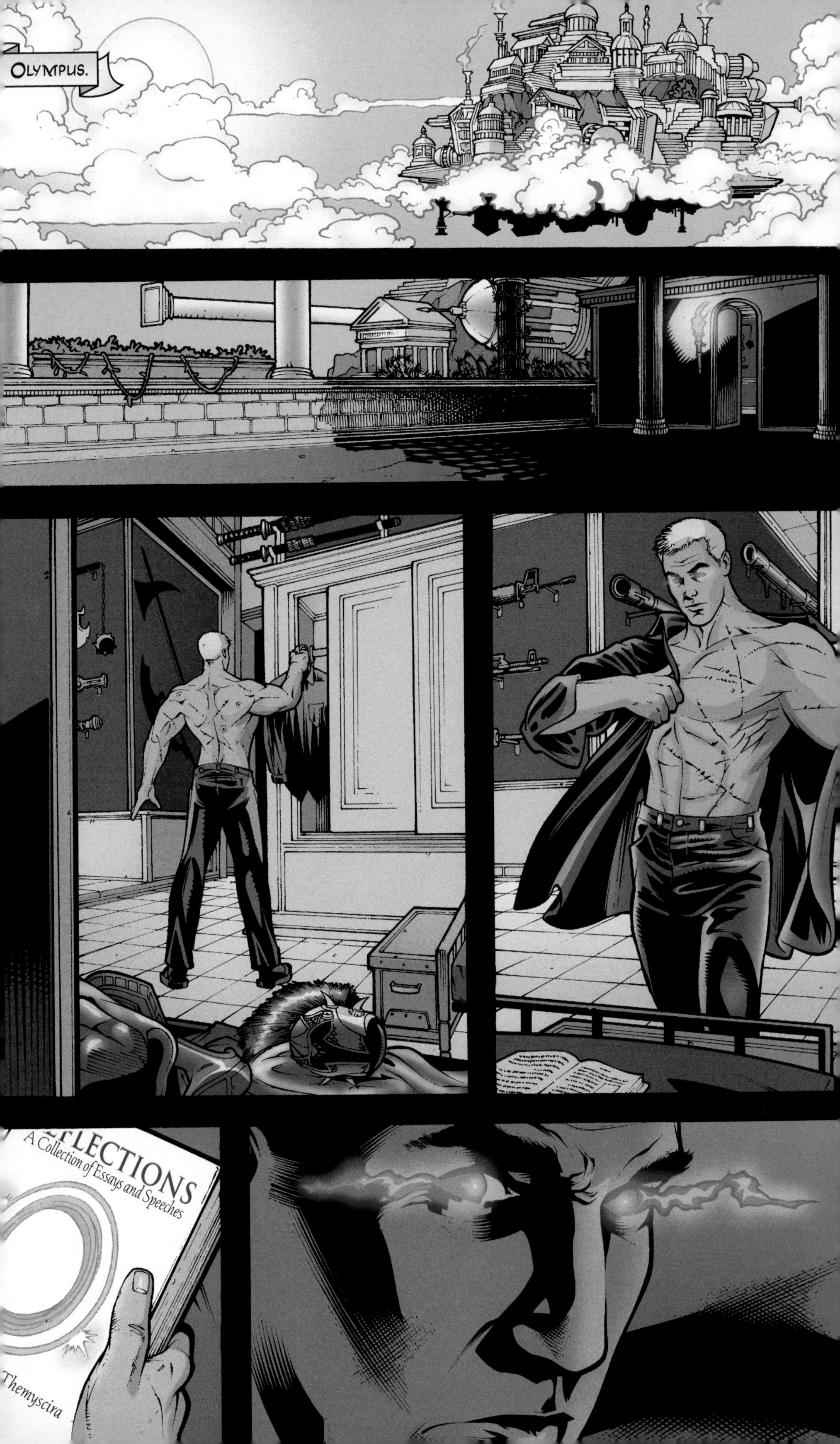
OLYMPUS.
...FLECTIONS
A Collection of Essays and Speeches
Themyscira

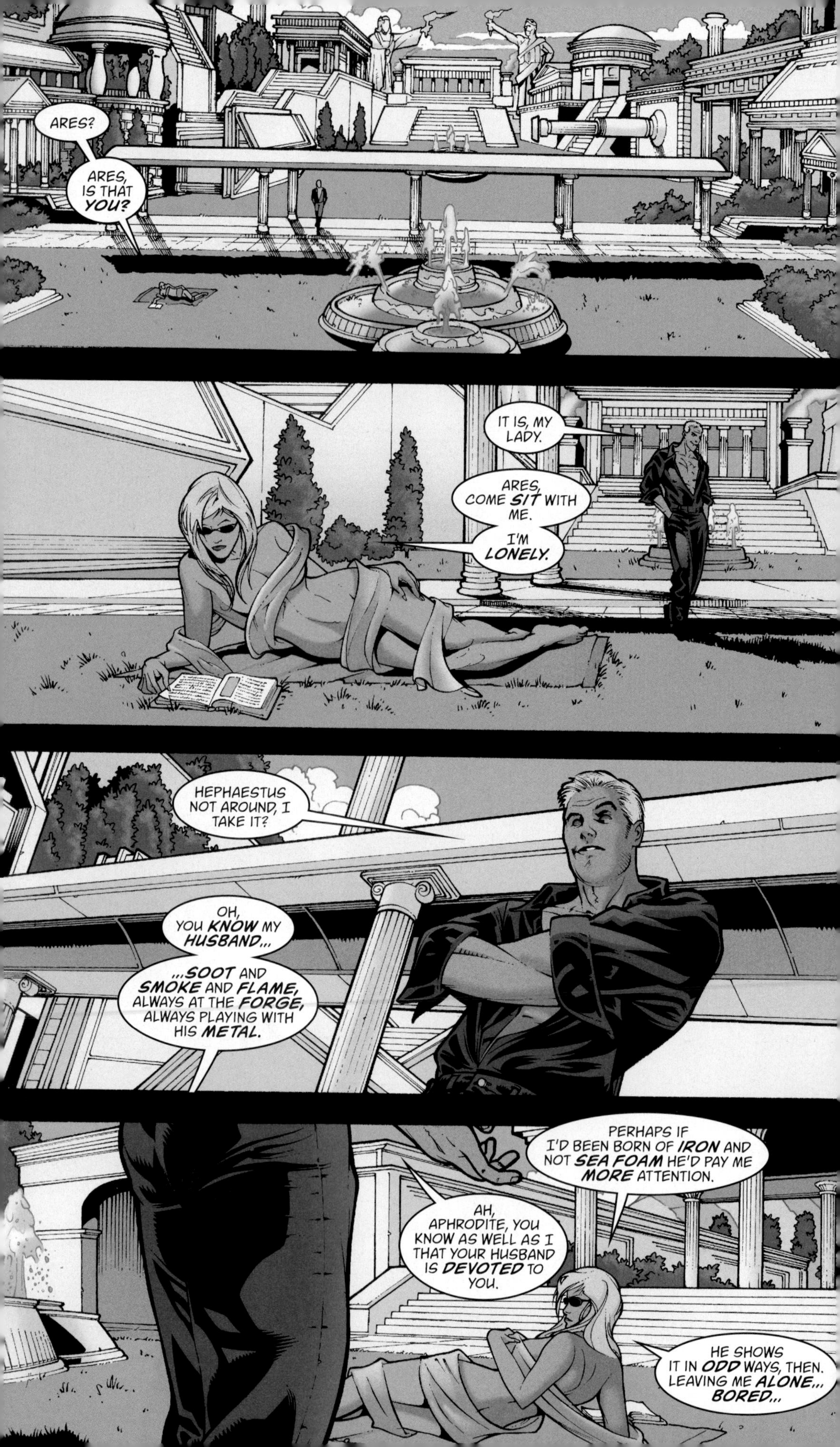
ARES?
ARES, IS THAT YOU?
IT IS, MY LADY.
ARES, COME SIT WITH ME.
I'M LONELY.
HEPHAESTUS NOT AROUND, I TAKE IT?
OH, YOU KNOW MY HUSBAND...
...SOOT AND SMOKE AND FLAME, ALWAYS AT THE FORGE, ALWAYS PLAYING WITH HIS METAL.
PERHAPS IF I'D BEEN BORN OF IRON AND NOT SEA FOAM HE'D PAY ME MORE ATTENTION.
AH, APHRODITE, YOU KNOW AS WELL AS I THAT YOUR HUSBAND IS DEVOTED TO YOU.
HE SHOWS IT IN ODD WAYS, THEN. LEAVING ME ALONE... BORED...

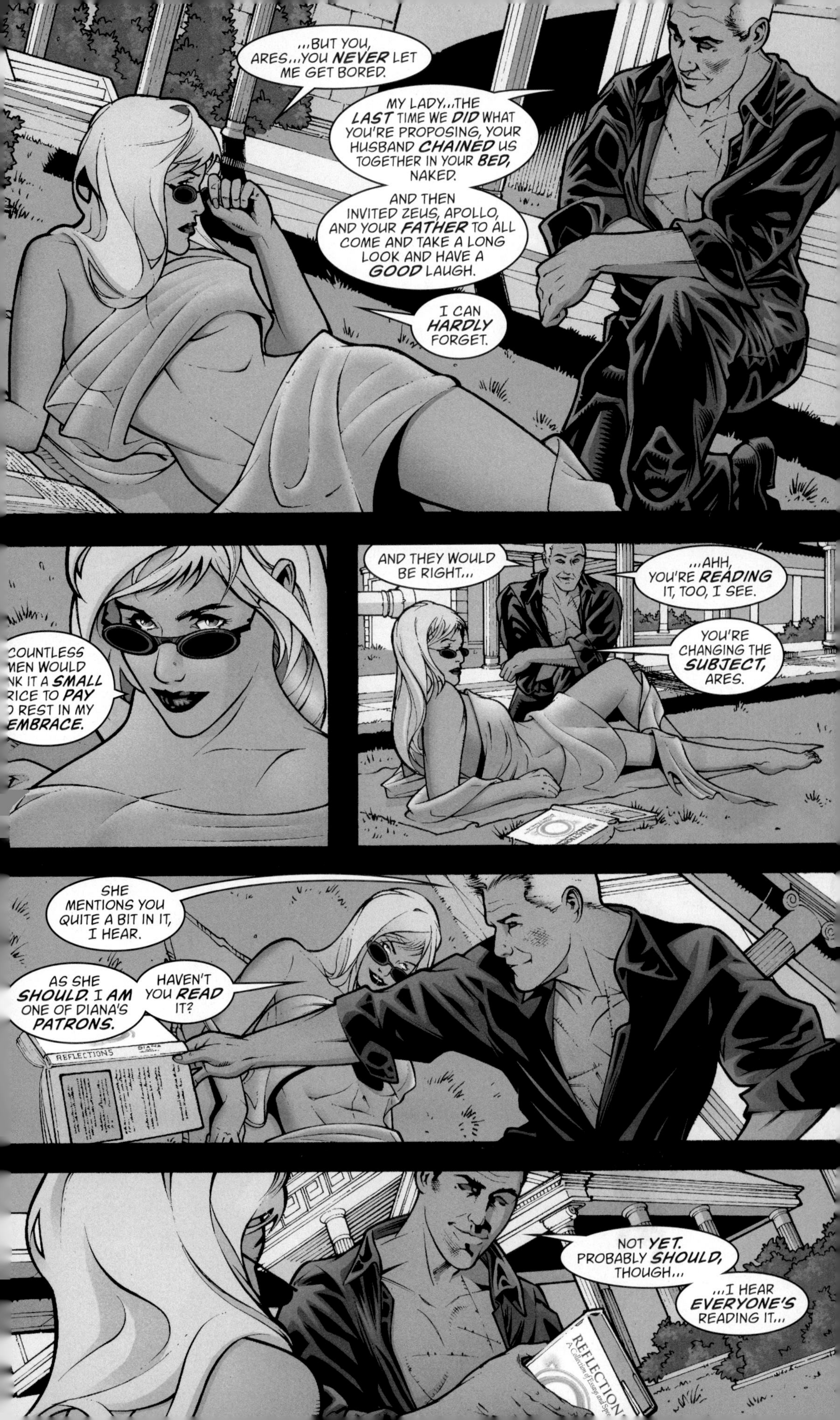
...BUT YOU, ARES...YOU **NEVER** LET ME GET BORED.
MY LADY...THE **LAST** TIME WE **DID** WHAT YOU'RE PROPOSING, YOUR HUSBAND **CHAINED** US TOGETHER IN YOUR **BED,** NAKED.
AND THEN INVITED ZEUS, APOLLO, AND YOUR **FATHER** TO ALL COME AND TAKE A LONG LOOK AND HAVE A **GOOD** LAUGH.
I CAN **HARDLY** FORGET.
COUNTLESS MEN WOULD NK IT A **SMALL** RICE TO **PAY** REST IN MY **EMBRACE.**
AND THEY WOULD BE RIGHT...
...AHH, YOU'RE **READING** IT, TOO, I SEE.
YOU'RE CHANGING THE **SUBJECT,** ARES.
SHE MENTIONS YOU QUITE A BIT IN IT, I HEAR.
AS SHE **SHOULD. I AM** ONE OF DIANA'S **PATRONS.**
HAVEN'T YOU **READ** IT?
NOT **YET.** PROBABLY **SHOULD,** THOUGH...
...I HEAR **EVERYONE'S** READING IT...

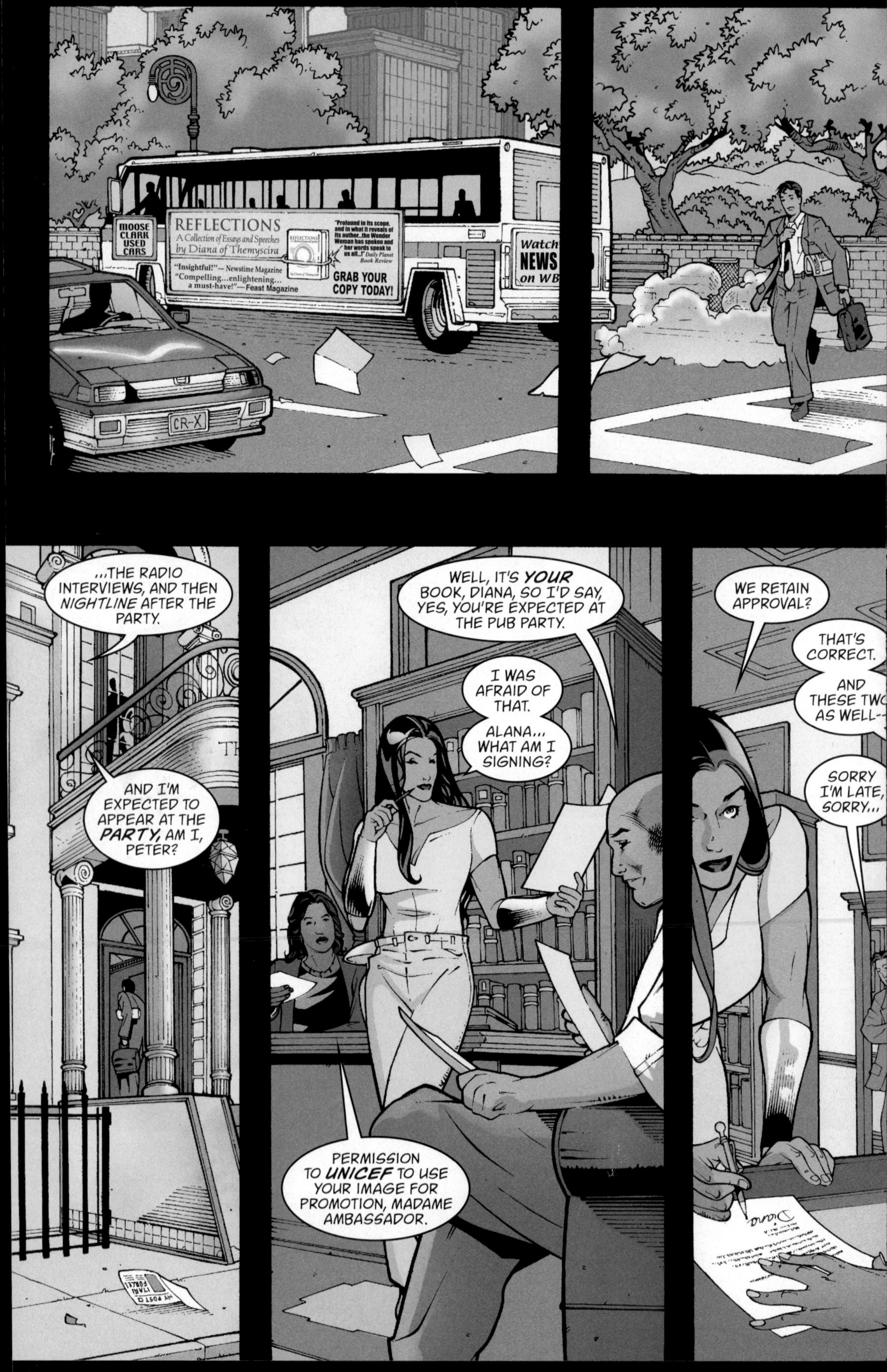
MOOSE CLARK USED CARS
REFLECTIONS
A Collection of Essays and Speeches by Diana of Themyscira
"Insightful!" — Newstime Magazine
"Compelling...enlightening... a must-have!" — Feast Magazine
"Profound in its scope, and in what it reveals of its author...the Wonder Woman has spoken and her words speak to us all...!" Daily Planet Book Review
GRAB YOUR COPY TODAY!
CR-X
...THE RADIO INTERVIEWS, AND THEN NIGHTLINE AFTER THE PARTY.
AND I'M EXPECTED TO APPEAR AT THE PARTY, AM I, PETER?
WELL, IT'S YOUR BOOK, DIANA, SO I'D SAY, YES, YOU'RE EXPECTED AT THE PUB PARTY.
I WAS AFRAID OF THAT.
ALANA... WHAT AM I SIGNING?
PERMISSION TO UNICEF TO USE YOUR IMAGE FOR PROMOTION, MADAME AMBASSADOR.
WE RETAIN APPROVAL?
THAT'S CORRECT.
AND THESE TWO AS WELL--
SORRY I'M LATE, SORRY...

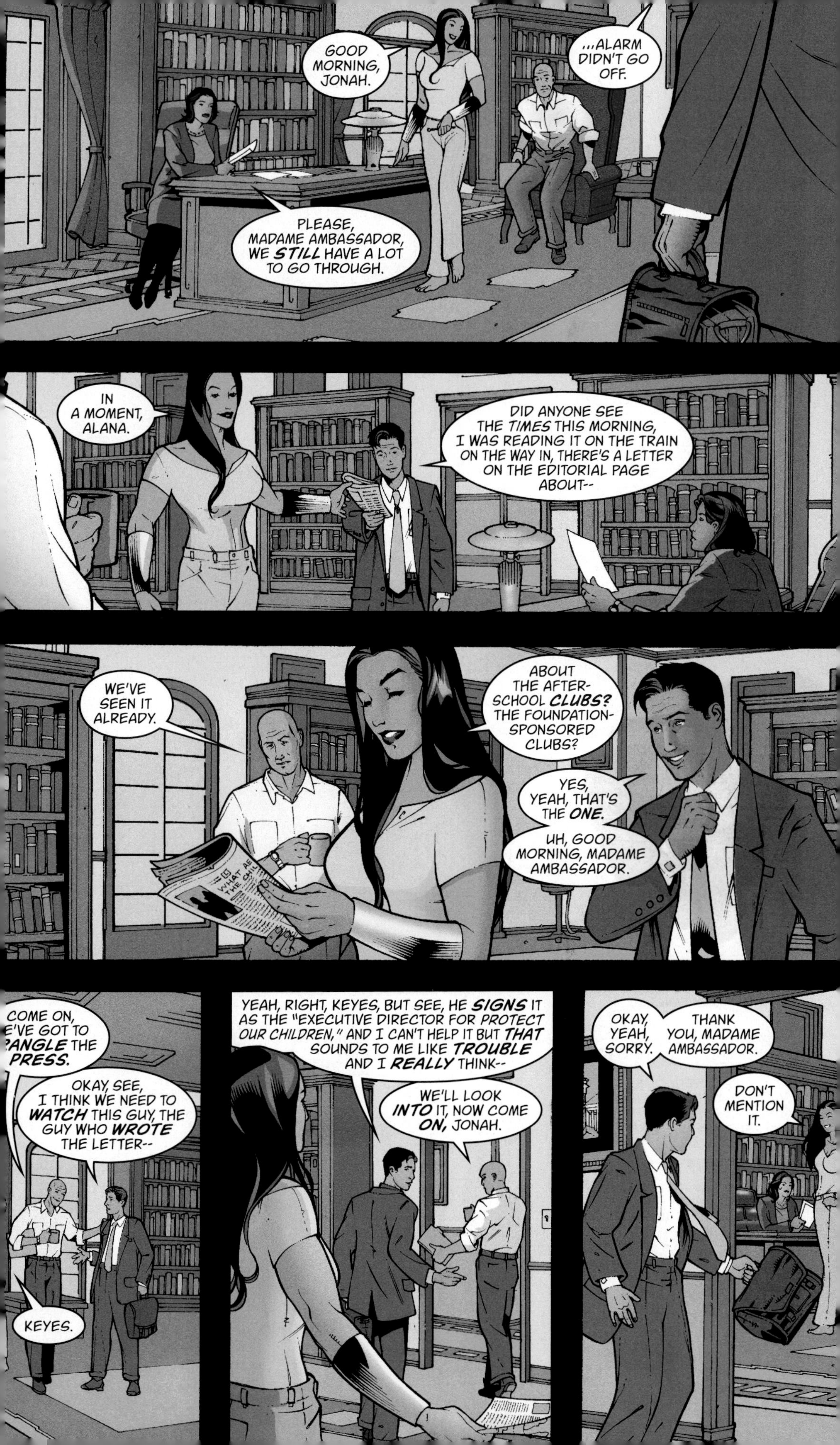

GOOD MORNING, JONAH.
...ALARM DIDN'T GO OFF.
PLEASE, MADAME AMBASSADOR, WE *STILL* HAVE A LOT TO GO THROUGH.
IN A MOMENT, ALANA.
DID ANYONE SEE THE *TIMES* THIS MORNING, I WAS READING IT ON THE TRAIN ON THE WAY IN, THERE'S A LETTER ON THE EDITORIAL PAGE ABOUT--
WE'VE SEEN IT ALREADY.
ABOUT THE AFTER-SCHOOL **CLUBS?** THE FOUNDATION-SPONSORED CLUBS?
YES, YEAH, THAT'S THE ***ONE.***
UH, GOOD MORNING, MADAME AMBASSADOR.
COME ON, 'VE GOT TO ANGLE THE PRESS.
OKAY, SEE, I THINK WE NEED TO ***WATCH*** THIS GUY, THE GUY WHO ***WROTE*** THE LETTER--
KEYES.
YEAH, RIGHT, KEYES, BUT SEE, HE ***SIGNS*** IT AS THE "EXECUTIVE DIRECTOR FOR *PROTECT OUR CHILDREN,*" AND I CAN'T HELP IT BUT ***THAT*** SOUNDS TO ME LIKE ***TROUBLE*** AND I ***REALLY*** THINK--
WE'LL LOOK ***INTO*** IT, NOW COME ***ON,*** JONAH.
OKAY, YEAH, SORRY.
THANK YOU, MADAME AMBASSADOR.
DON'T MENTION IT.

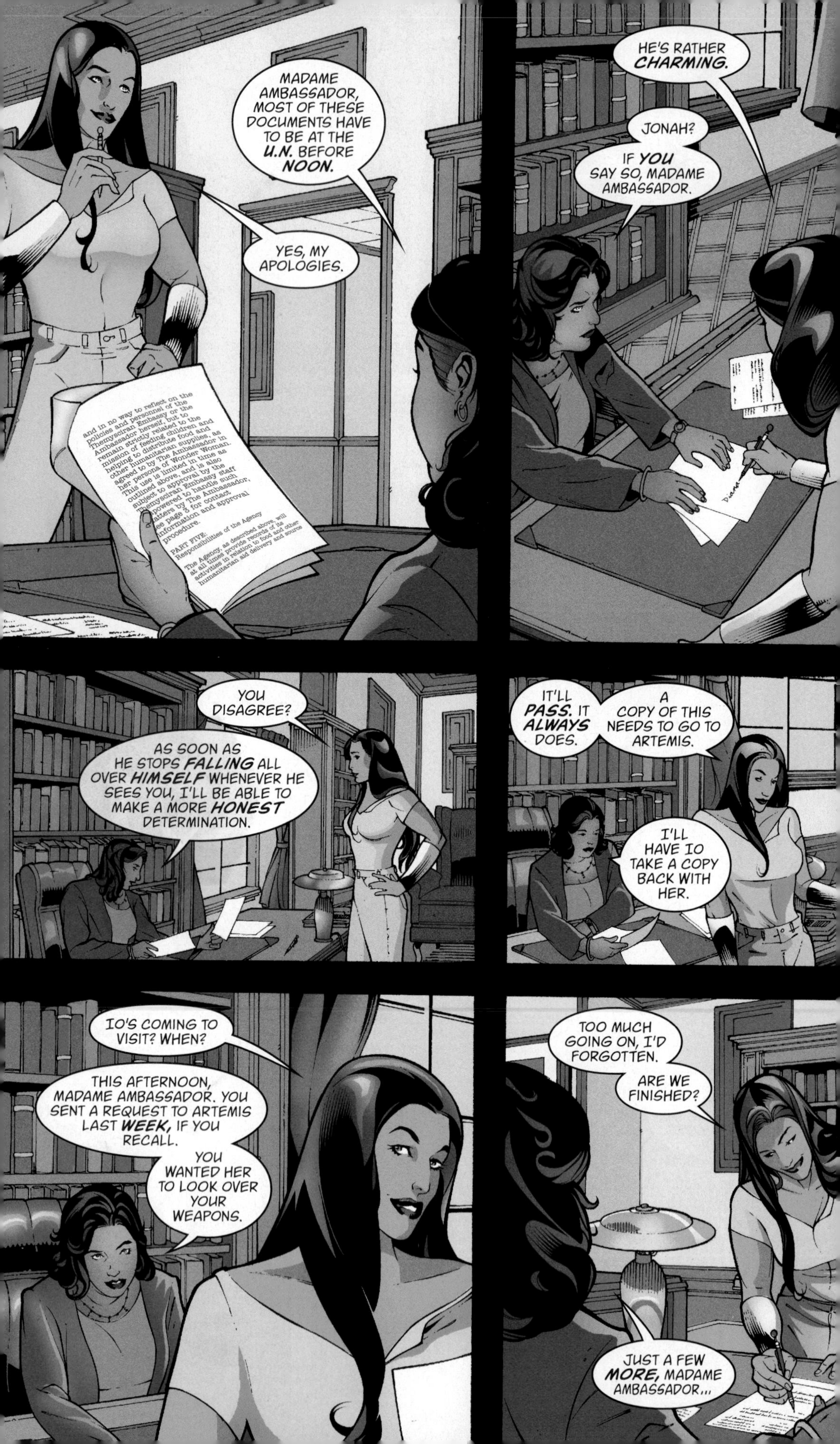
MADAME AMBASSADOR, MOST OF THESE DOCUMENTS HAVE TO BE AT THE U.N. BEFORE NOON.
YES, MY APOLOGIES.
and in no way to reflect on the policies and personnel of the Themysciran Embassy or the Ambassador herself, but to remain strictly related to the mission of feeding children and helping to distribute food and other humanitarian supplies, as agreed to by The Ambassador in her persona of Wonder Woman. This use is limited in time as outlined above, and is also subject to approval by the Themysciran Embassy staff empowered to handle such matters by The Ambassador. See page 3 for contact information and approval procedure.
PART FIVE: Responsibilities of the Agency
The Agency, as described above, will at all times provide records of its activities in relation to food and other humanitarian aid delivery and source
HE'S RATHER CHARMING.
JONAH?
IF YOU SAY SO, MADAME AMBASSADOR.
Diana
YOU DISAGREE?
AS SOON AS HE STOPS FALLING ALL OVER HIMSELF WHENEVER HE SEES YOU, I'LL BE ABLE TO MAKE A MORE HONEST DETERMINATION.
IT'LL PASS. IT ALWAYS DOES.
A COPY OF THIS NEEDS TO GO TO ARTEMIS.
I'LL HAVE IO TAKE A COPY BACK WITH HER.
IO'S COMING TO VISIT? WHEN?
THIS AFTERNOON, MADAME AMBASSADOR. YOU SENT A REQUEST TO ARTEMIS LAST WEEK, IF YOU RECALL.
YOU WANTED HER TO LOOK OVER YOUR WEAPONS.
TOO MUCH GOING ON, I'D FORGOTTEN.
ARE WE FINISHED?
JUST A FEW MORE, MADAME AMBASSADOR...

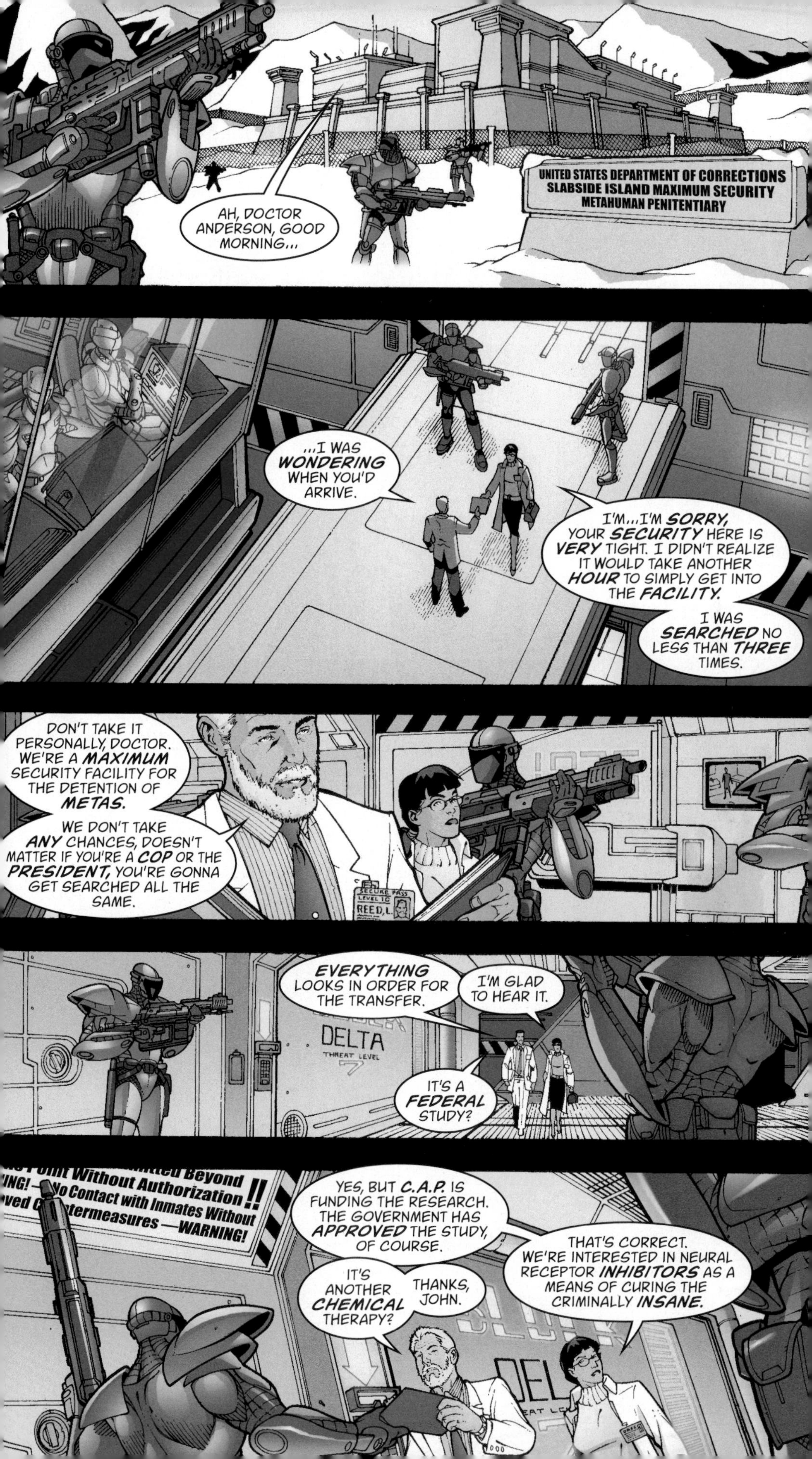

UNITED STATES DEPARTMENT OF CORRECTIONS
SLABSIDE ISLAND MAXIMUM SECURITY
METAHUMAN PENITENTIARY
AH, DOCTOR ANDERSON, GOOD MORNING...
...I WAS WONDERING WHEN YOU'D ARRIVE.
I'M...I'M SORRY, YOUR SECURITY HERE IS VERY TIGHT. I DIDN'T REALIZE IT WOULD TAKE ANOTHER HOUR TO SIMPLY GET INTO THE FACILITY.
I WAS SEARCHED NO LESS THAN THREE TIMES.
DON'T TAKE IT PERSONALLY, DOCTOR. WE'RE A MAXIMUM SECURITY FACILITY FOR THE DETENTION OF METAS.
WE DON'T TAKE ANY CHANCES, DOESN'T MATTER IF YOU'RE A COP OR THE PRESIDENT, YOU'RE GONNA GET SEARCHED ALL THE SAME.
SECURE PASS
REED, L.
EVERYTHING LOOKS IN ORDER FOR THE TRANSFER.
I'M GLAD TO HEAR IT.
DELTA
THREAT LEVEL
7
IT'S A FEDERAL STUDY?
Without Authorization!!
No Contact with Inmates Without
termeasures —WARNING!
YES, BUT C.A.P. IS FUNDING THE RESEARCH. THE GOVERNMENT HAS APPROVED THE STUDY, OF COURSE.
IT'S ANOTHER CHEMICAL THERAPY?
THANKS, JOHN.
THAT'S CORRECT. WE'RE INTERESTED IN NEURAL RECEPTOR INHIBITORS AS A MEANS OF CURING THE CRIMINALLY INSANE.

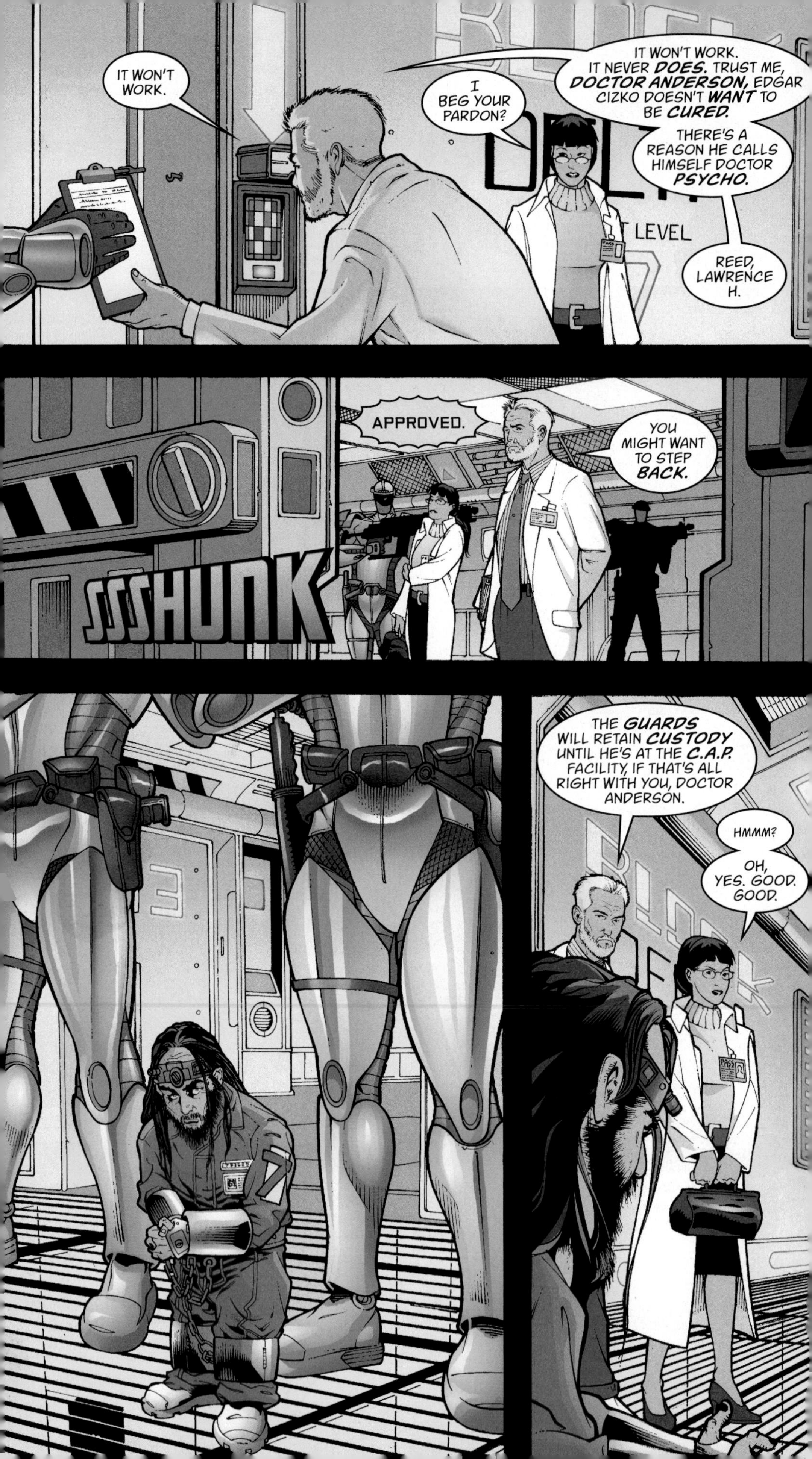
IT WON'T WORK.
I BEG YOUR PARDON?
IT WON'T WORK. IT NEVER DOES. TRUST ME, DOCTOR ANDERSON, EDGAR CIZKO DOESN'T WANT TO BE CURED.
THERE'S A REASON HE CALLS HIMSELF DOCTOR PSYCHO.
REED, LAWRENCE H.
APPROVED.
YOU MIGHT WANT TO STEP BACK.
SSSHUNK
THE GUARDS WILL RETAIN CUSTODY UNTIL HE'S AT THE C.A.P. FACILITY, IF THAT'S ALL RIGHT WITH YOU, DOCTOR ANDERSON.
HMMM?
OH, YES. GOOD. GOOD.

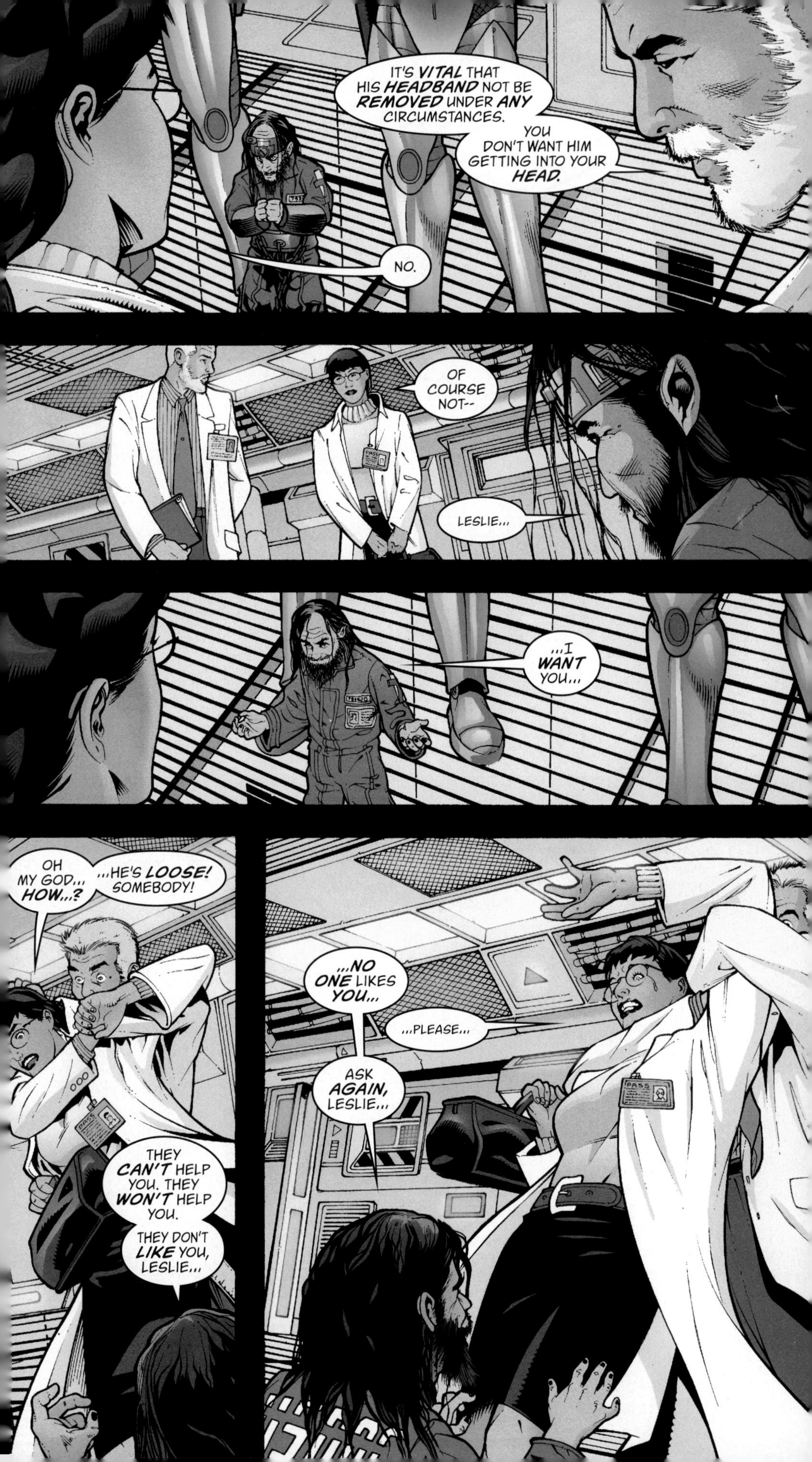
IT'S VITAL THAT HIS HEADBAND NOT BE REMOVED UNDER ANY CIRCUMSTANCES.
YOU DON'T WANT HIM GETTING INTO YOUR HEAD.
NO.
OF COURSE NOT--
LESLIE...
...I WANT YOU...
OH MY GOD... HOW...?
...HE'S LOOSE! SOMEBODY!
THEY CAN'T HELP YOU. THEY WON'T HELP YOU.
THEY DON'T LIKE YOU, LESLIE...
...NO ONE LIKES YOU...
...PLEASE...
ASK AGAIN, LESLIE...

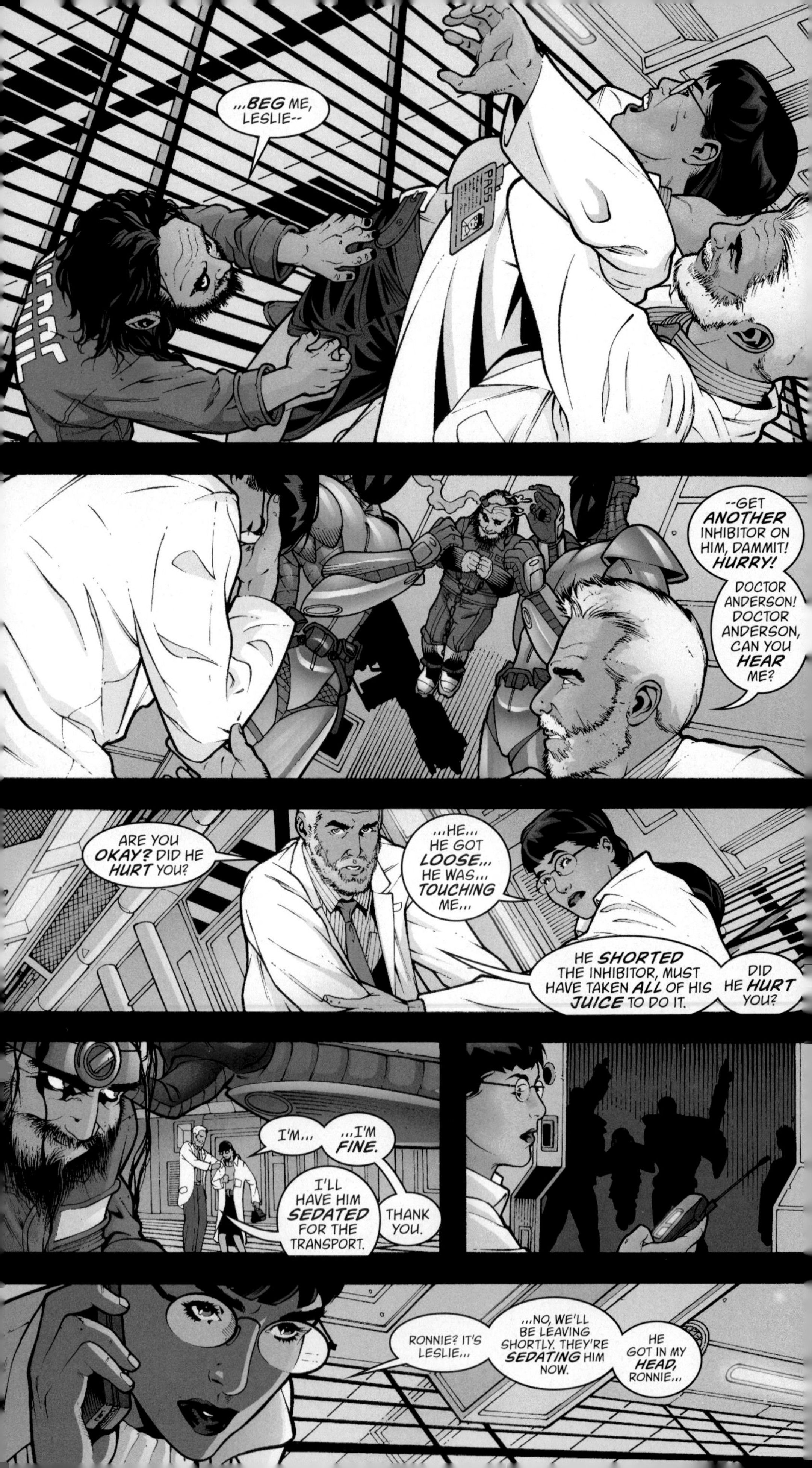
...BEG ME, LESLIE--
--GET ANOTHER INHIBITOR ON HIM, DAMMIT! HURRY!
DOCTOR ANDERSON! DOCTOR ANDERSON, CAN YOU HEAR ME?
ARE YOU OKAY? DID HE HURT YOU?
...HE... HE GOT LOOSE... HE WAS... TOUCHING ME...
HE SHORTED THE INHIBITOR, MUST HAVE TAKEN ALL OF HIS JUICE TO DO IT.
DID HE HURT YOU?
I'M...
...I'M FINE.
I'LL HAVE HIM SEDATED FOR THE TRANSPORT.
THANK YOU.
RONNIE? IT'S LESLIE...
...NO, WE'LL BE LEAVING SHORTLY. THEY'RE SEDATING HIM NOW.
HE GOT IN MY HEAD, RONNIE...

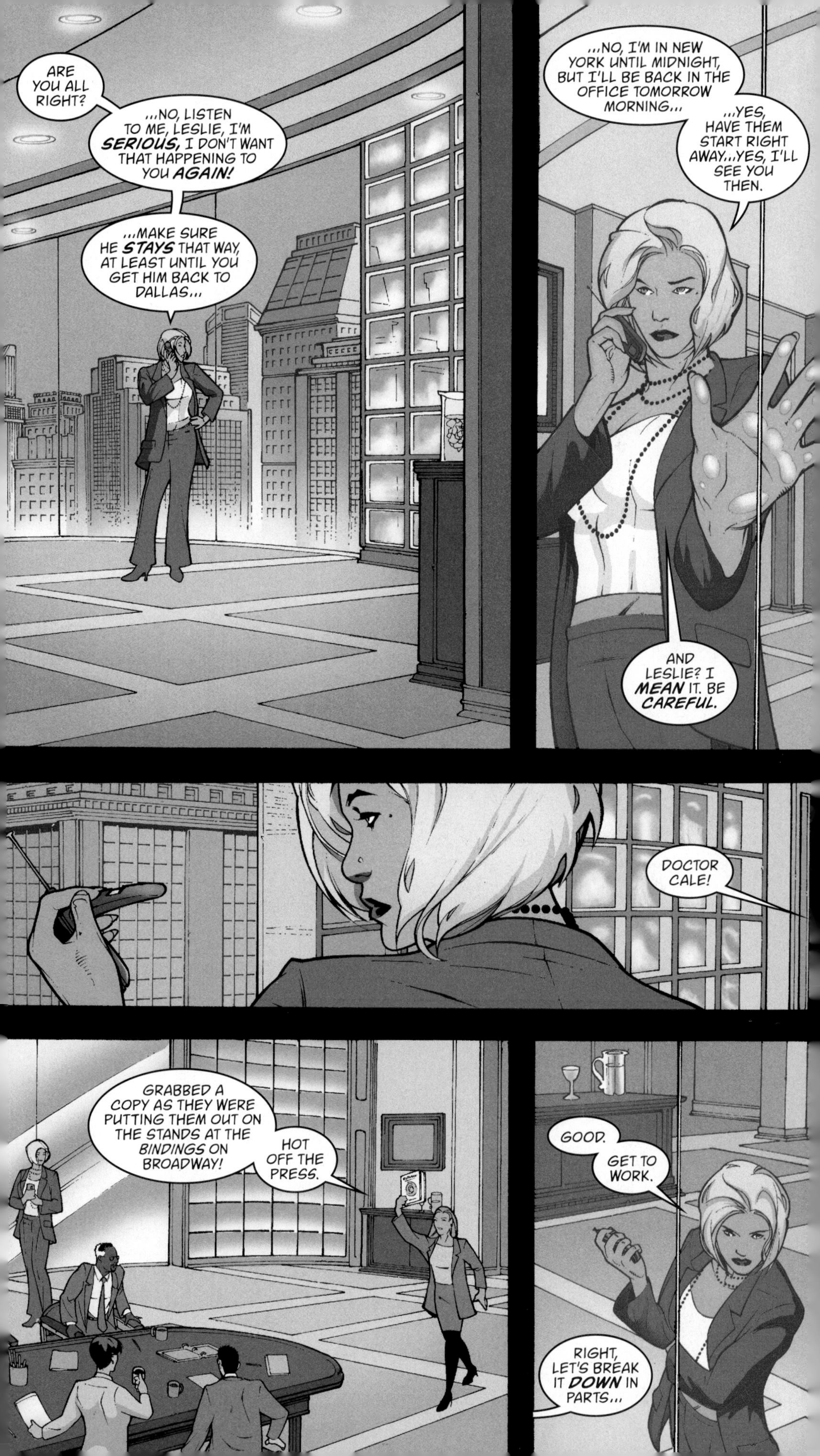
ARE YOU ALL RIGHT?
...NO, LISTEN TO ME, LESLIE, I'M **SERIOUS,** I DON'T WANT THAT HAPPENING TO YOU **AGAIN!**
...MAKE SURE HE **STAYS** THAT WAY, AT LEAST UNTIL YOU GET HIM BACK TO DALLAS...
...NO, I'M IN NEW YORK UNTIL MIDNIGHT, BUT I'LL BE BACK IN THE OFFICE TOMORROW MORNING...
...YES, HAVE THEM START RIGHT AWAY...YES, I'LL SEE YOU THEN.
AND LESLIE? I **MEAN** IT. BE **CAREFUL.**
DOCTOR CALE!
GRABBED A COPY AS THEY WERE PUTTING THEM OUT ON THE STANDS AT THE *BINDINGS* ON BROADWAY!
HOT OFF THE PRESS.
GOOD.
GET TO WORK.
RIGHT, LET'S BREAK IT **DOWN** IN PARTS...

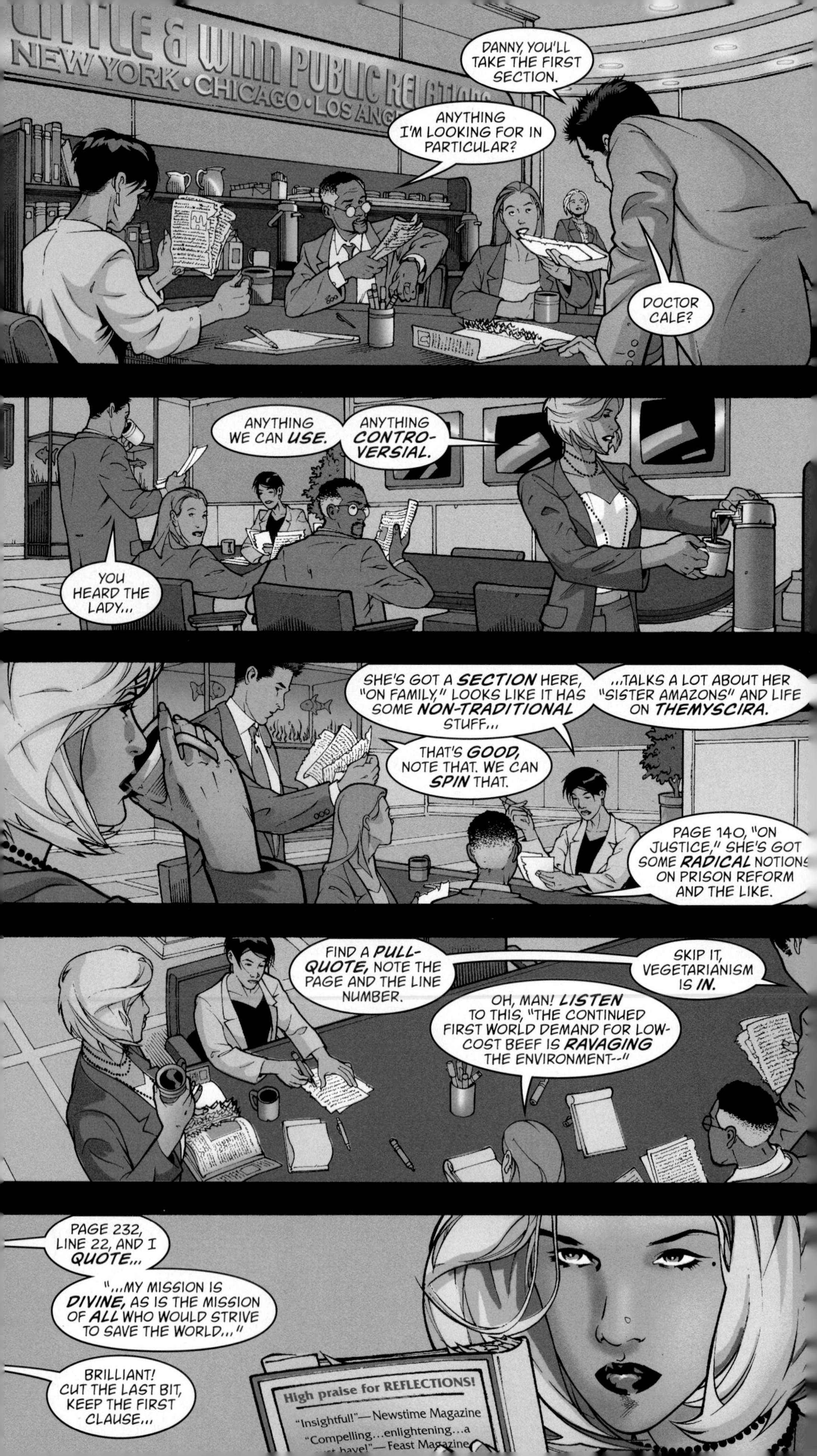
LITTLE & WINN PUBLIC RELATIONS
NEW YORK • CHICAGO • LOS ANG
DANNY, YOU'LL TAKE THE FIRST SECTION.
ANYTHING I'M LOOKING FOR IN PARTICULAR?
DOCTOR CALE?
ANYTHING WE CAN USE.
ANYTHING CONTRO-VERSIAL.
YOU HEARD THE LADY...
SHE'S GOT A SECTION HERE, "ON FAMILY," LOOKS LIKE IT HAS SOME NON-TRADITIONAL STUFF...
THAT'S GOOD, NOTE THAT. WE CAN SPIN THAT.
...TALKS A LOT ABOUT HER "SISTER AMAZONS" AND LIFE ON THEMYSCIRA.
PAGE 140, "ON JUSTICE," SHE'S GOT SOME RADICAL NOTIONS ON PRISON REFORM AND THE LIKE.
FIND A PULL-QUOTE, NOTE THE PAGE AND THE LINE NUMBER.
SKIP IT, VEGETARIANISM IS IN.
OH, MAN! LISTEN TO THIS, "THE CONTINUED FIRST WORLD DEMAND FOR LOW-COST BEEF IS RAVAGING THE ENVIRONMENT--"
PAGE 232, LINE 22, AND I QUOTE...
"...MY MISSION IS DIVINE, AS IS THE MISSION OF ALL WHO WOULD STRIVE TO SAVE THE WORLD..."
BRILLIANT! CUT THE LAST BIT, KEEP THE FIRST CLAUSE...
High praise for REFLECTIONS!
"Insightful!"—Newstime Magazine
"Compelling...enlightening...a
have!"—Feast Magazine

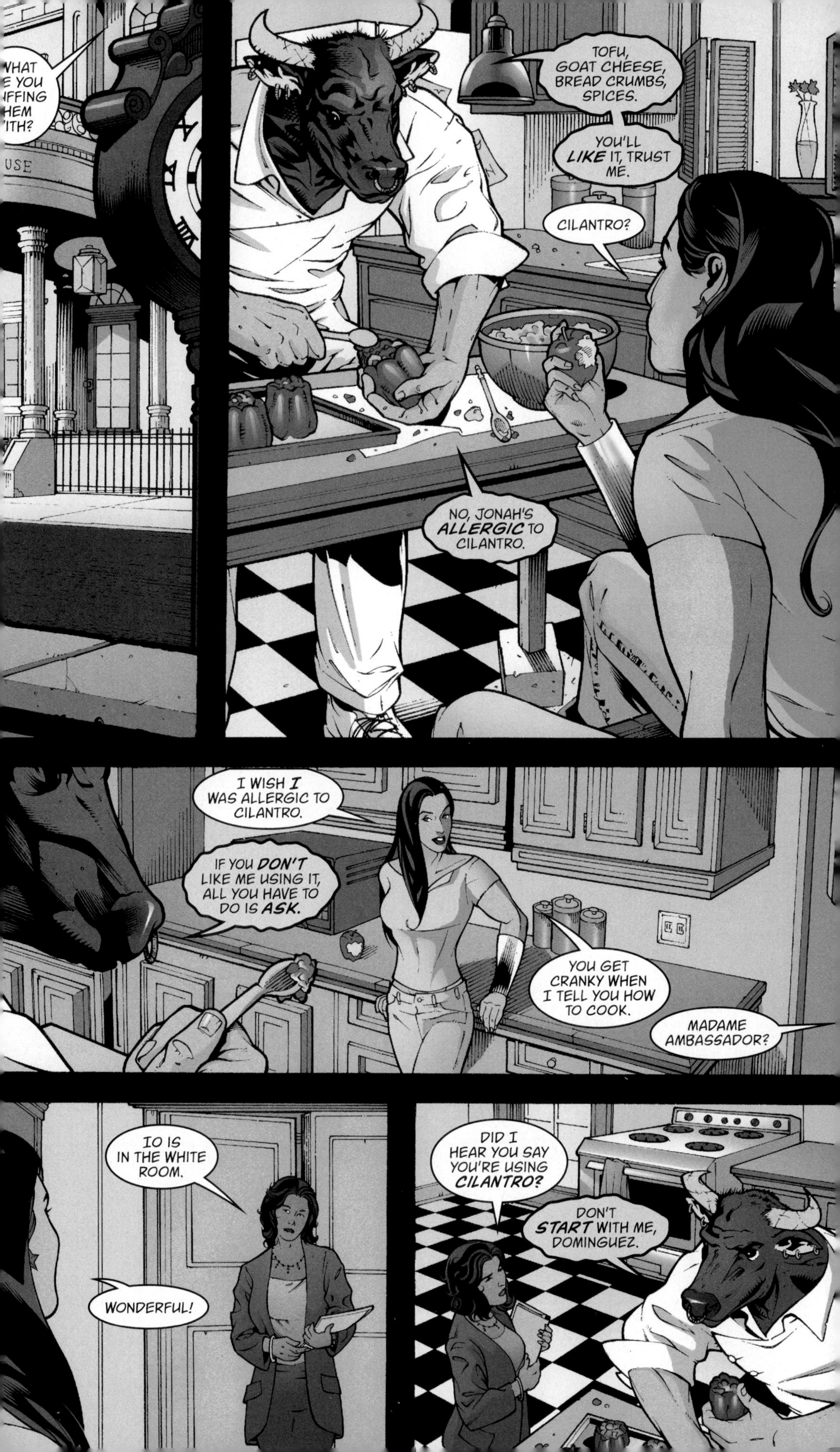
WHAT
E YOU
IFFING
HEM
ITH?
USE
TOFU, GOAT CHEESE, BREAD CRUMBS, SPICES.
YOU'LL LIKE IT, TRUST ME.
CILANTRO?
NO, JONAH'S ALLERGIC TO CILANTRO.
I WISH I WAS ALLERGIC TO CILANTRO.
IF YOU DON'T LIKE ME USING IT, ALL YOU HAVE TO DO IS ASK.
YOU GET CRANKY WHEN I TELL YOU HOW TO COOK.
MADAME AMBASSADOR?
IO IS IN THE WHITE ROOM.
WONDERFUL!
DID I HEAR YOU SAY YOU'RE USING CILANTRO?
DON'T START WITH ME, DOMINGUEZ.

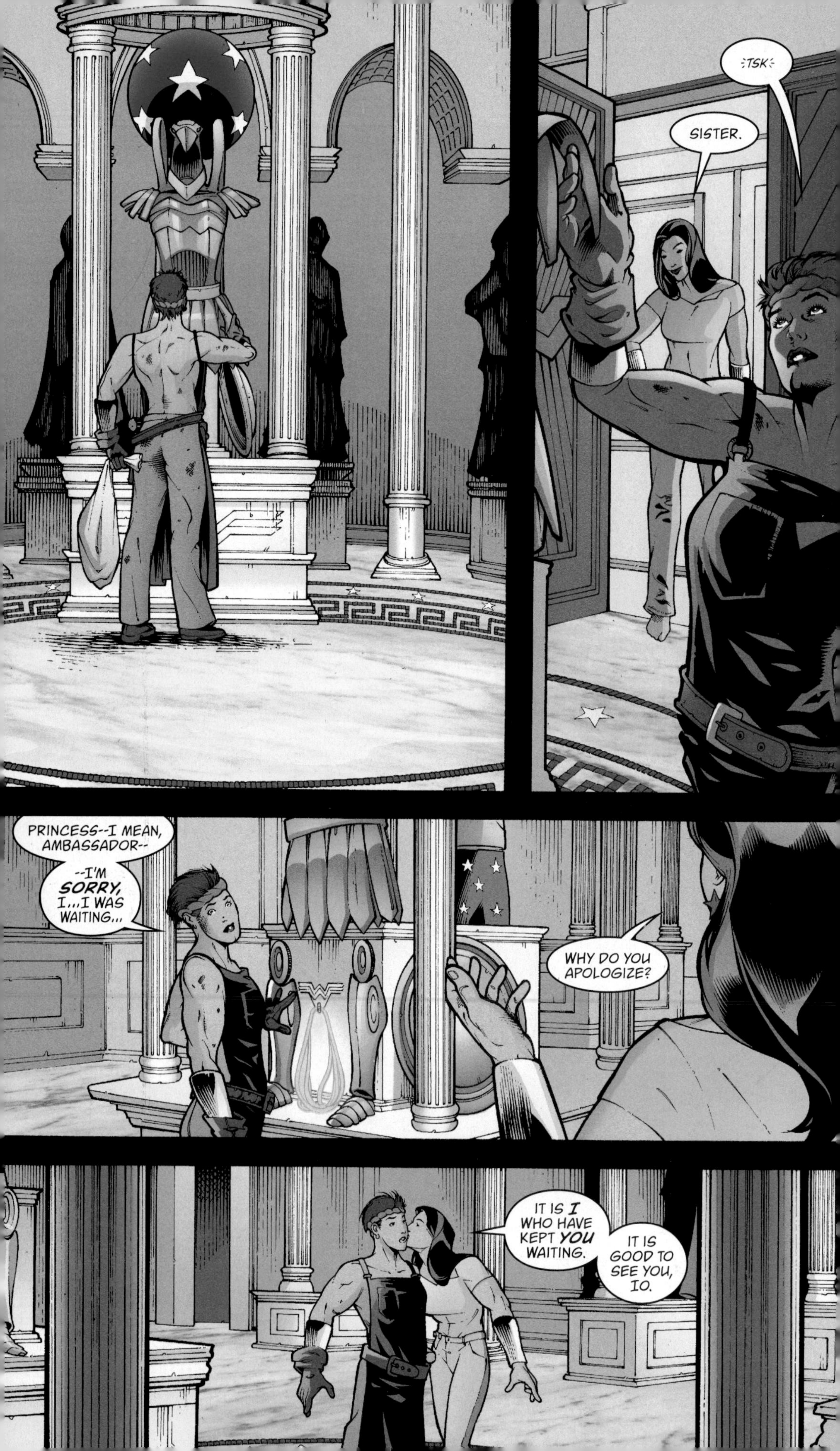
TSK
SISTER.
PRINCESS--I MEAN, AMBASSADOR--
--I'M SORRY, I...I WAS WAITING...
WHY DO YOU APOLOGIZE?
IT IS I WHO HAVE KEPT YOU WAITING.
IT IS GOOD TO SEE YOU, IO.

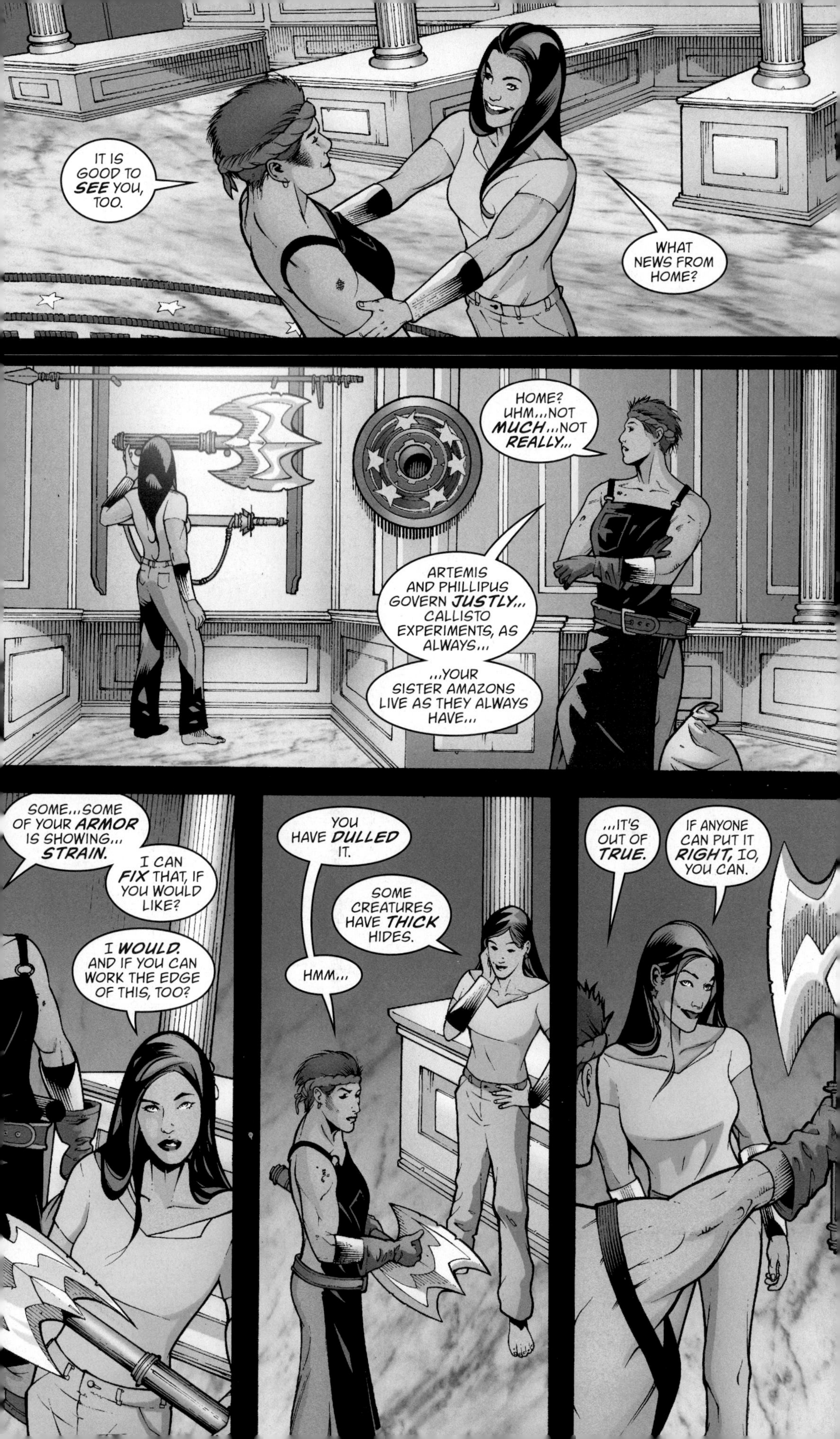
IT IS GOOD TO SEE YOU, TOO.
WHAT NEWS FROM HOME?
HOME? UHM...NOT MUCH...NOT REALLY...
ARTEMIS AND PHILLIPUS GOVERN JUSTLY... CALLISTO EXPERIMENTS, AS ALWAYS...
...YOUR SISTER AMAZONS LIVE AS THEY ALWAYS HAVE...
SOME...SOME OF YOUR ARMOR IS SHOWING... STRAIN.
I CAN FIX THAT, IF YOU WOULD LIKE?
I WOULD. AND IF YOU CAN WORK THE EDGE OF THIS, TOO?
YOU HAVE DULLED IT.
SOME CREATURES HAVE THICK HIDES.
HMM...
...IT'S OUT OF TRUE.
IF ANYONE CAN PUT IT RIGHT, IO, YOU CAN.

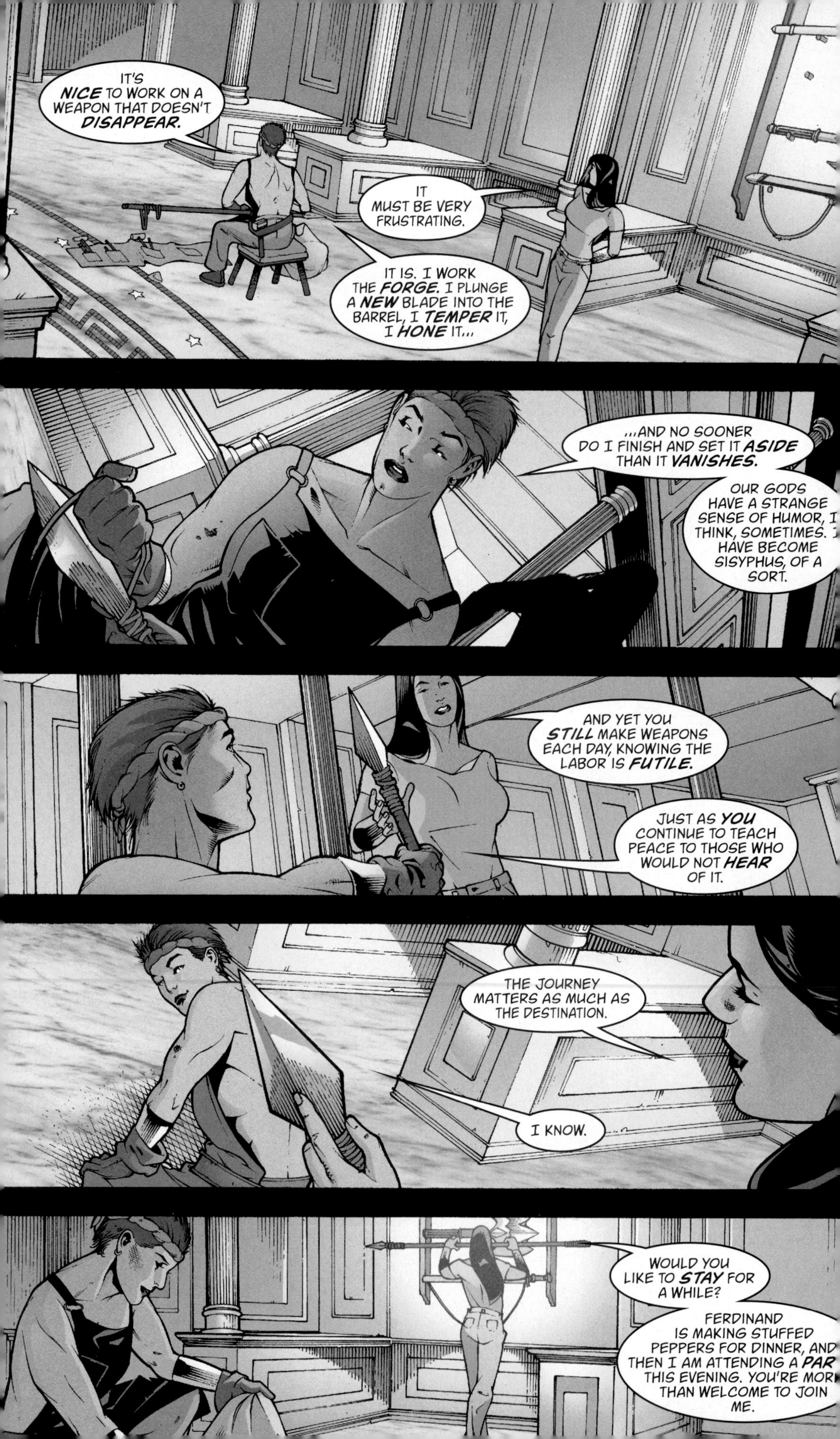
IT'S NICE TO WORK ON A WEAPON THAT DOESN'T DISAPPEAR.
IT MUST BE VERY FRUSTRATING.
IT IS. I WORK THE FORGE. I PLUNGE A NEW BLADE INTO THE BARREL, I TEMPER IT, I HONE IT...
...AND NO SOONER DO I FINISH AND SET IT ASIDE THAN IT VANISHES.
OUR GODS HAVE A STRANGE SENSE OF HUMOR, I THINK, SOMETIMES. I HAVE BECOME SISYPHUS, OF A SORT.
AND YET YOU STILL MAKE WEAPONS EACH DAY, KNOWING THE LABOR IS FUTILE.
JUST AS YOU CONTINUE TO TEACH PEACE TO THOSE WHO WOULD NOT HEAR OF IT.
THE JOURNEY MATTERS AS MUCH AS THE DESTINATION.
I KNOW.
WOULD YOU LIKE TO STAY FOR A WHILE?
FERDINAND IS MAKING STUFFED PEPPERS FOR DINNER, AND THEN I AM ATTENDING A PAR THIS EVENING. YOU'RE MOR THAN WELCOME TO JOIN ME.

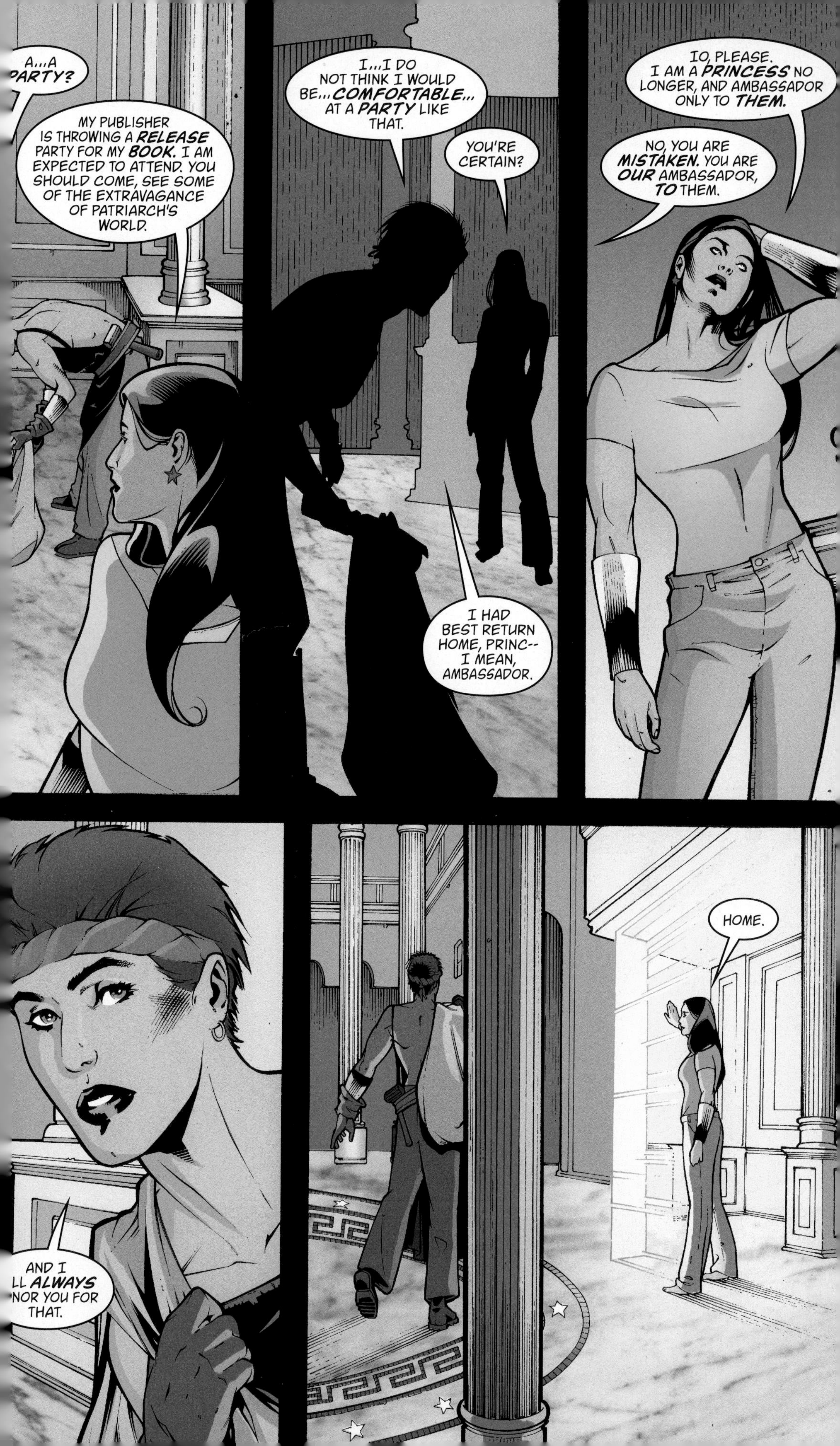
A...A PARTY?
MY PUBLISHER IS THROWING A RELEASE PARTY FOR MY BOOK. I AM EXPECTED TO ATTEND. YOU SHOULD COME, SEE SOME OF THE EXTRAVAGANCE OF PATRIARCH'S WORLD.
I...I DO NOT THINK I WOULD BE...COMFORTABLE... AT A PARTY LIKE THAT.
YOU'RE CERTAIN?
I HAD BEST RETURN HOME, PRINC-- I MEAN, AMBASSADOR.
IO, PLEASE. I AM A PRINCESS NO LONGER, AND AMBASSADOR ONLY TO THEM.
NO, YOU ARE MISTAKEN. YOU ARE OUR AMBASSADOR, TO THEM.
AND I LL ALWAYS NOR YOU FOR THAT.
HOME.

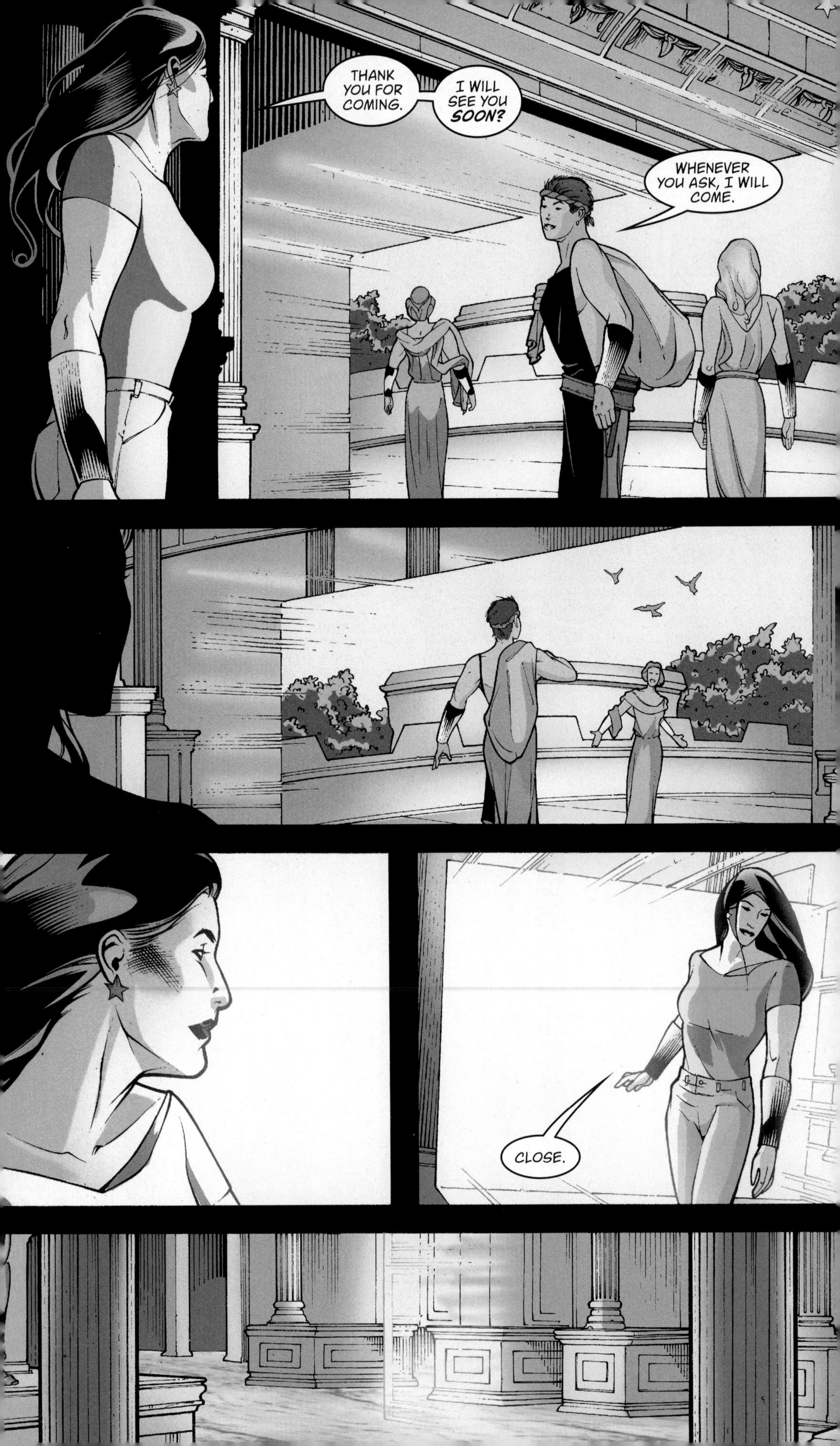
THANK YOU FOR COMING.
I WILL SEE YOU SOON?
WHENEVER YOU ASK, I WILL COME.
CLOSE.

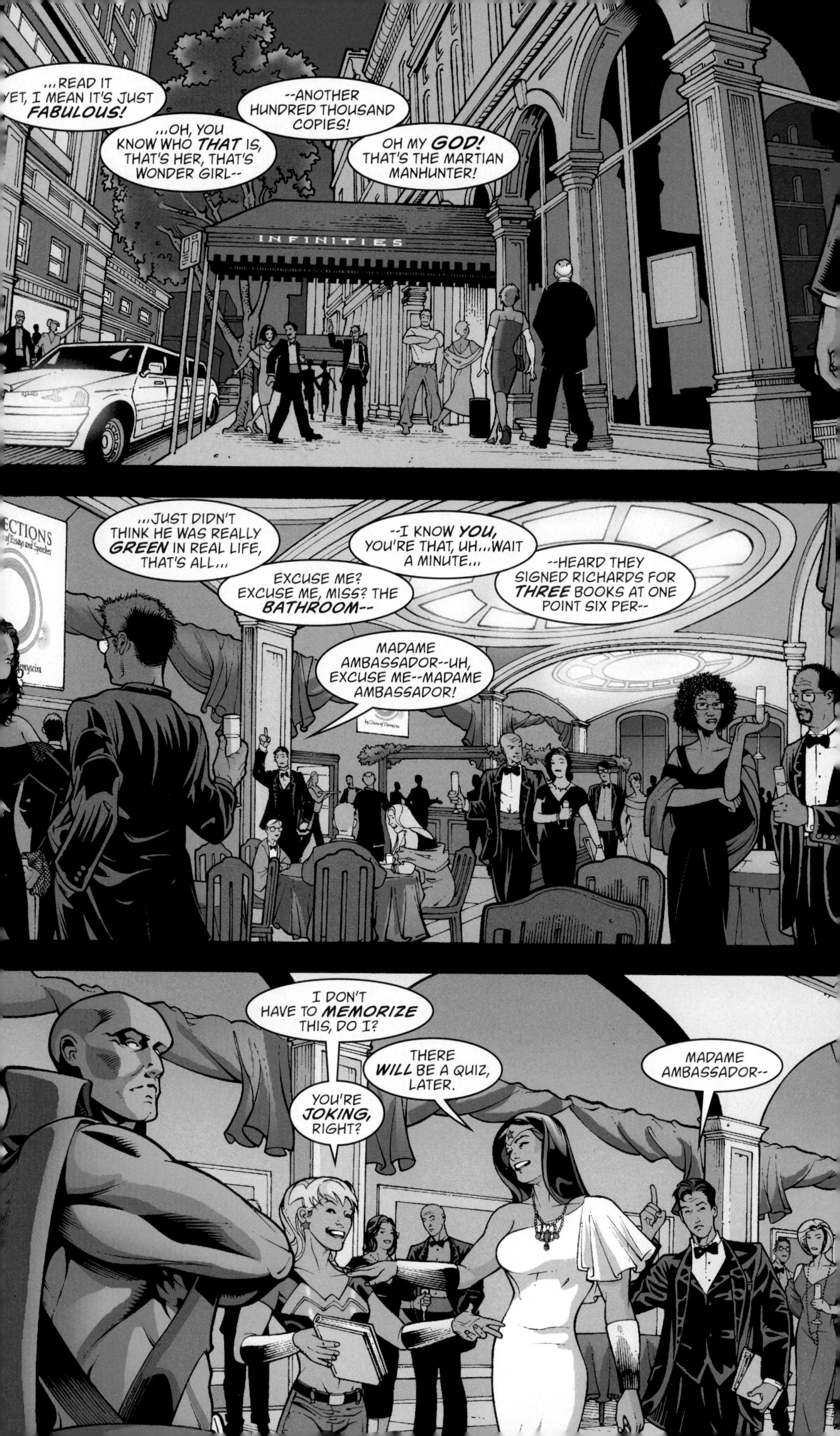
...READ IT YET, I MEAN IT'S JUST FABULOUS!
...OH, YOU KNOW WHO THAT IS, THAT'S HER, THAT'S WONDER GIRL--
--ANOTHER HUNDRED THOUSAND COPIES!
OH MY GOD! THAT'S THE MARTIAN MANHUNTER!
INFINITIES
...JUST DIDN'T THINK HE WAS REALLY GREEN IN REAL LIFE, THAT'S ALL...
EXCUSE ME? EXCUSE ME, MISS? THE BATHROOM--
--I KNOW YOU, YOU'RE THAT, UH...WAIT A MINUTE...
--HEARD THEY SIGNED RICHARDS FOR THREE BOOKS AT ONE POINT SIX PER--
MADAME AMBASSADOR--UH, EXCUSE ME--MADAME AMBASSADOR!
I DON'T HAVE TO MEMORIZE THIS, DO I?
THERE WILL BE A QUIZ, LATER.
YOU'RE JOKING, RIGHT?
MADAME AMBASSADOR--

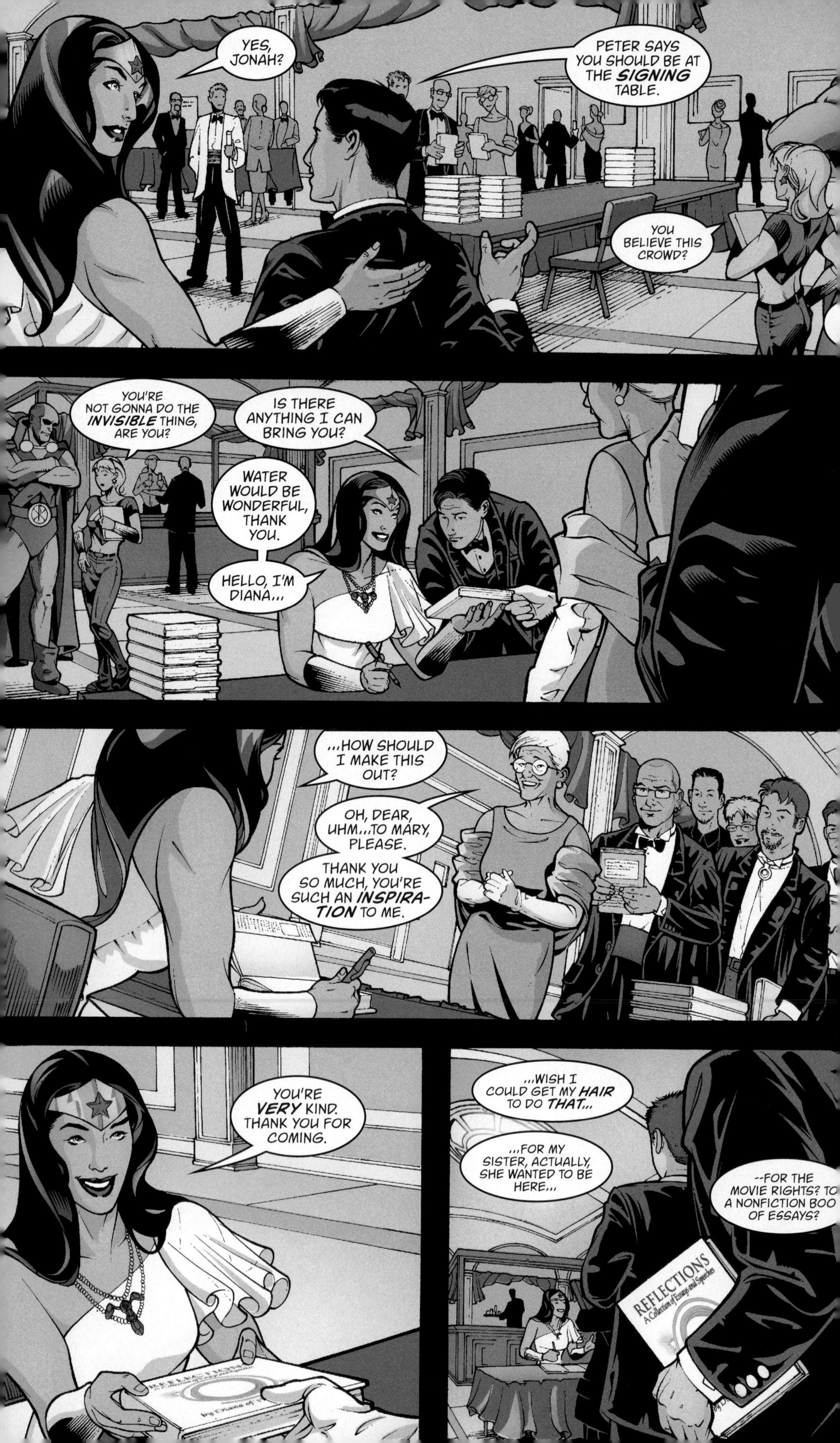
YES, JONAH?
PETER SAYS YOU SHOULD BE AT THE SIGNING TABLE.
YOU BELIEVE THIS CROWD?
YOU'RE NOT GONNA DO THE INVISIBLE THING, ARE YOU?
IS THERE ANYTHING I CAN BRING YOU?
WATER WOULD BE WONDERFUL, THANK YOU.
HELLO, I'M DIANA...
...HOW SHOULD I MAKE THIS OUT?
OH, DEAR, UHM...TO MARY, PLEASE.
THANK YOU SO MUCH, YOU'RE SUCH AN INSPIRATION TO ME.
YOU'RE VERY KIND. THANK YOU FOR COMING.
...WISH I COULD GET MY HAIR TO DO THAT...
...FOR MY SISTER, ACTUALLY, SHE WANTED TO BE HERE...
--FOR THE MOVIE RIGHTS? TO A NONFICTION BOO OF ESSAYS?
REFLECTIONS
A Collection of Essays and Speeches

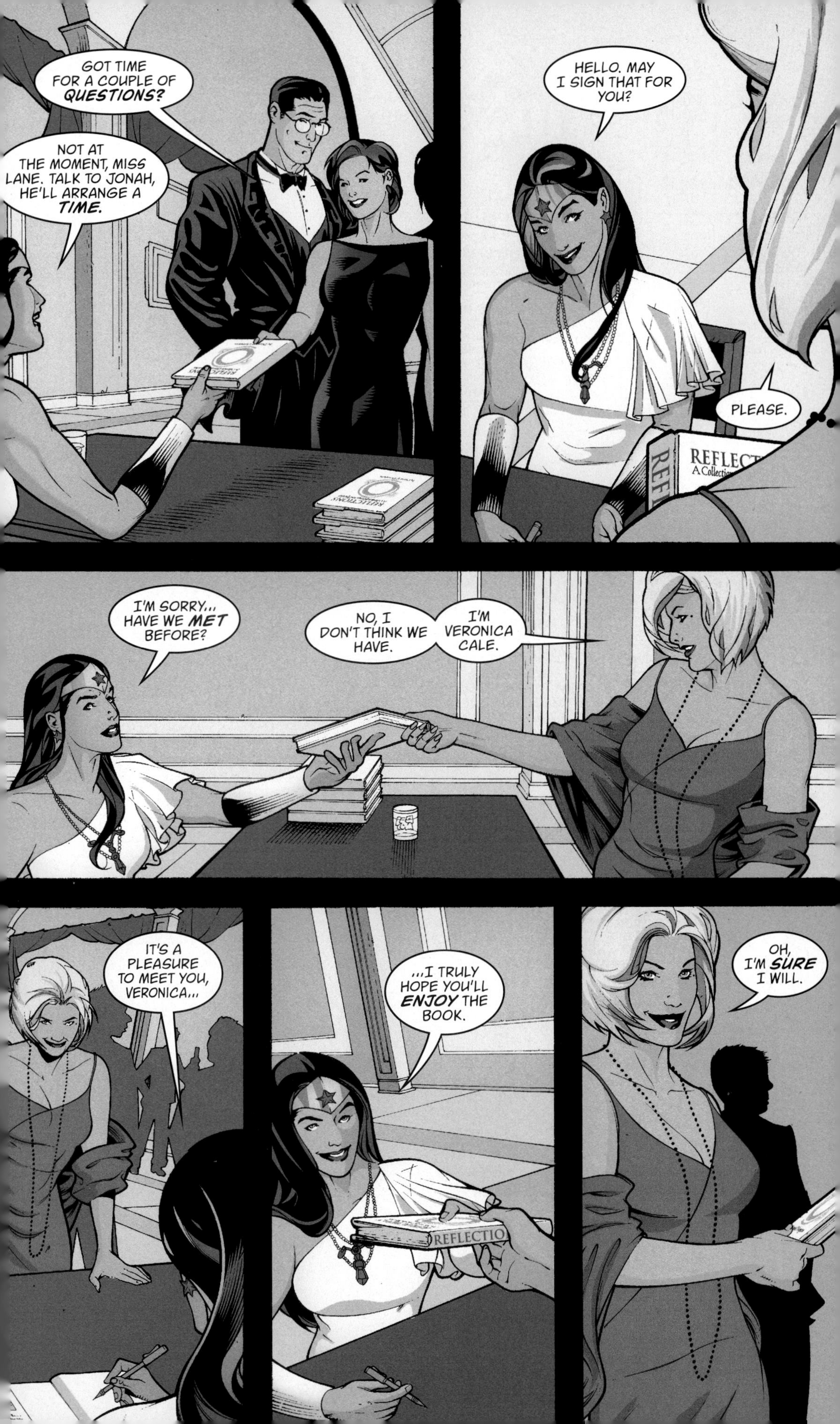
GOT TIME FOR A COUPLE OF QUESTIONS?
NOT AT THE MOMENT, MISS LANE. TALK TO JONAH, HE'LL ARRANGE A TIME.
HELLO. MAY I SIGN THAT FOR YOU?
PLEASE.
REFLECTI
A Collection
I'M SORRY... HAVE WE MET BEFORE?
NO, I DON'T THINK WE HAVE.
I'M VERONICA CALE.
IT'S A PLEASURE TO MEET YOU, VERONICA...
...I TRULY HOPE YOU'LL ENJOY THE BOOK.
REFLECTIO
OH, I'M SURE I WILL.

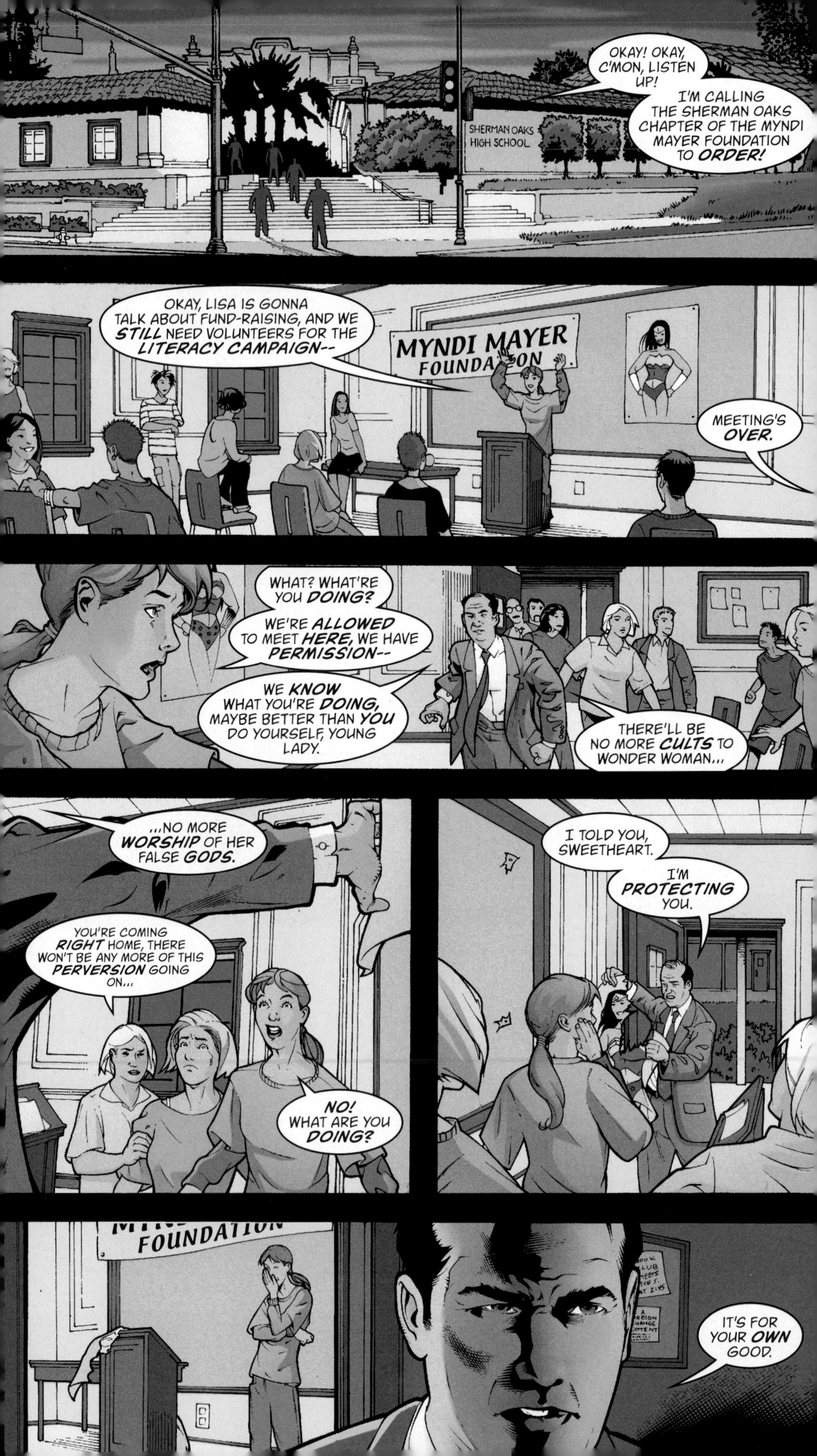

OKAY! OKAY, C'MON, LISTEN UP!
I'M CALLING THE SHERMAN OAKS CHAPTER OF THE MYNDI MAYER FOUNDATION TO ORDER!
SHERMAN OAKS HIGH SCHOOL
OKAY, LISA IS GONNA TALK ABOUT FUND-RAISING, AND WE STILL NEED VOLUNTEERS FOR THE LITERACY CAMPAIGN--
MYNDI MAYER FOUNDATION
MEETING'S OVER.
WHAT? WHAT'RE YOU DOING?
WE'RE ALLOWED TO MEET HERE, WE HAVE PERMISSION--
WE KNOW WHAT YOU'RE DOING, MAYBE BETTER THAN YOU DO YOURSELF, YOUNG LADY.
THERE'LL BE NO MORE CULTS TO WONDER WOMAN...
...NO MORE WORSHIP OF HER FALSE GODS.
YOU'RE COMING RIGHT HOME, THERE WON'T BE ANY MORE OF THIS PERVERSION GOING ON...
NO! WHAT ARE YOU DOING?
I TOLD YOU, SWEETHEART.
I'M PROTECTING YOU.
FOUNDATION
IT'S FOR YOUR OWN GOOD.

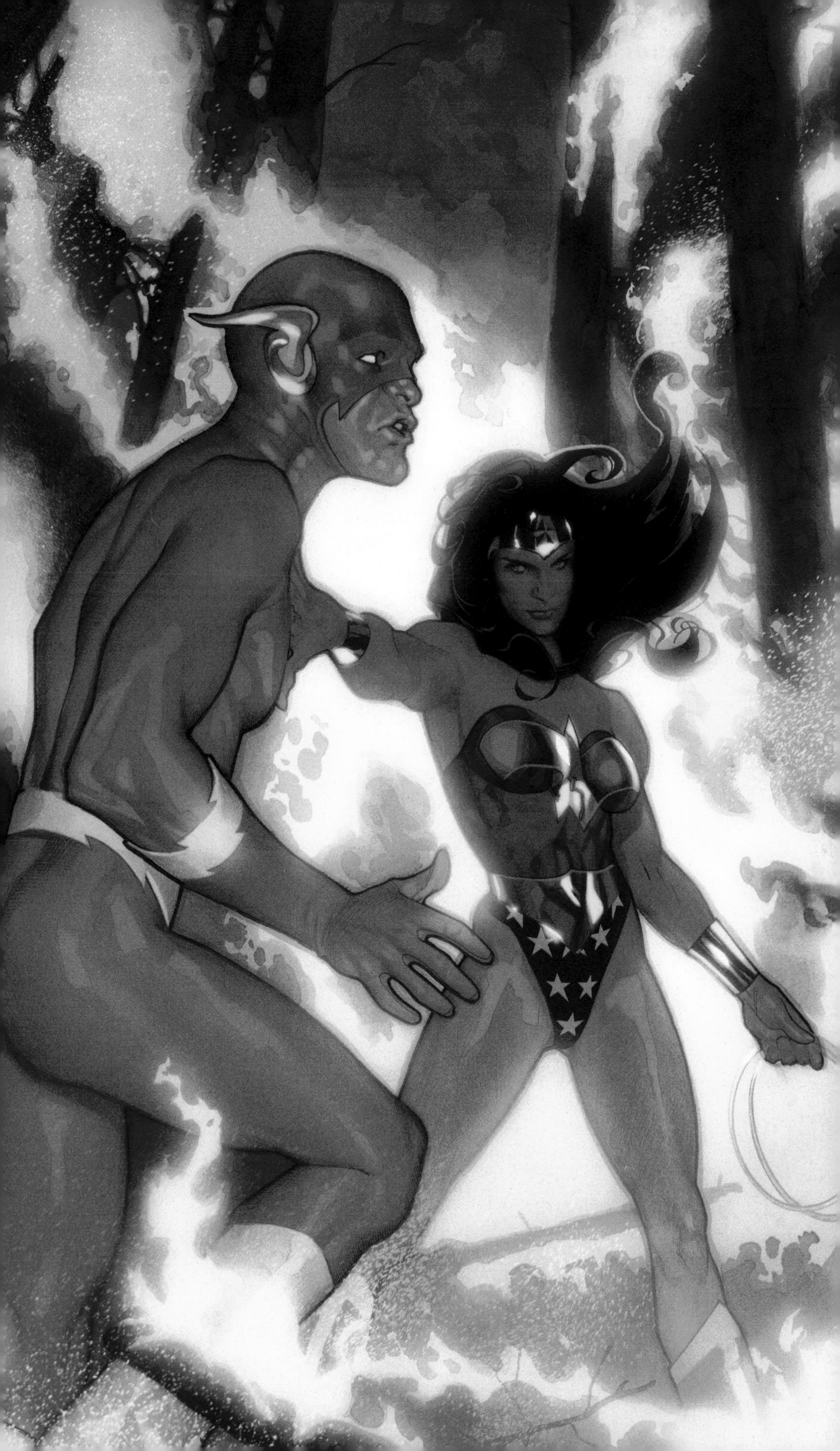

"DOWN TO EARTH: PART TWO"

Drew Johnson – *pencils*
Ray Snyder – *inks*
Trish Mulvihill - *colors*
Adam Hughes – *cover art*

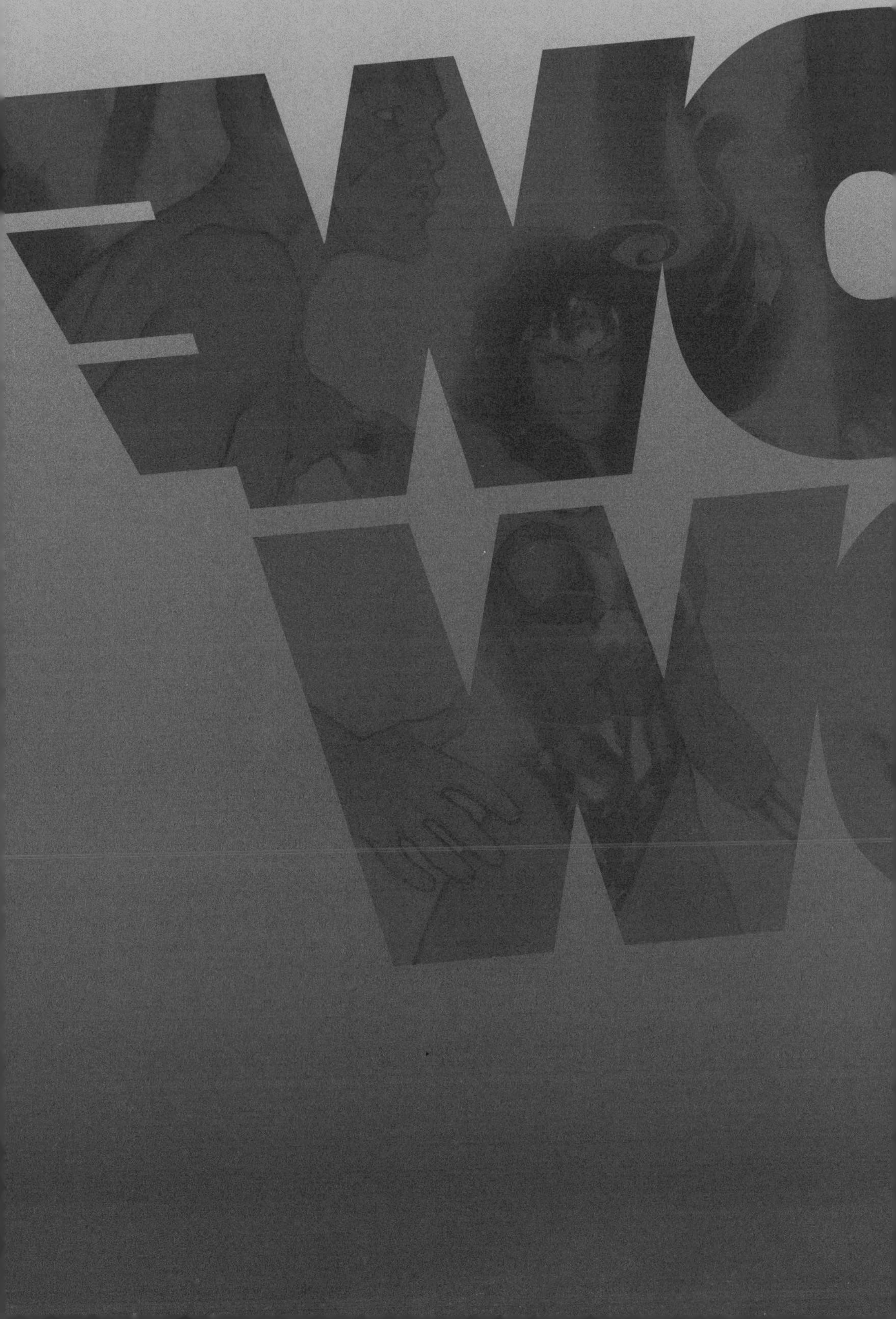

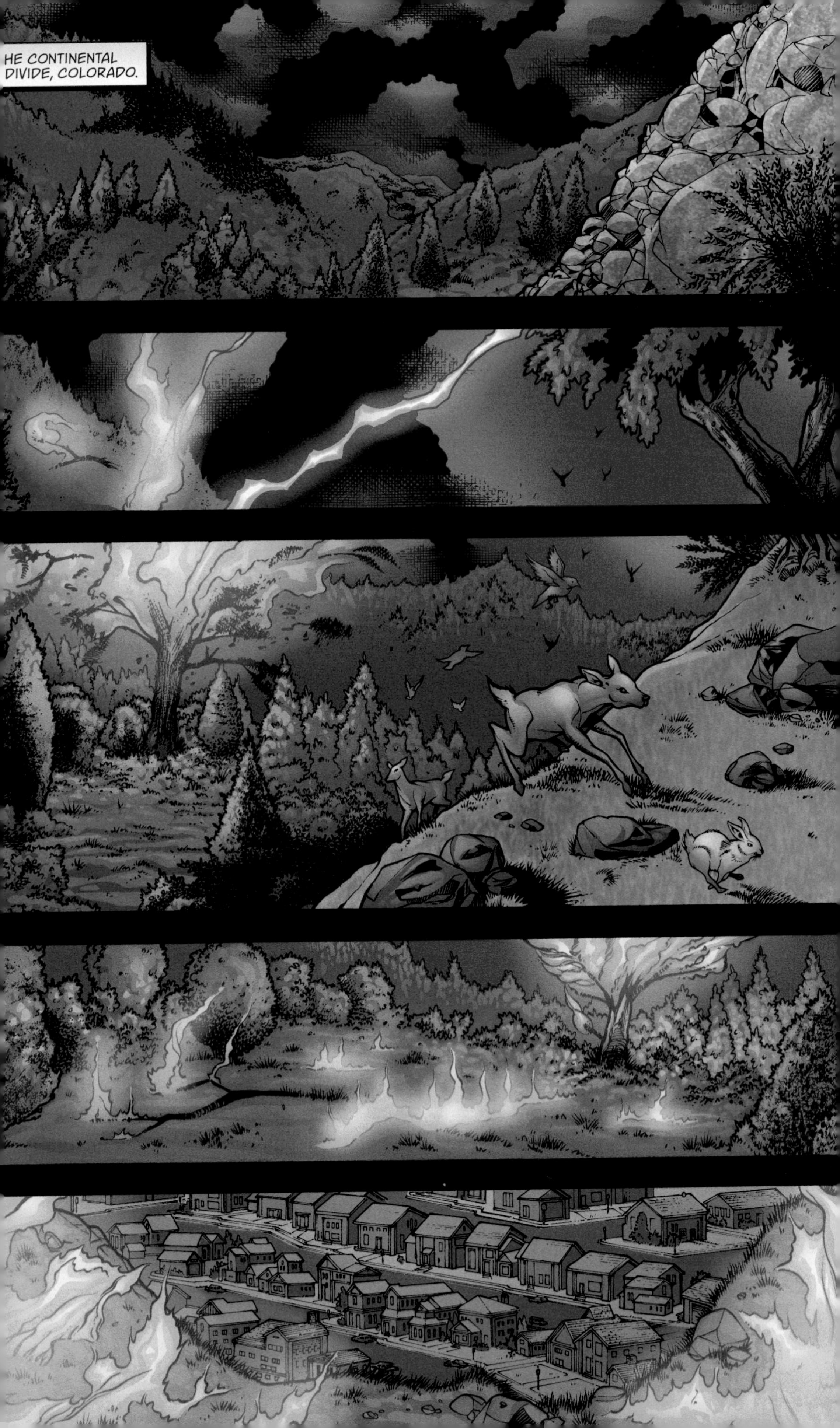
HE CONTINENTAL DIVIDE, COLORADO.

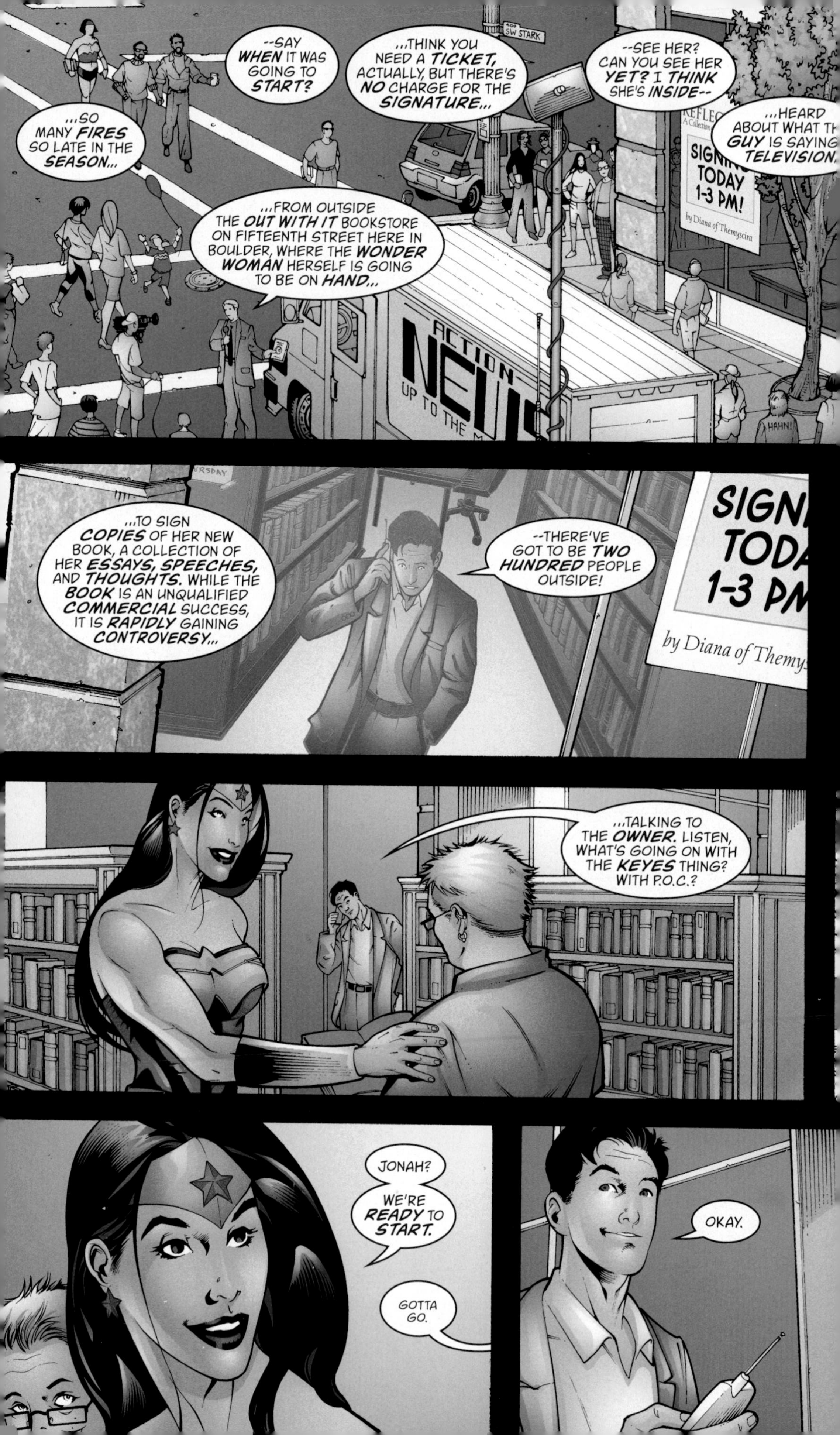
SW STARK
...SO MANY FIRES SO LATE IN THE SEASON...
--SAY WHEN IT WAS GOING TO START?
...THINK YOU NEED A TICKET, ACTUALLY, BUT THERE'S NO CHARGE FOR THE SIGNATURE...
--SEE HER? CAN YOU SEE HER YET? I THINK SHE'S INSIDE--
...HEARD ABOUT WHAT TH GUY IS SAYING TELEVISION
SIGNING TODAY 1-3 PM!
by Diana of Themyscira
...FROM OUTSIDE THE OUT WITH IT BOOKSTORE ON FIFTEENTH STREET HERE IN BOULDER, WHERE THE WONDER WOMAN HERSELF IS GOING TO BE ON HAND...
ACTION NEWS
HAHN!
...TO SIGN COPIES OF HER NEW BOOK, A COLLECTION OF HER ESSAYS, SPEECHES, AND THOUGHTS. WHILE THE BOOK IS AN UNQUALIFIED COMMERCIAL SUCCESS, IT IS RAPIDLY GAINING CONTROVERSY...
--THERE'VE GOT TO BE TWO HUNDRED PEOPLE OUTSIDE!
...TALKING TO THE OWNER. LISTEN, WHAT'S GOING ON WITH THE KEYES THING? WITH P.O.C.?
JONAH?
WE'RE READY TO START.
GOTTA GO.
OKAY.

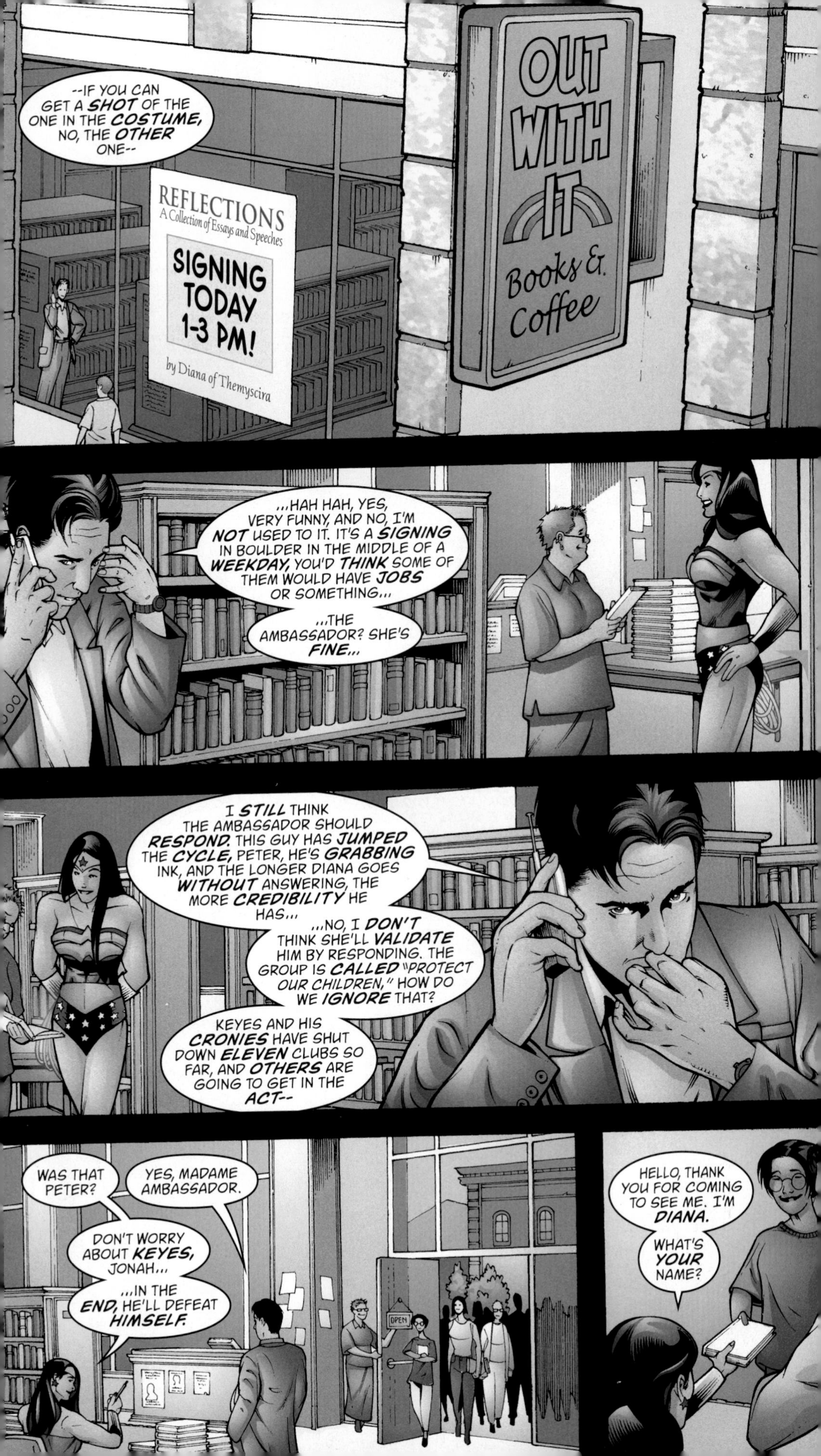
--IF YOU CAN GET A SHOT OF THE ONE IN THE COSTUME, NO, THE OTHER ONE--
REFLECTIONS
A Collection of Essays and Speeches
SIGNING TODAY 1-3 PM!
by Diana of Themyscira
OUT WITH IT
Books & Coffee
...HAH HAH, YES, VERY FUNNY, AND NO, I'M NOT USED TO IT. IT'S A SIGNING IN BOULDER IN THE MIDDLE OF A WEEKDAY, YOU'D THINK SOME OF THEM WOULD HAVE JOBS OR SOMETHING...
...THE AMBASSADOR? SHE'S FINE...
I STILL THINK THE AMBASSADOR SHOULD RESPOND. THIS GUY HAS JUMPED THE CYCLE, PETER, HE'S GRABBING INK, AND THE LONGER DIANA GOES WITHOUT ANSWERING, THE MORE CREDIBILITY HE HAS...
...NO, I DON'T THINK SHE'LL VALIDATE HIM BY RESPONDING. THE GROUP IS CALLED "PROTECT OUR CHILDREN," HOW DO WE IGNORE THAT?
KEYES AND HIS CRONIES HAVE SHUT DOWN ELEVEN CLUBS SO FAR, AND OTHERS ARE GOING TO GET IN THE ACT--
WAS THAT PETER?
YES, MADAME AMBASSADOR.
DON'T WORRY ABOUT KEYES, JONAH...
...IN THE END, HE'LL DEFEAT HIMSELF.
OPEN
HELLO, THANK YOU FOR COMING TO SEE ME. I'M DIANA.
WHAT'S YOUR NAME?

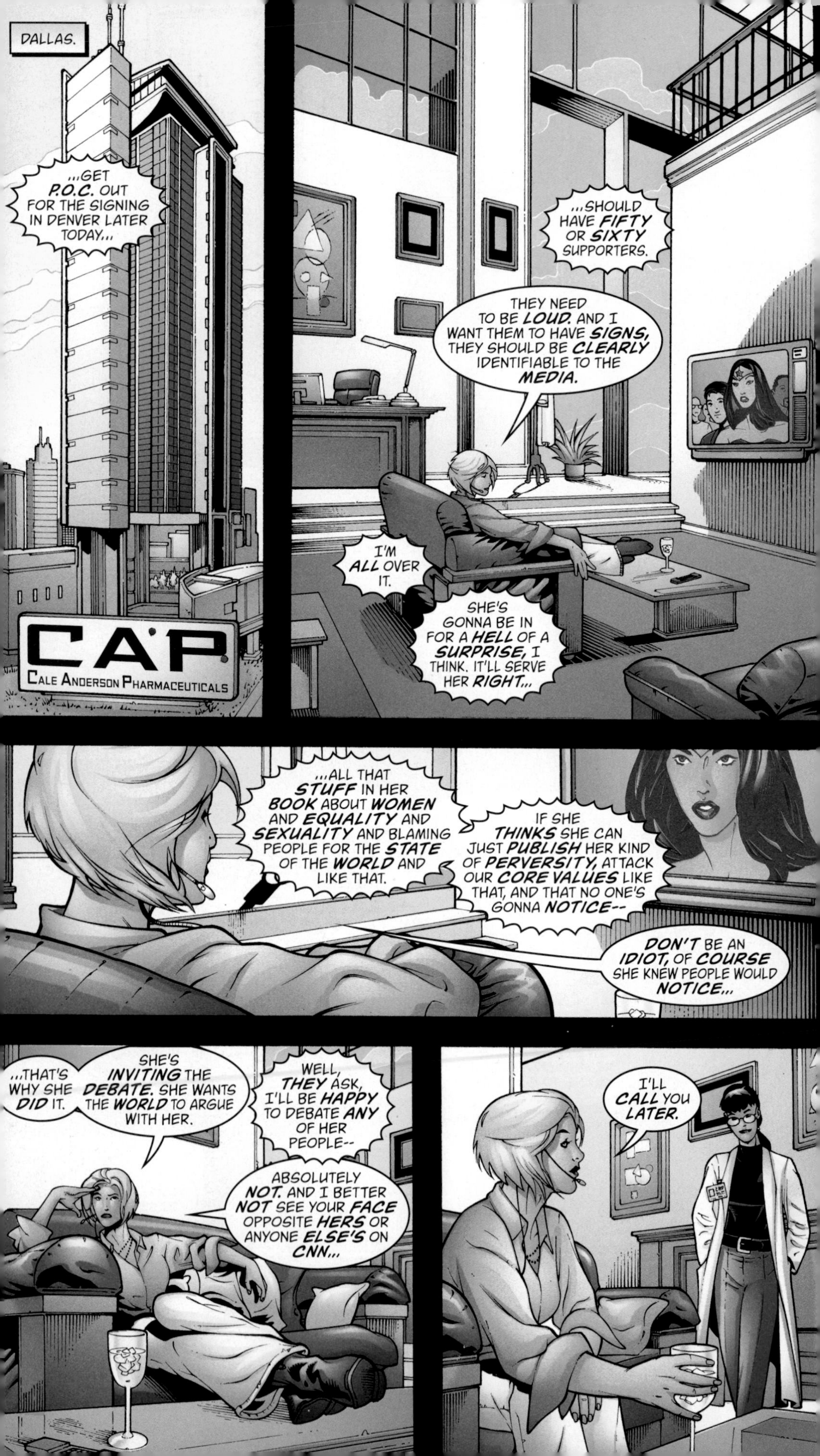

DALLAS.
...GET P.O.C. OUT FOR THE SIGNING IN DENVER LATER TODAY...
CAP
CALE ANDERSON PHARMACEUTICALS
...SHOULD HAVE FIFTY OR SIXTY SUPPORTERS.
THEY NEED TO BE LOUD. AND I WANT THEM TO HAVE SIGNS, THEY SHOULD BE CLEARLY IDENTIFIABLE TO THE MEDIA.
I'M ALL OVER IT.
SHE'S GONNA BE IN FOR A HELL OF A SURPRISE, I THINK. IT'LL SERVE HER RIGHT...
...ALL THAT STUFF IN HER BOOK ABOUT WOMEN AND EQUALITY AND SEXUALITY AND BLAMING PEOPLE FOR THE STATE OF THE WORLD AND LIKE THAT.
IF SHE THINKS SHE CAN JUST PUBLISH HER KIND OF PERVERSITY, ATTACK OUR CORE VALUES LIKE THAT, AND THAT NO ONE'S GONNA NOTICE--
DON'T BE AN IDIOT, OF COURSE SHE KNEW PEOPLE WOULD NOTICE...
...THAT'S WHY SHE DID IT.
SHE'S INVITING THE DEBATE. SHE WANTS THE WORLD TO ARGUE WITH HER.
WELL, THEY ASK, I'LL BE HAPPY TO DEBATE ANY OF HER PEOPLE--
ABSOLUTELY NOT. AND I BETTER NOT SEE YOUR FACE OPPOSITE HERS OR ANYONE ELSE'S ON CNN...
I'LL CALL YOU LATER.

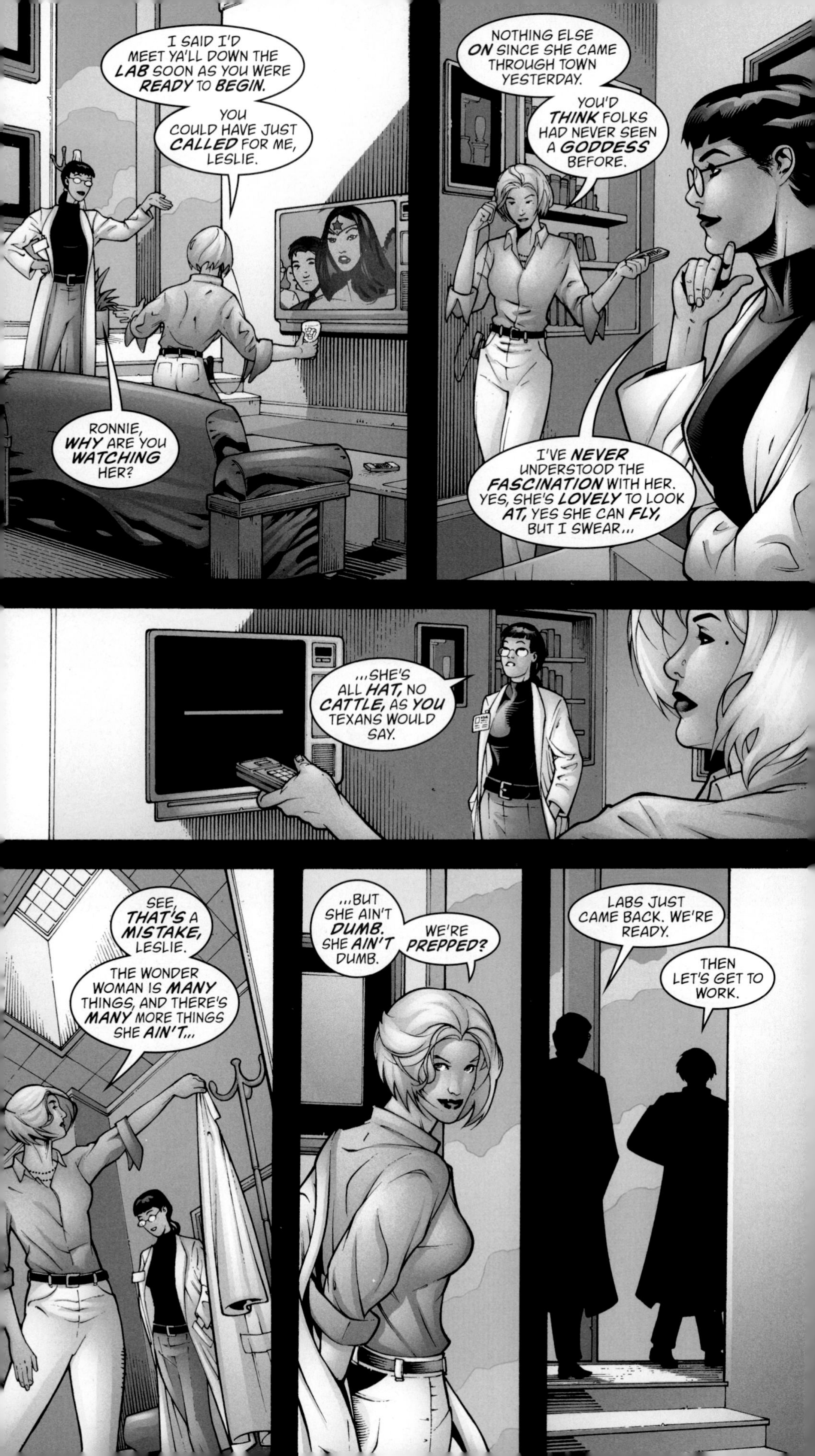

I SAID I'D MEET YA'LL DOWN THE LAB SOON AS YOU WERE READY TO BEGIN.
YOU COULD HAVE JUST CALLED FOR ME, LESLIE.
RONNIE, WHY ARE YOU WATCHING HER?
NOTHING ELSE ON SINCE SHE CAME THROUGH TOWN YESTERDAY.
YOU'D THINK FOLKS HAD NEVER SEEN A GODDESS BEFORE.
I'VE NEVER UNDERSTOOD THE FASCINATION WITH HER. YES, SHE'S LOVELY TO LOOK AT, YES SHE CAN FLY, BUT I SWEAR...
...SHE'S ALL HAT, NO CATTLE, AS YOU TEXANS WOULD SAY.
SEE, THAT'S A MISTAKE, LESLIE.
THE WONDER WOMAN IS MANY THINGS, AND THERE'S MANY MORE THINGS SHE AIN'T...
...BUT SHE AIN'T DUMB. SHE AIN'T DUMB.
WE'RE PREPPED?
LABS JUST CAME BACK. WE'RE READY.
THEN LET'S GET TO WORK.

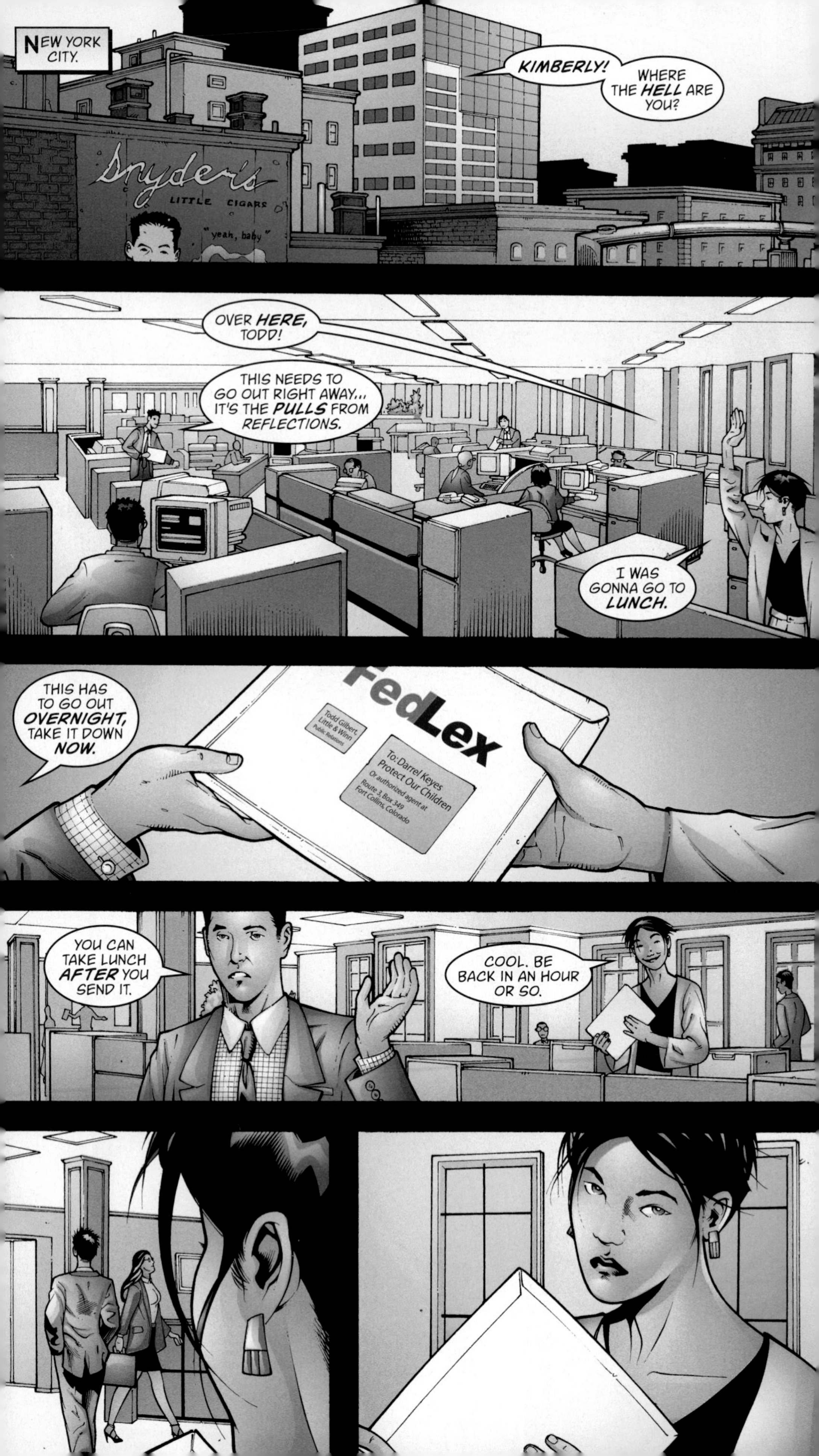
NEW YORK CITY.
Snyder's
LITTLE CIGARS
"yeah, baby"
KIMBERLY!
WHERE THE HELL ARE YOU?
OVER HERE, TODD!
THIS NEEDS TO GO OUT RIGHT AWAY... IT'S THE PULLS FROM REFLECTIONS.
I WAS GONNA GO TO LUNCH.
THIS HAS TO GO OUT OVERNIGHT, TAKE IT DOWN NOW.
FedLex
Todd Gilbert, Little & Winn
Public Relations
To: Darrel Keyes
Protect Our Children
Or authorized agent at
Route 3, Box 349
Fort Collins, Colorado
YOU CAN TAKE LUNCH AFTER YOU SEND IT.
COOL. BE BACK IN AN HOUR OR SO.

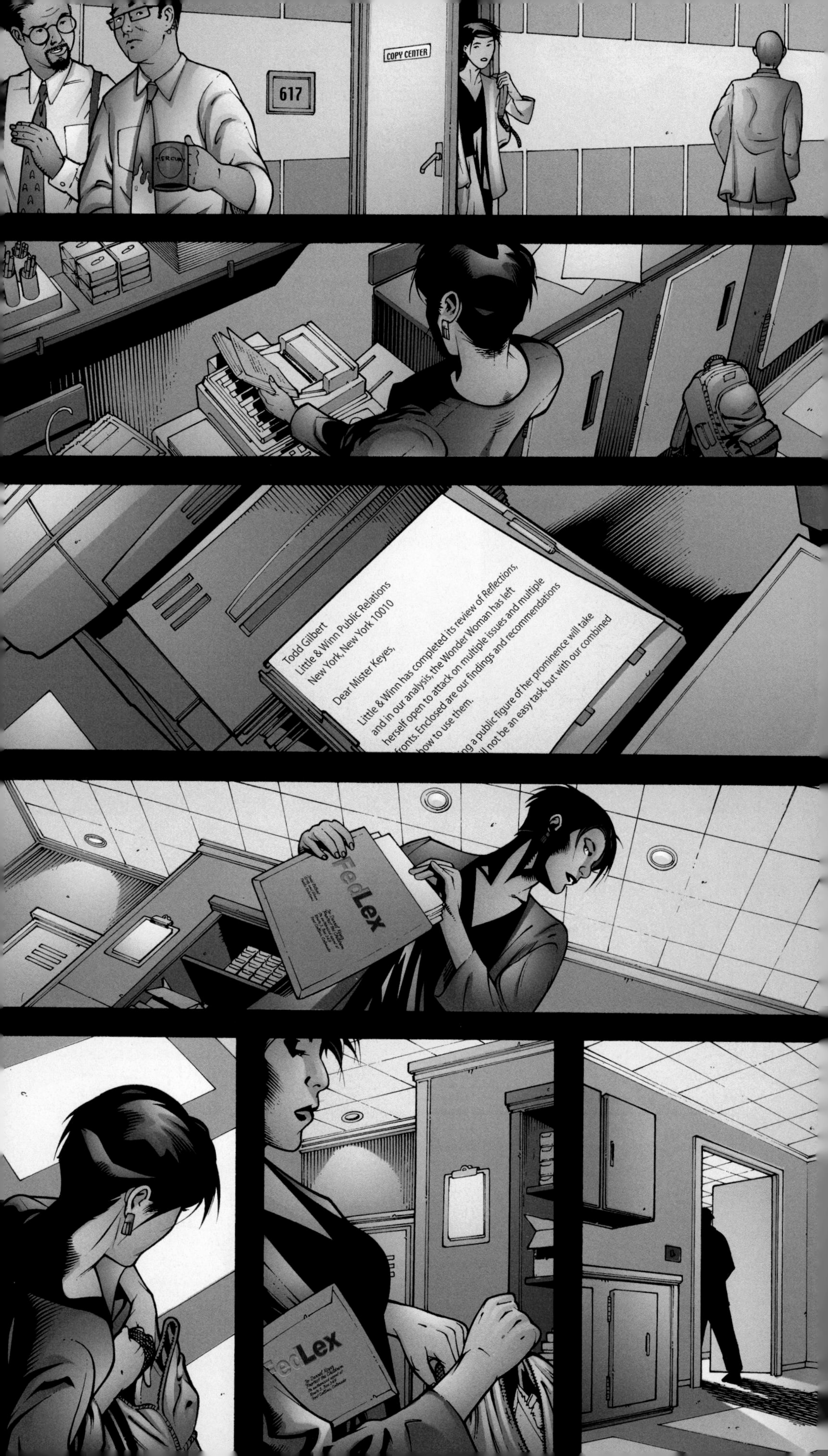
617
COPY CENTER
MERCURY
Todd Gilbert
Little & Winn Public Relations
New York, New York 10010
Dear Mister Keyes,
Little & Winn has completed its review of *Reflections*, and in our analysis, the Wonder Woman has left herself open to attack on multiple issues and multiple fronts. Enclosed are our findings and recommendations
how to use them.
a public figure of her prominence will take
not be an easy task, but with our combined
FedLex
FedLex

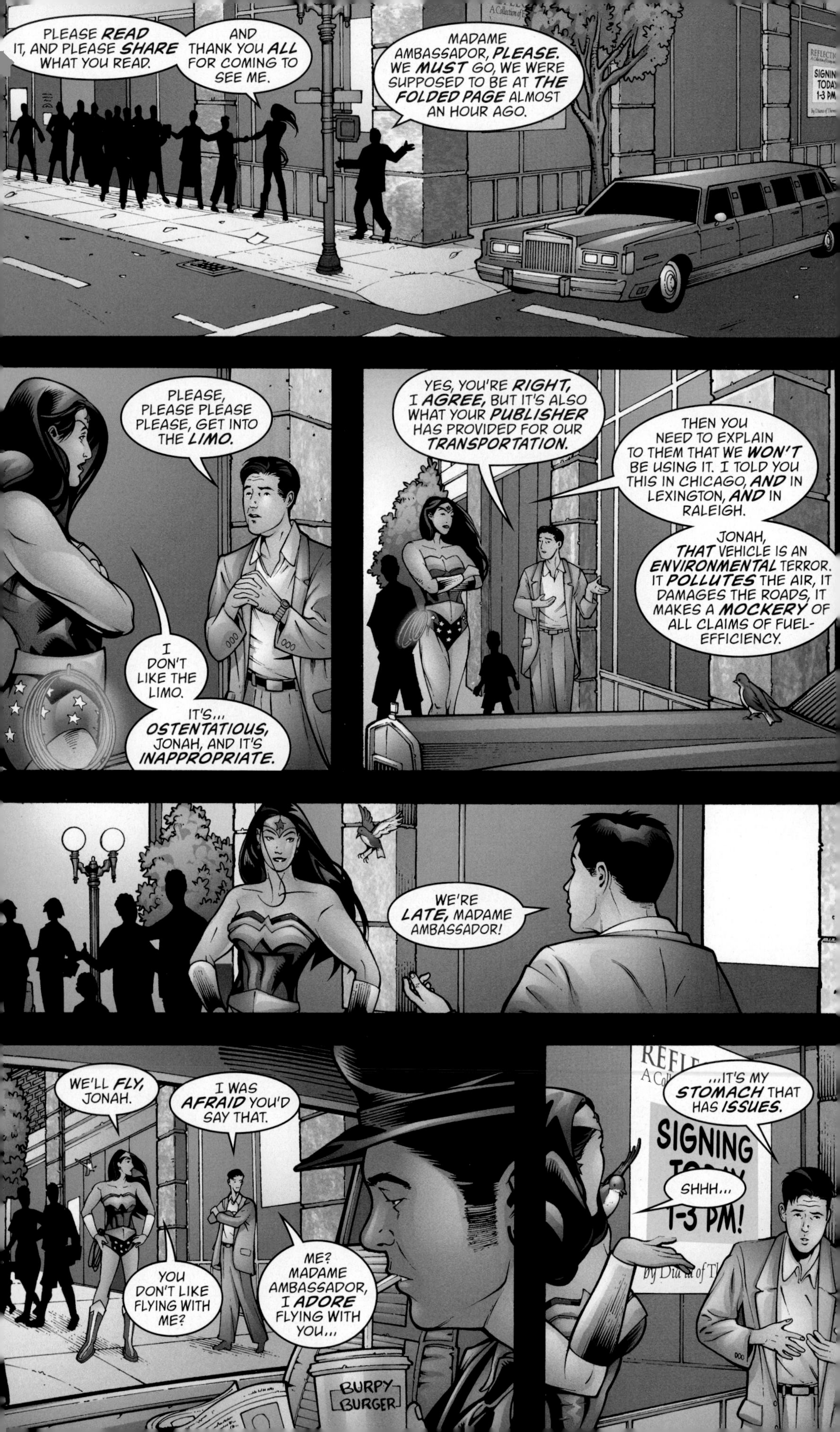
PLEASE READ IT, AND PLEASE SHARE WHAT YOU READ.
AND THANK YOU ALL FOR COMING TO SEE ME.
MADAME AMBASSADOR, PLEASE. WE MUST GO, WE WERE SUPPOSED TO BE AT THE FOLDED PAGE ALMOST AN HOUR AGO.
SIGNING TODAY 1-3 PM
PLEASE, PLEASE PLEASE PLEASE, GET INTO THE LIMO.
I DON'T LIKE THE LIMO.
IT'S... OSTENTATIOUS, JONAH, AND IT'S INAPPROPRIATE.
YES, YOU'RE RIGHT, I AGREE, BUT IT'S ALSO WHAT YOUR PUBLISHER HAS PROVIDED FOR OUR TRANSPORTATION.
THEN YOU NEED TO EXPLAIN TO THEM THAT WE WON'T BE USING IT. I TOLD YOU THIS IN CHICAGO, AND IN LEXINGTON, AND IN RALEIGH.
JONAH, THAT VEHICLE IS AN ENVIRONMENTAL TERROR. IT POLLUTES THE AIR, IT DAMAGES THE ROADS, IT MAKES A MOCKERY OF ALL CLAIMS OF FUEL-EFFICIENCY.
WE'RE LATE, MADAME AMBASSADOR!
WE'LL FLY, JONAH.
I WAS AFRAID YOU'D SAY THAT.
YOU DON'T LIKE FLYING WITH ME?
ME? MADAME AMBASSADOR, I ADORE FLYING WITH YOU...
BURPY BURGER
...IT'S MY STOMACH THAT HAS ISSUES.
SIGNING
1-3 PM!
SHHH...

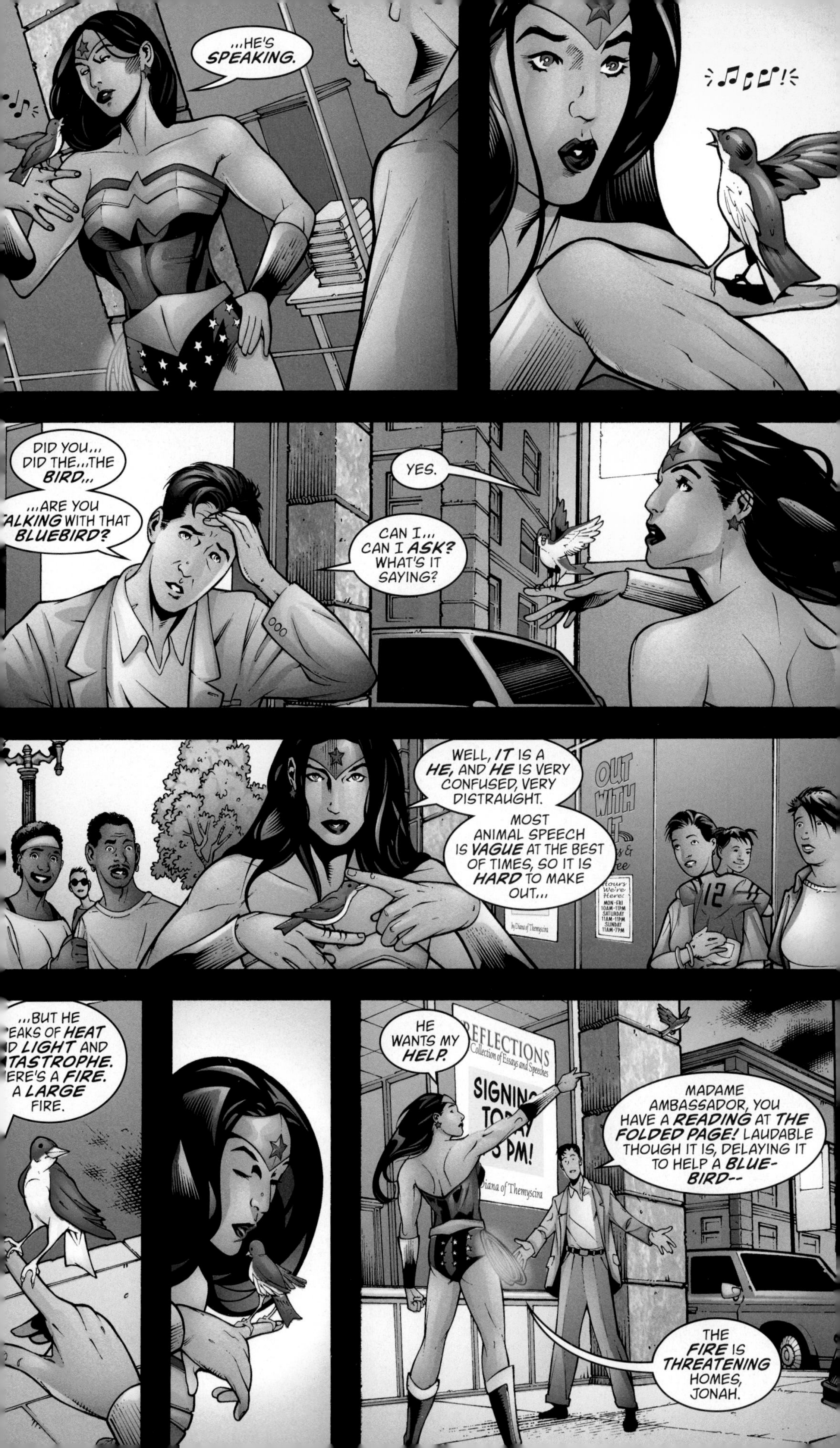
...HE'S SPEAKING.
DID YOU... DID THE...THE BIRD...
...ARE YOU TALKING WITH THAT BLUEBIRD?
YES.
CAN I... CAN I ASK? WHAT'S IT SAYING?
WELL, IT IS A HE, AND HE IS VERY CONFUSED, VERY DISTRAUGHT.
MOST ANIMAL SPEECH IS VAGUE AT THE BEST OF TIMES, SO IT IS HARD TO MAKE OUT...
OUT WITH IT
...BUT HE
HE WANTS MY HELP.
REFLECTIONS
Collection of Essays and Speeches
Diana of Themyscira
MADAME AMBASSADOR, YOU HAVE A READING AT THE FOLDED PAGE! LAUDABLE THOUGH IT IS, DELAYING IT TO HELP A BLUE-BIRD--
THE FIRE IS THREATENING HOMES, JONAH.

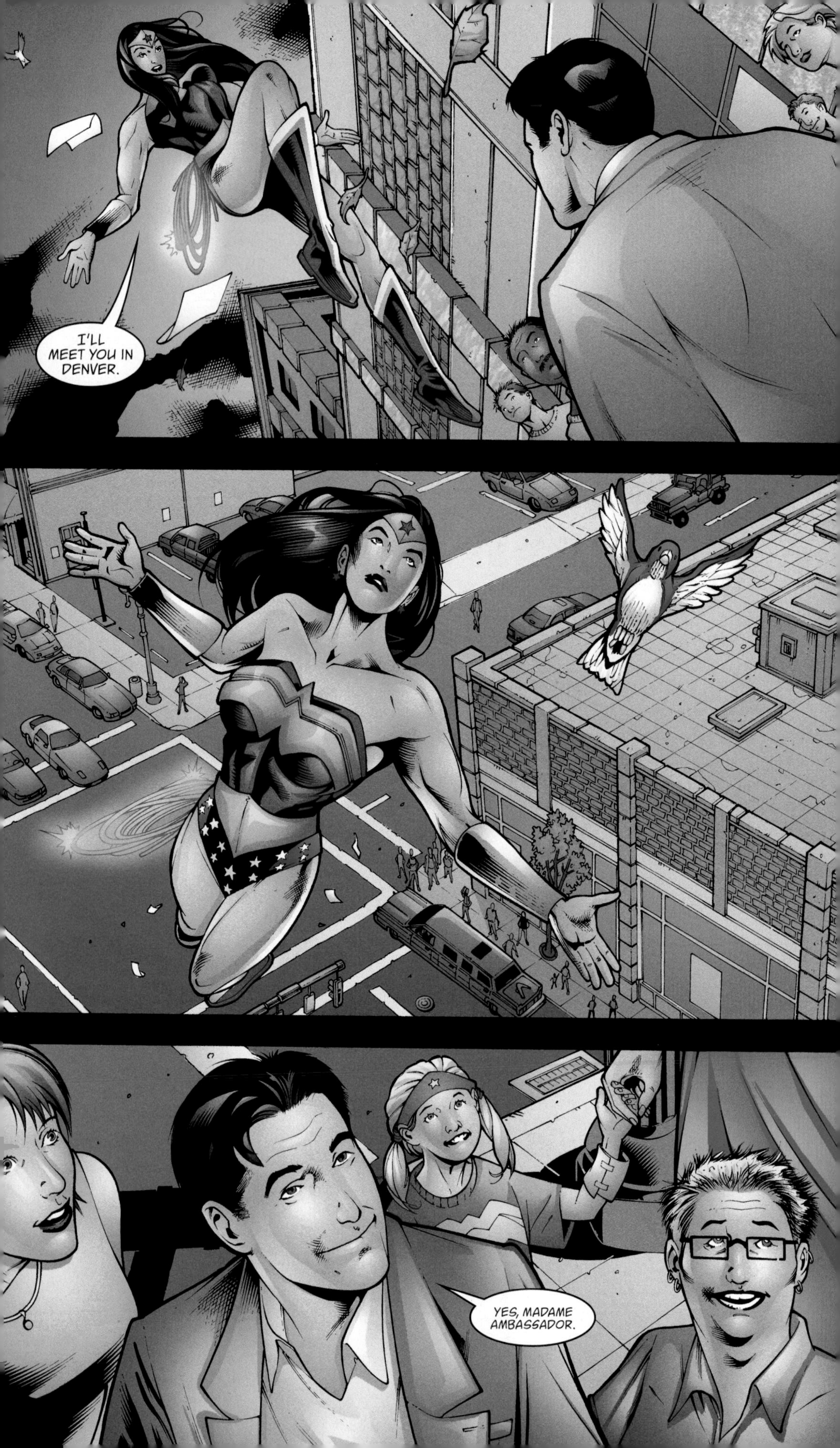
I'LL MEET YOU IN DENVER.
YES, MADAME AMBASSADOR.

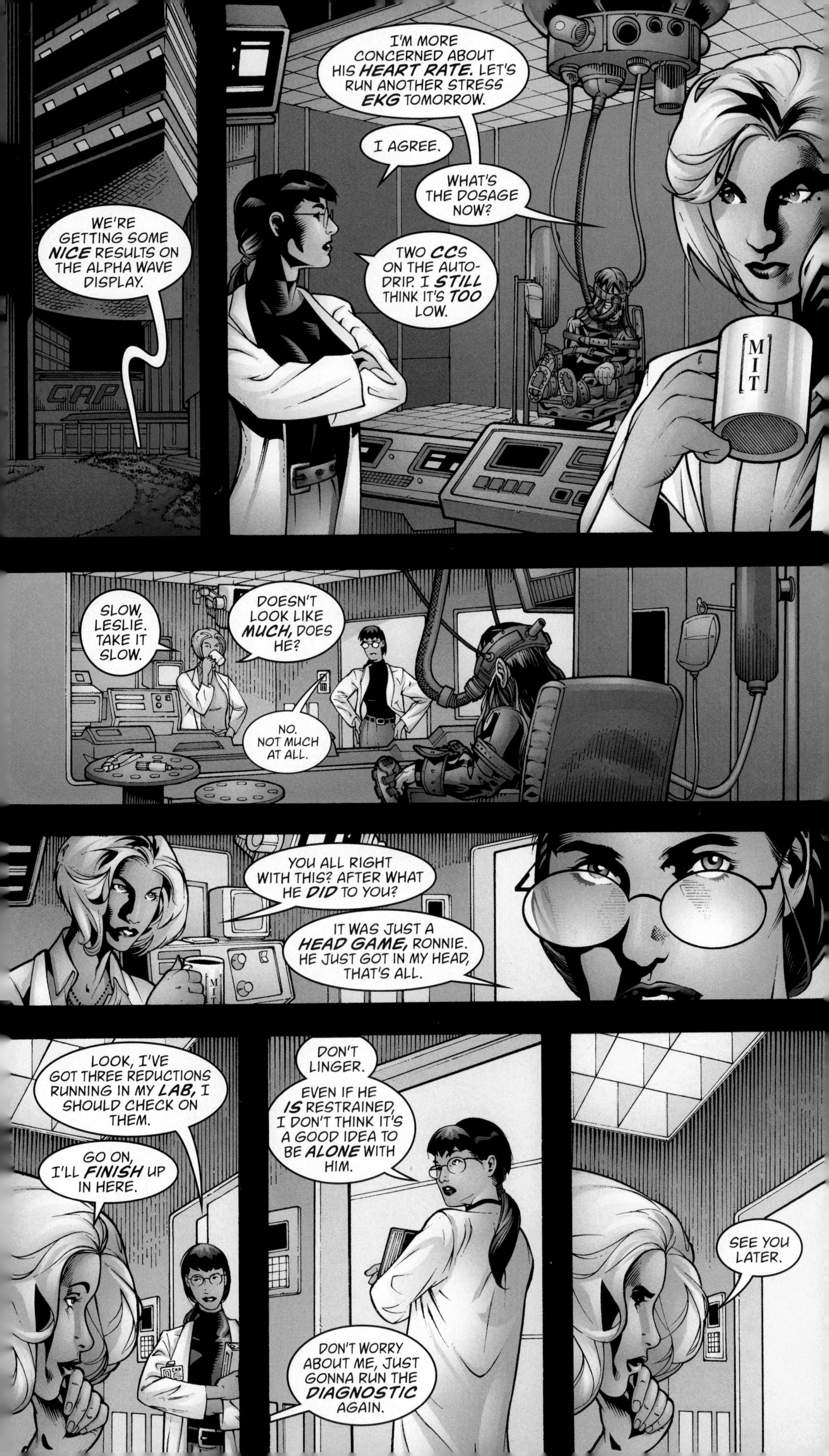
WE'RE GETTING SOME NICE RESULTS ON THE ALPHA WAVE DISPLAY.
I'M MORE CONCERNED ABOUT HIS HEART RATE. LET'S RUN ANOTHER STRESS EKG TOMORROW.
I AGREE.
WHAT'S THE DOSAGE NOW?
TWO CCS ON THE AUTO-DRIP. I STILL THINK IT'S TOO LOW.
MIT
SLOW, LESLIE. TAKE IT SLOW.
DOESN'T LOOK LIKE MUCH, DOES HE?
NO. NOT MUCH AT ALL.
YOU ALL RIGHT WITH THIS? AFTER WHAT HE DID TO YOU?
IT WAS JUST A HEAD GAME, RONNIE. HE JUST GOT IN MY HEAD, THAT'S ALL.
LOOK, I'VE GOT THREE REDUCTIONS RUNNING IN MY LAB, I SHOULD CHECK ON THEM.
GO ON, I'LL FINISH UP IN HERE.
DON'T LINGER.
EVEN IF HE IS RESTRAINED, I DON'T THINK IT'S A GOOD IDEA TO BE ALONE WITH HIM.
DON'T WORRY ABOUT ME, JUST GONNA RUN THE DIAGNOSTIC AGAIN.
SEE YOU LATER.

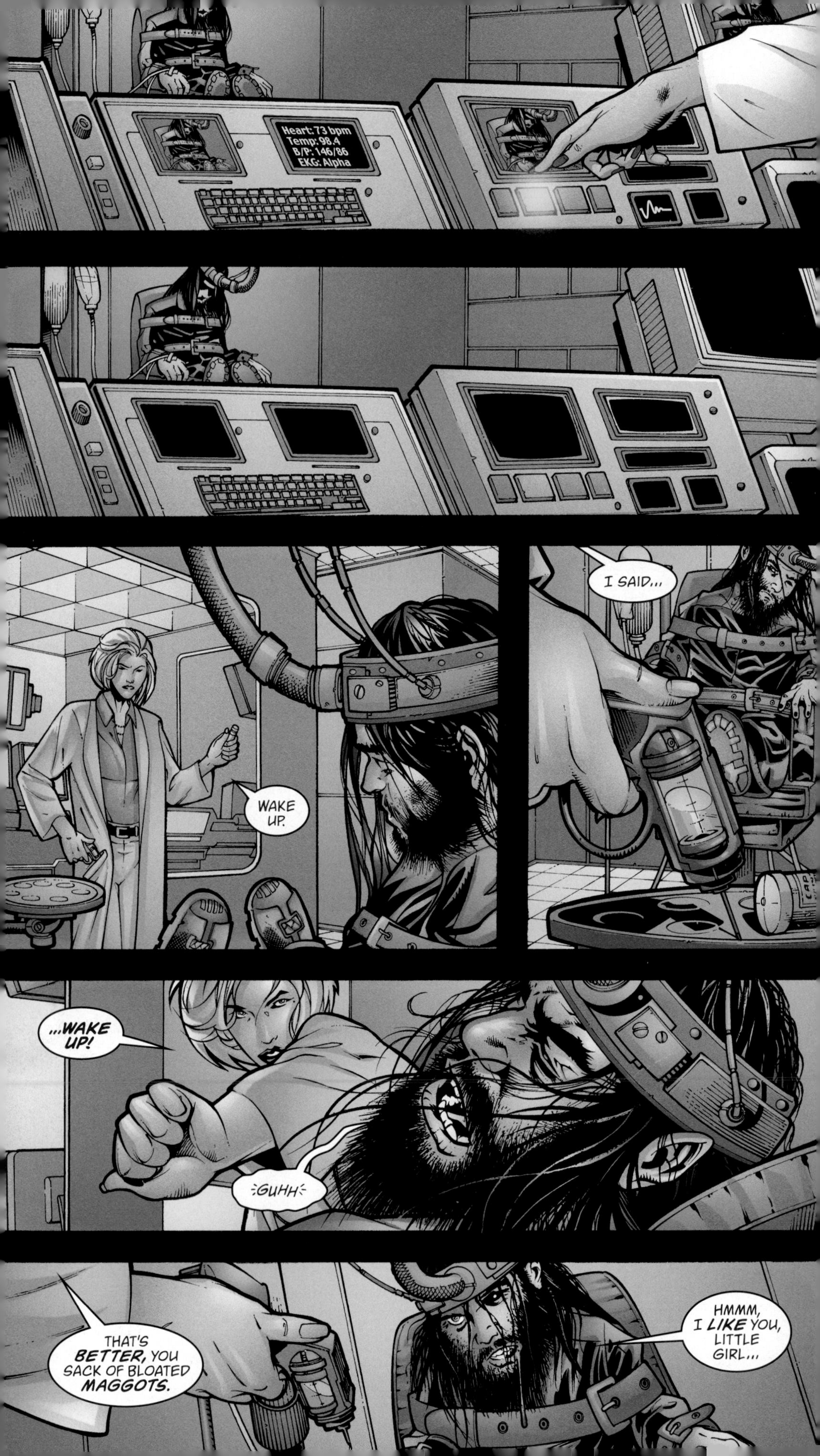
Heart: 73 bpm
Temp: 98.4
B/P: 146/86
EKG: Alpha
WAKE UP.
I SAID...
...WAKE UP!
GUHH
THAT'S BETTER, YOU SACK OF BLOATED MAGGOTS.
HMMM, I LIKE YOU, LITTLE GIRL...

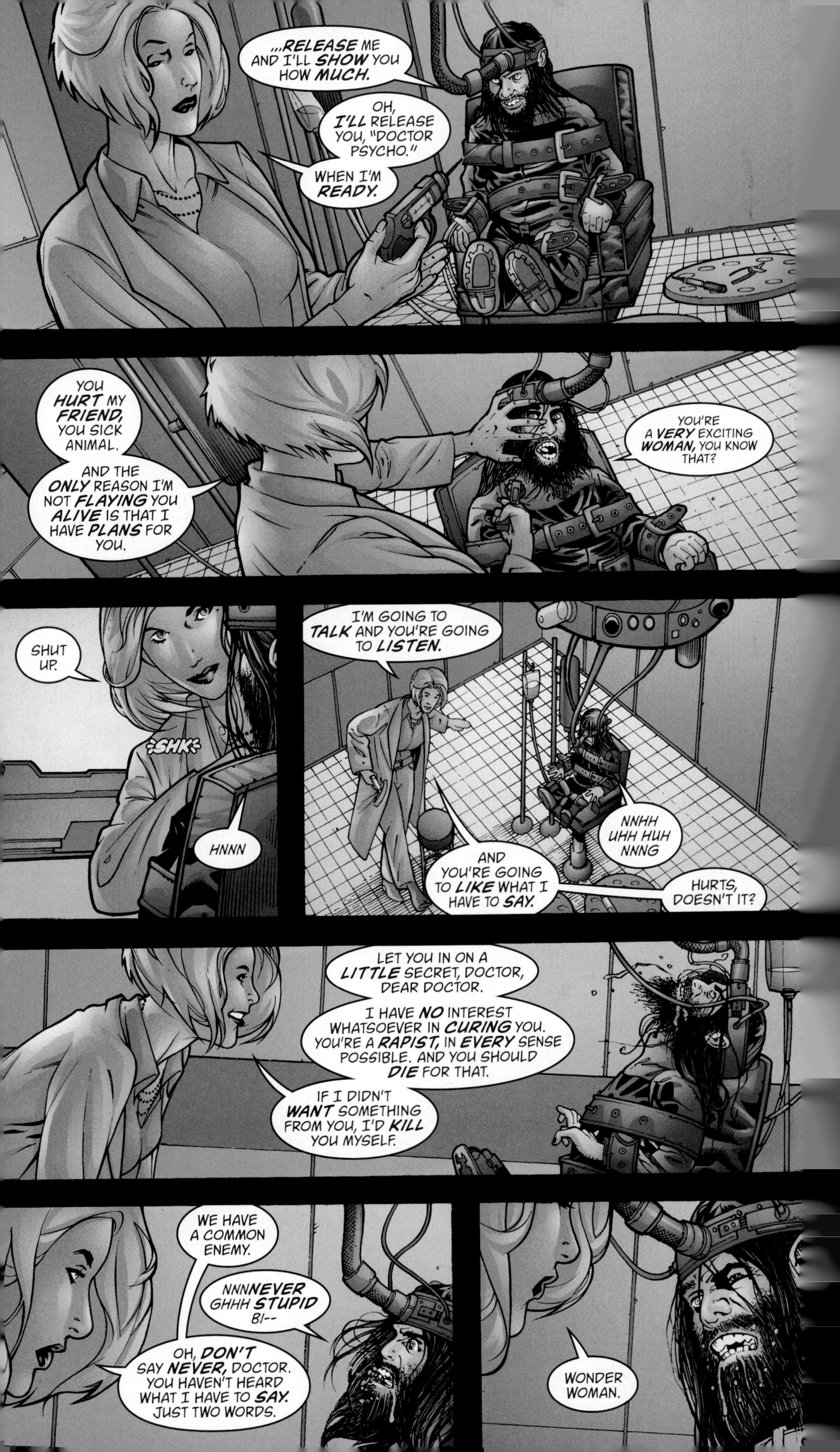
...RELEASE ME AND I'LL SHOW YOU HOW MUCH.
OH, I'LL RELEASE YOU, "DOCTOR PSYCHO."
WHEN I'M READY.
YOU HURT MY FRIEND, YOU SICK ANIMAL.
AND THE ONLY REASON I'M NOT FLAYING YOU ALIVE IS THAT I HAVE PLANS FOR YOU.
YOU'RE A VERY EXCITING WOMAN, YOU KNOW THAT?
SHUT UP.
SHK
HNNN
I'M GOING TO TALK AND YOU'RE GOING TO LISTEN.
NNHH UHH HUH NNNG
AND YOU'RE GOING TO LIKE WHAT I HAVE TO SAY.
HURTS, DOESN'T IT?
LET YOU IN ON A LITTLE SECRET, DOCTOR, DEAR DOCTOR.
I HAVE NO INTEREST WHATSOEVER IN CURING YOU. YOU'RE A RAPIST, IN EVERY SENSE POSSIBLE. AND YOU SHOULD DIE FOR THAT.
IF I DIDN'T WANT SOMETHING FROM YOU, I'D KILL YOU MYSELF.
WE HAVE A COMMON ENEMY.
NNNNEVER GHHH STUPID BI--
OH, DON'T SAY NEVER, DOCTOR. YOU HAVEN'T HEARD WHAT I HAVE TO SAY. JUST TWO WORDS.
WONDER WOMAN.

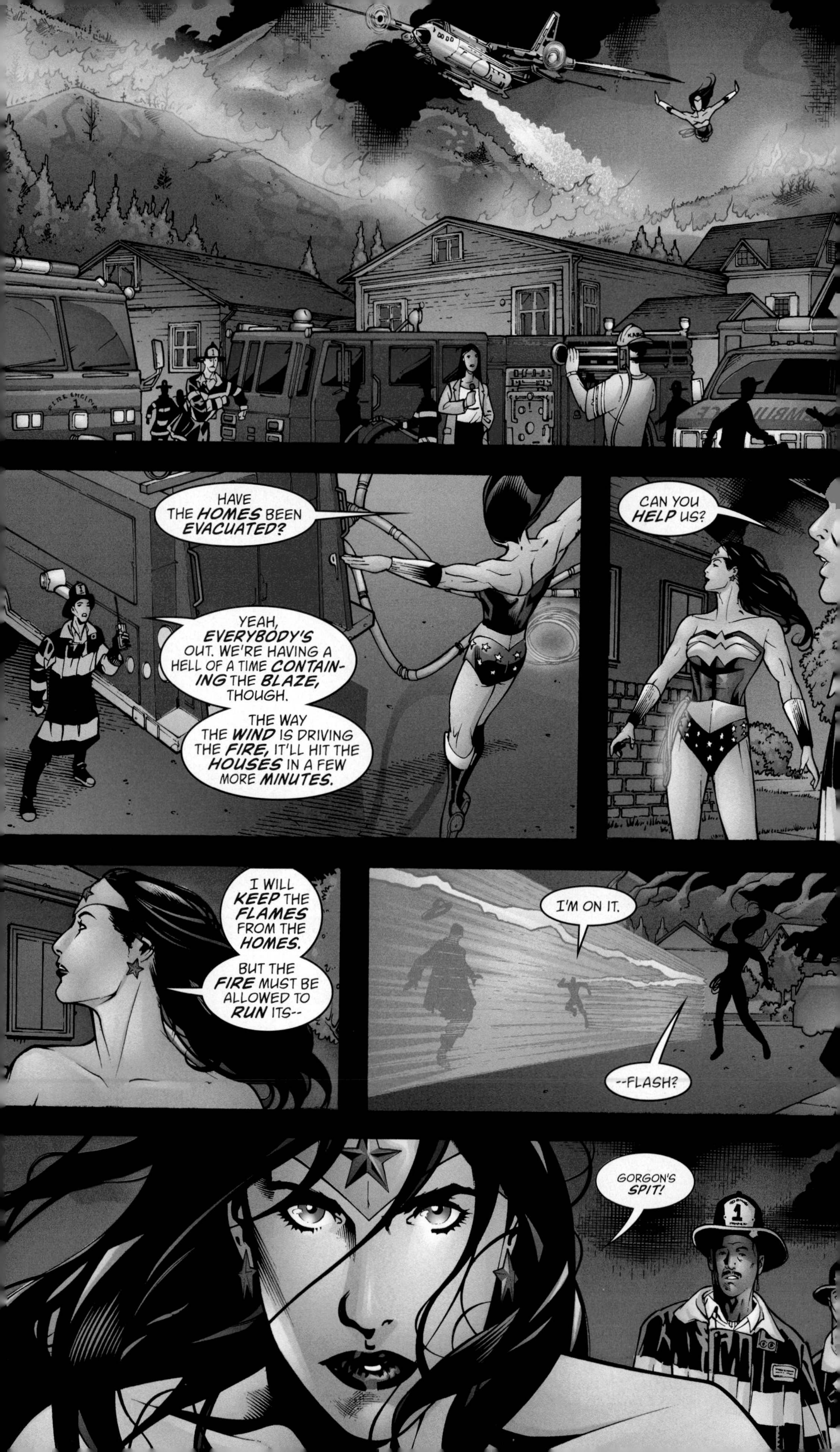
HAVE THE HOMES BEEN EVACUATED?
YEAH, EVERYBODY'S OUT. WE'RE HAVING A HELL OF A TIME CONTAINING THE BLAZE, THOUGH.
THE WAY THE WIND IS DRIVING THE FIRE, IT'LL HIT THE HOUSES IN A FEW MORE MINUTES.
CAN YOU HELP US?
I WILL KEEP THE FLAMES FROM THE HOMES.
BUT THE FIRE MUST BE ALLOWED TO RUN ITS--
I'M ON IT.
--FLASH?
GORGON'S SPIT!

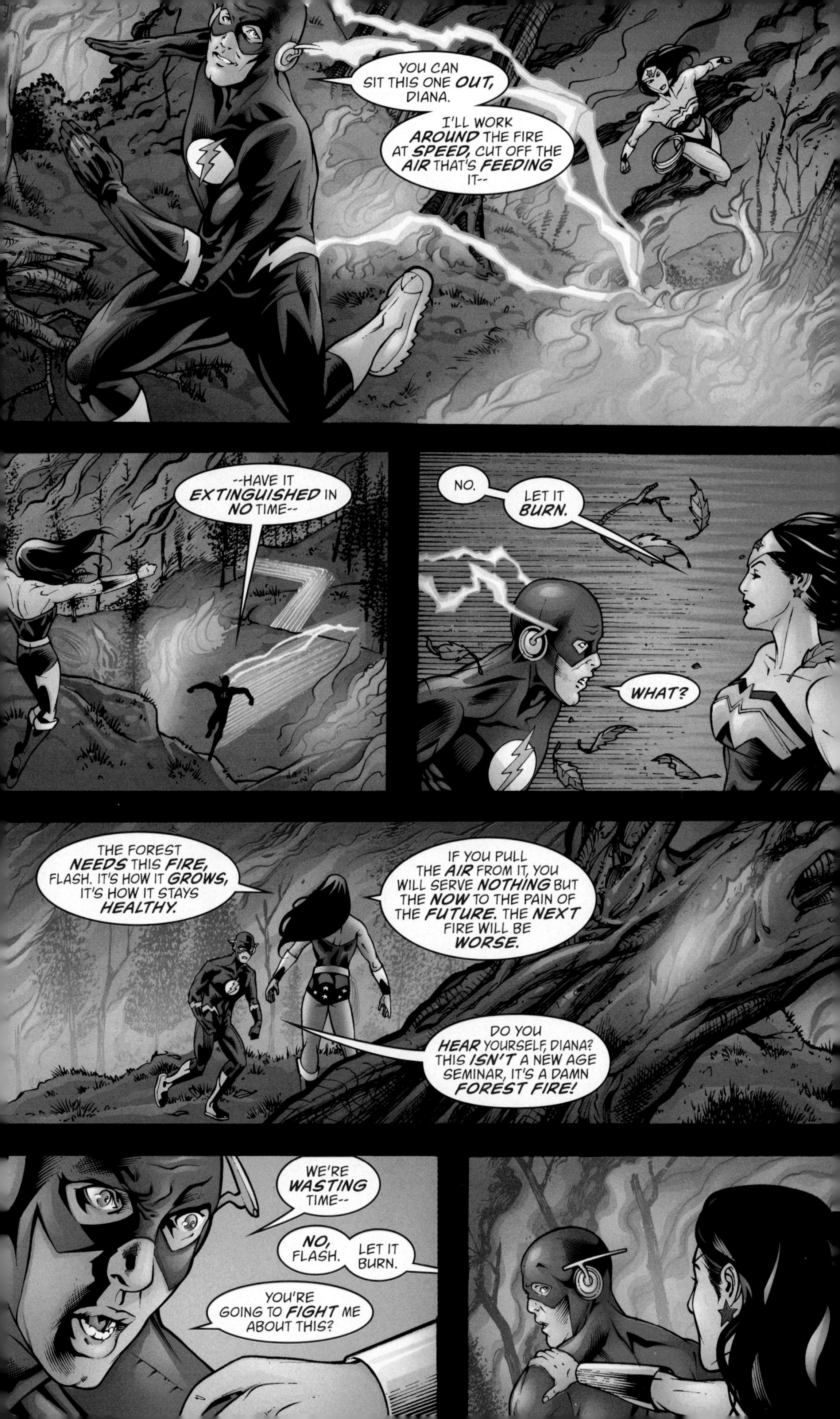
YOU CAN SIT THIS ONE OUT, DIANA.
I'LL WORK AROUND THE FIRE AT SPEED, CUT OFF THE AIR THAT'S FEEDING IT--
--HAVE IT EXTINGUISHED IN NO TIME--
NO.
LET IT BURN.
WHAT?
THE FOREST NEEDS THIS FIRE, FLASH. IT'S HOW IT GROWS, IT'S HOW IT STAYS HEALTHY.
IF YOU PULL THE AIR FROM IT, YOU WILL SERVE NOTHING BUT THE NOW TO THE PAIN OF THE FUTURE. THE NEXT FIRE WILL BE WORSE.
DO YOU HEAR YOURSELF, DIANA? THIS ISN'T A NEW AGE SEMINAR, IT'S A DAMN FOREST FIRE!
WE'RE WASTING TIME--
NO, FLASH.
LET IT BURN.
YOU'RE GOING TO FIGHT ME ABOUT THIS?

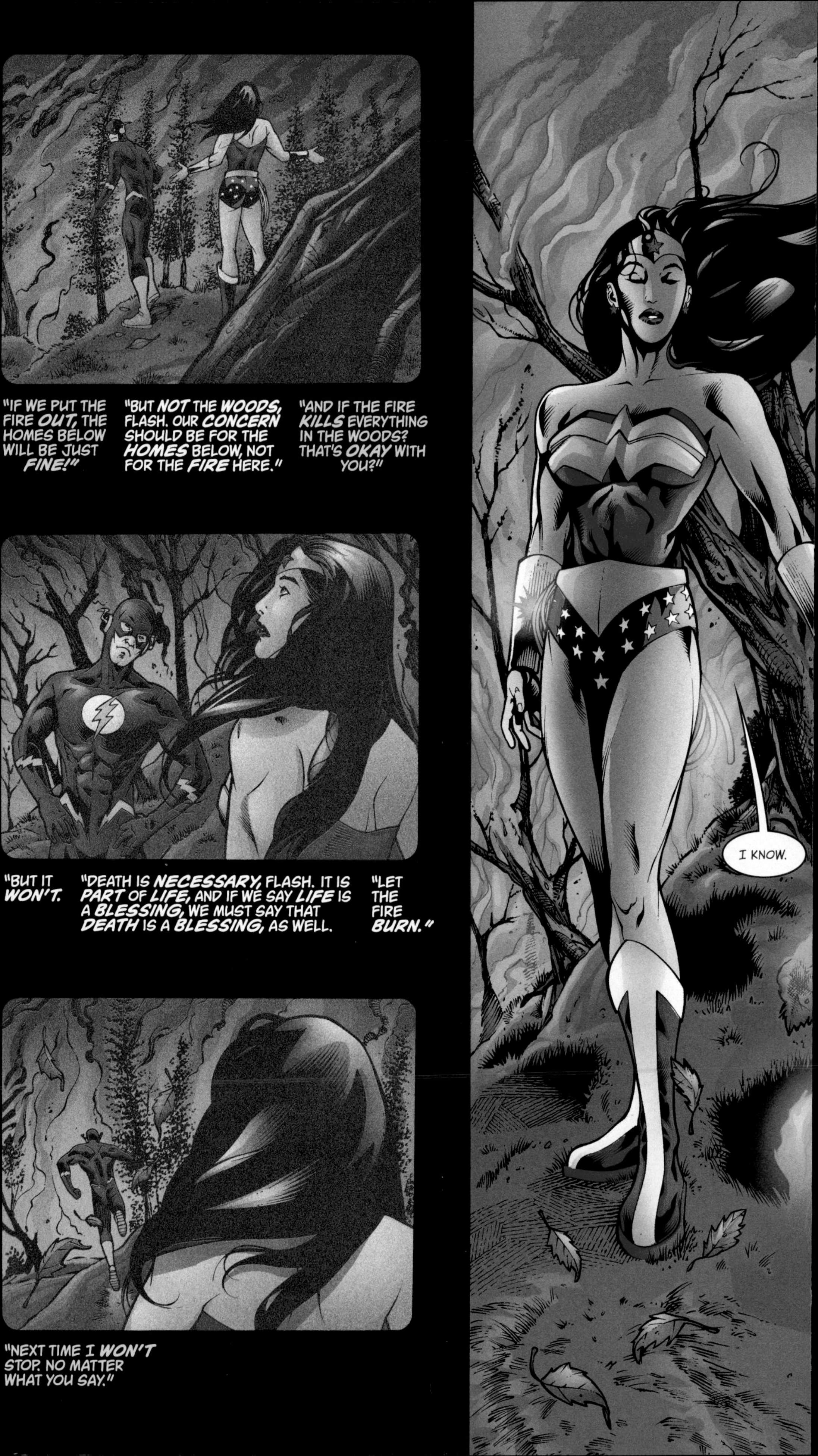
"IF WE PUT THE FIRE OUT, THE HOMES BELOW WILL BE JUST FINE!"
"BUT NOT THE WOODS, FLASH. OUR CONCERN SHOULD BE FOR THE HOMES BELOW, NOT FOR THE FIRE HERE."
"AND IF THE FIRE KILLS EVERYTHING IN THE WOODS? THAT'S OKAY WITH YOU?"
"BUT IT WON'T.
"DEATH IS NECESSARY, FLASH. IT IS PART OF LIFE, AND IF WE SAY LIFE IS A BLESSING, WE MUST SAY THAT DEATH IS A BLESSING, AS WELL.
"LET THE FIRE BURN."
"NEXT TIME I WON'T STOP. NO MATTER WHAT YOU SAY."
I KNOW.

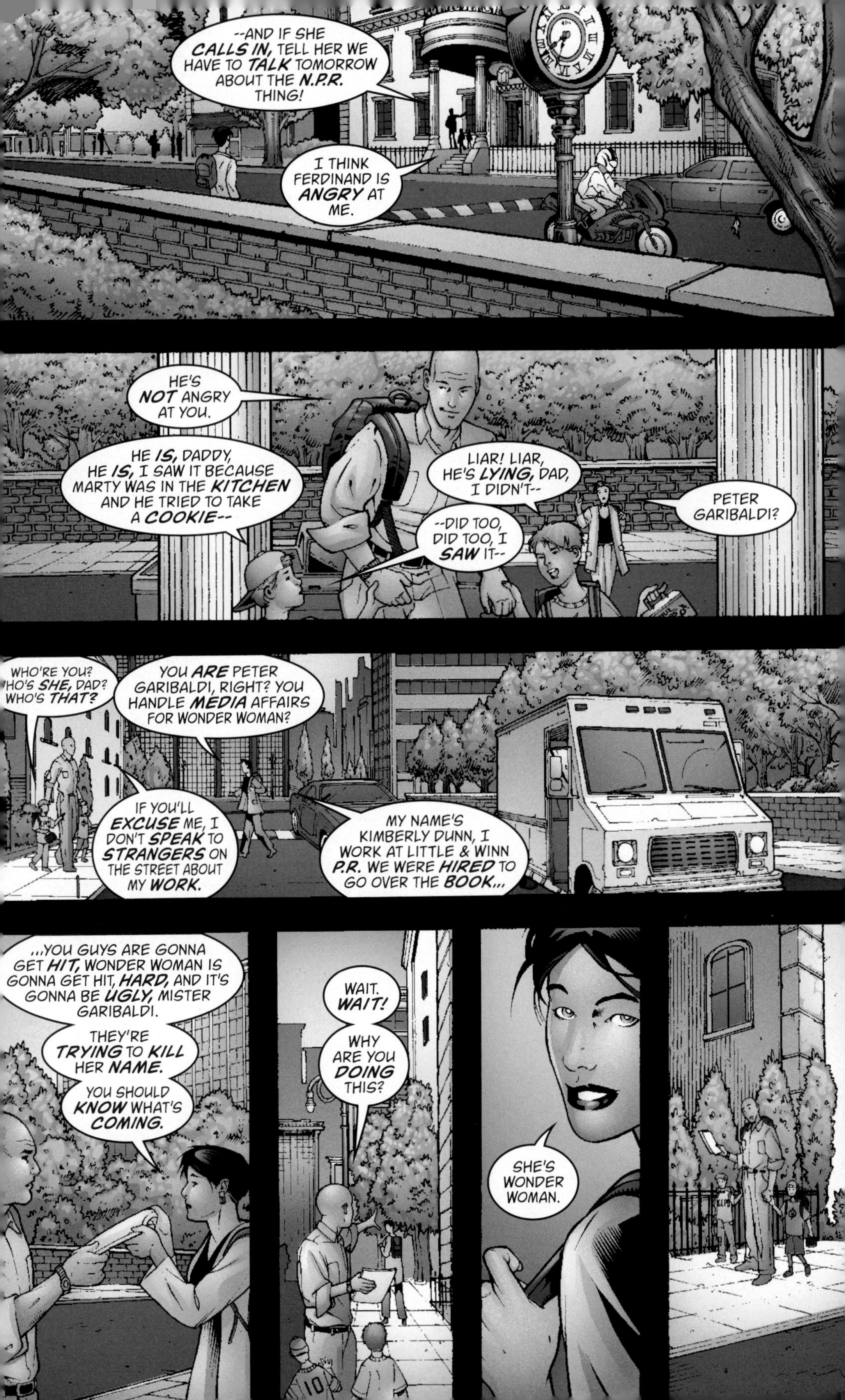
--AND IF SHE CALLS IN, TELL HER WE HAVE TO TALK TOMORROW ABOUT THE N.P.R. THING!
I THINK FERDINAND IS ANGRY AT ME.
HE'S NOT ANGRY AT YOU.
HE IS, DADDY, HE IS, I SAW IT BECAUSE MARTY WAS IN THE KITCHEN AND HE TRIED TO TAKE A COOKIE--
LIAR! LIAR, HE'S LYING, DAD, I DIDN'T--
--DID TOO, DID TOO, I SAW IT--
PETER GARIBALDI?
WHO'RE YOU? WHO'S SHE, DAD? WHO'S THAT?
YOU ARE PETER GARIBALDI, RIGHT? YOU HANDLE MEDIA AFFAIRS FOR WONDER WOMAN?
IF YOU'LL EXCUSE ME, I DON'T SPEAK TO STRANGERS ON THE STREET ABOUT MY WORK.
MY NAME'S KIMBERLY DUNN, I WORK AT LITTLE & WINN P.R. WE WERE HIRED TO GO OVER THE BOOK...
...YOU GUYS ARE GONNA GET HIT, WONDER WOMAN IS GONNA GET HIT, HARD, AND IT'S GONNA BE UGLY, MISTER GARIBALDI.
THEY'RE TRYING TO KILL HER NAME.
YOU SHOULD KNOW WHAT'S COMING.
WAIT. WAIT!
WHY ARE YOU DOING THIS?
SHE'S WONDER WOMAN.

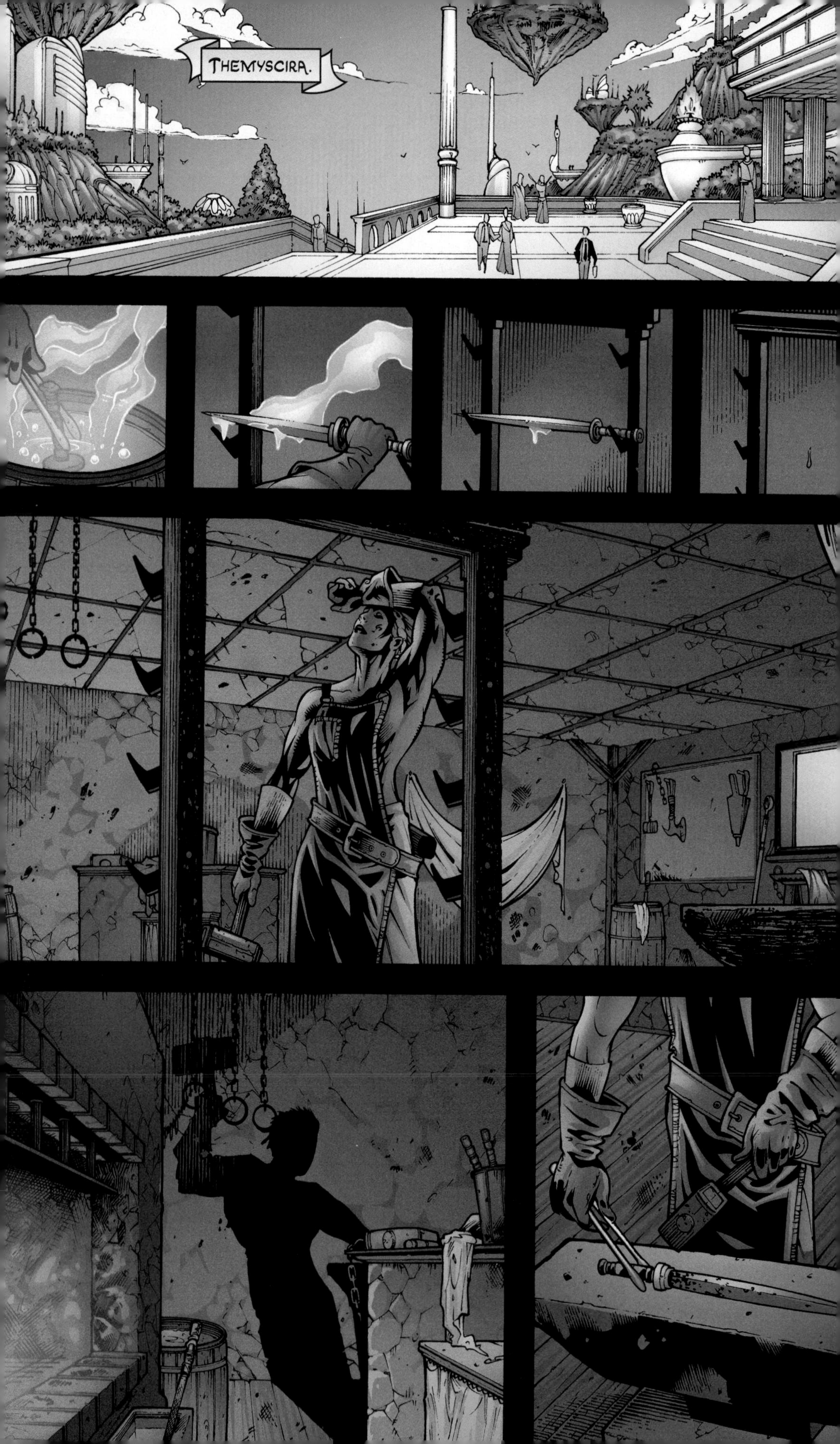
THEMYSCIRA.

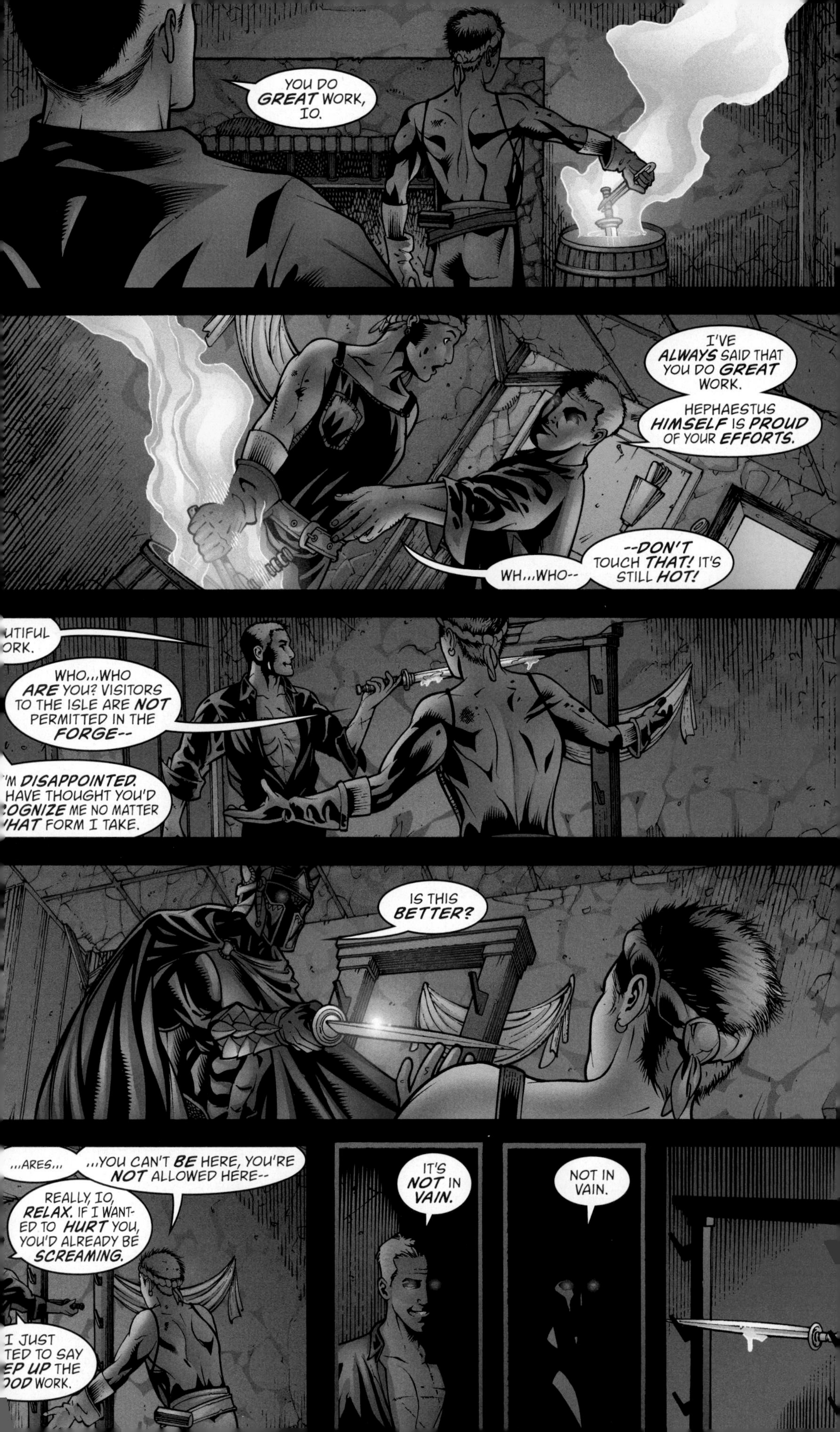
YOU DO GREAT WORK, IO.
I'VE ALWAYS SAID THAT YOU DO GREAT WORK.
HEPHAESTUS HIMSELF IS PROUD OF YOUR EFFORTS.
WH...WHO--
--DON'T TOUCH THAT! IT'S STILL HOT!
UTIFUL ORK.
WHO...WHO ARE YOU? VISITORS TO THE ISLE ARE NOT PERMITTED IN THE FORGE--
'M DISAPPOINTED. HAVE THOUGHT YOU'D COGNIZE ME NO MATTER WHAT FORM I TAKE.
IS THIS BETTER?
...ARES...
...YOU CAN'T BE HERE, YOU'RE NOT ALLOWED HERE--
REALLY, IO, RELAX. IF I WANTED TO HURT YOU, YOU'D ALREADY BE SCREAMING.
I JUST TED TO SAY EP UP THE OOD WORK.
IT'S NOT IN VAIN.
NOT IN VAIN.

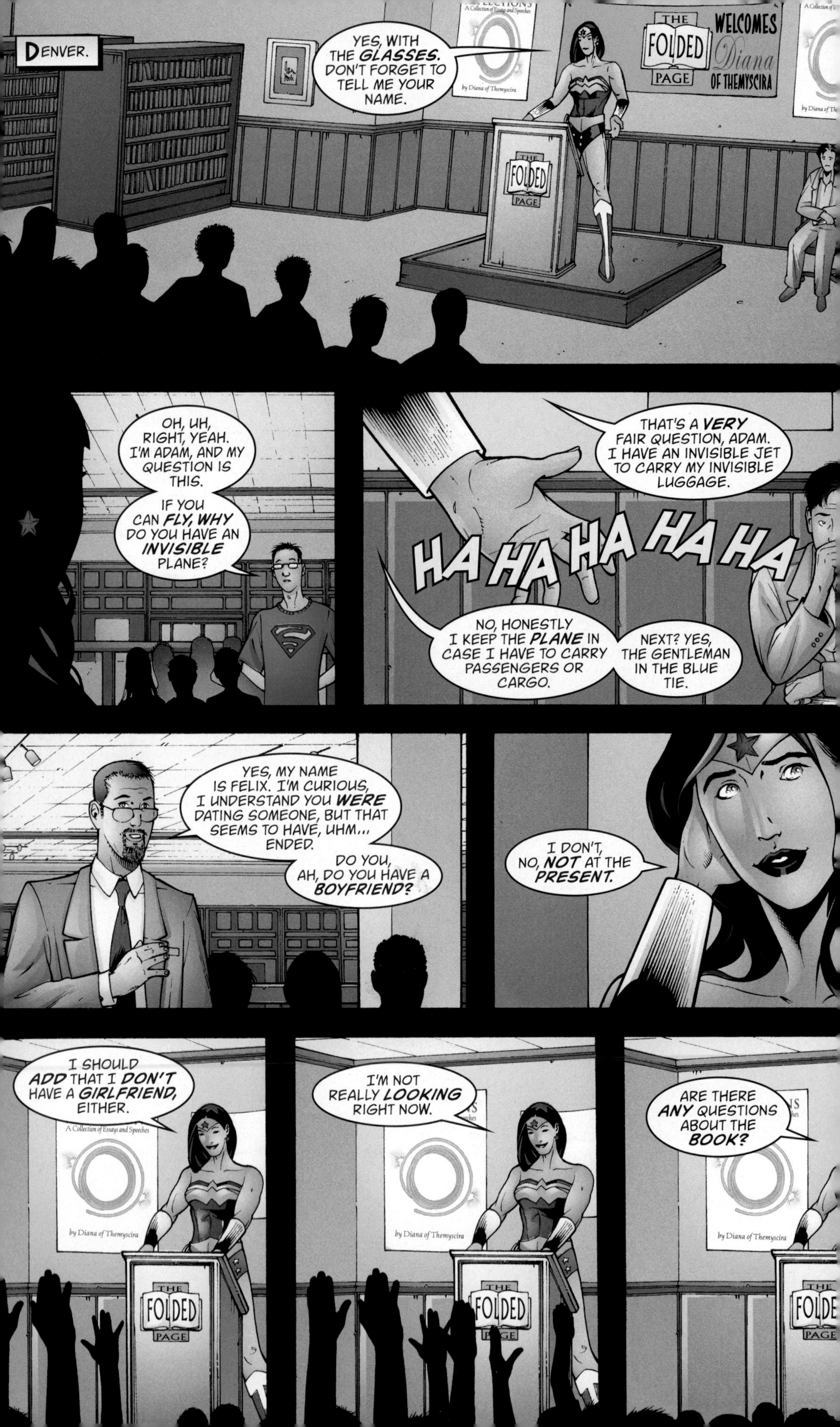
DENVER.
YES, WITH THE GLASSES. DON'T FORGET TO TELL ME YOUR NAME.
THE FOLDED PAGE WELCOMES Diana OF THEMYSCIRA
by Diana of Themyscira
OH, UH, RIGHT, YEAH. I'M ADAM, AND MY QUESTION IS THIS.
IF YOU CAN FLY, WHY DO YOU HAVE AN INVISIBLE PLANE?
THAT'S A VERY FAIR QUESTION, ADAM. I HAVE AN INVISIBLE JET TO CARRY MY INVISIBLE LUGGAGE.
HA HA HA HA HA HA
NO, HONESTLY I KEEP THE PLANE IN CASE I HAVE TO CARRY PASSENGERS OR CARGO.
NEXT? YES, THE GENTLEMAN IN THE BLUE TIE.
YES, MY NAME IS FELIX. I'M CURIOUS, I UNDERSTAND YOU WERE DATING SOMEONE, BUT THAT SEEMS TO HAVE, UHM... ENDED.
DO YOU, AH, DO YOU HAVE A BOYFRIEND?
I DON'T, NO, NOT AT THE PRESENT.
I SHOULD ADD THAT I DON'T HAVE A GIRLFRIEND, EITHER.
A Collection of Essays and Speeches
by Diana of Themyscira
I'M NOT REALLY LOOKING RIGHT NOW.
ARE THERE ANY QUESTIONS ABOUT THE BOOK?

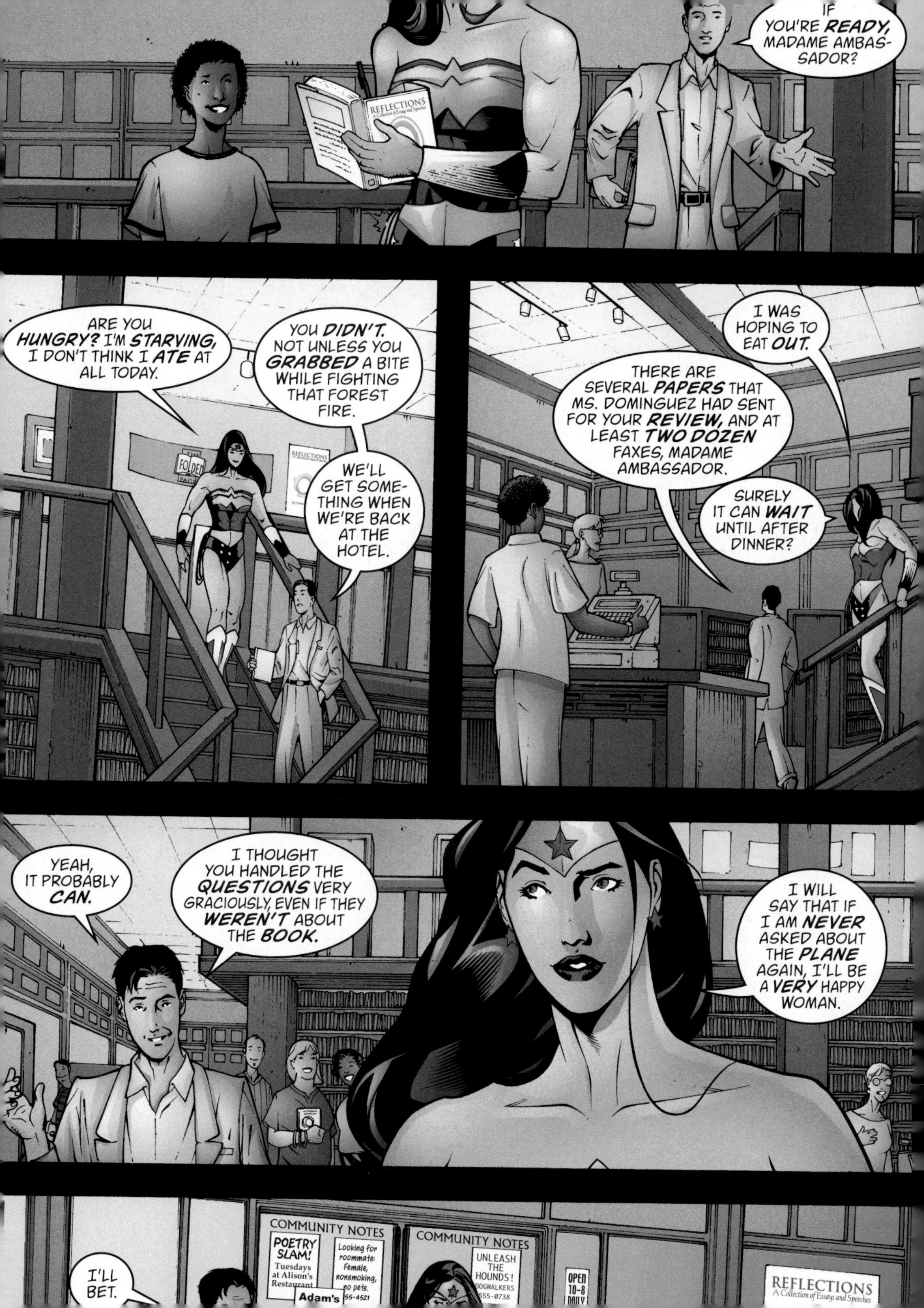
IF YOU'RE READY, MADAME AMBASSADOR?
REFLECTIONS A Collection of Essays and Speeches
ARE YOU HUNGRY? I'M STARVING, I DON'T THINK I ATE AT ALL TODAY.
YOU DIDN'T. NOT UNLESS YOU GRABBED A BITE WHILE FIGHTING THAT FOREST FIRE.
WE'LL GET SOMETHING WHEN WE'RE BACK AT THE HOTEL.
I WAS HOPING TO EAT OUT.
THERE ARE SEVERAL PAPERS THAT MS. DOMINGUEZ HAD SENT FOR YOUR REVIEW, AND AT LEAST TWO DOZEN FAXES, MADAME AMBASSADOR.
SURELY IT CAN WAIT UNTIL AFTER DINNER?
YEAH, IT PROBABLY CAN.
I THOUGHT YOU HANDLED THE QUESTIONS VERY GRACIOUSLY, EVEN IF THEY WEREN'T ABOUT THE BOOK.
I WILL SAY THAT IF I AM NEVER ASKED ABOUT THE PLANE AGAIN, I'LL BE A VERY HAPPY WOMAN.
COMMUNITY NOTES
POETRY SLAM! Tuesdays at Alison's Restaurant
Looking for roommate: Female, nonsmoking, no pets. 55-4521
Adam's
COMMUNITY NOTES
UNLEASH THE HOUNDS! DOGWALKERS 555-0738
OPEN 10-8
REFLECTIONS A Collection of Essays and Speeches
I'LL BET.

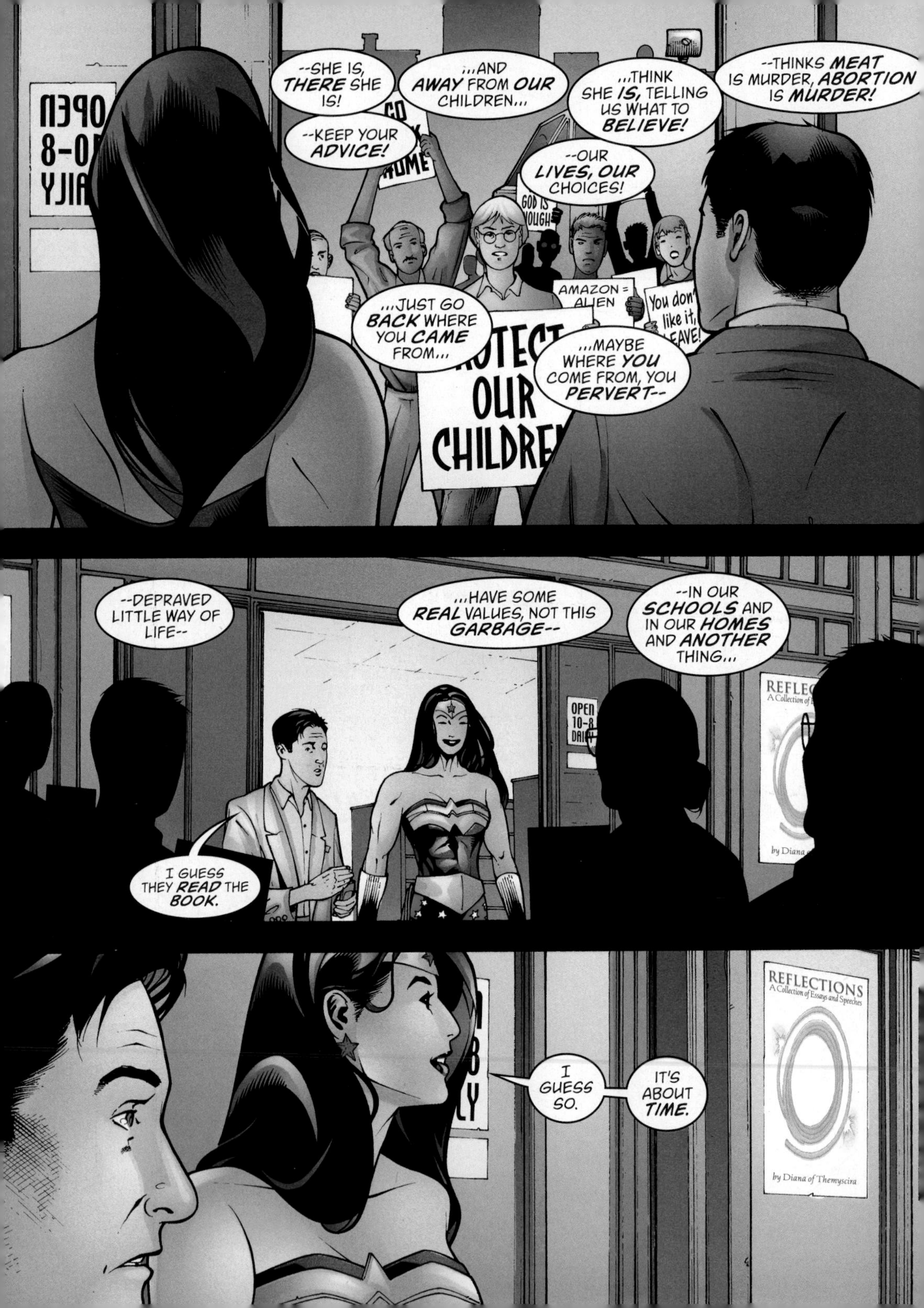
OPEN 8-0 DAILY
--SHE IS, THERE SHE IS!
--KEEP YOUR ADVICE!
...AND AWAY FROM OUR CHILDREN...
...THINK SHE IS, TELLING US WHAT TO BELIEVE!
--THINKS MEAT IS MURDER, ABORTION IS MURDER!
--OUR LIVES, OUR CHOICES!
GOD IS
AMAZON = ALIEN
You don't like it, LEAVE!
...JUST GO BACK WHERE YOU CAME FROM...
...MAYBE WHERE YOU COME FROM, YOU PERVERT--
PROTECT OUR CHILDREN
--DEPRAVED LITTLE WAY OF LIFE--
...HAVE SOME REAL VALUES, NOT THIS GARBAGE--
--IN OUR SCHOOLS AND IN OUR HOMES AND ANOTHER THING...
OPEN 10-8 DAILY
I GUESS THEY READ THE BOOK.
I GUESS SO.
IT'S ABOUT TIME.
REFLECTIONS
A Collection of Essays and Speeches
by Diana of Themyscira

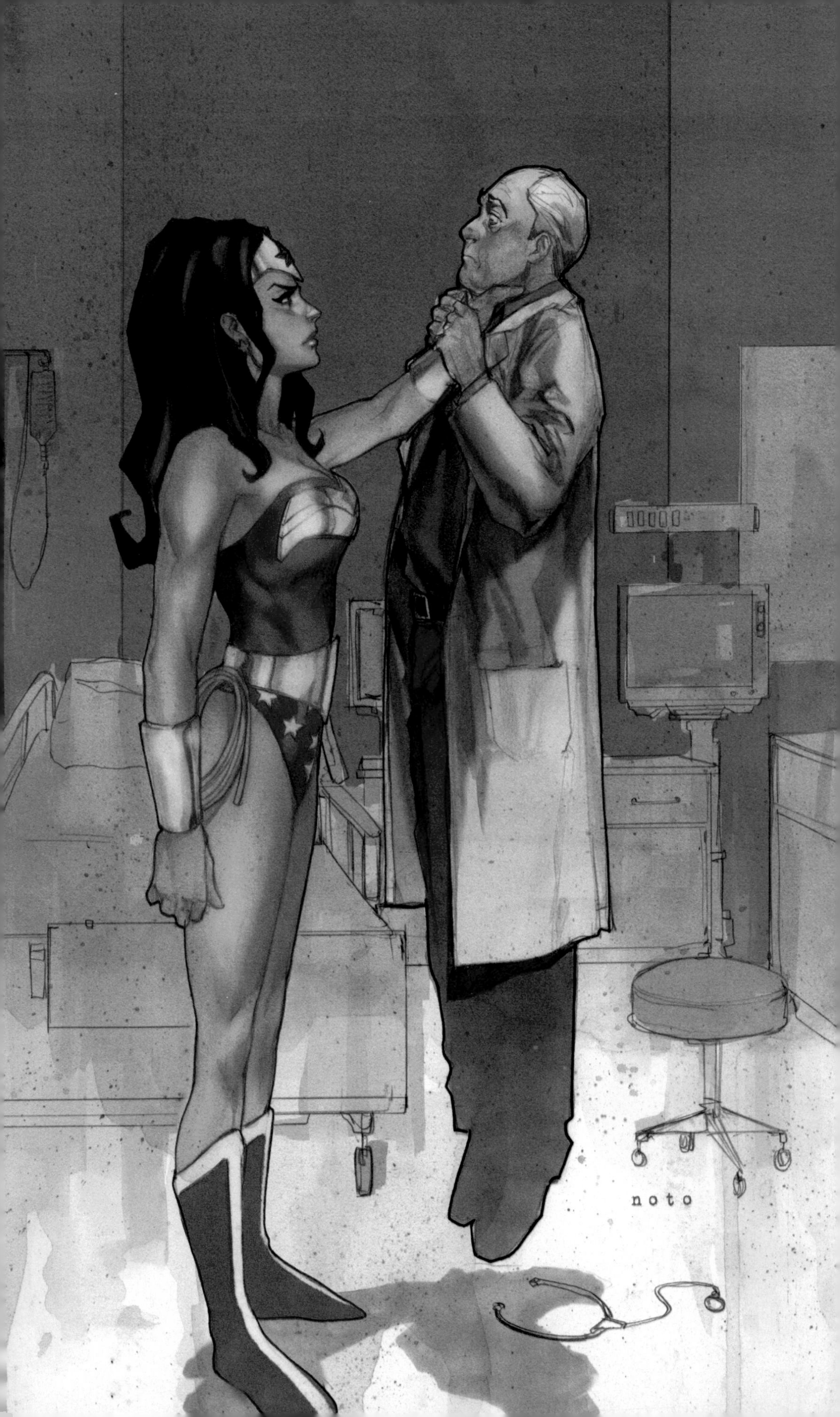
noto

"DOWN TO EARTH: PART THREE"

Drew Johnson – *pencils*
Ray Snyder – *inks*
Richard Horie, Tanya Horie - *colors*
Phil Noto – *cover art*

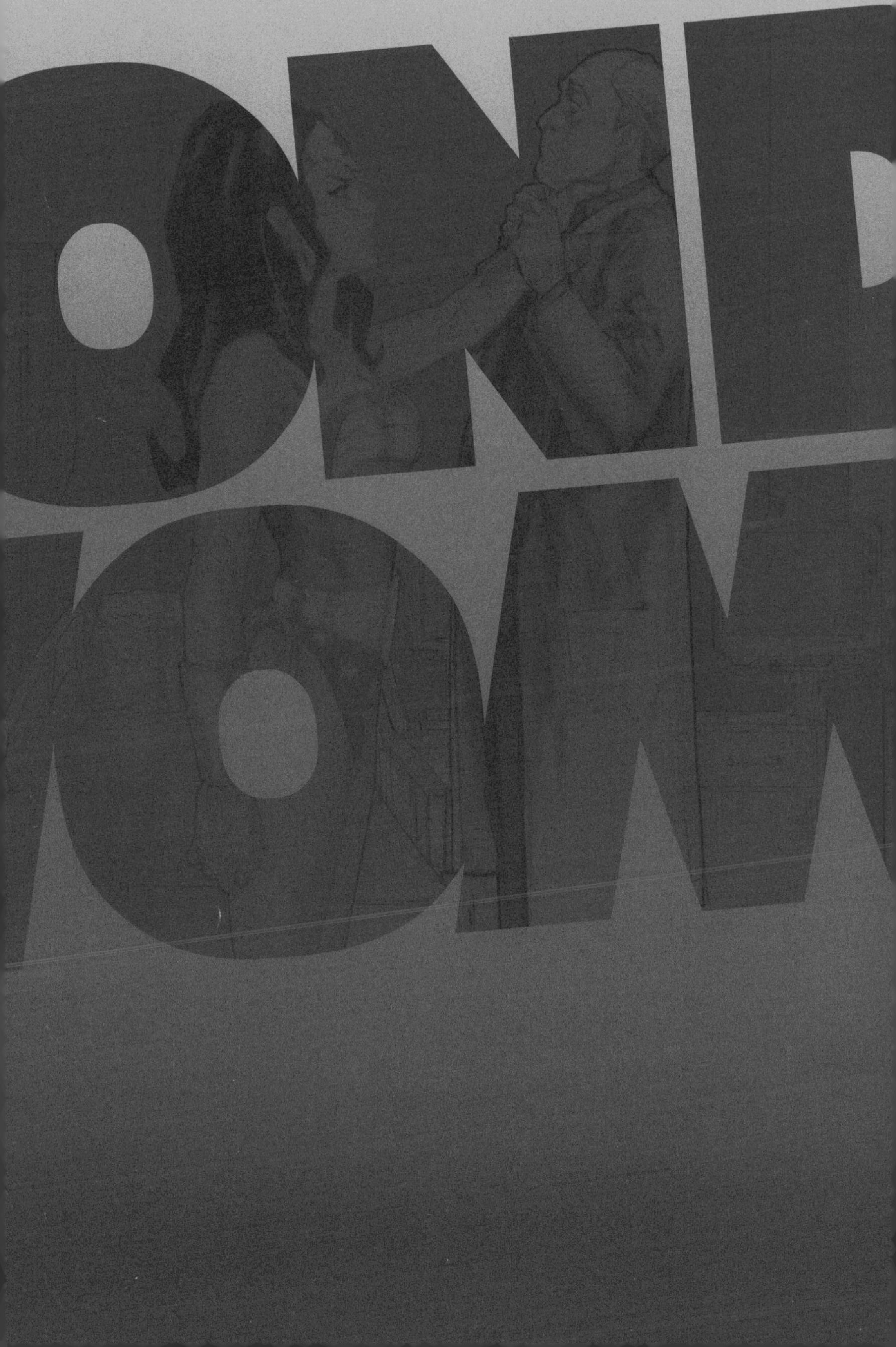

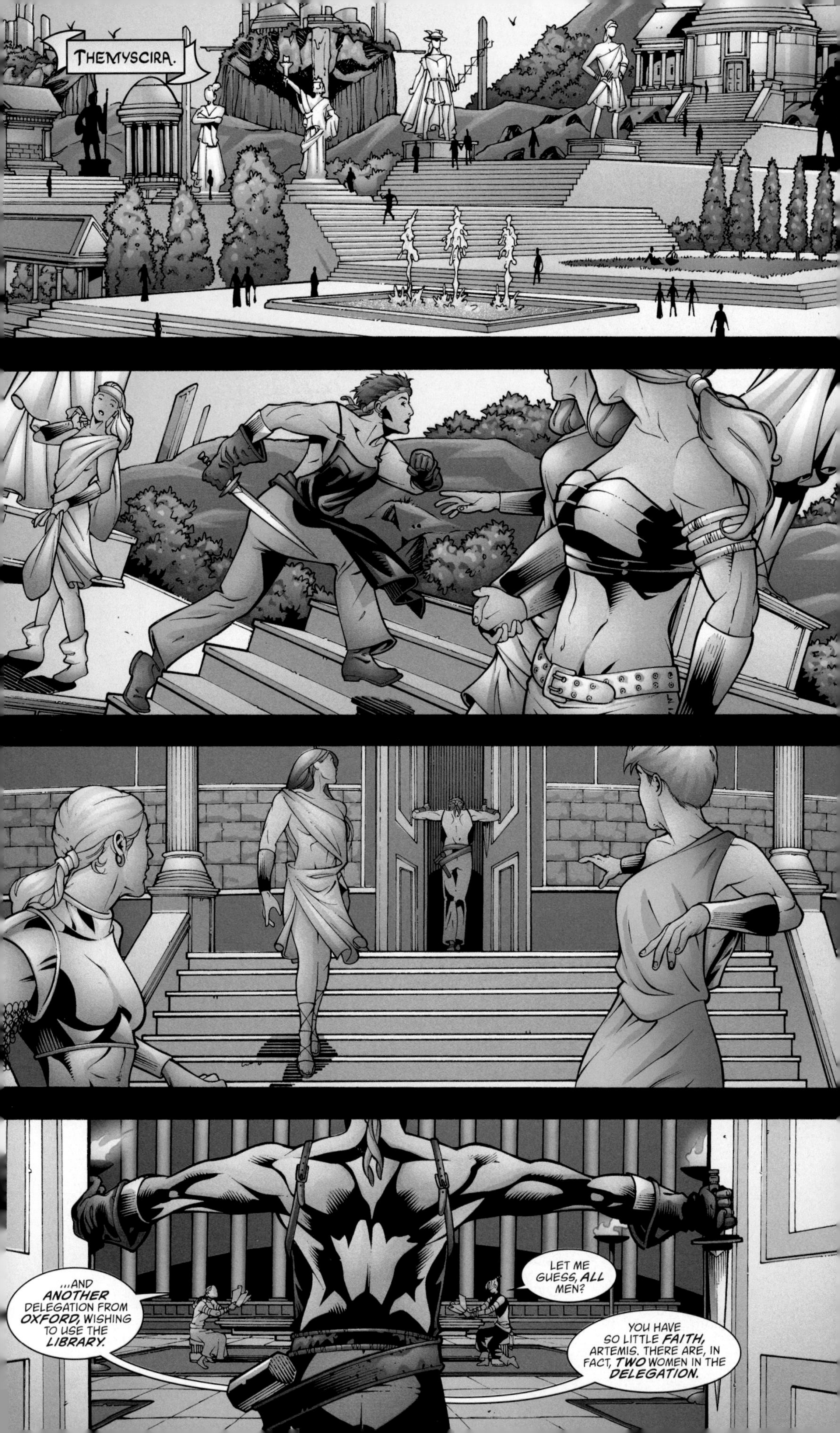
THEMYSCIRA.
...AND ANOTHER DELEGATION FROM OXFORD, WISHING TO USE THE LIBRARY.
LET ME GUESS, ALL MEN?
YOU HAVE SO LITTLE FAITH, ARTEMIS. THERE ARE, IN FACT, TWO WOMEN IN THE DELEGATION.

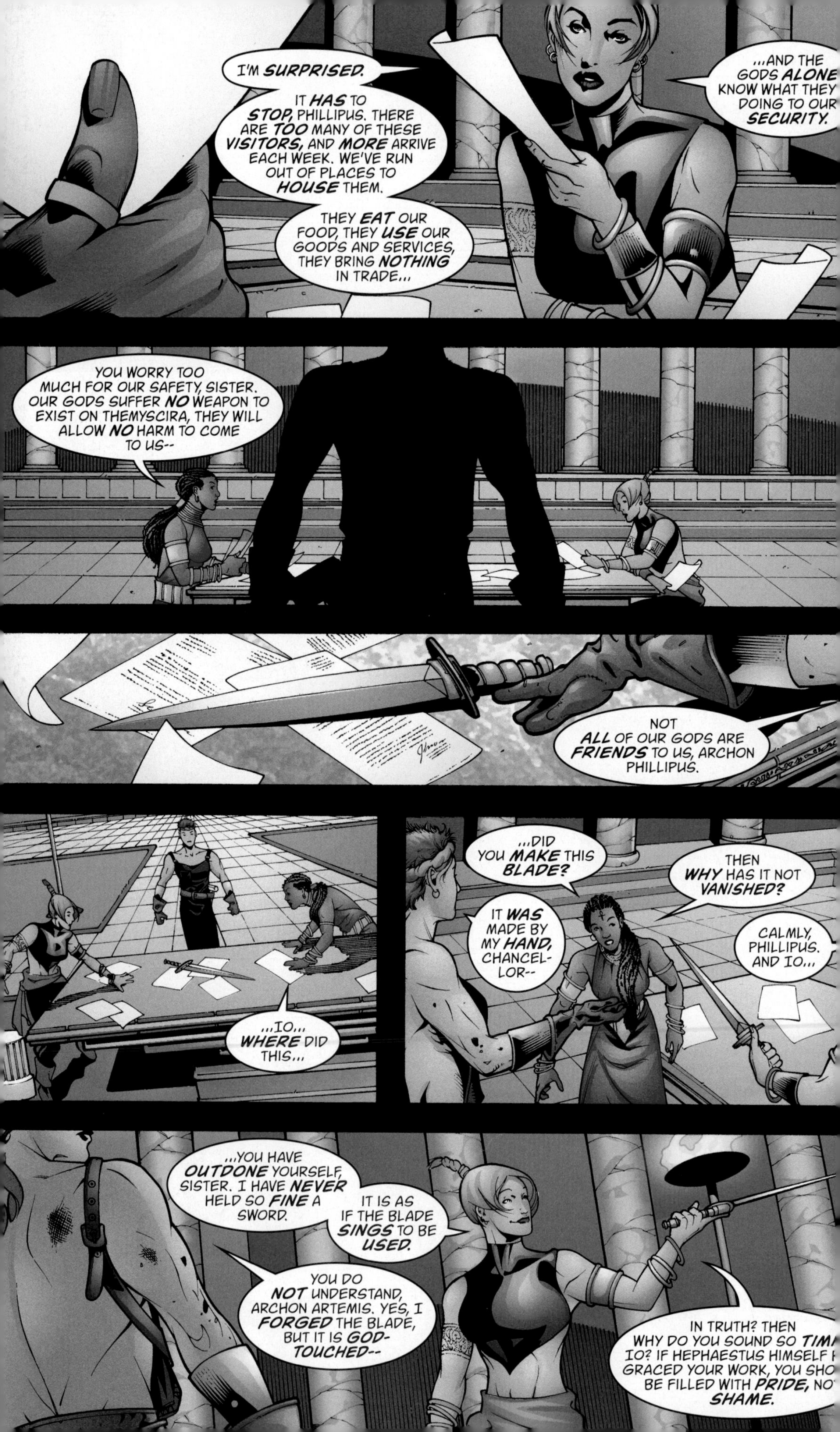
I'M SURPRISED.
IT HAS TO STOP, PHILLIPUS. THERE ARE TOO MANY OF THESE VISITORS, AND MORE ARRIVE EACH WEEK. WE'VE RUN OUT OF PLACES TO HOUSE THEM.
THEY EAT OUR FOOD, THEY USE OUR GOODS AND SERVICES, THEY BRING NOTHING IN TRADE...
...AND THE GODS ALONE KNOW WHAT THEY DOING TO OUR SECURITY.
YOU WORRY TOO MUCH FOR OUR SAFETY, SISTER. OUR GODS SUFFER NO WEAPON TO EXIST ON THEMYSCIRA, THEY WILL ALLOW NO HARM TO COME TO US--
NOT ALL OF OUR GODS ARE FRIENDS TO US, ARCHON PHILLIPUS.
...IO... WHERE DID THIS...
...DID YOU MAKE THIS BLADE?
IT WAS MADE BY MY HAND, CHANCEL-LOR--
THEN WHY HAS IT NOT VANISHED?
CALMLY, PHILLIPUS. AND IO...
...YOU HAVE OUTDONE YOURSELF, SISTER. I HAVE NEVER HELD SO FINE A SWORD.
IT IS AS IF THE BLADE SINGS TO BE USED.
YOU DO NOT UNDERSTAND, ARCHON ARTEMIS. YES, I FORGED THE BLADE, BUT IT IS GOD-TOUCHED--
IN TRUTH? THEN WHY DO YOU SOUND SO TIM IO? IF HEPHAESTUS HIMSELF GRACED YOUR WORK, YOU SHO BE FILLED WITH PRIDE, NO SHAME.

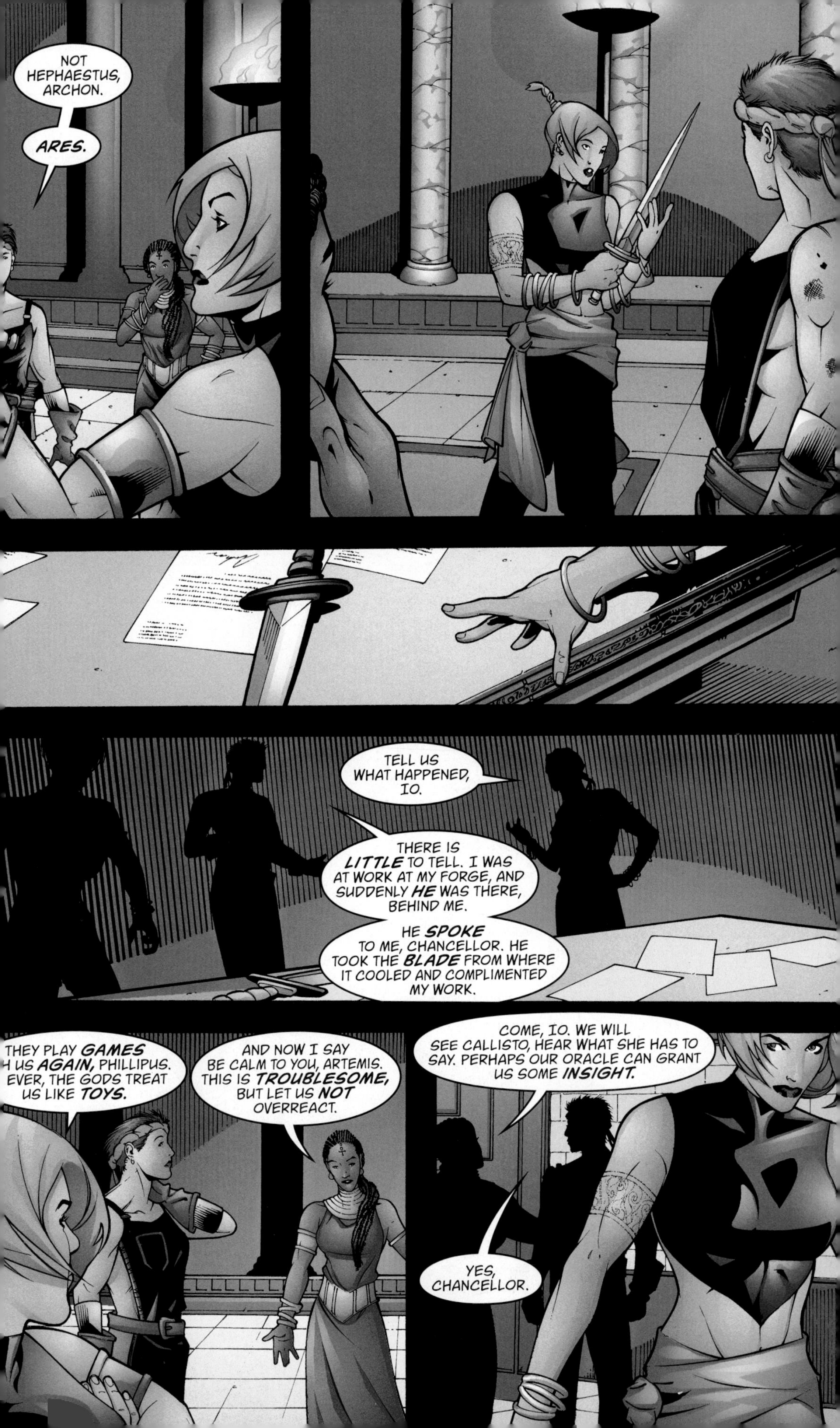
NOT HEPHAESTUS, ARCHON.
ARES.
TELL US WHAT HAPPENED, IO.
THERE IS LITTLE TO TELL. I WAS AT WORK AT MY FORGE, AND SUDDENLY HE WAS THERE, BEHIND ME.
HE SPOKE TO ME, CHANCELLOR. HE TOOK THE BLADE FROM WHERE IT COOLED AND COMPLIMENTED MY WORK.
THEY PLAY GAMES H US AGAIN, PHILLIPUS. EVER, THE GODS TREAT US LIKE TOYS.
AND NOW I SAY BE CALM TO YOU, ARTEMIS. THIS IS TROUBLESOME, BUT LET US NOT OVERREACT.
COME, IO. WE WILL SEE CALLISTO, HEAR WHAT SHE HAS TO SAY. PERHAPS OUR ORACLE CAN GRANT US SOME INSIGHT.
YES, CHANCELLOR.

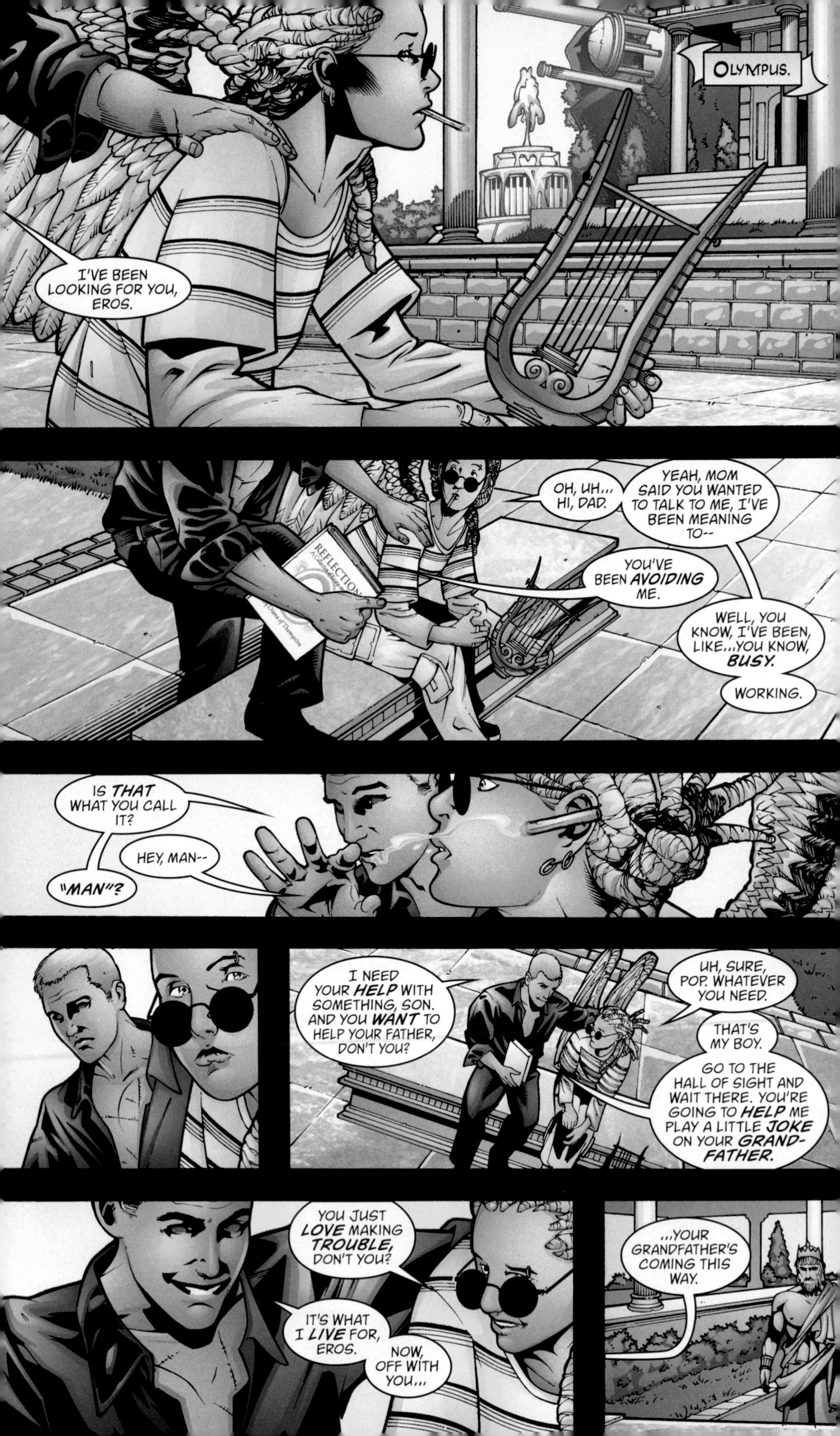
OLYMPUS.
I'VE BEEN LOOKING FOR YOU, EROS.
OH, UH... HI, DAD.
YEAH, MOM SAID YOU WANTED TO TALK TO ME, I'VE BEEN MEANING TO--
YOU'VE BEEN AVOIDING ME.
WELL, YOU KNOW, I'VE BEEN, LIKE...YOU KNOW, BUSY.
WORKING.
REFLECTIONS
IS THAT WHAT YOU CALL IT?
HEY, MAN--
"MAN"?
I NEED YOUR HELP WITH SOMETHING, SON. AND YOU WANT TO HELP YOUR FATHER, DON'T YOU?
UH, SURE, POP. WHATEVER YOU NEED.
THAT'S MY BOY.
GO TO THE HALL OF SIGHT AND WAIT THERE. YOU'RE GOING TO HELP ME PLAY A LITTLE JOKE ON YOUR GRAND-FATHER.
YOU JUST LOVE MAKING TROUBLE, DON'T YOU?
IT'S WHAT I LIVE FOR, EROS.
NOW, OFF WITH YOU...
...YOUR GRANDFATHER'S COMING THIS WAY.

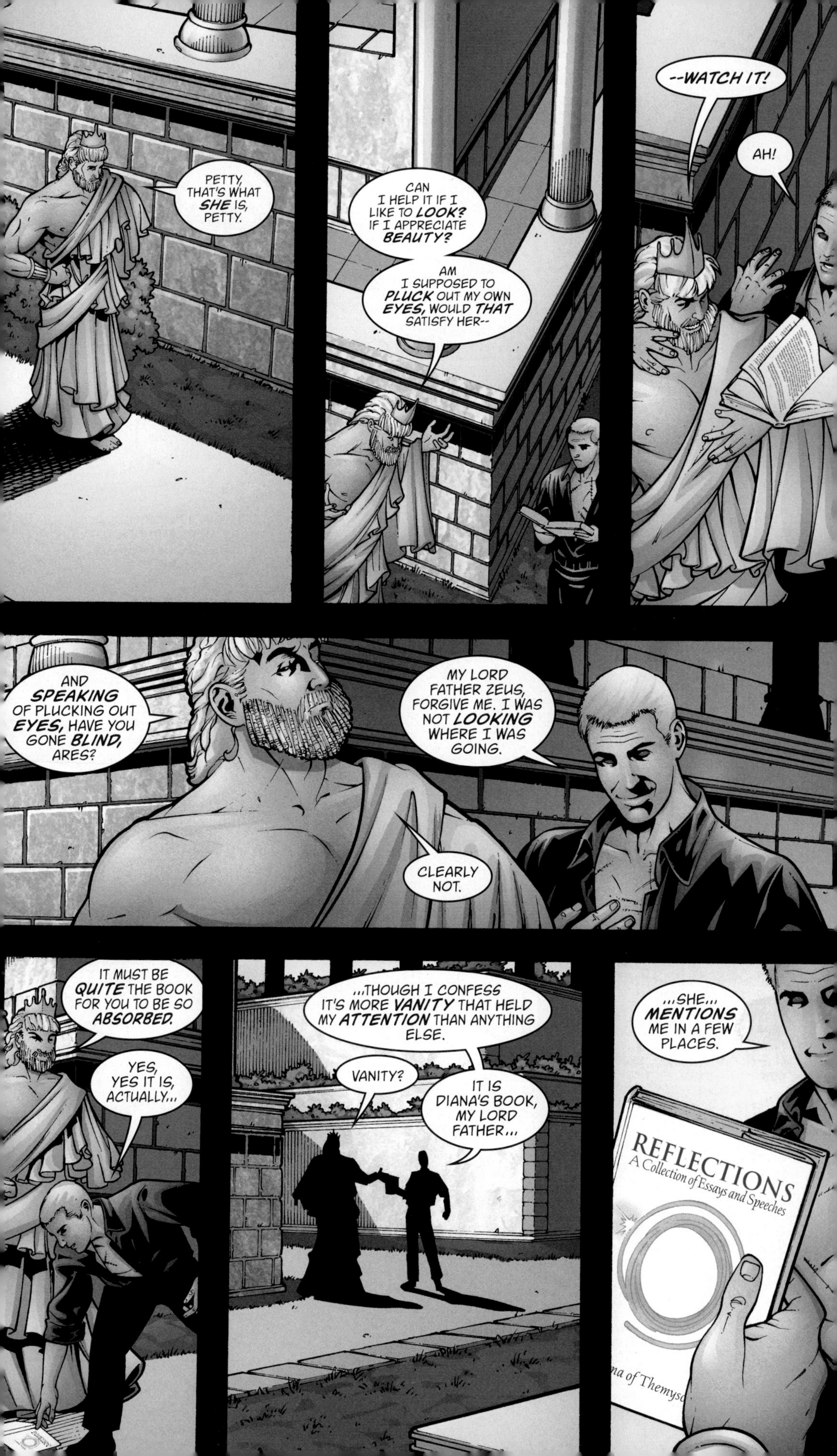
PETTY, THAT'S WHAT SHE IS, PETTY.
CAN I HELP IT IF I LIKE TO LOOK? IF I APPRECIATE BEAUTY?
AM I SUPPOSED TO PLUCK OUT MY OWN EYES, WOULD THAT SATISFY HER--
--WATCH IT!
AH!
AND SPEAKING OF PLUCKING OUT EYES, HAVE YOU GONE BLIND, ARES?
MY LORD FATHER ZEUS, FORGIVE ME. I WAS NOT LOOKING WHERE I WAS GOING.
CLEARLY NOT.
IT MUST BE QUITE THE BOOK FOR YOU TO BE SO ABSORBED.
YES, YES IT IS, ACTUALLY...
...THOUGH I CONFESS IT'S MORE VANITY THAT HELD MY ATTENTION THAN ANYTHING ELSE.
VANITY?
IT IS DIANA'S BOOK, MY LORD FATHER...
...SHE... MENTIONS ME IN A FEW PLACES.
REFLECTIONS
A Collection of Essays and Speeches

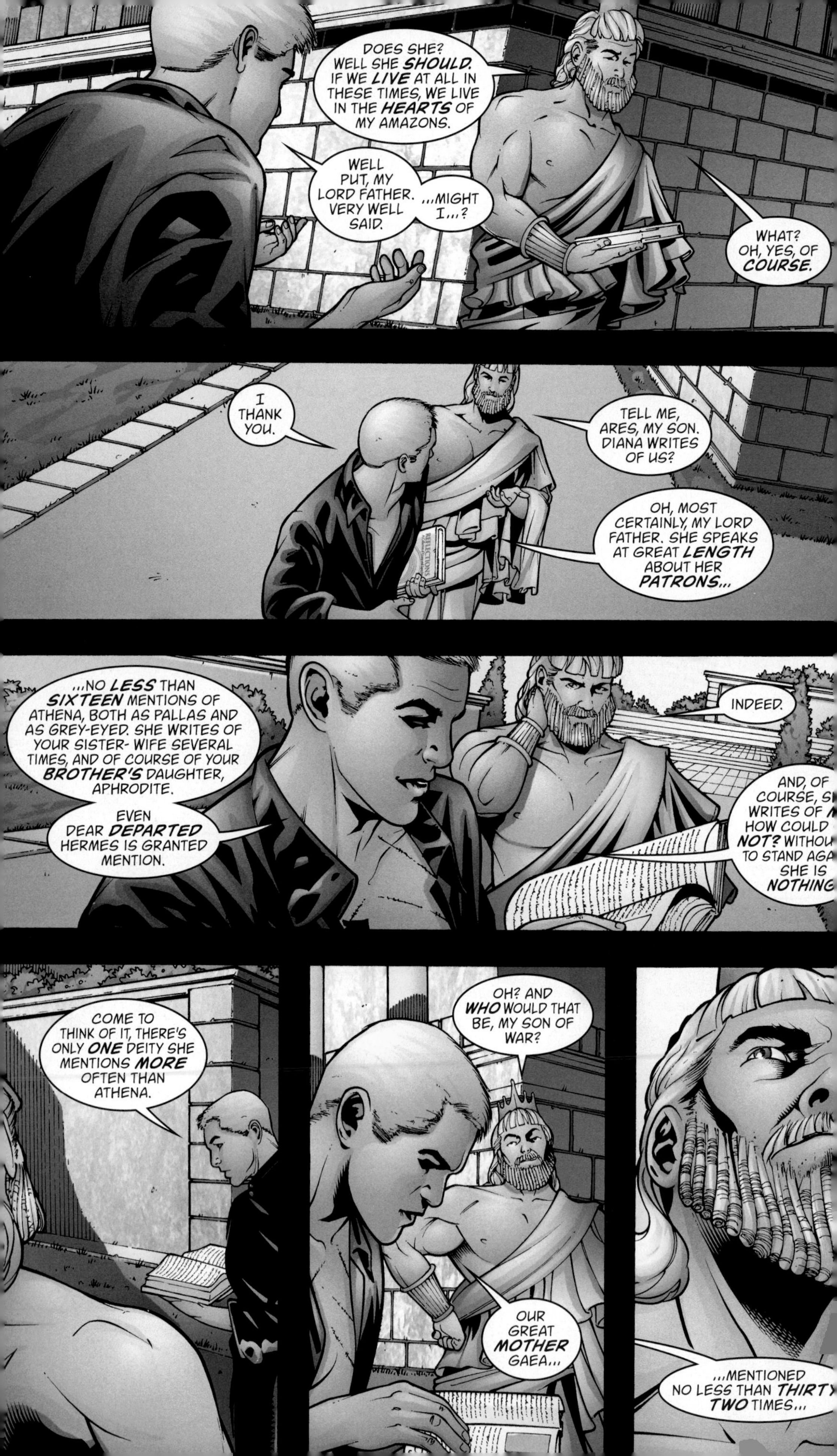
DOES SHE? WELL SHE SHOULD. IF WE LIVE AT ALL IN THESE TIMES, WE LIVE IN THE HEARTS OF MY AMAZONS.
WELL PUT, MY LORD FATHER. VERY WELL SAID.
...MIGHT I...?
WHAT? OH, YES, OF COURSE.
I THANK YOU.
TELL ME, ARES, MY SON. DIANA WRITES OF US?
OH, MOST CERTAINLY, MY LORD FATHER. SHE SPEAKS AT GREAT LENGTH ABOUT HER PATRONS...
...NO LESS THAN SIXTEEN MENTIONS OF ATHENA, BOTH AS PALLAS AND AS GREY-EYED. SHE WRITES OF YOUR SISTER-WIFE SEVERAL TIMES, AND OF COURSE OF YOUR BROTHER'S DAUGHTER, APHRODITE.
EVEN DEAR DEPARTED HERMES IS GRANTED MENTION.
INDEED.
COME TO THINK OF IT, THERE'S ONLY ONE DEITY SHE MENTIONS MORE OFTEN THAN ATHENA.
OH? AND WHO WOULD THAT BE, MY SON OF WAR?
OUR GREAT MOTHER GAEA...

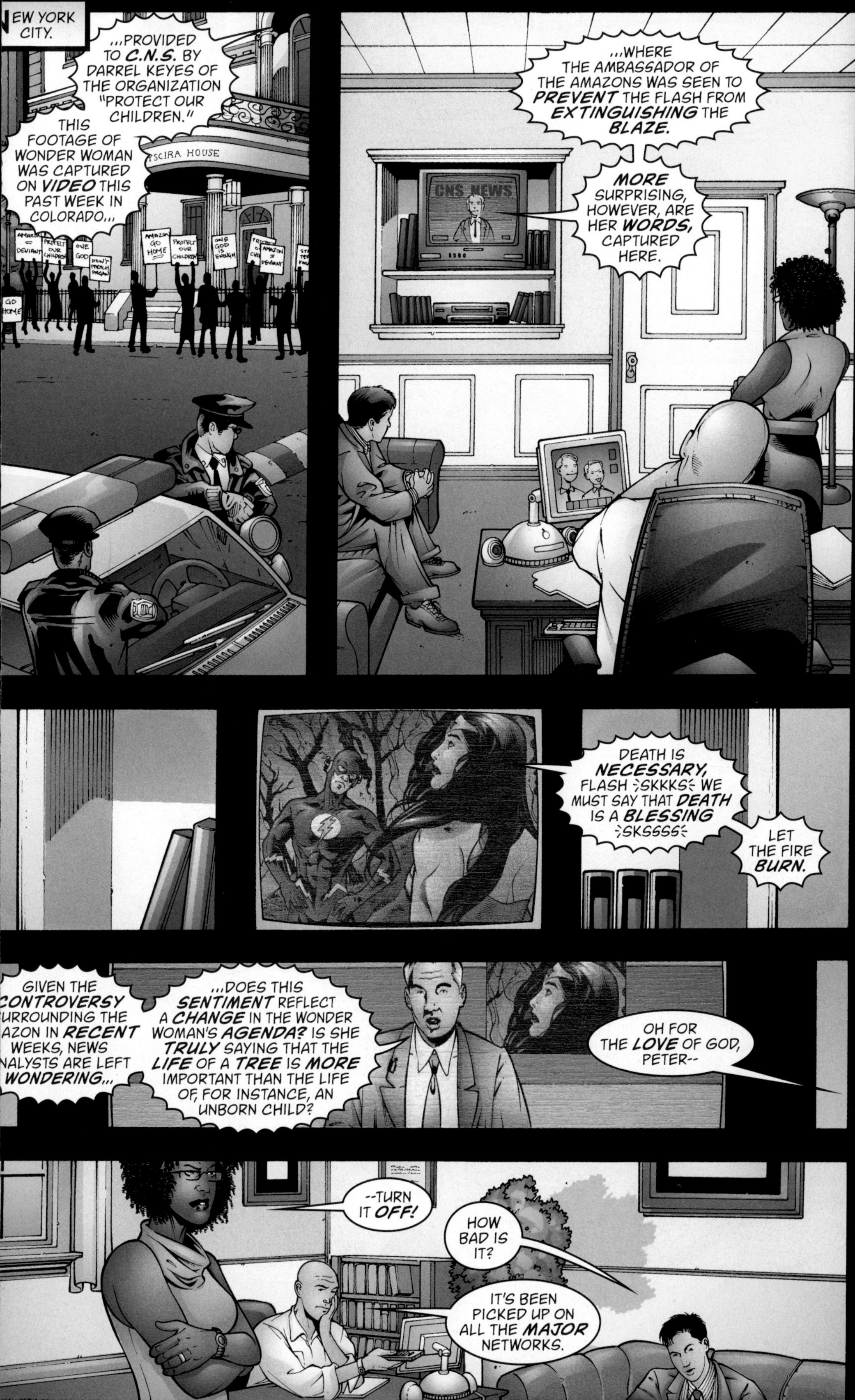
NEW YORK CITY.
...PROVIDED TO C.N.S. BY DARREL KEYES OF THE ORGANIZATION "PROTECT OUR CHILDREN."
THIS FOOTAGE OF WONDER WOMAN WAS CAPTURED ON VIDEO THIS PAST WEEK IN COLORADO...
SCIRA HOUSE
AMAZON GO HOME
PROTECT OUR CHILDREN
ONE GOD IS ENOUGH
AMAZON = DEVIANT
ONE GOD
GO HOME
...WHERE THE AMBASSADOR OF THE AMAZONS WAS SEEN TO PREVENT THE FLASH FROM EXTINGUISHING THE BLAZE.
CNS NEWS
MORE SURPRISING, HOWEVER, ARE HER WORDS, CAPTURED HERE.
DEATH IS NECESSARY, FLASH -SKKKS- WE MUST SAY THAT DEATH IS A BLESSING -SKSSSS-
LET THE FIRE BURN.
GIVEN THE CONTROVERSY SURROUNDING THE AMAZON IN RECENT WEEKS, NEWS ANALYSTS ARE LEFT WONDERING...
...DOES THIS SENTIMENT REFLECT A CHANGE IN THE WONDER WOMAN'S AGENDA? IS SHE TRULY SAYING THAT THE LIFE OF A TREE IS MORE IMPORTANT THAN THE LIFE OF, FOR INSTANCE, AN UNBORN CHILD?
OH FOR THE LOVE OF GOD, PETER--
--TURN IT OFF!
HOW BAD IS IT?
IT'S BEEN PICKED UP ON ALL THE MAJOR NETWORKS.

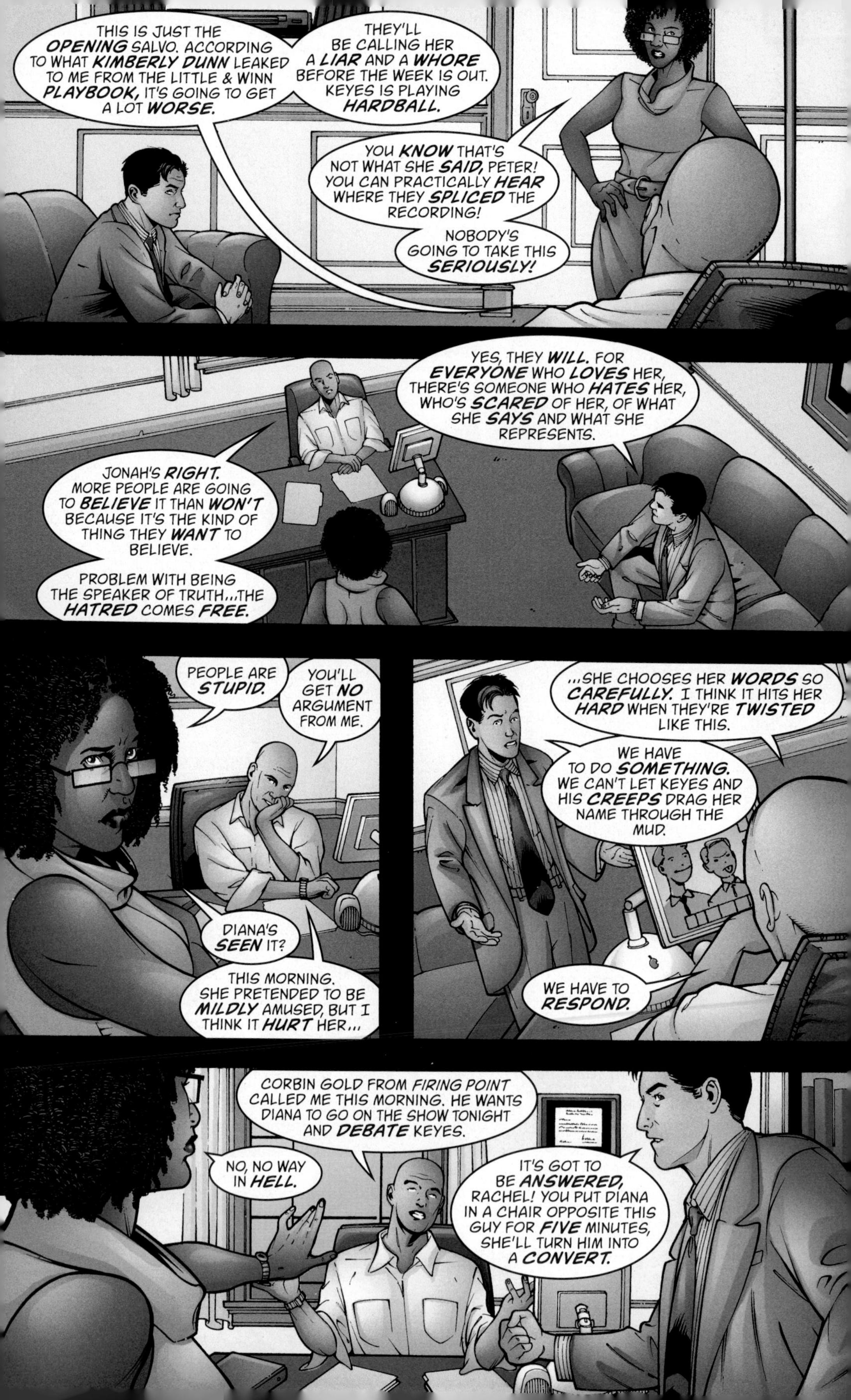
THIS IS JUST THE OPENING SALVO. ACCORDING TO WHAT KIMBERLY DUNN LEAKED TO ME FROM THE LITTLE & WINN PLAYBOOK, IT'S GOING TO GET A LOT WORSE.
THEY'LL BE CALLING HER A LIAR AND A WHORE BEFORE THE WEEK IS OUT. KEYES IS PLAYING HARDBALL.
YOU KNOW THAT'S NOT WHAT SHE SAID, PETER! YOU CAN PRACTICALLY HEAR WHERE THEY SPLICED THE RECORDING!
NOBODY'S GOING TO TAKE THIS SERIOUSLY!
YES, THEY WILL. FOR EVERYONE WHO LOVES HER, THERE'S SOMEONE WHO HATES HER, WHO'S SCARED OF HER, OF WHAT SHE SAYS AND WHAT SHE REPRESENTS.
JONAH'S RIGHT. MORE PEOPLE ARE GOING TO BELIEVE IT THAN WON'T BECAUSE IT'S THE KIND OF THING THEY WANT TO BELIEVE.
PROBLEM WITH BEING THE SPEAKER OF TRUTH...THE HATRED COMES FREE.
PEOPLE ARE STUPID.
YOU'LL GET NO ARGUMENT FROM ME.
DIANA'S SEEN IT?
THIS MORNING. SHE PRETENDED TO BE MILDLY AMUSED, BUT I THINK IT HURT HER...
...SHE CHOOSES HER WORDS SO CAREFULLY. I THINK IT HITS HER HARD WHEN THEY'RE TWISTED LIKE THIS.
WE HAVE TO DO SOMETHING. WE CAN'T LET KEYES AND HIS CREEPS DRAG HER NAME THROUGH THE MUD.
WE HAVE TO RESPOND.
CORBIN GOLD FROM FIRING POINT CALLED ME THIS MORNING. HE WANTS DIANA TO GO ON THE SHOW TONIGHT AND DEBATE KEYES.
NO, NO WAY IN HELL.
IT'S GOT TO BE ANSWERED, RACHEL! YOU PUT DIANA IN A CHAIR OPPOSITE THIS GUY FOR FIVE MINUTES, SHE'LL TURN HIM INTO A CONVERT.

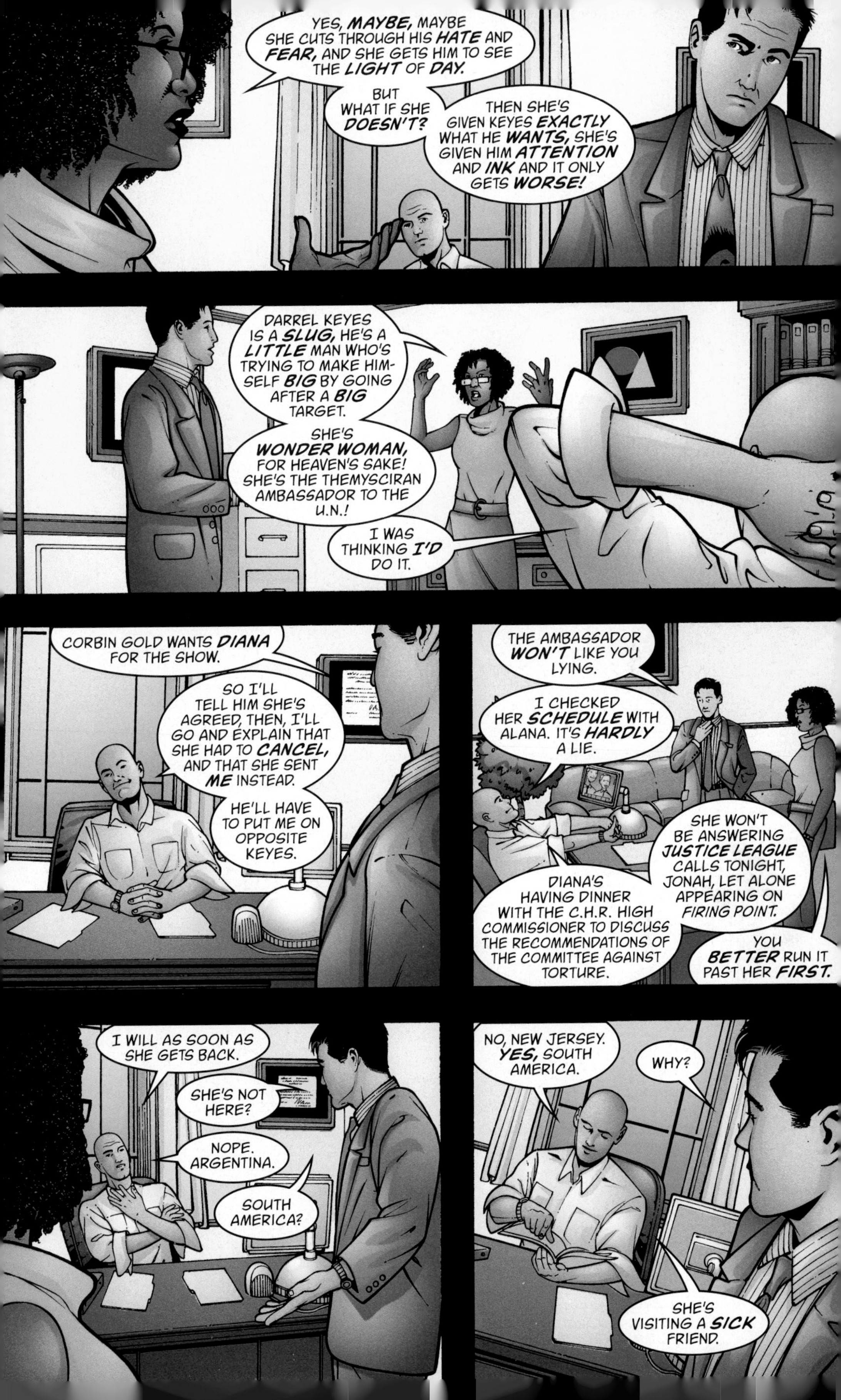
YES, MAYBE, MAYBE SHE CUTS THROUGH HIS HATE AND FEAR, AND SHE GETS HIM TO SEE THE LIGHT OF DAY.
BUT WHAT IF SHE DOESN'T?
THEN SHE'S GIVEN KEYES EXACTLY WHAT HE WANTS, SHE'S GIVEN HIM ATTENTION AND INK AND IT ONLY GETS WORSE!
DARREL KEYES IS A SLUG, HE'S A LITTLE MAN WHO'S TRYING TO MAKE HIM-SELF BIG BY GOING AFTER A BIG TARGET.
SHE'S WONDER WOMAN, FOR HEAVEN'S SAKE! SHE'S THE THEMYSCIRAN AMBASSADOR TO THE U.N.!
I WAS THINKING I'D DO IT.
CORBIN GOLD WANTS DIANA FOR THE SHOW.
SO I'LL TELL HIM SHE'S AGREED, THEN, I'LL GO AND EXPLAIN THAT SHE HAD TO CANCEL, AND THAT SHE SENT ME INSTEAD.
HE'LL HAVE TO PUT ME ON OPPOSITE KEYES.
THE AMBASSADOR WON'T LIKE YOU LYING.
I CHECKED HER SCHEDULE WITH ALANA. IT'S HARDLY A LIE.
DIANA'S HAVING DINNER WITH THE C.H.R. HIGH COMMISSIONER TO DISCUSS THE RECOMMENDATIONS OF THE COMMITTEE AGAINST TORTURE.
SHE WON'T BE ANSWERING JUSTICE LEAGUE CALLS TONIGHT, JONAH, LET ALONE APPEARING ON FIRING POINT.
YOU BETTER RUN IT PAST HER FIRST.
I WILL AS SOON AS SHE GETS BACK.
SHE'S NOT HERE?
NOPE. ARGENTINA.
SOUTH AMERICA?
NO, NEW JERSEY. YES, SOUTH AMERICA.
WHY?
SHE'S VISITING A SICK FRIEND.

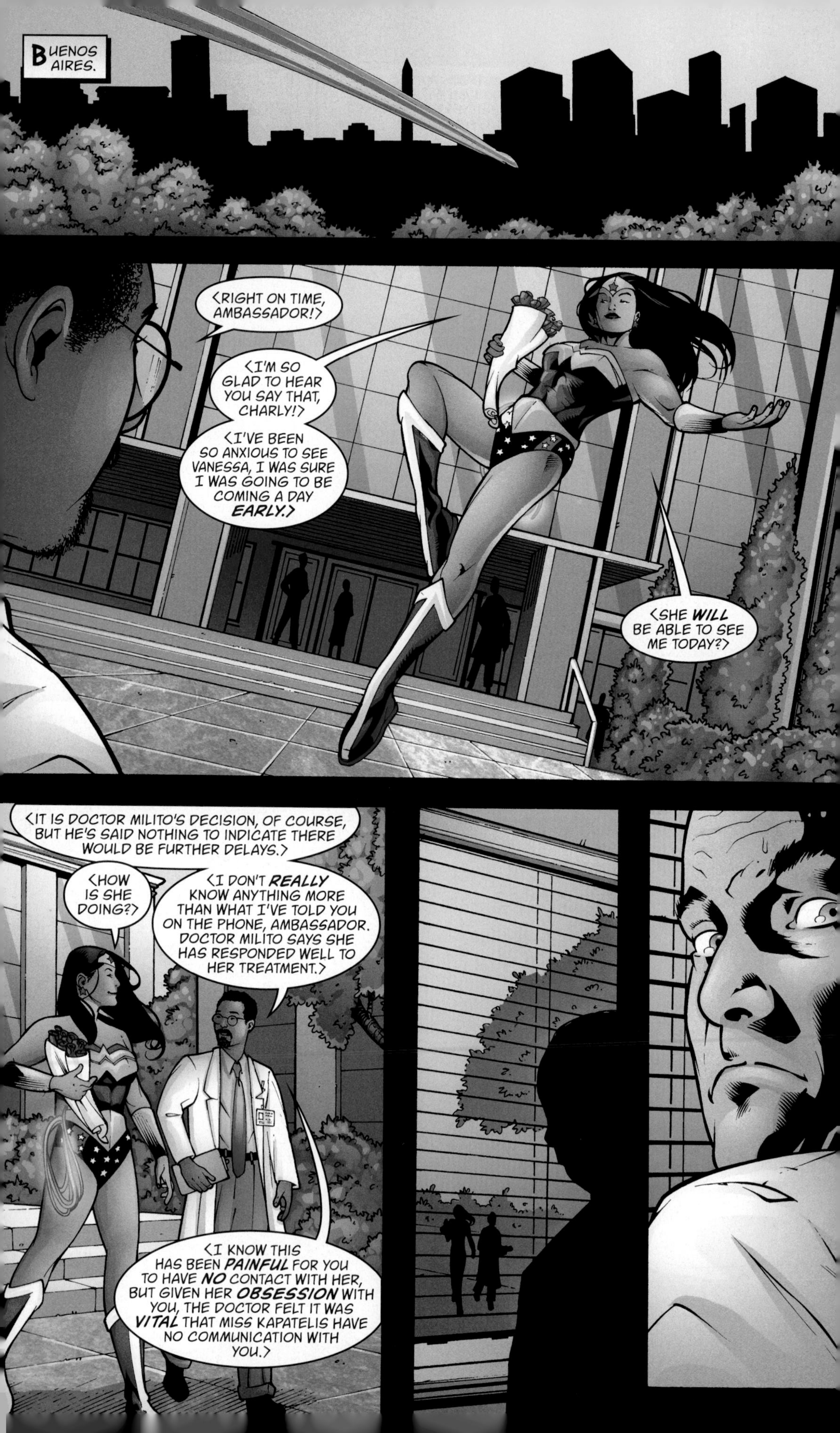

BUENOS AIRES.
<RIGHT ON TIME, AMBASSADOR!>
<I'M SO GLAD TO HEAR YOU SAY THAT, CHARLY!>
<I'VE BEEN SO ANXIOUS TO SEE VANESSA, I WAS SURE I WAS GOING TO BE COMING A DAY EARLY.>
<SHE WILL BE ABLE TO SEE ME TODAY?>
<IT IS DOCTOR MILITO'S DECISION, OF COURSE, BUT HE'S SAID NOTHING TO INDICATE THERE WOULD BE FURTHER DELAYS.>
<HOW IS SHE DOING?>
<I DON'T REALLY KNOW ANYTHING MORE THAN WHAT I'VE TOLD YOU ON THE PHONE, AMBASSADOR. DOCTOR MILITO SAYS SHE HAS RESPONDED WELL TO HER TREATMENT.>
<I KNOW THIS HAS BEEN PAINFUL FOR YOU TO HAVE NO CONTACT WITH HER, BUT GIVEN HER OBSESSION WITH YOU, THE DOCTOR FELT IT WAS VITAL THAT MISS KAPATELIS HAVE NO COMMUNICATION WITH YOU.>

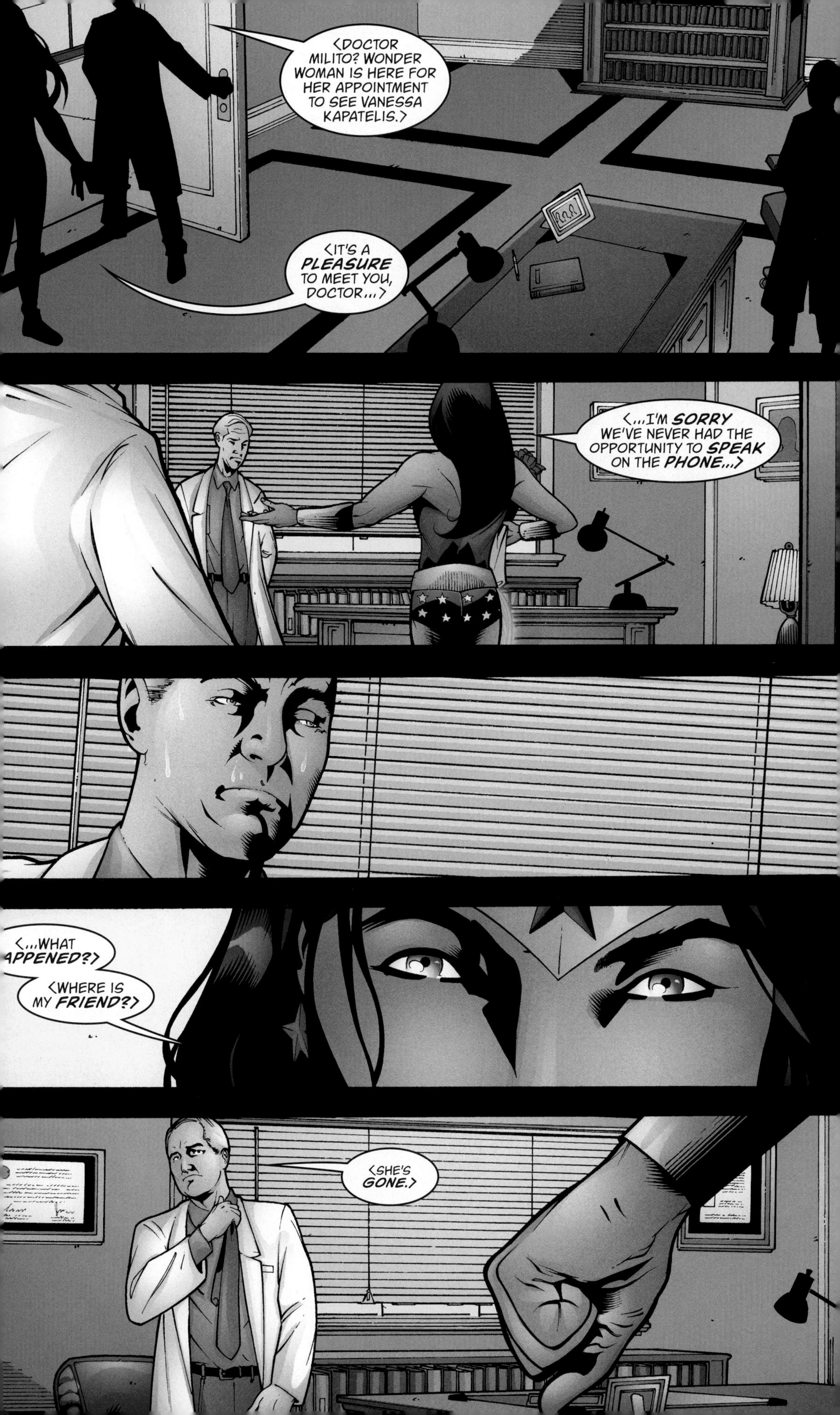

<DOCTOR MILITO? WONDER WOMAN IS HERE FOR HER APPOINTMENT TO SEE VANESSA KAPATELIS.>
<IT'S A PLEASURE TO MEET YOU, DOCTOR...>
<...I'M SORRY WE'VE NEVER HAD THE OPPORTUNITY TO SPEAK ON THE PHONE...>
<...WHAT APPENED?>
<WHERE IS MY FRIEND?>
<SHE'S GONE.>

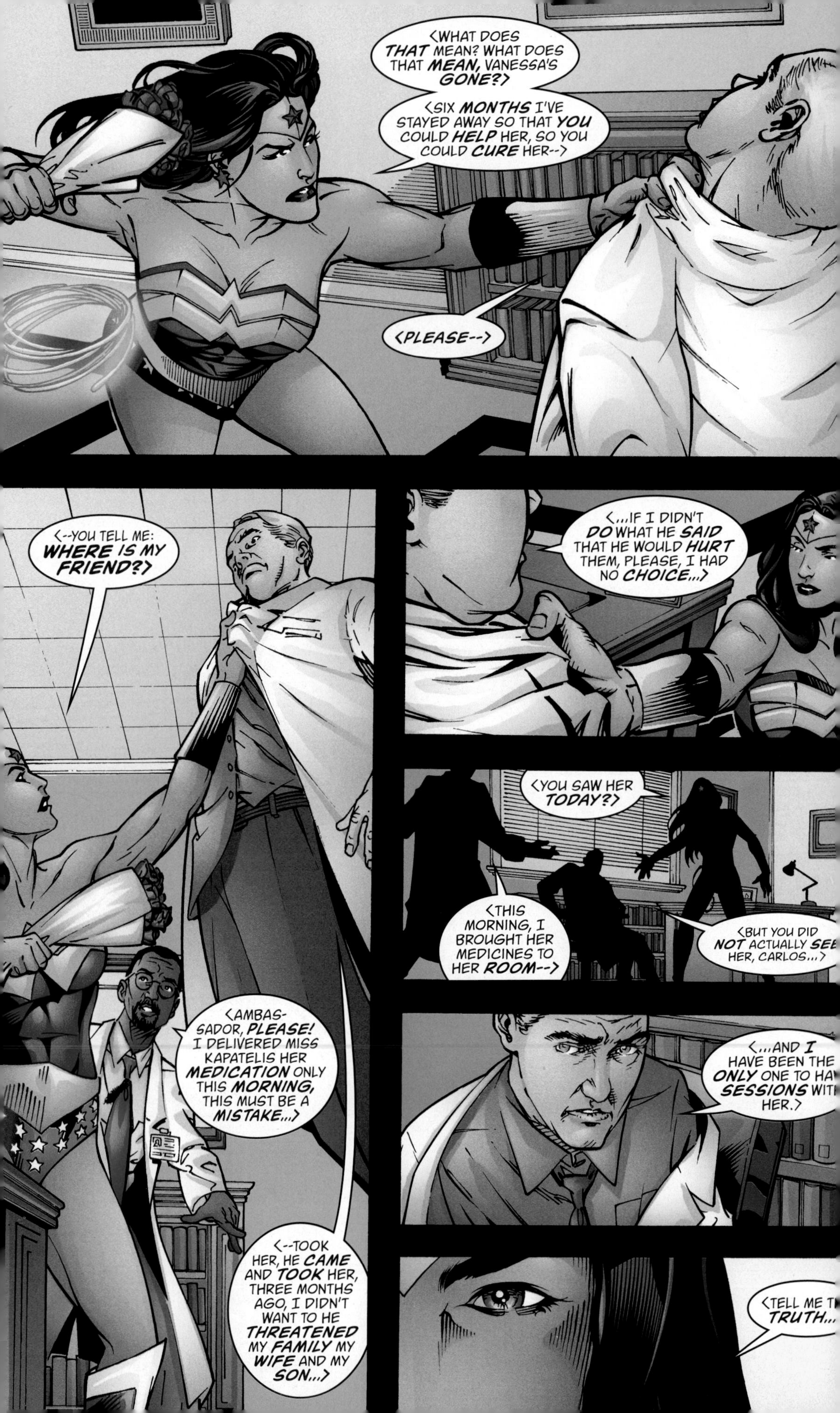

<WHAT DOES THAT MEAN? WHAT DOES THAT MEAN, VANESSA'S GONE?>
<SIX MONTHS I'VE STAYED AWAY SO THAT YOU COULD HELP HER, SO YOU COULD CURE HER-->
<PLEASE-->
<--YOU TELL ME: WHERE IS MY FRIEND?>
<AMBASSADOR, PLEASE! I DELIVERED MISS KAPATELIS HER MEDICATION ONLY THIS MORNING, THIS MUST BE A MISTAKE...>
<--TOOK HER, HE CAME AND TOOK HER, THREE MONTHS AGO, I DIDN'T WANT TO HE THREATENED MY FAMILY MY WIFE AND MY SON...>
<...IF I DIDN'T DO WHAT HE SAID THAT HE WOULD HURT THEM, PLEASE, I HAD NO CHOICE...>
<YOU SAW HER TODAY?>
<THIS MORNING, I BROUGHT HER MEDICINES TO HER ROOM-->
<BUT YOU DID NOT ACTUALLY SEE HER, CARLOS...>
<...AND I HAVE BEEN THE ONLY ONE TO HA SESSIONS WIT HER.>
<TELL ME T TRUTH...

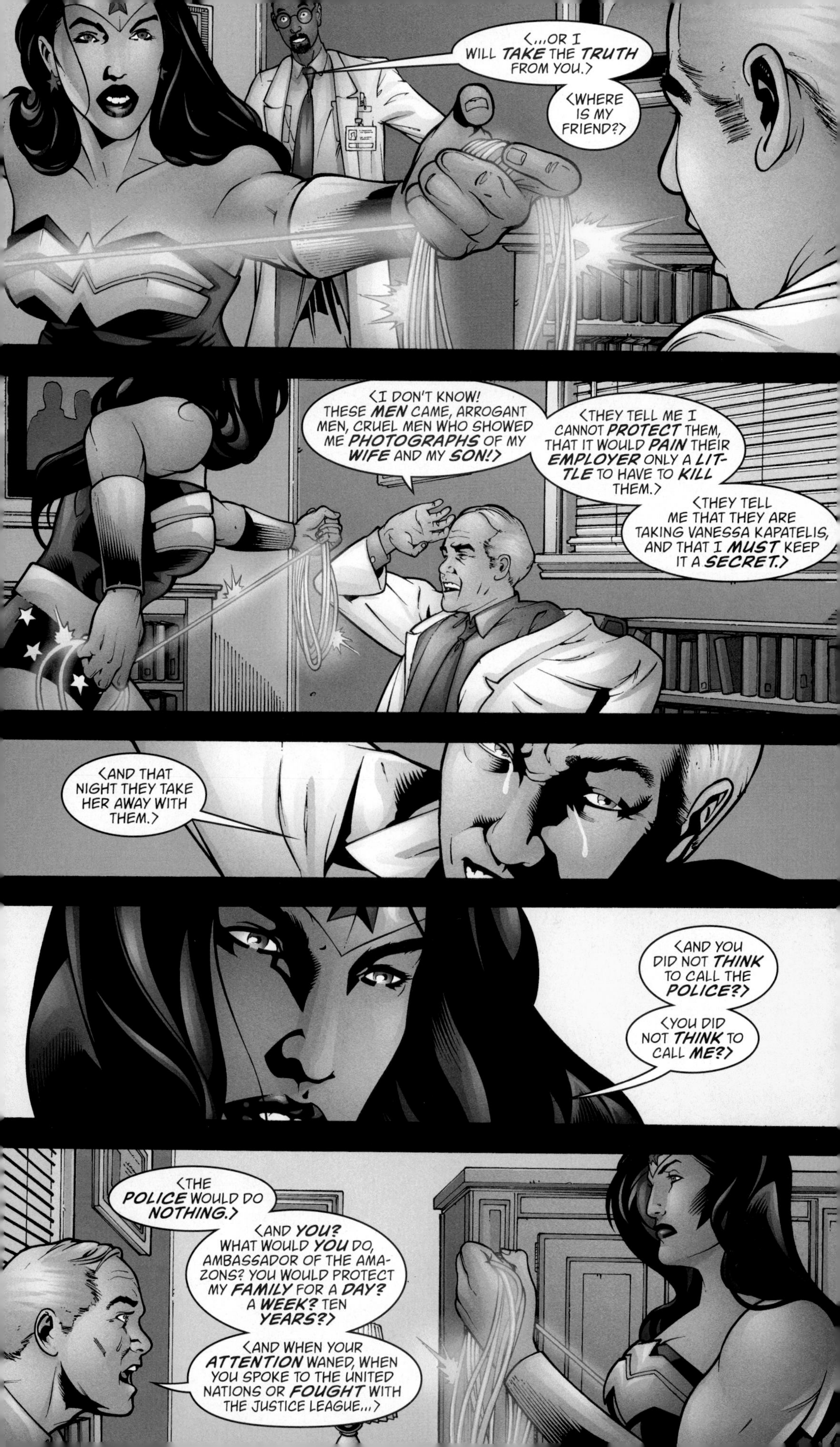
<...OR I WILL TAKE THE TRUTH FROM YOU.>
<WHERE IS MY FRIEND?>
<I DON'T KNOW! THESE MEN CAME, ARROGANT MEN, CRUEL MEN WHO SHOWED ME PHOTOGRAPHS OF MY WIFE AND MY SON!>
<THEY TELL ME I CANNOT PROTECT THEM, THAT IT WOULD PAIN THEIR EMPLOYER ONLY A LIT-TLE TO HAVE TO KILL THEM.>
<THEY TELL ME THAT THEY ARE TAKING VANESSA KAPATELIS, AND THAT I MUST KEEP IT A SECRET.>
<AND THAT NIGHT THEY TAKE HER AWAY WITH THEM.>
<AND YOU DID NOT THINK TO CALL THE POLICE?>
<YOU DID NOT THINK TO CALL ME?>
<THE POLICE WOULD DO NOTHING.>
<AND YOU? WHAT WOULD YOU DO, AMBASSADOR OF THE AMA-ZONS? YOU WOULD PROTECT MY FAMILY FOR A DAY? A WEEK? TEN YEARS?>
<AND WHEN YOUR ATTENTION WANED, WHEN YOU SPOKE TO THE UNITED NATIONS OR FOUGHT WITH THE JUSTICE LEAGUE...>

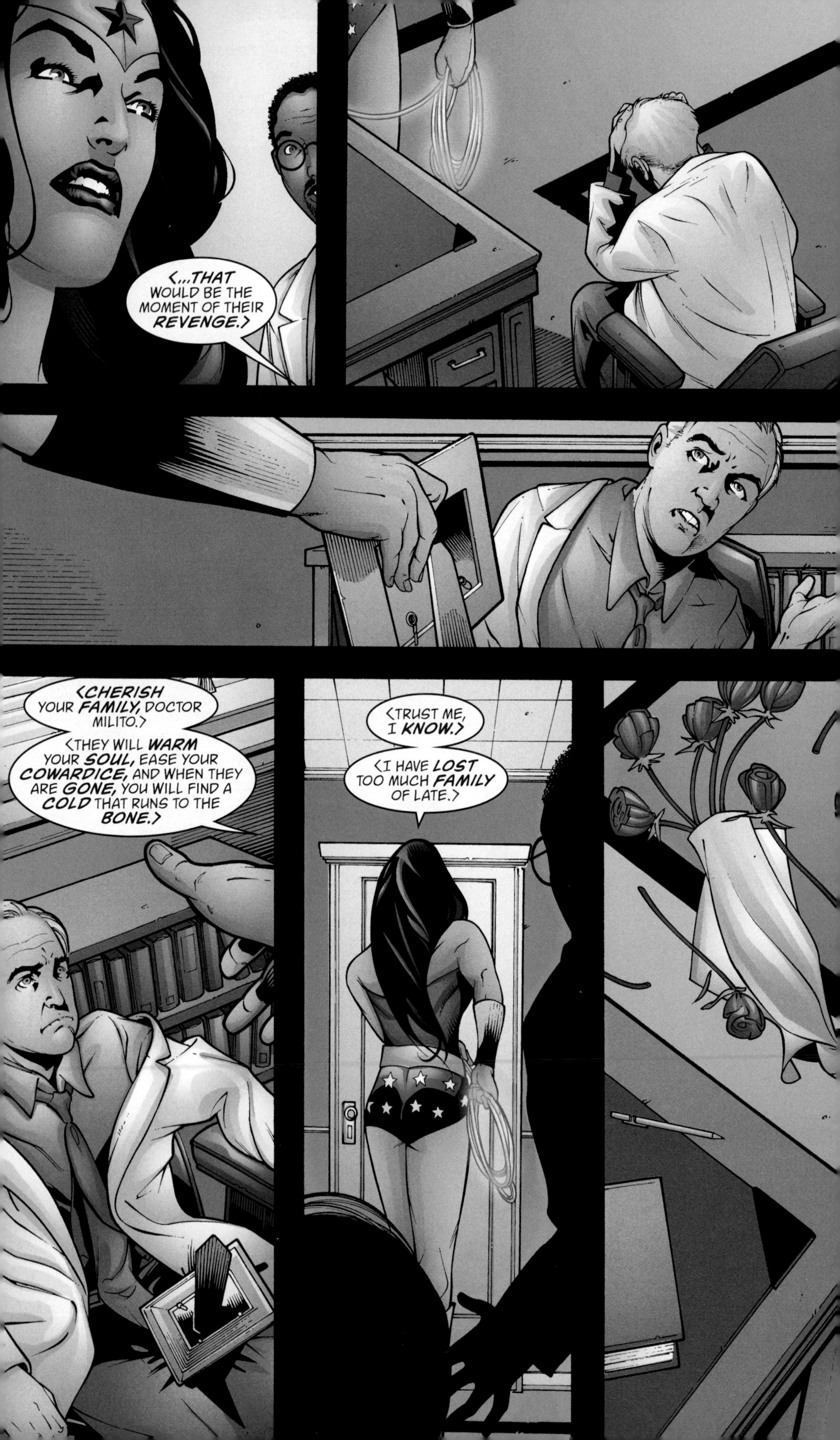

<...THAT WOULD BE THE MOMENT OF THEIR REVENGE.>
<CHERISH YOUR FAMILY, DOCTOR MILITO.>
<THEY WILL WARM YOUR SOUL, EASE YOUR COWARDICE, AND WHEN THEY ARE GONE, YOU WILL FIND A COLD THAT RUNS TO THE BONE.>
<TRUST ME, I KNOW.>
<I HAVE LOST TOO MUCH FAMILY OF LATE.>

...AMBASSADOR EXTENDS HER *REGRETS*, BUT UNFORTUNATELY SHE HAD A *PREVIOUS* ENGAGEMENT.

I *KNEW* SHE'D *CHICKEN* OUT.

THE AMBASSADOR FELT HER DINNER WITH THE HIGH COMMISSIONER ON HUMAN RIGHTS WAS *MORE* PRESSING THAN THE SHOW, I'M AFRAID.

SHE ASKED ME TO SEND HER REGARDS, AND HER *REGRETS*.

SHE CAN HAVE THE REGRETS *LATER*, WHEN THE SHOW'S *OVER*.

GUESS WE'LL HAVE TO WAIT AND SEE.

FIFTEEN SECONDS!

KEEP IT *CIVIL*, BOYS.

HEATED, BUT *CIVIL*.

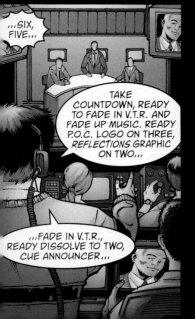

...SIX, FIVE...

TAKE COUNTDOWN, READY TO FADE IN V.T.R. AND FADE UP MUSIC. READY P.O.C. LOGO ON THREE, REFLECTIONS GRAPHIC ON TWO...

...FADE IN V.T.R., READY DISSOLVE TO TWO, CUE ANNOUNCER...

...DISSOLVE TO TWO, FADE DOWN MUSIC, CUE ANNOUNCER...

FIRING POINT, WITH *CORBIN GOLD!*

FIRING POINT
with
Corbin Gold

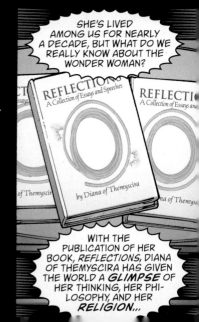

SHE'S LIVED AMONG US FOR NEARLY A DECADE, BUT WHAT DO WE REALLY KNOW ABOUT THE WONDER WOMAN?

REFLECTIONS
A Collection of Essays and Speeches

by Diana of Themyscira

WITH THE PUBLICATION OF HER BOOK, *REFLECTIONS*, DIANA OF THEMYSCIRA HAS GIVEN THE WORLD A *GLIMPSE* OF HER THINKING, HER PHILOSOPHY, AND HER *RELIGION*...

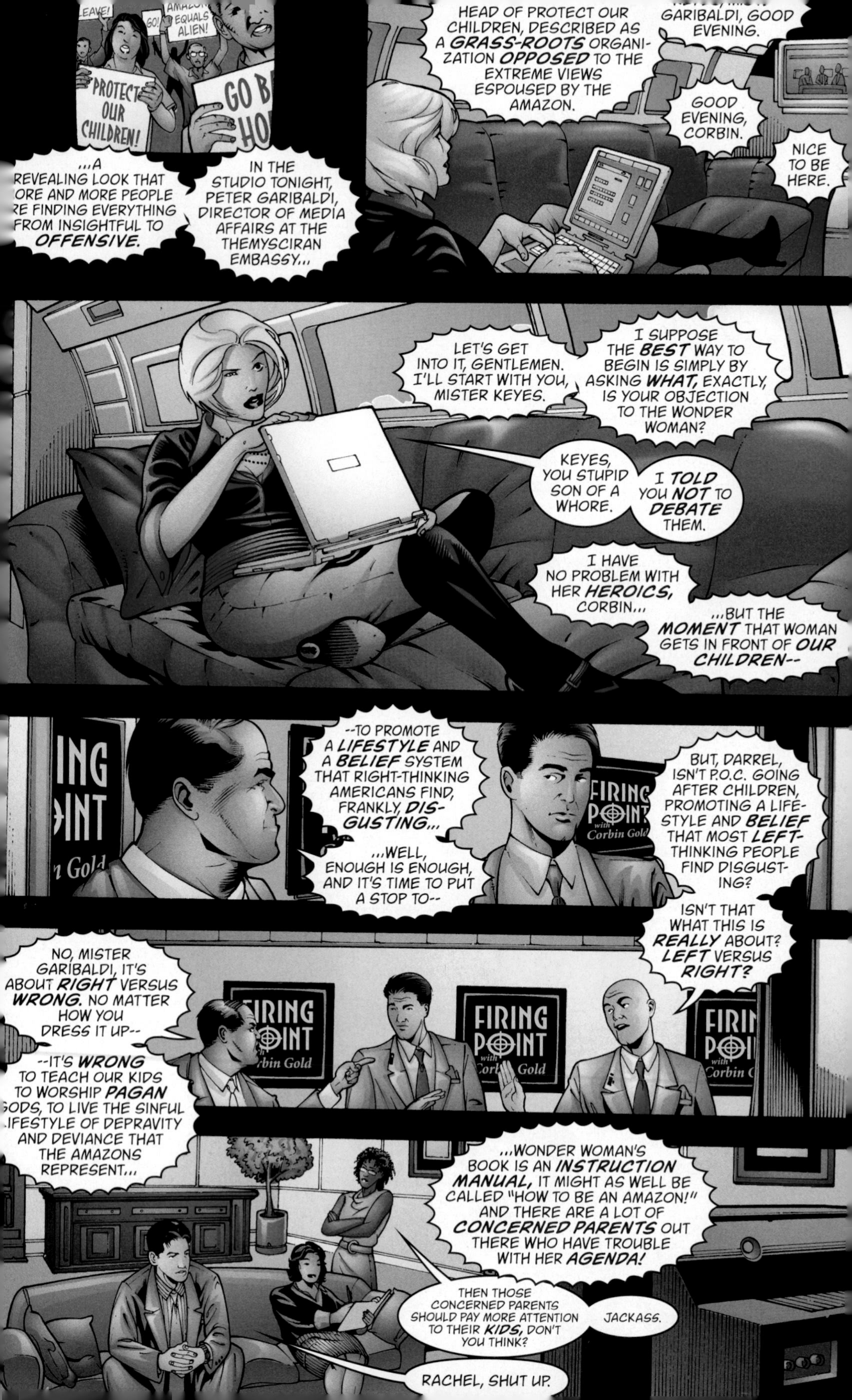
LEAVE!
GO!
EQUALS ALIEN!
PROTECT OUR CHILDREN!
...A REVEALING LOOK THAT ORE AND MORE PEOPLE RE FINDING EVERYTHING FROM INSIGHTFUL TO OFFENSIVE.
IN THE STUDIO TONIGHT, PETER GARIBALDI, DIRECTOR OF MEDIA AFFAIRS AT THE THEMYSCIRAN EMBASSY...
HEAD OF PROTECT OUR CHILDREN, DESCRIBED AS A GRASS-ROOTS ORGANIZATION OPPOSED TO THE EXTREME VIEWS ESPOUSED BY THE AMAZON.
GARIBALDI, GOOD EVENING.
GOOD EVENING, CORBIN.
NICE TO BE HERE.
LET'S GET INTO IT, GENTLEMEN. I'LL START WITH YOU, MISTER KEYES.
I SUPPOSE THE BEST WAY TO BEGIN IS SIMPLY BY ASKING WHAT, EXACTLY, IS YOUR OBJECTION TO THE WONDER WOMAN?
KEYES, YOU STUPID SON OF A WHORE.
I TOLD YOU NOT TO DEBATE THEM.
I HAVE NO PROBLEM WITH HER HEROICS, CORBIN...
...BUT THE MOMENT THAT WOMAN GETS IN FRONT OF OUR CHILDREN--
--TO PROMOTE A LIFESTYLE AND A BELIEF SYSTEM THAT RIGHT-THINKING AMERICANS FIND, FRANKLY, DISGUSTING...
...WELL, ENOUGH IS ENOUGH, AND IT'S TIME TO PUT A STOP TO--
FIRING POINT with Corbin Gold
BUT, DARREL, ISN'T P.O.C. GOING AFTER CHILDREN, PROMOTING A LIFESTYLE AND BELIEF THAT MOST LEFT-THINKING PEOPLE FIND DISGUSTING?
ISN'T THAT WHAT THIS IS REALLY ABOUT? LEFT VERSUS RIGHT?
NO, MISTER GARIBALDI, IT'S ABOUT RIGHT VERSUS WRONG. NO MATTER HOW YOU DRESS IT UP--
--IT'S WRONG TO TEACH OUR KIDS TO WORSHIP PAGAN GODS, TO LIVE THE SINFUL LIFESTYLE OF DEPRAVITY AND DEVIANCE THAT THE AMAZONS REPRESENT...
FIRING POINT with Corbin Gold
...WONDER WOMAN'S BOOK IS AN INSTRUCTION MANUAL, IT MIGHT AS WELL BE CALLED "HOW TO BE AN AMAZON!" AND THERE ARE A LOT OF CONCERNED PARENTS OUT THERE WHO HAVE TROUBLE WITH HER AGENDA!
THEN THOSE CONCERNED PARENTS SHOULD PAY MORE ATTENTION TO THEIR KIDS, DON'T YOU THINK?
JACKASS.
RACHEL, SHUT UP.

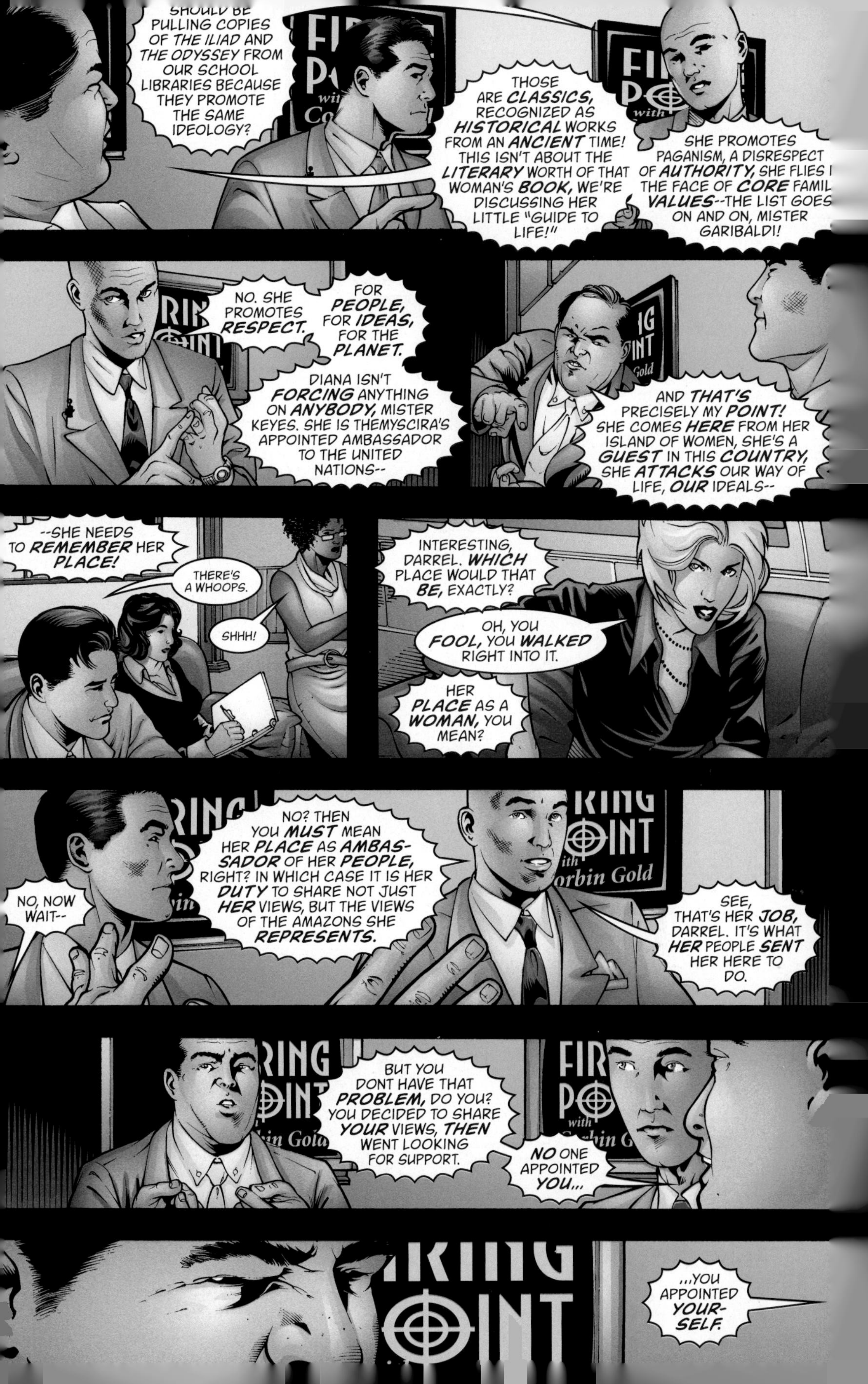
SHOULD BE PULLING COPIES OF THE ILIAD AND THE ODYSSEY FROM OUR SCHOOL LIBRARIES BECAUSE THEY PROMOTE THE SAME IDEOLOGY?
THOSE ARE CLASSICS, RECOGNIZED AS HISTORICAL WORKS FROM AN ANCIENT TIME! THIS ISN'T ABOUT THE LITERARY WORTH OF THAT WOMAN'S BOOK, WE'RE DISCUSSING HER LITTLE "GUIDE TO LIFE!"
SHE PROMOTES PAGANISM, A DISRESPECT OF AUTHORITY, SHE FLIES I THE FACE OF CORE FAMIL VALUES--THE LIST GOES ON AND ON, MISTER GARIBALDI!
NO. SHE PROMOTES RESPECT.
FOR PEOPLE, FOR IDEAS, FOR THE PLANET.
DIANA ISN'T FORCING ANYTHING ON ANYBODY, MISTER KEYES. SHE IS THEMYSCIRA'S APPOINTED AMBASSADOR TO THE UNITED NATIONS--
AND THAT'S PRECISELY MY POINT! SHE COMES HERE FROM HER ISLAND OF WOMEN, SHE'S A GUEST IN THIS COUNTRY, SHE ATTACKS OUR WAY OF LIFE, OUR IDEALS--
--SHE NEEDS TO REMEMBER HER PLACE!
THERE'S A WHOOPS.
SHHH!
INTERESTING, DARREL. WHICH PLACE WOULD THAT BE, EXACTLY?
OH, YOU FOOL, YOU WALKED RIGHT INTO IT.
HER PLACE AS A WOMAN, YOU MEAN?
NO? THEN YOU MUST MEAN HER PLACE AS AMBAS-SADOR OF HER PEOPLE, RIGHT? IN WHICH CASE IT IS HER DUTY TO SHARE NOT JUST HER VIEWS, BUT THE VIEWS OF THE AMAZONS SHE REPRESENTS.
NO, NOW WAIT--
SEE, THAT'S HER JOB, DARREL. IT'S WHAT HER PEOPLE SENT HER HERE TO DO.
BUT YOU DONT HAVE THAT PROBLEM, DO YOU? YOU DECIDED TO SHARE YOUR VIEWS, THEN WENT LOOKING FOR SUPPORT.
NO ONE APPOINTED YOU...
...YOU APPOINTED YOUR-SELF.

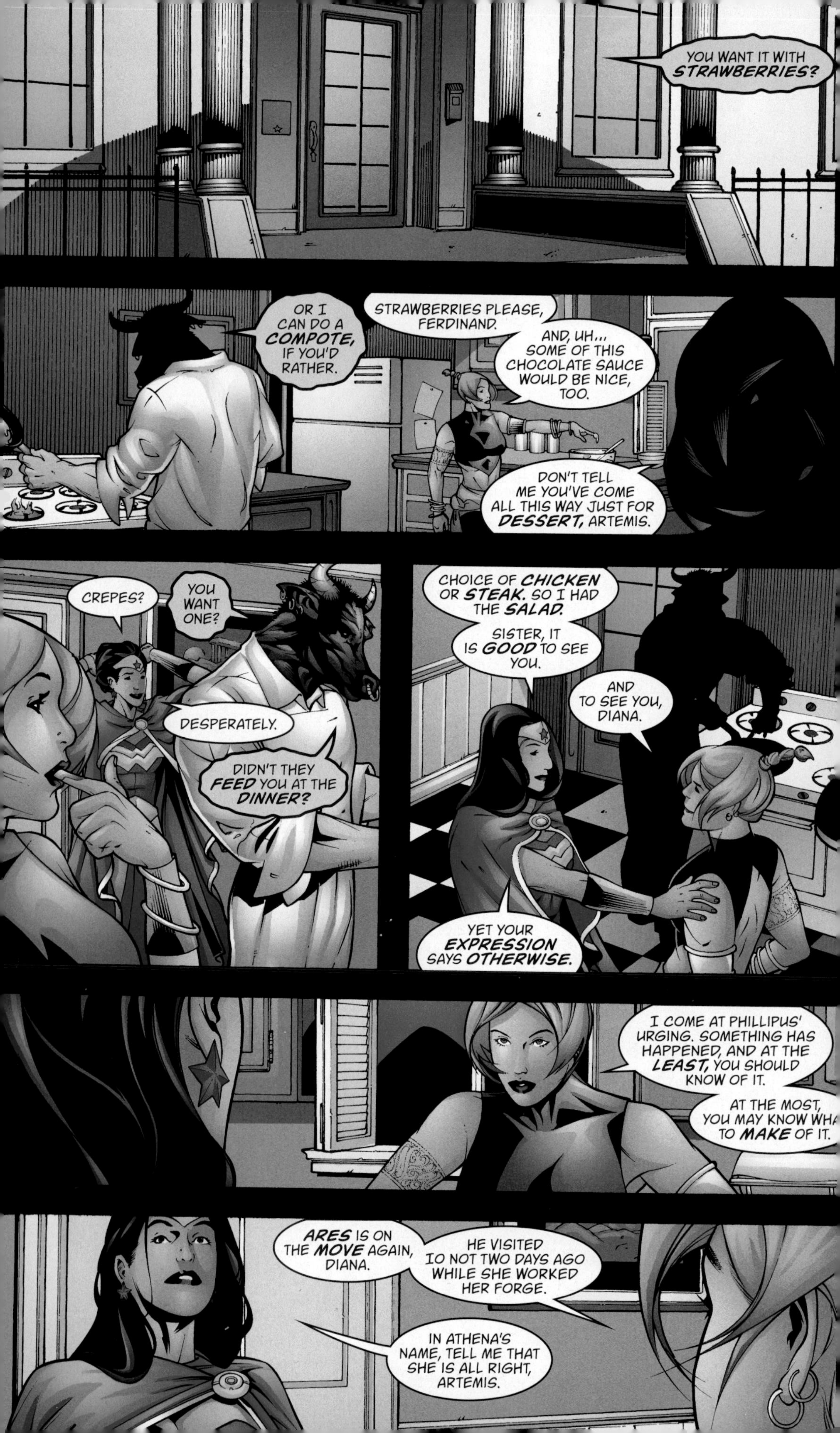
YOU WANT IT WITH STRAWBERRIES?
OR I CAN DO A COMPOTE, IF YOU'D RATHER.
STRAWBERRIES PLEASE, FERDINAND.
AND, UH... SOME OF THIS CHOCOLATE SAUCE WOULD BE NICE, TOO.
DON'T TELL ME YOU'VE COME ALL THIS WAY JUST FOR DESSERT, ARTEMIS.
CREPES?
YOU WANT ONE?
DESPERATELY.
DIDN'T THEY FEED YOU AT THE DINNER?
CHOICE OF CHICKEN OR STEAK. SO I HAD THE SALAD.
SISTER, IT IS GOOD TO SEE YOU.
AND TO SEE YOU, DIANA.
YET YOUR EXPRESSION SAYS OTHERWISE.
I COME AT PHILLIPUS' URGING. SOMETHING HAS HAPPENED, AND AT THE LEAST, YOU SHOULD KNOW OF IT.
AT THE MOST, YOU MAY KNOW WHA TO MAKE OF IT.
ARES IS ON THE MOVE AGAIN, DIANA.
HE VISITED IO NOT TWO DAYS AGO WHILE SHE WORKED HER FORGE.
IN ATHENA'S NAME, TELL ME THAT SHE IS ALL RIGHT, ARTEMIS.

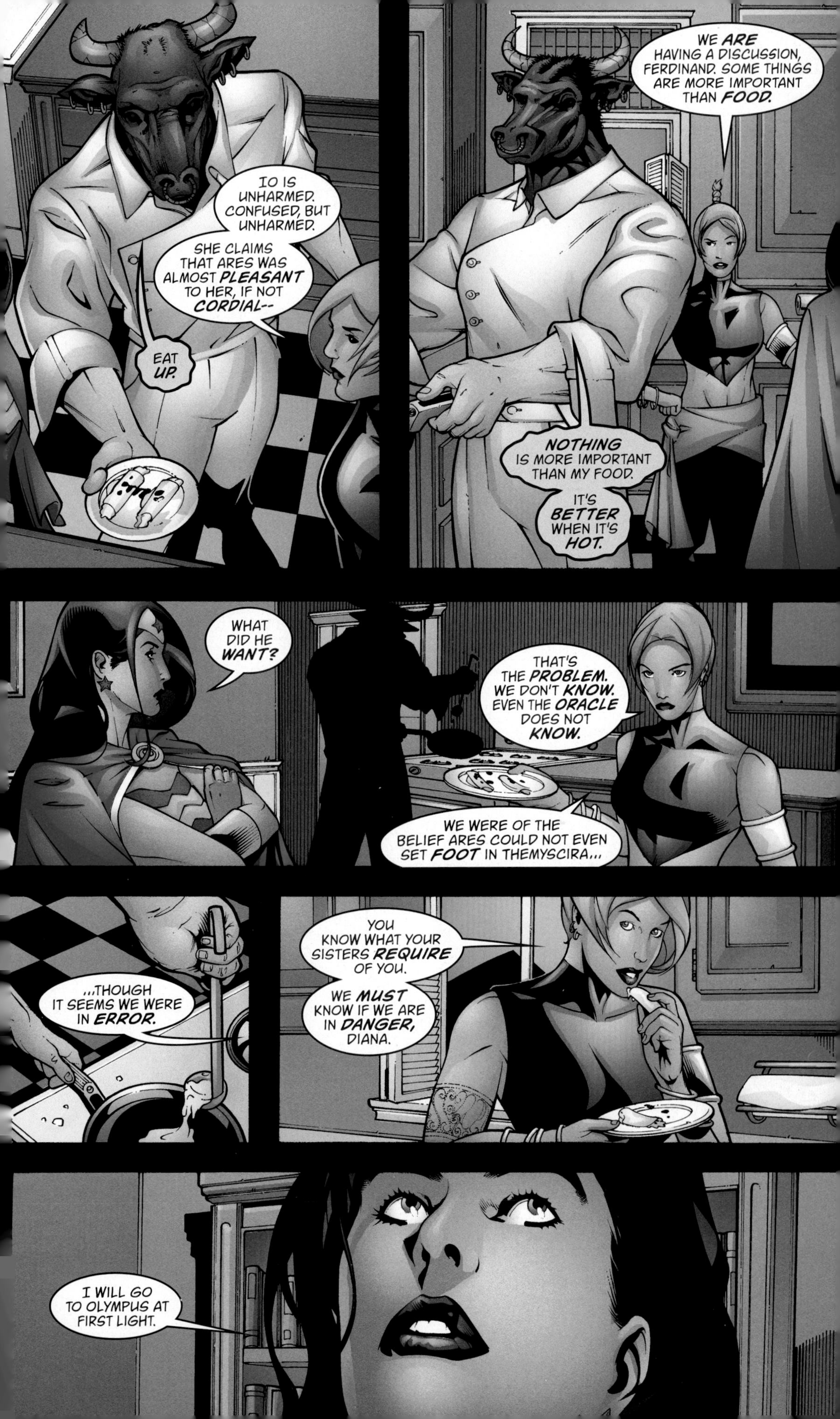
IO IS UNHARMED. CONFUSED, BUT UNHARMED.
SHE CLAIMS THAT ARES WAS ALMOST PLEASANT TO HER, IF NOT CORDIAL--
EAT UP.
WE ARE HAVING A DISCUSSION, FERDINAND. SOME THINGS ARE MORE IMPORTANT THAN FOOD.
NOTHING IS MORE IMPORTANT THAN MY FOOD.
IT'S BETTER WHEN IT'S HOT.
WHAT DID HE WANT?
THAT'S THE PROBLEM. WE DON'T KNOW. EVEN THE ORACLE DOES NOT KNOW.
WE WERE OF THE BELIEF ARES COULD NOT EVEN SET FOOT IN THEMYSCIRA...
...THOUGH IT SEEMS WE WERE IN ERROR.
YOU KNOW WHAT YOUR SISTERS REQUIRE OF YOU.
WE MUST KNOW IF WE ARE IN DANGER, DIANA.
I WILL GO TO OLYMPUS AT FIRST LIGHT.

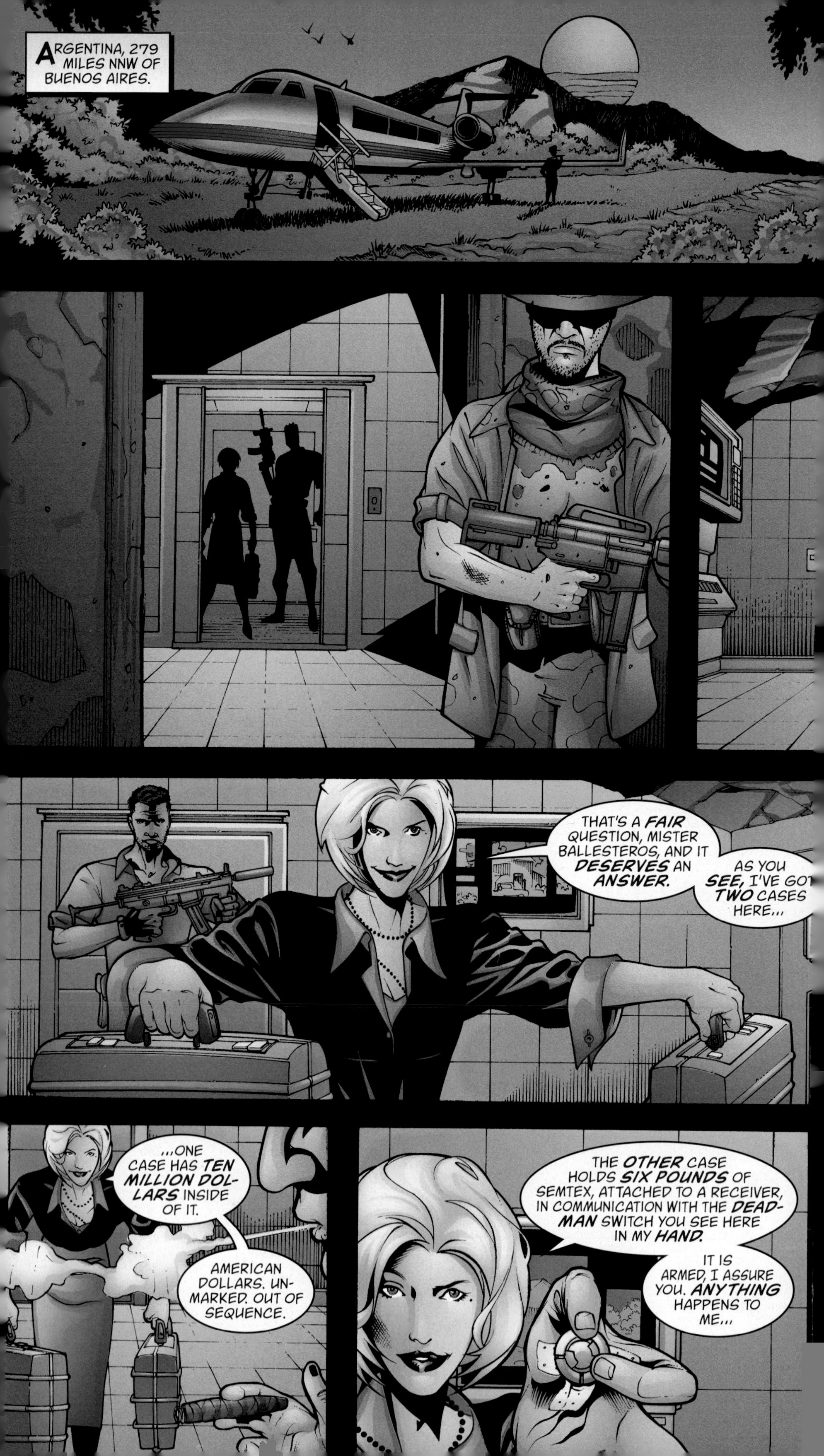
ARGENTINA, 279 MILES NNW OF BUENOS AIRES.
THAT'S A FAIR QUESTION, MISTER BALLESTEROS, AND IT DESERVES AN ANSWER.
AS YOU SEE, I'VE GOT TWO CASES HERE...
...ONE CASE HAS TEN MILLION DOLLARS INSIDE OF IT.
AMERICAN DOLLARS. UNMARKED. OUT OF SEQUENCE.
THE OTHER CASE HOLDS SIX POUNDS OF SEMTEX, ATTACHED TO A RECEIVER, IN COMMUNICATION WITH THE DEAD-MAN SWITCH YOU SEE HERE IN MY HAND.
IT IS ARMED, I ASSURE YOU. ANYTHING HAPPENS TO ME...

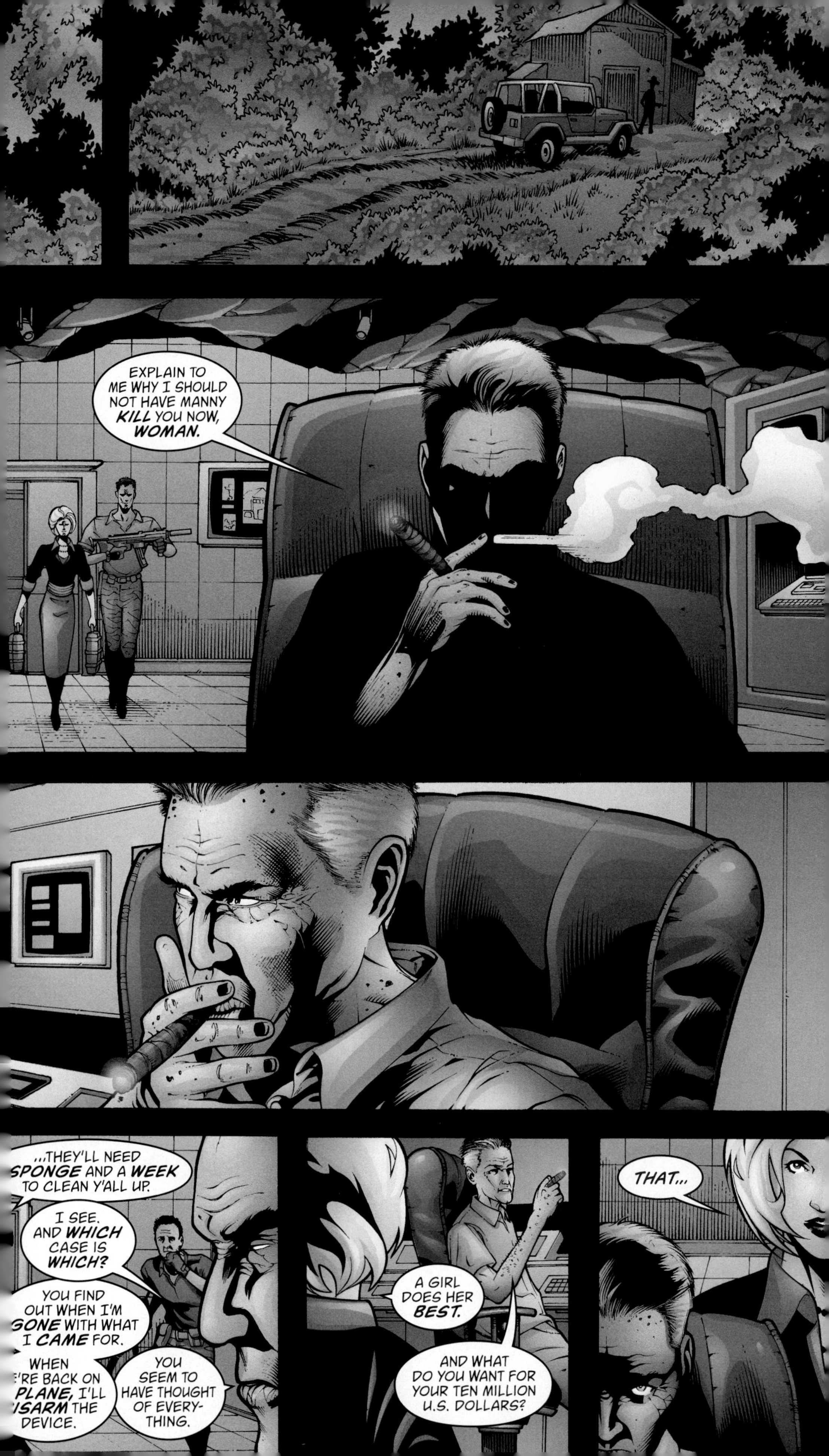

EXPLAIN TO ME WHY I SHOULD NOT HAVE MANNY KILL YOU NOW, WOMAN.
...THEY'LL NEED SPONGE AND A WEEK TO CLEAN Y'ALL UP.
I SEE. AND WHICH CASE IS WHICH?
YOU FIND OUT WHEN I'M GONE WITH WHAT I CAME FOR.
WHEN 'RE BACK ON PLANE, I'LL ISARM THE DEVICE.
YOU SEEM TO HAVE THOUGHT OF EVERY-THING.
A GIRL DOES HER BEST.
AND WHAT DO YOU WANT FOR YOUR TEN MILLION U.S. DOLLARS?
THAT...

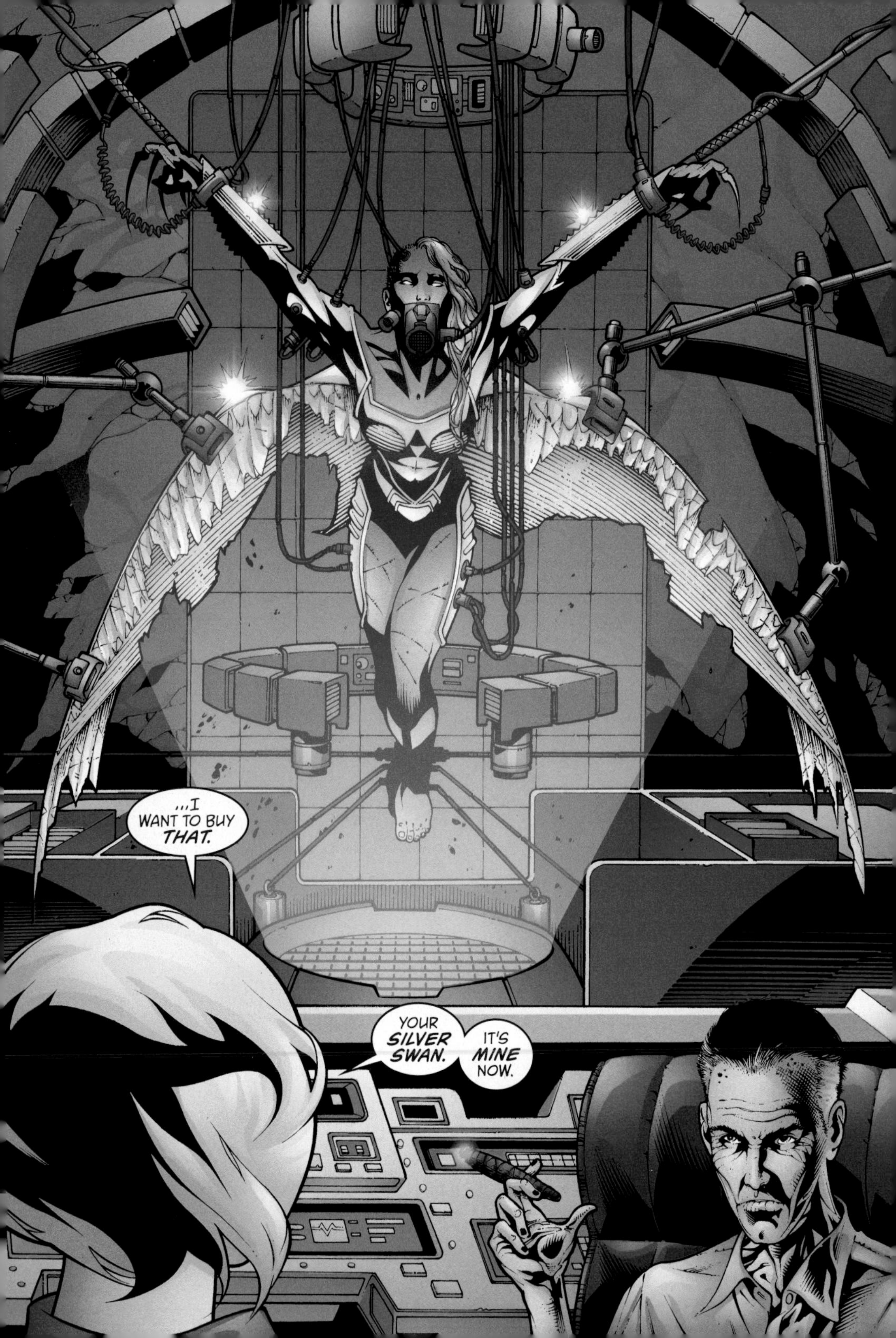
...I WANT TO BUY THAT.
YOUR SILVER SWAN.
IT'S MINE NOW.

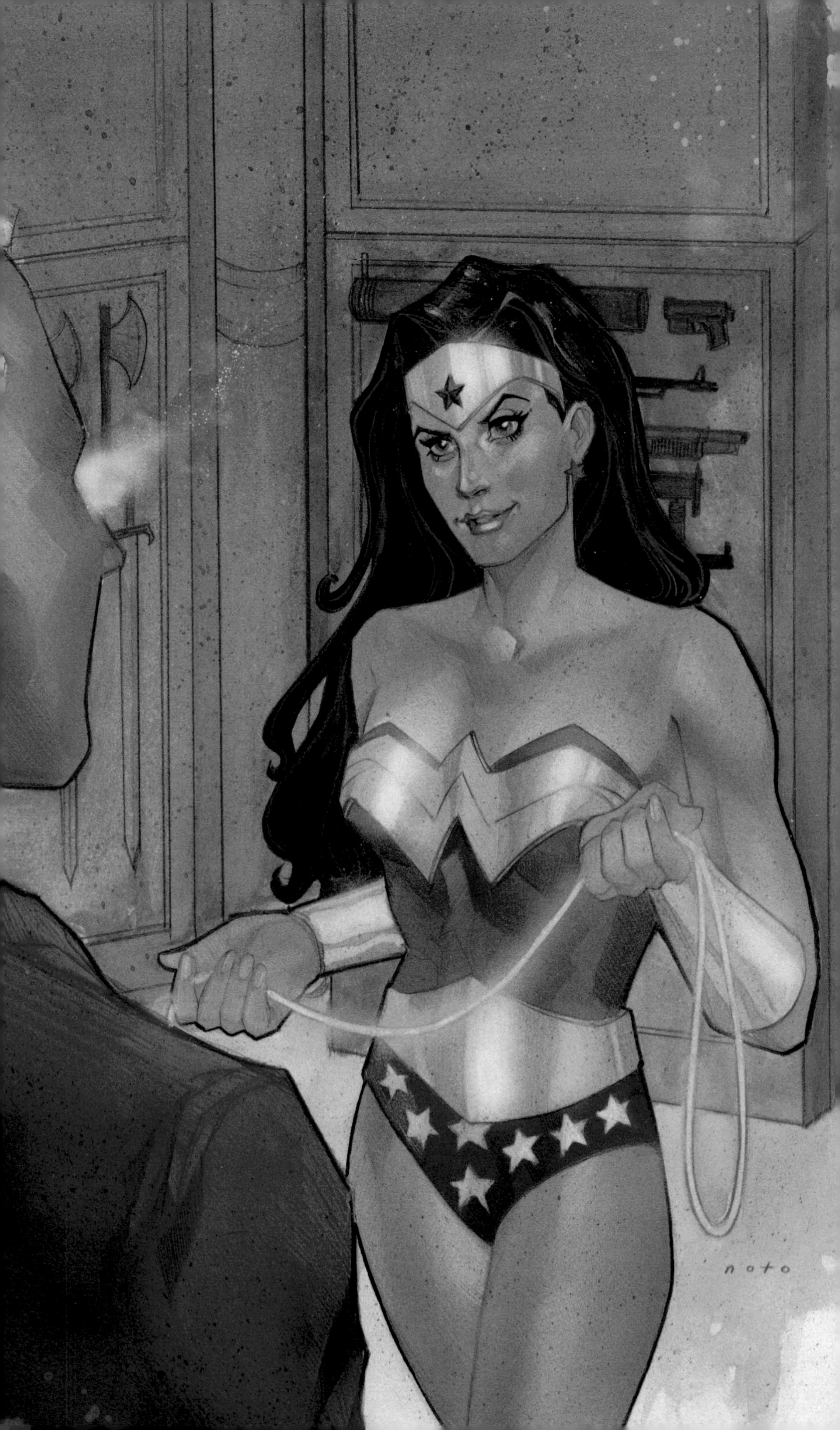
noto

"DOWN TO EARTH: PART FOUR"

Drew Johnson – *pencils*
Ray Snyder – *inks*
Richard Horie, Tanya Horie - *colors*
Phil Noto – *cover art*

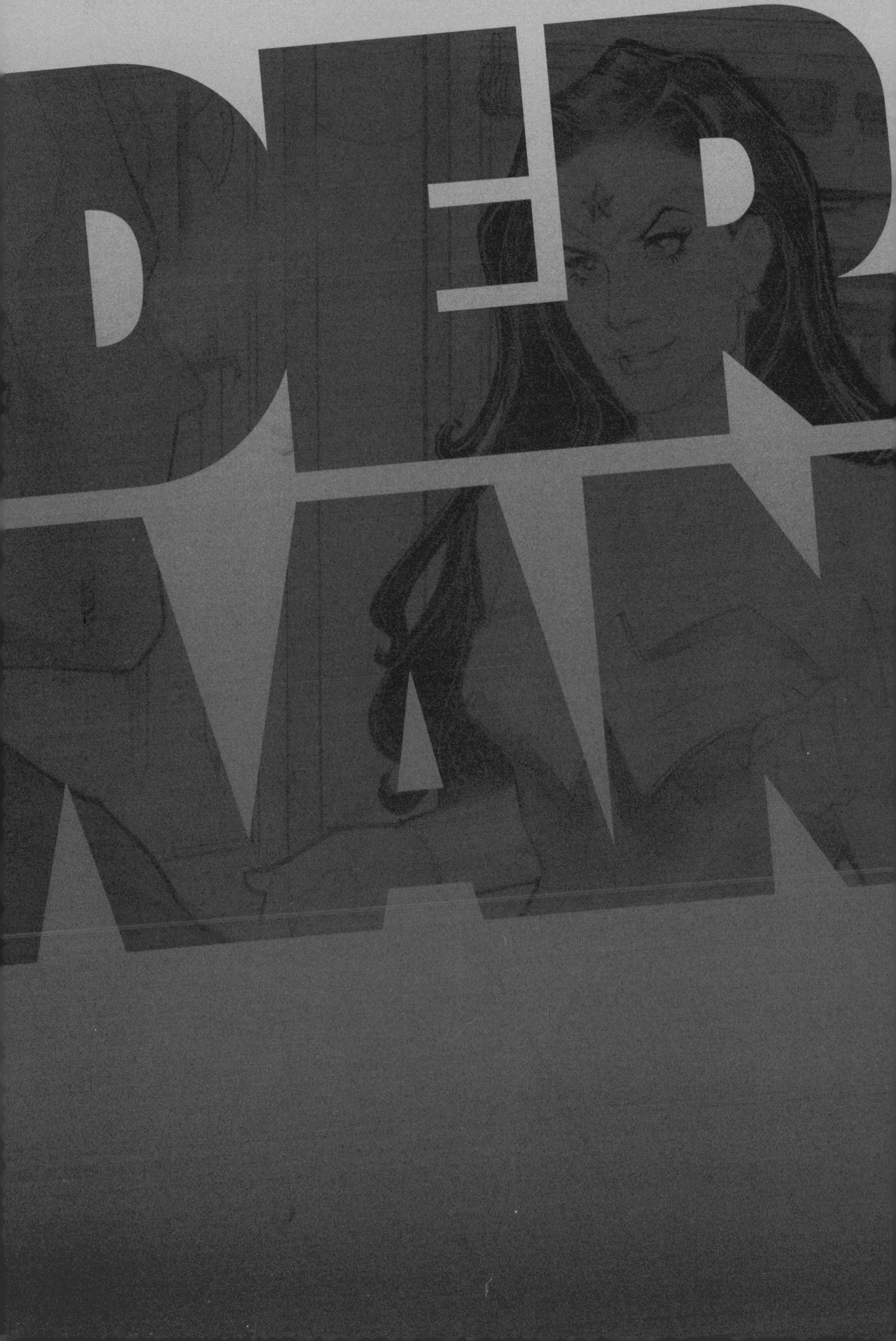

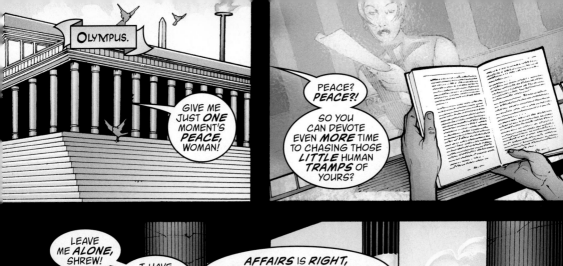

OLYMPUS.

GIVE ME JUST **ONE** MOMENT'S **PEACE**, WOMAN!

PEACE? **PEACE?!**

SO YOU CAN DEVOTE EVEN **MORE** TIME TO CHASING THOSE **LITTLE** HUMAN **TRAMPS** OF YOURS?

LEAVE ME **ALONE**, SHREW!

I HAVE **AFFAIRS** TO **ATTEND** TO!

AFFAIRS IS **RIGHT**, MY **BROTHER-HUSBAND!** MAYBE THERE'S SOMEONE YOU'D CARE TO **VISIT** AS A **SWAN?**

I SWEAR, HERA, YOU **PURSUE** THAT AT YOUR **PERIL!** LEDA WAS **THOUSANDS** OF YEARS AGO, LET IT **BE!**

AH, BUT THAT LITTLE **TART** FROM HALKIDIKI, THAT WAS ONLY **YESTERDAY**, WASN'T IT? AND THERE YOU WERE, DOING YOUR **BIRD** IMPRESSION ALL OVER **AGAIN!**

SHE CALLED OUT IN PRAYER TO **ME**, YOU KNOW HOW **RARE** THAT IS THESE DAYS!

I WAS ONLY **ANSWER**-ING A MORTAL SUMMONS--

REALLY, **DEAR** HUSBAND, DEAR **BROTHER**, IT'S **BEEN** THREE THOUSAND **YEARS!**

PERHAPS IT'S TIME YOU TRIED ON A **NEW** ANIMAL, MY **WANDERING-EYED MATE....**

...A **SWINE**, FOR INSTANCE!

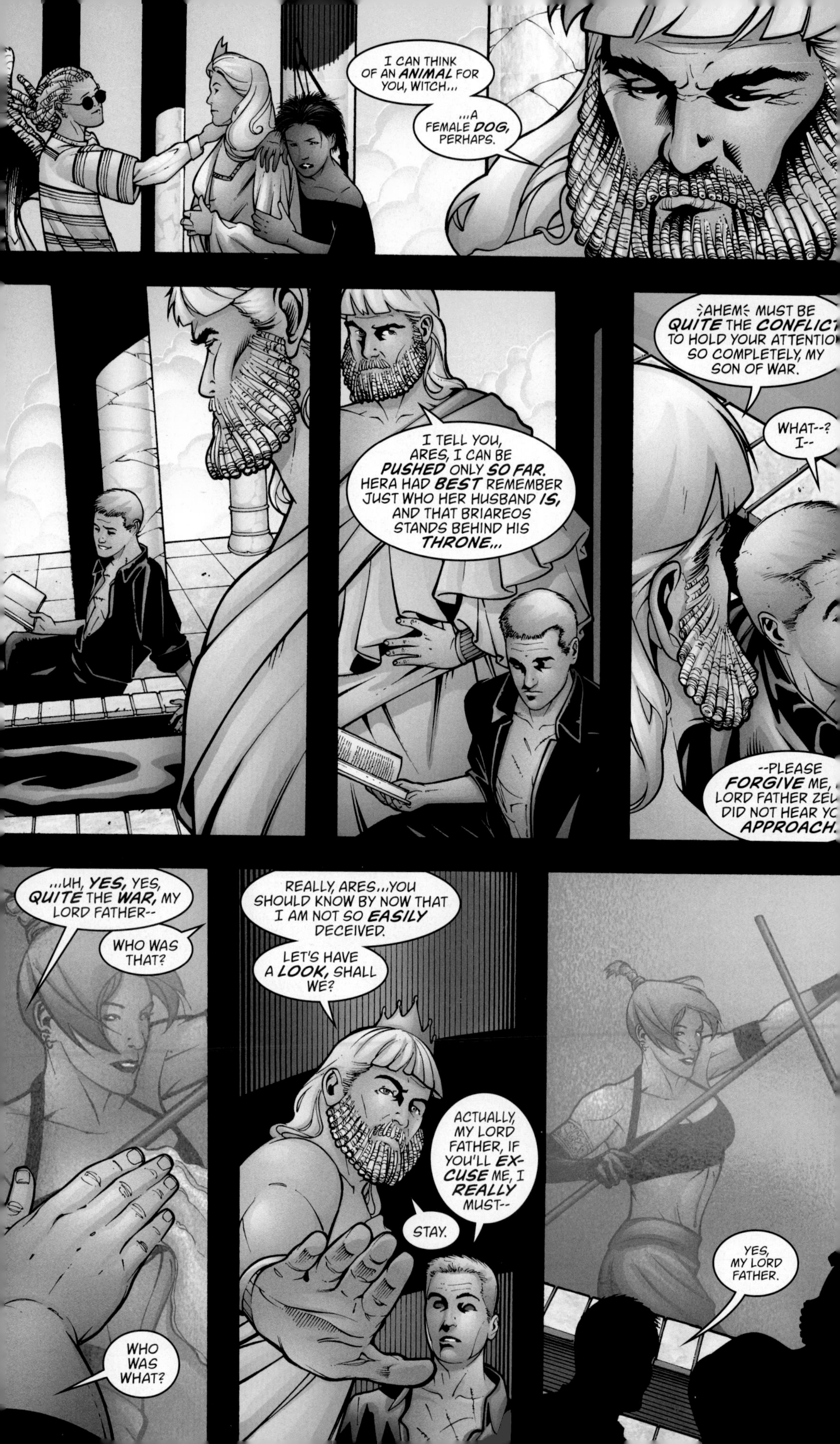
I CAN THINK OF AN ANIMAL FOR YOU, WITCH...
...A FEMALE DOG, PERHAPS.
I TELL YOU, ARES, I CAN BE PUSHED ONLY SO FAR. HERA HAD BEST REMEMBER JUST WHO HER HUSBAND IS, AND THAT BRIAREOS STANDS BEHIND HIS THRONE...
AHEM MUST BE QUITE THE CONFLICT TO HOLD YOUR ATTENTION SO COMPLETELY, MY SON OF WAR.
WHAT--? I--
--PLEASE FORGIVE ME, LORD FATHER ZEU DID NOT HEAR YO APPROACH.
...UH, YES, YES, QUITE THE WAR, MY LORD FATHER--
WHO WAS THAT?
WHO WAS WHAT?
REALLY, ARES...YOU SHOULD KNOW BY NOW THAT I AM NOT SO EASILY DECEIVED.
LET'S HAVE A LOOK, SHALL WE?
ACTUALLY, MY LORD FATHER, IF YOU'LL EXCUSE ME, I REALLY MUST--
STAY.
YES, MY LORD FATHER.

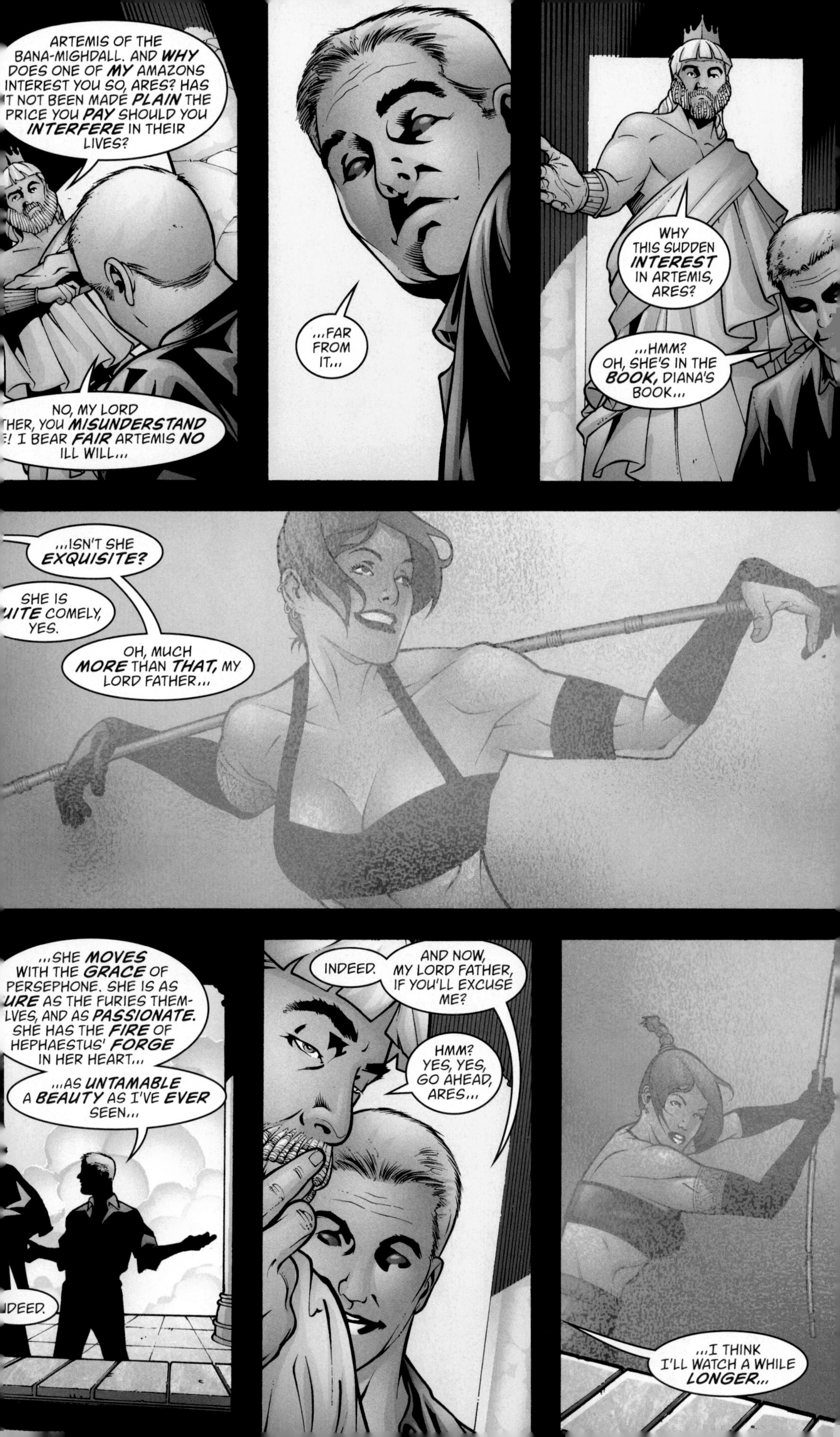

ARTEMIS OF THE BANA-MIGHDALL. AND WHY DOES ONE OF MY AMAZONS INTEREST YOU SO, ARES? HAS IT NOT BEEN MADE PLAIN THE PRICE YOU PAY SHOULD YOU INTERFERE IN THEIR LIVES?
NO, MY LORD FATHER, YOU MISUNDERSTAND ME! I BEAR FAIR ARTEMIS NO ILL WILL...
...FAR FROM IT...
WHY THIS SUDDEN INTEREST IN ARTEMIS, ARES?
...HMM? OH, SHE'S IN THE BOOK, DIANA'S BOOK...
...ISN'T SHE EXQUISITE?
SHE IS QUITE COMELY, YES.
OH, MUCH MORE THAN THAT, MY LORD FATHER...
...SHE MOVES WITH THE GRACE OF PERSEPHONE. SHE IS AS PURE AS THE FURIES THEMSELVES, AND AS PASSIONATE. SHE HAS THE FIRE OF HEPHAESTUS' FORGE IN HER HEART...
...AS UNTAMABLE A BEAUTY AS I'VE EVER SEEN...
INDEED.
INDEED.
AND NOW, MY LORD FATHER, IF YOU'LL EXCUSE ME?
HMM? YES, YES, GO AHEAD, ARES...
...I THINK I'LL WATCH A WHILE LONGER...

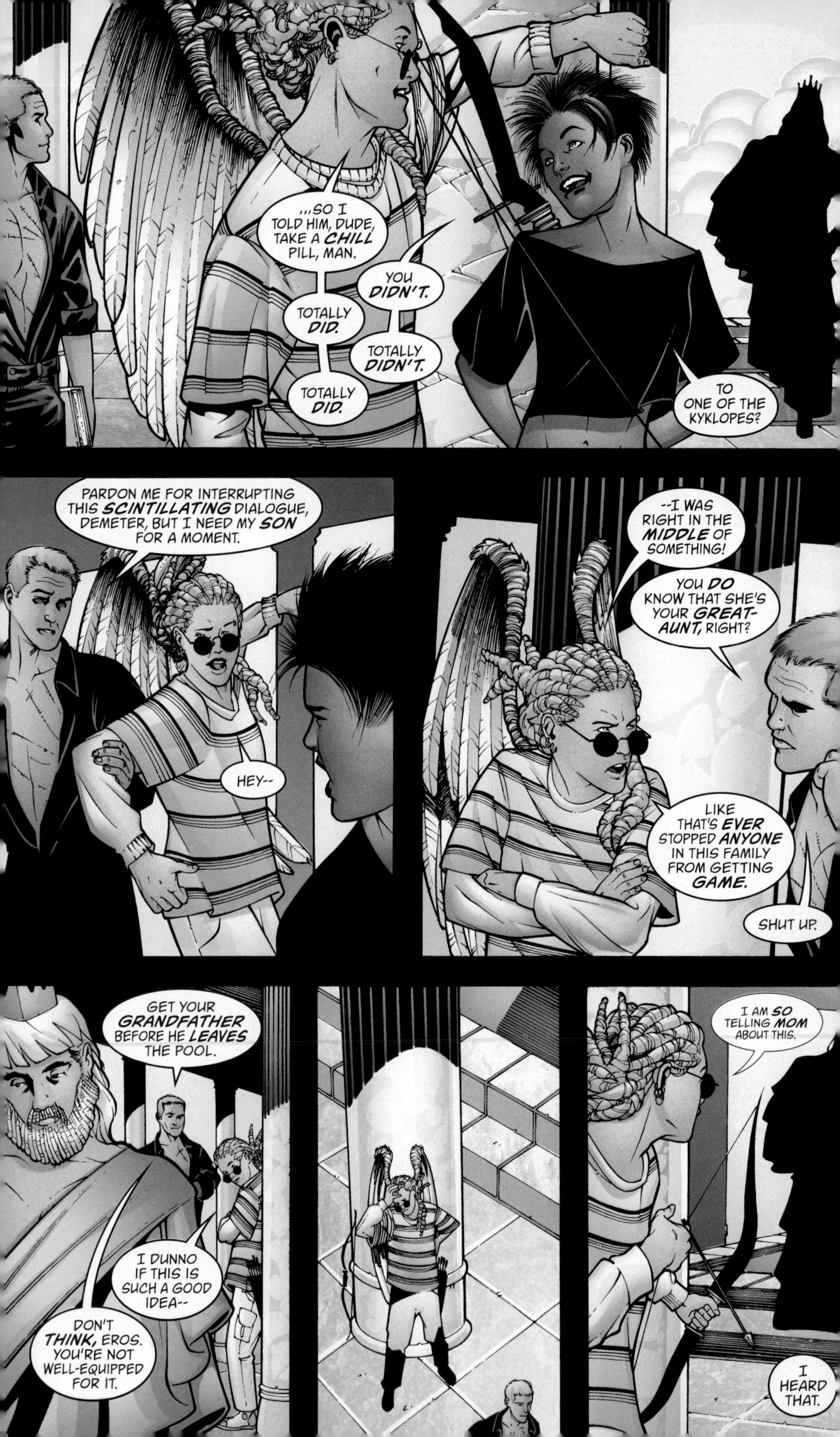
...SO I TOLD HIM, DUDE, TAKE A CHILL PILL, MAN.
YOU DIDN'T.
TOTALLY DID.
TOTALLY DIDN'T.
TOTALLY DID.
TO ONE OF THE KYKLOPES?
PARDON ME FOR INTERRUPTING THIS SCINTILLATING DIALOGUE, DEMETER, BUT I NEED MY SON FOR A MOMENT.
HEY--
--I WAS RIGHT IN THE MIDDLE OF SOMETHING!
YOU DO KNOW THAT SHE'S YOUR GREAT-AUNT, RIGHT?
LIKE THAT'S EVER STOPPED ANYONE IN THIS FAMILY FROM GETTING GAME.
SHUT UP.
GET YOUR GRANDFATHER BEFORE HE LEAVES THE POOL.
I DUNNO IF THIS IS SUCH A GOOD IDEA--
DON'T THINK, EROS. YOU'RE NOT WELL-EQUIPPED FOR IT.
I AM SO TELLING MOM ABOUT THIS.
I HEARD THAT.

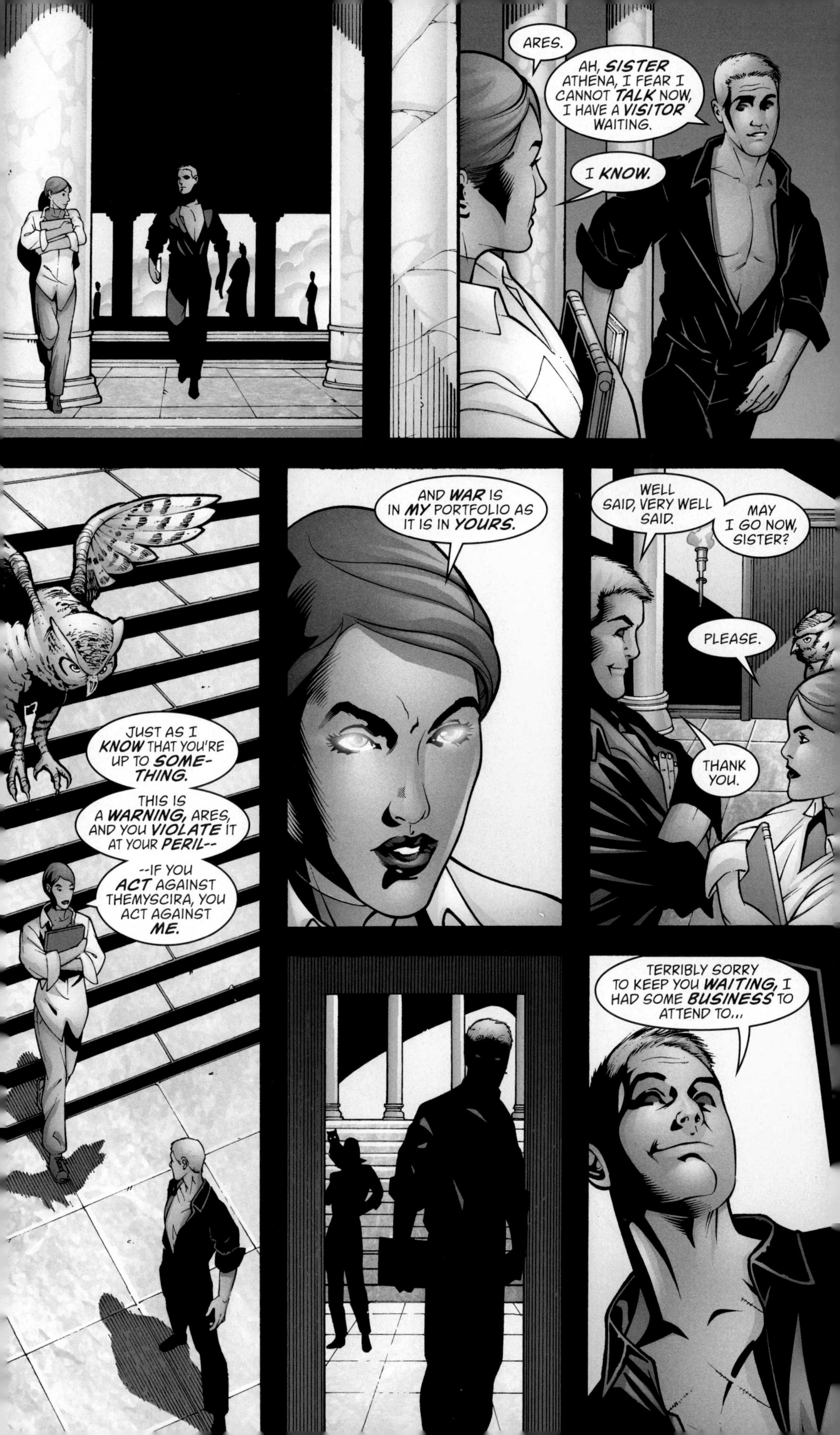
ARES.
AH, SISTER ATHENA, I FEAR I CANNOT TALK NOW, I HAVE A VISITOR WAITING.
I KNOW.
JUST AS I KNOW THAT YOU'RE UP TO SOME-THING.
THIS IS A WARNING, ARES, AND YOU VIOLATE IT AT YOUR PERIL--
--IF YOU ACT AGAINST THEMYSCIRA, YOU ACT AGAINST ME.
AND WAR IS IN MY PORTFOLIO AS IT IS IN YOURS.
WELL SAID, VERY WELL SAID.
MAY I GO NOW, SISTER?
PLEASE.
THANK YOU.
TERRIBLY SORRY TO KEEP YOU WAITING, I HAD SOME BUSINESS TO ATTEND TO...

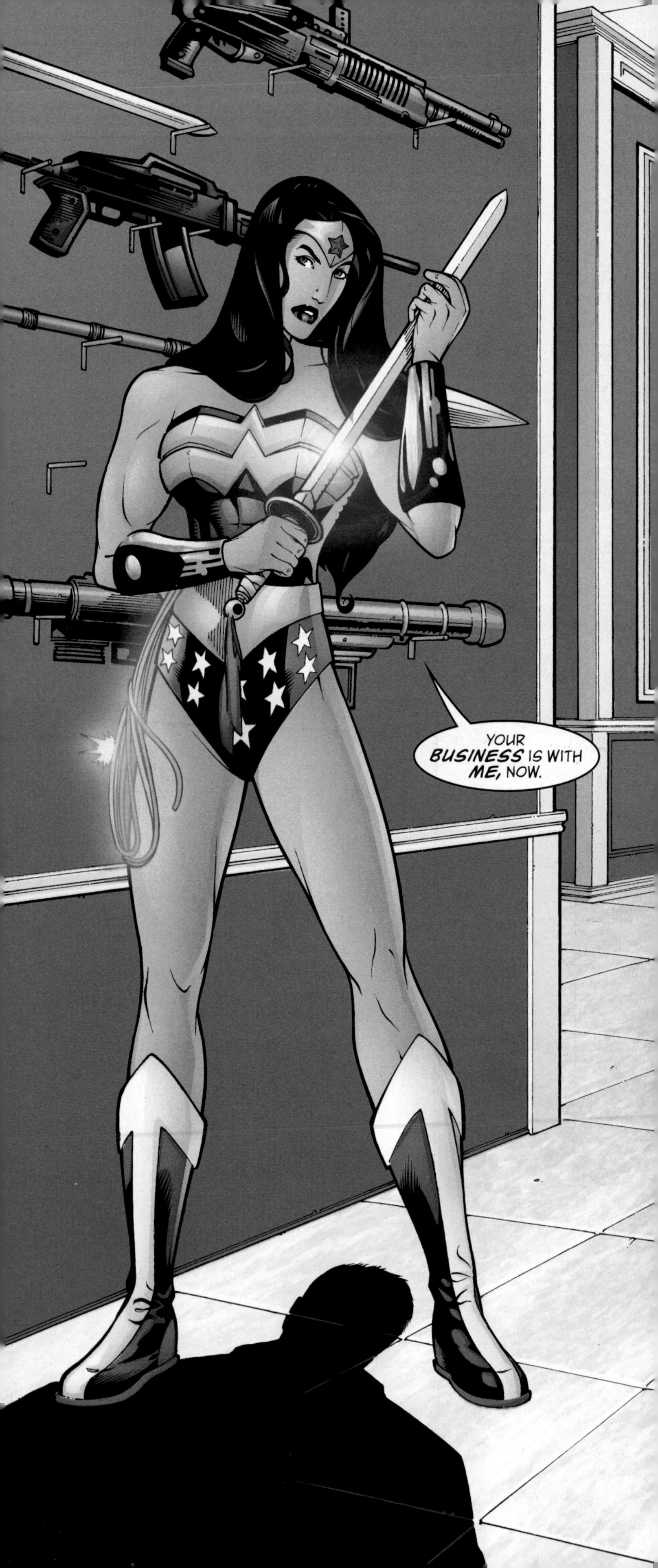
YOUR BUSINESS IS WITH ME, NOW.

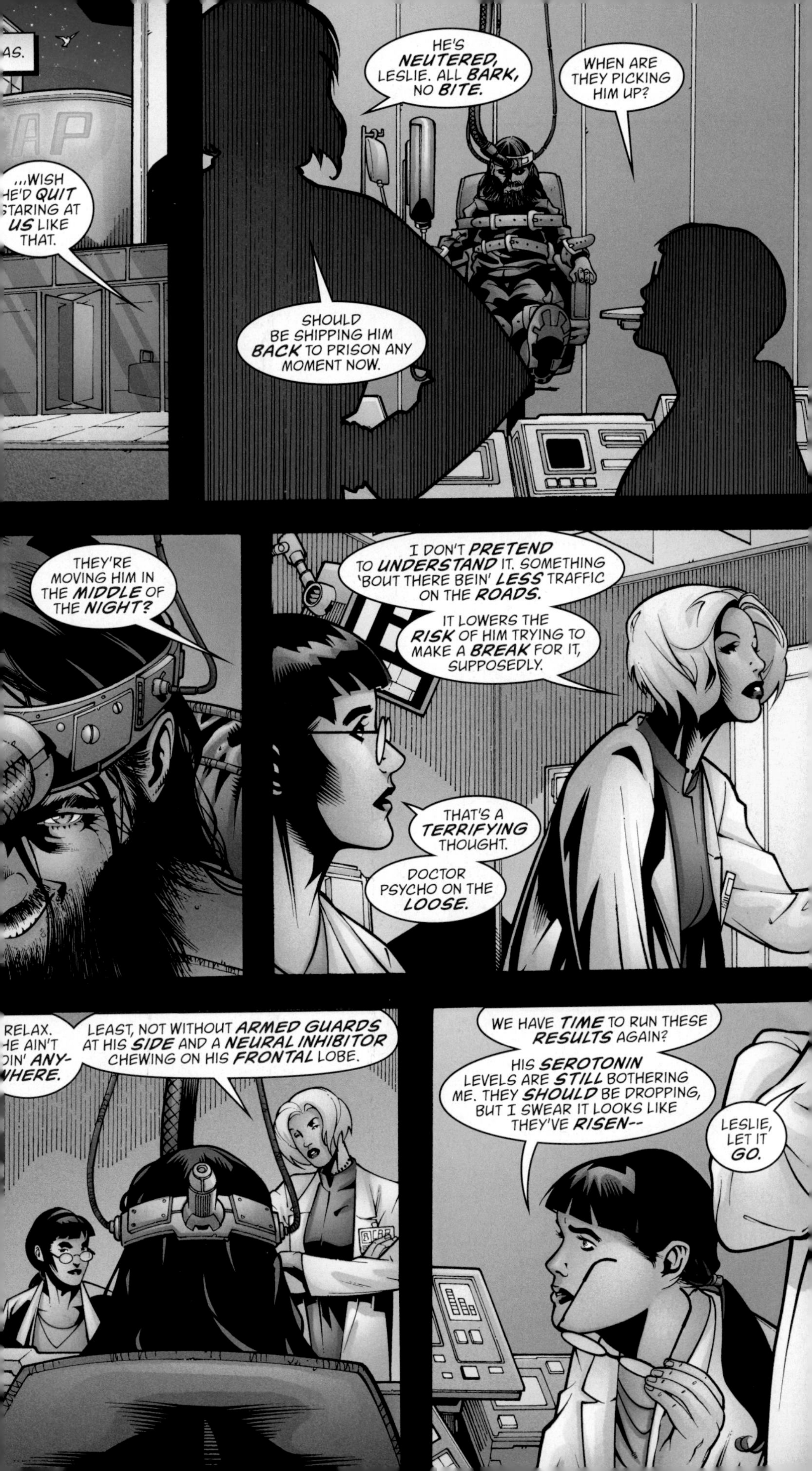
AS.
...WISH HE'D QUIT STARING AT US LIKE THAT.
HE'S NEUTERED, LESLIE. ALL BARK, NO BITE.
WHEN ARE THEY PICKING HIM UP?
SHOULD BE SHIPPING HIM BACK TO PRISON ANY MOMENT NOW.
THEY'RE MOVING HIM IN THE MIDDLE OF THE NIGHT?
I DON'T PRETEND TO UNDERSTAND IT. SOMETHING 'BOUT THERE BEIN' LESS TRAFFIC ON THE ROADS.
IT LOWERS THE RISK OF HIM TRYING TO MAKE A BREAK FOR IT, SUPPOSEDLY.
THAT'S A TERRIFYING THOUGHT.
DOCTOR PSYCHO ON THE LOOSE.
RELAX. HE AIN'T GOIN' ANYWHERE.
LEAST, NOT WITHOUT ARMED GUARDS AT HIS SIDE AND A NEURAL INHIBITOR CHEWING ON HIS FRONTAL LOBE.
WE HAVE TIME TO RUN THESE RESULTS AGAIN?
HIS SEROTONIN LEVELS ARE STILL BOTHERING ME. THEY SHOULD BE DROPPING, BUT I SWEAR IT LOOKS LIKE THEY'VE RISEN--
LESLIE, LET IT GO.

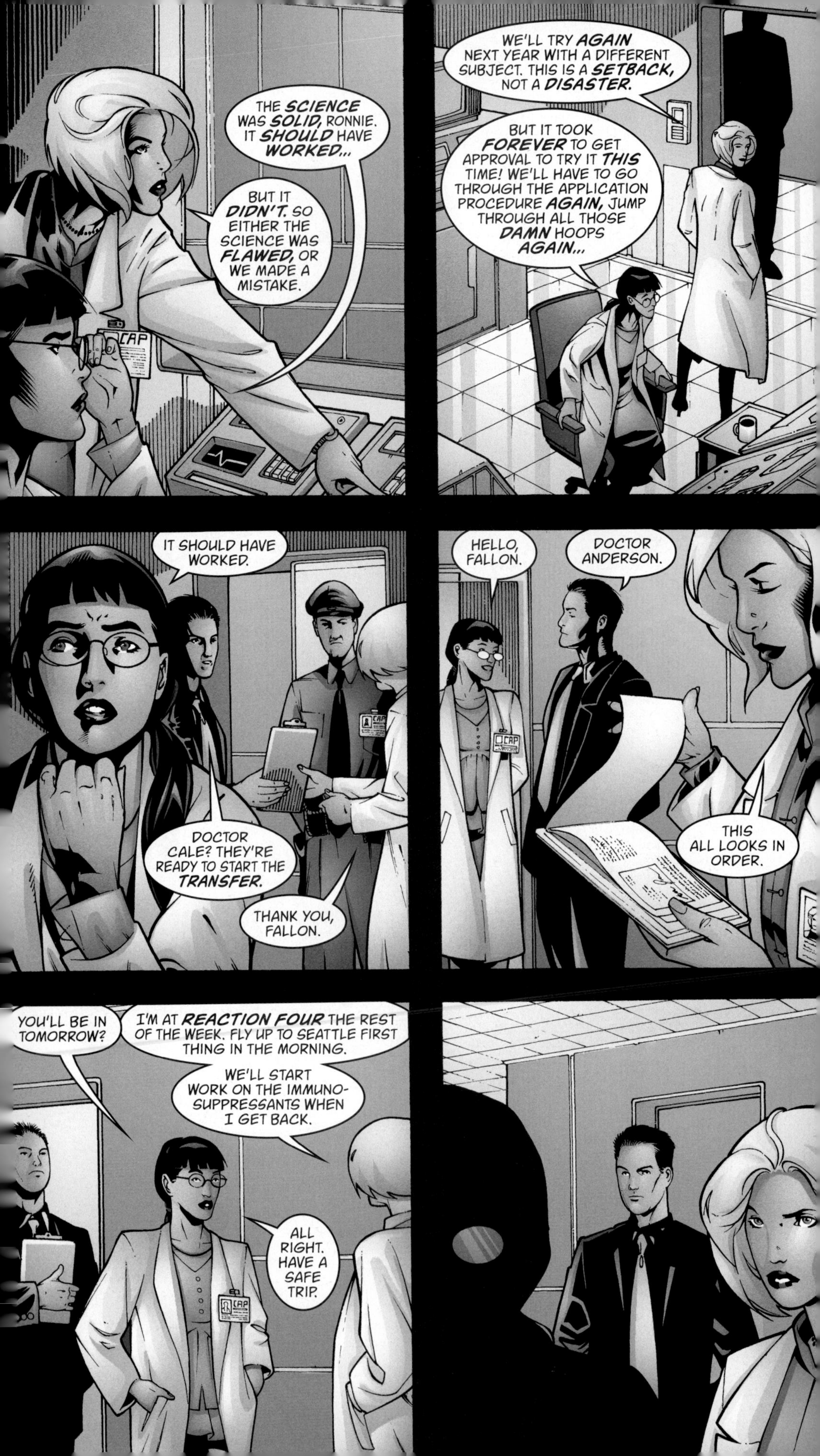
THE SCIENCE WAS SOLID, RONNIE. IT SHOULD HAVE WORKED...
BUT IT DIDN'T. SO EITHER THE SCIENCE WAS FLAWED, OR WE MADE A MISTAKE.
WE'LL TRY AGAIN NEXT YEAR WITH A DIFFERENT SUBJECT. THIS IS A SETBACK, NOT A DISASTER.
BUT IT TOOK FOREVER TO GET APPROVAL TO TRY IT THIS TIME! WE'LL HAVE TO GO THROUGH THE APPLICATION PROCEDURE AGAIN, JUMP THROUGH ALL THOSE DAMN HOOPS AGAIN...
IT SHOULD HAVE WORKED.
DOCTOR CALE? THEY'RE READY TO START THE TRANSFER.
THANK YOU, FALLON.
HELLO, FALLON.
DOCTOR ANDERSON.
THIS ALL LOOKS IN ORDER.
YOU'LL BE IN TOMORROW?
I'M AT REACTION FOUR THE REST OF THE WEEK. FLY UP TO SEATTLE FIRST THING IN THE MORNING.
WE'LL START WORK ON THE IMMUNO-SUPPRESSANTS WHEN I GET BACK.
ALL RIGHT. HAVE A SAFE TRIP.

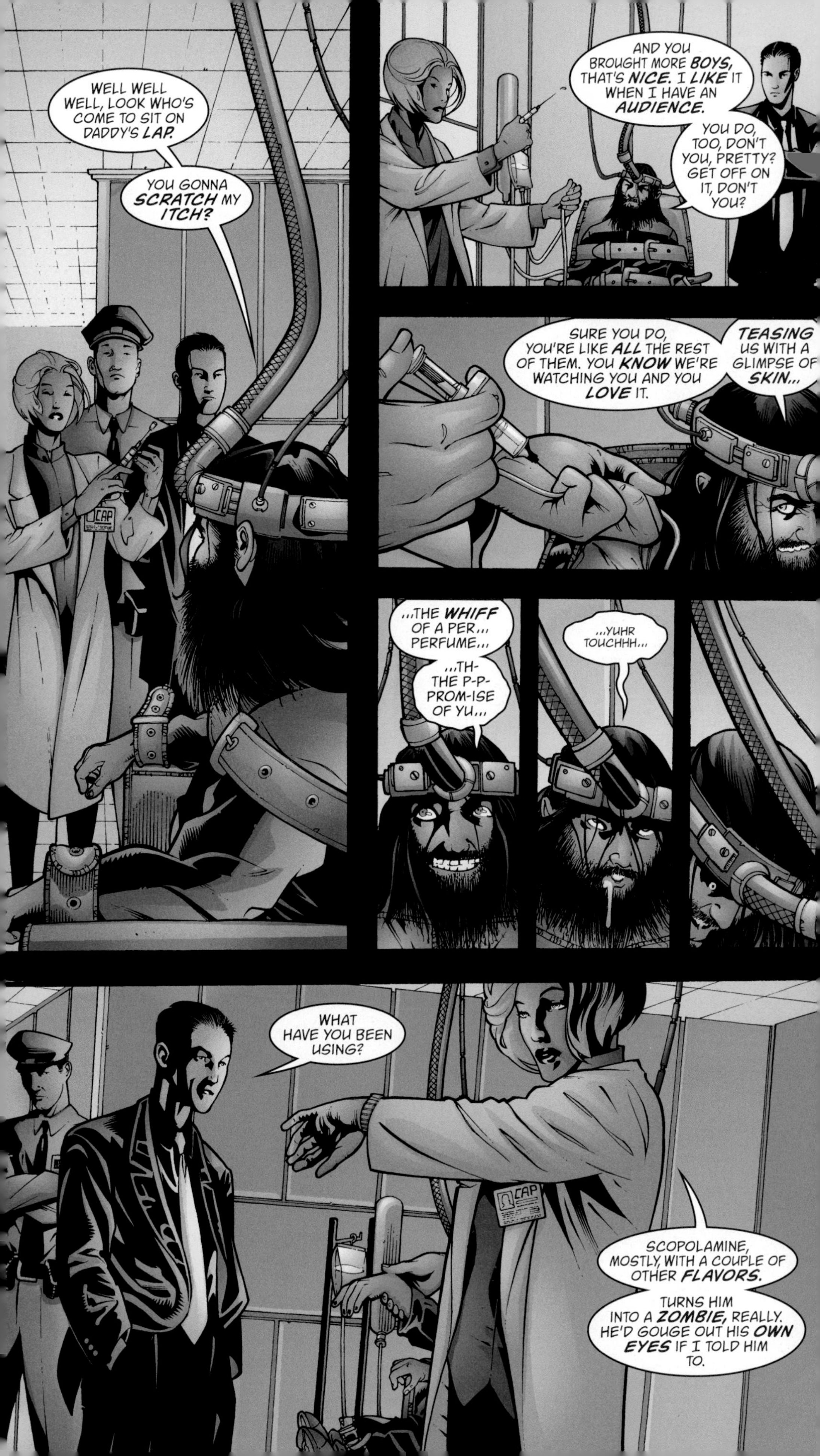

WELL WELL WELL, LOOK WHO'S COME TO SIT ON DADDY'S **LAP.**
YOU GONNA **SCRATCH** MY **ITCH?**
AND YOU BROUGHT MORE **BOYS,** THAT'S **NICE.** I **LIKE** IT WHEN I HAVE AN **AUDIENCE.**
YOU DO, TOO, DON'T YOU, PRETTY? GET OFF ON IT, DON'T YOU?
SURE YOU DO, YOU'RE LIKE **ALL** THE REST OF THEM. YOU **KNOW** WE'RE WATCHING YOU AND YOU **LOVE** IT.
TEASING US WITH A GLIMPSE OF **SKIN...**
...THE **WHIFF** OF A PER... PERFUME...
...TH-THE P-P-PROM-ISE OF YU...
...YUHR TOUCHHH...
WHAT HAVE YOU BEEN USING?
SCOPOLAMINE, MOSTLY, WITH A COUPLE OF OTHER **FLAVORS.**
TURNS HIM INTO A **ZOMBIE,** REALLY. HE'D GOUGE OUT HIS **OWN EYES** IF I TOLD HIM TO.

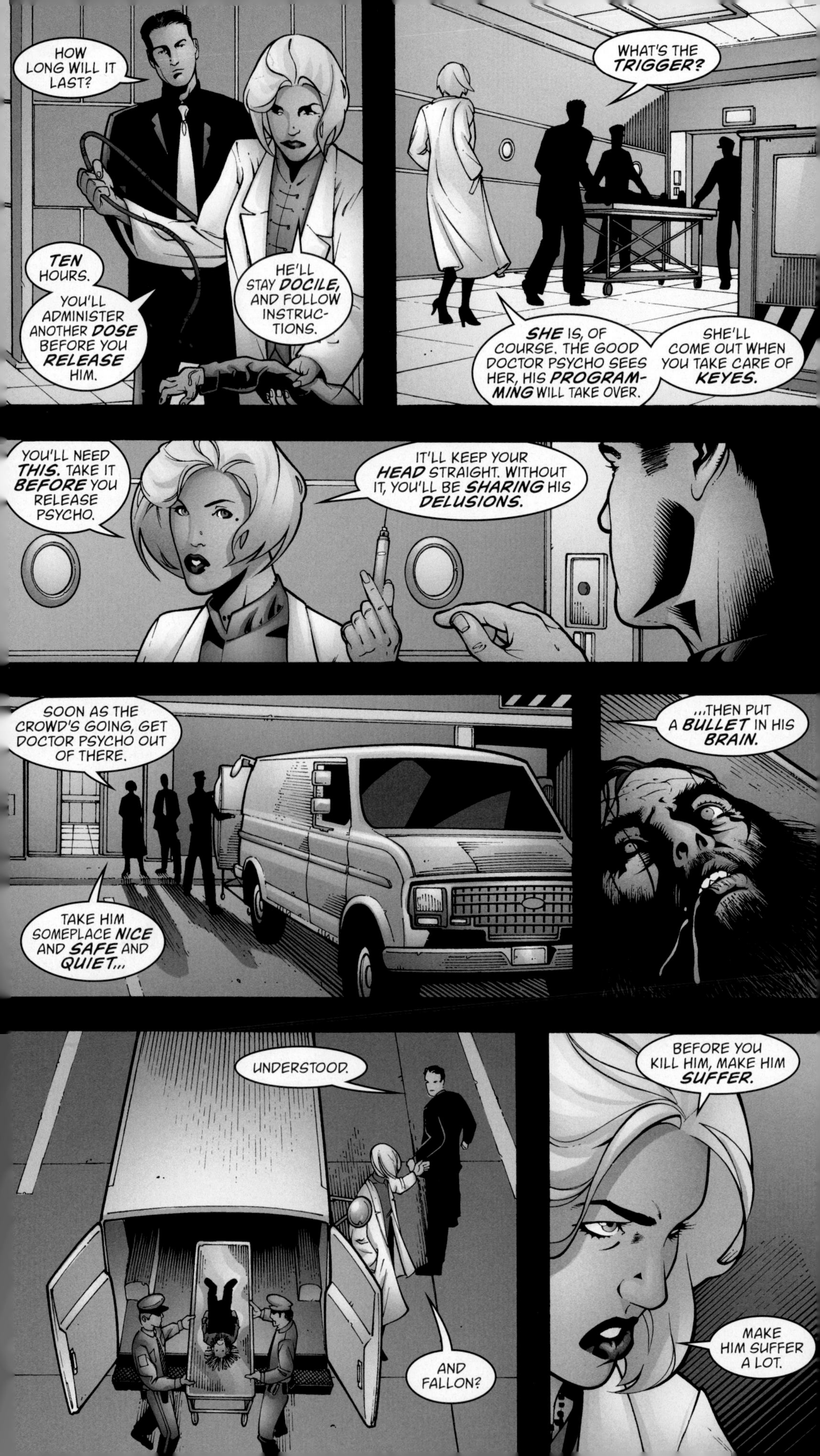
HOW LONG WILL IT LAST?
TEN HOURS.
YOU'LL ADMINISTER ANOTHER DOSE BEFORE YOU RELEASE HIM.
HE'LL STAY DOCILE, AND FOLLOW INSTRUC-TIONS.
WHAT'S THE TRIGGER?
SHE IS, OF COURSE. THE GOOD DOCTOR PSYCHO SEES HER, HIS PROGRAM-MING WILL TAKE OVER.
SHE'LL COME OUT WHEN YOU TAKE CARE OF KEYES.
YOU'LL NEED THIS. TAKE IT BEFORE YOU RELEASE PSYCHO.
IT'LL KEEP YOUR HEAD STRAIGHT. WITHOUT IT, YOU'LL BE SHARING HIS DELUSIONS.
SOON AS THE CROWD'S GOING, GET DOCTOR PSYCHO OUT OF THERE.
TAKE HIM SOMEPLACE NICE AND SAFE AND QUIET...
...THEN PUT A BULLET IN HIS BRAIN.
UNDERSTOOD.
AND FALLON?
BEFORE YOU KILL HIM, MAKE HIM SUFFER.
MAKE HIM SUFFER A LOT.

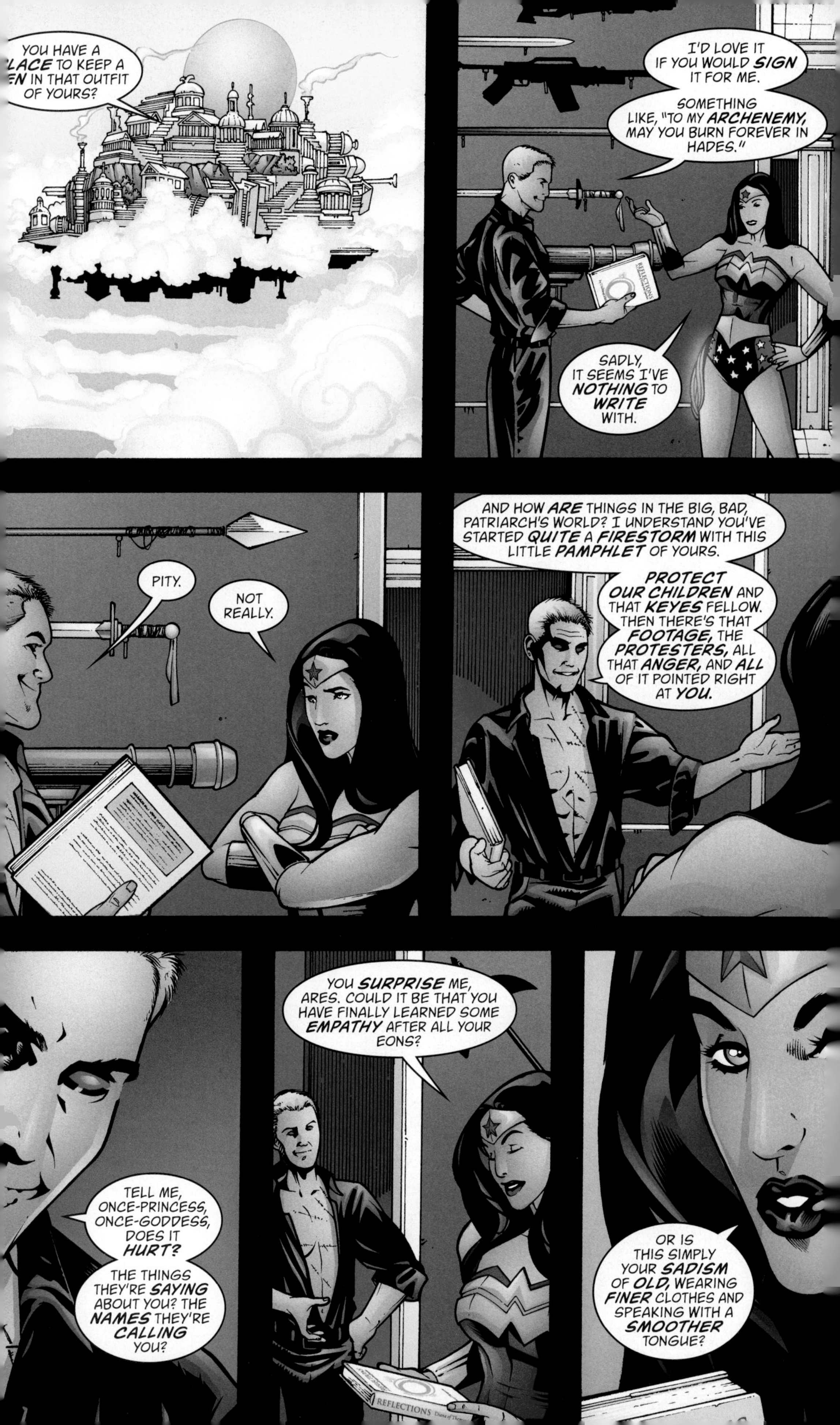

YOU HAVE A LACE TO KEEP A EN IN THAT OUTFIT OF YOURS?
I'D LOVE IT IF YOU WOULD SIGN IT FOR ME.
SOMETHING LIKE, "TO MY ARCHENEMY, MAY YOU BURN FOREVER IN HADES."
SADLY, IT SEEMS I'VE NOTHING TO WRITE WITH.
REFLECTIONS
PITY.
NOT REALLY.
AND HOW ARE THINGS IN THE BIG, BAD, PATRIARCH'S WORLD? I UNDERSTAND YOU'VE STARTED QUITE A FIRESTORM WITH THIS LITTLE PAMPHLET OF YOURS.
PROTECT OUR CHILDREN AND THAT KEYES FELLOW. THEN THERE'S THAT FOOTAGE, THE PROTESTERS, ALL THAT ANGER, AND ALL OF IT POINTED RIGHT AT YOU.
TELL ME, ONCE-PRINCESS, ONCE-GODDESS, DOES IT HURT?
THE THINGS THEY'RE SAYING ABOUT YOU? THE NAMES THEY'RE CALLING YOU?
YOU SURPRISE ME, ARES. COULD IT BE THAT YOU HAVE FINALLY LEARNED SOME EMPATHY AFTER ALL YOUR EONS?
OR IS THIS SIMPLY YOUR SADISM OF OLD, WEARING FINER CLOTHES AND SPEAKING WITH A SMOOTHER TONGUE?
REFLECTIONS

THIS IS ABOUT MY *VISIT* TO THEMYSCIRA, I ASSUME?

IT *WAS* AT FIRST, BUT NO LONGER.

LISTENING TO YOU NOW, I AM FORCED TO WONDER JUST HOW *MUCH* OF A *HAND* YOU HAVE BEEN PLAYING IN MY *AFFAIRS* OF LATE.

IF THE *DISAPPEARANCE* OF VANESSA KAPATELIS IS *YOUR* DOING, FOR INSTAN

KAPATELIS HOLDS *NO* INTEREST FOR ME, AND I GAVE UP *MEDDLING* WITH *MORTALS* LONG AGO.

YOU VISITED IO, YOU WENT TO THEMYSCIRA.

THE *AMAZONS* ARE *HARDLY* MORTALS, DIANA.

YOU MADE A *VOW.* YOU SWORE TO *LEAVE* THE EARTH *ALONE--*

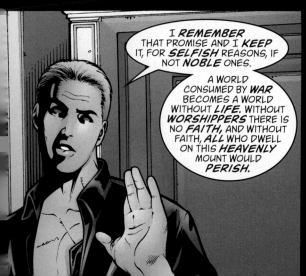

I *REMEMBER* THAT PROMISE AND I *KEEP* IT, FOR *SELFISH* REASONS, IF NOT *NOBLE* ONES.

A WORLD CONSUMED BY *WAR* BECOMES A WORLD WITHOUT *LIFE.* WITHOUT *WORSHIPPERS* THERE IS NO *FAITH,* AND WITHOUT FAITH, *ALL* WHO DWELL ON THIS *HEAVENLY* MOUNT WOULD *PERISH.*

I REMEMBER THE *LESSON* YOU TAUGHT ME *WELL,* AS YOU CAN SEE.

THE OLD *DOG* OF *WAR* HAS LEARNED *NEW* TRICKS, OR HAVEN'T YOU NOTICED?

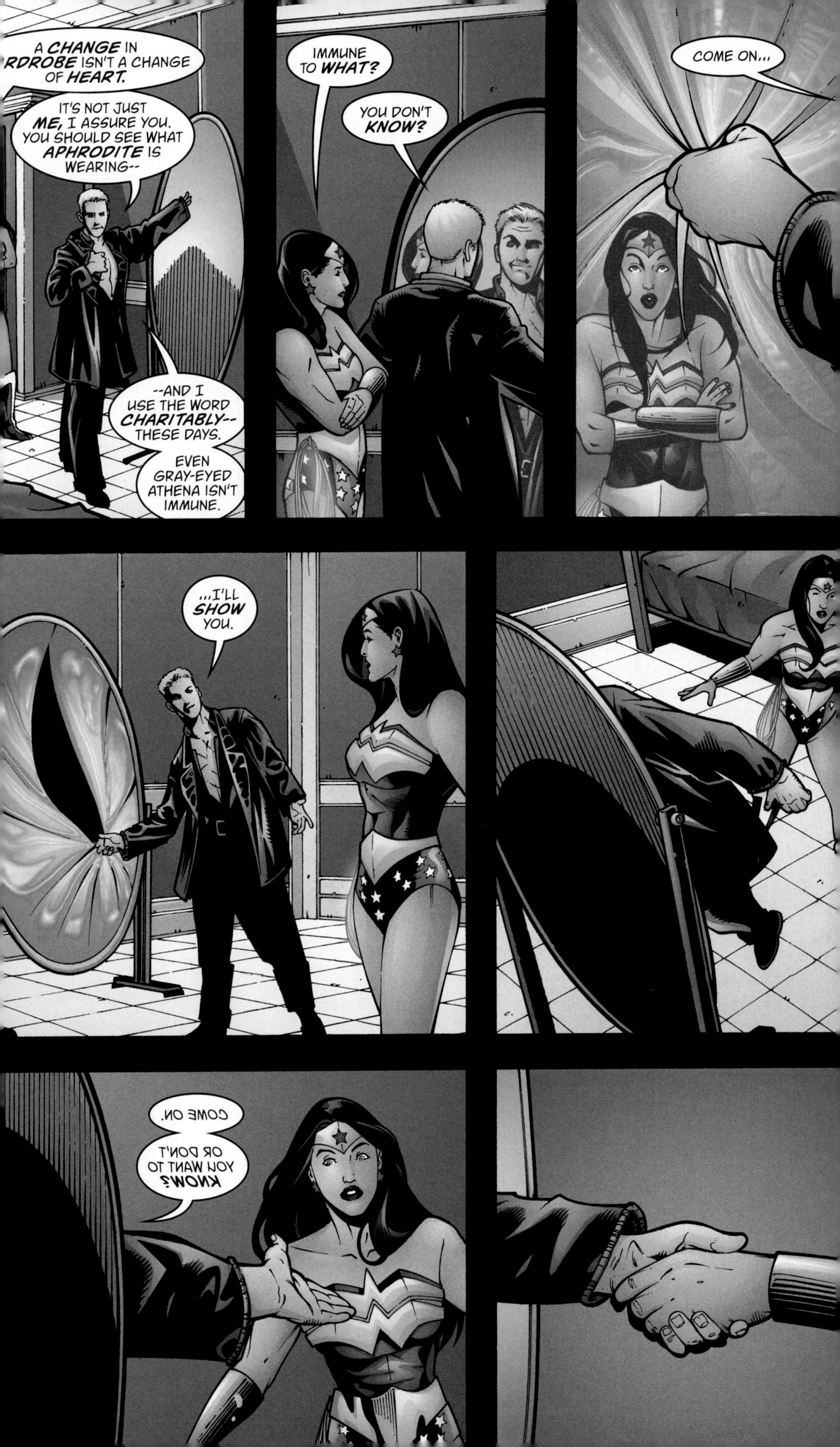
A CHANGE IN RDROBE ISN'T A CHANGE OF HEART.
IT'S NOT JUST ME, I ASSURE YOU. YOU SHOULD SEE WHAT APHRODITE IS WEARING--
--AND I USE THE WORD CHARITABLY-- THESE DAYS.
EVEN GRAY-EYED ATHENA ISN'T IMMUNE.
IMMUNE TO WHAT?
YOU DON'T KNOW?
COME ON...
...I'LL SHOW YOU.
COME ON.
OR DON'T YOU WANT TO KNOW?

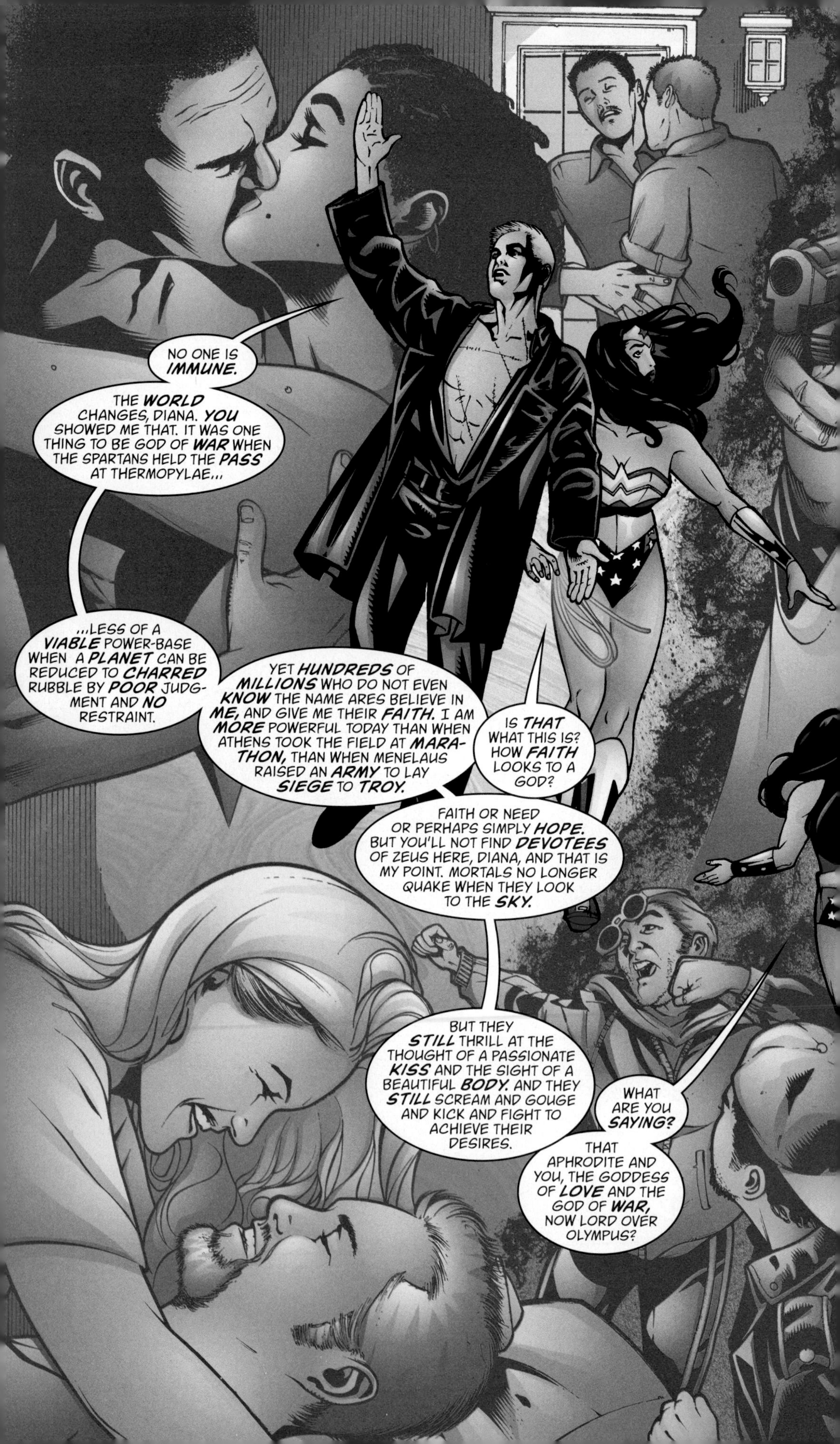
NO ONE IS IMMUNE.
THE WORLD CHANGES, DIANA. YOU SHOWED ME THAT. IT WAS ONE THING TO BE GOD OF WAR WHEN THE SPARTANS HELD THE PASS AT THERMOPYLAE...
...LESS OF A VIABLE POWER-BASE WHEN A PLANET CAN BE REDUCED TO CHARRED RUBBLE BY POOR JUDGMENT AND NO RESTRAINT.
YET HUNDREDS OF MILLIONS WHO DO NOT EVEN KNOW THE NAME ARES BELIEVE IN ME, AND GIVE ME THEIR FAITH. I AM MORE POWERFUL TODAY THAN WHEN ATHENS TOOK THE FIELD AT MARATHON, THAN WHEN MENELAUS RAISED AN ARMY TO LAY SIEGE TO TROY.
IS THAT WHAT THIS IS? HOW FAITH LOOKS TO A GOD?
FAITH OR NEED OR PERHAPS SIMPLY HOPE. BUT YOU'LL NOT FIND DEVOTEES OF ZEUS HERE, DIANA, AND THAT IS MY POINT. MORTALS NO LONGER QUAKE WHEN THEY LOOK TO THE SKY.
BUT THEY STILL THRILL AT THE THOUGHT OF A PASSIONATE KISS AND THE SIGHT OF A BEAUTIFUL BODY. AND THEY STILL SCREAM AND GOUGE AND KICK AND FIGHT TO ACHIEVE THEIR DESIRES.
WHAT ARE YOU SAYING?
THAT APHRODITE AND YOU, THE GODDESS OF LOVE AND THE GOD OF WAR, NOW LORD OVER OLYMPUS?

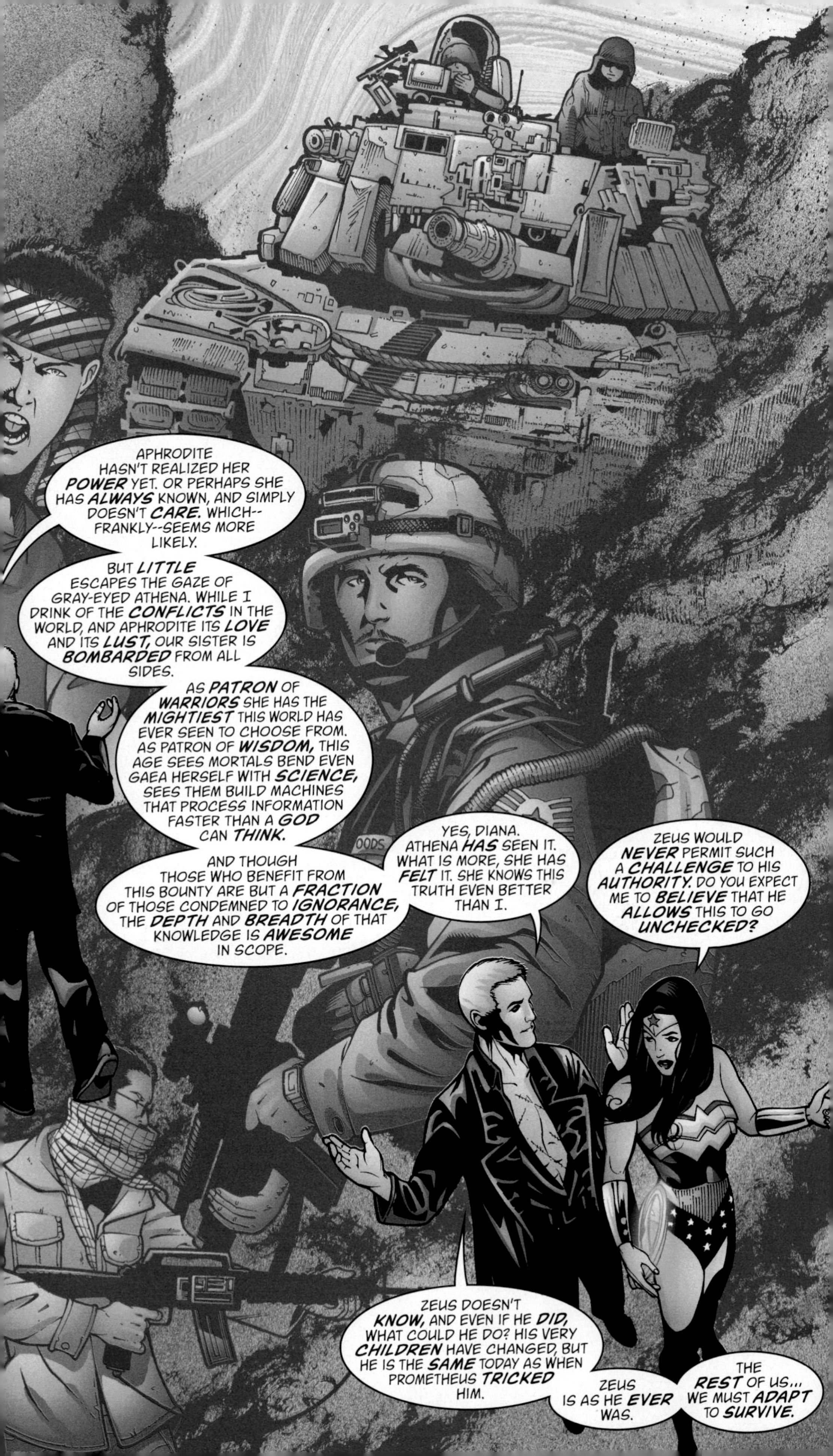
APHRODITE HASN'T REALIZED HER POWER YET. OR PERHAPS SHE HAS ALWAYS KNOWN, AND SIMPLY DOESN'T CARE. WHICH--FRANKLY--SEEMS MORE LIKELY.
BUT LITTLE ESCAPES THE GAZE OF GRAY-EYED ATHENA. WHILE I DRINK OF THE CONFLICTS IN THE WORLD, AND APHRODITE ITS LOVE AND ITS LUST, OUR SISTER IS BOMBARDED FROM ALL SIDES.
AS PATRON OF WARRIORS SHE HAS THE MIGHTIEST THIS WORLD HAS EVER SEEN TO CHOOSE FROM. AS PATRON OF WISDOM, THIS AGE SEES MORTALS BEND EVEN GAEA HERSELF WITH SCIENCE, SEES THEM BUILD MACHINES THAT PROCESS INFORMATION FASTER THAN A GOD CAN THINK.
AND THOUGH THOSE WHO BENEFIT FROM THIS BOUNTY ARE BUT A FRACTION OF THOSE CONDEMNED TO IGNORANCE, THE DEPTH AND BREADTH OF THAT KNOWLEDGE IS AWESOME IN SCOPE.
YES, DIANA. ATHENA HAS SEEN IT. WHAT IS MORE, SHE HAS FELT IT. SHE KNOWS THIS TRUTH EVEN BETTER THAN I.
ZEUS WOULD NEVER PERMIT SUCH A CHALLENGE TO HIS AUTHORITY. DO YOU EXPECT ME TO BELIEVE THAT HE ALLOWS THIS TO GO UNCHECKED?
ZEUS DOESN'T KNOW, AND EVEN IF HE DID, WHAT COULD HE DO? HIS VERY CHILDREN HAVE CHANGED, BUT HE IS THE SAME TODAY AS WHEN PROMETHEUS TRICKED HIM.
ZEUS IS AS HE EVER WAS.
THE REST OF US... WE MUST ADAPT TO SURVIVE.

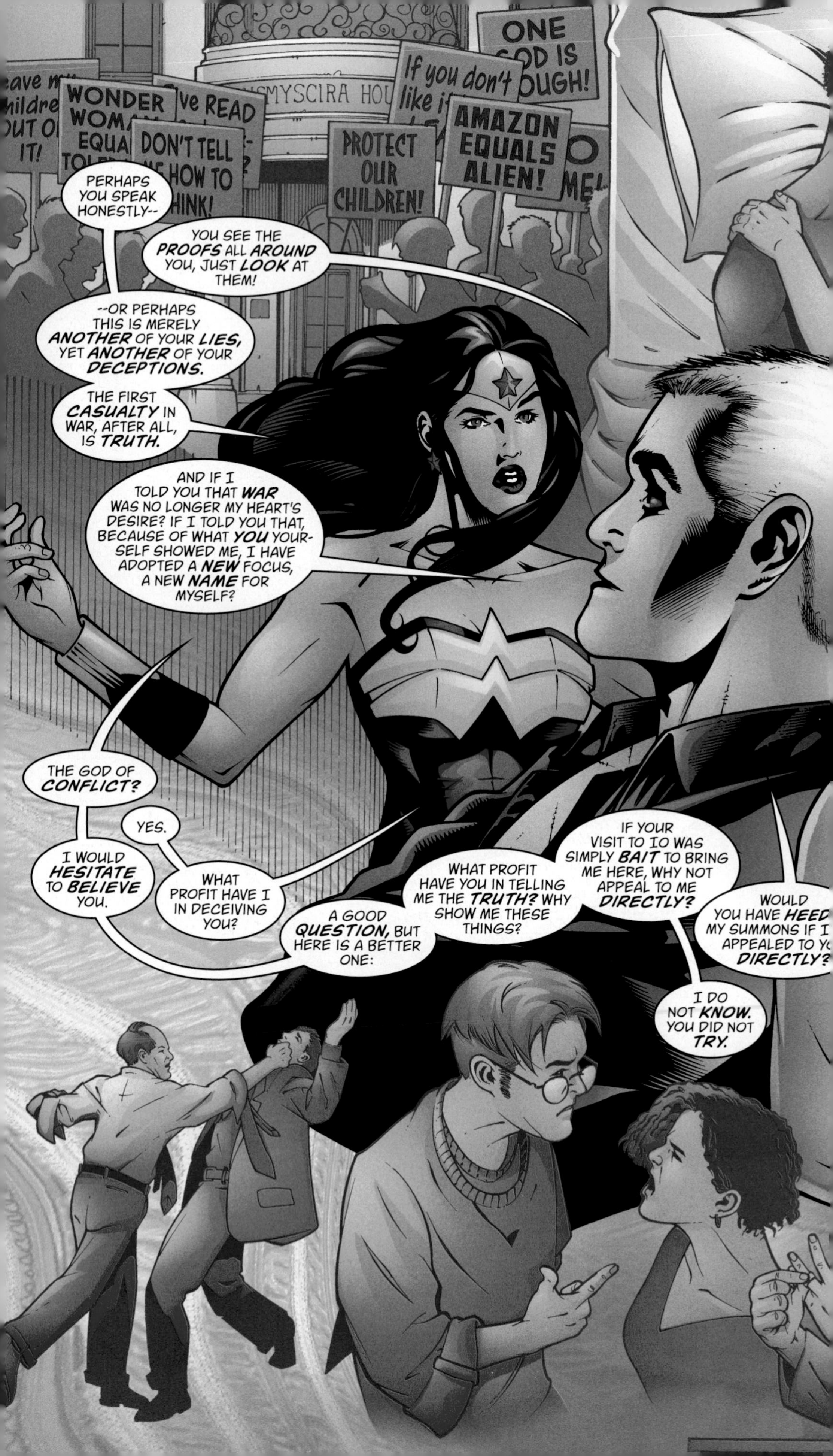
WONDER WOMAN EQUA
DON'T TELL ME HOW TO THINK!
PROTECT OUR CHILDREN!
If you don't like it
AMAZON EQUALS ALIEN!
ONE GOD IS ENOUGH!
PERHAPS YOU SPEAK HONESTLY--
YOU SEE THE PROOFS ALL AROUND YOU, JUST LOOK AT THEM!
--OR PERHAPS THIS IS MERELY ANOTHER OF YOUR LIES, YET ANOTHER OF YOUR DECEPTIONS.
THE FIRST CASUALTY IN WAR, AFTER ALL, IS TRUTH.
AND IF I TOLD YOU THAT WAR WAS NO LONGER MY HEART'S DESIRE? IF I TOLD YOU THAT, BECAUSE OF WHAT YOU YOURSELF SHOWED ME, I HAVE ADOPTED A NEW FOCUS, A NEW NAME FOR MYSELF?
THE GOD OF CONFLICT?
YES.
I WOULD HESITATE TO BELIEVE YOU.
WHAT PROFIT HAVE I IN DECEIVING YOU?
A GOOD QUESTION, BUT HERE IS A BETTER ONE:
WHAT PROFIT HAVE YOU IN TELLING ME THE TRUTH? WHY SHOW ME THESE THINGS?
IF YOUR VISIT TO IO WAS SIMPLY BAIT TO BRING ME HERE, WHY NOT APPEAL TO ME DIRECTLY?
I DO NOT KNOW. YOU DID NOT TRY.

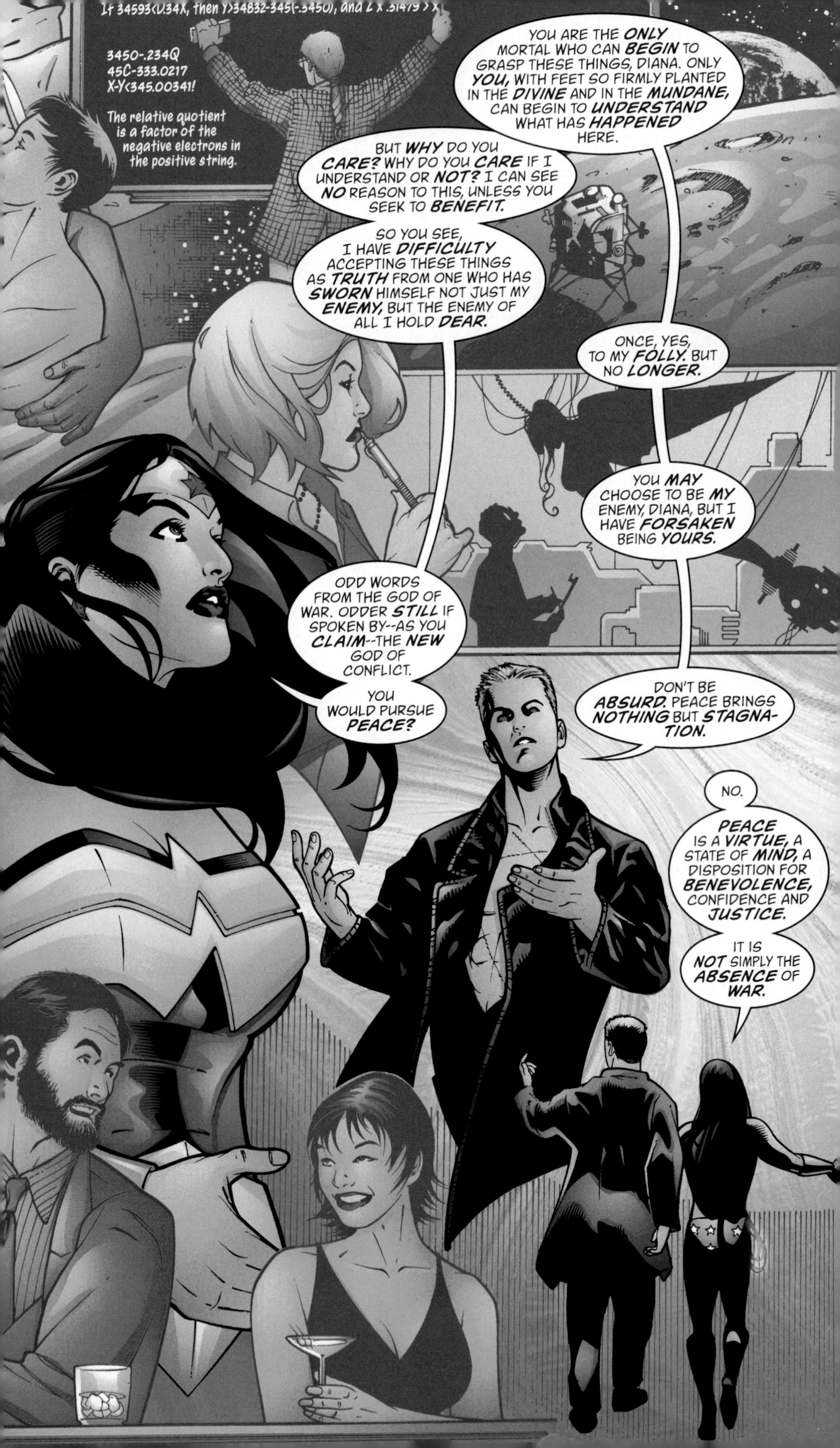
3450-.234Q
45C-333.0217
X-Y<345.00341!
The relative quotient is a factor of the negative electrons in the positive string.
YOU ARE THE ONLY MORTAL WHO CAN BEGIN TO GRASP THESE THINGS, DIANA. ONLY YOU, WITH FEET SO FIRMLY PLANTED IN THE DIVINE AND IN THE MUNDANE, CAN BEGIN TO UNDERSTAND WHAT HAS HAPPENED HERE.
BUT WHY DO YOU CARE? WHY DO YOU CARE IF I UNDERSTAND OR NOT? I CAN SEE NO REASON TO THIS, UNLESS YOU SEEK TO BENEFIT.
SO YOU SEE, I HAVE DIFFICULTY ACCEPTING THESE THINGS AS TRUTH FROM ONE WHO HAS SWORN HIMSELF NOT JUST MY ENEMY, BUT THE ENEMY OF ALL I HOLD DEAR.
ONCE, YES, TO MY FOLLY. BUT NO LONGER.
YOU MAY CHOOSE TO BE MY ENEMY, DIANA, BUT I HAVE FORSAKEN BEING YOURS.
ODD WORDS FROM THE GOD OF WAR. ODDER STILL IF SPOKEN BY--AS YOU CLAIM--THE NEW GOD OF CONFLICT.
YOU WOULD PURSUE PEACE?
DON'T BE ABSURD. PEACE BRINGS NOTHING BUT STAGNATION.
NO.
PEACE IS A VIRTUE, A STATE OF MIND, A DISPOSITION FOR BENEVOLENCE, CONFIDENCE AND JUSTICE.
IT IS NOT SIMPLY THE ABSENCE OF WAR.

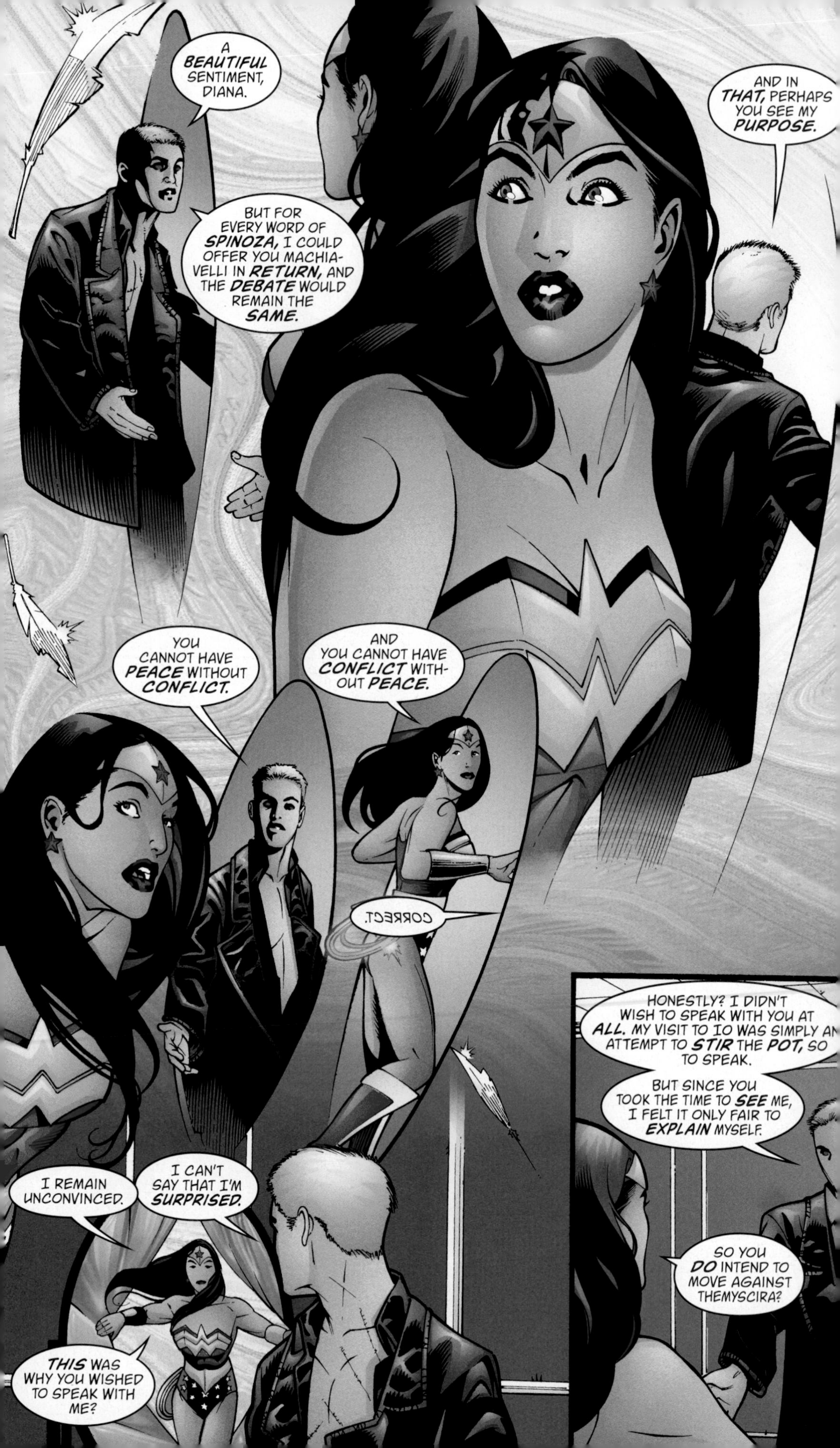
A BEAUTIFUL SENTIMENT, DIANA.
BUT FOR EVERY WORD OF SPINOZA, I COULD OFFER YOU MACHIAVELLI IN RETURN, AND THE DEBATE WOULD REMAIN THE SAME.
AND IN THAT, PERHAPS YOU SEE MY PURPOSE.
YOU CANNOT HAVE PEACE WITHOUT CONFLICT.
AND YOU CANNOT HAVE CONFLICT WITHOUT PEACE.
CORRECT.
I REMAIN UNCONVINCED.
I CAN'T SAY THAT I'M SURPRISED.
THIS WAS WHY YOU WISHED TO SPEAK WITH ME?
HONESTLY? I DIDN'T WISH TO SPEAK WITH YOU AT ALL. MY VISIT TO IO WAS SIMPLY AN ATTEMPT TO STIR THE POT, SO TO SPEAK.
BUT SINCE YOU TOOK THE TIME TO SEE ME, I FELT IT ONLY FAIR TO EXPLAIN MYSELF.
SO YOU DO INTEND TO MOVE AGAINST THEMYSCIRA?

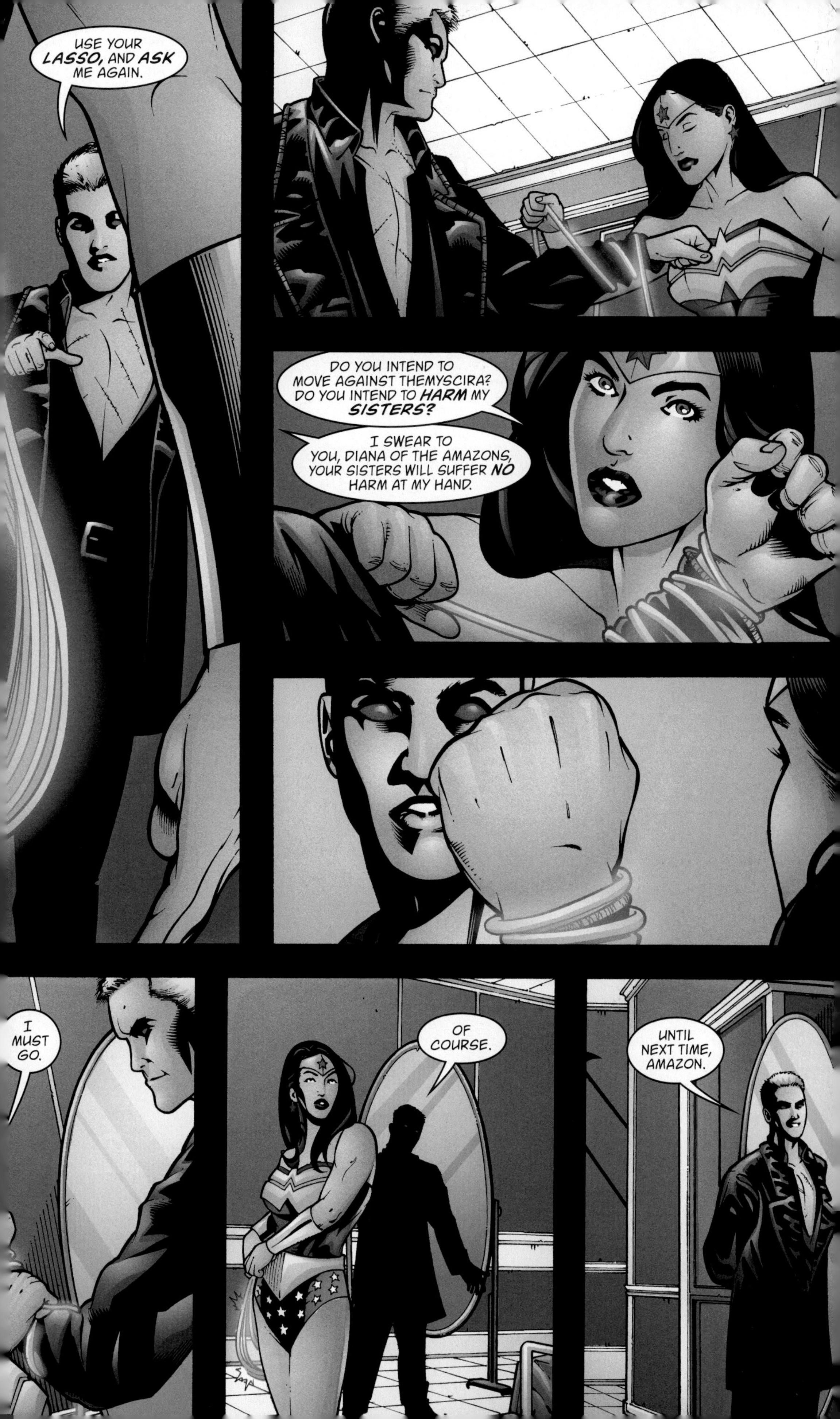
USE YOUR LASSO, AND ASK ME AGAIN.
DO YOU INTEND TO MOVE AGAINST THEMYSCIRA? DO YOU INTEND TO HARM MY SISTERS?
I SWEAR TO YOU, DIANA OF THE AMAZONS, YOUR SISTERS WILL SUFFER NO HARM AT MY HAND.
I MUST GO.
OF COURSE.
UNTIL NEXT TIME, AMAZON.

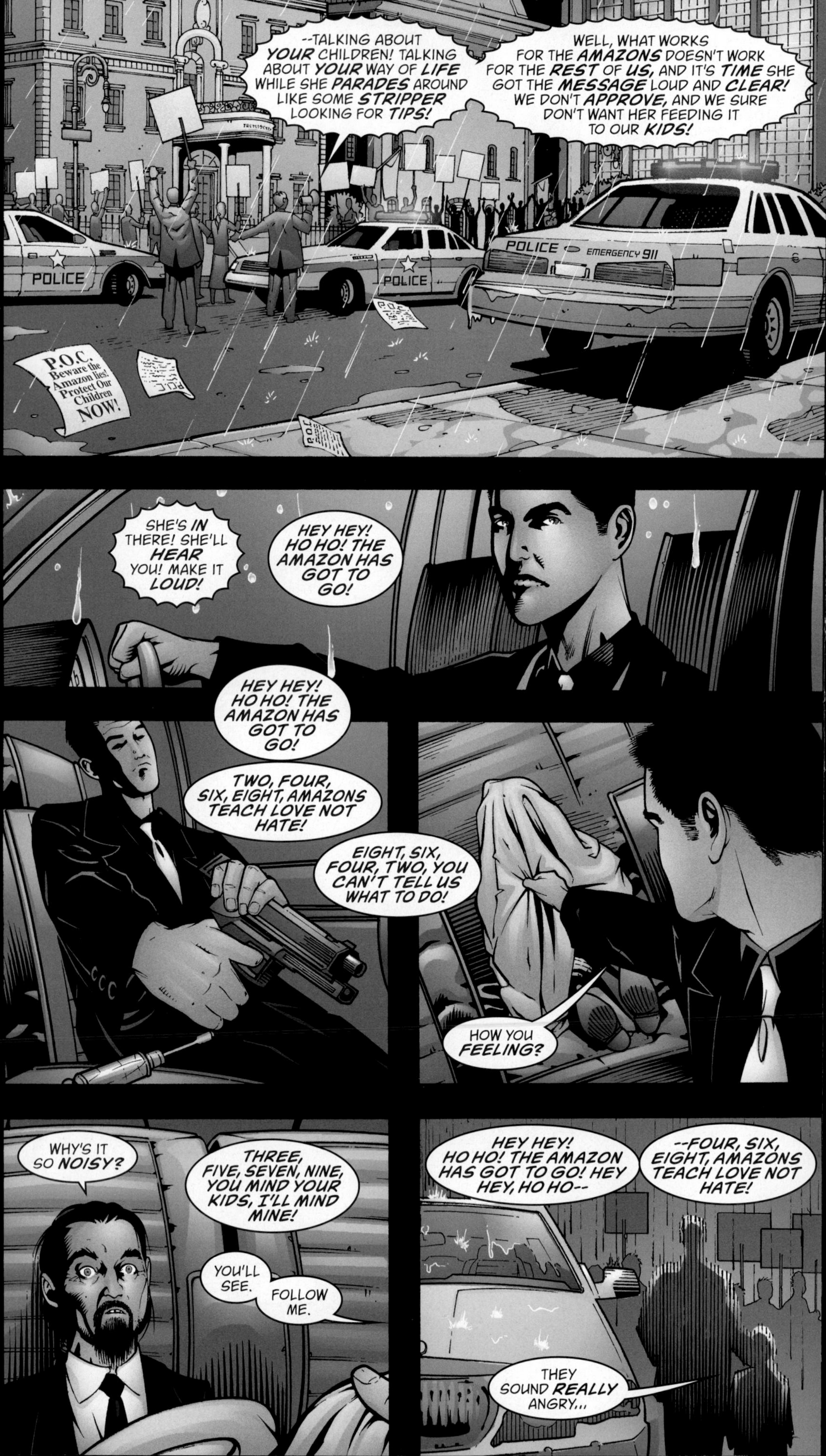
--TALKING ABOUT YOUR CHILDREN! TALKING ABOUT YOUR WAY OF LIFE WHILE SHE PARADES AROUND LIKE SOME STRIPPER LOOKING FOR TIPS!
WELL, WHAT WORKS FOR THE AMAZONS DOESN'T WORK FOR THE REST OF US, AND IT'S TIME SHE GOT THE MESSAGE LOUD AND CLEAR! WE DON'T APPROVE, AND WE SURE DON'T WANT HER FEEDING IT TO OUR KIDS!
POLICE
POLICE
POLICE
EMERGENCY 911
P.O.C. Beware the Amazon lies! Protect Our Children NOW!
SHE'S IN THERE! SHE'LL HEAR YOU! MAKE IT LOUD!
HEY HEY! HO HO! THE AMAZON HAS GOT TO GO!
HEY HEY! HO HO! THE AMAZON HAS GOT TO GO!
TWO, FOUR, SIX, EIGHT, AMAZONS TEACH LOVE NOT HATE!
EIGHT, SIX, FOUR, TWO, YOU CAN'T TELL US WHAT TO DO!
HOW YOU FEELING?
WHY'S IT SO NOISY?
THREE, FIVE, SEVEN, NINE, YOU MIND YOUR KIDS, I'LL MIND MINE!
YOU'LL SEE.
FOLLOW ME.
HEY HEY! HO HO! THE AMAZON HAS GOT TO GO! HEY HEY, HO HO--
--FOUR, SIX, EIGHT, AMAZONS TEACH LOVE NOT HATE!
THEY SOUND REALLY ANGRY...

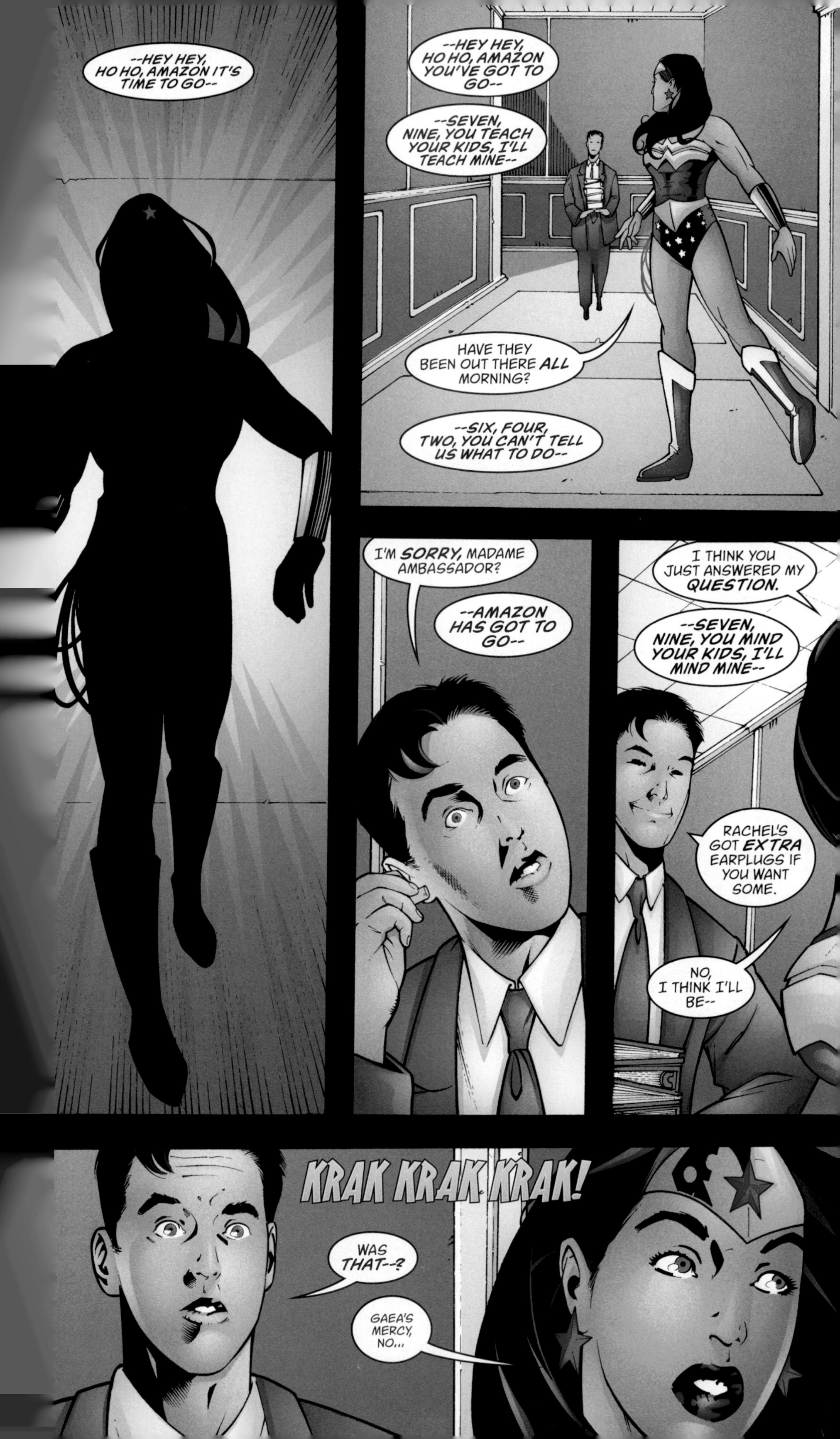
--HEY HEY, HO HO, AMAZON IT'S TIME TO GO--
--HEY HEY, HO HO, AMAZON YOU'VE GOT TO GO--
--SEVEN, NINE, YOU TEACH YOUR KIDS, I'LL TEACH MINE--
HAVE THEY BEEN OUT THERE ALL MORNING?
--SIX, FOUR, TWO, YOU CAN'T TELL US WHAT TO DO--
I'M SORRY, MADAME AMBASSADOR?
--AMAZON HAS GOT TO GO--
I THINK YOU JUST ANSWERED MY QUESTION.
--SEVEN, NINE, YOU MIND YOUR KIDS, I'LL MIND MINE--
RACHEL'S GOT EXTRA EARPLUGS IF YOU WANT SOME.
NO, I THINK I'LL BE--
KRAK KRAK KRAK!
WAS THAT--?
GAEA'S MERCY, NO...

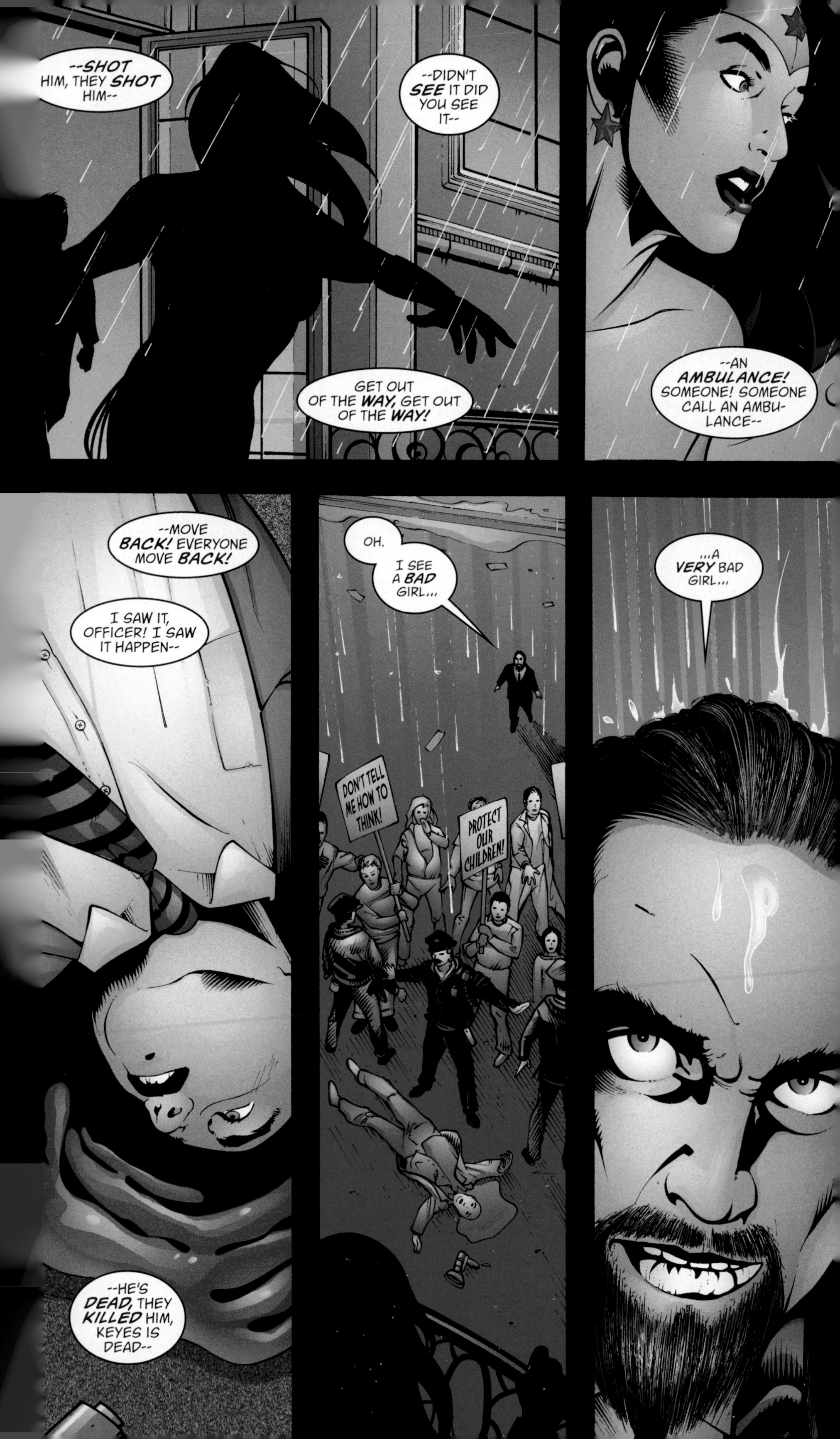
--SHOT HIM, THEY SHOT HIM--
--DIDN'T SEE IT DID YOU SEE IT--
GET OUT OF THE WAY, GET OUT OF THE WAY!
--AN AMBULANCE! SOMEONE! SOMEONE CALL AN AMBU-LANCE--
--MOVE BACK! EVERYONE MOVE BACK!
I SAW IT, OFFICER! I SAW IT HAPPEN--
--HE'S DEAD, THEY KILLED HIM, KEYES IS DEAD--
OH.
I SEE A BAD GIRL...
DON'T TELL ME HOW TO THINK!
PROTECT OUR CHILDREN!
...A VERY BAD GIRL...

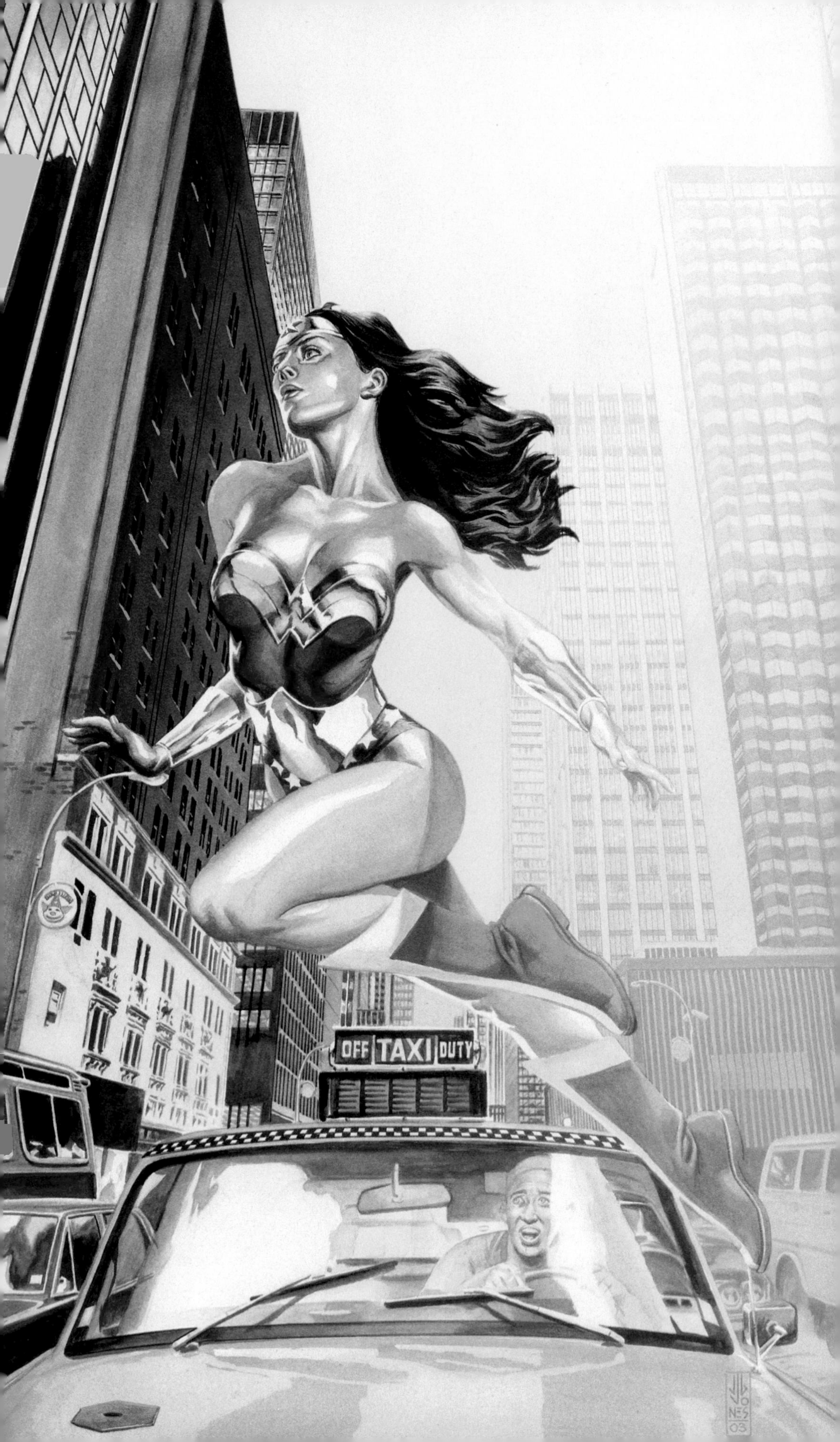
OFF TAXI DUTY

"DOWN TO EARTH: CONCLUSION"

Drew Johnson – *pencils*
Ray Snyder – *inks*
Richard Horie, Tanya Horie - *colors*
J.G. Jones – *cover art*

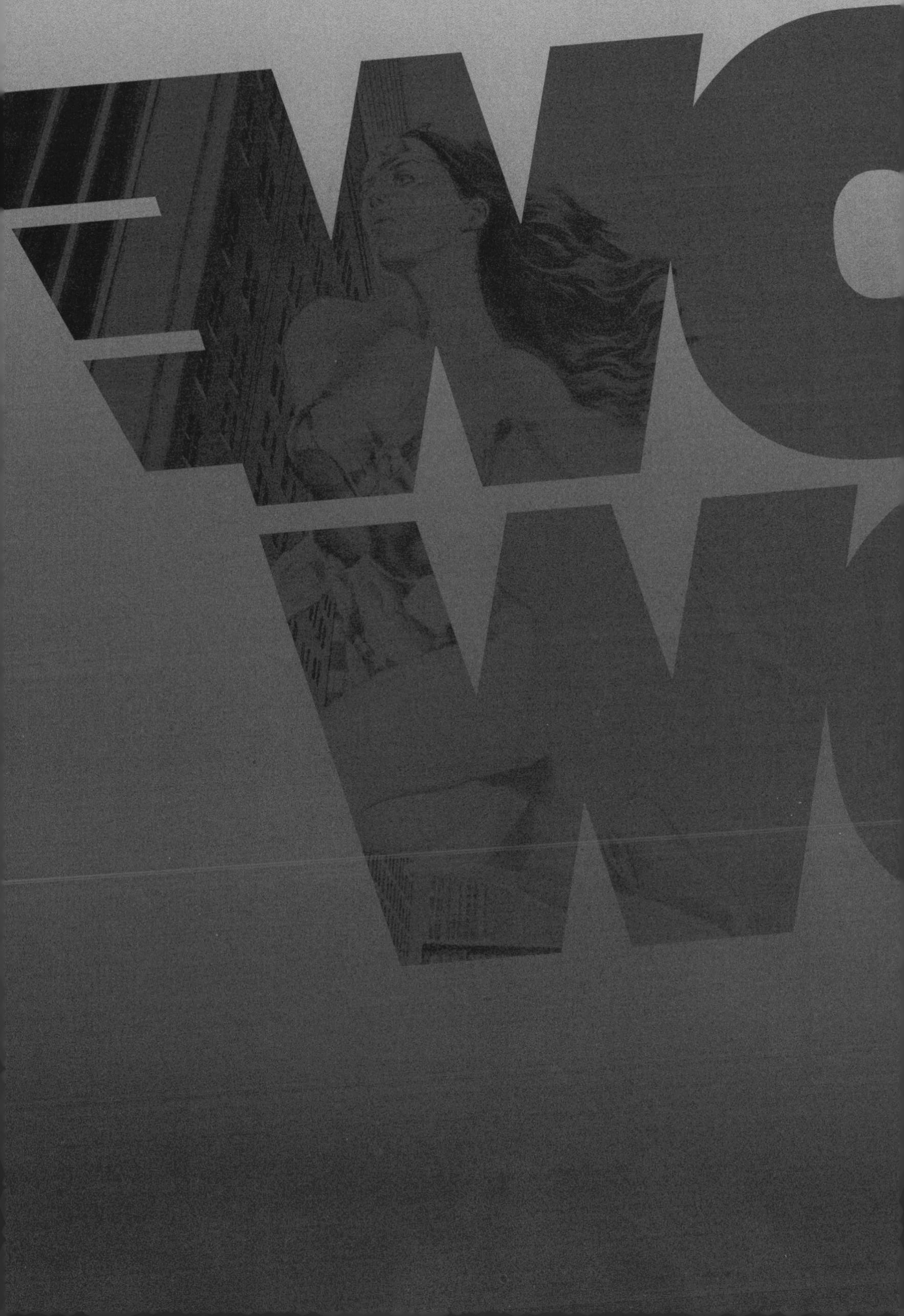

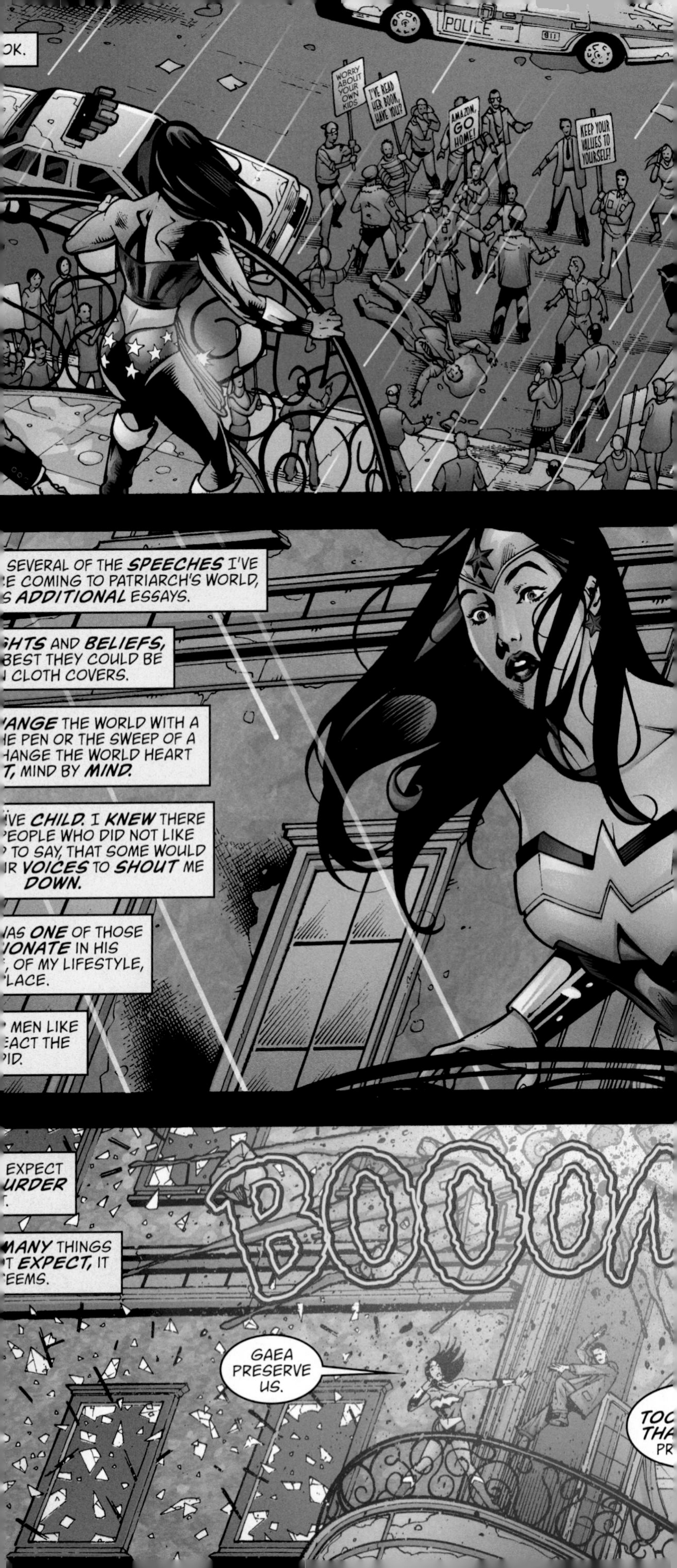
OK.
POLICE
WORRY ABOUT YOUR OWN KIDS
I'VE READ HER BOOK, HAVE YOU?
AMAZON, GO HOME!
KEEP YOUR VALUES TO YOURSELF!
SEVERAL OF THE SPEECHES I'VE
E COMING TO PATRIARCH'S WORLD,
S ADDITIONAL ESSAYS.
GHTS AND BELIEFS,
BEST THEY COULD BE
CLOTH COVERS.
ANGE THE WORLD WITH A
E PEN OR THE SWEEP OF A
HANGE THE WORLD HEART
T, MIND BY MIND.
IVE CHILD. I KNEW THERE
PEOPLE WHO DID NOT LIKE
TO SAY, THAT SOME WOULD
R VOICES TO SHOUT ME
DOWN.
AS ONE OF THOSE
IONATE IN HIS
, OF MY LIFESTYLE,
LACE.
MEN LIKE
ACT THE
ID.
EXPECT
URDER
MANY THINGS
T EXPECT, IT
EEMS.
BOOO
GAEA PRESERVE US.
TOO
THA
PR

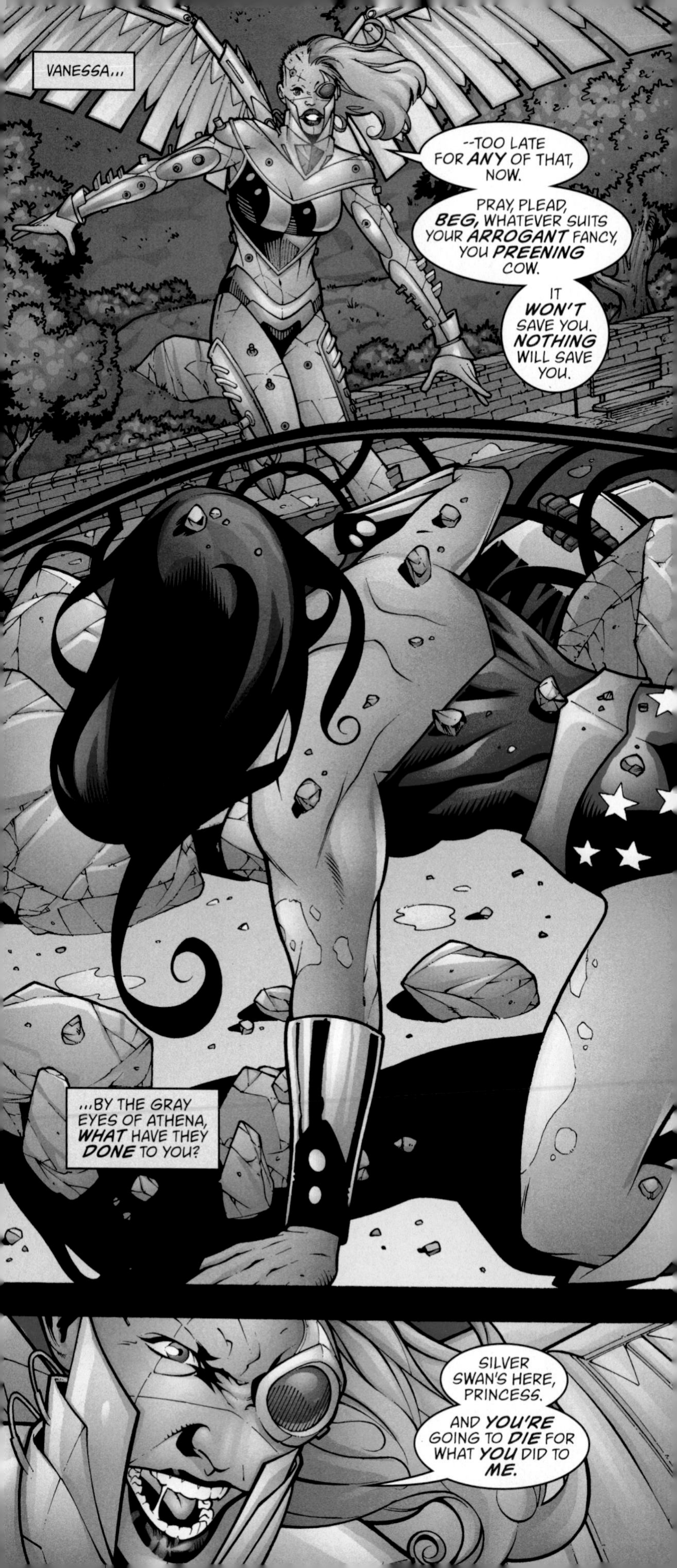
VANESSA...
--TOO LATE FOR ANY OF THAT, NOW.
PRAY, PLEAD, BEG, WHATEVER SUITS YOUR ARROGANT FANCY, YOU PREENING COW.
IT WON'T SAVE YOU. NOTHING WILL SAVE YOU.
...BY THE GRAY EYES OF ATHENA, WHAT HAVE THEY DONE TO YOU?
SILVER SWAN'S HERE, PRINCESS.
AND YOU'RE GOING TO DIE FOR WHAT YOU DID TO ME.

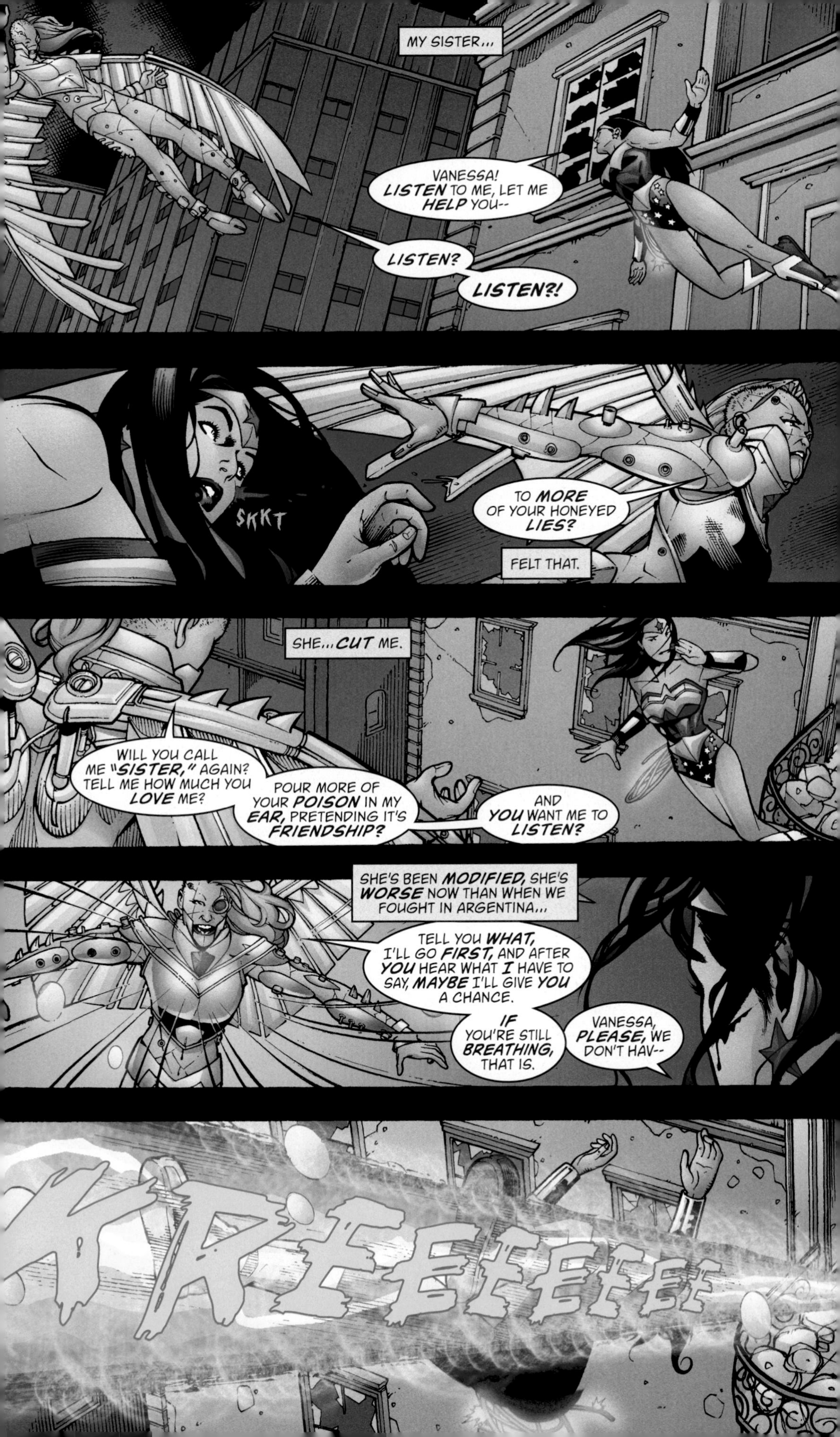
MY SISTER...
VANESSA! LISTEN TO ME, LET ME HELP YOU--
LISTEN?
LISTEN?!
SKKT
TO MORE OF YOUR HONEYED LIES?
FELT THAT.
SHE...CUT ME.
WILL YOU CALL ME "SISTER," AGAIN? TELL ME HOW MUCH YOU LOVE ME?
POUR MORE OF YOUR POISON IN MY EAR, PRETENDING IT'S FRIENDSHIP?
AND YOU WANT ME TO LISTEN?
SHE'S BEEN MODIFIED, SHE'S WORSE NOW THAN WHEN WE FOUGHT IN ARGENTINA...
TELL YOU WHAT, I'LL GO FIRST, AND AFTER YOU HEAR WHAT I HAVE TO SAY, MAYBE I'LL GIVE YOU A CHANCE.
IF YOU'RE STILL BREATHING, THAT IS.
VANESSA, PLEASE, WE DON'T HAV--
KREEEEEE

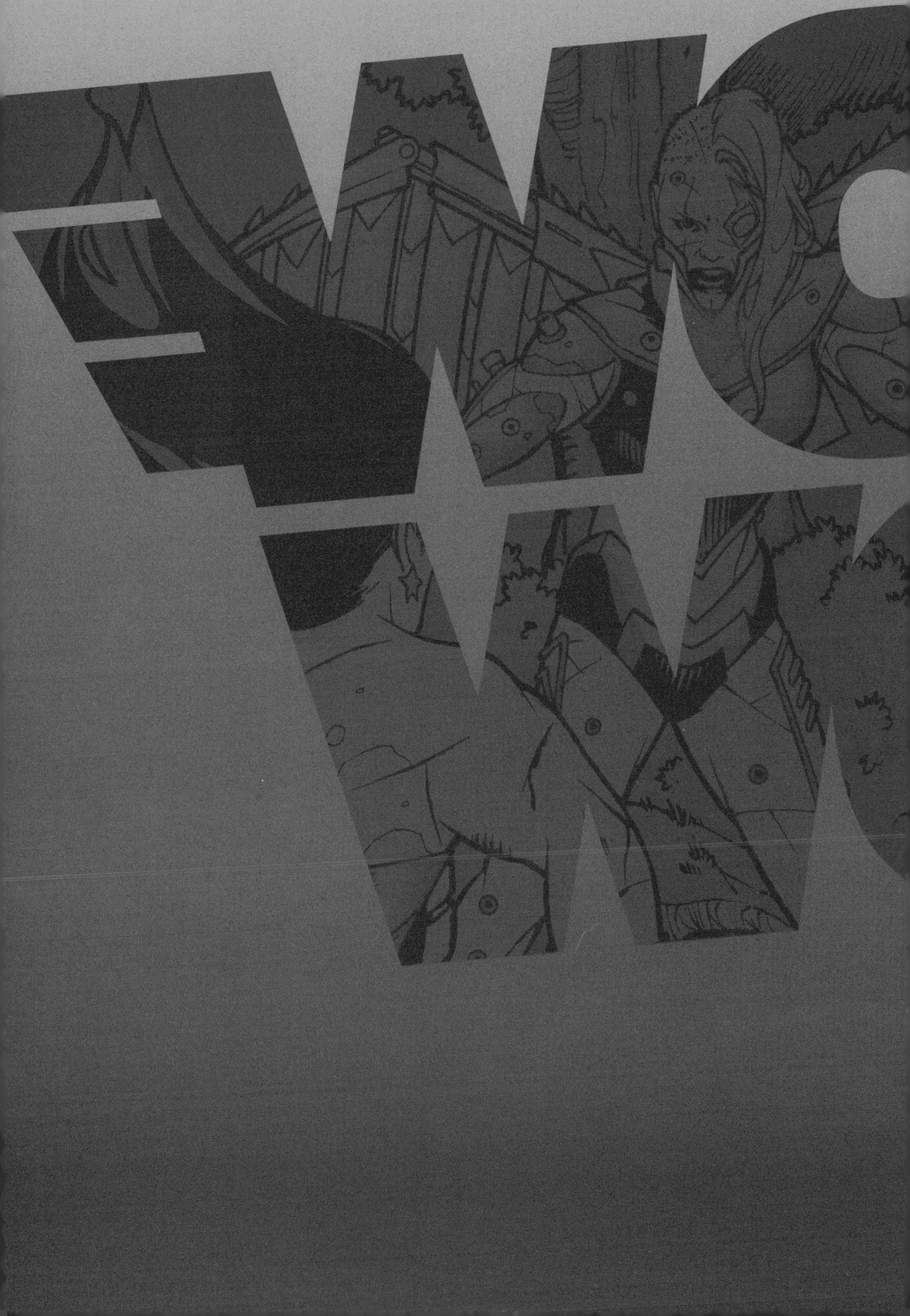

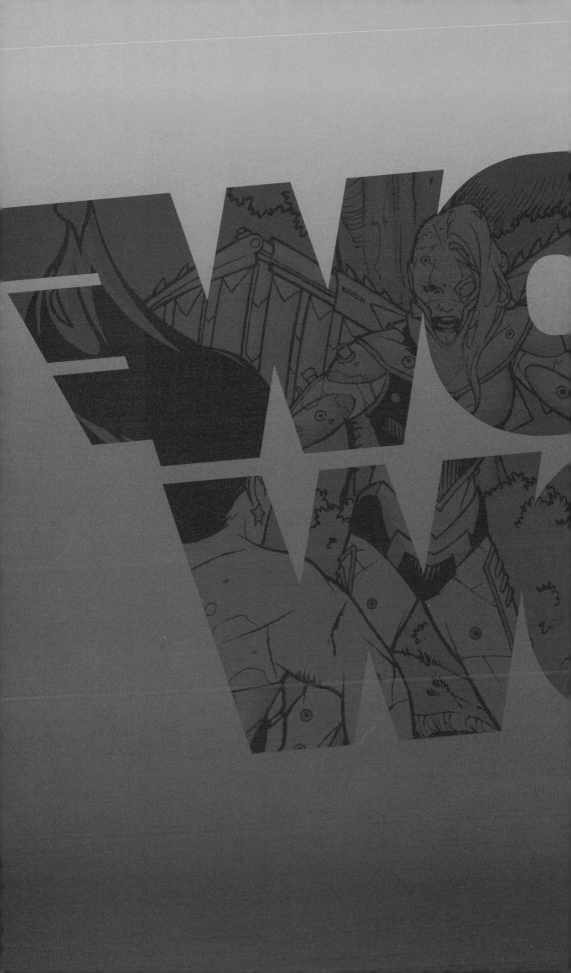

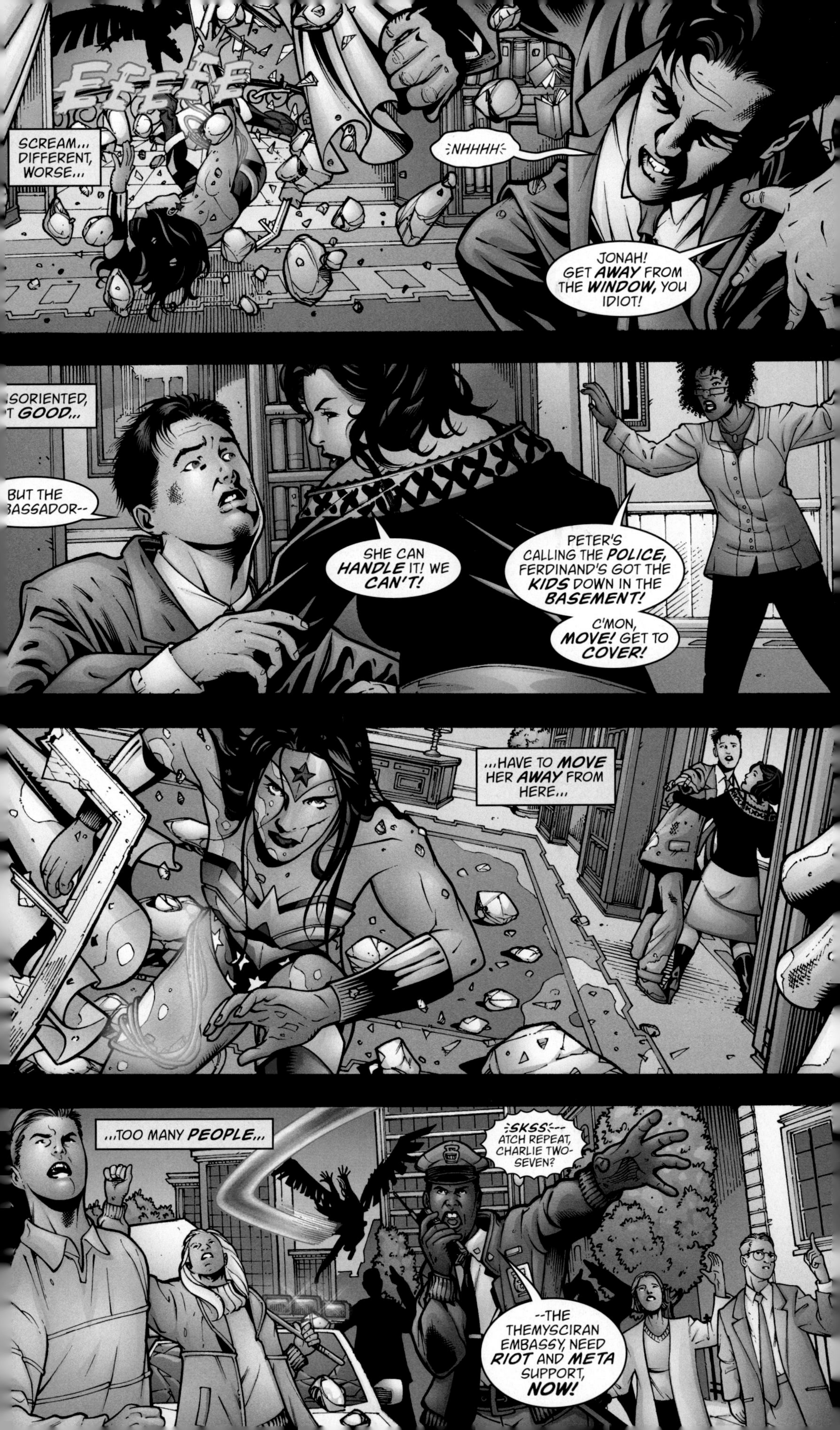

EEEEE
SCREAM... DIFFERENT, WORSE...
NHHHH
JONAH! GET AWAY FROM THE WINDOW, YOU IDIOT!
SORIENTED, T GOOD...
BUT THE BASSADOR--
SHE CAN HANDLE IT! WE CAN'T!
PETER'S CALLING THE POLICE, FERDINAND'S GOT THE KIDS DOWN IN THE BASEMENT!
C'MON, MOVE! GET TO COVER!
...HAVE TO MOVE HER AWAY FROM HERE...
...TOO MANY PEOPLE...
SKSS-- ATCH REPEAT, CHARLIE TWO-SEVEN?
--THE THEMYSCIRAN EMBASSY, NEED RIOT AND META SUPPORT, NOW!

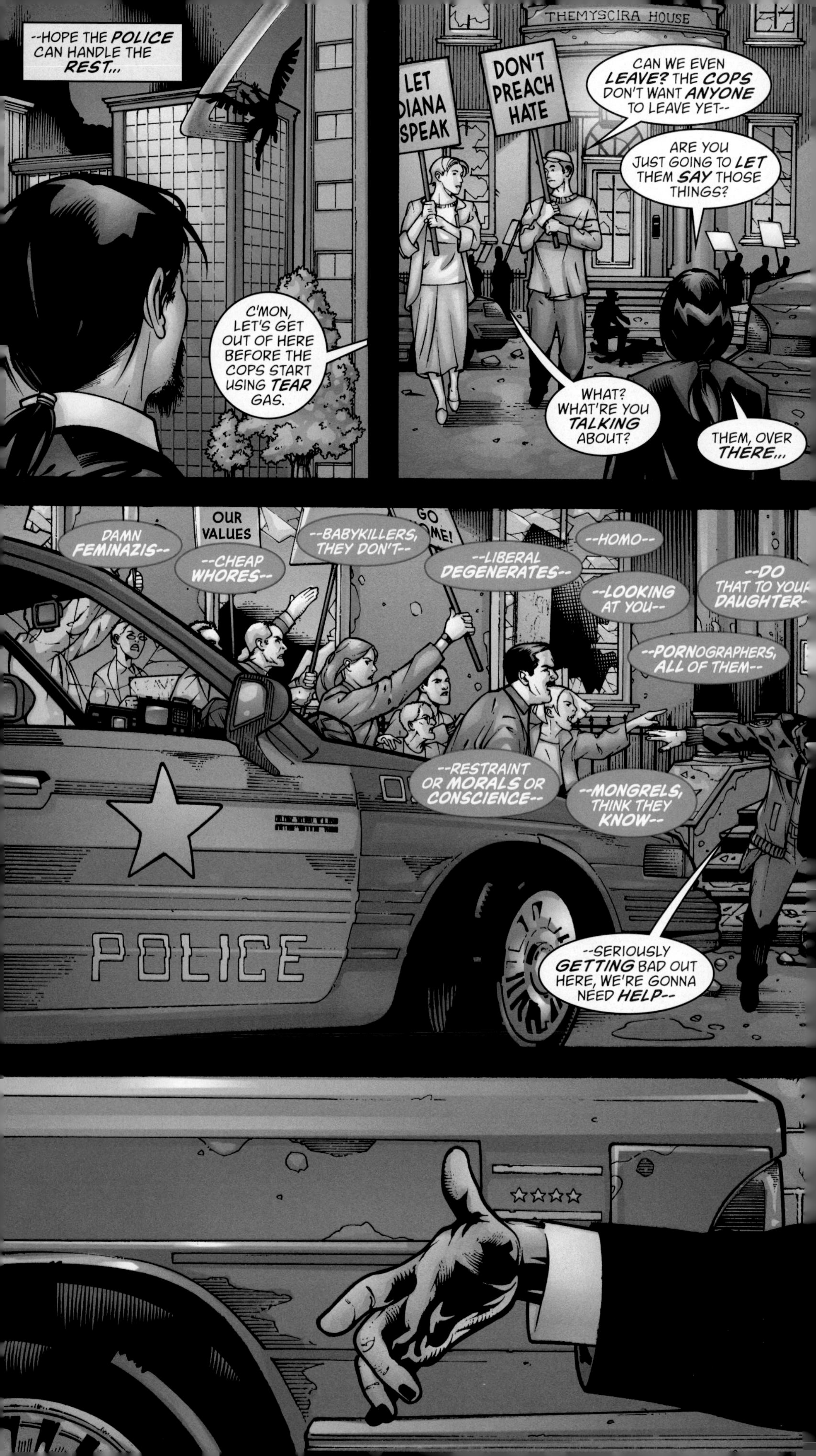
--HOPE THE POLICE CAN HANDLE THE REST...
C'MON, LET'S GET OUT OF HERE BEFORE THE COPS START USING TEAR GAS.
THEMYSCIRA HOUSE
LET DIANA SPEAK
DON'T PREACH HATE
CAN WE EVEN LEAVE? THE COPS DON'T WANT ANYONE TO LEAVE YET--
ARE YOU JUST GOING TO LET THEM SAY THOSE THINGS?
WHAT? WHAT'RE YOU TALKING ABOUT?
THEM, OVER THERE...
OUR VALUES
GO HOME!
DAMN FEMINAZIS--
--CHEAP WHORES--
--BABYKILLERS, THEY DON'T--
--LIBERAL DEGENERATES--
--HOMO--
--LOOKING AT YOU--
--DO THAT TO YOUR DAUGHTER--
--PORNOGRAPHERS, ALL OF THEM--
--RESTRAINT OR MORALS OR CONSCIENCE--
--MONGRELS, THINK THEY KNOW--
POLICE
--SERIOUSLY GETTING BAD OUT HERE, WE'RE GONNA NEED HELP--

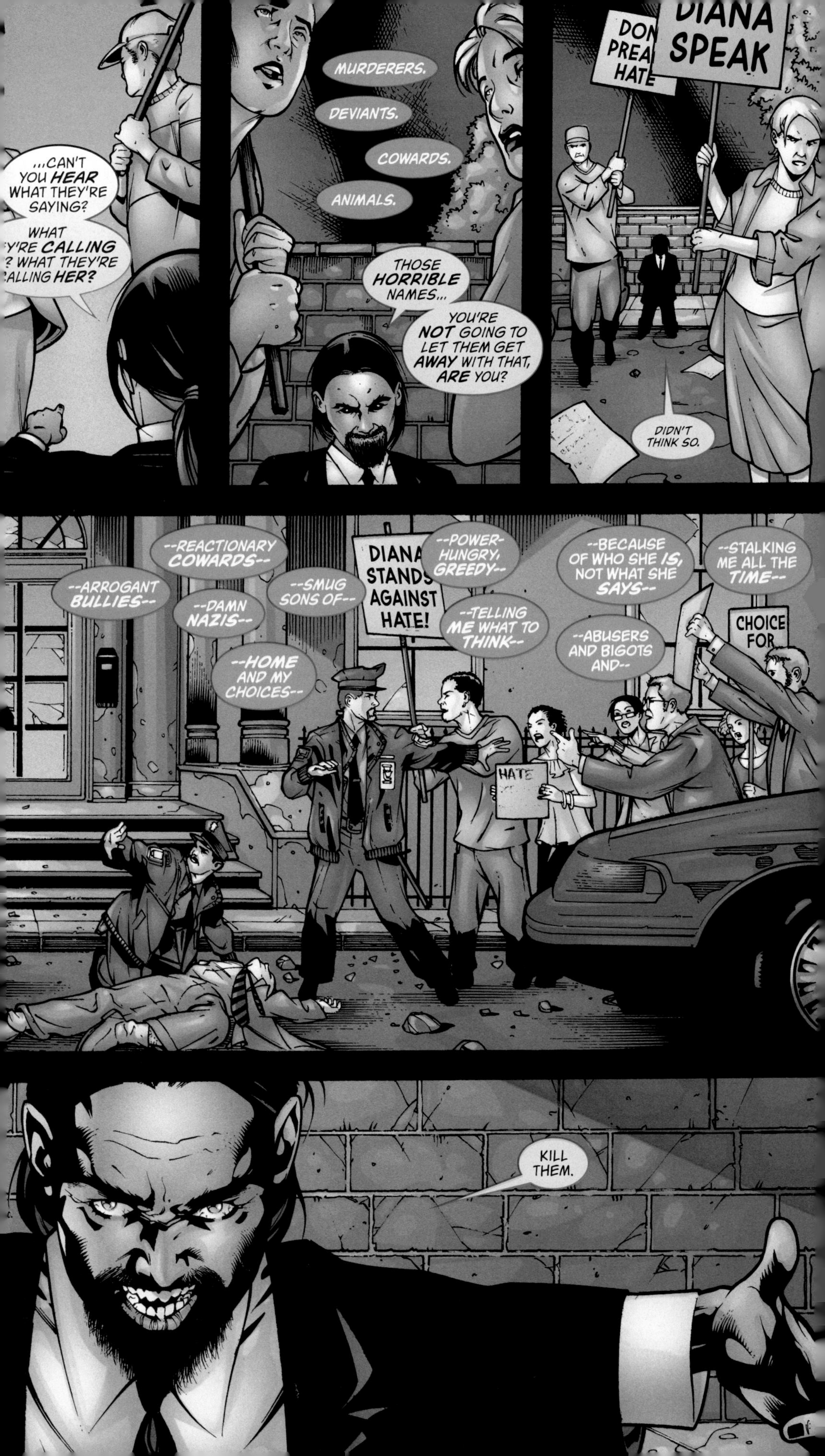

...CAN'T YOU HEAR WHAT THEY'RE SAYING?
WHAT ...Y'RE CALLING ...? WHAT THEY'RE ...ALLING HER?
MURDERERS.
DEVIANTS.
COWARDS.
ANIMALS.
THOSE HORRIBLE NAMES...
YOU'RE NOT GOING TO LET THEM GET AWAY WITH THAT, ARE YOU?
DON PREA HATE
DIANA SPEAK
DIDN'T THINK SO.
--REACTIONARY COWARDS--
--ARROGANT BULLIES--
--DAMN NAZIS--
--SMUG SONS OF--
DIANA STANDS AGAINST HATE!
--POWER-HUNGRY, GREEDY--
--TELLING ME WHAT TO THINK--
--HOME AND MY CHOICES--
--BECAUSE OF WHO SHE IS, NOT WHAT SHE SAYS--
--ABUSERS AND BIGOTS AND--
--STALKING ME ALL THE TIME--
CHOICE FOR
HATE
KILL THEM.

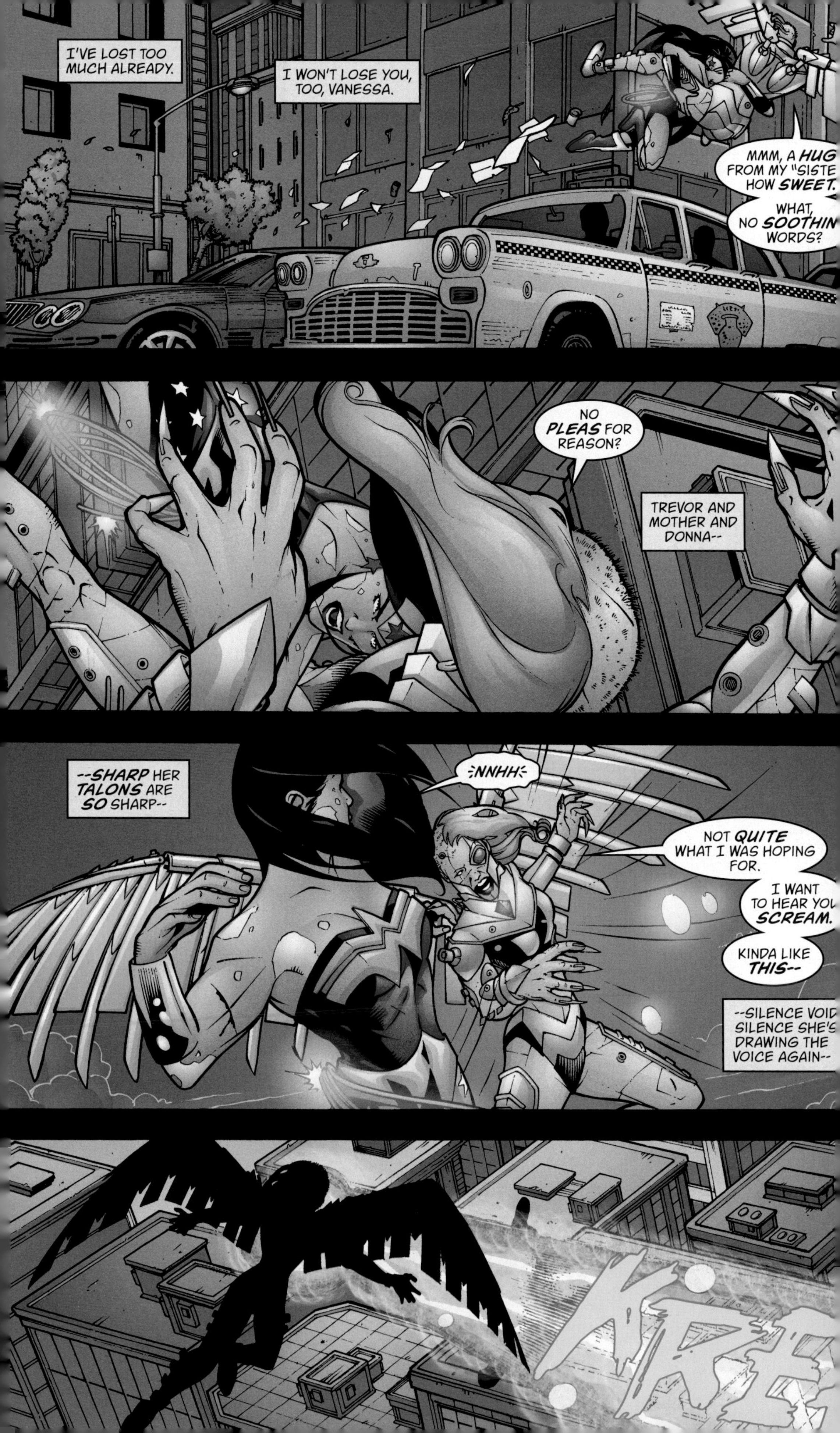
I'VE LOST TOO MUCH ALREADY.
I WON'T LOSE YOU, TOO, VANESSA.
MMM, A HUG FROM MY "SISTE
HOW SWEET.
WHAT, NO SOOTHIN WORDS?
NO PLEAS FOR REASON?
TREVOR AND MOTHER AND DONNA--
--SHARP HER TALONS ARE SO SHARP--
NNHH
NOT QUITE WHAT I WAS HOPING FOR.
I WANT TO HEAR YOU SCREAM.
KINDA LIKE THIS--
--SILENCE VOID SILENCE SHE'S DRAWING THE VOICE AGAIN--

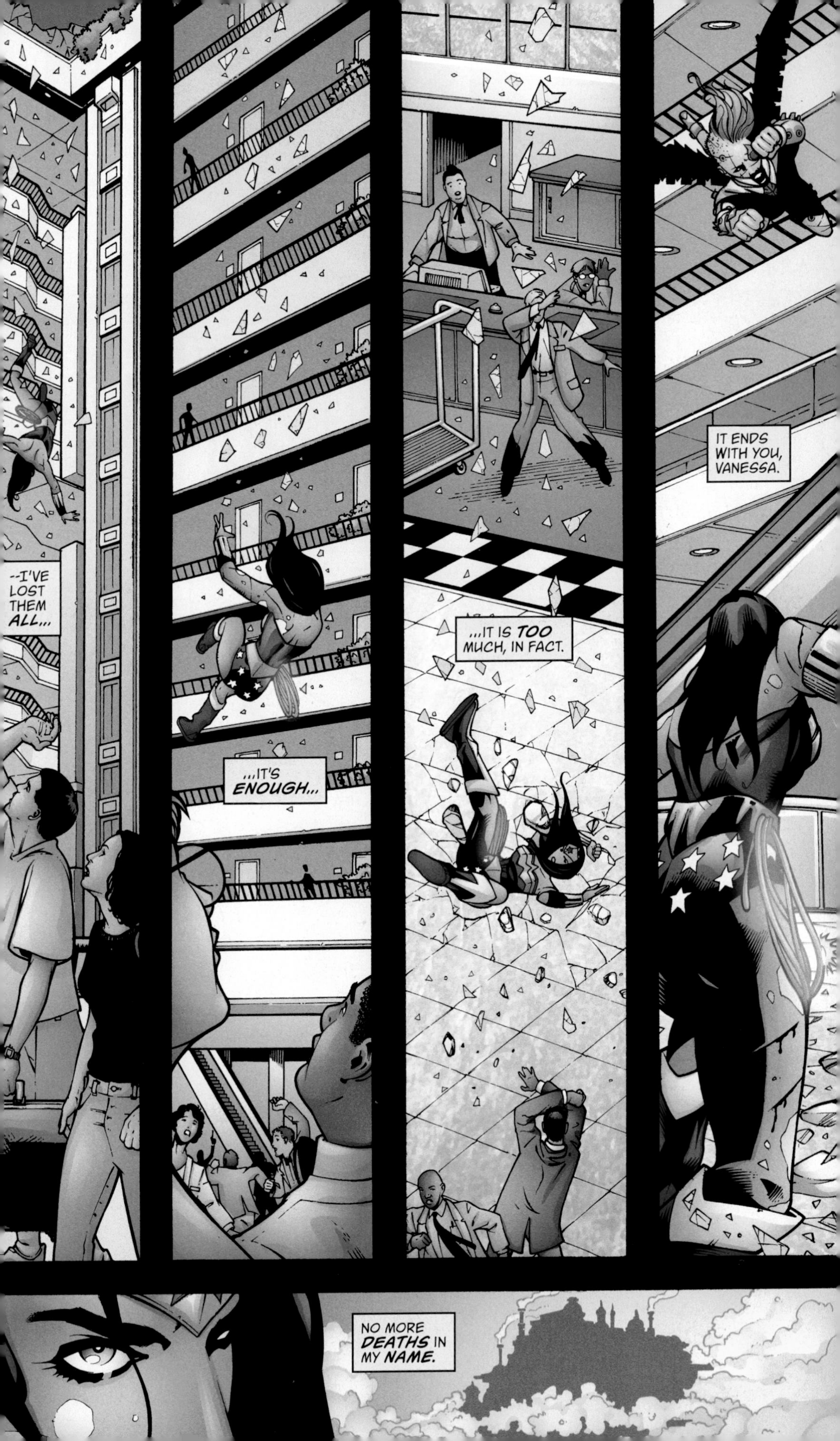
--I'VE LOST THEM *ALL*...
...IT'S *ENOUGH*...
...IT IS *TOO* MUCH, IN FACT.
IT ENDS WITH YOU, VANESSA.
NO MORE *DEATHS* IN MY *NAME*.

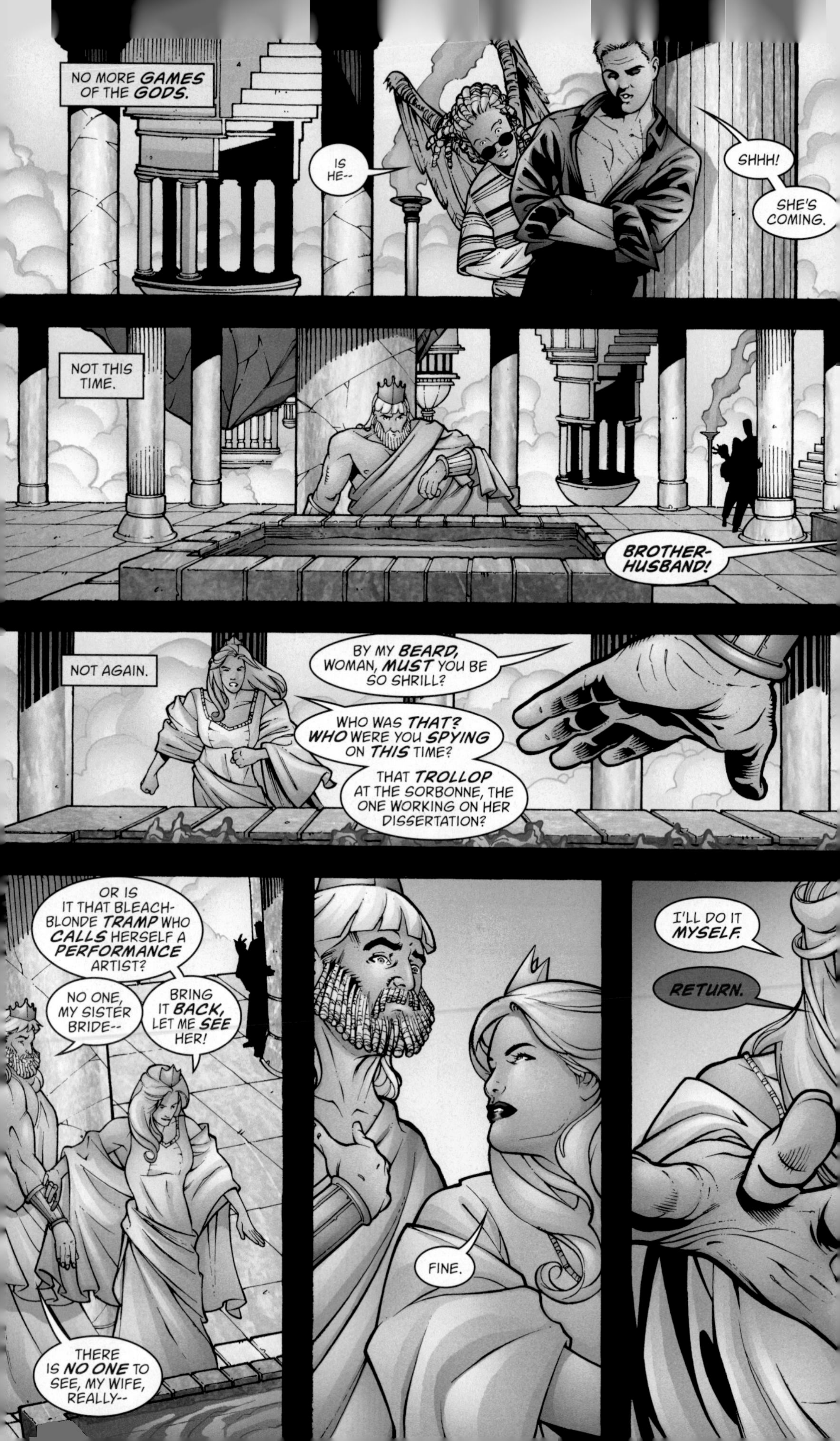
NO MORE GAMES OF THE GODS.
IS HE--
SHHH!
SHE'S COMING.
NOT THIS TIME.
BROTHER-HUSBAND!
NOT AGAIN.
BY MY BEARD, WOMAN, MUST YOU BE SO SHRILL?
WHO WAS THAT? WHO WERE YOU SPYING ON THIS TIME?
THAT TROLLOP AT THE SORBONNE, THE ONE WORKING ON HER DISSERTATION?
OR IS IT THAT BLEACH-BLONDE TRAMP WHO CALLS HERSELF A PERFORMANCE ARTIST?
NO ONE, MY SISTER BRIDE--
BRING IT BACK, LET ME SEE HER!
THERE IS NO ONE TO SEE, MY WIFE, REALLY--
FINE.
I'LL DO IT MYSELF.
RETURN.

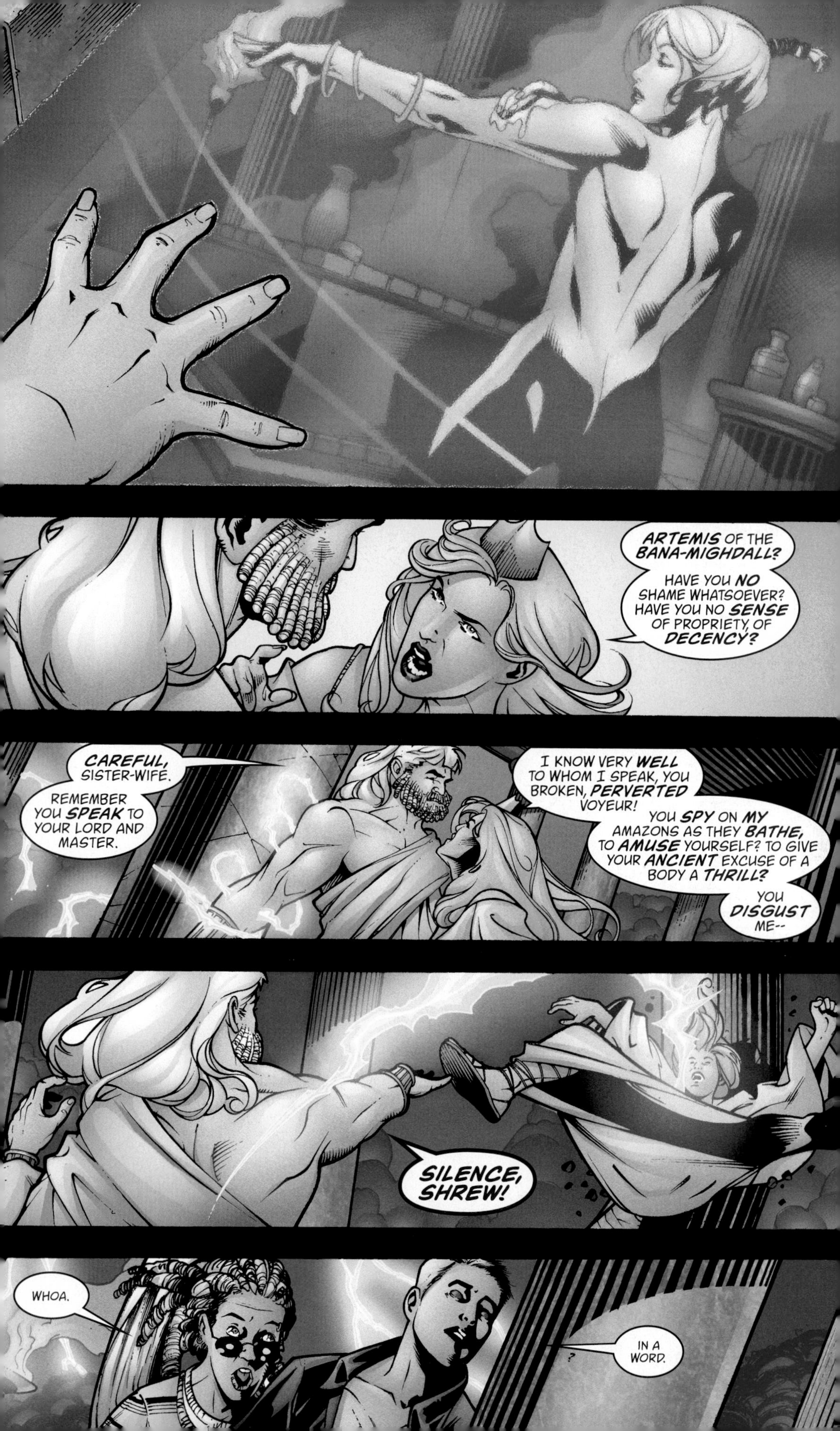
ARTEMIS OF THE BANA-MIGHDALL?
HAVE YOU NO SHAME WHATSOEVER? HAVE YOU NO SENSE OF PROPRIETY, OF DECENCY?
CAREFUL, SISTER-WIFE.
REMEMBER YOU SPEAK TO YOUR LORD AND MASTER.
I KNOW VERY WELL TO WHOM I SPEAK, YOU BROKEN, PERVERTED VOYEUR!
YOU SPY ON MY AMAZONS AS THEY BATHE, TO AMUSE YOURSELF? TO GIVE YOUR ANCIENT EXCUSE OF A BODY A THRILL?
YOU DISGUST ME--
SILENCE, SHREW!
WHOA.
IN A WORD.

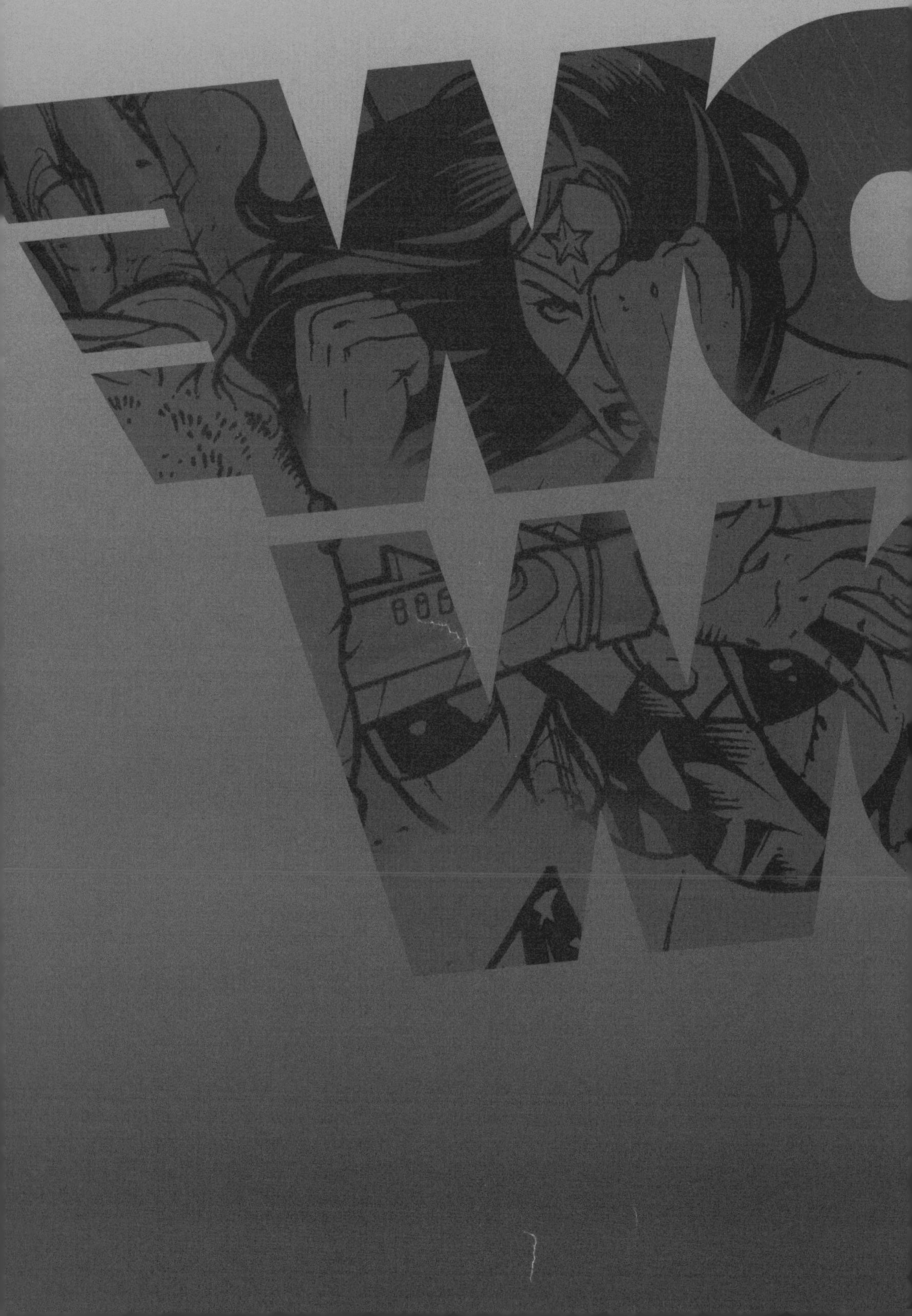

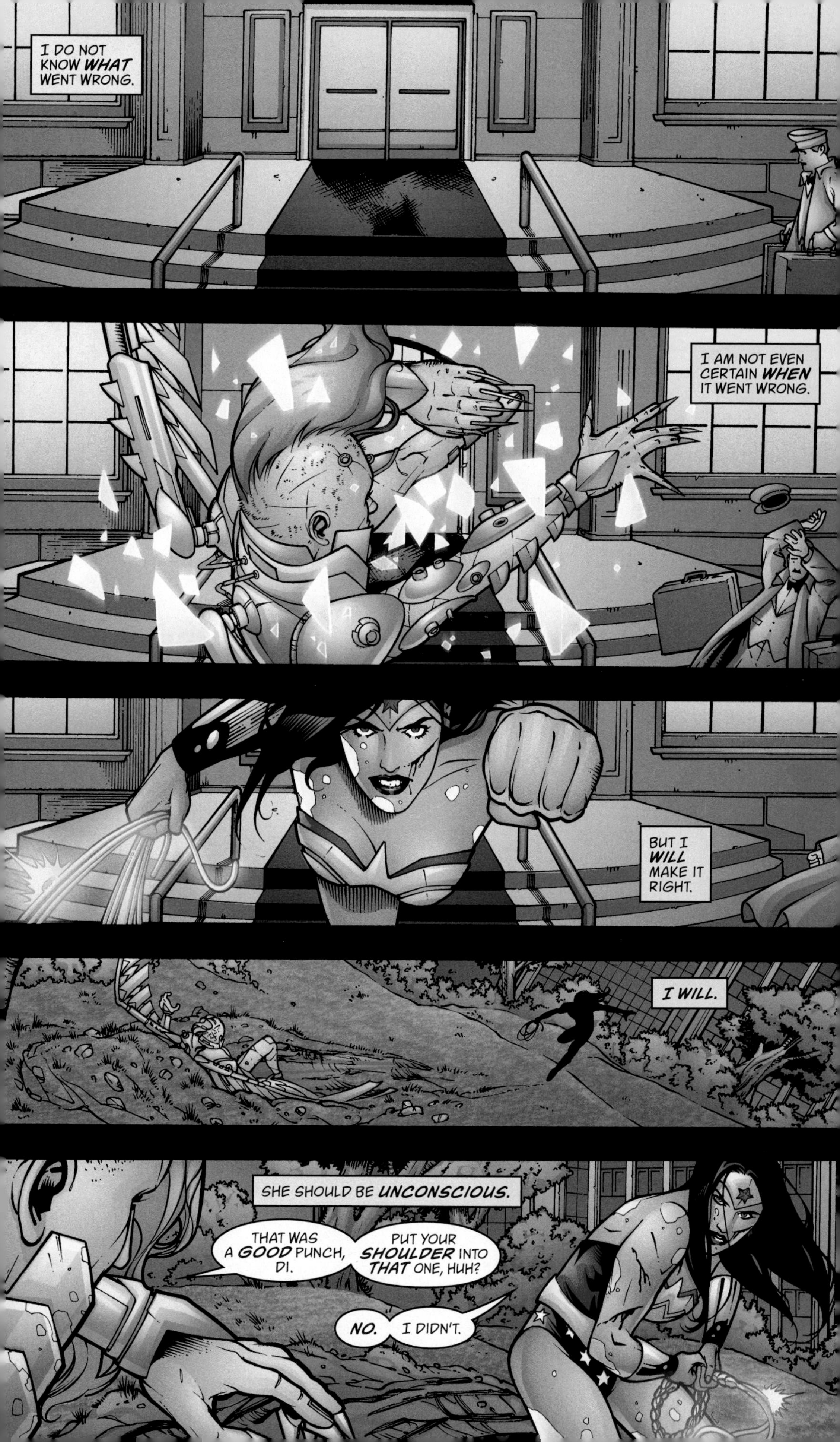
I DO NOT KNOW WHAT WENT WRONG.
I AM NOT EVEN CERTAIN WHEN IT WENT WRONG.
BUT I WILL MAKE IT RIGHT.
I WILL.
SHE SHOULD BE UNCONSCIOUS.
THAT WAS A GOOD PUNCH, DI.
PUT YOUR SHOULDER INTO THAT ONE, HUH?
NO.
I DIDN'T.

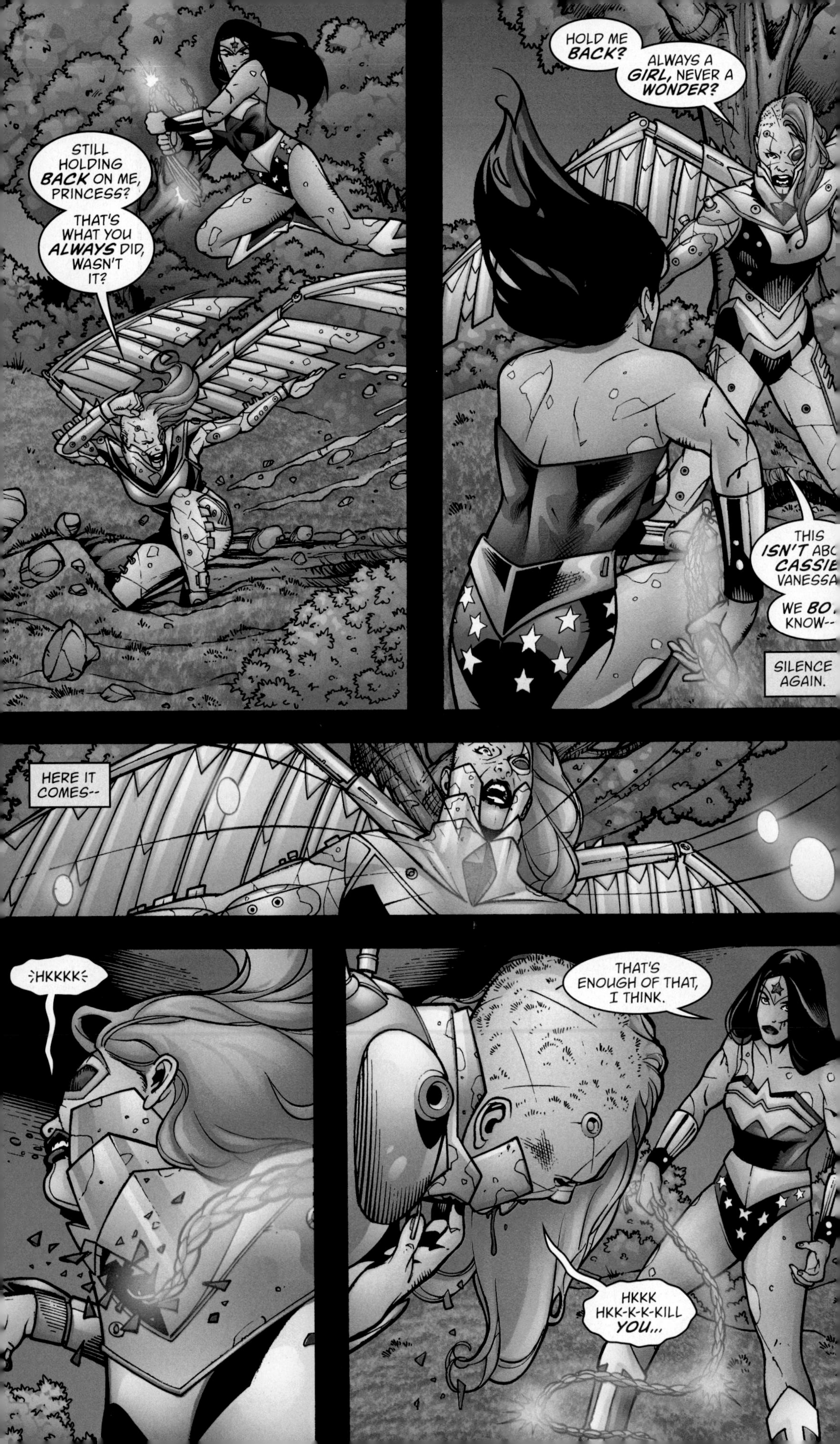
STILL HOLDING BACK ON ME, PRINCESS?
THAT'S WHAT YOU ALWAYS DID, WASN'T IT?
HOLD ME BACK?
ALWAYS A GIRL, NEVER A WONDER?
THIS ISN'T ABO CASSIE VANESSA
WE BO KNOW--
SILENCE AGAIN.
HERE IT COMES--
HKKKK
THAT'S ENOUGH OF THAT, I THINK.
HKKK HKK-K-K-KILL YOU...

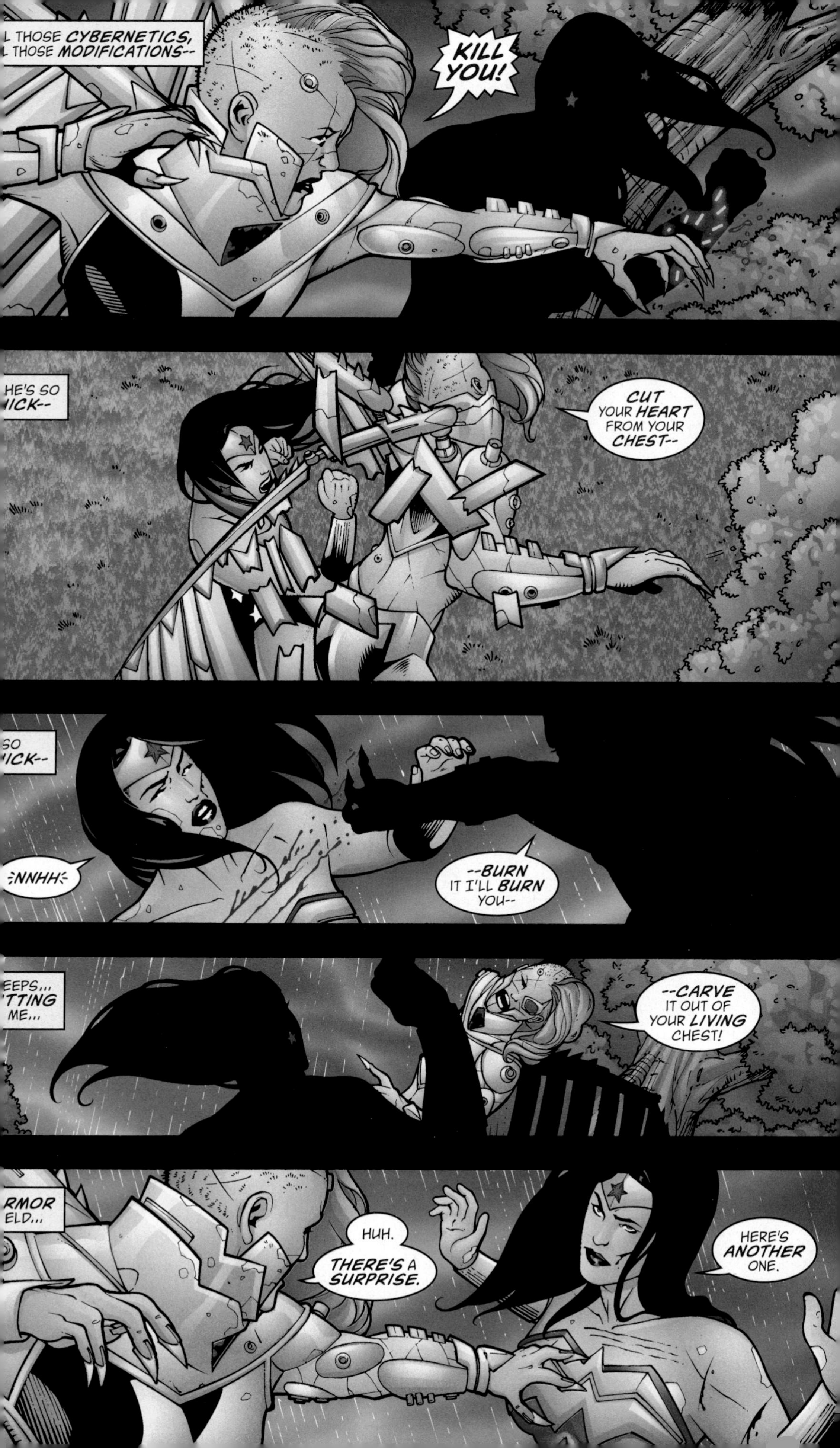
L THOSE CYBERNETICS,
L THOSE MODIFICATIONS--
KILL YOU!
HE'S SO
ICK--
CUT YOUR HEART FROM YOUR CHEST--
SO
ICK--
NNHH
--BURN IT I'LL BURN YOU--
EEPS...
TTING
ME...
--CARVE IT OUT OF YOUR LIVING CHEST!
RMOR
ELD...
HUH.
THERE'S A SURPRISE.
HERE'S ANOTHER ONE.

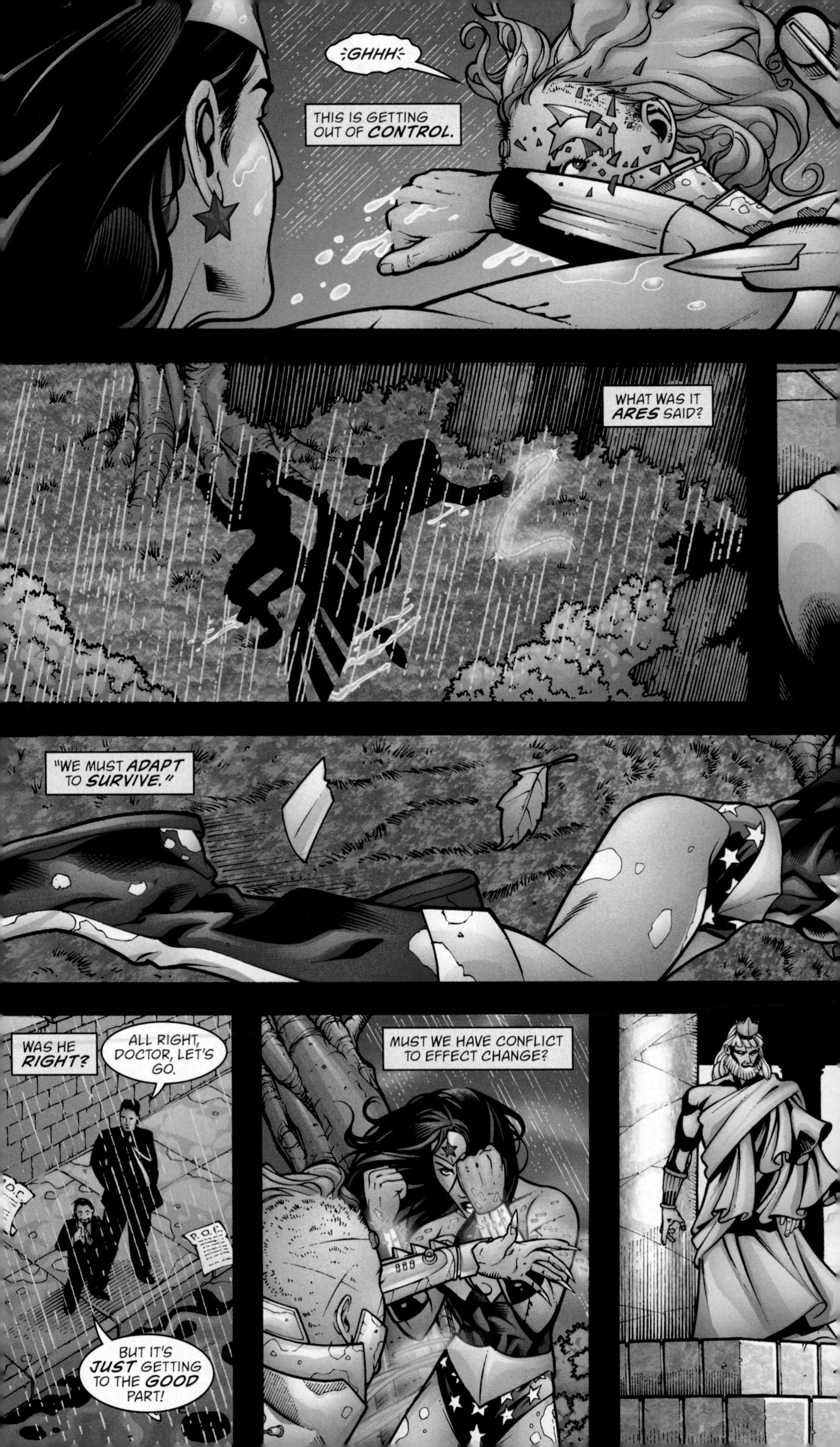

GHHH
THIS IS GETTING OUT OF CONTROL.
WHAT WAS IT ARES SAID?
"WE MUST ADAPT TO SURVIVE."
WAS HE RIGHT?
ALL RIGHT, DOCTOR, LET'S GO.
BUT IT'S JUST GETTING TO THE GOOD PART!
MUST WE HAVE CONFLICT TO EFFECT CHANGE?

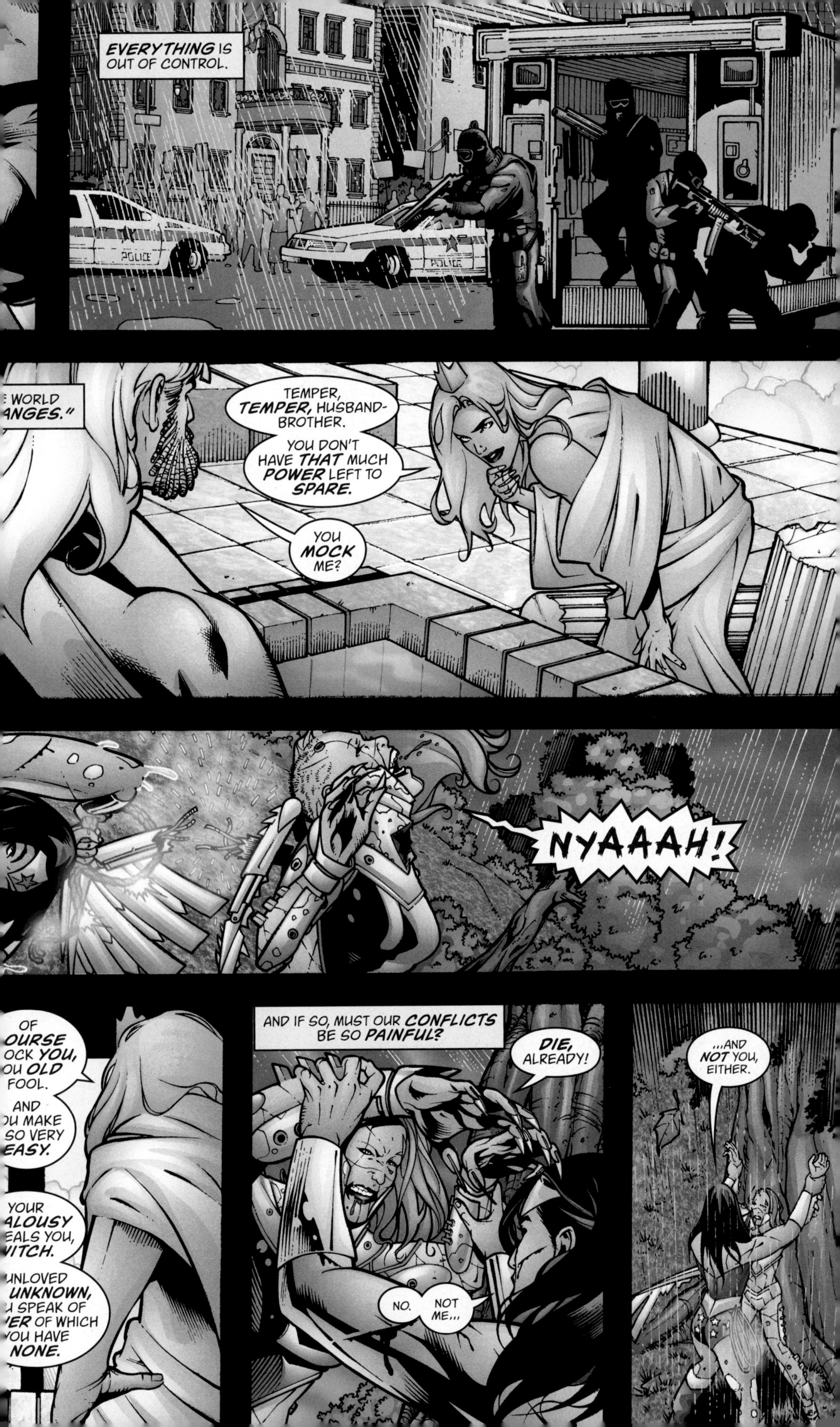
EVERYTHING IS OUT OF CONTROL.
WORLD ANGES."
TEMPER, TEMPER, HUSBAND-BROTHER.
YOU DON'T HAVE THAT MUCH POWER LEFT TO SPARE.
YOU MOCK ME?
NYAAAH!
OF OURSE OCK YOU, OU OLD FOOL.
AND OU MAKE SO VERY EASY.
YOUR ALOUSY EALS YOU, WITCH.
UNLOVED UNKNOWN, SPEAK OF ER OF WHICH YOU HAVE NONE.
AND IF SO, MUST OUR CONFLICTS BE SO PAINFUL?
DIE, ALREADY!
NO.
NOT ME...
...AND NOT YOU, EITHER.

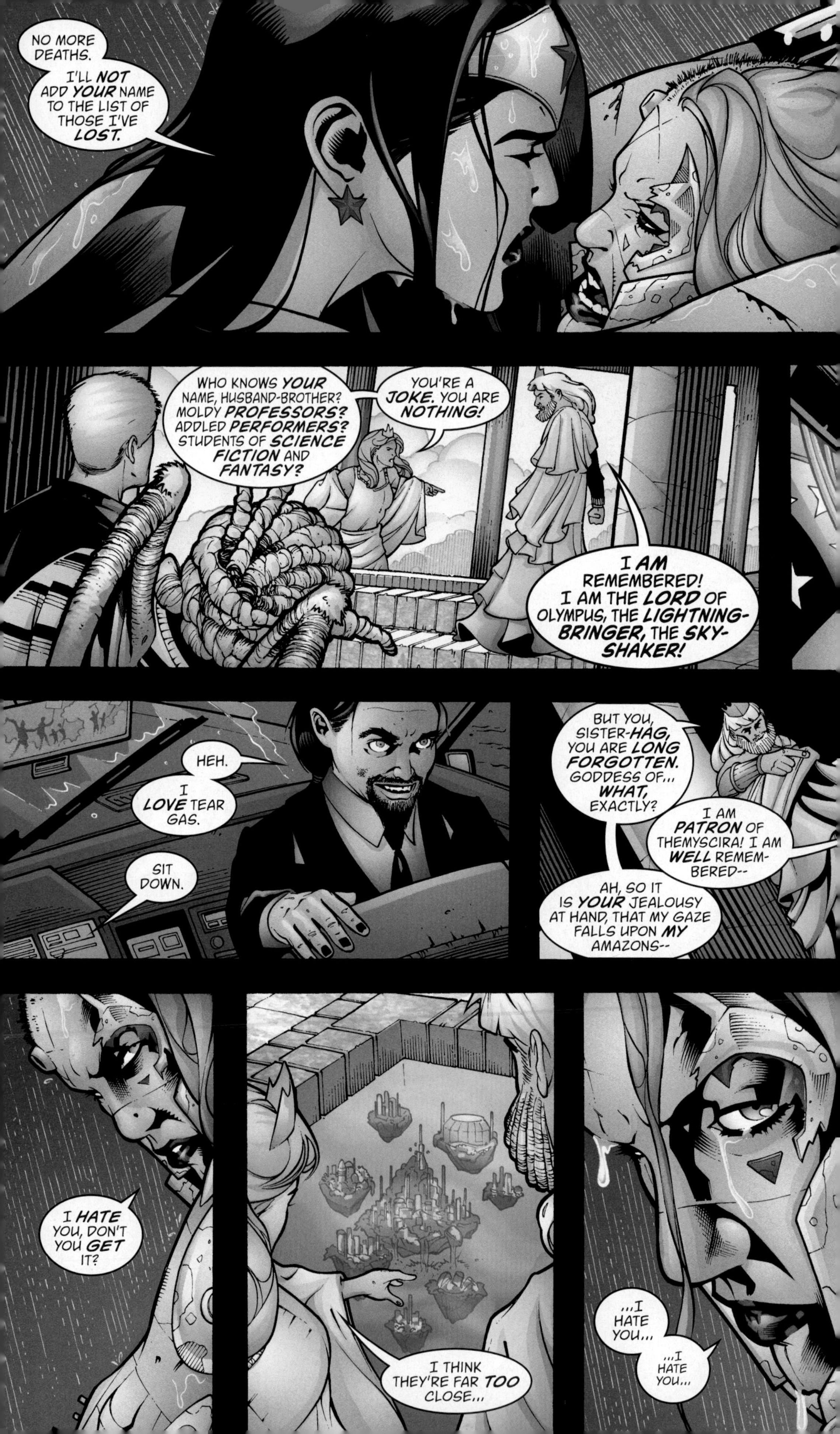
NO MORE DEATHS.
I'LL NOT ADD YOUR NAME TO THE LIST OF THOSE I'VE LOST.
WHO KNOWS YOUR NAME, HUSBAND-BROTHER? MOLDY PROFESSORS? ADDLED PERFORMERS? STUDENTS OF SCIENCE FICTION AND FANTASY?
YOU'RE A JOKE. YOU ARE NOTHING!
I AM REMEMBERED! I AM THE LORD OF OLYMPUS, THE LIGHTNING-BRINGER, THE SKY-SHAKER!
HEH.
I LOVE TEAR GAS.
SIT DOWN.
BUT YOU, SISTER-HAG, YOU ARE LONG FORGOTTEN. GODDESS OF... WHAT, EXACTLY?
I AM PATRON OF THEMYSCIRA! I AM WELL REMEMBERED--
AH, SO IT IS YOUR JEALOUSY AT HAND, THAT MY GAZE FALLS UPON MY AMAZONS--
I HATE YOU, DON'T YOU GET IT?
I THINK THEY'RE FAR TOO CLOSE...
...I HATE YOU...
...I HATE YOU...

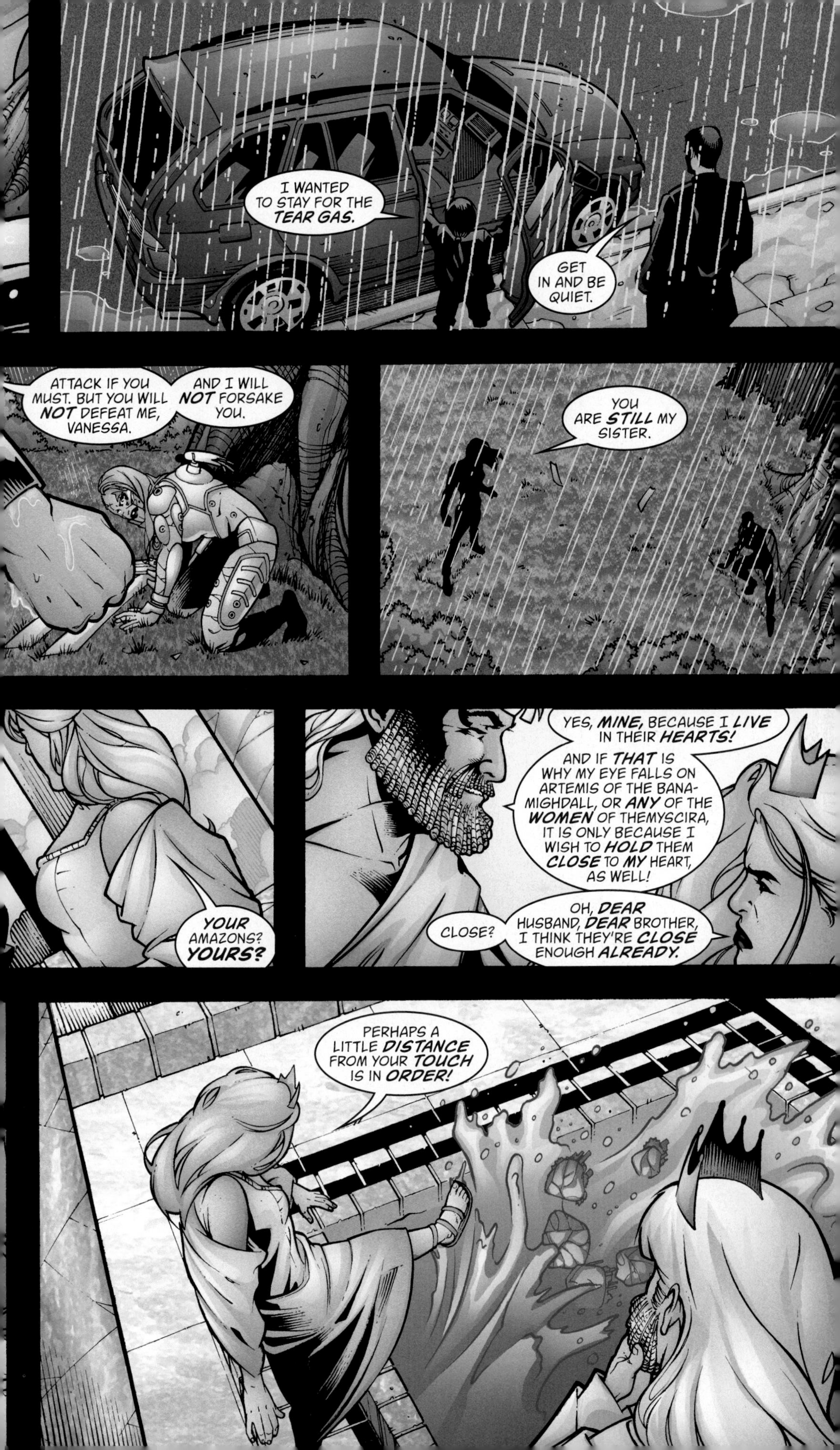
I WANTED TO STAY FOR THE TEAR GAS.
GET IN AND BE QUIET.
ATTACK IF YOU MUST. BUT YOU WILL NOT DEFEAT ME, VANESSA.
AND I WILL NOT FORSAKE YOU.
YOU ARE STILL MY SISTER.
YOUR AMAZONS? YOURS?
YES, MINE, BECAUSE I LIVE IN THEIR HEARTS!
AND IF THAT IS WHY MY EYE FALLS ON ARTEMIS OF THE BANA-MIGHDALL, OR ANY OF THE WOMEN OF THEMYSCIRA, IT IS ONLY BECAUSE I WISH TO HOLD THEM CLOSE TO MY HEART, AS WELL!
CLOSE?
OH, DEAR HUSBAND, DEAR BROTHER, I THINK THEY'RE CLOSE ENOUGH ALREADY.
PERHAPS A LITTLE DISTANCE FROM YOUR TOUCH IS IN ORDER!

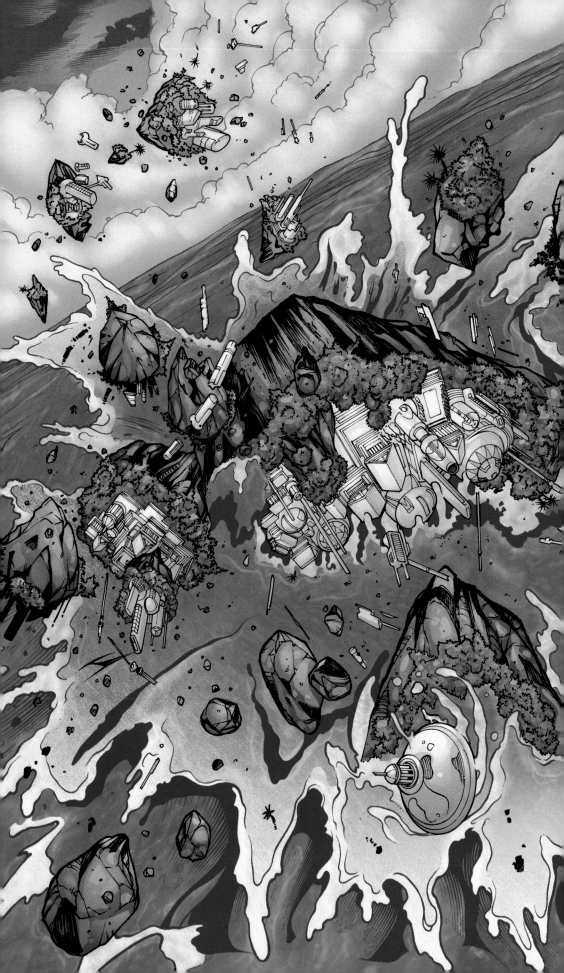

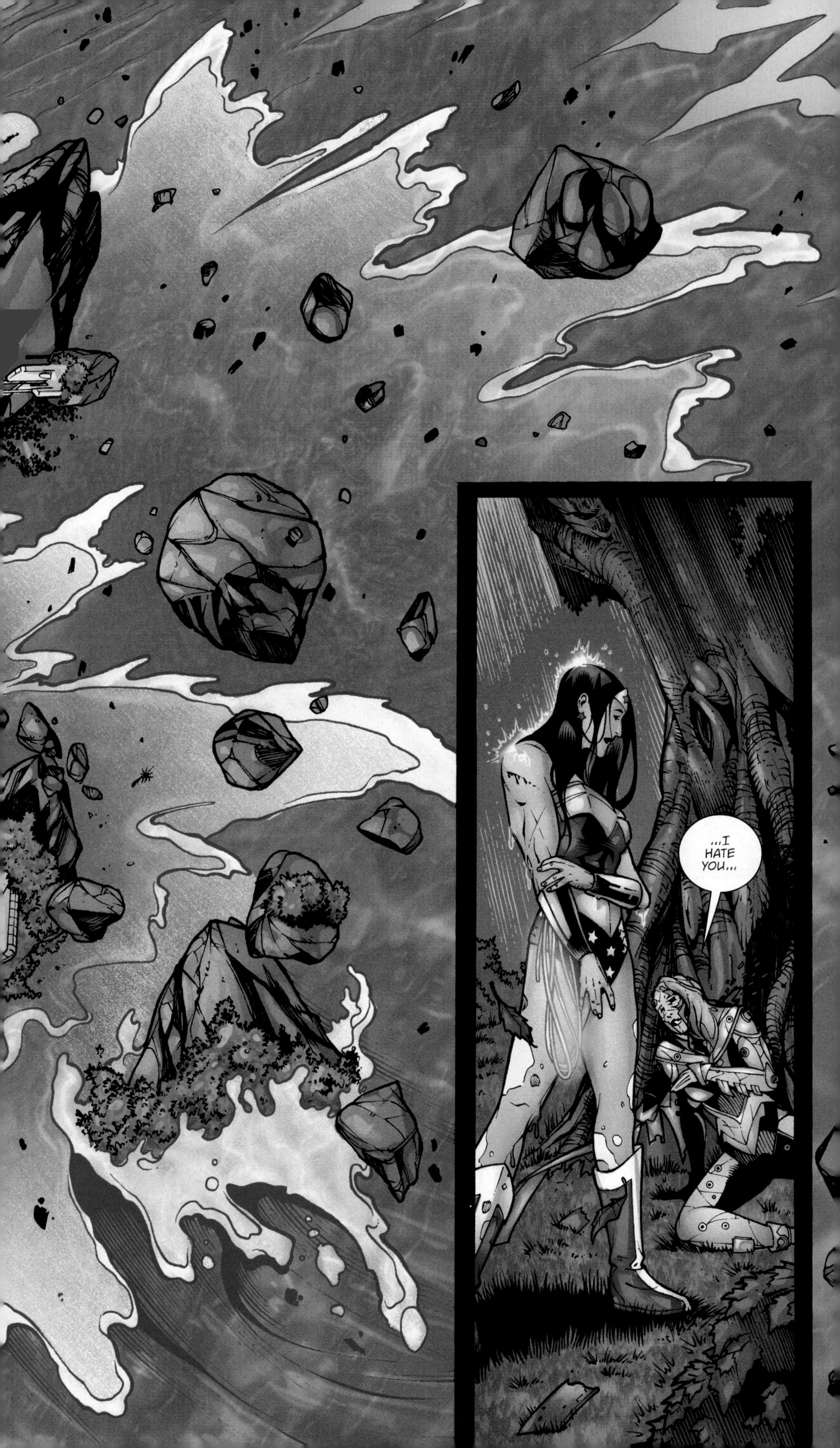
...I HATE YOU...

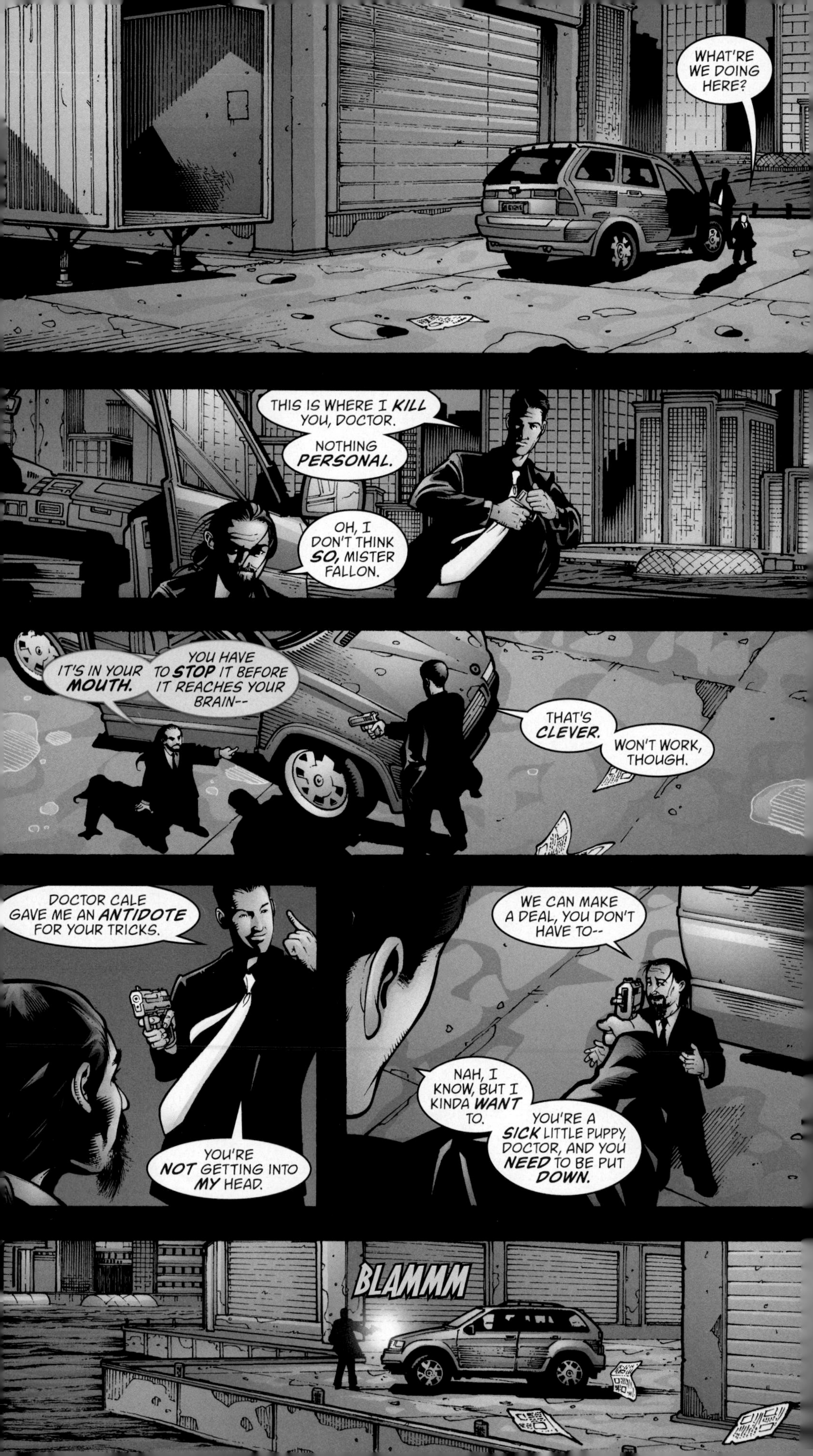

WHAT'RE WE DOING HERE?
THIS IS WHERE I KILL YOU, DOCTOR.
NOTHING PERSONAL.
OH, I DON'T THINK SO, MISTER FALLON.
IT'S IN YOUR MOUTH.
YOU HAVE TO STOP IT BEFORE IT REACHES YOUR BRAIN--
THAT'S CLEVER.
WON'T WORK, THOUGH.
DOCTOR CALE GAVE ME AN ANTIDOTE FOR YOUR TRICKS.
YOU'RE NOT GETTING INTO MY HEAD.
WE CAN MAKE A DEAL, YOU DON'T HAVE TO--
NAH, I KNOW, BUT I KINDA WANT TO.
YOU'RE A SICK LITTLE PUPPY, DOCTOR, AND YOU NEED TO BE PUT DOWN.
BLAMMM

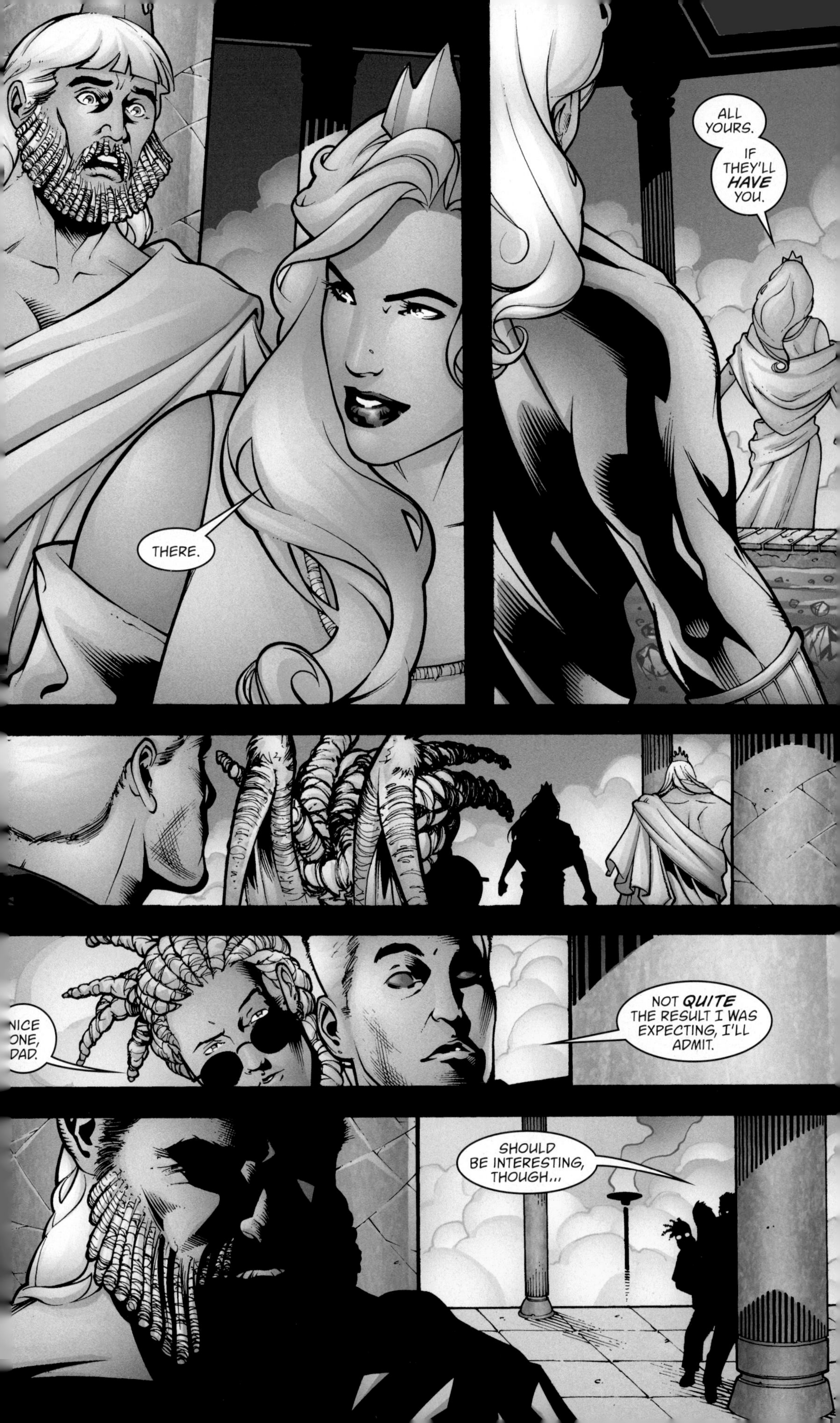
THERE.
ALL YOURS.
IF THEY'LL *HAVE* YOU.
NICE ONE, DAD.
NOT *QUITE* THE RESULT I WAS EXPECTING, I'LL ADMIT.
SHOULD BE INTERESTING, THOUGH...

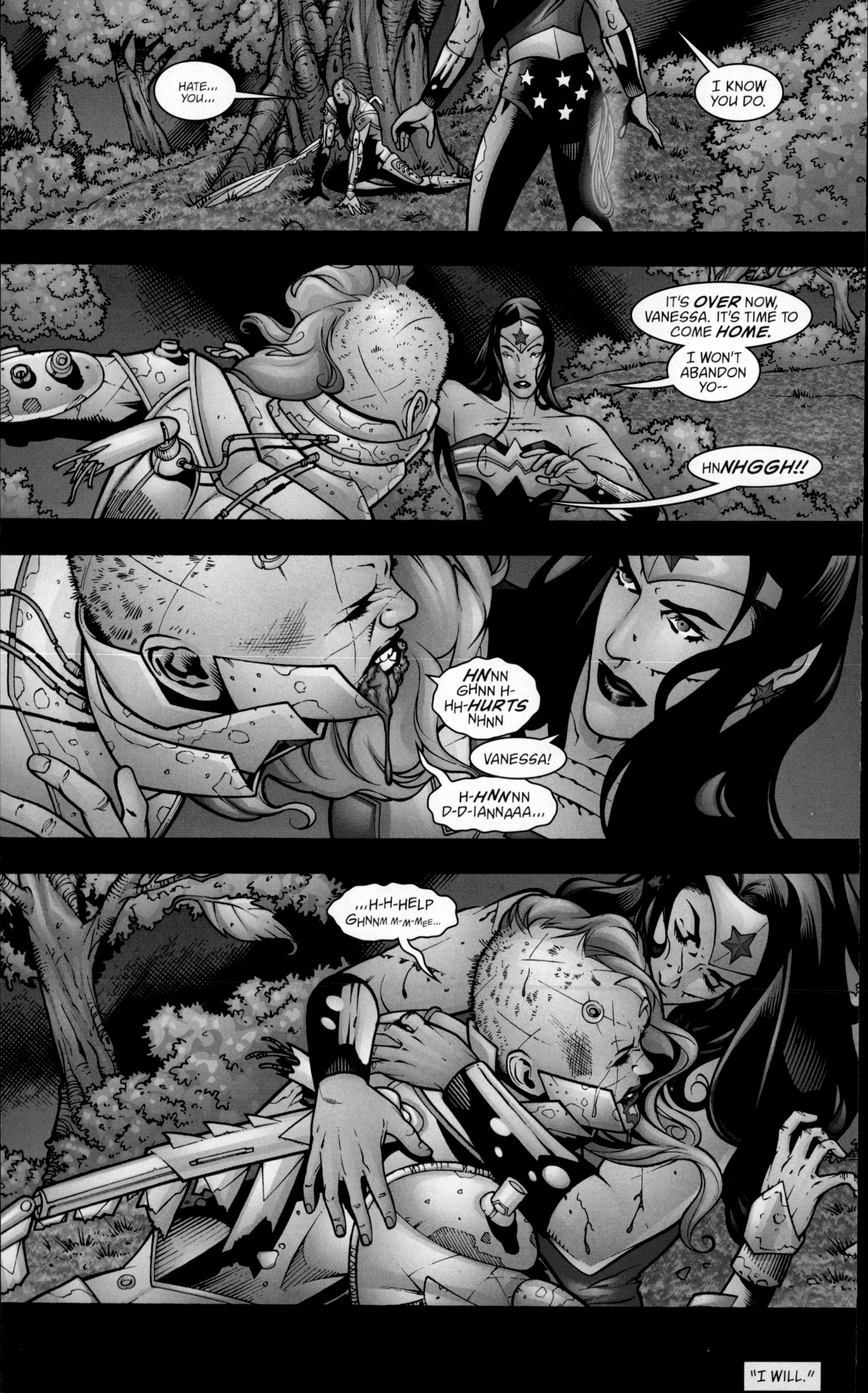
HATE... YOU...
I KNOW YOU DO.
IT'S OVER NOW, VANESSA. IT'S TIME TO COME HOME.
I WON'T ABANDON YO--
HNNHGGH!!
HNNN GHNN H-HH-HURTS NHNN
VANESSA!
H-HNNNN D-D-IANNAAA...
...H-H-HELP GHNNM M-M-MEE...
"I WILL."

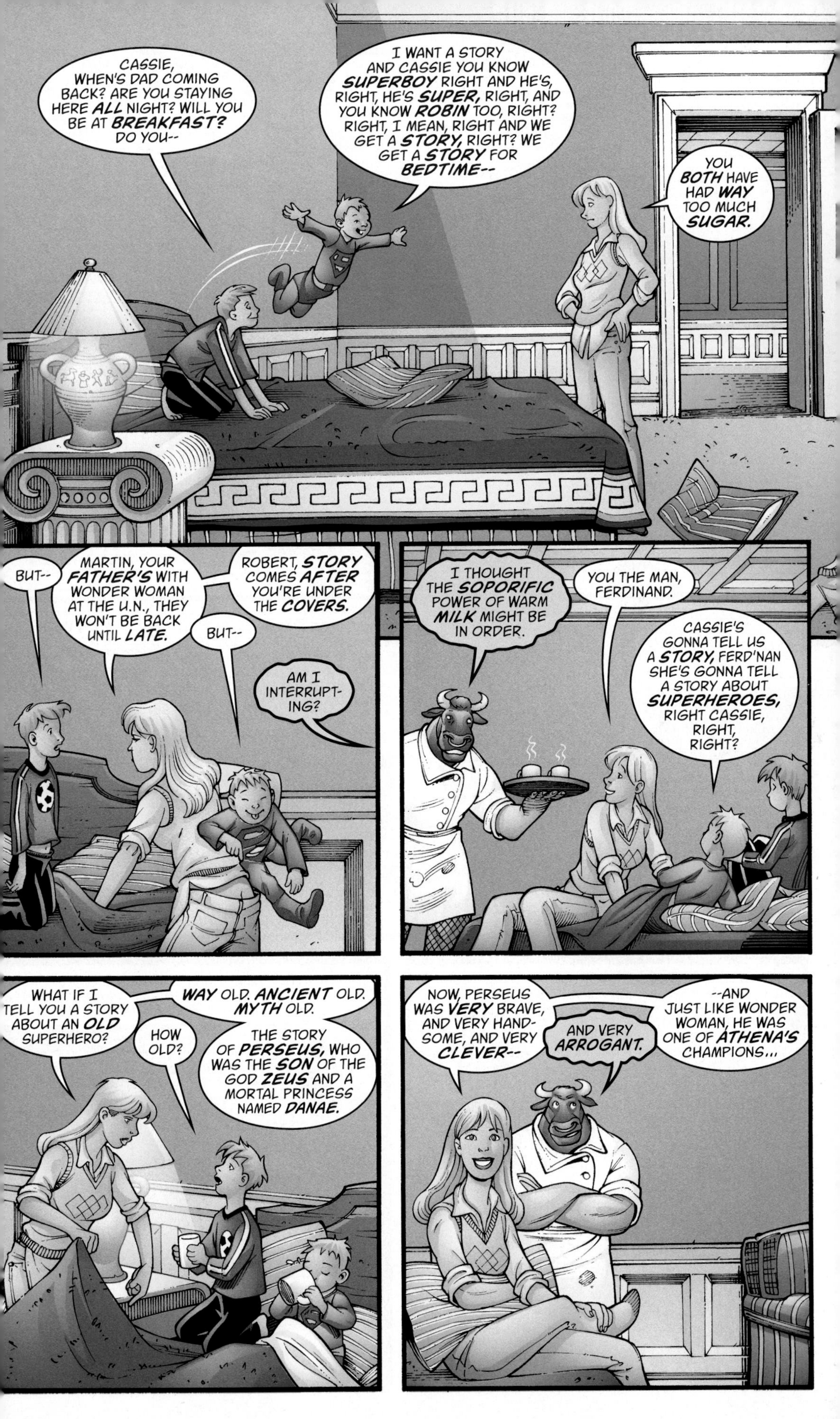

CASSIE, WHEN'S DAD COMING BACK? ARE YOU STAYING HERE ALL NIGHT? WILL YOU BE AT BREAKFAST? DO YOU--
I WANT A STORY AND CASSIE YOU KNOW SUPERBOY RIGHT AND HE'S, RIGHT, HE'S SUPER, RIGHT, AND YOU KNOW ROBIN TOO, RIGHT? RIGHT, I MEAN, RIGHT AND WE GET A STORY, RIGHT? WE GET A STORY FOR BEDTIME--
YOU BOTH HAVE HAD WAY TOO MUCH SUGAR.
BUT--
MARTIN, YOUR FATHER'S WITH WONDER WOMAN AT THE U.N., THEY WON'T BE BACK UNTIL LATE.
ROBERT, STORY COMES AFTER YOU'RE UNDER THE COVERS.
BUT--
AM I INTERRUPT-ING?
I THOUGHT THE SOPORIFIC POWER OF WARM MILK MIGHT BE IN ORDER.
YOU THE MAN, FERDINAND.
CASSIE'S GONNA TELL US A STORY, FERD'NAN SHE'S GONNA TELL A STORY ABOUT SUPERHEROES, RIGHT CASSIE, RIGHT, RIGHT?
WHAT IF I TELL YOU A STORY ABOUT AN OLD SUPERHERO?
HOW OLD?
WAY OLD. ANCIENT OLD. MYTH OLD.
THE STORY OF PERSEUS, WHO WAS THE SON OF THE GOD ZEUS AND A MORTAL PRINCESS NAMED DANAE.
NOW, PERSEUS WAS VERY BRAVE, AND VERY HAND-SOME, AND VERY CLEVER--
AND VERY ARROGANT.
--AND JUST LIKE WONDER WOMAN, HE WAS ONE OF ATHENA'S CHAMPIONS...

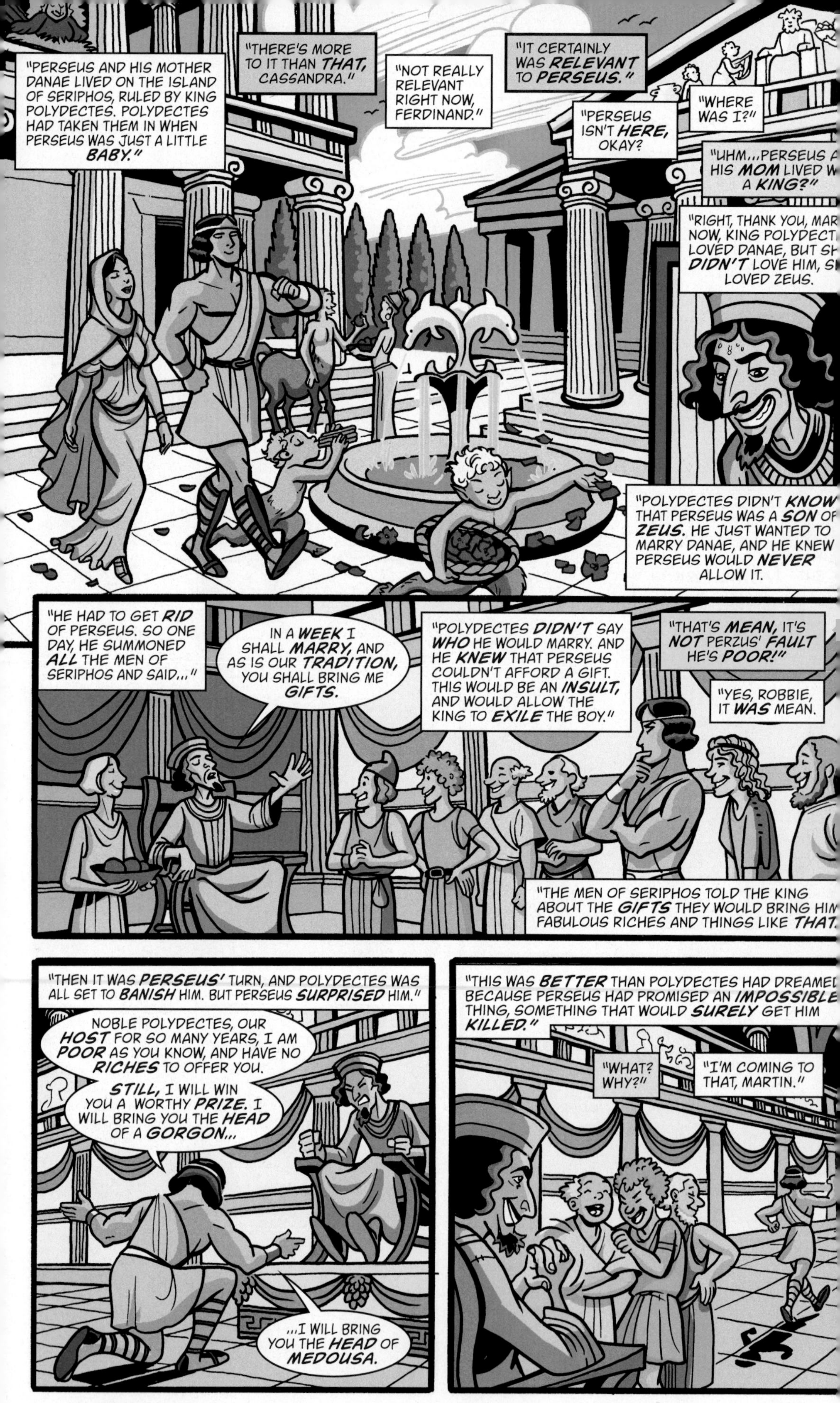
"PERSEUS AND HIS MOTHER DANAE LIVED ON THE ISLAND OF SERIPHOS, RULED BY KING POLYDECTES. POLYDECTES HAD TAKEN THEM IN WHEN PERSEUS WAS JUST A LITTLE BABY."
"THERE'S MORE TO IT THAN THAT, CASSANDRA."
"NOT REALLY RELEVANT RIGHT NOW, FERDINAND."
"IT CERTAINLY WAS RELEVANT TO PERSEUS."
"PERSEUS ISN'T HERE, OKAY?
"WHERE WAS I?"
"UHM...PERSEUS A HIS MOM LIVED W A KING?"
"RIGHT, THANK YOU, MAR NOW, KING POLYDECT LOVED DANAE, BUT SH DIDN'T LOVE HIM, SH LOVED ZEUS.
"POLYDECTES DIDN'T KNOW THAT PERSEUS WAS A SON OF ZEUS. HE JUST WANTED TO MARRY DANAE, AND HE KNEW PERSEUS WOULD NEVER ALLOW IT.
"HE HAD TO GET RID OF PERSEUS. SO ONE DAY, HE SUMMONED ALL THE MEN OF SERIPHOS AND SAID..."
IN A WEEK I SHALL MARRY, AND AS IS OUR TRADITION, YOU SHALL BRING ME GIFTS.
"POLYDECTES DIDN'T SAY WHO HE WOULD MARRY. AND HE KNEW THAT PERSEUS COULDN'T AFFORD A GIFT. THIS WOULD BE AN INSULT, AND WOULD ALLOW THE KING TO EXILE THE BOY."
"THAT'S MEAN, IT'S NOT PERZUS' FAULT HE'S POOR!"
"YES, ROBBIE, IT WAS MEAN.
"THE MEN OF SERIPHOS TOLD THE KING ABOUT THE GIFTS THEY WOULD BRING HIM FABULOUS RICHES AND THINGS LIKE THAT.
"THEN IT WAS PERSEUS' TURN, AND POLYDECTES WAS ALL SET TO BANISH HIM. BUT PERSEUS SURPRISED HIM."
NOBLE POLYDECTES, OUR HOST FOR SO MANY YEARS, I AM POOR AS YOU KNOW, AND HAVE NO RICHES TO OFFER YOU.
STILL, I WILL WIN YOU A WORTHY PRIZE. I WILL BRING YOU THE HEAD OF A GORGON...
...I WILL BRING YOU THE HEAD OF MEDOUSA.
"THIS WAS BETTER THAN POLYDECTES HAD DREAMED BECAUSE PERSEUS HAD PROMISED AN IMPOSSIBLE THING, SOMETHING THAT WOULD SURELY GET HIM KILLED."
"WHAT? WHY?"
"I'M COMING TO THAT, MARTIN."

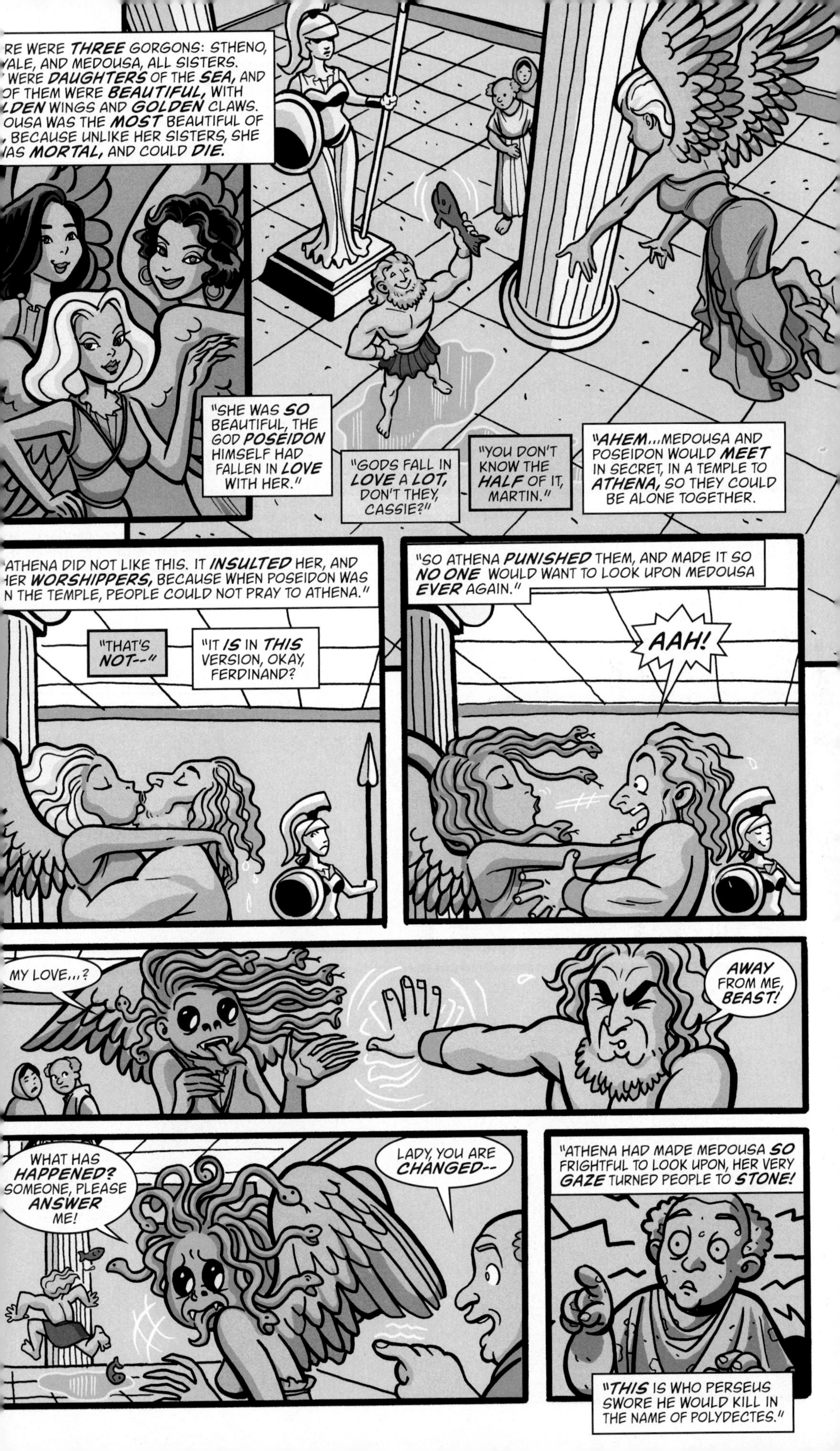
RE WERE THREE GORGONS: STHENO, YALE, AND MEDOUSA, ALL SISTERS. WERE DAUGHTERS OF THE SEA, AND OF THEM WERE BEAUTIFUL, WITH LDEN WINGS AND GOLDEN CLAWS. OUSA WAS THE MOST BEAUTIFUL OF , BECAUSE UNLIKE HER SISTERS, SHE AS MORTAL, AND COULD DIE.
"SHE WAS SO BEAUTIFUL, THE GOD POSEIDON HIMSELF HAD FALLEN IN LOVE WITH HER."
"GODS FALL IN LOVE A LOT, DON'T THEY, CASSIE?"
"YOU DON'T KNOW THE HALF OF IT, MARTIN."
"AHEM...MEDOUSA AND POSEIDON WOULD MEET IN SECRET, IN A TEMPLE TO ATHENA, SO THEY COULD BE ALONE TOGETHER.
ATHENA DID NOT LIKE THIS. IT INSULTED HER, AND HER WORSHIPPERS, BECAUSE WHEN POSEIDON WAS N THE TEMPLE, PEOPLE COULD NOT PRAY TO ATHENA."
"THAT'S NOT--"
"IT IS IN THIS VERSION, OKAY, FERDINAND?
"SO ATHENA PUNISHED THEM, AND MADE IT SO NO ONE WOULD WANT TO LOOK UPON MEDOUSA EVER AGAIN."
AAH!
MY LOVE...?
AWAY FROM ME, BEAST!
WHAT HAS HAPPENED? SOMEONE, PLEASE ANSWER ME!
LADY, YOU ARE CHANGED--
"ATHENA HAD MADE MEDOUSA SO FRIGHTFUL TO LOOK UPON, HER VERY GAZE TURNED PEOPLE TO STONE!
"THIS IS WHO PERSEUS SWORE HE WOULD KILL IN THE NAME OF POLYDECTES."

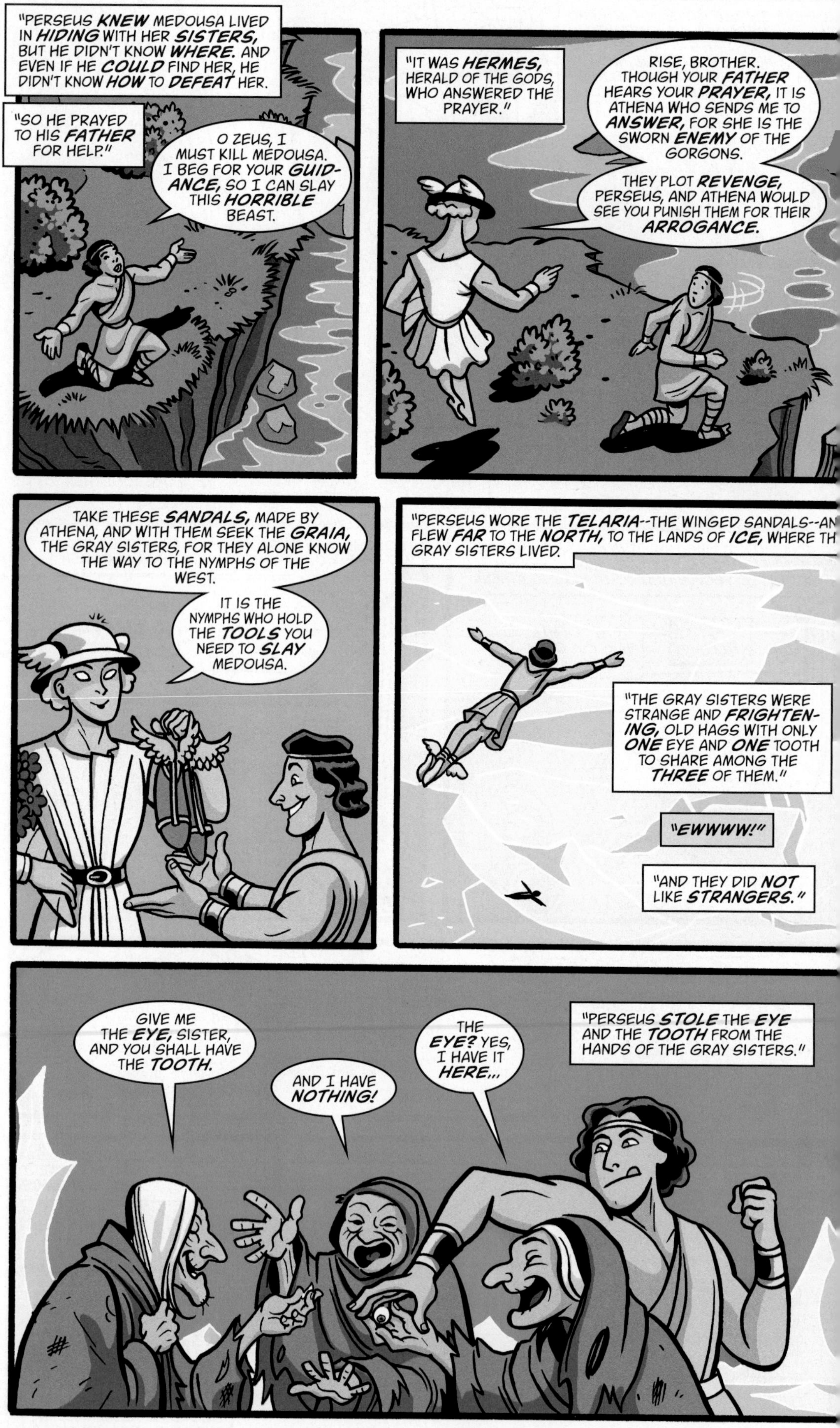
"PERSEUS KNEW MEDOUSA LIVED IN HIDING WITH HER SISTERS, BUT HE DIDN'T KNOW WHERE. AND EVEN IF HE COULD FIND HER, HE DIDN'T KNOW HOW TO DEFEAT HER.
"SO HE PRAYED TO HIS FATHER FOR HELP."
O ZEUS, I MUST KILL MEDOUSA. I BEG FOR YOUR GUIDANCE, SO I CAN SLAY THIS HORRIBLE BEAST.
"IT WAS HERMES, HERALD OF THE GODS, WHO ANSWERED THE PRAYER."
RISE, BROTHER. THOUGH YOUR FATHER HEARS YOUR PRAYER, IT IS ATHENA WHO SENDS ME TO ANSWER, FOR SHE IS THE SWORN ENEMY OF THE GORGONS.
THEY PLOT REVENGE, PERSEUS, AND ATHENA WOULD SEE YOU PUNISH THEM FOR THEIR ARROGANCE.
TAKE THESE SANDALS, MADE BY ATHENA, AND WITH THEM SEEK THE GRAIA, THE GRAY SISTERS, FOR THEY ALONE KNOW THE WAY TO THE NYMPHS OF THE WEST.
IT IS THE NYMPHS WHO HOLD THE TOOLS YOU NEED TO SLAY MEDOUSA.
"PERSEUS WORE THE TELARIA--THE WINGED SANDALS--AN FLEW FAR TO THE NORTH, TO THE LANDS OF ICE, WHERE TH GRAY SISTERS LIVED.
"THE GRAY SISTERS WERE STRANGE AND FRIGHTENING, OLD HAGS WITH ONLY ONE EYE AND ONE TOOTH TO SHARE AMONG THE THREE OF THEM."
"EWWWW!"
"AND THEY DID NOT LIKE STRANGERS."
GIVE ME THE EYE, SISTER, AND YOU SHALL HAVE THE TOOTH.
AND I HAVE NOTHING!
THE EYE? YES, I HAVE IT HERE...
"PERSEUS STOLE THE EYE AND THE TOOTH FROM THE HANDS OF THE GRAY SISTERS."

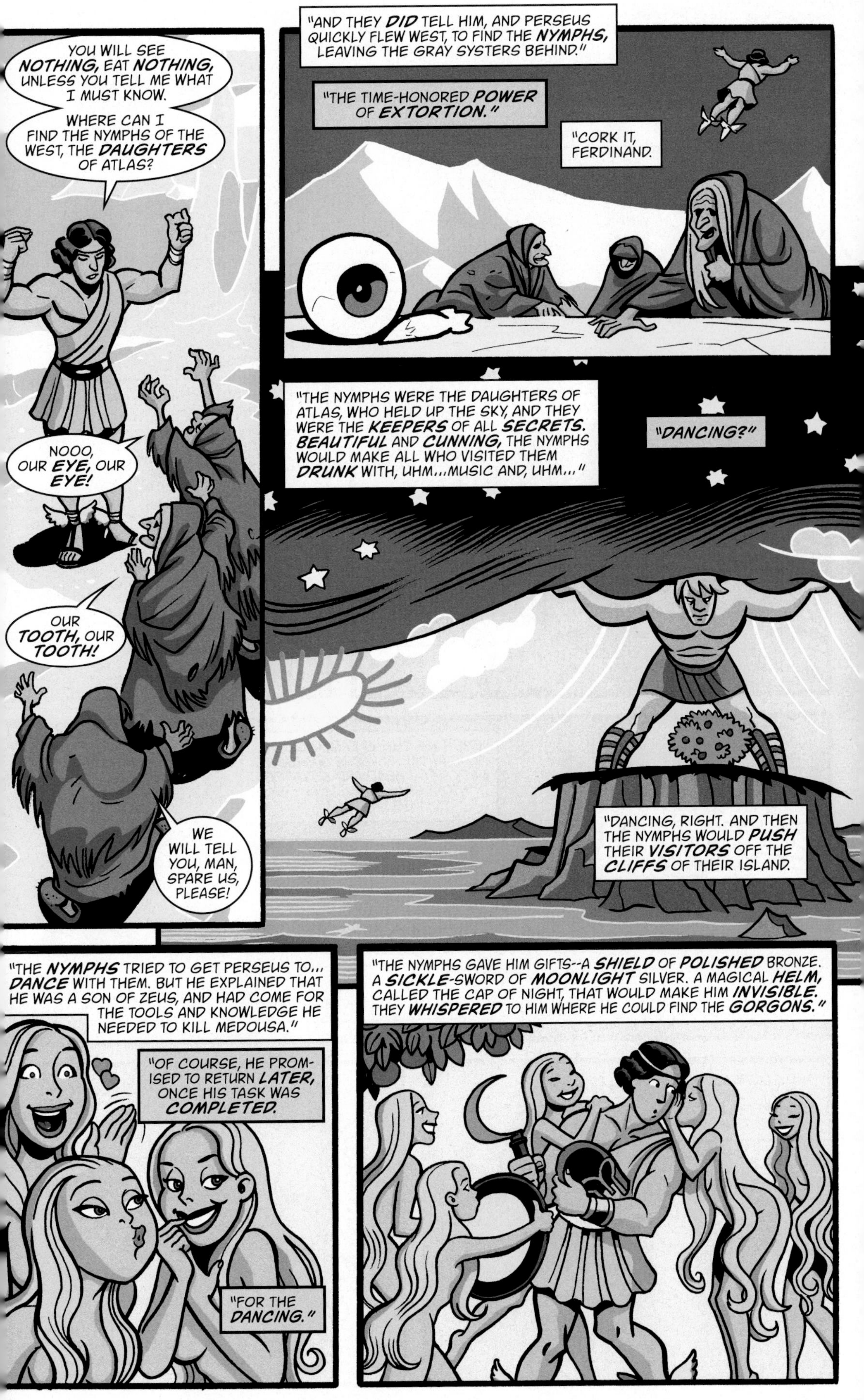

YOU WILL SEE NOTHING, EAT NOTHING, UNLESS YOU TELL ME WHAT I MUST KNOW.
WHERE CAN I FIND THE NYMPHS OF THE WEST, THE DAUGHTERS OF ATLAS?
NOOO, OUR EYE, OUR EYE!
OUR TOOTH, OUR TOOTH!
WE WILL TELL YOU, MAN, SPARE US, PLEASE!
"AND THEY DID TELL HIM, AND PERSEUS QUICKLY FLEW WEST, TO FIND THE NYMPHS, LEAVING THE GRAY SYSTERS BEHIND."
"THE TIME-HONORED POWER OF EXTORTION."
"CORK IT, FERDINAND.
"THE NYMPHS WERE THE DAUGHTERS OF ATLAS, WHO HELD UP THE SKY, AND THEY WERE THE KEEPERS OF ALL SECRETS. BEAUTIFUL AND CUNNING, THE NYMPHS WOULD MAKE ALL WHO VISITED THEM DRUNK WITH, UHM...MUSIC AND, UHM..."
"DANCING?"
"DANCING, RIGHT. AND THEN THE NYMPHS WOULD PUSH THEIR VISITORS OFF THE CLIFFS OF THEIR ISLAND.
"THE NYMPHS TRIED TO GET PERSEUS TO... DANCE WITH THEM. BUT HE EXPLAINED THAT HE WAS A SON OF ZEUS, AND HAD COME FOR THE TOOLS AND KNOWLEDGE HE NEEDED TO KILL MEDOUSA."
"OF COURSE, HE PROMISED TO RETURN LATER, ONCE HIS TASK WAS COMPLETED.
"FOR THE DANCING."
"THE NYMPHS GAVE HIM GIFTS--A SHIELD OF POLISHED BRONZE. A SICKLE-SWORD OF MOONLIGHT SILVER. A MAGICAL HELM, CALLED THE CAP OF NIGHT, THAT WOULD MAKE HIM INVISIBLE. THEY WHISPERED TO HIM WHERE HE COULD FIND THE GORGONS."

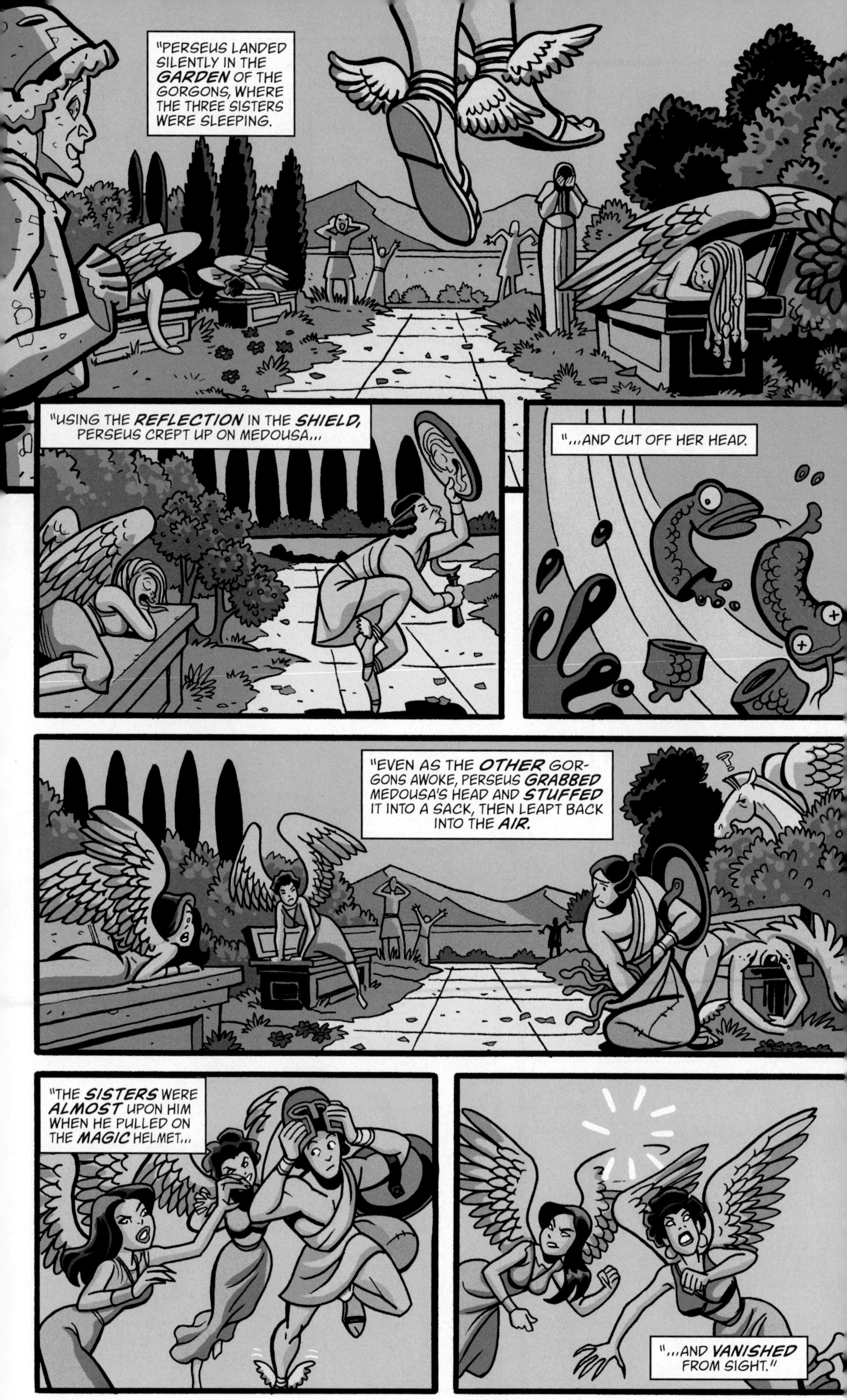

"PERSEUS LANDED SILENTLY IN THE GARDEN OF THE GORGONS, WHERE THE THREE SISTERS WERE SLEEPING.
"USING THE REFLECTION IN THE SHIELD, PERSEUS CREPT UP ON MEDOUSA...
"...AND CUT OFF HER HEAD.
"EVEN AS THE OTHER GORGONS AWOKE, PERSEUS GRABBED MEDOUSA'S HEAD AND STUFFED IT INTO A SACK, THEN LEAPT BACK INTO THE AIR.
"THE SISTERS WERE ALMOST UPON HIM WHEN HE PULLED ON THE MAGIC HELMET...
"...AND VANISHED FROM SIGHT."

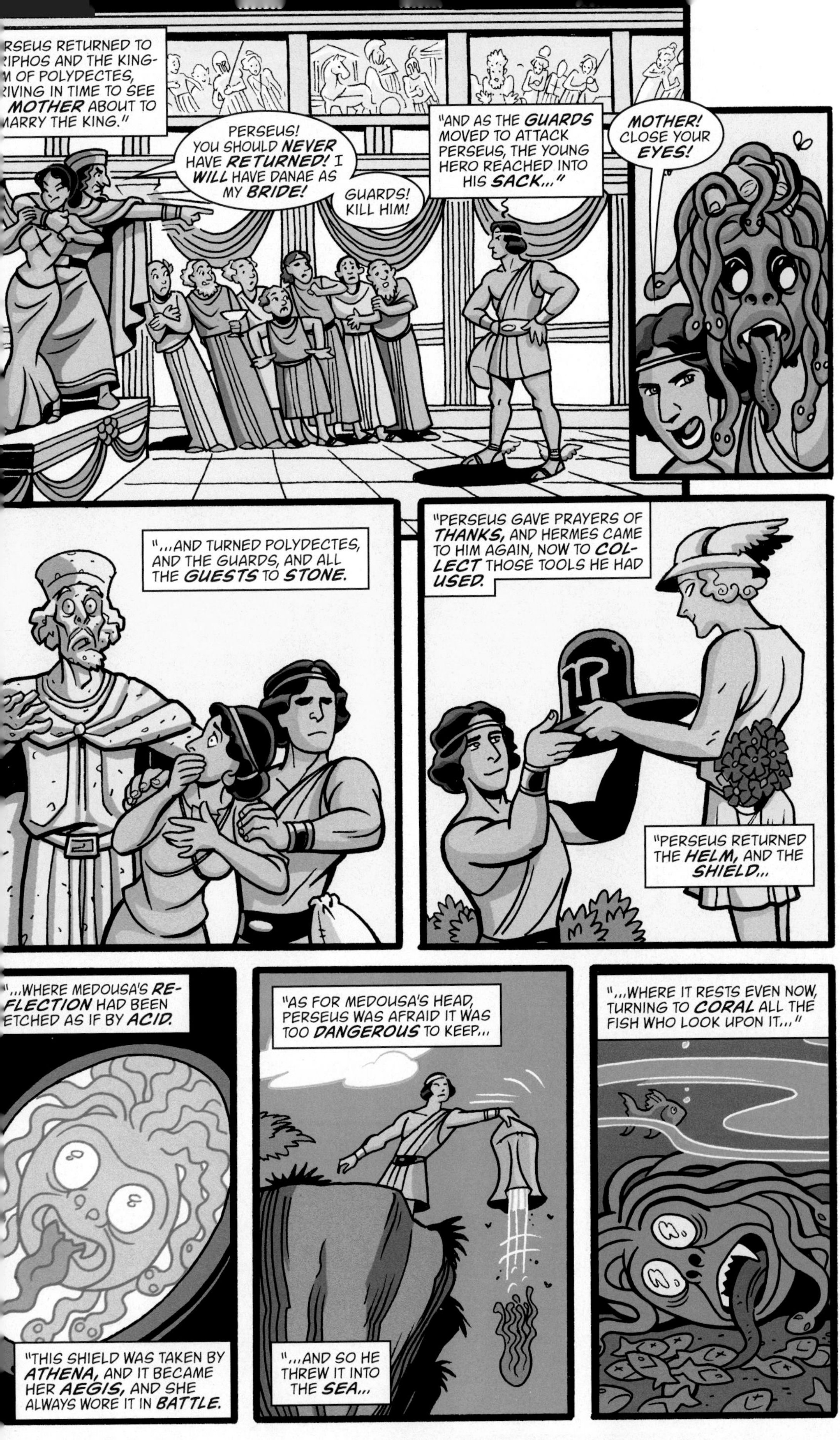
RSEUS RETURNED TO
RIPHOS AND THE KING-
M OF POLYDECTES,
RIVING IN TIME TO SEE
MOTHER ABOUT TO
MARRY THE KING."
PERSEUS! YOU SHOULD NEVER HAVE RETURNED! I WILL HAVE DANAE AS MY BRIDE!
GUARDS! KILL HIM!
"AND AS THE GUARDS MOVED TO ATTACK PERSEUS, THE YOUNG HERO REACHED INTO HIS SACK..."
MOTHER! CLOSE YOUR EYES!
"...AND TURNED POLYDECTES, AND THE GUARDS, AND ALL THE GUESTS TO STONE.
"PERSEUS GAVE PRAYERS OF THANKS, AND HERMES CAME TO HIM AGAIN, NOW TO COLLECT THOSE TOOLS HE HAD USED.
"PERSEUS RETURNED THE HELM, AND THE SHIELD...
"...WHERE MEDOUSA'S RE-
FLECTION HAD BEEN
ETCHED AS IF BY ACID.
"THIS SHIELD WAS TAKEN BY ATHENA, AND IT BECAME HER AEGIS, AND SHE ALWAYS WORE IT IN BATTLE.
"AS FOR MEDOUSA'S HEAD, PERSEUS WAS AFRAID IT WAS TOO DANGEROUS TO KEEP...
"...AND SO HE THREW IT INTO THE SEA...
"...WHERE IT RESTS EVEN NOW, TURNING TO CORAL ALL THE FISH WHO LOOK UPON IT..."

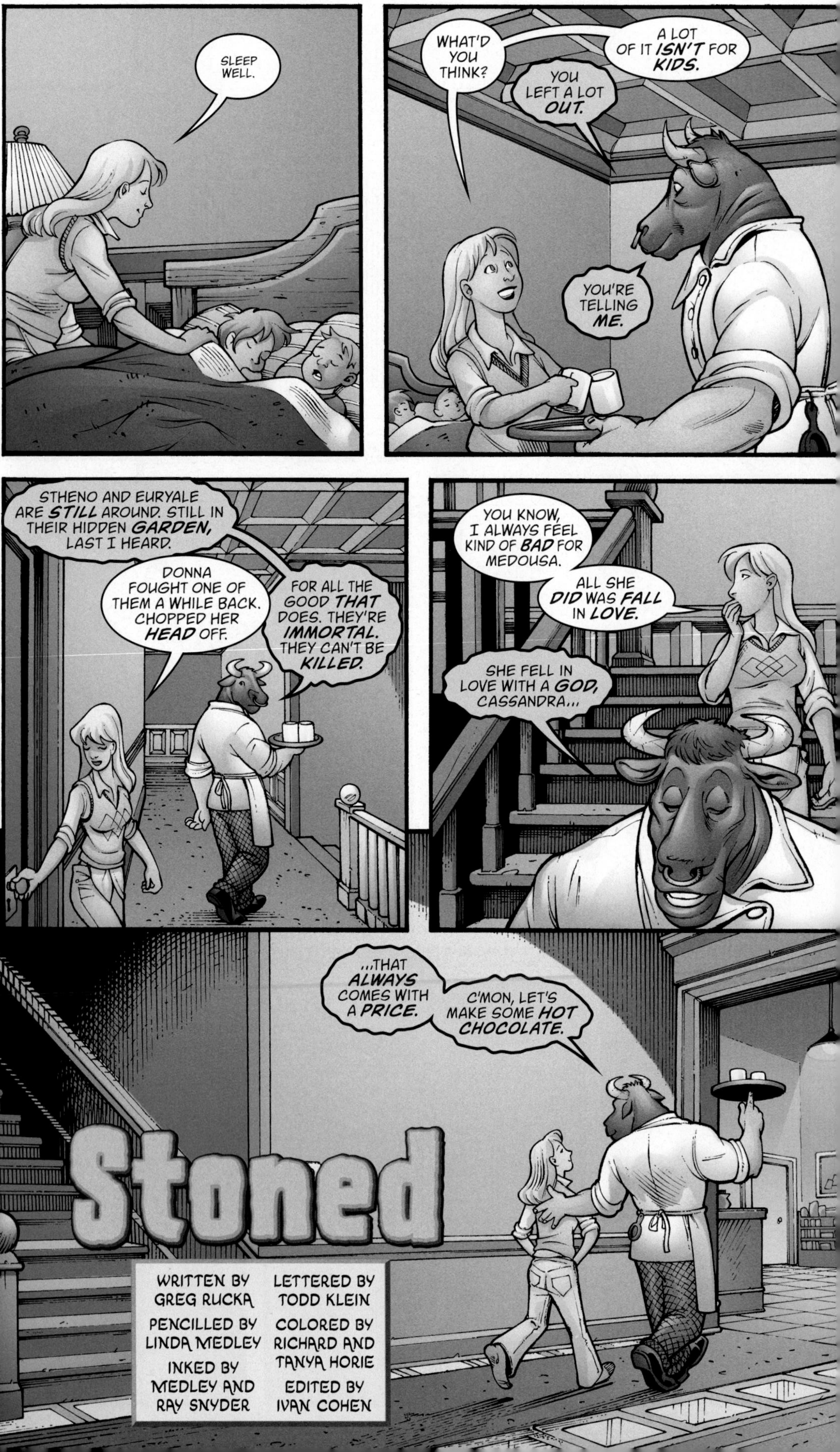
SLEEP WELL.
WHAT'D YOU THINK?
A LOT OF IT ISN'T FOR KIDS.
YOU LEFT A LOT OUT.
YOU'RE TELLING ME.
STHENO AND EURYALE ARE STILL AROUND. STILL IN THEIR HIDDEN GARDEN, LAST I HEARD.
DONNA FOUGHT ONE OF THEM A WHILE BACK. CHOPPED HER HEAD OFF.
FOR ALL THE GOOD THAT DOES. THEY'RE IMMORTAL. THEY CAN'T BE KILLED.
YOU KNOW, I ALWAYS FEEL KIND OF BAD FOR MEDOUSA.
ALL SHE DID WAS FALL IN LOVE.
SHE FELL IN LOVE WITH A GOD, CASSANDRA...
...THAT ALWAYS COMES WITH A PRICE.
C'MON, LET'S MAKE SOME HOT CHOCOLATE.
Stoned
WRITTEN BY GREG RUCKA
PENCILLED BY LINDA MEDLEY
INKED BY MEDLEY AND RAY SNYDER
LETTERED BY TODD KLEIN
COLORED BY RICHARD AND TANYA HORIE
EDITED BY IVAN COHEN

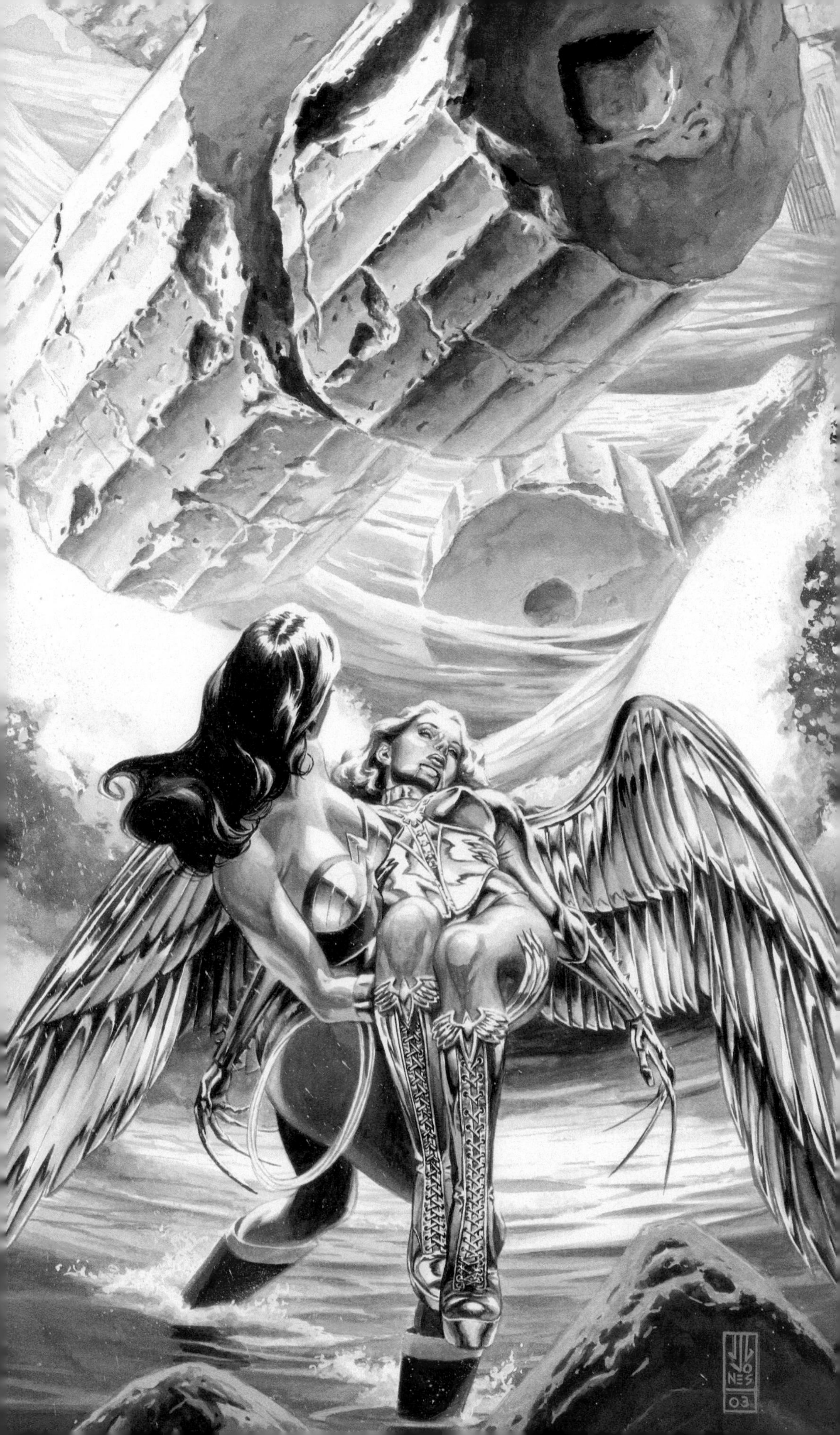

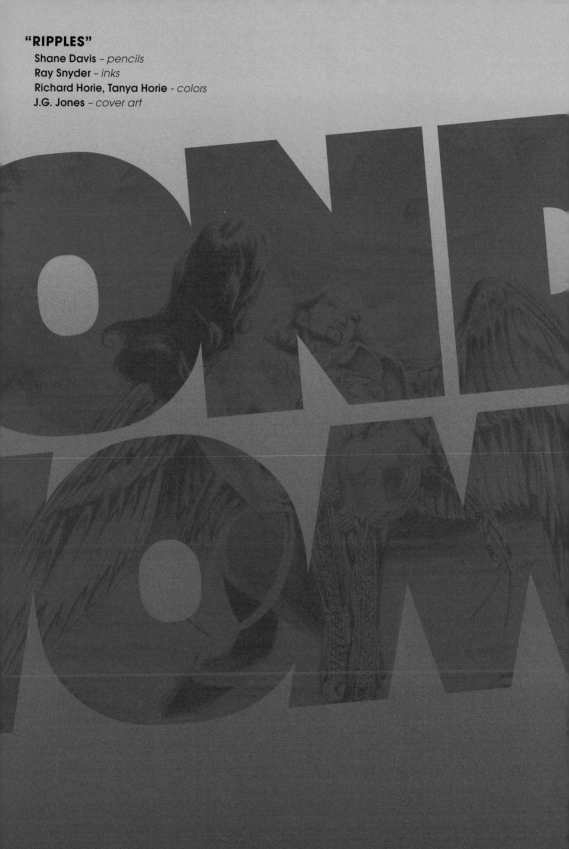

"RIPPLES"

Shane Davis – *pencils*
Ray Snyder – *inks*
Richard Horie, Tanya Horie - *colors*
J.G. Jones – *cover art*

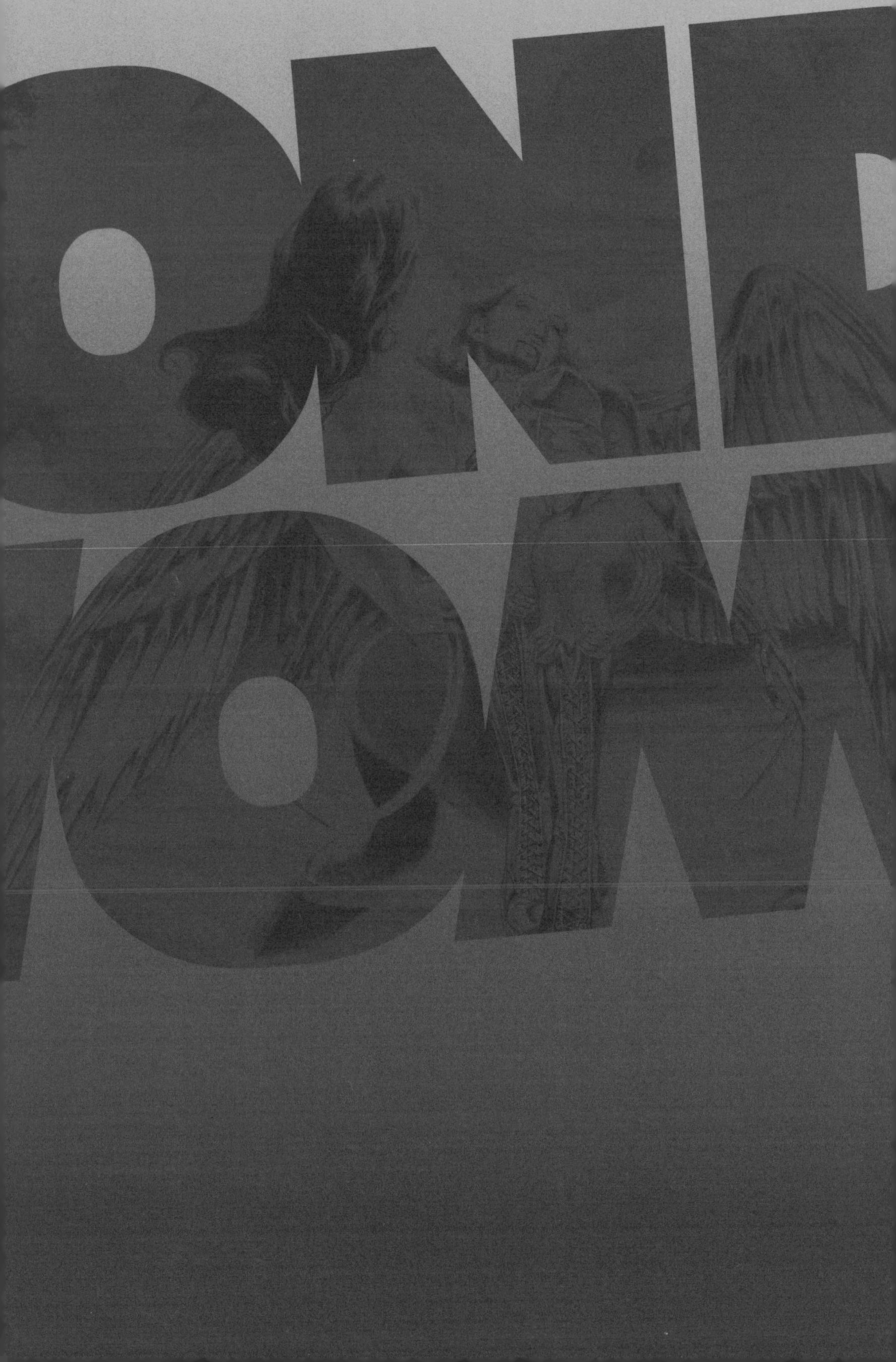

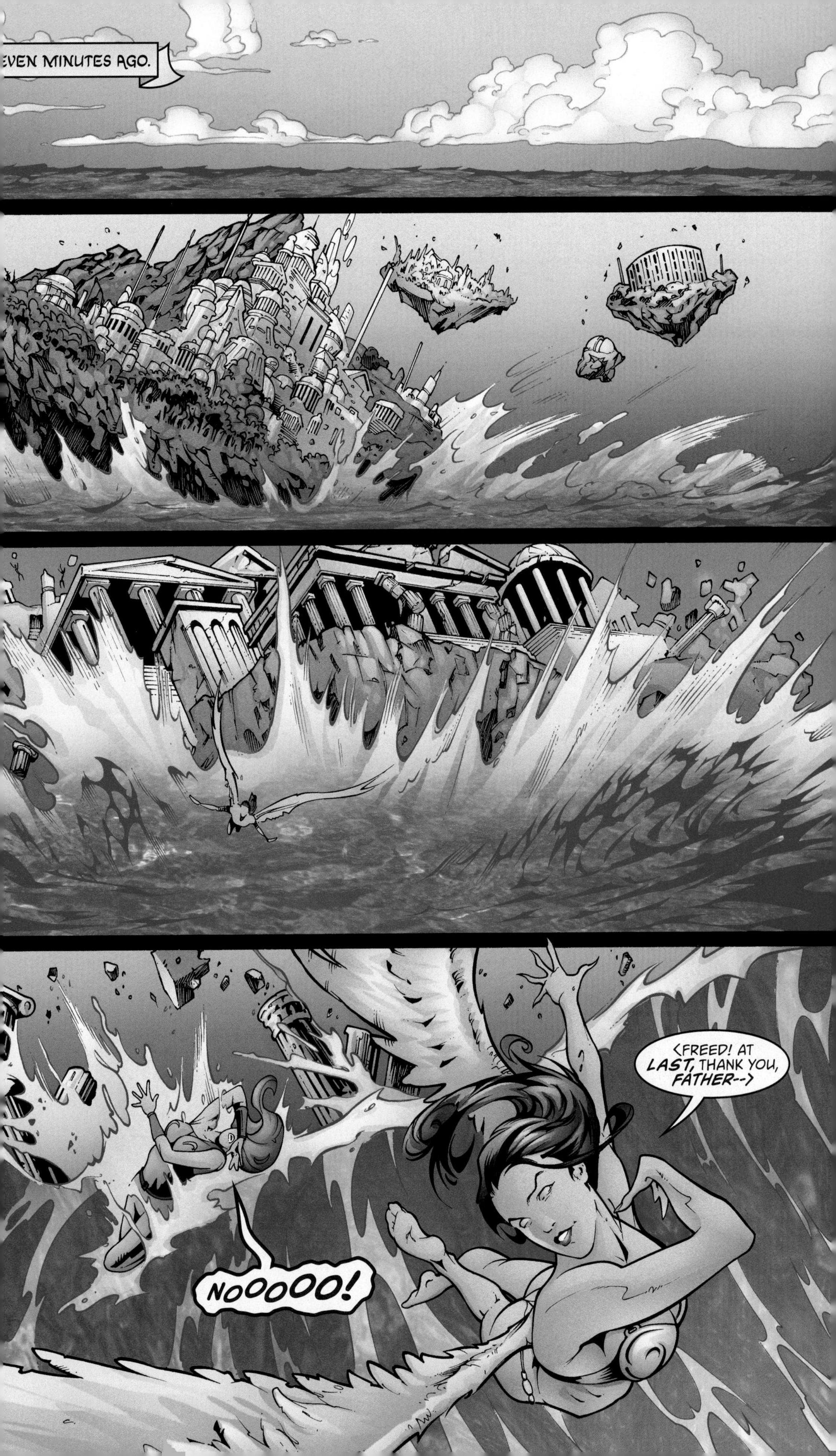
EVEN MINUTES AGO.
<FREED! AT LAST, THANK YOU, FATHER-->
NOOOOO!

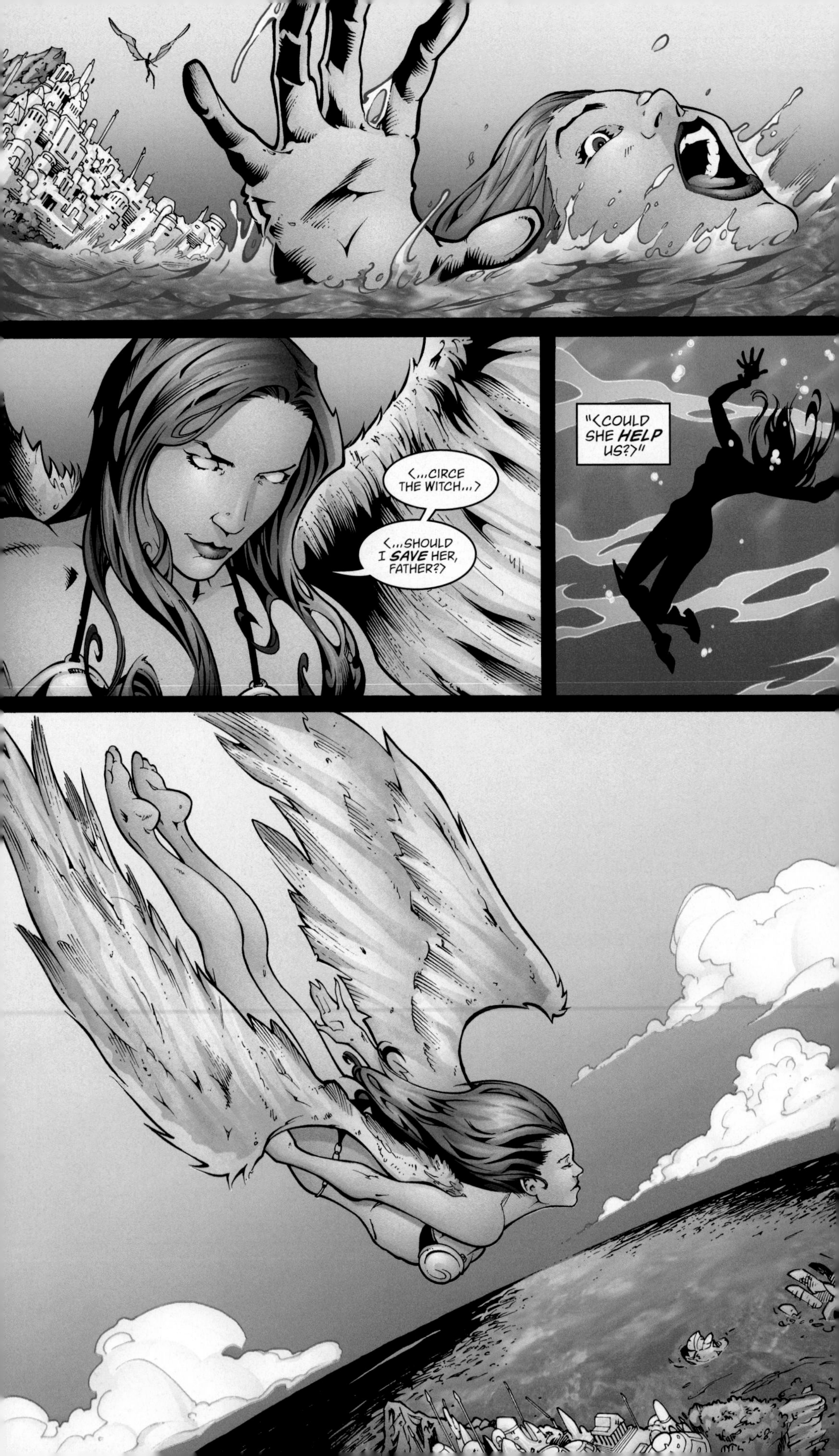
<...CIRCE THE WITCH...>
<...SHOULD I SAVE HER, FATHER?>
"<COULD SHE HELP US?>"

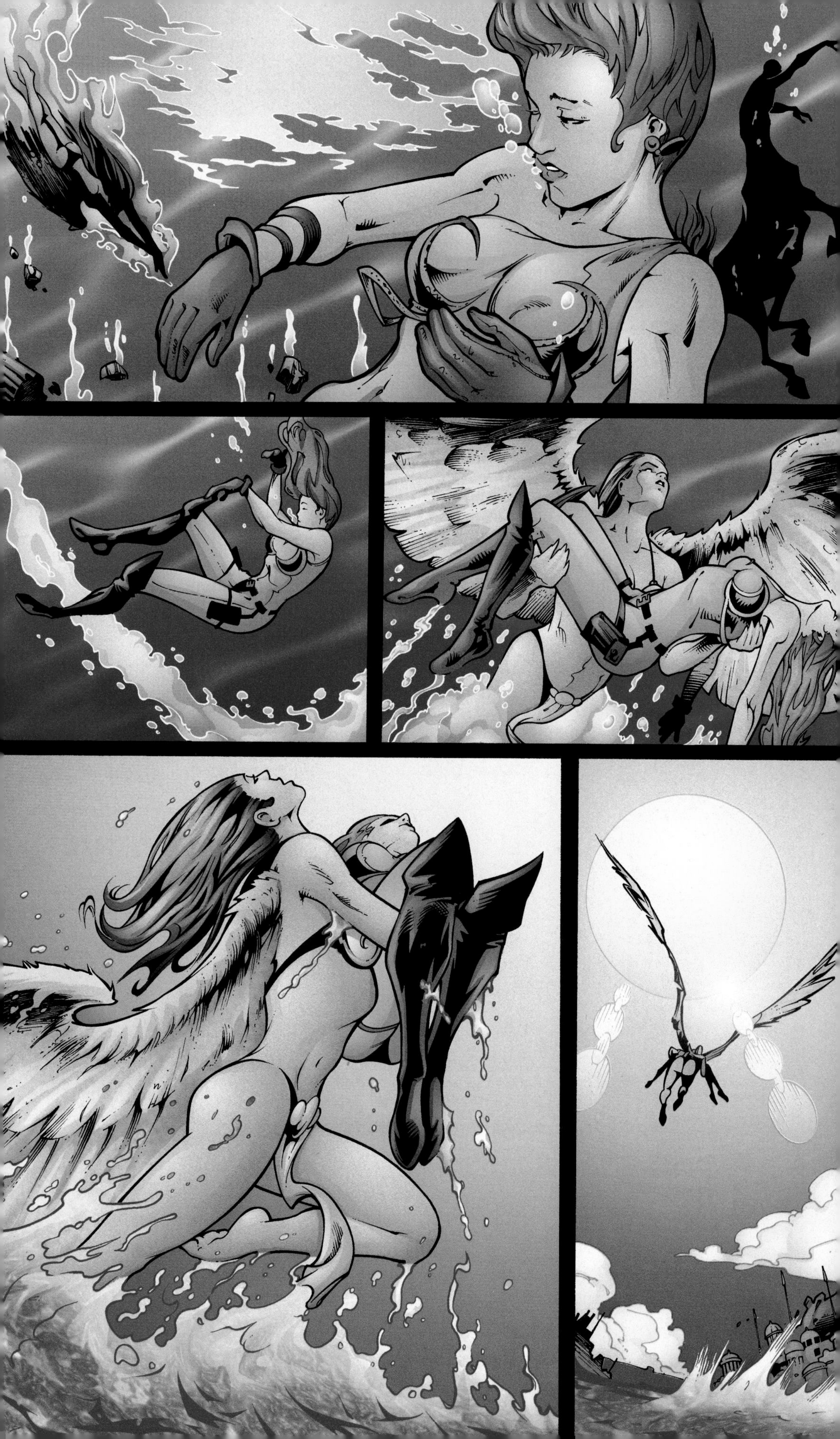

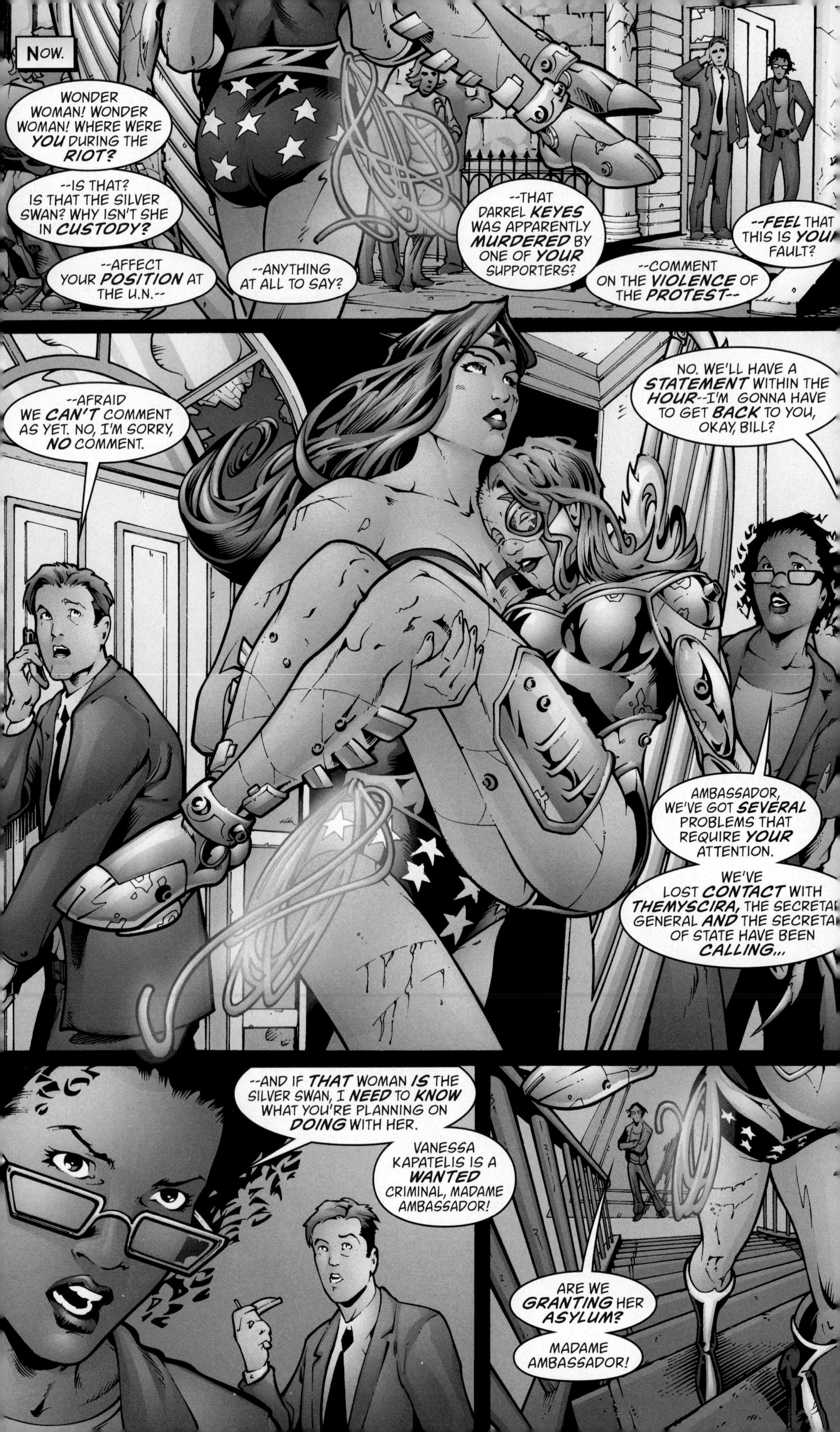
NOW.
WONDER WOMAN! WONDER WOMAN! WHERE WERE YOU DURING THE RIOT?
--IS THAT? IS THAT THE SILVER SWAN? WHY ISN'T SHE IN CUSTODY?
--AFFECT YOUR POSITION AT THE U.N.--
--ANYTHING AT ALL TO SAY?
--THAT DARREL KEYES WAS APPARENTLY MURDERED BY ONE OF YOUR SUPPORTERS?
--COMMENT ON THE VIOLENCE OF THE PROTEST--
--FEEL THAT THIS IS YOUR FAULT?
--AFRAID WE CAN'T COMMENT AS YET. NO, I'M SORRY, NO COMMENT.
NO. WE'LL HAVE A STATEMENT WITHIN THE HOUR--I'M GONNA HAVE TO GET BACK TO YOU, OKAY, BILL?
AMBASSADOR, WE'VE GOT SEVERAL PROBLEMS THAT REQUIRE YOUR ATTENTION.
WE'VE LOST CONTACT WITH THEMYSCIRA, THE SECRETARY GENERAL AND THE SECRETARY OF STATE HAVE BEEN CALLING...
--AND IF THAT WOMAN IS THE SILVER SWAN, I NEED TO KNOW WHAT YOU'RE PLANNING ON DOING WITH HER.
VANESSA KAPATELIS IS A WANTED CRIMINAL, MADAME AMBASSADOR!
ARE WE GRANTING HER ASYLUM?
MADAME AMBASSADOR!

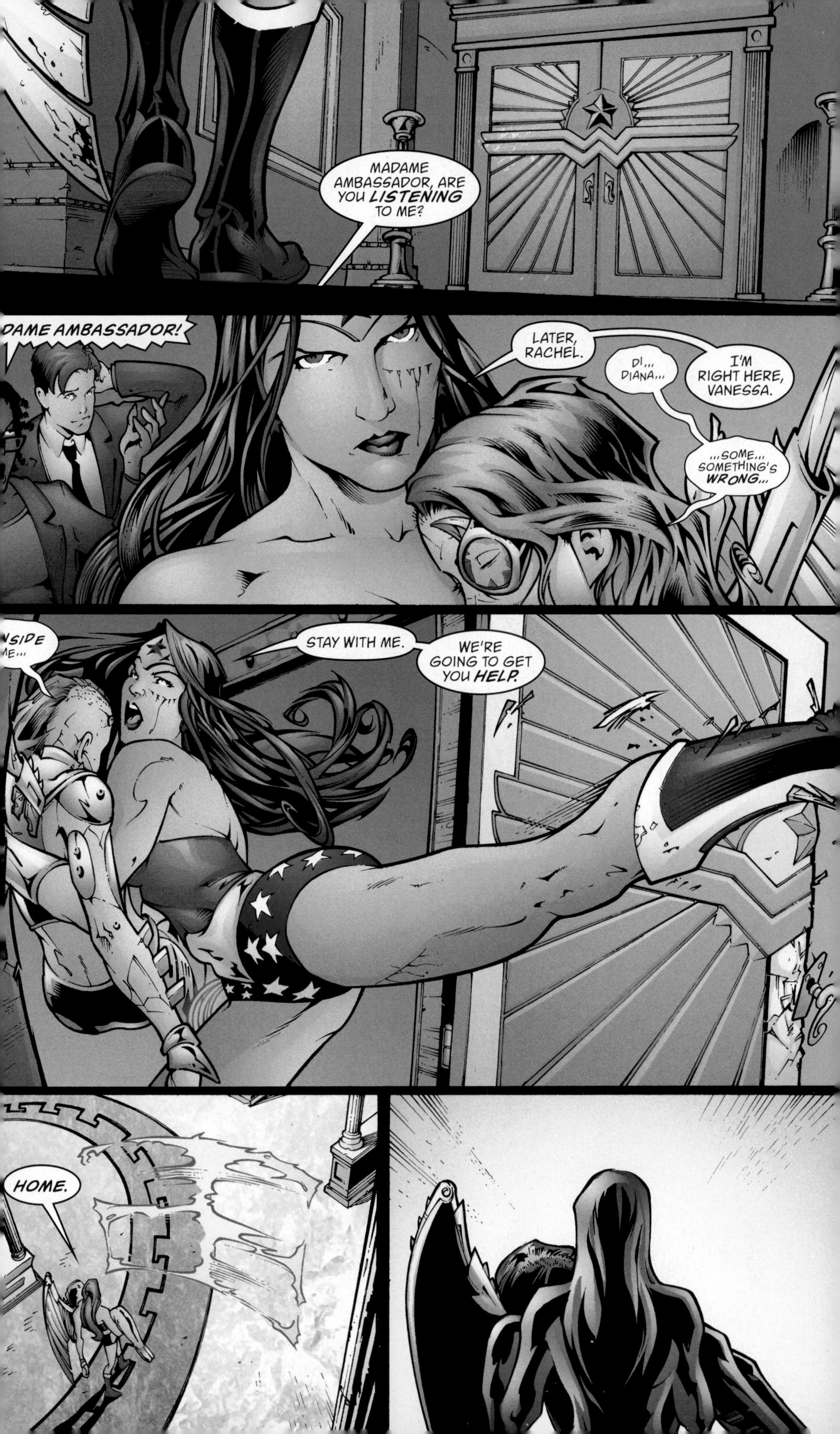
MADAME AMBASSADOR, ARE YOU **LISTENING** TO ME?
DAME AMBASSADOR!
LATER, RACHEL.
DI... DIANA...
I'M RIGHT HERE, VANESSA.
...SOME... SOMETHING'S **WRONG**...
NSIDE
STAY WITH ME.
WE'RE GOING TO GET YOU **HELP.**
HOME.

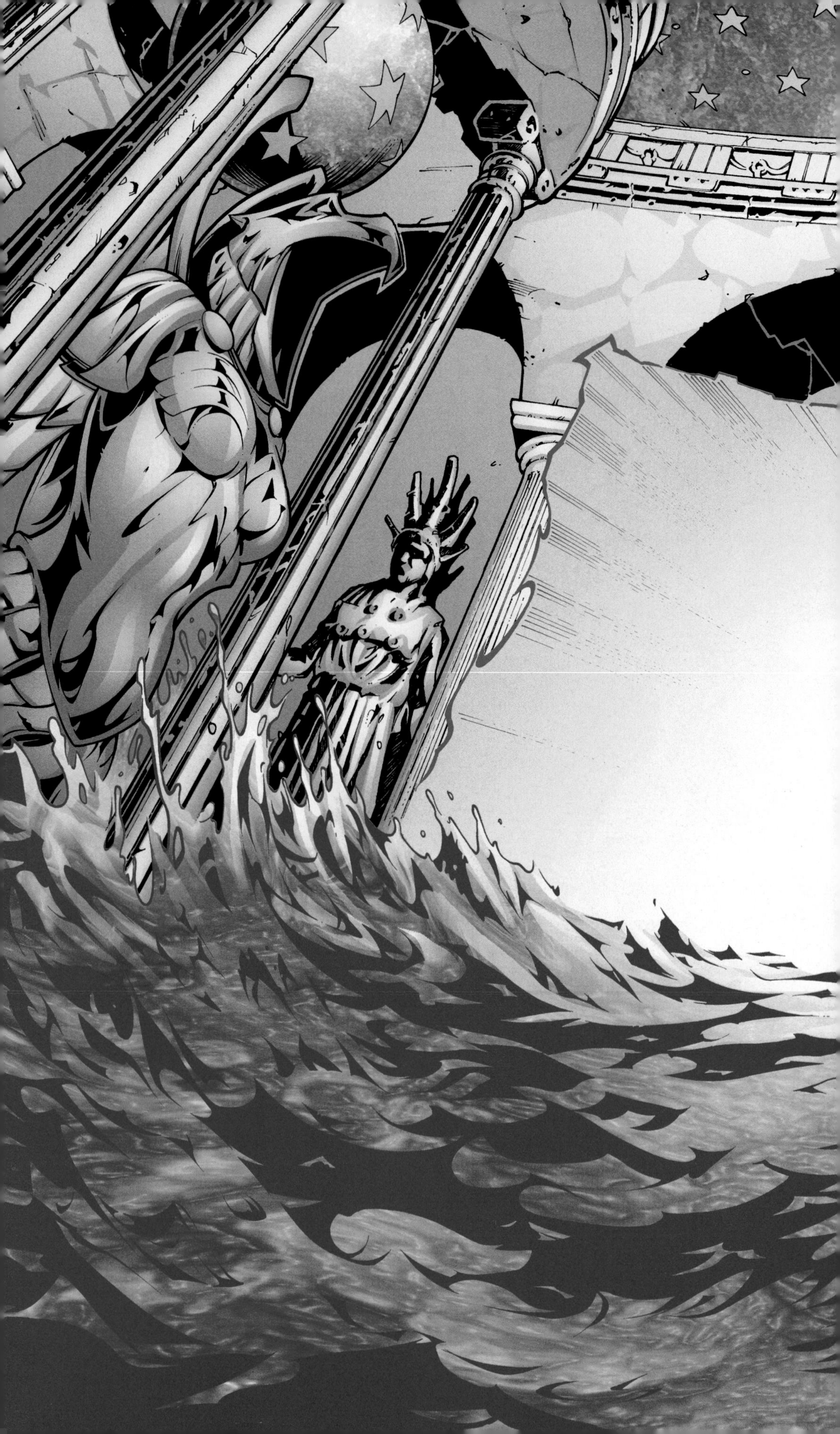

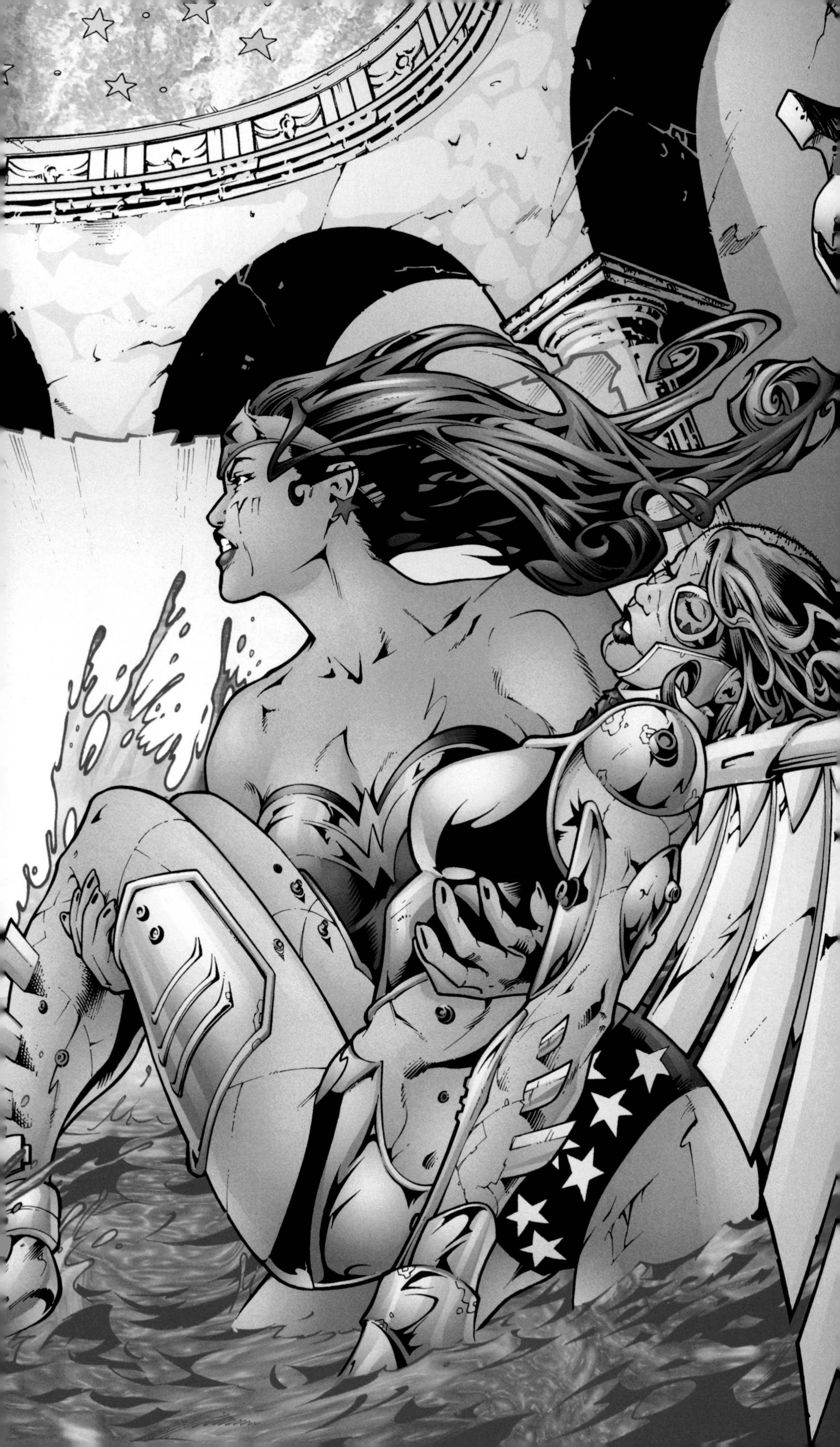

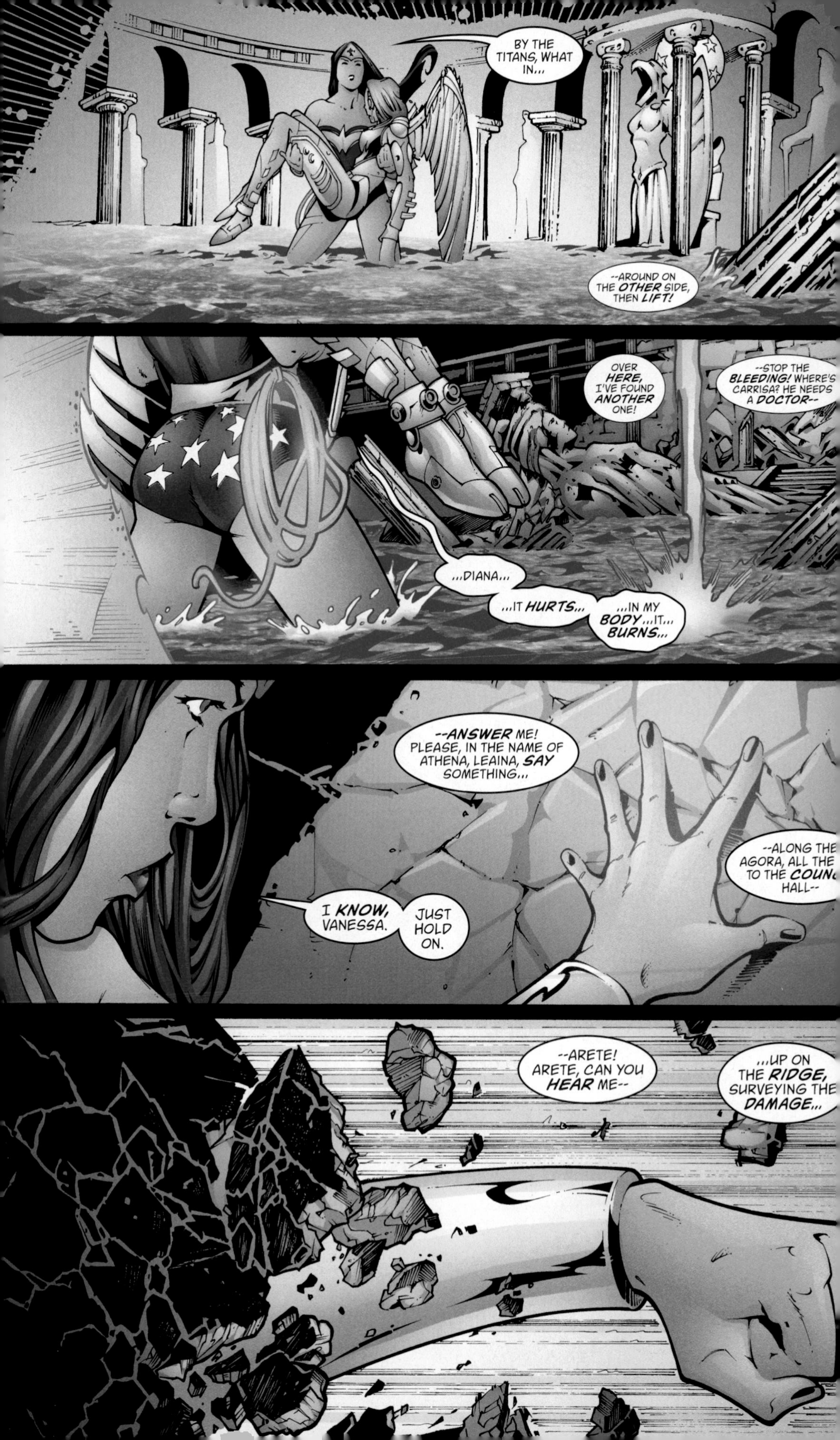
BY THE TITANS, WHAT IN...
--AROUND ON THE OTHER SIDE, THEN LIFT!
OVER HERE, I'VE FOUND ANOTHER ONE!
--STOP THE BLEEDING! WHERE'S CARRISA? HE NEEDS A DOCTOR--
...DIANA...
...IT HURTS...
...IN MY BODY...IT... BURNS...
--ANSWER ME! PLEASE, IN THE NAME OF ATHENA, LEAINA, SAY SOMETHING...
--ALONG THE AGORA, ALL THE TO THE COUN HALL--
I KNOW, VANESSA.
JUST HOLD ON.
--ARETE! ARETE, CAN YOU HEAR ME--
...UP ON THE RIDGE, SURVEYING THE DAMAGE...

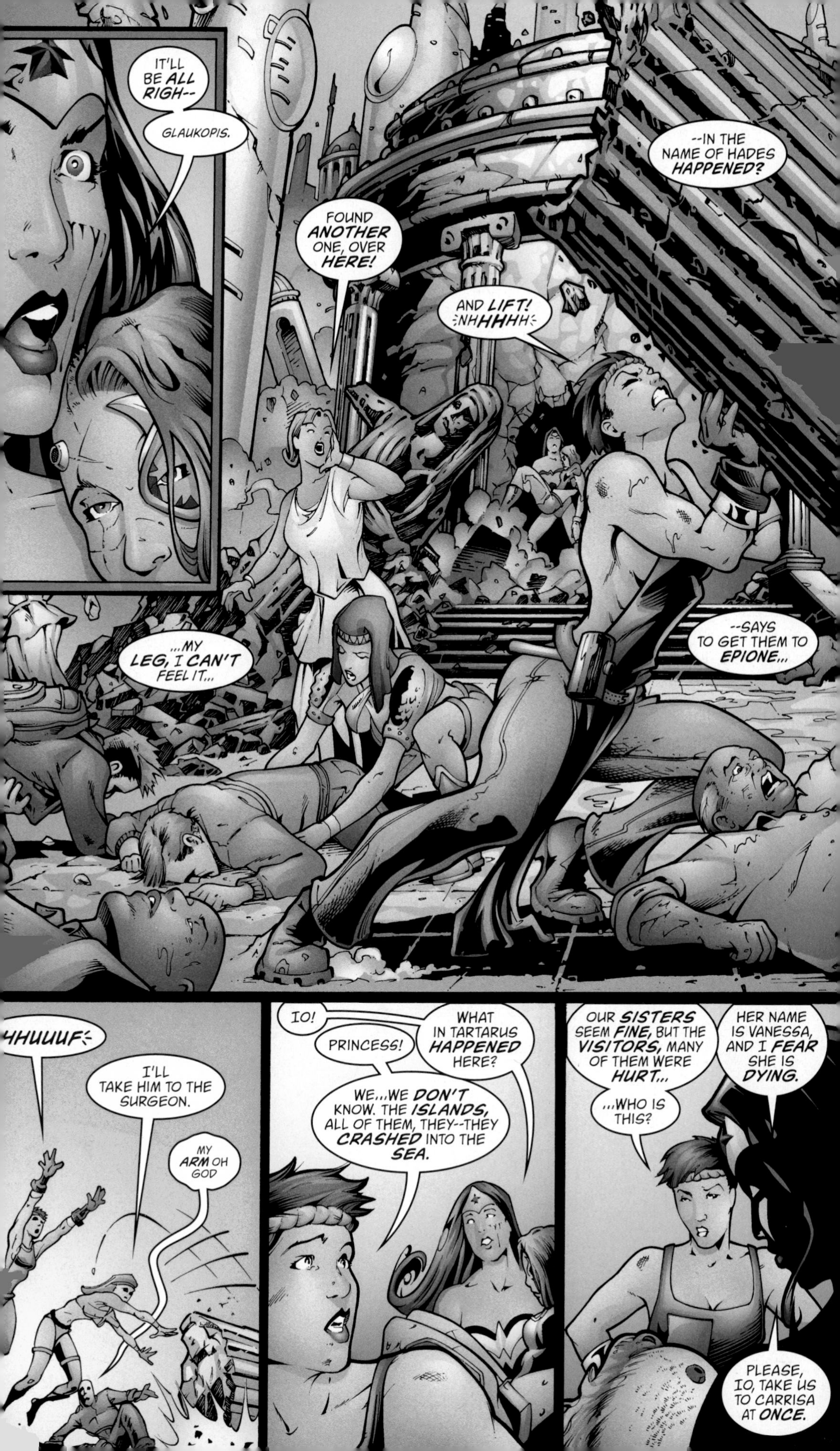

IT'LL BE ALL RIGH--
GLAUKOPIS.
FOUND ANOTHER ONE, OVER HERE!
--IN THE NAME OF HADES HAPPENED?
AND LIFT! NHHHHH
...MY LEG, I CAN'T FEEL IT...
--SAYS TO GET THEM TO EPIONE...
HHUUUF
I'LL TAKE HIM TO THE SURGEON.
MY ARM OH GOD
IO!
WHAT IN TARTARUS HAPPENED HERE?
PRINCESS!
WE...WE DON'T KNOW. THE ISLANDS, ALL OF THEM, THEY--THEY CRASHED INTO THE SEA.
OUR SISTERS SEEM FINE, BUT THE VISITORS, MANY OF THEM WERE HURT...
...WHO IS THIS?
HER NAME IS VANESSA, AND I FEAR SHE IS DYING.
PLEASE, IO, TAKE US TO CARRISA AT ONCE.

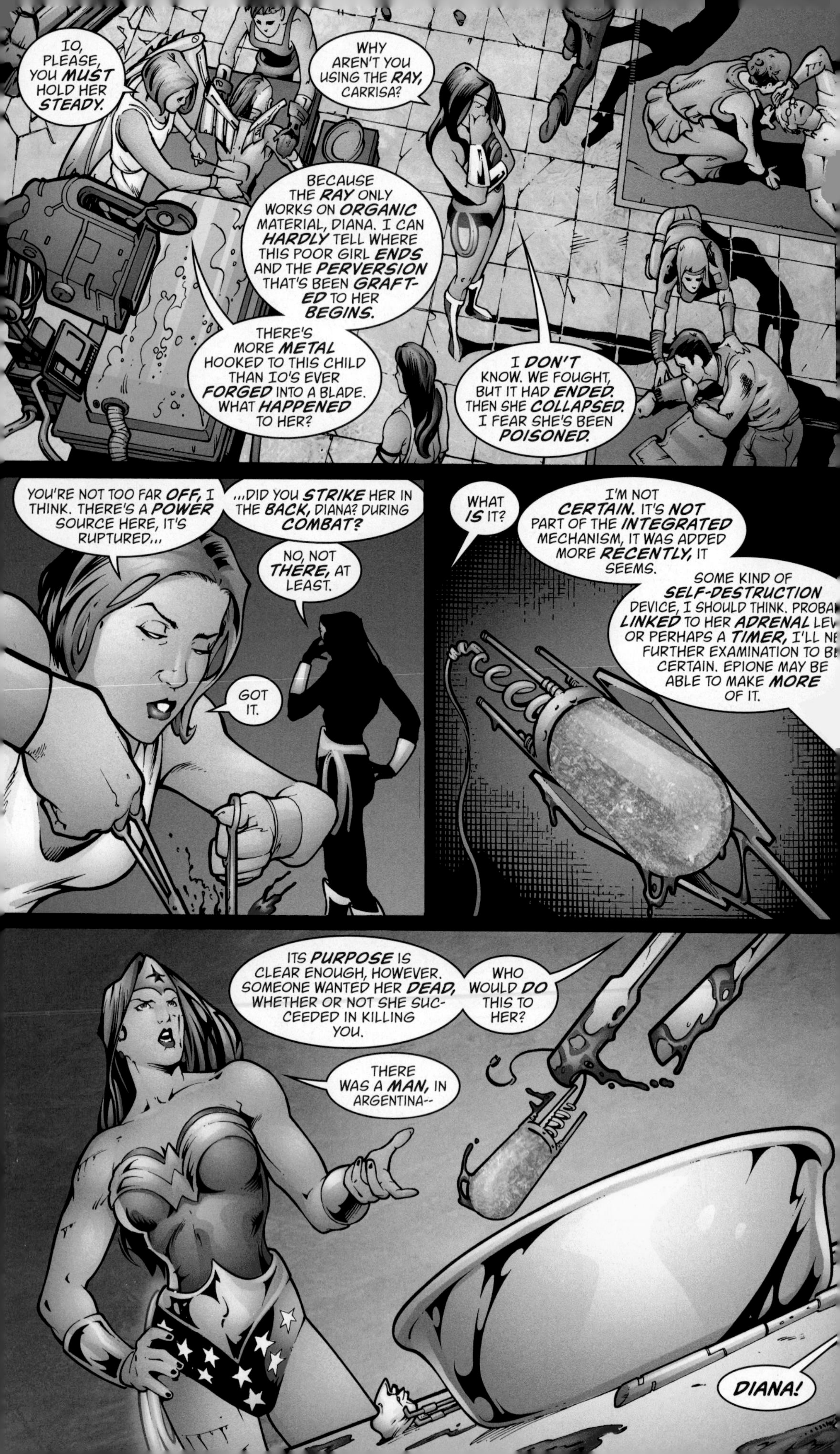
IO, PLEASE, YOU MUST HOLD HER STEADY.
WHY AREN'T YOU USING THE RAY, CARRISA?
BECAUSE THE RAY ONLY WORKS ON ORGANIC MATERIAL, DIANA. I CAN HARDLY TELL WHERE THIS POOR GIRL ENDS AND THE PERVERSION THAT'S BEEN GRAFT-ED TO HER BEGINS.
THERE'S MORE METAL HOOKED TO THIS CHILD THAN IO'S EVER FORGED INTO A BLADE. WHAT HAPPENED TO HER?
I DON'T KNOW. WE FOUGHT, BUT IT HAD ENDED. THEN SHE COLLAPSED. I FEAR SHE'S BEEN POISONED.
YOU'RE NOT TOO FAR OFF, I THINK. THERE'S A POWER SOURCE HERE, IT'S RUPTURED...
...DID YOU STRIKE HER IN THE BACK, DIANA? DURING COMBAT?
NO, NOT THERE, AT LEAST.
GOT IT.
WHAT IS IT?
I'M NOT CERTAIN. IT'S NOT PART OF THE INTEGRATED MECHANISM, IT WAS ADDED MORE RECENTLY, IT SEEMS.
SOME KIND OF SELF-DESTRUCTION DEVICE, I SHOULD THINK. PROBA LINKED TO HER ADRENAL LEV OR PERHAPS A TIMER, I'LL NE FURTHER EXAMINATION TO BE CERTAIN. EPIONE MAY BE ABLE TO MAKE MORE OF IT.
ITS PURPOSE IS CLEAR ENOUGH, HOWEVER. SOMEONE WANTED HER DEAD, WHETHER OR NOT SHE SUC-CEEDED IN KILLING YOU.
WHO WOULD DO THIS TO HER?
THERE WAS A MAN, IN ARGENTINA--
DIANA!

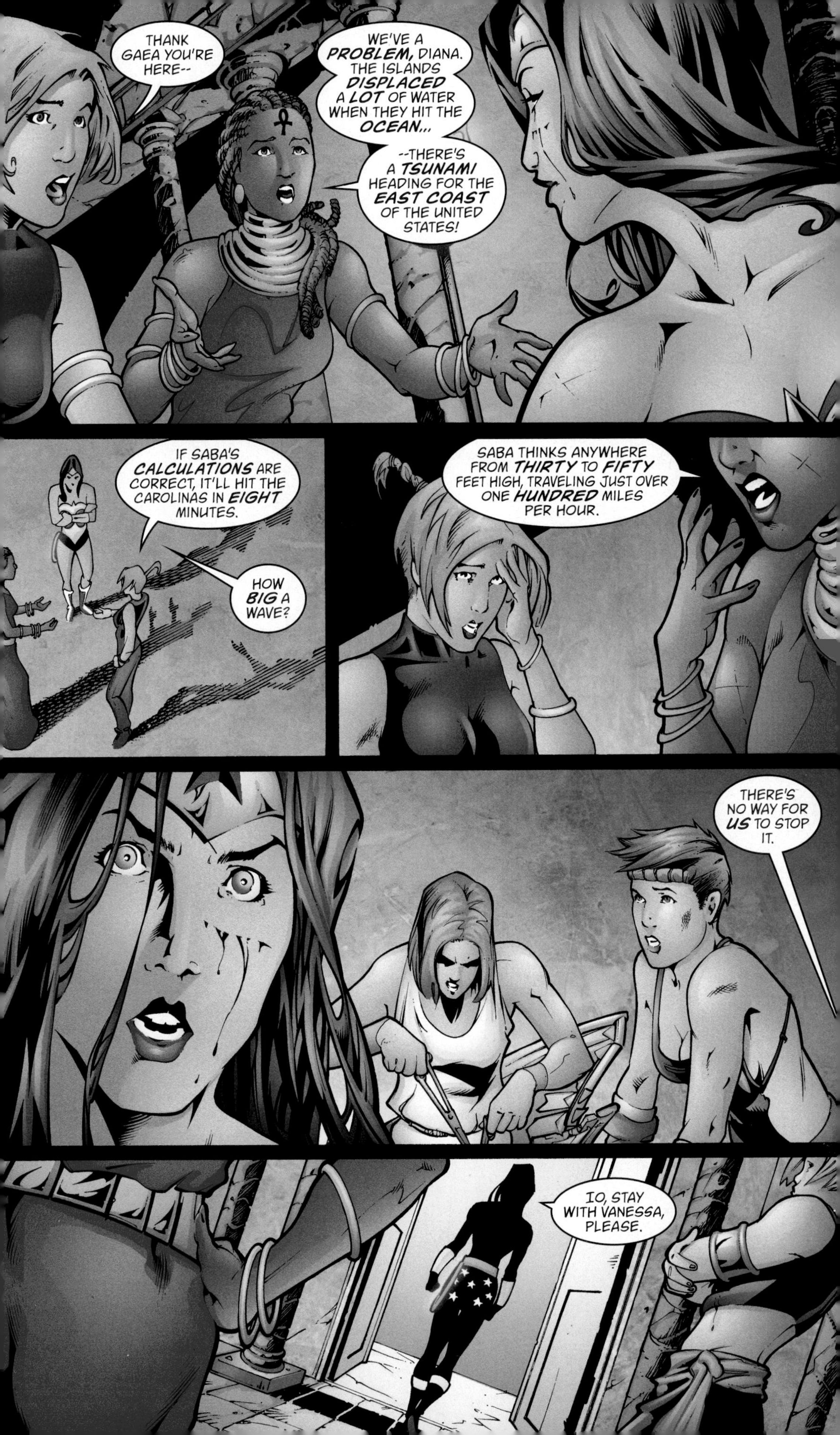
THANK GAEA YOU'RE HERE--
WE'VE A PROBLEM, DIANA. THE ISLANDS DISPLACED A LOT OF WATER WHEN THEY HIT THE OCEAN...
--THERE'S A TSUNAMI HEADING FOR THE EAST COAST OF THE UNITED STATES!
IF SABA'S CALCULATIONS ARE CORRECT, IT'LL HIT THE CAROLINAS IN EIGHT MINUTES.
HOW BIG A WAVE?
SABA THINKS ANYWHERE FROM THIRTY TO FIFTY FEET HIGH, TRAVELING JUST OVER ONE HUNDRED MILES PER HOUR.
THERE'S NO WAY FOR US TO STOP IT.
IO, STAY WITH VANESSA, PLEASE.

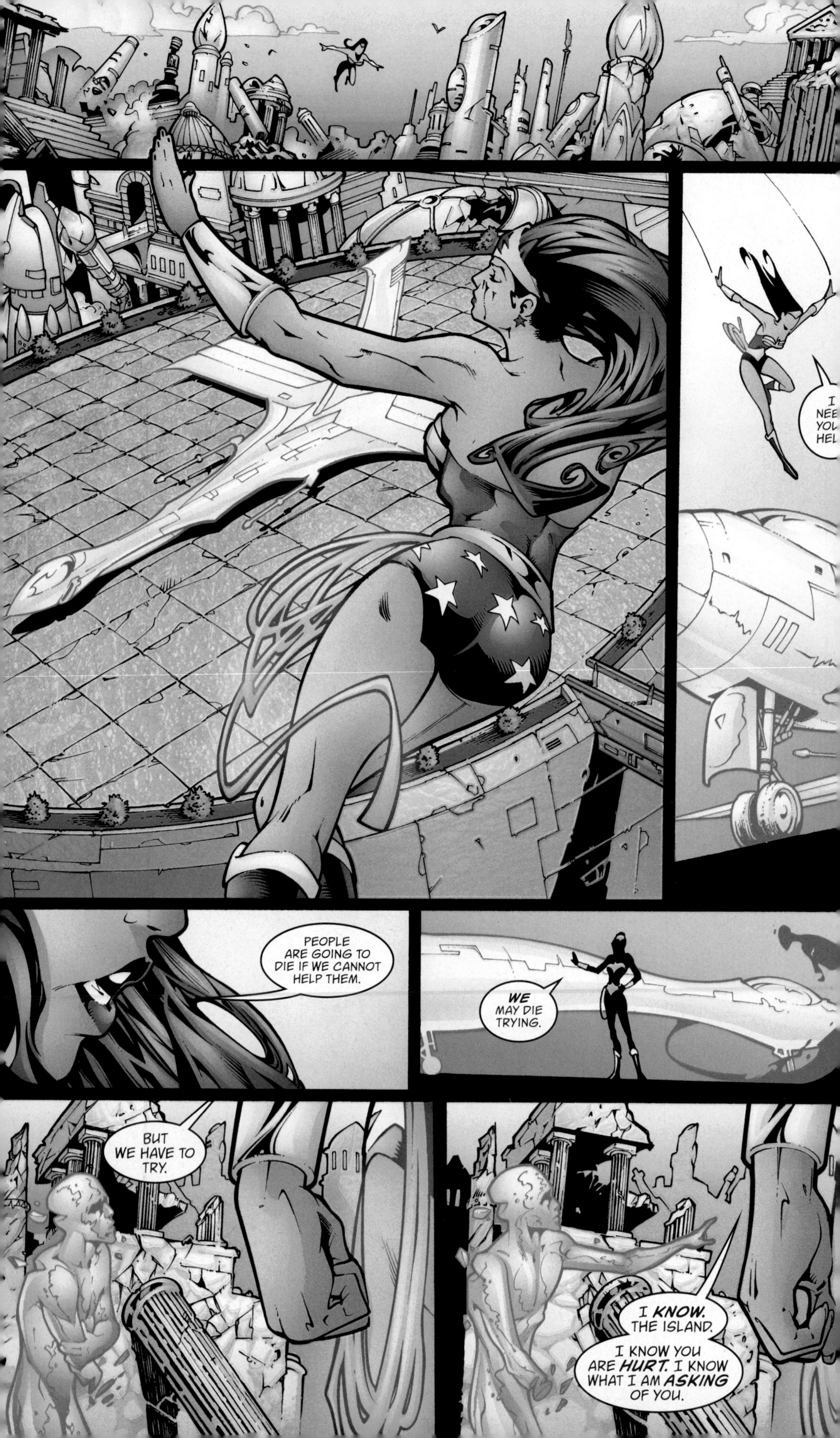
PEOPLE ARE GOING TO DIE IF WE CANNOT HELP THEM.
WE MAY DIE TRYING.
BUT WE HAVE TO TRY.
I KNOW. THE ISLAND.
I KNOW YOU ARE HURT. I KNOW WHAT I AM ASKING OF YOU.

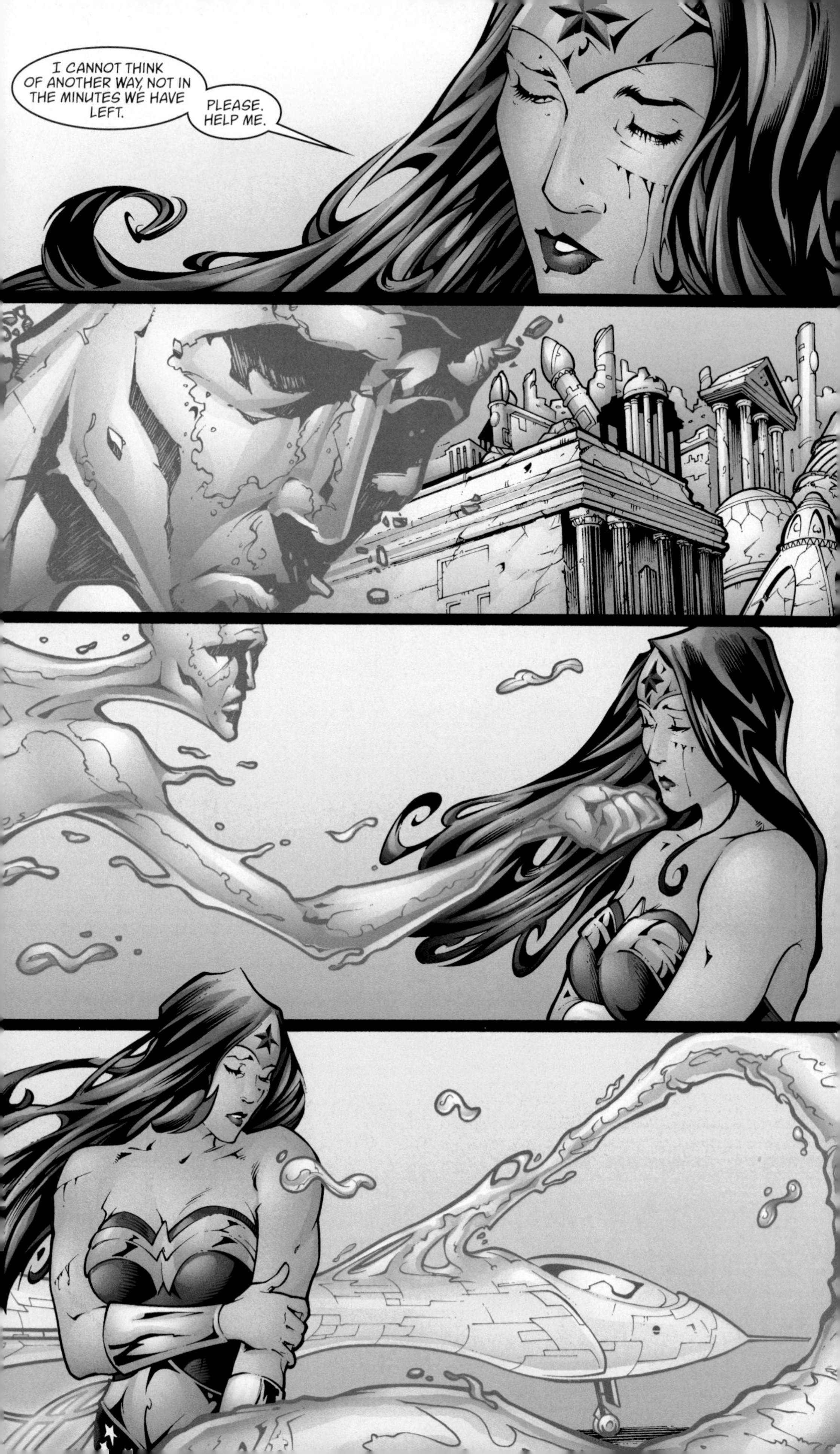
I CANNOT THINK OF ANOTHER WAY, NOT IN THE MINUTES WE HAVE LEFT.
PLEASE. HELP ME.

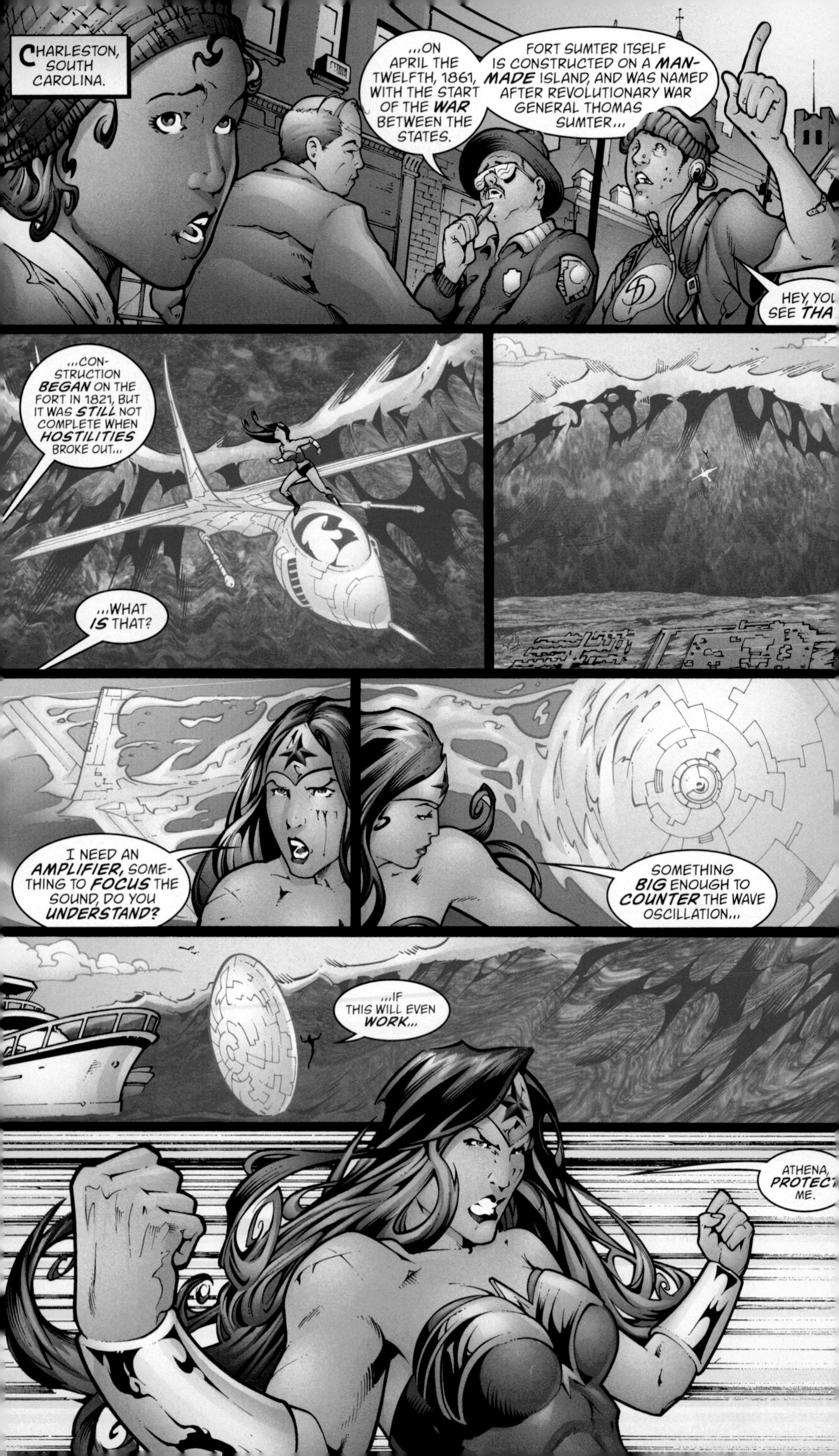
CHARLESTON, SOUTH CAROLINA.
...ON APRIL THE TWELFTH, 1861, WITH THE START OF THE WAR BETWEEN THE STATES.
FORT SUMTER ITSELF IS CONSTRUCTED ON A MAN-MADE ISLAND, AND WAS NAMED AFTER REVOLUTIONARY WAR GENERAL THOMAS SUMTER...
HEY, YOU SEE THA
...CONSTRUCTION BEGAN ON THE FORT IN 1821, BUT IT WAS STILL NOT COMPLETE WHEN HOSTILITIES BROKE OUT...
...WHAT IS THAT?
I NEED AN AMPLIFIER, SOMETHING TO FOCUS THE SOUND, DO YOU UNDERSTAND?
SOMETHING BIG ENOUGH TO COUNTER THE WAVE OSCILLATION...
...IF THIS WILL EVEN WORK...
ATHENA, PROTECT ME.

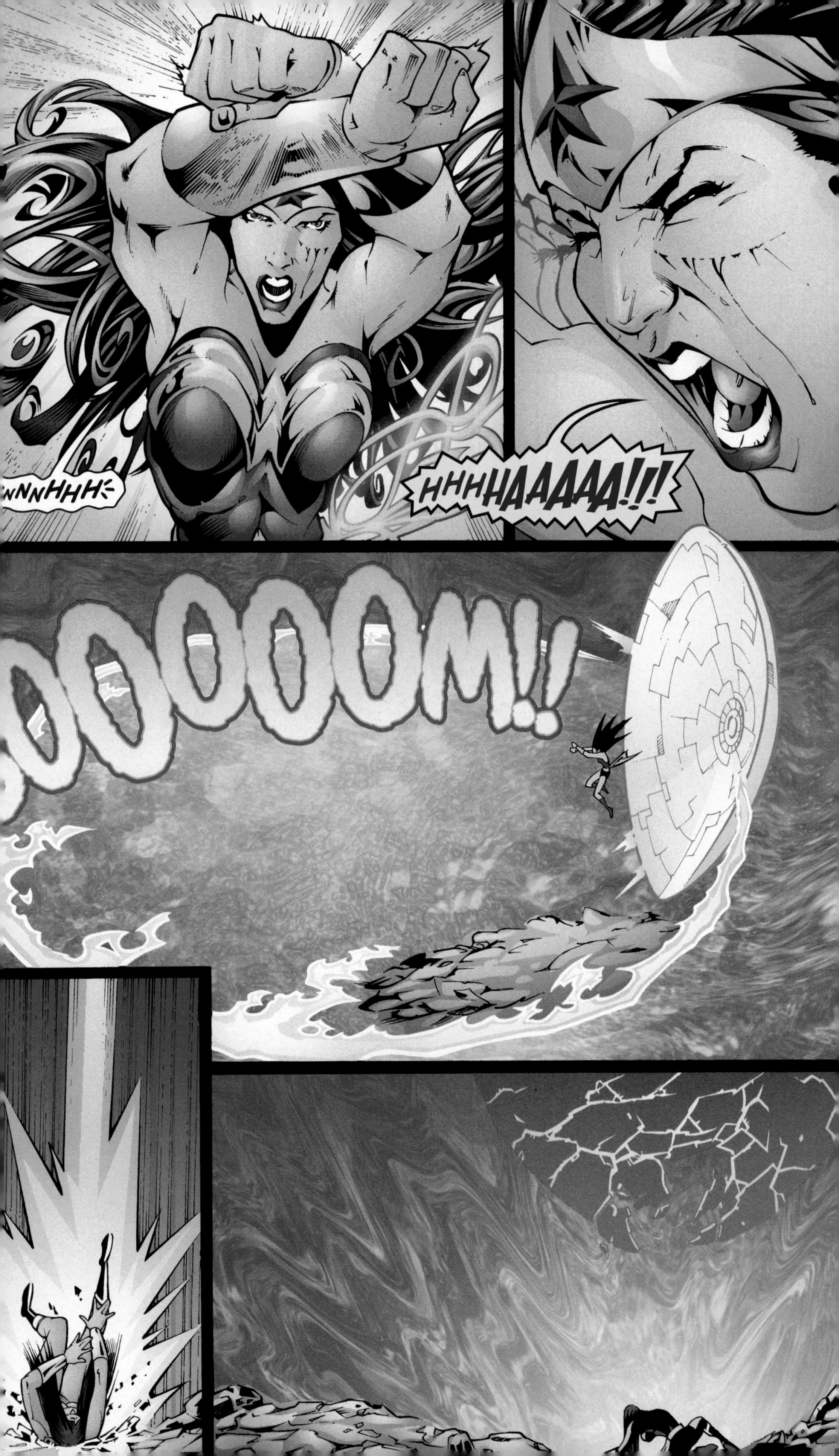
NNNHHH
HHHHAAAAA!!!
OOOOOM!!

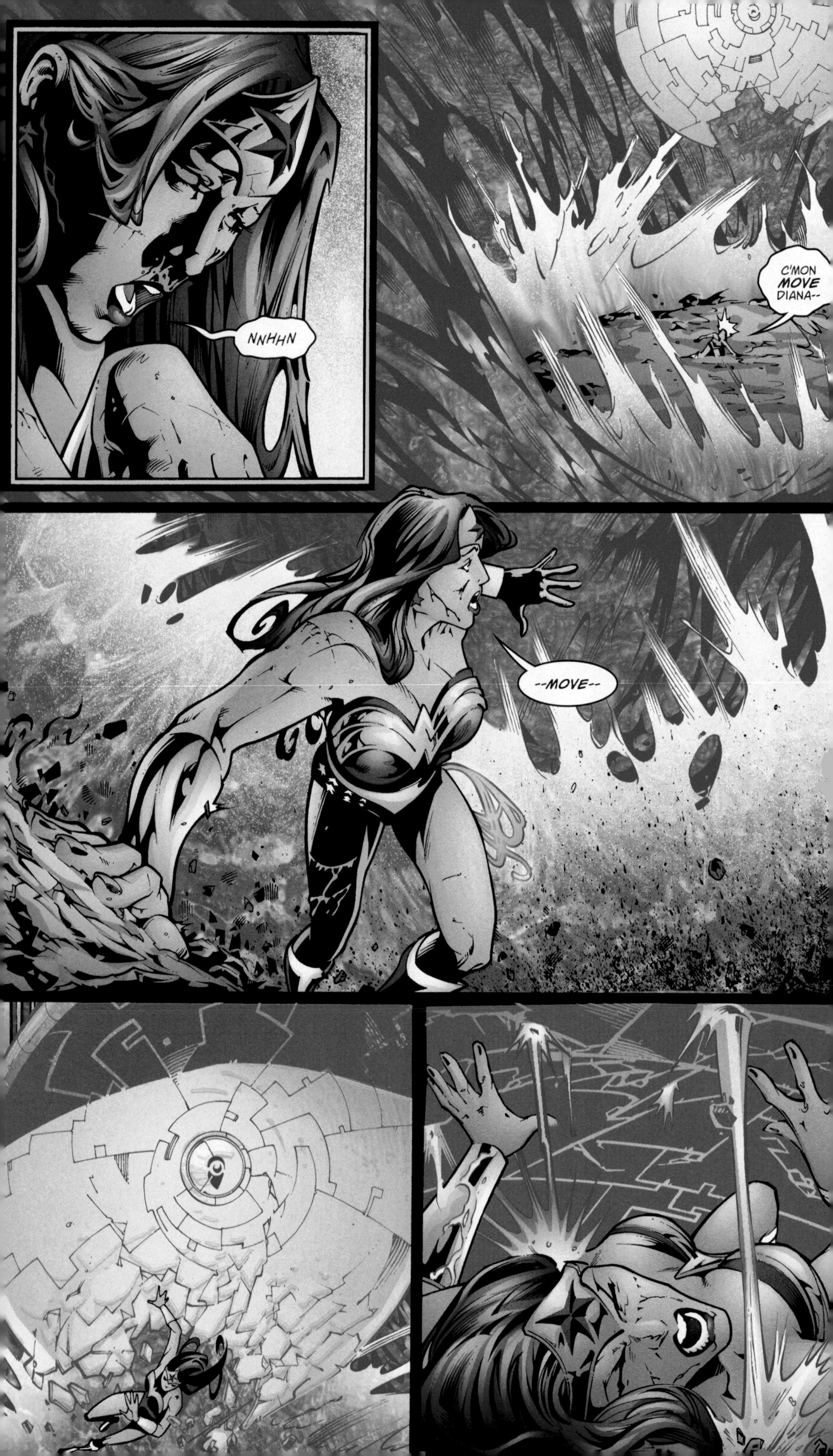
NNHHN
C'MON MOVE DIANA--
--MOVE--

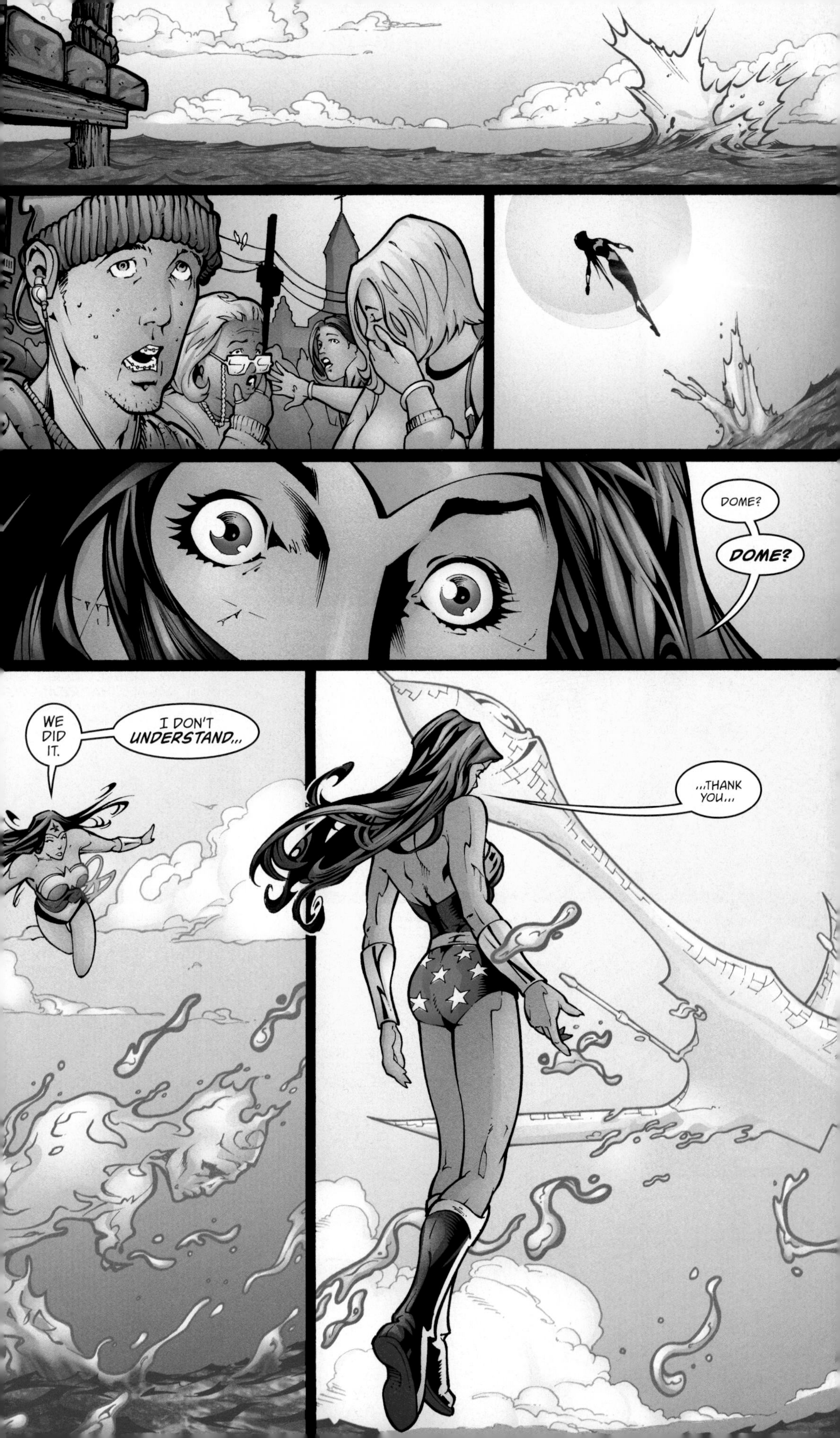
DOME?
DOME?
WE DID IT.
I DON'T UNDERSTAND...
...THANK YOU...

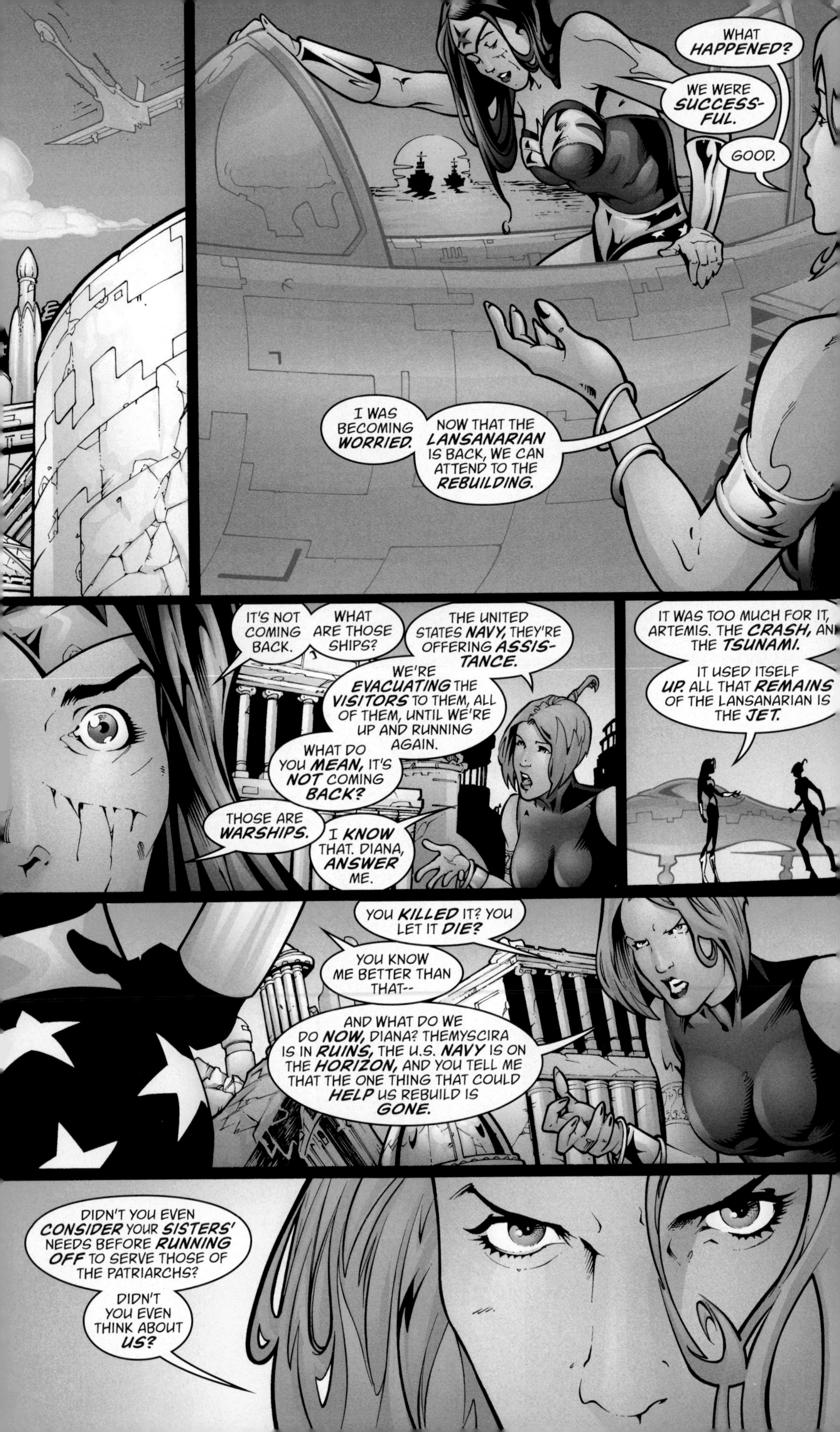
WHAT HAPPENED?
WE WERE SUCCESS-FUL.
GOOD.
I WAS BECOMING WORRIED.
NOW THAT THE LANSANARIAN IS BACK, WE CAN ATTEND TO THE REBUILDING.
IT'S NOT COMING BACK.
WHAT ARE THOSE SHIPS?
THE UNITED STATES NAVY, THEY'RE OFFERING ASSIS-TANCE.
WE'RE EVACUATING THE VISITORS TO THEM, ALL OF THEM, UNTIL WE'RE UP AND RUNNING AGAIN.
WHAT DO YOU MEAN, IT'S NOT COMING BACK?
THOSE ARE WARSHIPS.
I KNOW THAT. DIANA, ANSWER ME.
IT WAS TOO MUCH FOR IT, ARTEMIS. THE CRASH, AN THE TSUNAMI.
IT USED ITSELF UP. ALL THAT REMAINS OF THE LANSANARIAN IS THE JET.
YOU KILLED IT? YOU LET IT DIE?
YOU KNOW ME BETTER THAN THAT--
AND WHAT DO WE DO NOW, DIANA? THEMYSCIRA IS IN RUINS, THE U.S. NAVY IS ON THE HORIZON, AND YOU TELL ME THAT THE ONE THING THAT COULD HELP US REBUILD IS GONE.
DIDN'T YOU EVEN CONSIDER YOUR SISTERS' NEEDS BEFORE RUNNING OFF TO SERVE THOSE OF THE PATRIARCHS?
DIDN'T YOU EVEN THINK ABOUT US?

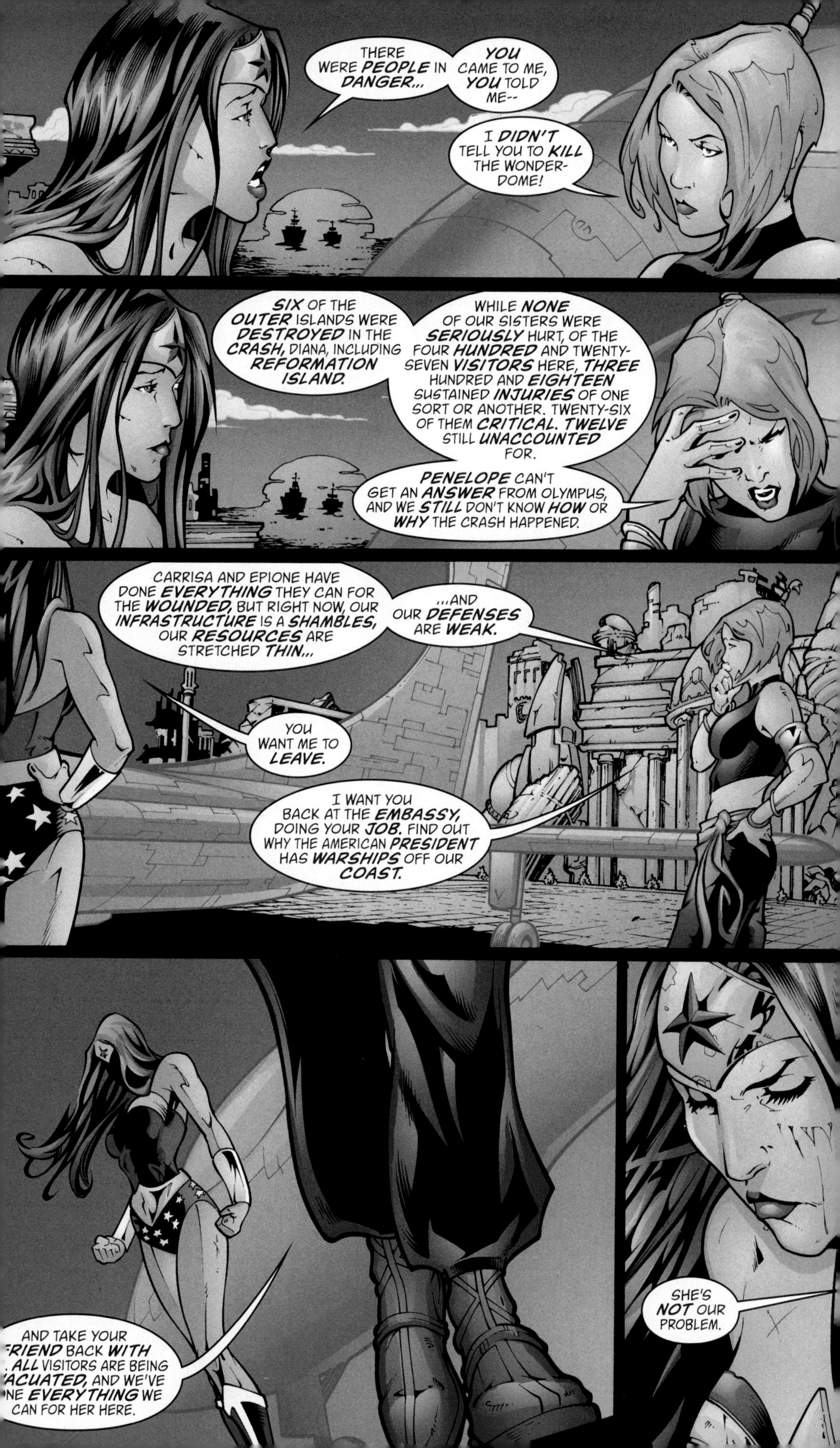
THERE WERE PEOPLE IN DANGER...
YOU CAME TO ME, YOU TOLD ME--
I DIDN'T TELL YOU TO KILL THE WONDER-DOME!
SIX OF THE OUTER ISLANDS WERE DESTROYED IN THE CRASH, DIANA, INCLUDING REFORMATION ISLAND.
WHILE NONE OF OUR SISTERS WERE SERIOUSLY HURT, OF THE FOUR HUNDRED AND TWENTY-SEVEN VISITORS HERE, THREE HUNDRED AND EIGHTEEN SUSTAINED INJURIES OF ONE SORT OR ANOTHER. TWENTY-SIX OF THEM CRITICAL. TWELVE STILL UNACCOUNTED FOR.
PENELOPE CAN'T GET AN ANSWER FROM OLYMPUS, AND WE STILL DON'T KNOW HOW OR WHY THE CRASH HAPPENED.
CARRISA AND EPIONE HAVE DONE EVERYTHING THEY CAN FOR THE WOUNDED, BUT RIGHT NOW, OUR INFRASTRUCTURE IS A SHAMBLES, OUR RESOURCES ARE STRETCHED THIN...
...AND OUR DEFENSES ARE WEAK.
YOU WANT ME TO LEAVE.
I WANT YOU BACK AT THE EMBASSY, DOING YOUR JOB. FIND OUT WHY THE AMERICAN PRESIDENT HAS WARSHIPS OFF OUR COAST.
AND TAKE YOUR FRIEND BACK WITH . ALL VISITORS ARE BEING ACUATED, AND WE'VE NE EVERYTHING WE CAN FOR HER HERE.
SHE'S NOT OUR PROBLEM.

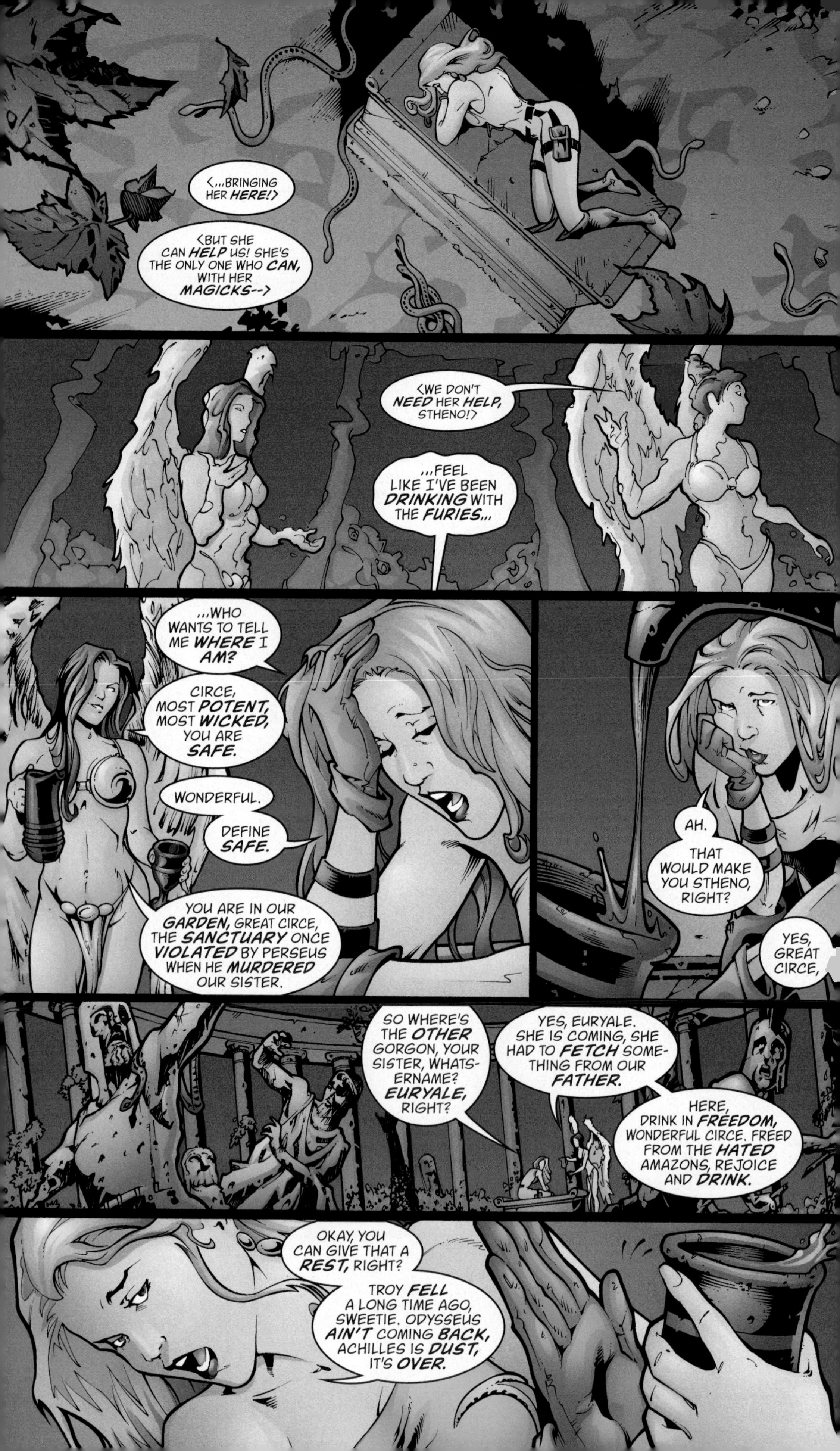

<...BRINGING HER HERE!>
<BUT SHE CAN HELP US! SHE'S THE ONLY ONE WHO CAN, WITH HER MAGICKS-->
<WE DON'T NEED HER HELP, STHENO!>
...FEEL LIKE I'VE BEEN DRINKING WITH THE FURIES...
...WHO WANTS TO TELL ME WHERE I AM?
CIRCE, MOST POTENT, MOST WICKED, YOU ARE SAFE.
WONDERFUL.
DEFINE SAFE.
YOU ARE IN OUR GARDEN, GREAT CIRCE, THE SANCTUARY ONCE VIOLATED BY PERSEUS WHEN HE MURDERED OUR SISTER.
AH.
THAT WOULD MAKE YOU STHENO, RIGHT?
YES, GREAT CIRCE,
SO WHERE'S THE OTHER GORGON, YOUR SISTER, WHATS-ERNAME? EURYALE, RIGHT?
YES, EURYALE. SHE IS COMING, SHE HAD TO FETCH SOME-THING FROM OUR FATHER.
HERE, DRINK IN FREEDOM, WONDERFUL CIRCE. FREED FROM THE HATED AMAZONS, REJOICE AND DRINK.
OKAY, YOU CAN GIVE THAT A REST, RIGHT?
TROY FELL A LONG TIME AGO, SWEETIE. ODYSSEUS AIN'T COMING BACK, ACHILLES IS DUST, IT'S OVER.

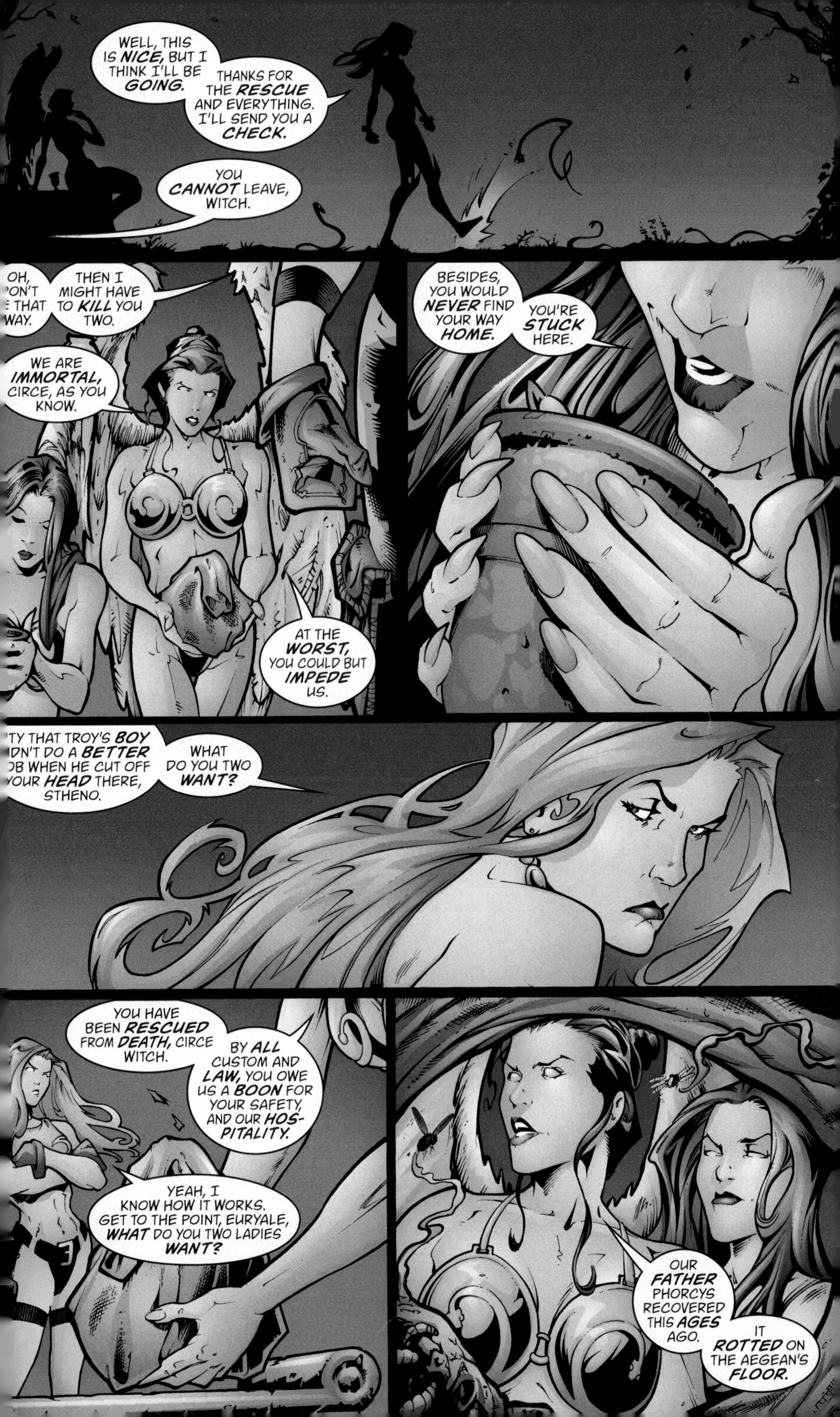
WELL, THIS IS NICE, BUT I THINK I'LL BE GOING.
THANKS FOR THE RESCUE AND EVERYTHING. I'LL SEND YOU A CHECK.
YOU CANNOT LEAVE, WITCH.
OH, 'ON'T E THAT WAY.
THEN I MIGHT HAVE TO KILL YOU TWO.
WE ARE IMMORTAL, CIRCE, AS YOU KNOW.
AT THE WORST, YOU COULD BUT IMPEDE US.
BESIDES, YOU WOULD NEVER FIND YOUR WAY HOME.
YOU'RE STUCK HERE.
TY THAT TROY'S BOY IDN'T DO A BETTER OB WHEN HE CUT OFF YOUR HEAD THERE, STHENO.
WHAT DO YOU TWO WANT?
YOU HAVE BEEN RESCUED FROM DEATH, CIRCE WITCH.
BY ALL CUSTOM AND LAW, YOU OWE US A BOON FOR YOUR SAFETY, AND OUR HOS-PITALITY.
YEAH, I KNOW HOW IT WORKS. GET TO THE POINT, EURYALE, WHAT DO YOU TWO LADIES WANT?
OUR FATHER PHORCYS RECOVERED THIS AGES AGO.
IT ROTTED ON THE AEGEAN'S FLOOR.

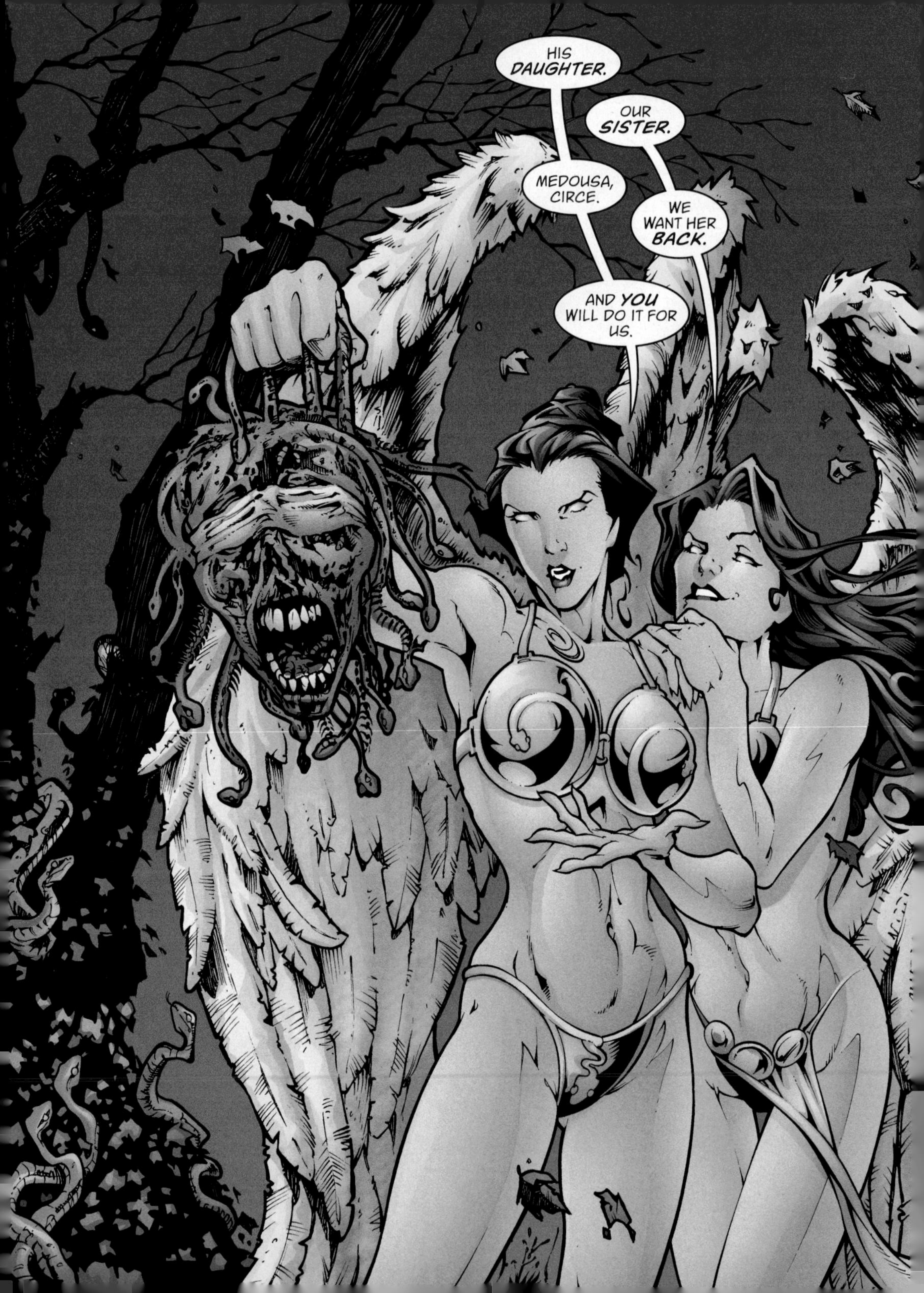
HIS DAUGHTER.
OUR SISTER.
MEDOUSA, CIRCE.
WE WANT HER BACK.
AND YOU WILL DO IT FOR US.

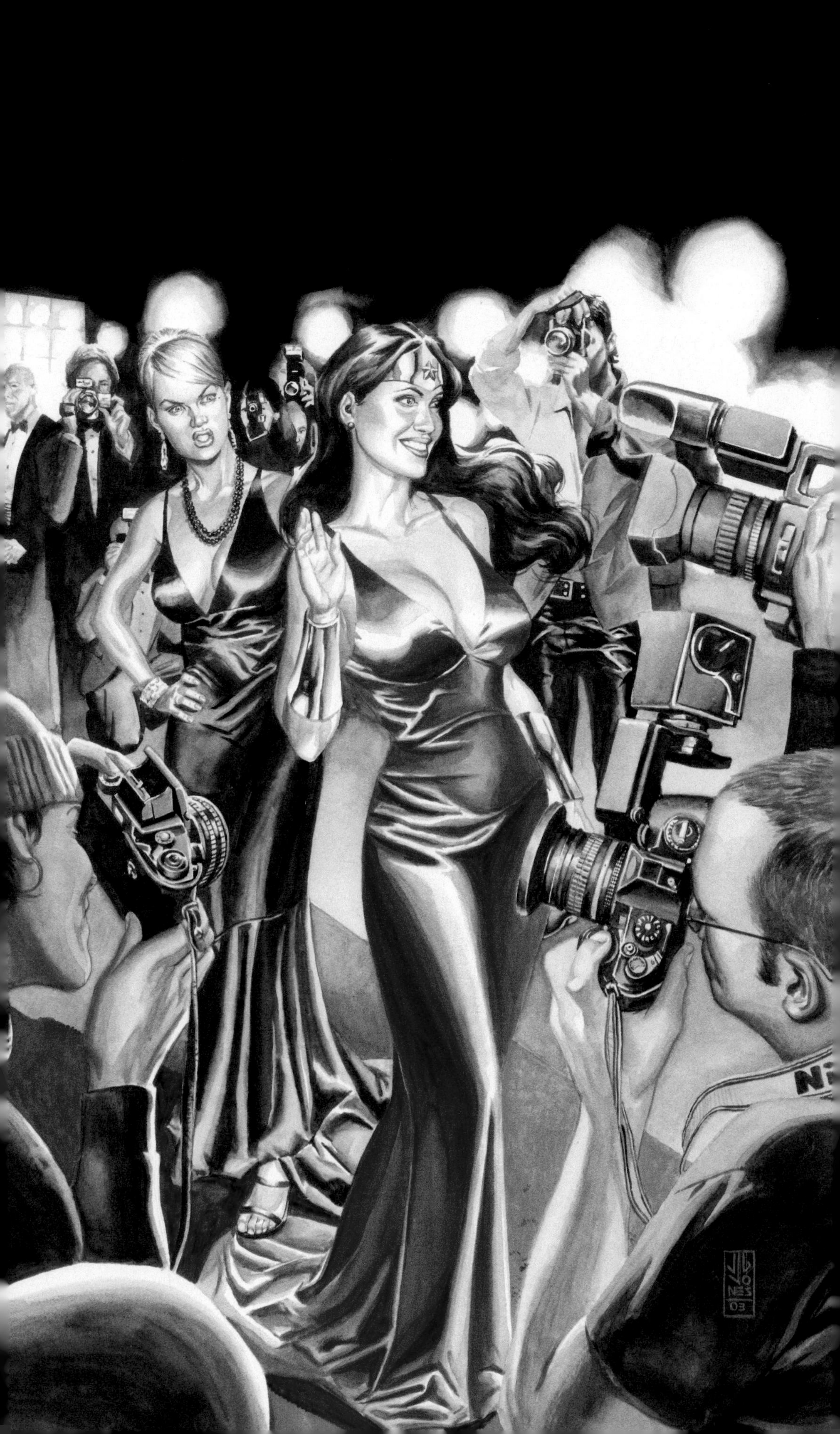

"LEAKS"

Stephen Sadowski – *pencils*
Andrew Currie – *inks*
Richard Horie, Tanya Horie - *colors*
J.G. Jones – *cover art*

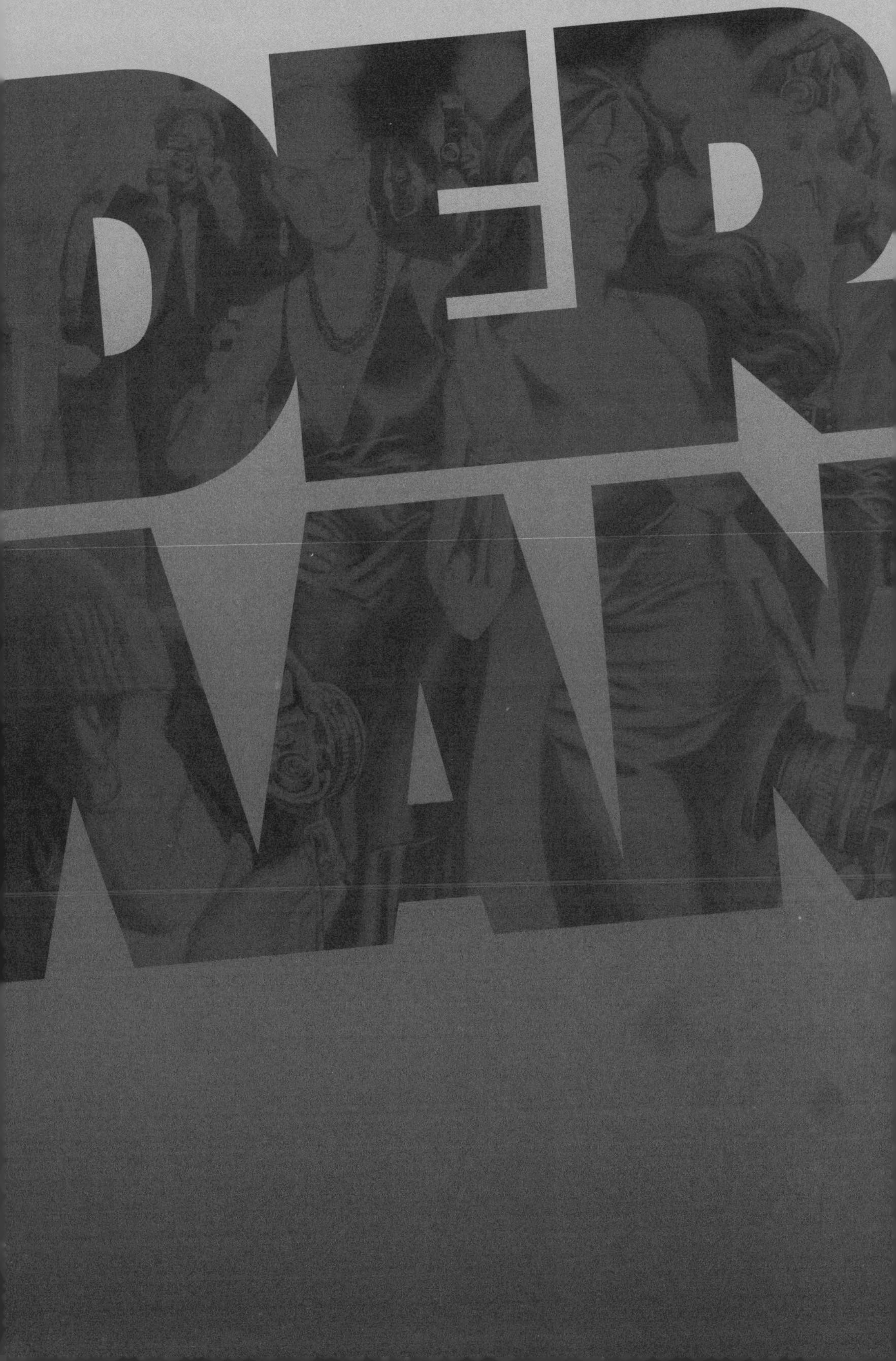

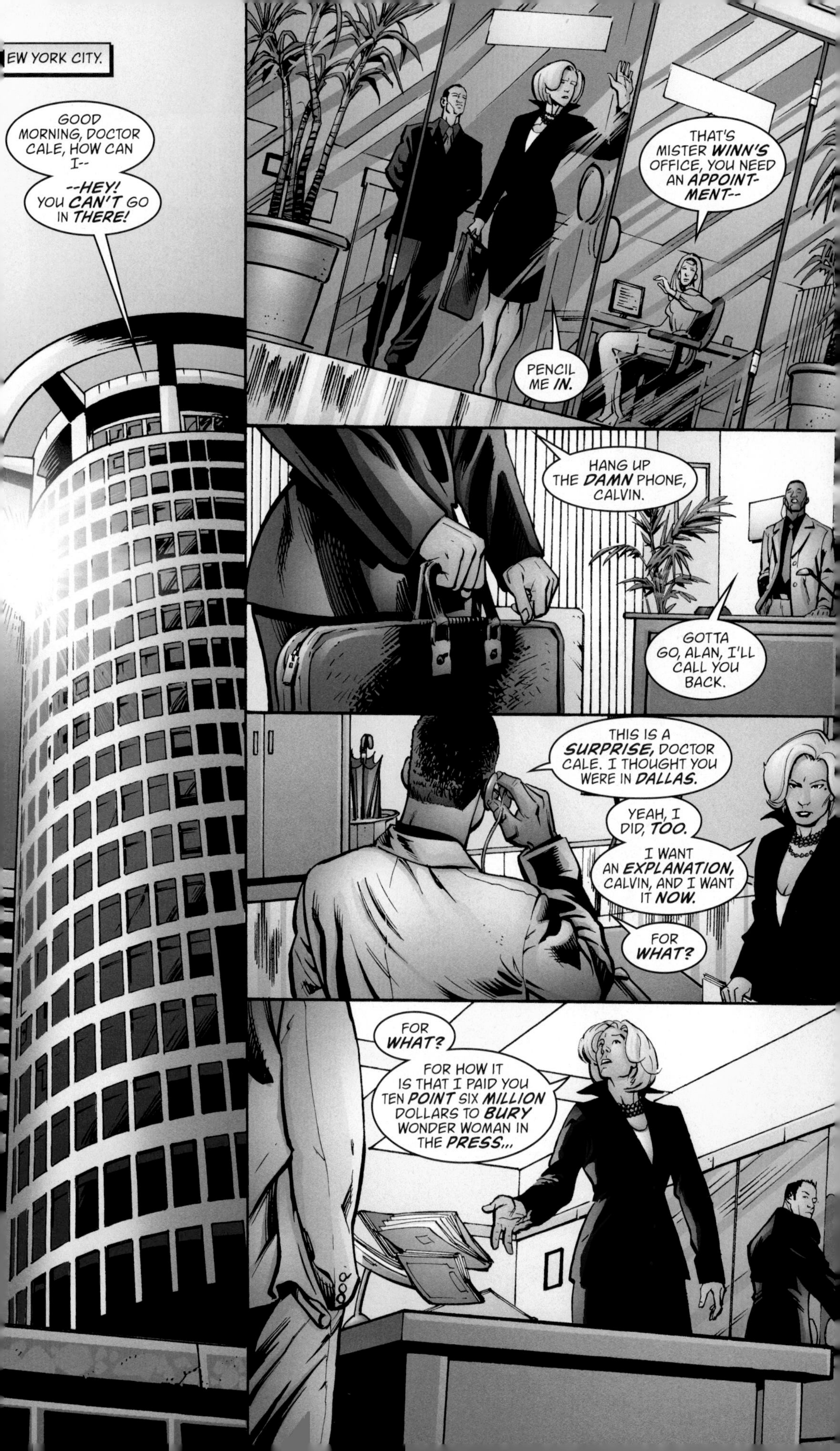

EW YORK CITY.
GOOD MORNING, DOCTOR CALE, HOW CAN I--
--HEY! YOU CAN'T GO IN THERE!
THAT'S MISTER WINN'S OFFICE, YOU NEED AN APPOINTMENT--
PENCIL ME IN.
HANG UP THE DAMN PHONE, CALVIN.
GOTTA GO, ALAN, I'LL CALL YOU BACK.
THIS IS A SURPRISE, DOCTOR CALE. I THOUGHT YOU WERE IN DALLAS.
YEAH, I DID, TOO.
I WANT AN EXPLANATION, CALVIN, AND I WANT IT NOW.
FOR WHAT?
FOR WHAT?
FOR HOW IT IS THAT I PAID YOU TEN POINT SIX MILLION DOLLARS TO BURY WONDER WOMAN IN THE PRESS...

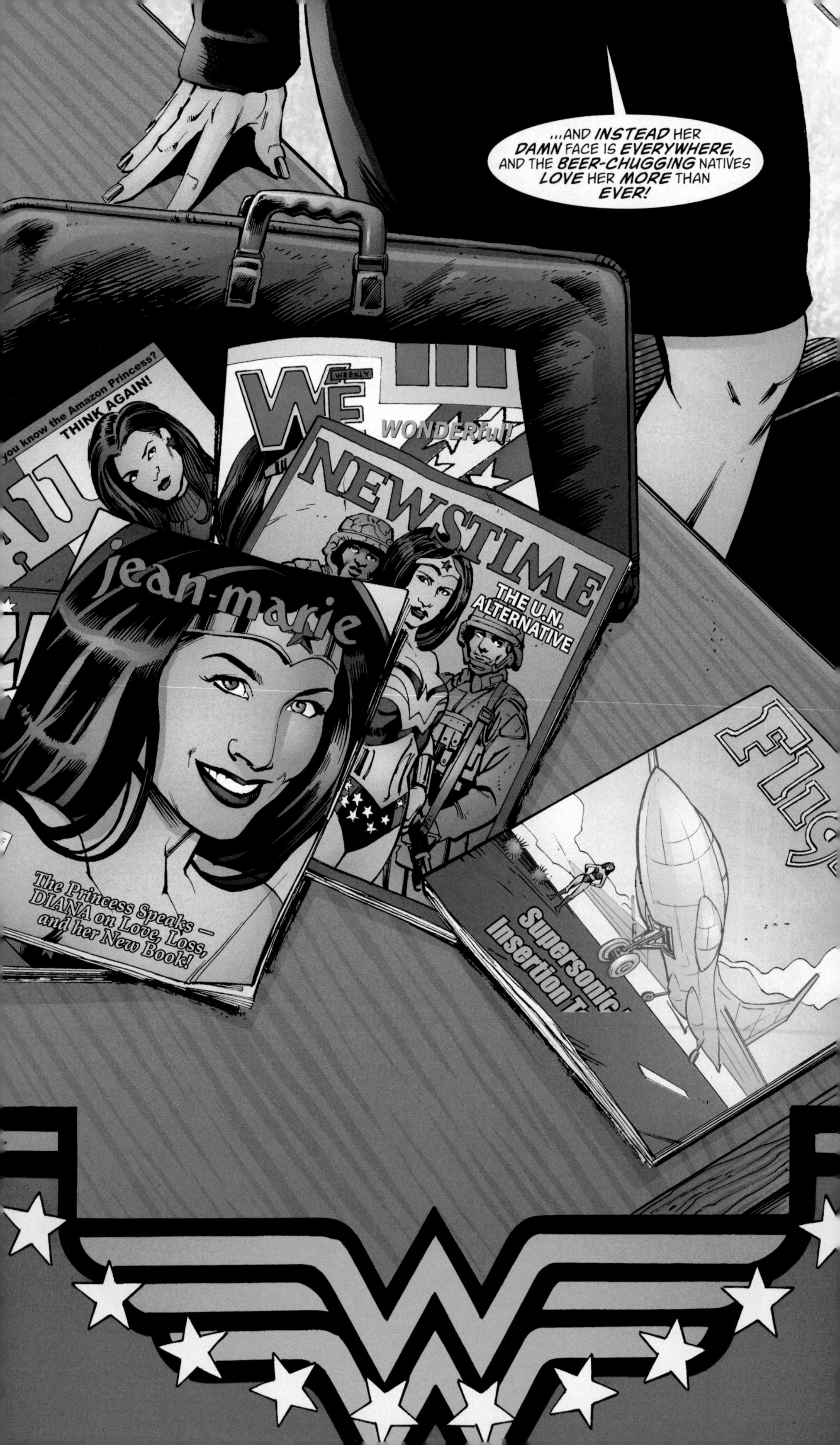
...AND INSTEAD HER DAMN FACE IS EVERYWHERE, AND THE BEER-CHUGGING NATIVES LOVE HER MORE THAN EVER!
you know the Amazon Princess?
THINK AGAIN!
WE
WEEKLY
WONDERful!
NEWSTIME
THE U.N. ALTERNATIVE
jean-marie
The Princess Speaks — DIANA on Love, Loss, and her New Book!
Supersonic
Insertion

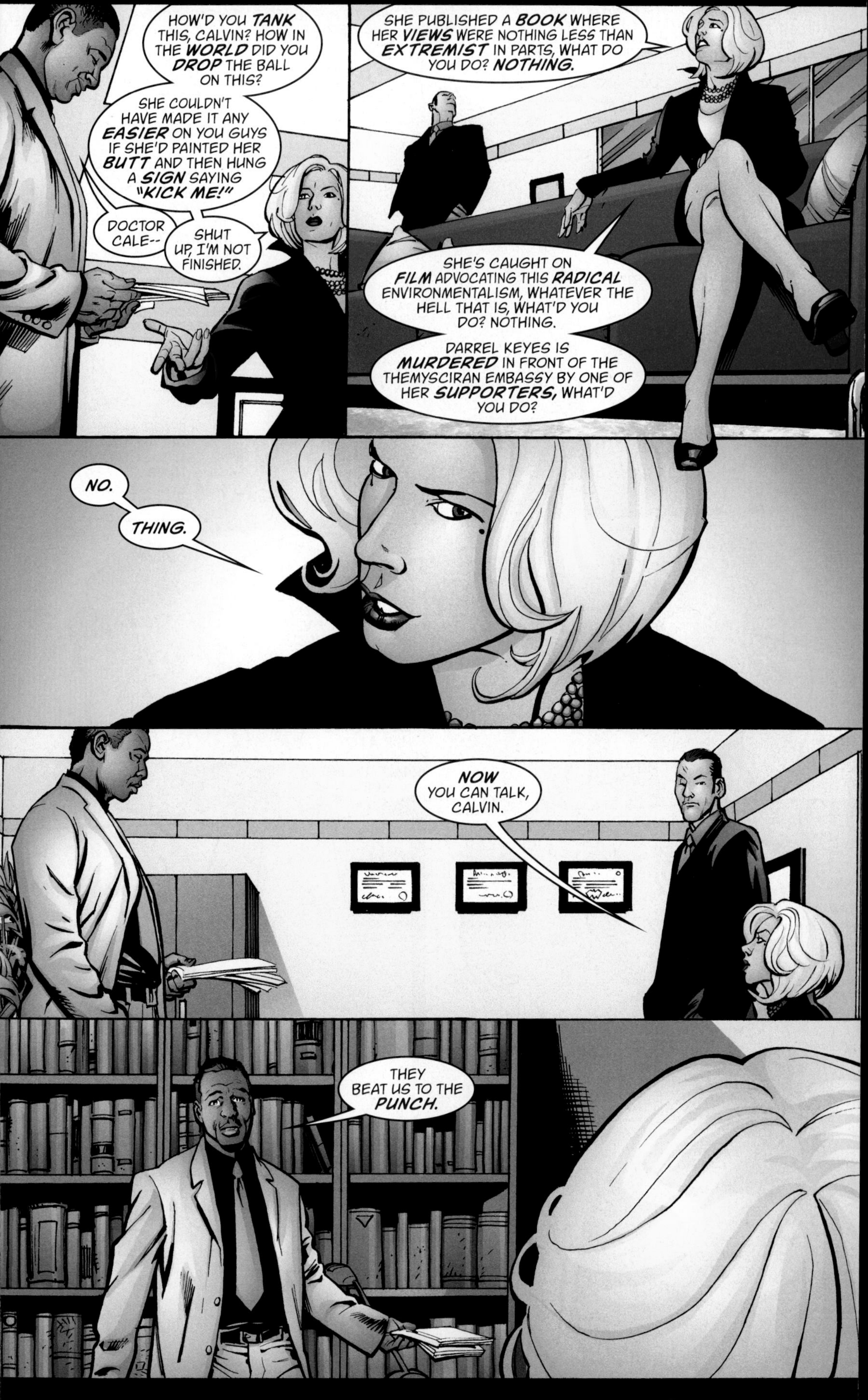

HOW'D YOU TANK THIS, CALVIN? HOW IN THE WORLD DID YOU DROP THE BALL ON THIS?
SHE COULDN'T HAVE MADE IT ANY EASIER ON YOU GUYS IF SHE'D PAINTED HER BUTT AND THEN HUNG A SIGN SAYING "KICK ME!"
DOCTOR CALE--
SHUT UP, I'M NOT FINISHED.
SHE PUBLISHED A BOOK WHERE HER VIEWS WERE NOTHING LESS THAN EXTREMIST IN PARTS, WHAT DO YOU DO? NOTHING.
SHE'S CAUGHT ON FILM ADVOCATING THIS RADICAL ENVIRONMENTALISM, WHATEVER THE HELL THAT IS, WHAT'D YOU DO? NOTHING.
DARREL KEYES IS MURDERED IN FRONT OF THE THEMYSCIRAN EMBASSY BY ONE OF HER SUPPORTERS, WHAT'D YOU DO?
NO.
THING.
NOW YOU CAN TALK, CALVIN.
THEY BEAT US TO THE PUNCH.

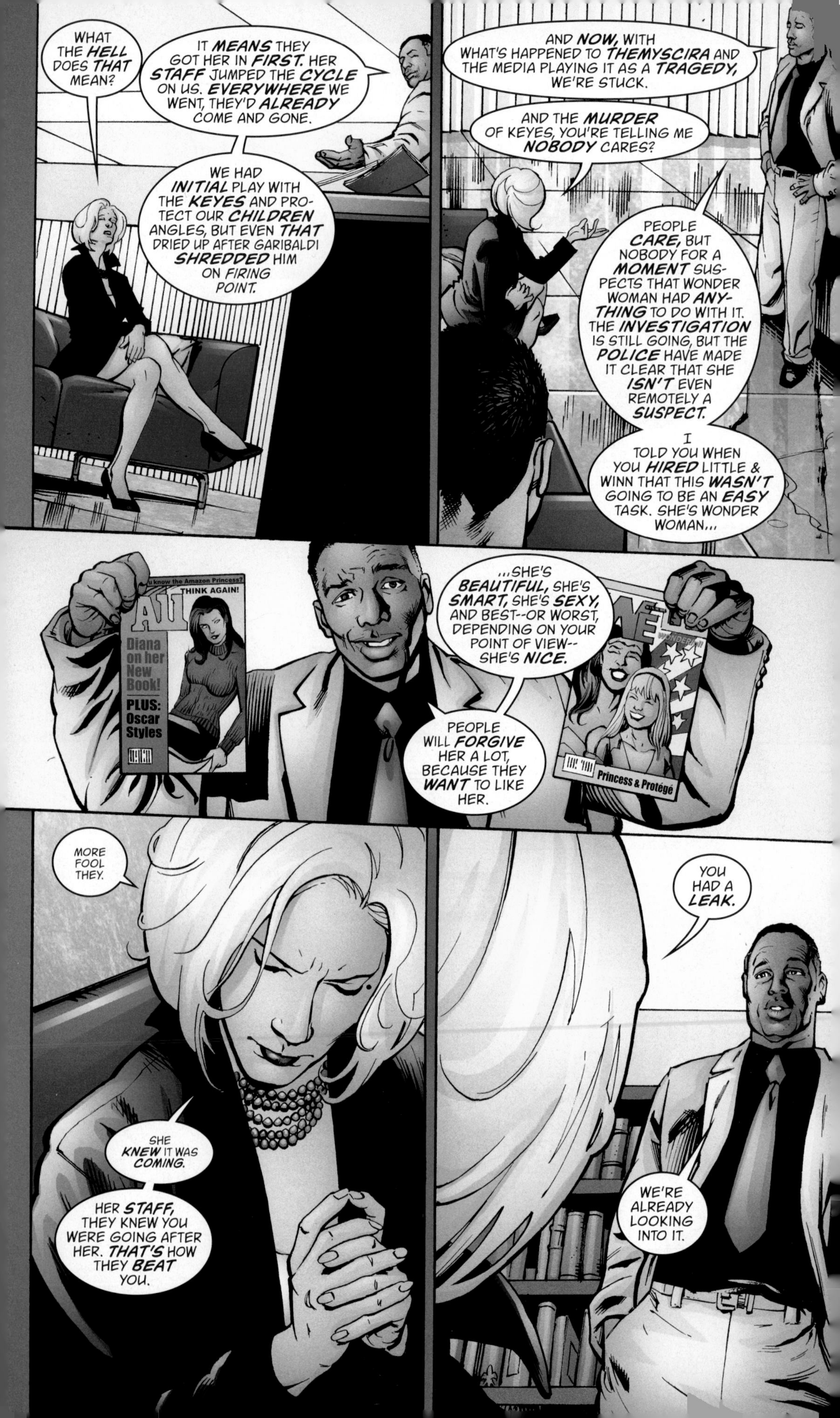
WHAT THE HELL DOES THAT MEAN?
IT MEANS THEY GOT HER IN FIRST. HER STAFF JUMPED THE CYCLE ON US. EVERYWHERE WE WENT, THEY'D ALREADY COME AND GONE.
WE HAD INITIAL PLAY WITH THE KEYES AND PROTECT OUR CHILDREN ANGLES, BUT EVEN THAT DRIED UP AFTER GARIBALDI SHREDDED HIM ON FIRING POINT.
AND NOW, WITH WHAT'S HAPPENED TO THEMYSCIRA AND THE MEDIA PLAYING IT AS A TRAGEDY, WE'RE STUCK.
AND THE MURDER OF KEYES, YOU'RE TELLING ME NOBODY CARES?
PEOPLE CARE, BUT NOBODY FOR A MOMENT SUSPECTS THAT WONDER WOMAN HAD ANYTHING TO DO WITH IT. THE INVESTIGATION IS STILL GOING, BUT THE POLICE HAVE MADE IT CLEAR THAT SHE ISN'T EVEN REMOTELY A SUSPECT.
I TOLD YOU WHEN YOU HIRED LITTLE & WINN THAT THIS WASN'T GOING TO BE AN EASY TASK. SHE'S WONDER WOMAN...
...SHE'S BEAUTIFUL, SHE'S SMART, SHE'S SEXY, AND BEST--OR WORST, DEPENDING ON YOUR POINT OF VIEW--SHE'S NICE.
PEOPLE WILL FORGIVE HER A LOT, BECAUSE THEY WANT TO LIKE HER.
THINK AGAIN!
Diana on her New Book!
PLUS: Oscar Styles
Princess & Protégé
MORE FOOL THEY.
SHE KNEW IT WAS COMING.
HER STAFF, THEY KNEW YOU WERE GOING AFTER HER. THAT'S HOW THEY BEAT YOU.
YOU HAD A LEAK.
WE'RE ALREADY LOOKING INTO IT.

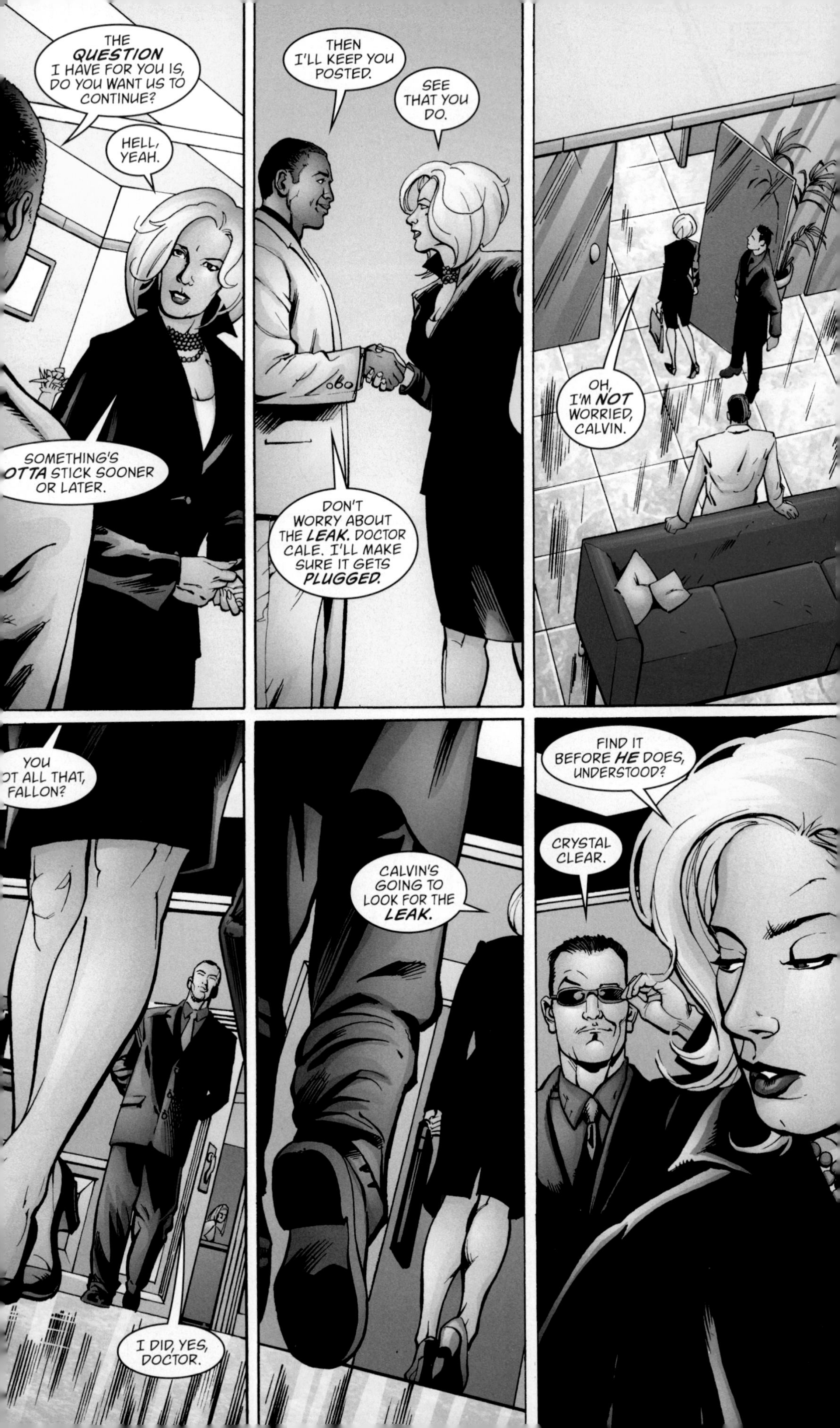
THE QUESTION I HAVE FOR YOU IS, DO YOU WANT US TO CONTINUE?
HELL, YEAH.
SOMETHING'S OTTA STICK SOONER OR LATER.
THEN I'LL KEEP YOU POSTED.
SEE THAT YOU DO.
DON'T WORRY ABOUT THE LEAK. DOCTOR CALE. I'LL MAKE SURE IT GETS PLUGGED.
OH, I'M NOT WORRIED, CALVIN.
YOU OT ALL THAT, FALLON?
I DID, YES, DOCTOR.
CALVIN'S GOING TO LOOK FOR THE LEAK.
FIND IT BEFORE HE DOES, UNDERSTOOD?
CRYSTAL CLEAR.

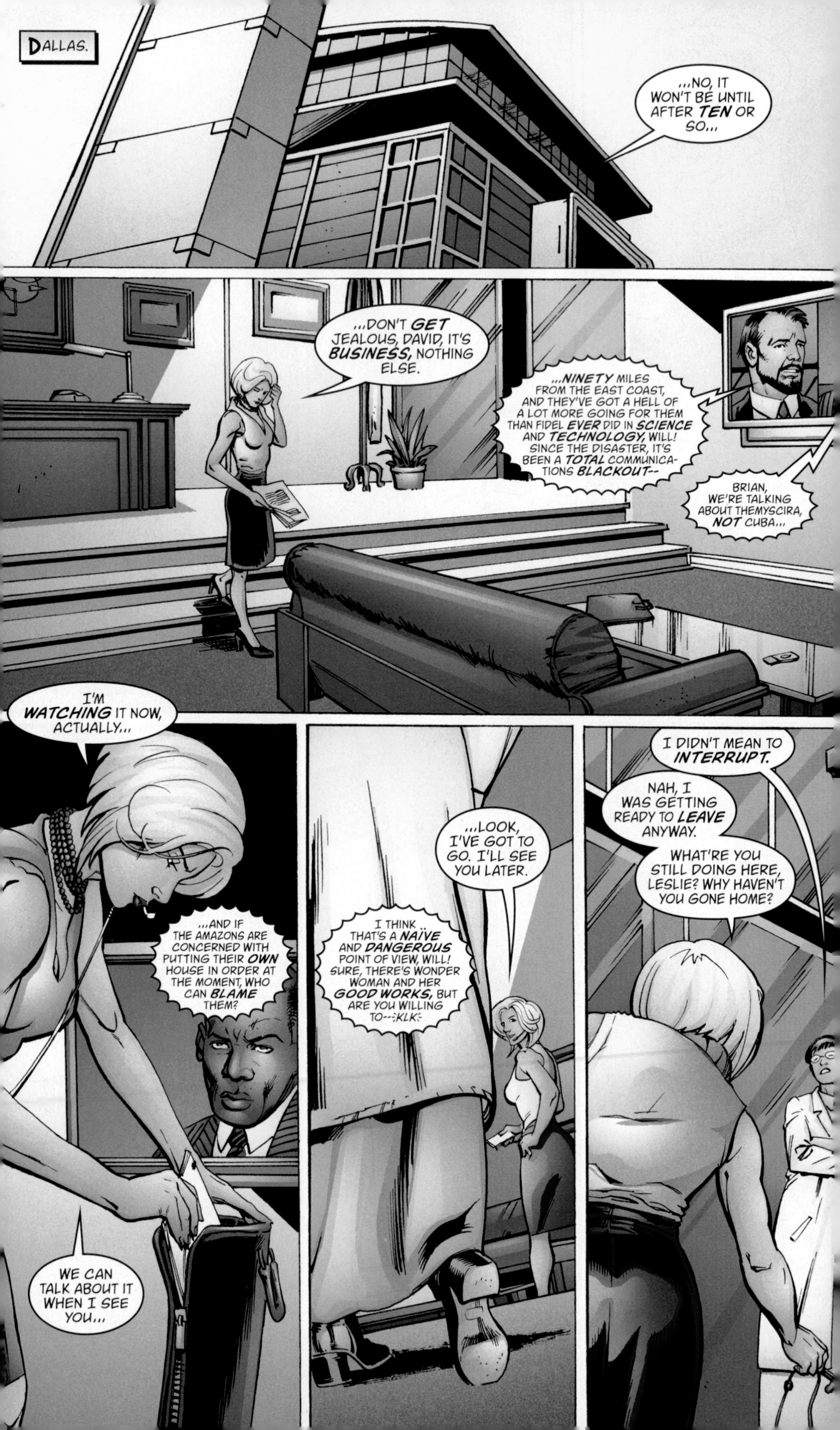
DALLAS.
...NO, IT WON'T BE UNTIL AFTER TEN OR SO...
...DON'T GET JEALOUS, DAVID, IT'S BUSINESS, NOTHING ELSE.
...NINETY MILES FROM THE EAST COAST, AND THEY'VE GOT A HELL OF A LOT MORE GOING FOR THEM THAN FIDEL EVER DID IN SCIENCE AND TECHNOLOGY, WILL! SINCE THE DISASTER, IT'S BEEN A TOTAL COMMUNICATIONS BLACKOUT--
BRIAN, WE'RE TALKING ABOUT THEMYSCIRA, NOT CUBA...
I'M WATCHING IT NOW, ACTUALLY...
...AND IF THE AMAZONS ARE CONCERNED WITH PUTTING THEIR OWN HOUSE IN ORDER AT THE MOMENT, WHO CAN BLAME THEM?
WE CAN TALK ABOUT IT WHEN I SEE YOU...
...LOOK, I'VE GOT TO GO. I'LL SEE YOU LATER.
I THINK THAT'S A NAÏVE AND DANGEROUS POINT OF VIEW, WILL! SURE, THERE'S WONDER WOMAN AND HER GOOD WORKS, BUT ARE YOU WILLING TO--KLK
I DIDN'T MEAN TO INTERRUPT.
NAH, I WAS GETTING READY TO LEAVE ANYWAY.
WHAT'RE YOU STILL DOING HERE, LESLIE? WHY HAVEN'T YOU GONE HOME?

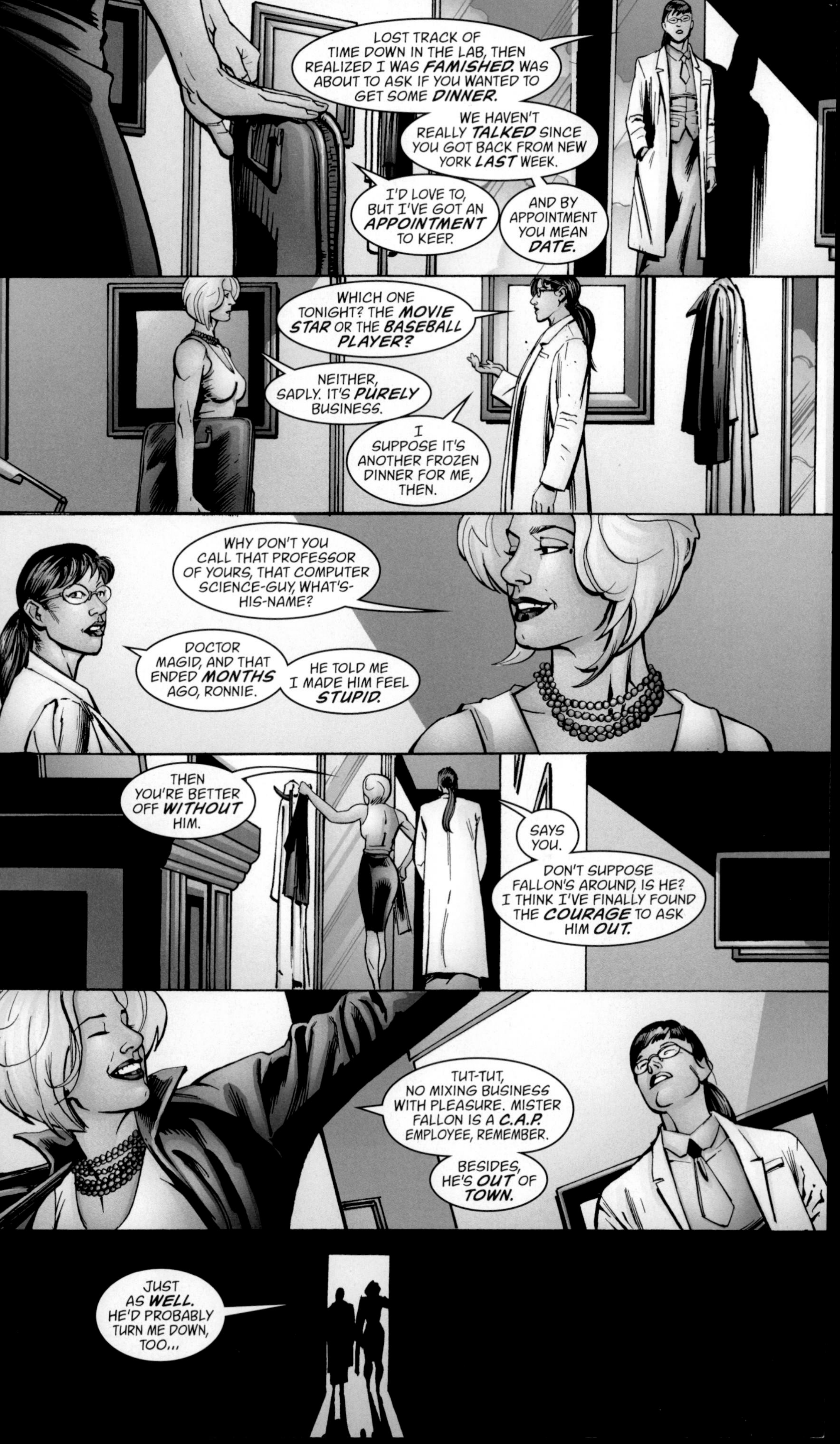

LOST TRACK OF TIME DOWN IN THE LAB, THEN REALIZED I WAS FAMISHED. WAS ABOUT TO ASK IF YOU WANTED TO GET SOME DINNER.
WE HAVEN'T REALLY TALKED SINCE YOU GOT BACK FROM NEW YORK LAST WEEK.
I'D LOVE TO, BUT I'VE GOT AN APPOINTMENT TO KEEP.
AND BY APPOINTMENT YOU MEAN DATE.
WHICH ONE TONIGHT? THE MOVIE STAR OR THE BASEBALL PLAYER?
NEITHER, SADLY. IT'S PURELY BUSINESS.
I SUPPOSE IT'S ANOTHER FROZEN DINNER FOR ME, THEN.
WHY DON'T YOU CALL THAT PROFESSOR OF YOURS, THAT COMPUTER SCIENCE-GUY, WHAT'S-HIS-NAME?
DOCTOR MAGID, AND THAT ENDED MONTHS AGO, RONNIE.
HE TOLD ME I MADE HIM FEEL STUPID.
THEN YOU'RE BETTER OFF WITHOUT HIM.
SAYS YOU.
DON'T SUPPOSE FALLON'S AROUND, IS HE? I THINK I'VE FINALLY FOUND THE COURAGE TO ASK HIM OUT.
TUT-TUT, NO MIXING BUSINESS WITH PLEASURE. MISTER FALLON IS A C.A.P. EMPLOYEE, REMEMBER.
BESIDES, HE'S OUT OF TOWN.
JUST AS WELL. HE'D PROBABLY TURN ME DOWN, TOO...

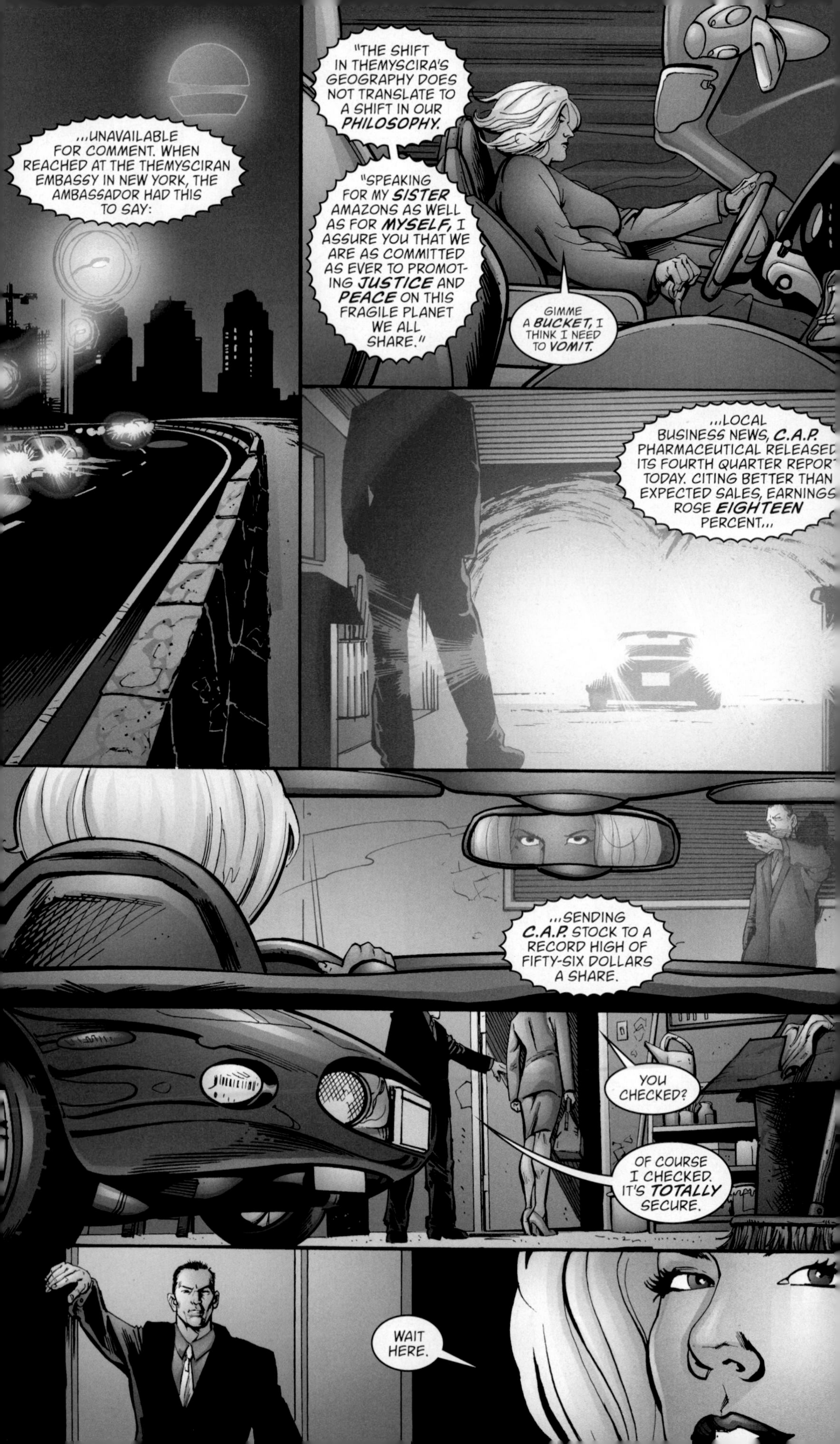
...UNAVAILABLE FOR COMMENT. WHEN REACHED AT THE THEMYSCIRAN EMBASSY IN NEW YORK, THE AMBASSADOR HAD THIS TO SAY:
"THE SHIFT IN THEMYSCIRA'S GEOGRAPHY DOES NOT TRANSLATE TO A SHIFT IN OUR PHILOSOPHY.
"SPEAKING FOR MY SISTER AMAZONS AS WELL AS FOR MYSELF, I ASSURE YOU THAT WE ARE AS COMMITTED AS EVER TO PROMOTING JUSTICE AND PEACE ON THIS FRAGILE PLANET WE ALL SHARE."
GIMME A BUCKET, I THINK I NEED TO VOMIT.
...LOCAL BUSINESS NEWS, C.A.P. PHARMACEUTICAL RELEASED ITS FOURTH QUARTER REPORT TODAY. CITING BETTER THAN EXPECTED SALES, EARNINGS ROSE EIGHTEEN PERCENT...
...SENDING C.A.P. STOCK TO A RECORD HIGH OF FIFTY-SIX DOLLARS A SHARE.
YOU CHECKED?
OF COURSE I CHECKED. IT'S TOTALLY SECURE.
WAIT HERE.

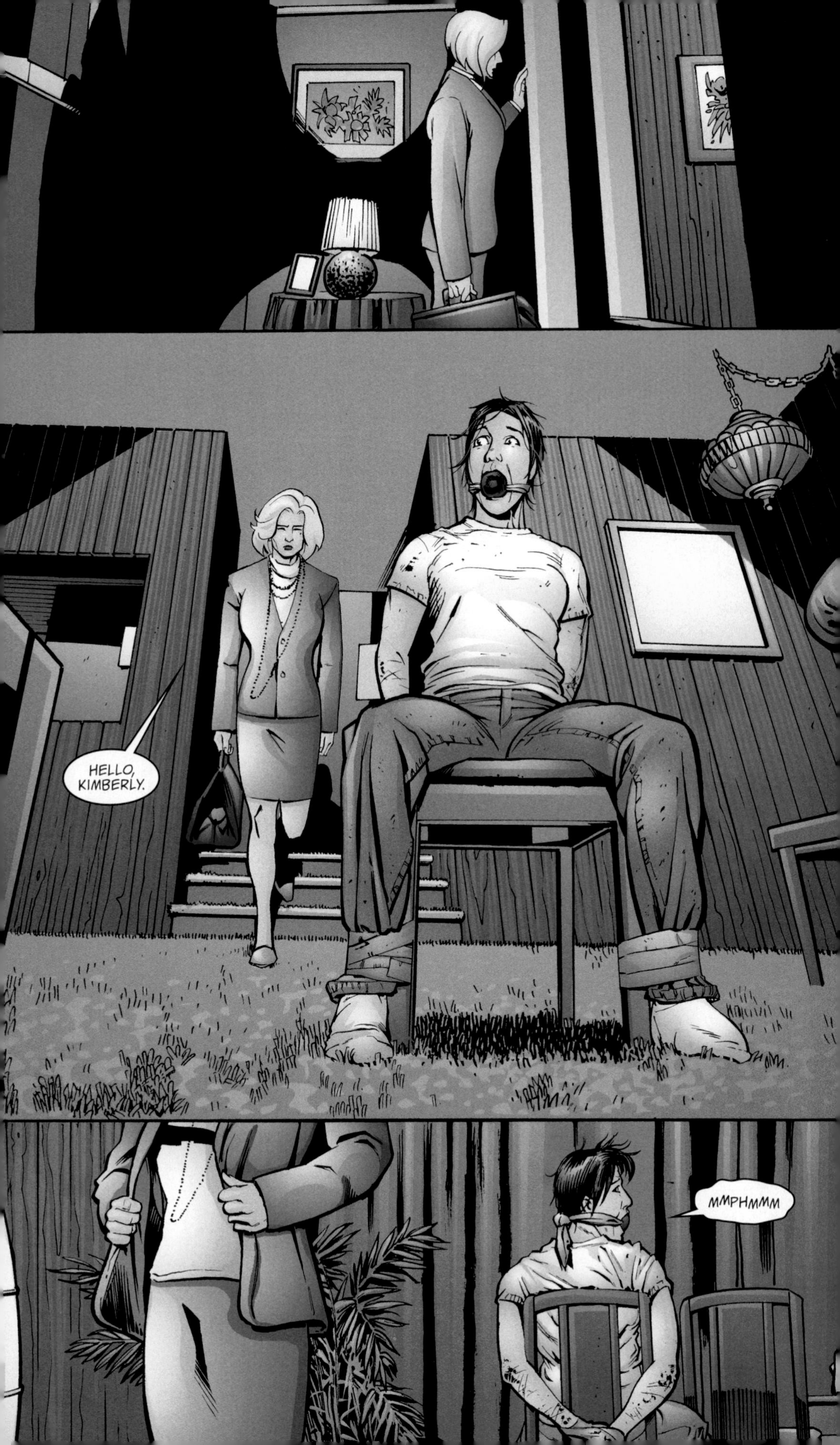
HELLO, KIMBERLY.
MMPHMMM

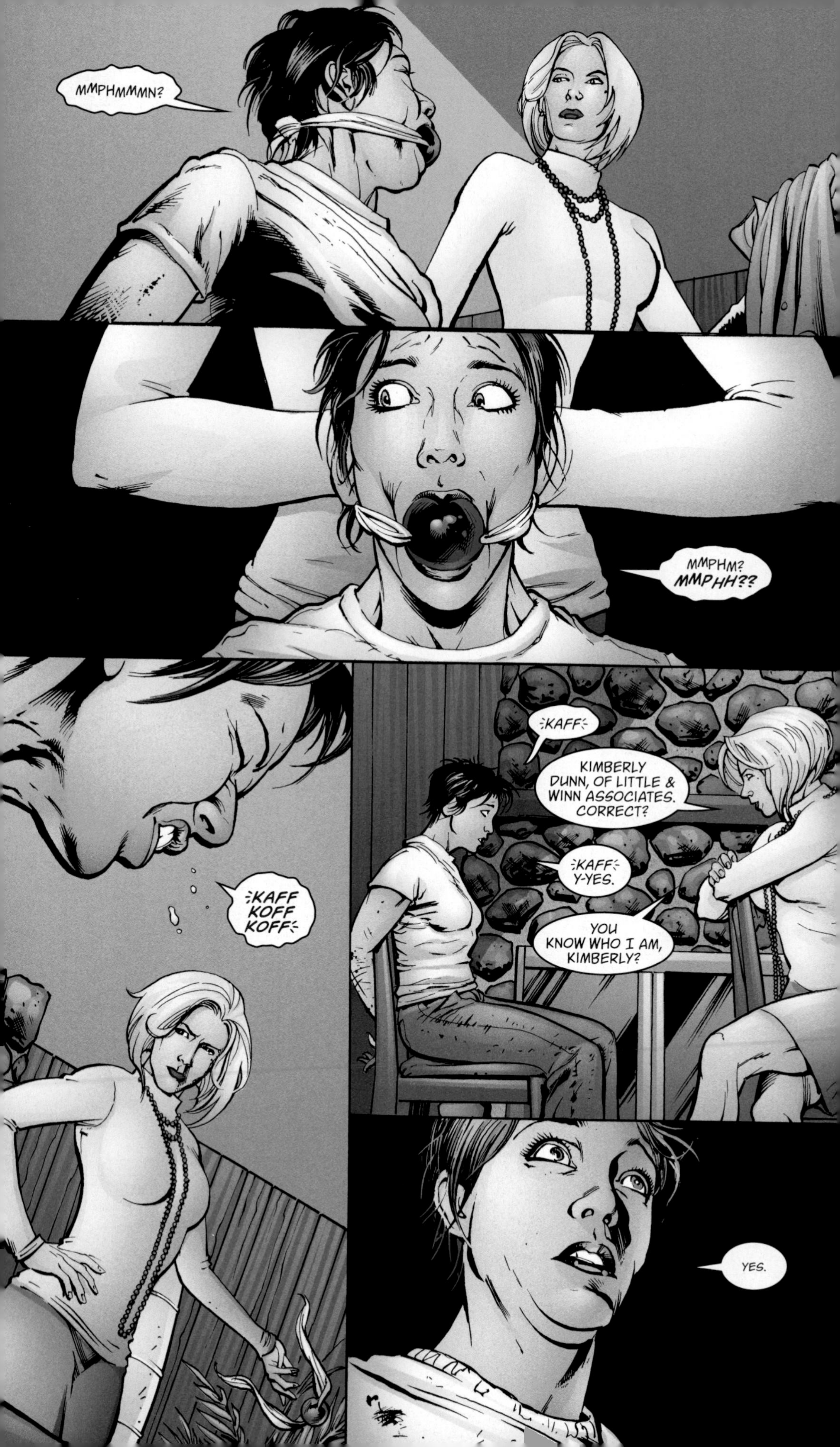
MMPHMMMN?
MMPHM? MMPHH??
KAFF KOFF KOFF
KAFF
KIMBERLY DUNN, OF LITTLE & WINN ASSOCIATES. CORRECT?
KAFF Y-YES.
YOU KNOW WHO I AM, KIMBERLY?
YES.

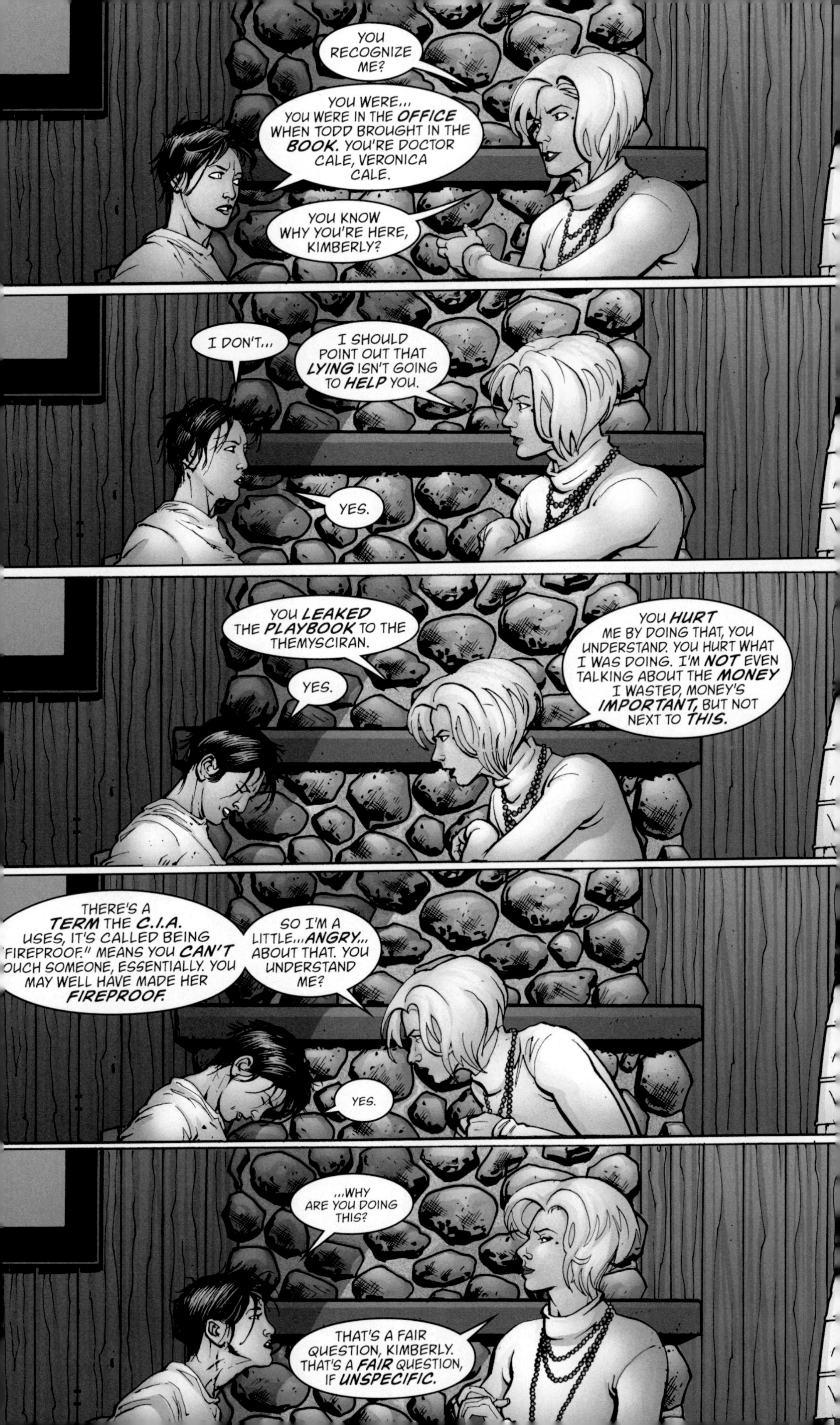
YOU RECOGNIZE ME?
YOU WERE... YOU WERE IN THE OFFICE WHEN TODD BROUGHT IN THE BOOK. YOU'RE DOCTOR CALE, VERONICA CALE.
YOU KNOW WHY YOU'RE HERE, KIMBERLY?
I DON'T...
I SHOULD POINT OUT THAT LYING ISN'T GOING TO HELP YOU.
YES.
YOU LEAKED THE PLAYBOOK TO THE THEMYSCIRAN.
YES.
YOU HURT ME BY DOING THAT, YOU UNDERSTAND. YOU HURT WHAT I WAS DOING. I'M NOT EVEN TALKING ABOUT THE MONEY I WASTED, MONEY'S IMPORTANT, BUT NOT NEXT TO THIS.
THERE'S A TERM THE C.I.A. USES, IT'S CALLED BEING "FIREPROOF." MEANS YOU CAN'T TOUCH SOMEONE, ESSENTIALLY. YOU MAY WELL HAVE MADE HER FIREPROOF.
SO I'M A LITTLE...ANGRY... ABOUT THAT. YOU UNDERSTAND ME?
YES.
...WHY ARE YOU DOING THIS?
THAT'S A FAIR QUESTION, KIMBERLY. THAT'S A FAIR QUESTION, IF UNSPECIFIC.

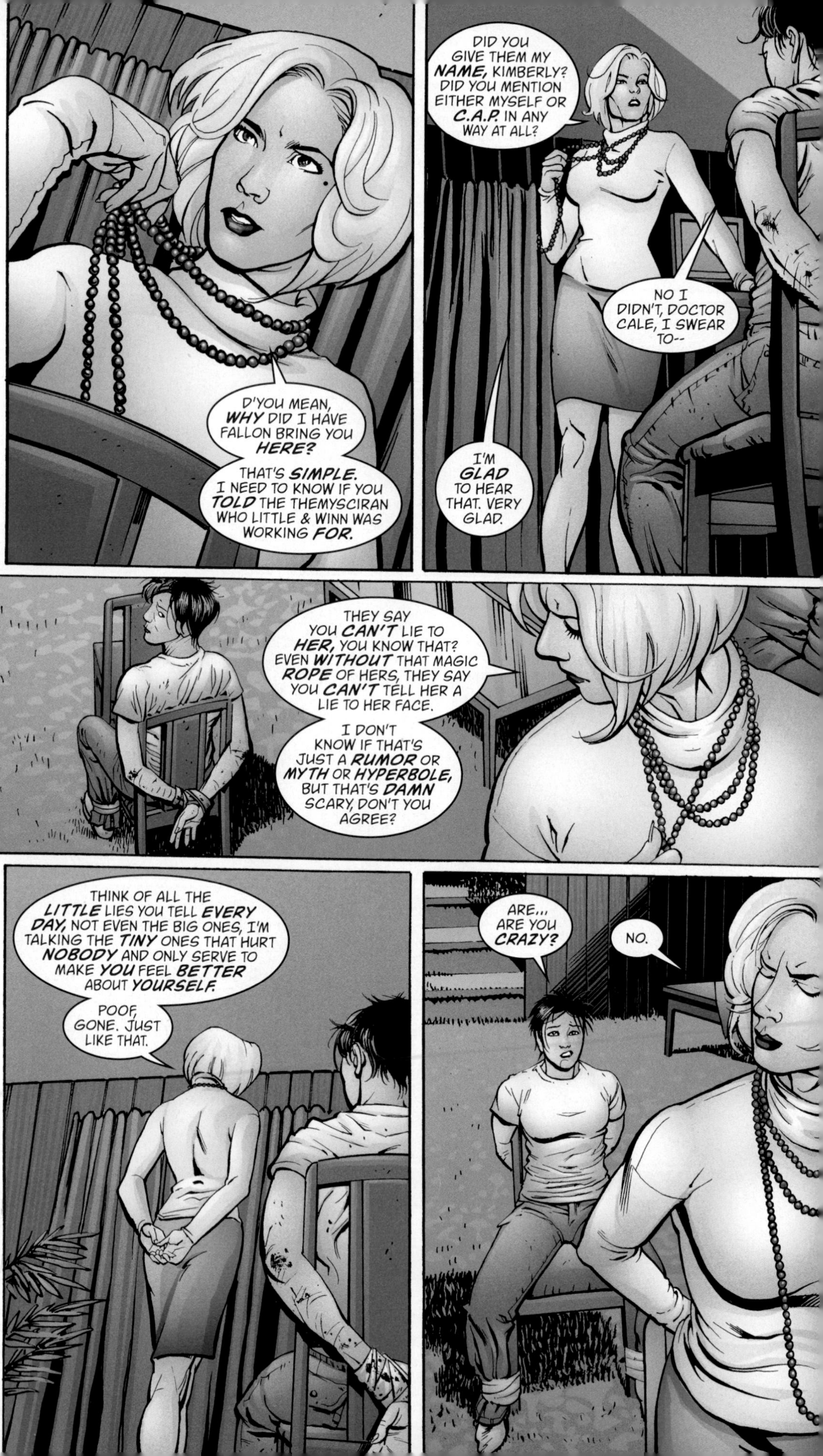
D'YOU MEAN, WHY DID I HAVE FALLON BRING YOU HERE?
THAT'S SIMPLE. I NEED TO KNOW IF YOU TOLD THE THEMYSCIRAN WHO LITTLE & WINN WAS WORKING FOR.
DID YOU GIVE THEM MY NAME, KIMBERLY? DID YOU MENTION EITHER MYSELF OR C.A.P. IN ANY WAY AT ALL?
NO I DIDN'T, DOCTOR CALE, I SWEAR TO--
I'M GLAD TO HEAR THAT. VERY GLAD.
THEY SAY YOU CAN'T LIE TO HER, YOU KNOW THAT? EVEN WITHOUT THAT MAGIC ROPE OF HERS, THEY SAY YOU CAN'T TELL HER A LIE TO HER FACE.
I DON'T KNOW IF THAT'S JUST A RUMOR OR MYTH OR HYPERBOLE, BUT THAT'S DAMN SCARY, DON'T YOU AGREE?
THINK OF ALL THE LITTLE LIES YOU TELL EVERY DAY, NOT EVEN THE BIG ONES, I'M TALKING THE TINY ONES THAT HURT NOBODY AND ONLY SERVE TO MAKE YOU FEEL BETTER ABOUT YOURSELF.
POOF, GONE. JUST LIKE THAT.
ARE... ARE YOU CRAZY?
NO.

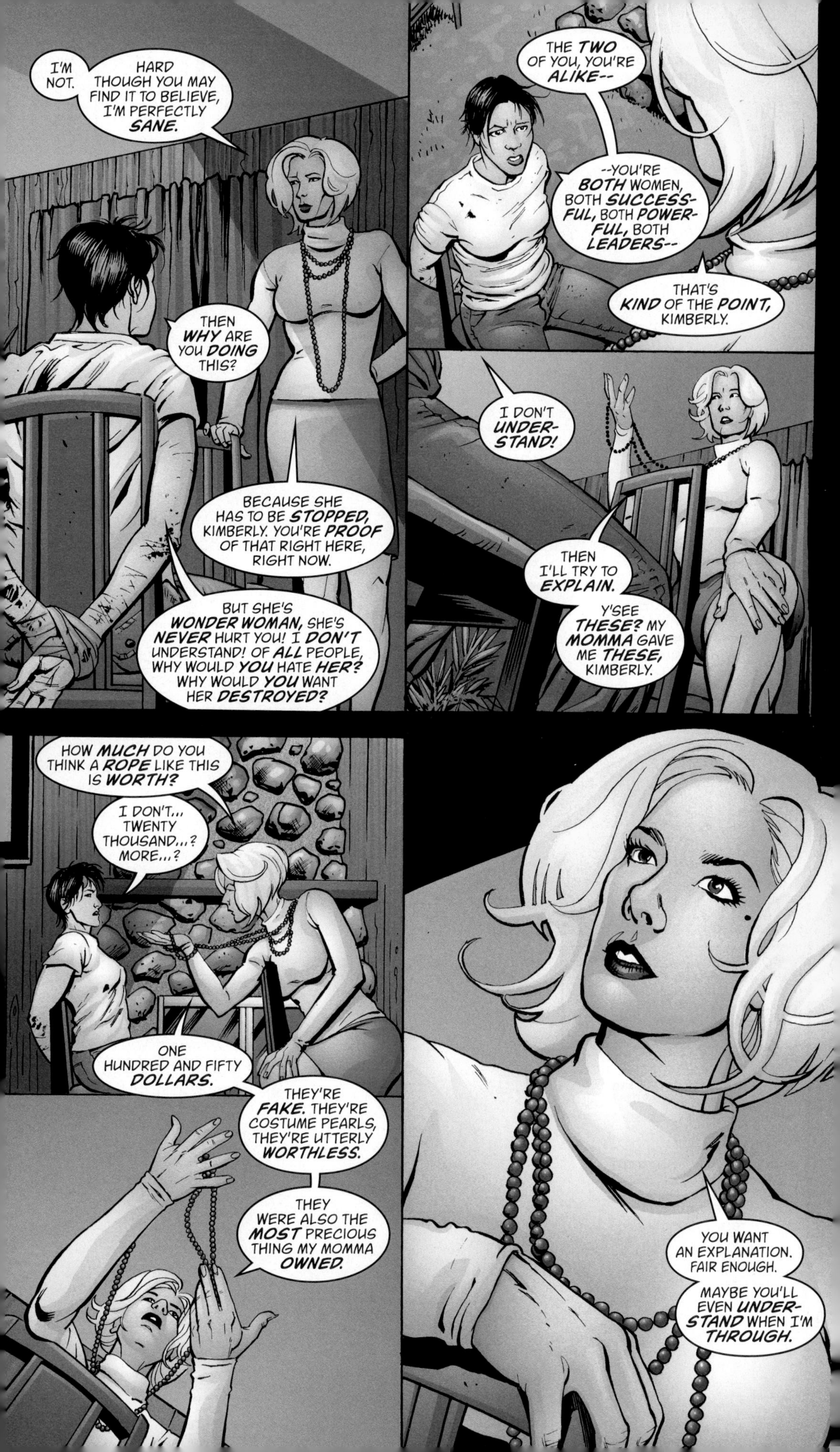
I'M NOT.
HARD THOUGH YOU MAY FIND IT TO BELIEVE, I'M PERFECTLY **SANE.**
THEN **WHY** ARE YOU **DOING** THIS?
BECAUSE SHE HAS TO BE **STOPPED,** KIMBERLY. YOU'RE **PROOF** OF THAT RIGHT HERE, RIGHT NOW.
BUT SHE'S **WONDER WOMAN,** SHE'S **NEVER** HURT YOU! I **DON'T** UNDERSTAND! OF **ALL** PEOPLE, WHY WOULD **YOU** HATE **HER?** WHY WOULD **YOU** WANT HER **DESTROYED?**
THE **TWO** OF YOU, YOU'RE **ALIKE--**
--YOU'RE **BOTH** WOMEN, BOTH **SUCCESS-FUL,** BOTH **POWER-FUL,** BOTH **LEADERS--**
THAT'S **KIND** OF THE **POINT,** KIMBERLY.
I DON'T **UNDER-STAND!**
THEN I'LL TRY TO **EXPLAIN.**
Y'SEE **THESE?** MY **MOMMA** GAVE ME **THESE,** KIMBERLY.
HOW **MUCH** DO YOU THINK A **ROPE** LIKE THIS IS **WORTH?**
I DON'T... TWENTY THOUSAND...? MORE...?
ONE HUNDRED AND FIFTY **DOLLARS.**
THEY'RE **FAKE.** THEY'RE COSTUME PEARLS, THEY'RE UTTERLY **WORTHLESS.**
THEY WERE ALSO THE **MOST** PRECIOUS THING MY MOMMA **OWNED.**
YOU WANT AN EXPLANATION. FAIR ENOUGH.
MAYBE YOU'LL EVEN **UNDER-STAND** WHEN I'M **THROUGH.**

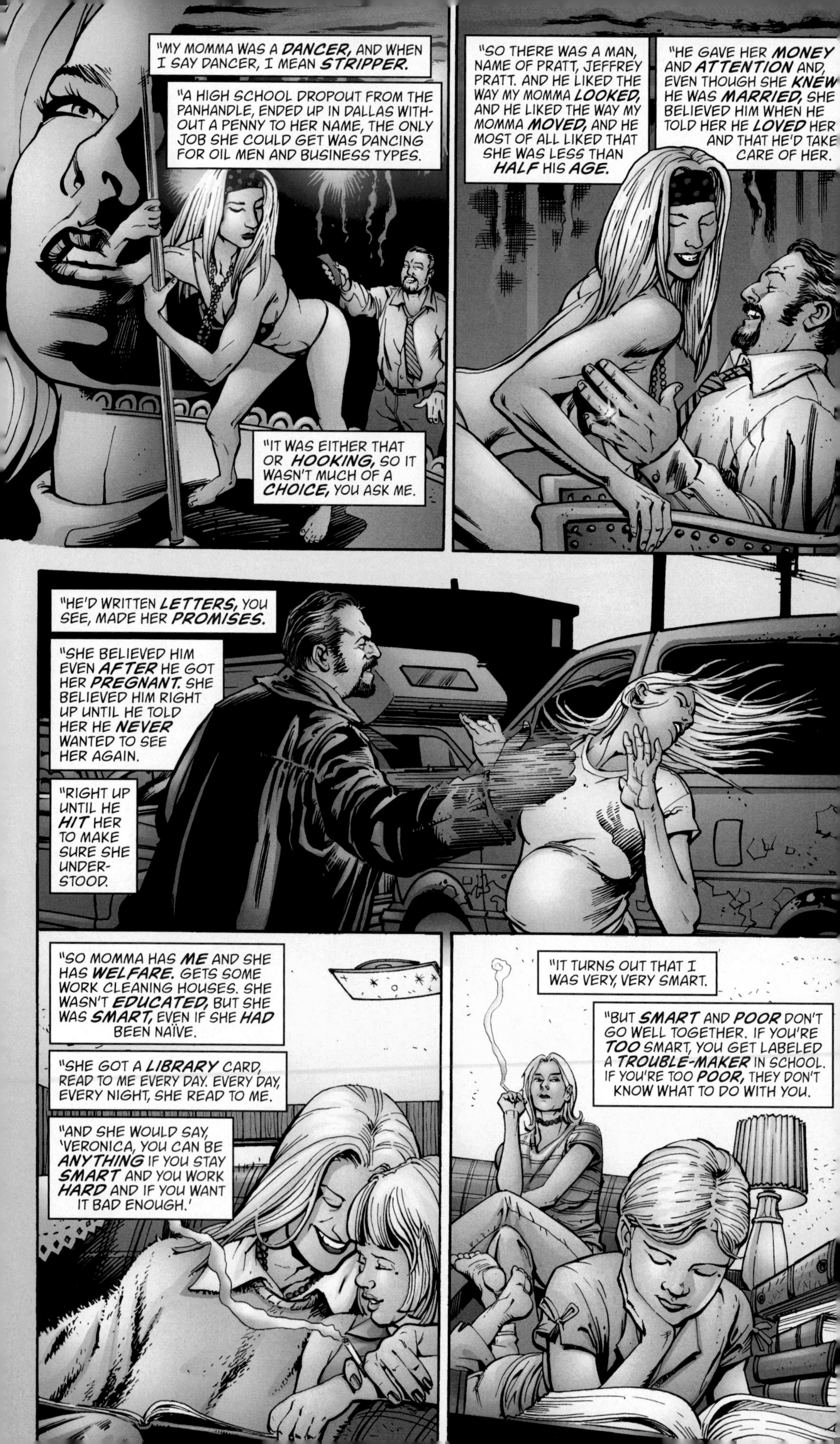
"MY MOMMA WAS A DANCER, AND WHEN I SAY DANCER, I MEAN STRIPPER.
"A HIGH SCHOOL DROPOUT FROM THE PANHANDLE, ENDED UP IN DALLAS WITHOUT A PENNY TO HER NAME, THE ONLY JOB SHE COULD GET WAS DANCING FOR OIL MEN AND BUSINESS TYPES.
"IT WAS EITHER THAT OR HOOKING, SO IT WASN'T MUCH OF A CHOICE, YOU ASK ME.
"SO THERE WAS A MAN, NAME OF PRATT, JEFFREY PRATT. AND HE LIKED THE WAY MY MOMMA LOOKED, AND HE LIKED THE WAY MY MOMMA MOVED, AND HE MOST OF ALL LIKED THAT SHE WAS LESS THAN HALF HIS AGE.
"HE GAVE HER MONEY AND ATTENTION AND, EVEN THOUGH SHE KNEW HE WAS MARRIED, SHE BELIEVED HIM WHEN HE TOLD HER HE LOVED HER AND THAT HE'D TAKE CARE OF HER.
"HE'D WRITTEN LETTERS, YOU SEE, MADE HER PROMISES.
"SHE BELIEVED HIM EVEN AFTER HE GOT HER PREGNANT. SHE BELIEVED HIM RIGHT UP UNTIL HE TOLD HER HE NEVER WANTED TO SEE HER AGAIN.
"RIGHT UP UNTIL HE HIT HER TO MAKE SURE SHE UNDERSTOOD.
"SO MOMMA HAS ME AND SHE HAS WELFARE. GETS SOME WORK CLEANING HOUSES. SHE WASN'T EDUCATED, BUT SHE WAS SMART, EVEN IF SHE HAD BEEN NAÏVE.
"SHE GOT A LIBRARY CARD, READ TO ME EVERY DAY. EVERY DAY, EVERY NIGHT, SHE READ TO ME.
"AND SHE WOULD SAY, 'VERONICA, YOU CAN BE ANYTHING IF YOU STAY SMART AND YOU WORK HARD AND IF YOU WANT IT BAD ENOUGH.'
"IT TURNS OUT THAT I WAS VERY, VERY SMART.
"BUT SMART AND POOR DON'T GO WELL TOGETHER. IF YOU'RE TOO SMART, YOU GET LABELED A TROUBLE-MAKER IN SCHOOL. IF YOU'RE TOO POOR, THEY DON'T KNOW WHAT TO DO WITH YOU.

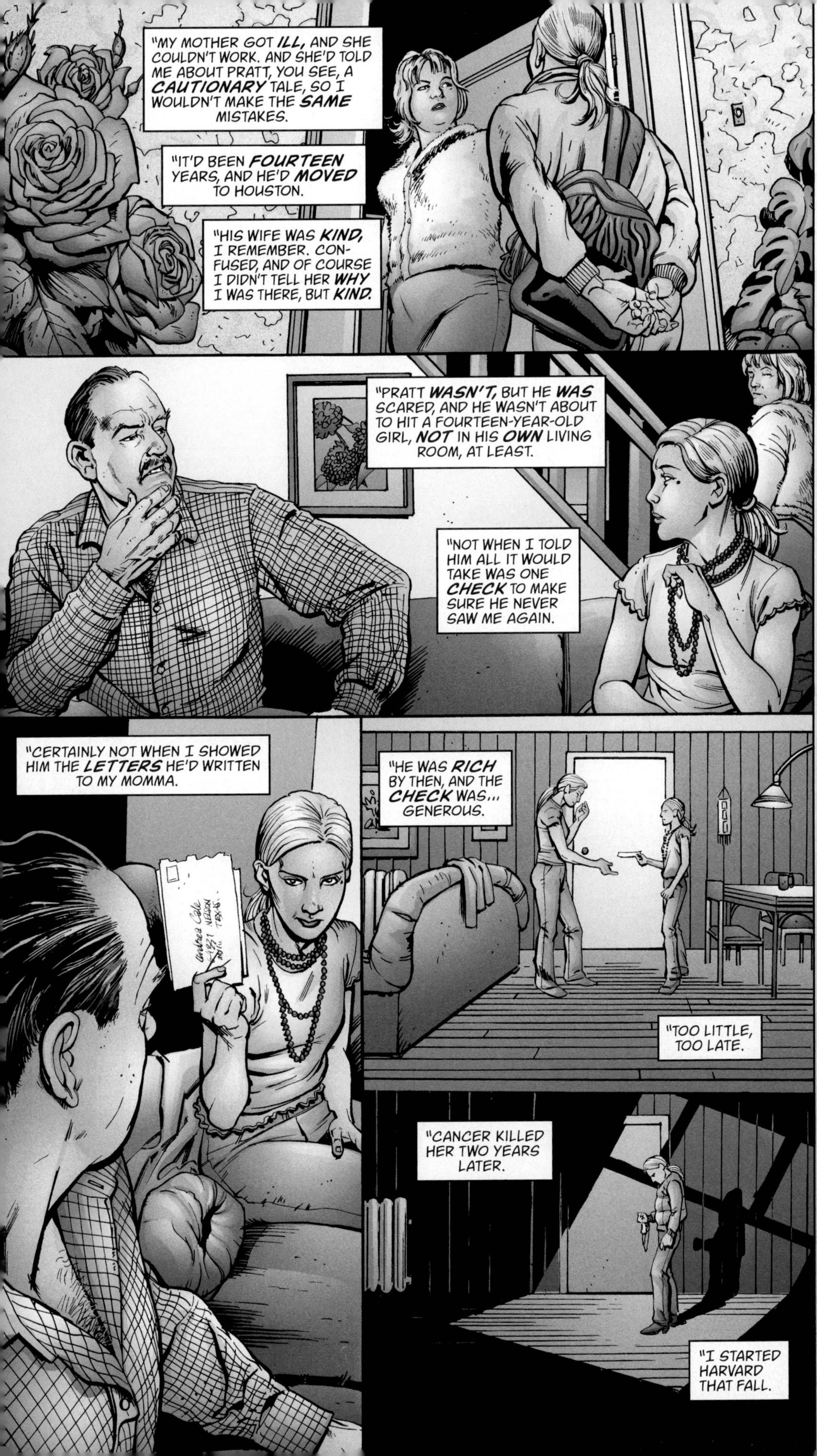
"MY MOTHER GOT ILL, AND SHE COULDN'T WORK. AND SHE'D TOLD ME ABOUT PRATT, YOU SEE, A CAUTIONARY TALE, SO I WOULDN'T MAKE THE SAME MISTAKES.
"IT'D BEEN FOURTEEN YEARS, AND HE'D MOVED TO HOUSTON.
"HIS WIFE WAS KIND, I REMEMBER. CON-FUSED, AND OF COURSE I DIDN'T TELL HER WHY I WAS THERE, BUT KIND.
"PRATT WASN'T, BUT HE WAS SCARED, AND HE WASN'T ABOUT TO HIT A FOURTEEN-YEAR-OLD GIRL, NOT IN HIS OWN LIVING ROOM, AT LEAST.
"NOT WHEN I TOLD HIM ALL IT WOULD TAKE WAS ONE CHECK TO MAKE SURE HE NEVER SAW ME AGAIN.
"CERTAINLY NOT WHEN I SHOWED HIM THE LETTERS HE'D WRITTEN TO MY MOMMA.
"HE WAS RICH BY THEN, AND THE CHECK WAS... GENEROUS.
"TOO LITTLE, TOO LATE.
"CANCER KILLED HER TWO YEARS LATER.
"I STARTED HARVARD THAT FALL.

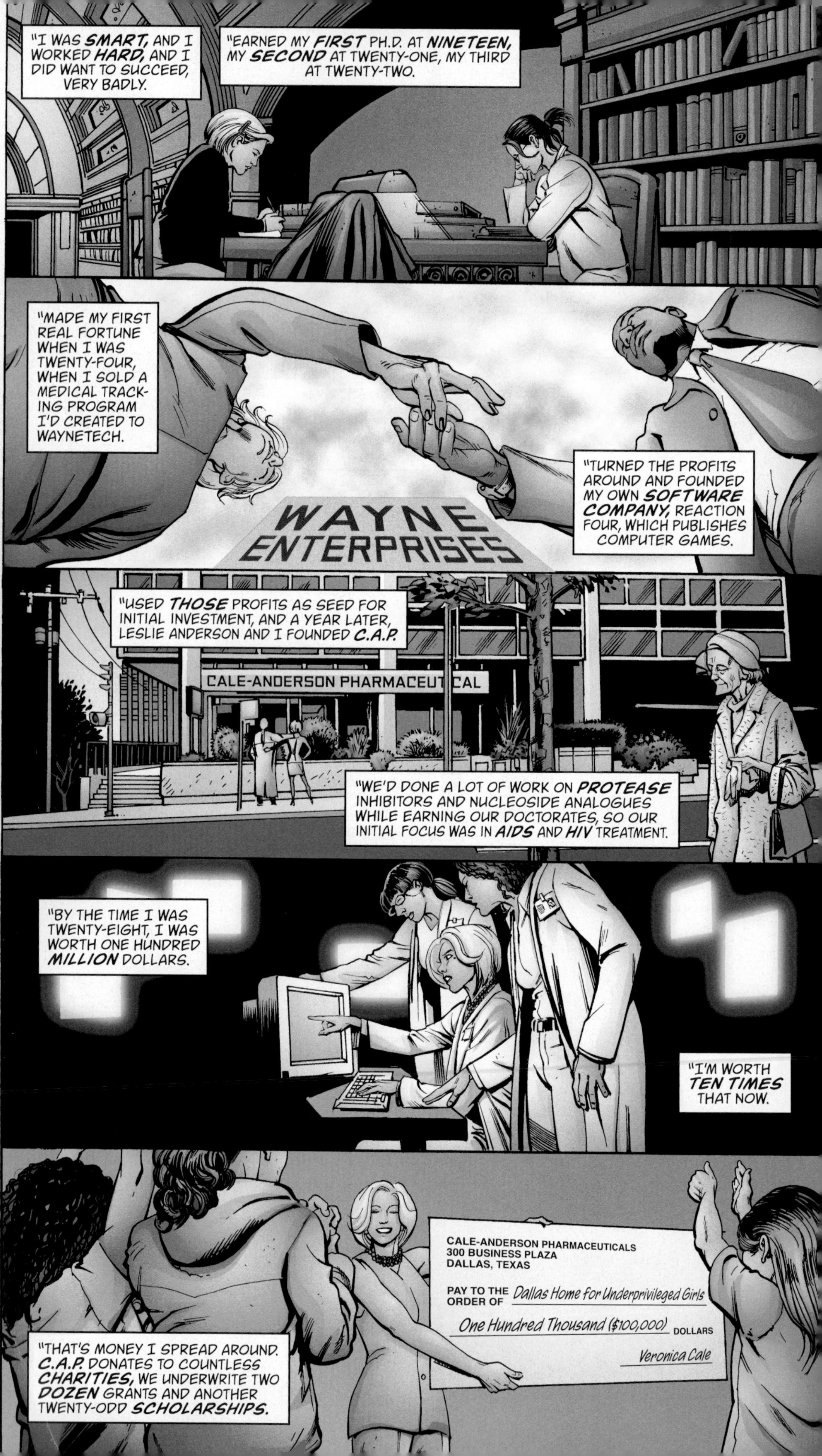
"I WAS SMART, AND I WORKED HARD, AND I DID WANT TO SUCCEED, VERY BADLY.
"EARNED MY FIRST PH.D. AT NINETEEN, MY SECOND AT TWENTY-ONE, MY THIRD AT TWENTY-TWO.
"MADE MY FIRST REAL FORTUNE WHEN I WAS TWENTY-FOUR, WHEN I SOLD A MEDICAL TRACKING PROGRAM I'D CREATED TO WAYNETECH.
WAYNE ENTERPRISES
"TURNED THE PROFITS AROUND AND FOUNDED MY OWN SOFTWARE COMPANY, REACTION FOUR, WHICH PUBLISHES COMPUTER GAMES.
"USED THOSE PROFITS AS SEED FOR INITIAL INVESTMENT, AND A YEAR LATER, LESLIE ANDERSON AND I FOUNDED C.A.P.
CALE-ANDERSON PHARMACEUTICAL
"WE'D DONE A LOT OF WORK ON PROTEASE INHIBITORS AND NUCLEOSIDE ANALOGUES WHILE EARNING OUR DOCTORATES, SO OUR INITIAL FOCUS WAS IN AIDS AND HIV TREATMENT.
"BY THE TIME I WAS TWENTY-EIGHT, I WAS WORTH ONE HUNDRED MILLION DOLLARS.
"I'M WORTH TEN TIMES THAT NOW.
CALE-ANDERSON PHARMACEUTICALS
300 BUSINESS PLAZA
DALLAS, TEXAS
PAY TO THE ORDER OF Dallas Home for Underprivileged Girls
One Hundred Thousand ($100,000) DOLLARS
Veronica Cale
"THAT'S MONEY I SPREAD AROUND. C.A.P. DONATES TO COUNTLESS CHARITIES, WE UNDERWRITE TWO DOZEN GRANTS AND ANOTHER TWENTY-ODD SCHOLARSHIPS.

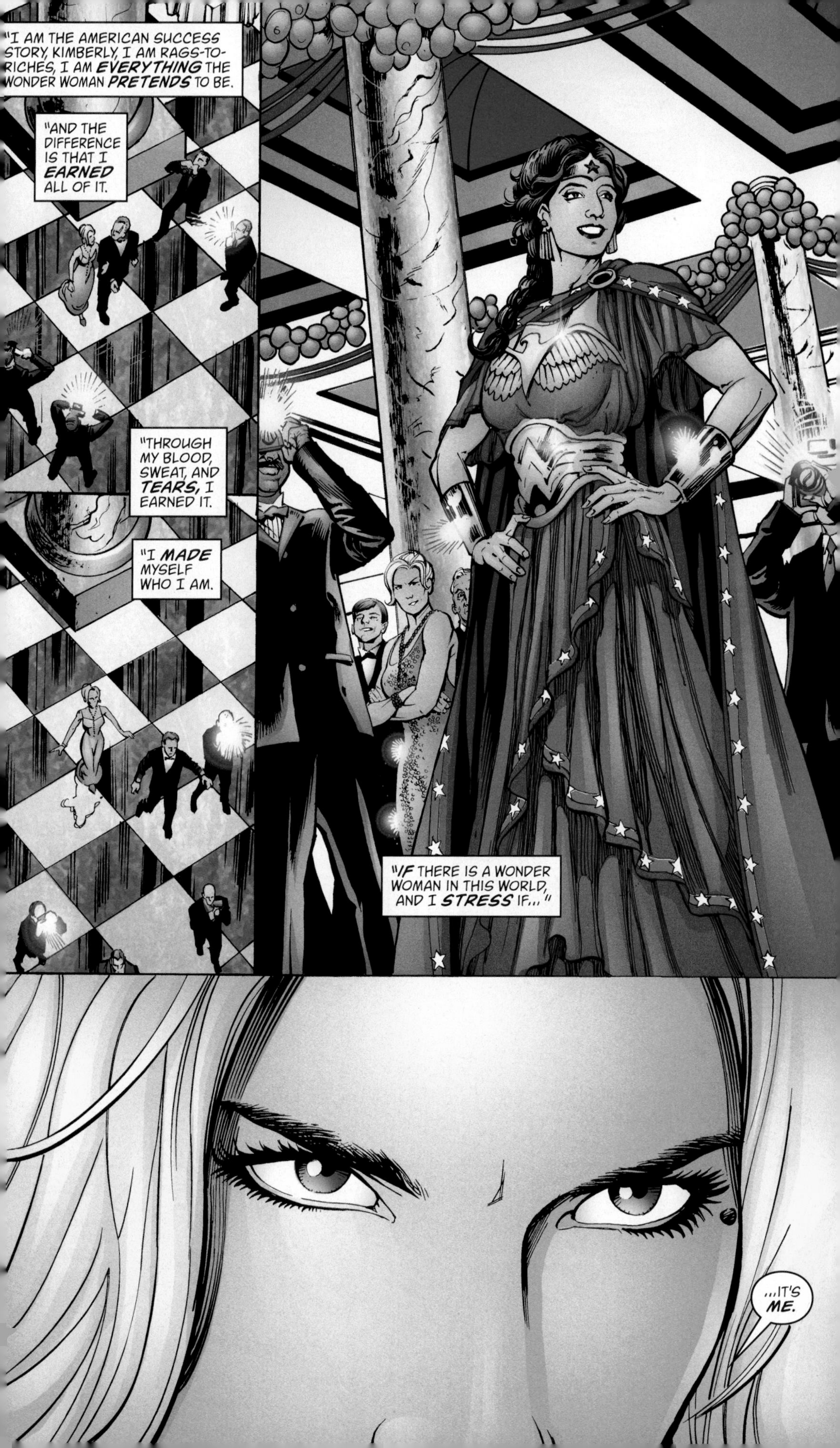
"I AM THE AMERICAN SUCCESS STORY, KIMBERLY. I AM RAGS-TO-RICHES. I AM EVERYTHING THE WONDER WOMAN PRETENDS TO BE.
"AND THE DIFFERENCE IS THAT I EARNED ALL OF IT.
"THROUGH MY BLOOD, SWEAT, AND TEARS, I EARNED IT.
"I MADE MYSELF WHO I AM.
"IF THERE IS A WONDER WOMAN IN THIS WORLD, AND I STRESS IF..."
...IT'S ME.

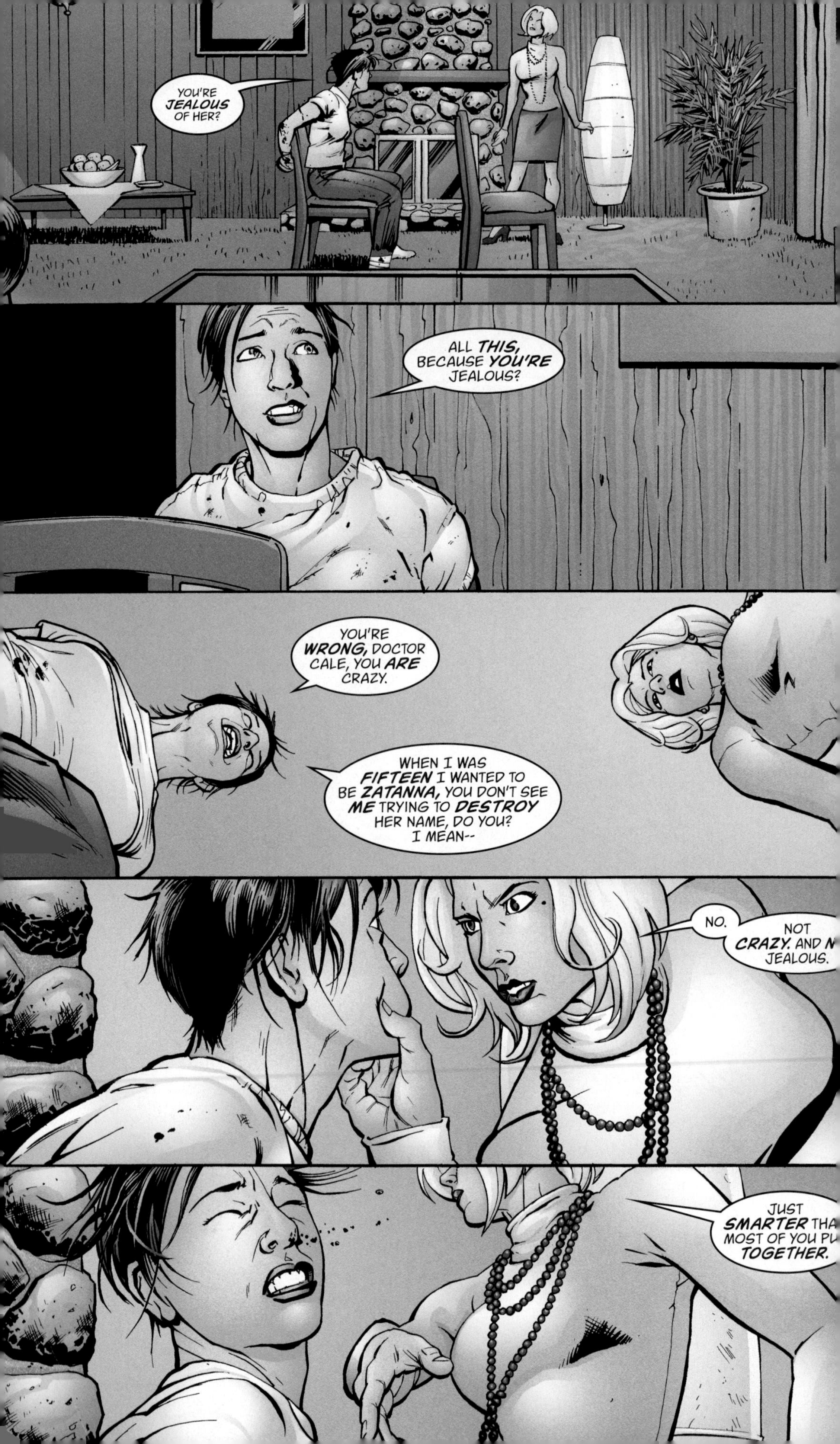

YOU'RE JEALOUS OF HER?
ALL THIS, BECAUSE YOU'RE JEALOUS?
YOU'RE WRONG, DOCTOR CALE, YOU ARE CRAZY.
WHEN I WAS FIFTEEN I WANTED TO BE ZATANNA, YOU DON'T SEE ME TRYING TO DESTROY HER NAME, DO YOU? I MEAN--
NO.
NOT CRAZY. AND
JEALOUS.
JUST SMARTER THA
MOST OF YOU PU
TOGETHER.

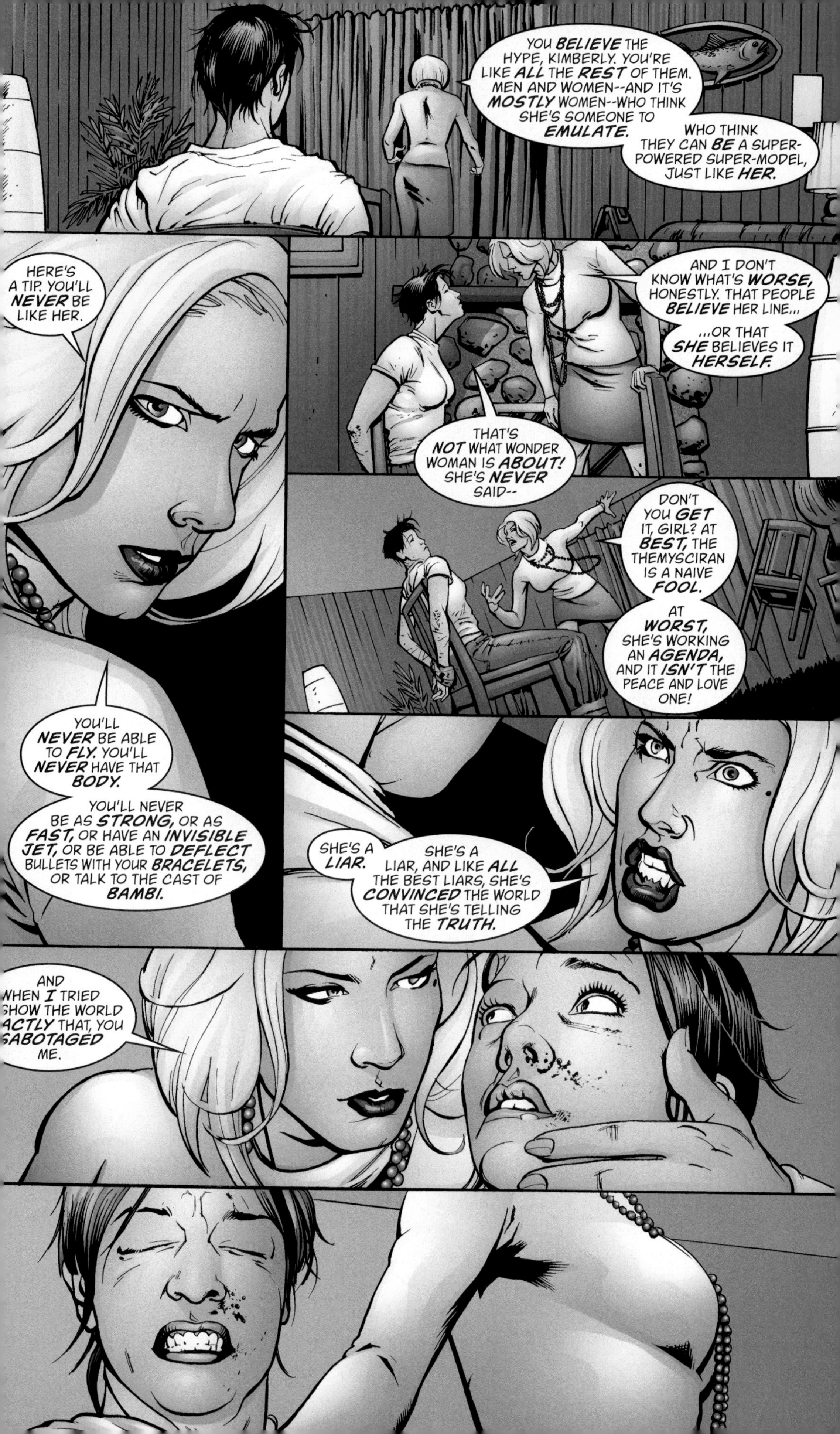
YOU BELIEVE THE HYPE, KIMBERLY. YOU'RE LIKE ALL THE REST OF THEM. MEN AND WOMEN--AND IT'S MOSTLY WOMEN--WHO THINK SHE'S SOMEONE TO EMULATE.
WHO THINK THEY CAN BE A SUPER-POWERED SUPER-MODEL, JUST LIKE HER.
HERE'S A TIP. YOU'LL NEVER BE LIKE HER.
AND I DON'T KNOW WHAT'S WORSE, HONESTLY. THAT PEOPLE BELIEVE HER LINE...
...OR THAT SHE BELIEVES IT HERSELF.
THAT'S NOT WHAT WONDER WOMAN IS ABOUT! SHE'S NEVER SAID--
DON'T YOU GET IT, GIRL? AT BEST, THE THEMYSCIRAN IS A NAIVE FOOL.
AT WORST, SHE'S WORKING AN AGENDA, AND IT ISN'T THE PEACE AND LOVE ONE!
YOU'LL NEVER BE ABLE TO FLY. YOU'LL NEVER HAVE THAT BODY.
YOU'LL NEVER BE AS STRONG, OR AS FAST, OR HAVE AN INVISIBLE JET, OR BE ABLE TO DEFLECT BULLETS WITH YOUR BRACELETS, OR TALK TO THE CAST OF BAMBI.
SHE'S A LIAR.
SHE'S A LIAR, AND LIKE ALL THE BEST LIARS, SHE'S CONVINCED THE WORLD THAT SHE'S TELLING THE TRUTH.
AND WHEN I TRIED SHOW THE WORLD ACTLY THAT, YOU SABOTAGED ME.

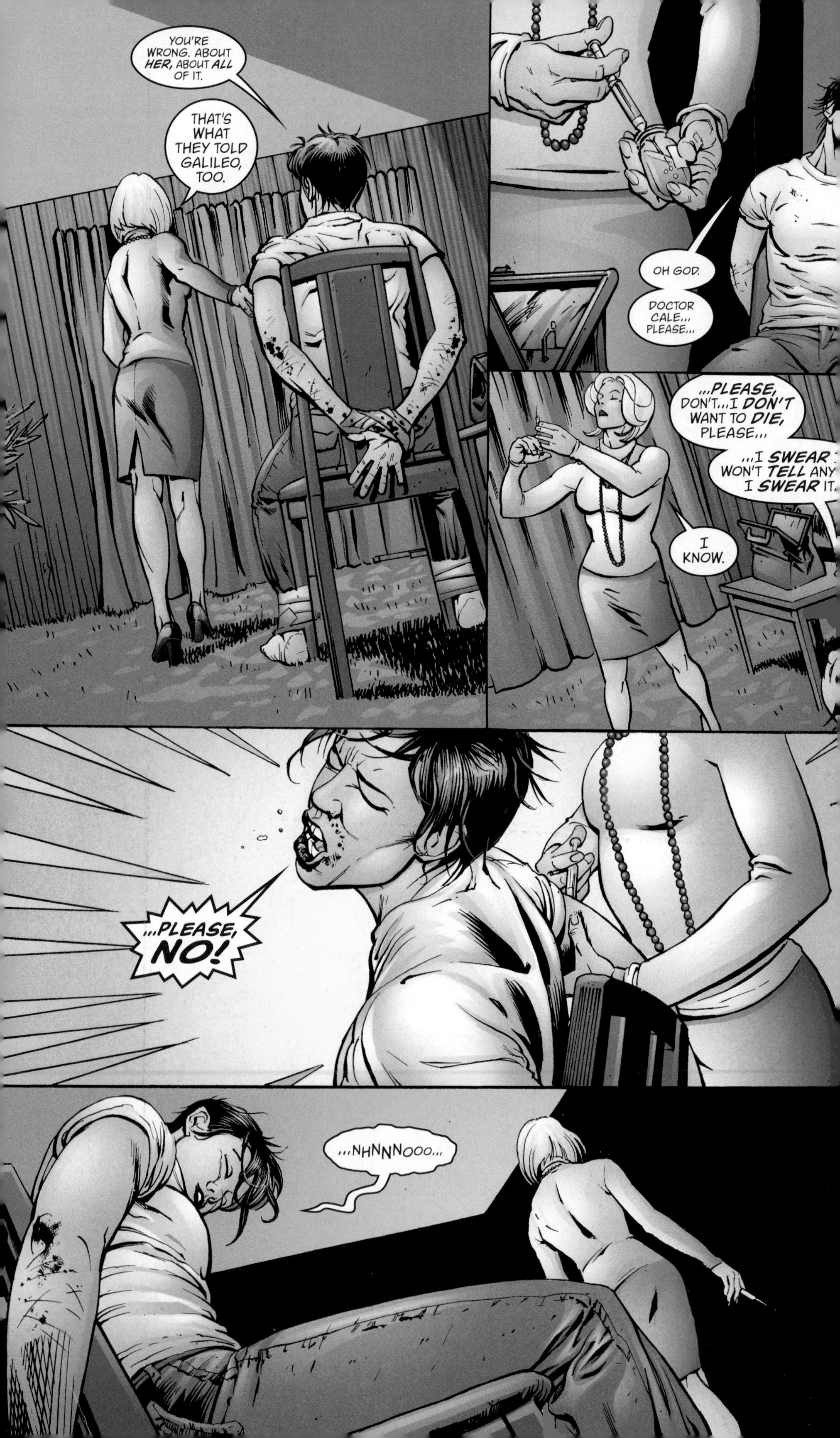
YOU'RE WRONG. ABOUT HER, ABOUT ALL OF IT.
THAT'S WHAT THEY TOLD GALILEO, TOO.
OH GOD.
DOCTOR CALE... PLEASE...
...PLEASE, DON'T...I DON'T WANT TO DIE, PLEASE...
...I SWEAR WON'T TELL ANY I SWEAR IT.
I KNOW.
...PLEASE, NO!
...NHNNNOOO...

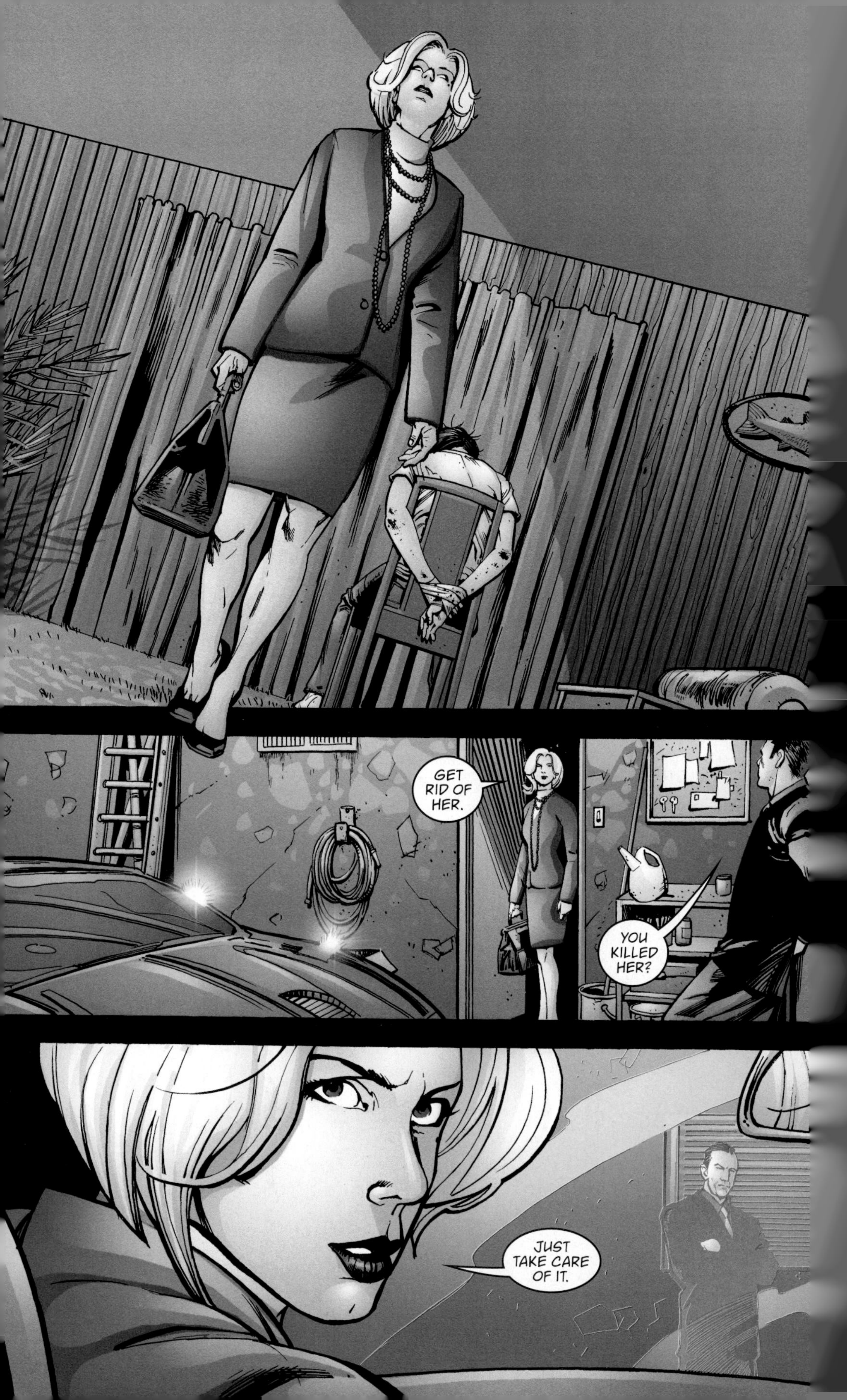
GET RID OF HER.
YOU KILLED HER?
JUST TAKE CARE OF IT.

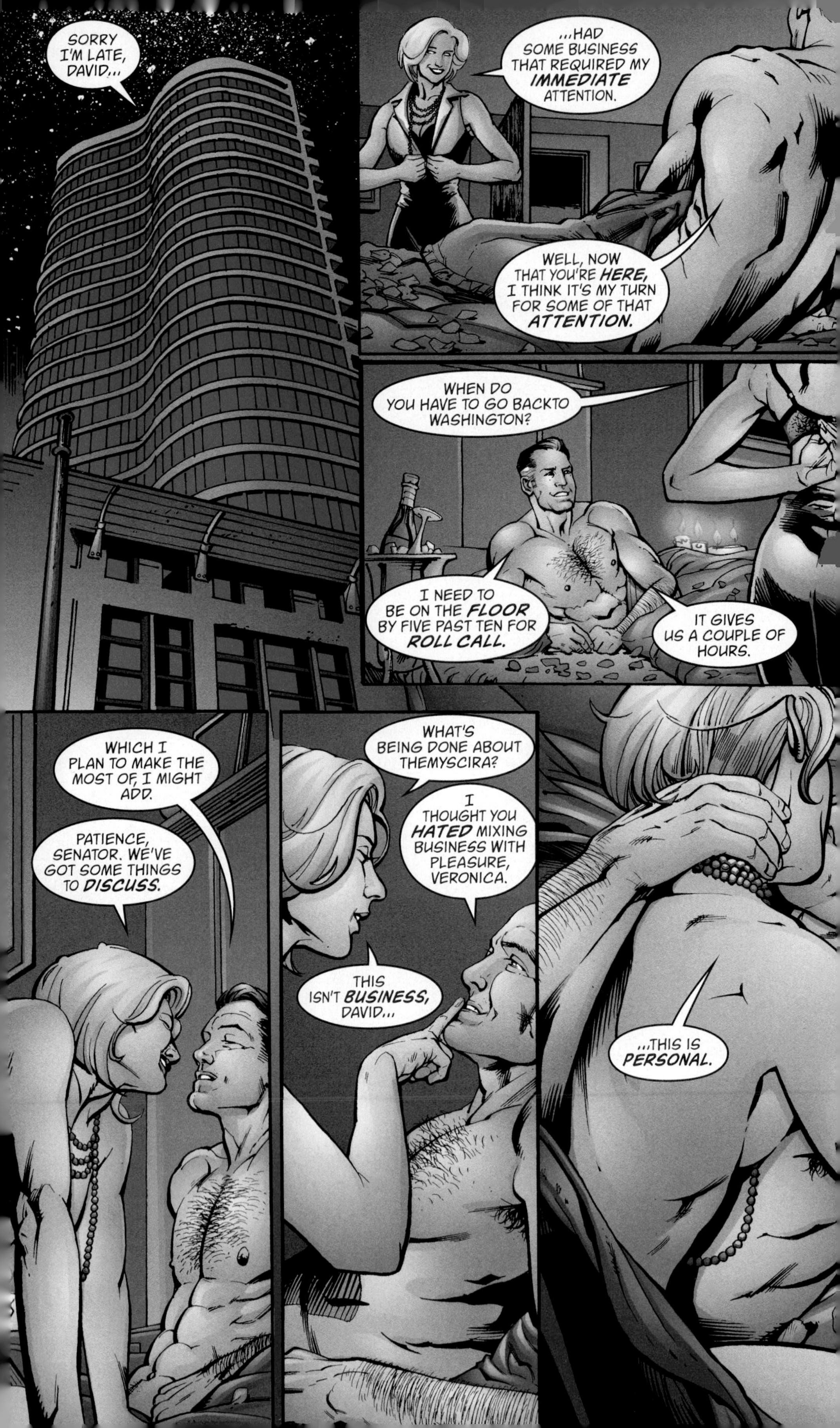
SORRY I'M LATE, DAVID...
...HAD SOME BUSINESS THAT REQUIRED MY IMMEDIATE ATTENTION.
WELL, NOW THAT YOU'RE HERE, I THINK IT'S MY TURN FOR SOME OF THAT ATTENTION.
WHEN DO YOU HAVE TO GO BACKTO WASHINGTON?
I NEED TO BE ON THE FLOOR BY FIVE PAST TEN FOR ROLL CALL.
IT GIVES US A COUPLE OF HOURS.
WHICH I PLAN TO MAKE THE MOST OF, I MIGHT ADD.
PATIENCE, SENATOR. WE'VE GOT SOME THINGS TO DISCUSS.
WHAT'S BEING DONE ABOUT THEMYSCIRA?
I THOUGHT YOU HATED MIXING BUSINESS WITH PLEASURE, VERONICA.
THIS ISN'T BUSINESS, DAVID...
...THIS IS PERSONAL.

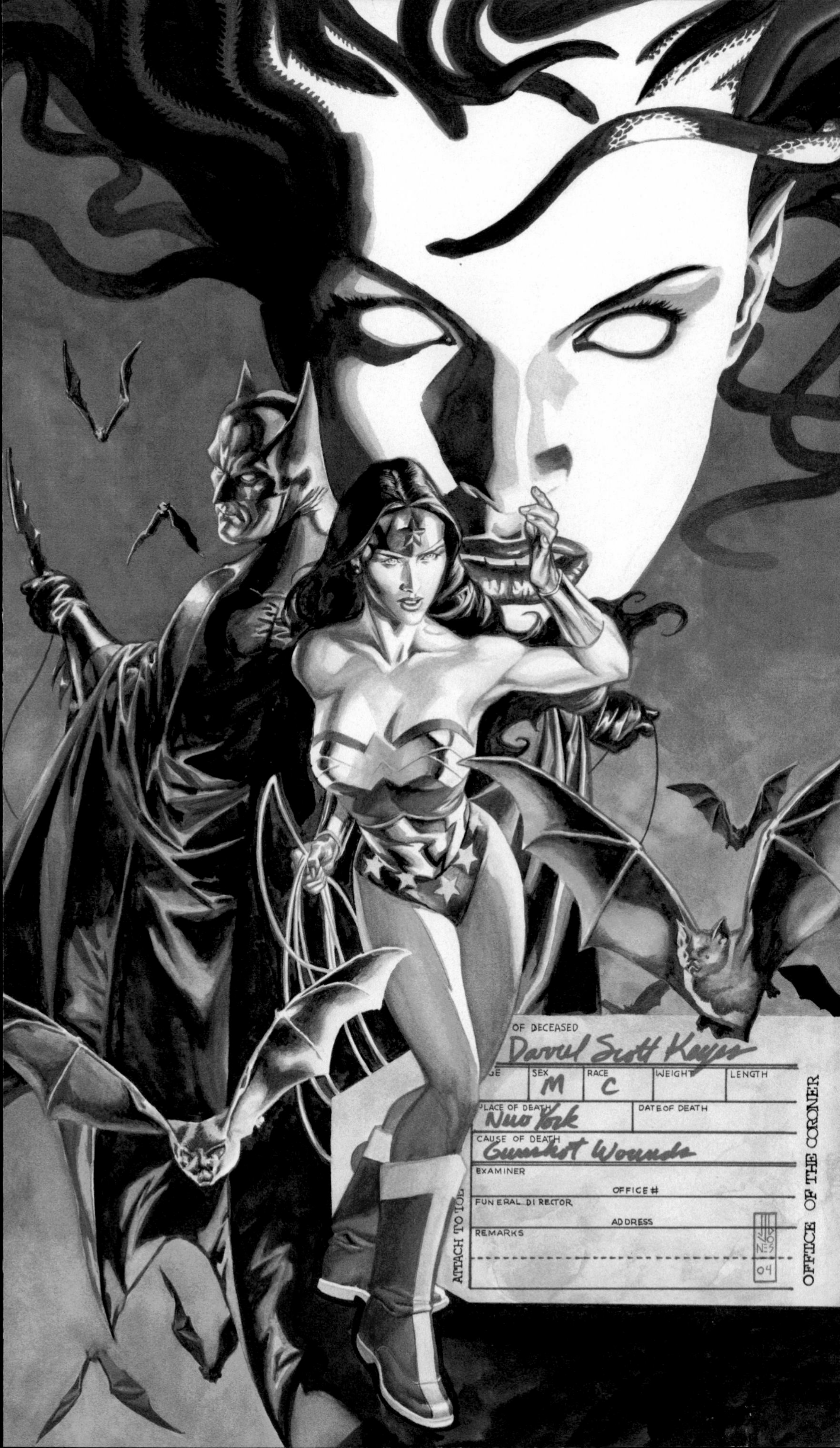
OF DECEASED
SEX
M
RACE
C
WEIGHT
LENGTH
PLACE OF DEATH
DATE OF DEATH
CAUSE OF DEATH
Gunshot Wounds
EXAMINER
OFFICE #
FUNERAL DIRECTOR
ADDRESS
REMARKS
ATTACH TO TOE
OFFICE OF THE CORONER
JG JONES 04

"BITTER PILLS: PART ONE"

Drew Johnson – *pencils*
Ray Snyder – *inks*
Richard Horie, Tanya Horie - *colors*
J.G. Jones – *cover art*

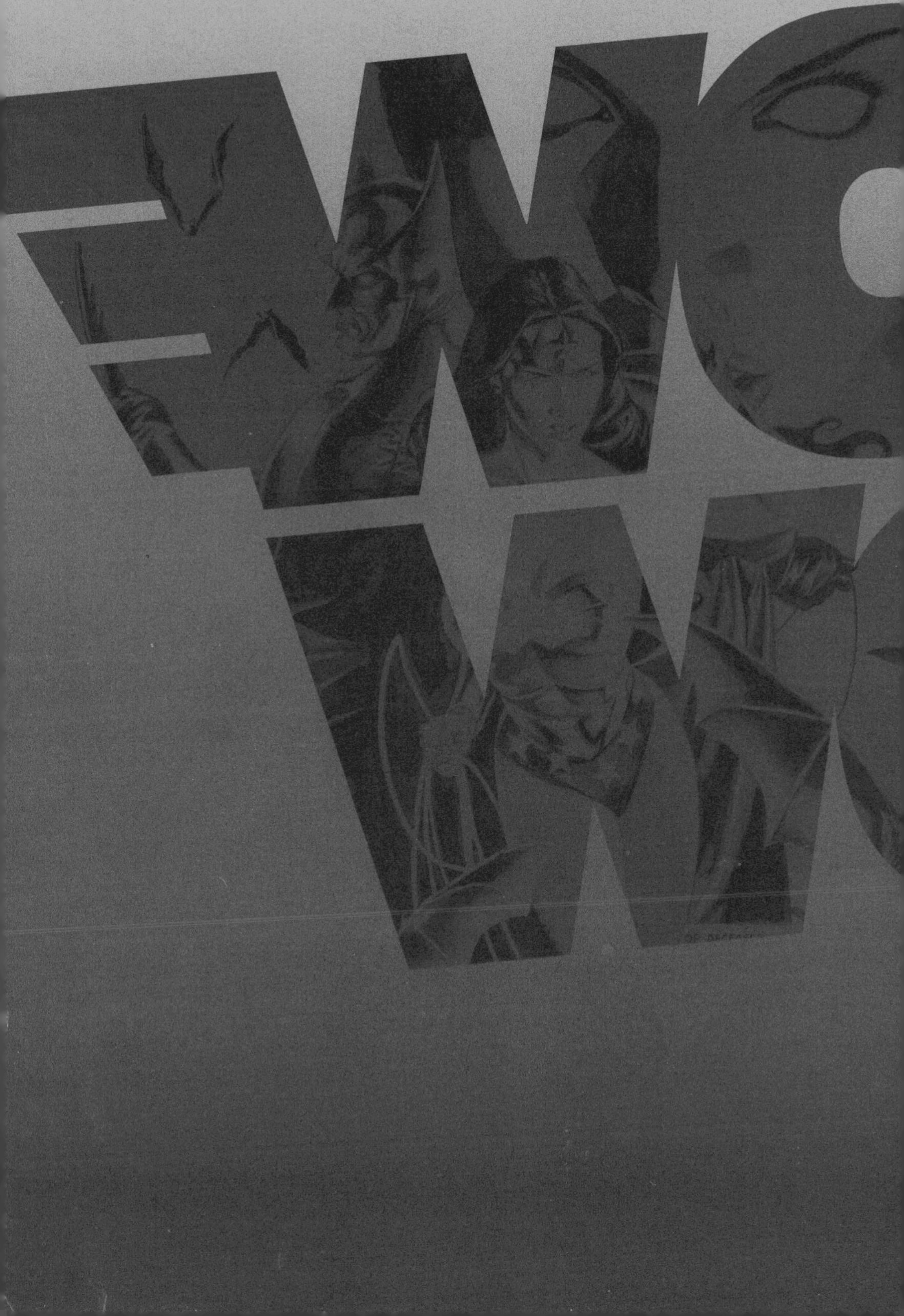

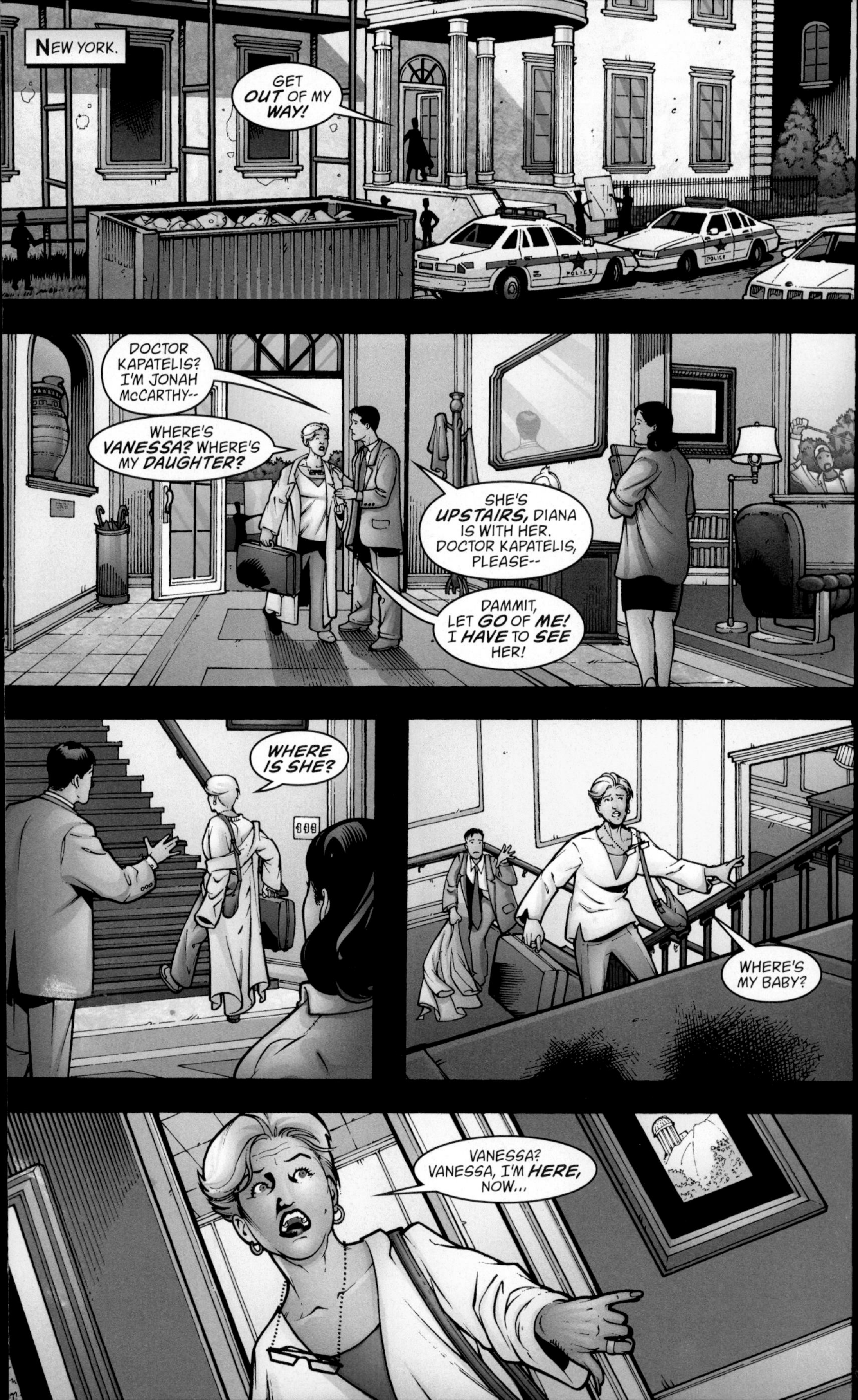
NEW YORK.
GET OUT OF MY WAY!
DOCTOR KAPATELIS? I'M JONAH McCARTHY--
WHERE'S VANESSA? WHERE'S MY DAUGHTER?
SHE'S UPSTAIRS, DIANA IS WITH HER. DOCTOR KAPATELIS, PLEASE--
DAMMIT, LET GO OF ME! I HAVE TO SEE HER!
WHERE IS SHE?
WHERE'S MY BABY?
VANESSA? VANESSA, I'M HERE, NOW...

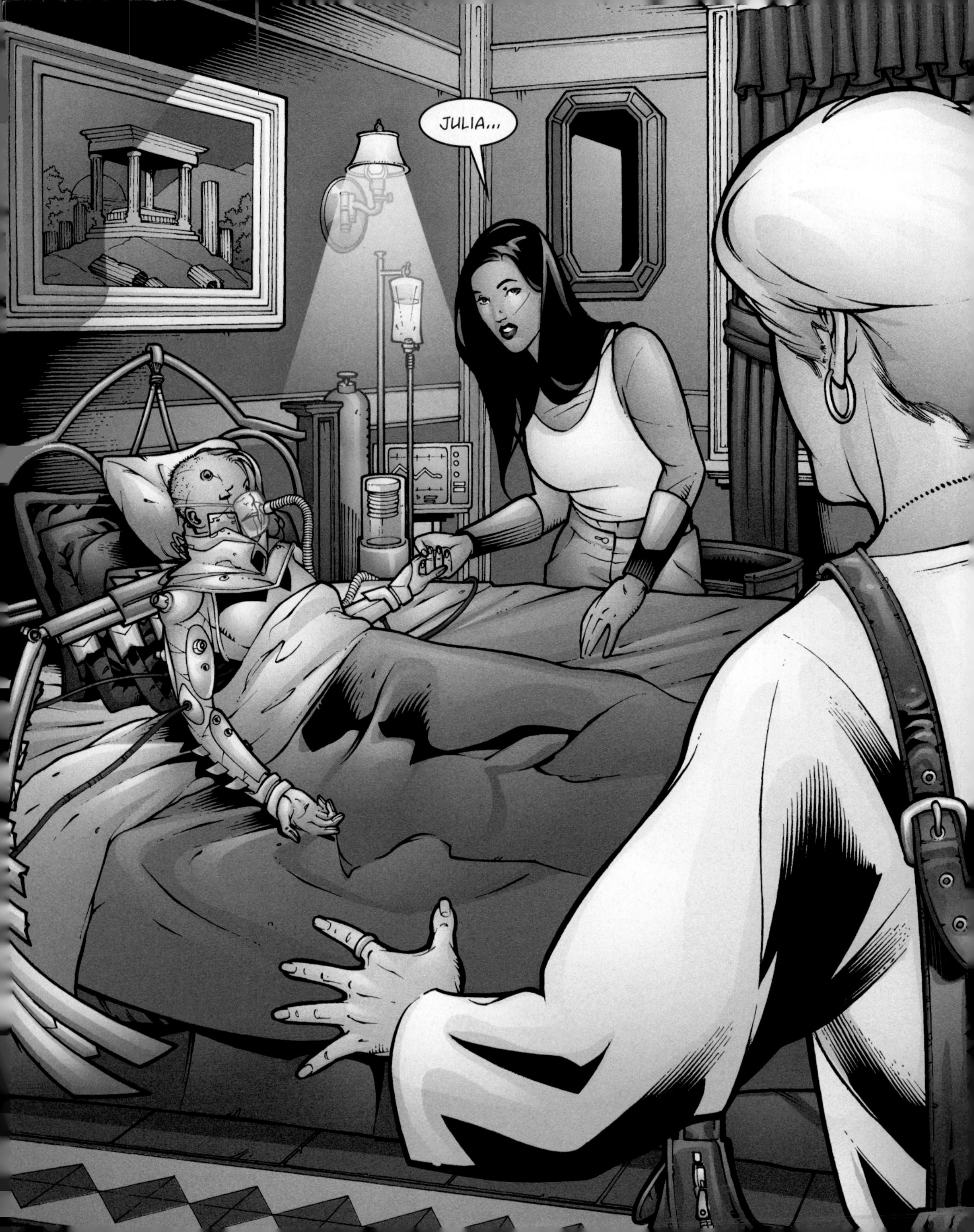
JULIA...

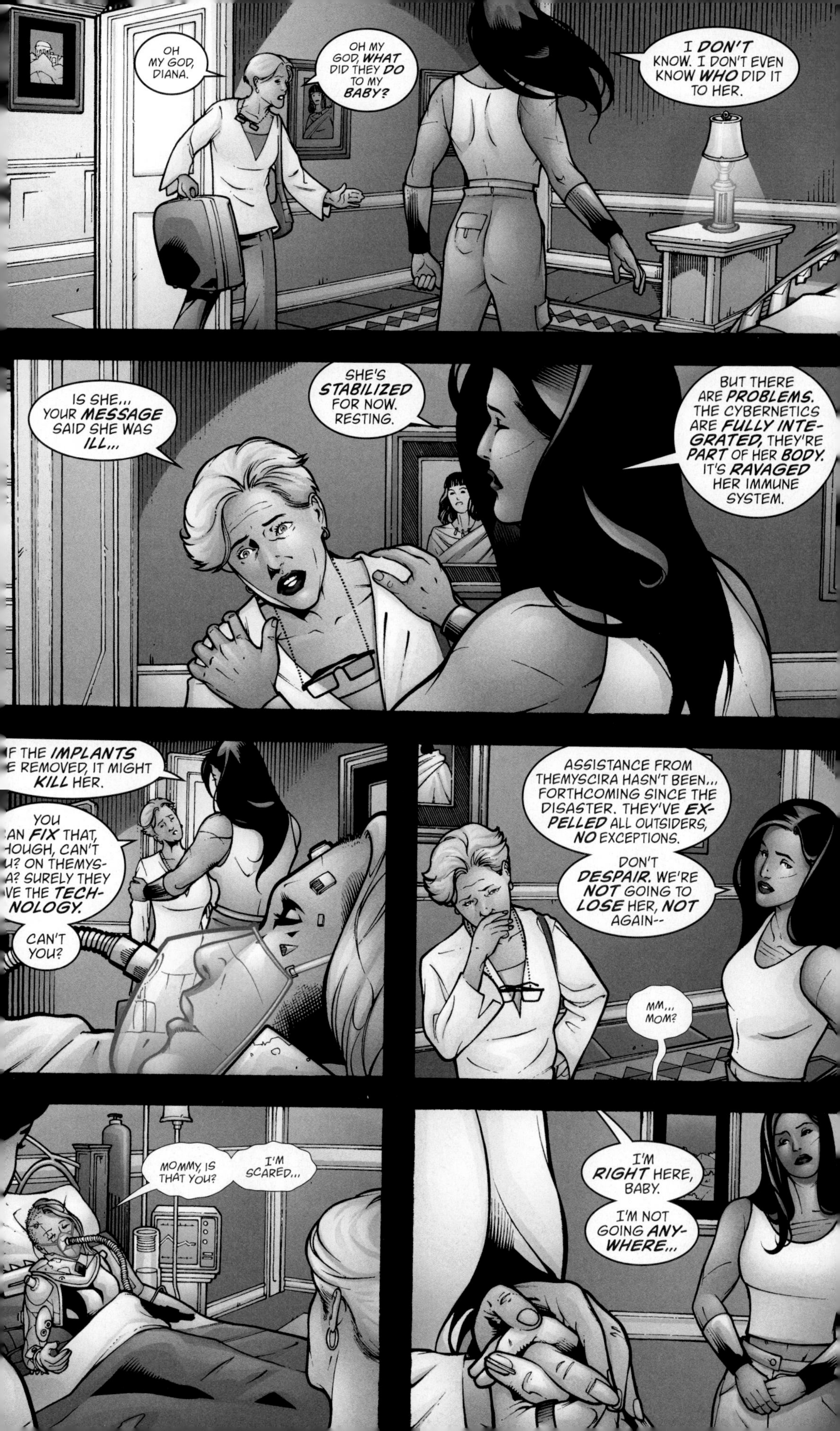
OH MY GOD, DIANA.
OH MY GOD, WHAT DID THEY DO TO MY BABY?
I DON'T KNOW. I DON'T EVEN KNOW WHO DID IT TO HER.
IS SHE... YOUR MESSAGE SAID SHE WAS ILL...
SHE'S STABILIZED FOR NOW. RESTING.
BUT THERE ARE PROBLEMS. THE CYBERNETICS ARE FULLY INTEGRATED, THEY'RE PART OF HER BODY. IT'S RAVAGED HER IMMUNE SYSTEM.
F THE IMPLANTS E REMOVED, IT MIGHT KILL HER.
YOU AN FIX THAT, HOUGH, CAN'T U? ON THEMYS- A? SURELY THEY VE THE TECH- NOLOGY.
CAN'T YOU?
ASSISTANCE FROM THEMYSCIRA HASN'T BEEN... FORTHCOMING SINCE THE DISASTER. THEY'VE EX- PELLED ALL OUTSIDERS, NO EXCEPTIONS.
DON'T DESPAIR. WE'RE NOT GOING TO LOSE HER, NOT AGAIN--
MM... MOM?
MOMMY, IS THAT YOU?
I'M SCARED...
I'M RIGHT HERE, BABY.
I'M NOT GOING ANY- WHERE...

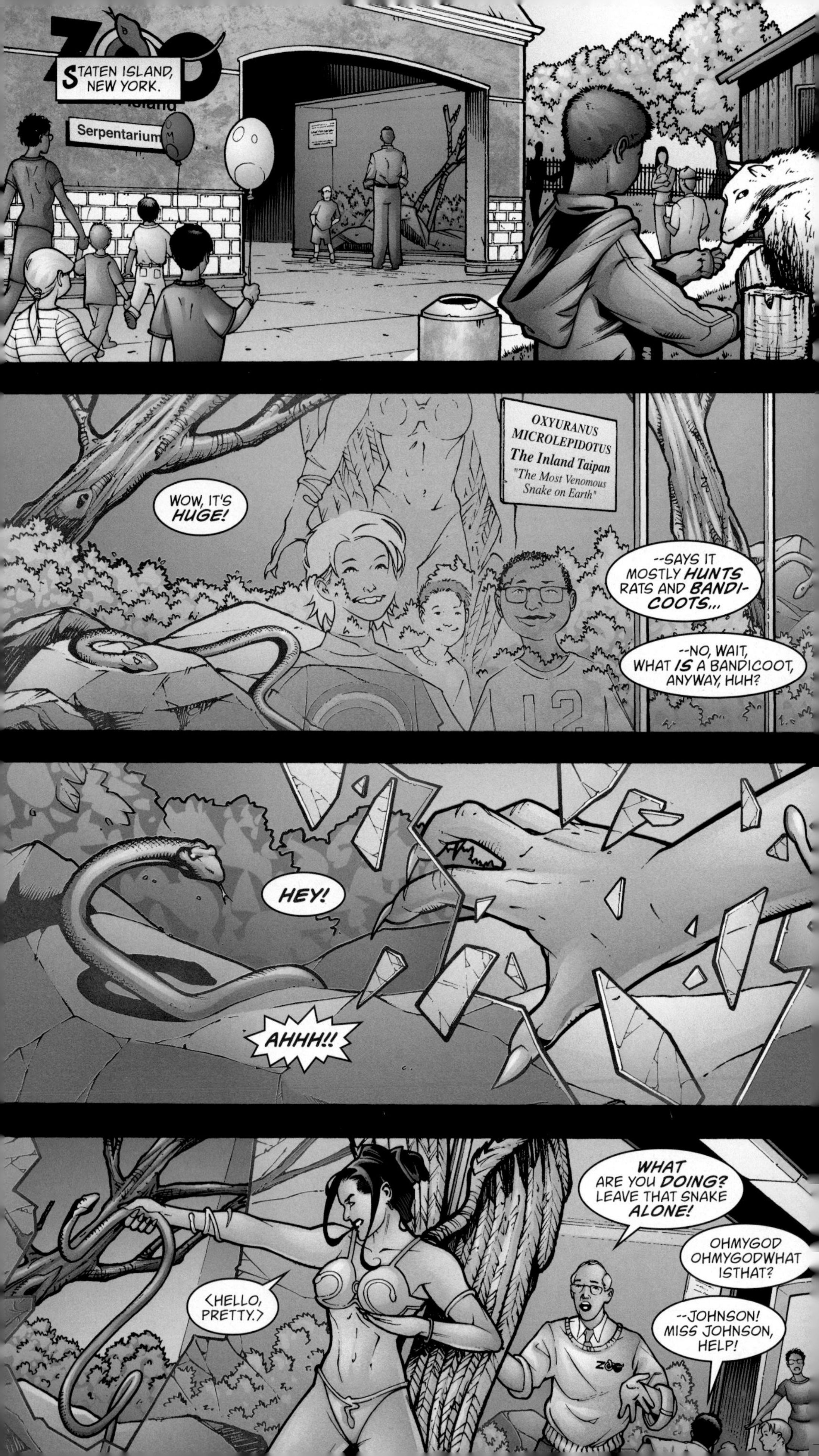
ZOO
STATEN ISLAND, NEW YORK.
Serpentarium
OXYURANUS MICROLEPIDOTUS
The Inland Taipan
"The Most Venomous Snake on Earth"
WOW, IT'S HUGE!
--SAYS IT MOSTLY HUNTS RATS AND BANDICOOTS...
--NO, WAIT, WHAT IS A BANDICOOT, ANYWAY, HUH?
HEY!
AHHH!!
WHAT ARE YOU DOING? LEAVE THAT SNAKE ALONE!
OHMYGOD OHMYGODWHAT ISTHAT?
<HELLO, PRETTY.>
--JOHNSON! MISS JOHNSON, HELP!

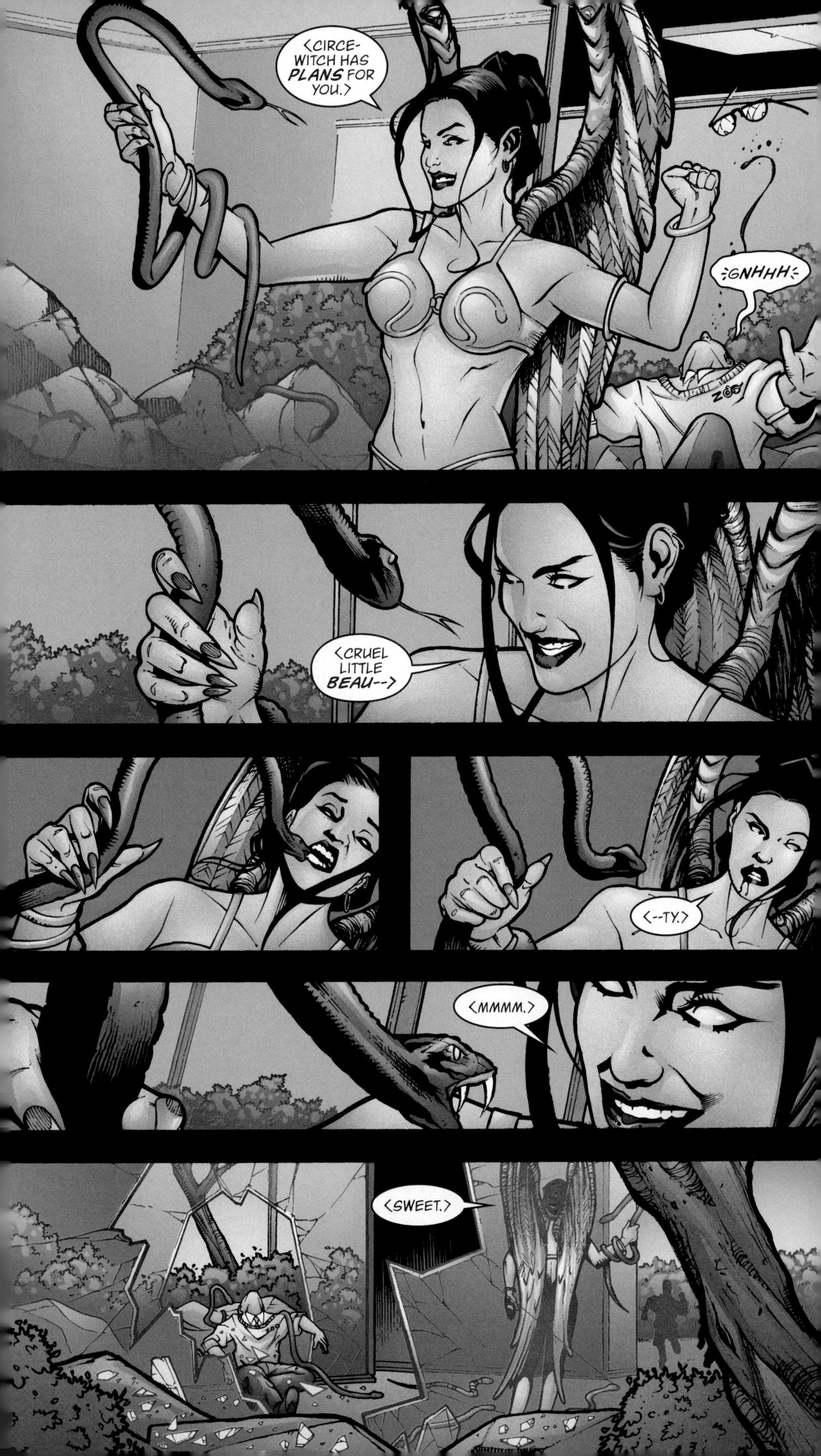

<CIRCE-WITCH HAS PLANS FOR YOU.>
GNHHH
<CRUEL LITTLE BEAU-->
<--TY.>
<MMMM.>
<SWEET.>

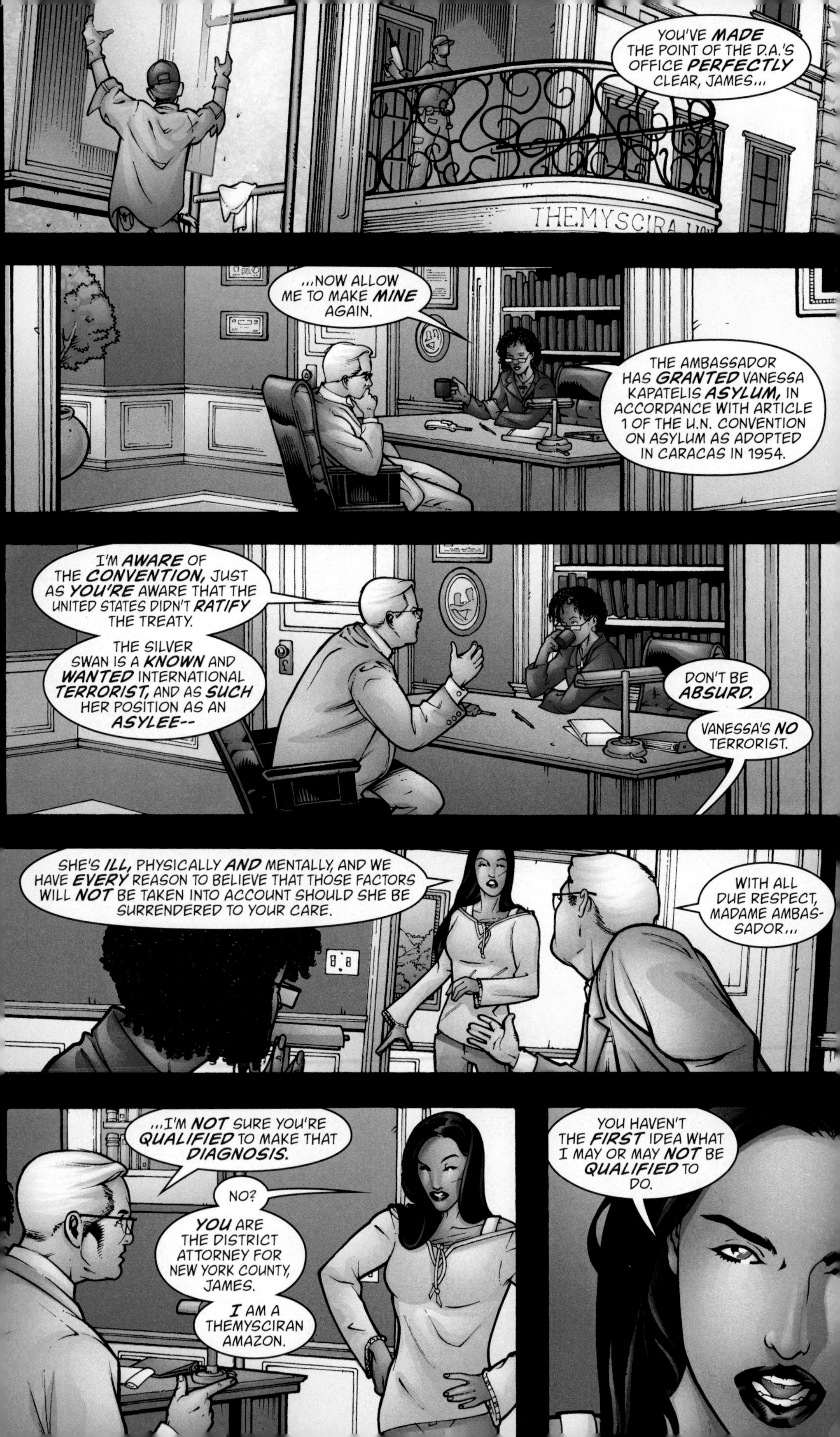
YOU'VE MADE THE POINT OF THE D.A.'S OFFICE PERFECTLY CLEAR, JAMES...
THEMYSCIRA
...NOW ALLOW ME TO MAKE MINE AGAIN.
THE AMBASSADOR HAS GRANTED VANESSA KAPATELIS ASYLUM, IN ACCORDANCE WITH ARTICLE 1 OF THE U.N. CONVENTION ON ASYLUM AS ADOPTED IN CARACAS IN 1954.
I'M AWARE OF THE CONVENTION, JUST AS YOU'RE AWARE THAT THE UNITED STATES DIDN'T RATIFY THE TREATY.
THE SILVER SWAN IS A KNOWN AND WANTED INTERNATIONAL TERRORIST, AND AS SUCH HER POSITION AS AN ASYLEE--
DON'T BE ABSURD.
VANESSA'S NO TERRORIST.
SHE'S ILL, PHYSICALLY AND MENTALLY, AND WE HAVE EVERY REASON TO BELIEVE THAT THOSE FACTORS WILL NOT BE TAKEN INTO ACCOUNT SHOULD SHE BE SURRENDERED TO YOUR CARE.
WITH ALL DUE RESPECT, MADAME AMBASSADOR...
...I'M NOT SURE YOU'RE QUALIFIED TO MAKE THAT DIAGNOSIS.
NO?
YOU ARE THE DISTRICT ATTORNEY FOR NEW YORK COUNTY, JAMES.
I AM A THEMYSCIRAN AMAZON.
YOU HAVEN'T THE FIRST IDEA WHAT I MAY OR MAY NOT BE QUALIFIED TO DO.

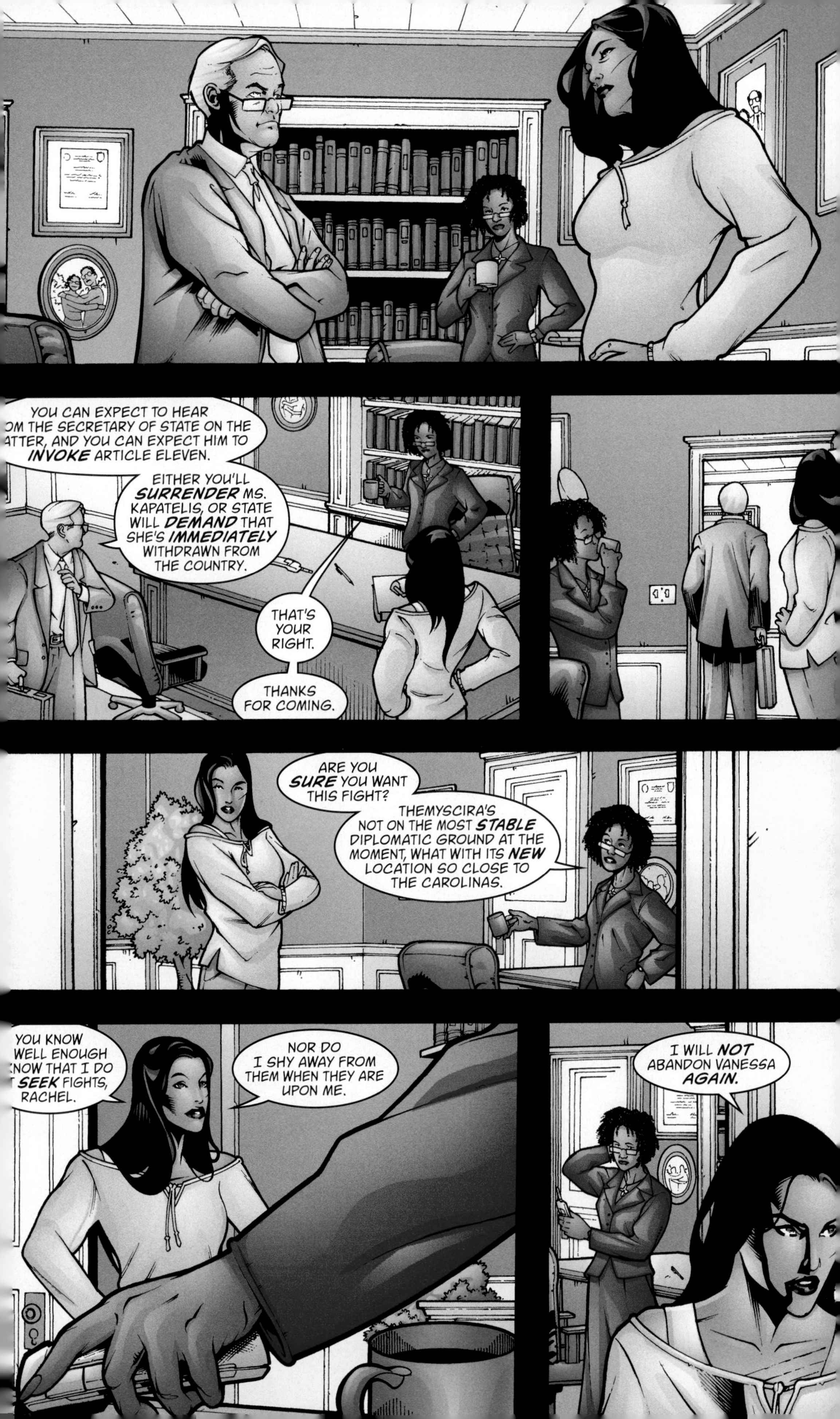
YOU CAN EXPECT TO HEAR
OM THE SECRETARY OF STATE ON THE
ATTER, AND YOU CAN EXPECT HIM TO
INVOKE ARTICLE ELEVEN.
EITHER YOU'LL SURRENDER MS. KAPATELIS, OR STATE WILL DEMAND THAT SHE'S IMMEDIATELY WITHDRAWN FROM THE COUNTRY.
THAT'S YOUR RIGHT.
THANKS FOR COMING.
ARE YOU SURE YOU WANT THIS FIGHT?
THEMYSCIRA'S NOT ON THE MOST STABLE DIPLOMATIC GROUND AT THE MOMENT, WHAT WITH ITS NEW LOCATION SO CLOSE TO THE CAROLINAS.
YOU KNOW
WELL ENOUGH
KNOW THAT I DO
SEEK FIGHTS,
RACHEL.
NOR DO I SHY AWAY FROM THEM WHEN THEY ARE UPON ME.
I WILL NOT ABANDON VANESSA AGAIN.

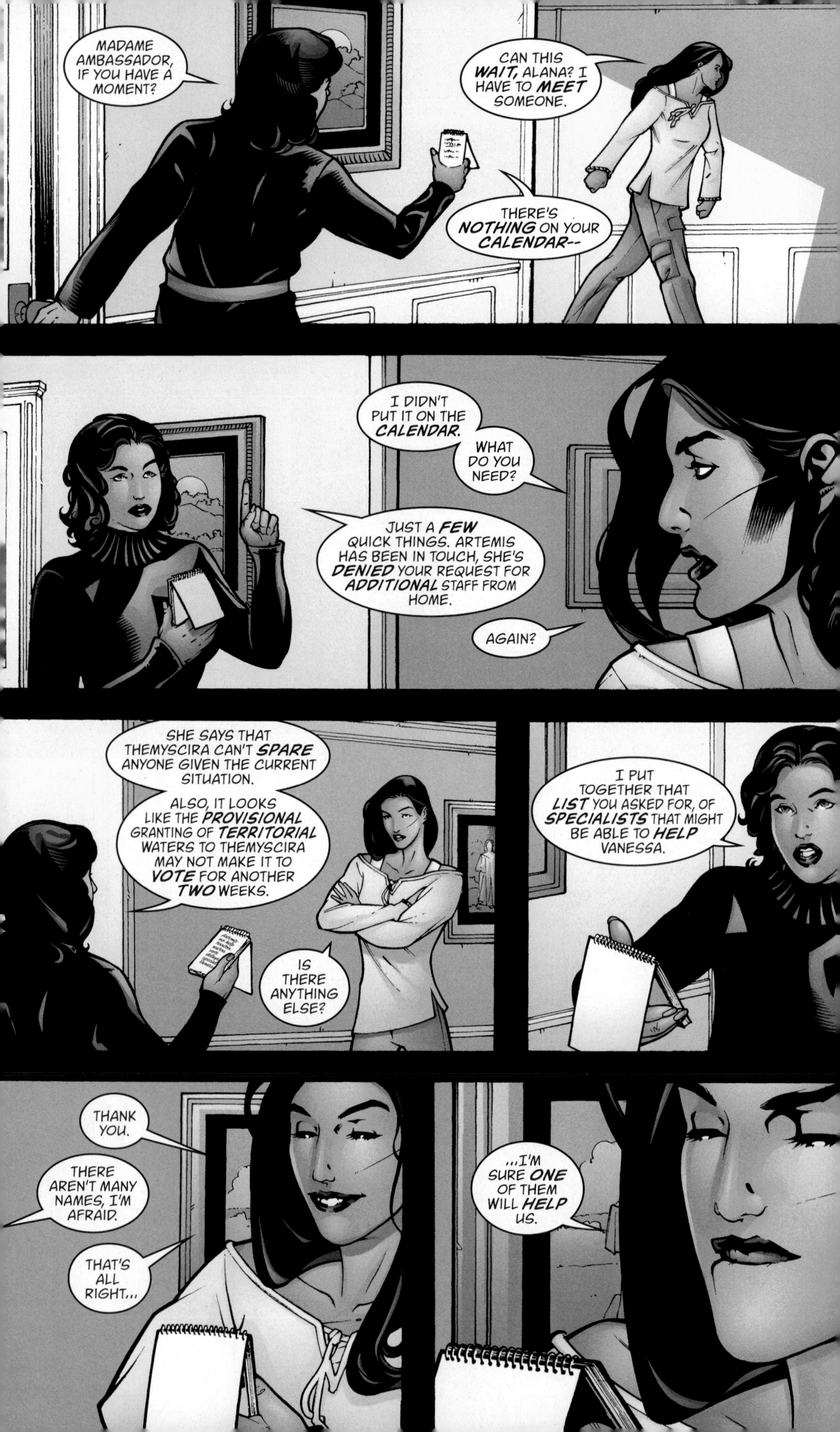
MADAME AMBASSADOR, IF YOU HAVE A MOMENT?
CAN THIS *WAIT,* ALANA? I HAVE TO *MEET* SOMEONE.
THERE'S *NOTHING* ON YOUR *CALENDAR--*
I DIDN'T PUT IT ON THE *CALENDAR.*
WHAT DO YOU NEED?
JUST A *FEW* QUICK THINGS. ARTEMIS HAS BEEN IN TOUCH, SHE'S *DENIED* YOUR REQUEST FOR *ADDITIONAL* STAFF FROM HOME.
AGAIN?
SHE SAYS THAT THEMYSCIRA CAN'T *SPARE* ANYONE GIVEN THE CURRENT SITUATION.
ALSO, IT LOOKS LIKE THE *PROVISIONAL* GRANTING OF *TERRITORIAL* WATERS TO THEMYSCIRA MAY NOT MAKE IT TO *VOTE* FOR ANOTHER *TWO* WEEKS.
IS THERE ANYTHING ELSE?
I PUT TOGETHER THAT *LIST* YOU ASKED FOR, OF *SPECIALISTS* THAT MIGHT BE ABLE TO *HELP* VANESSA.
THANK YOU.
THERE AREN'T MANY NAMES, I'M AFRAID.
THAT'S ALL RIGHT...
...I'M SURE *ONE* OF THEM WILL *HELP* US.

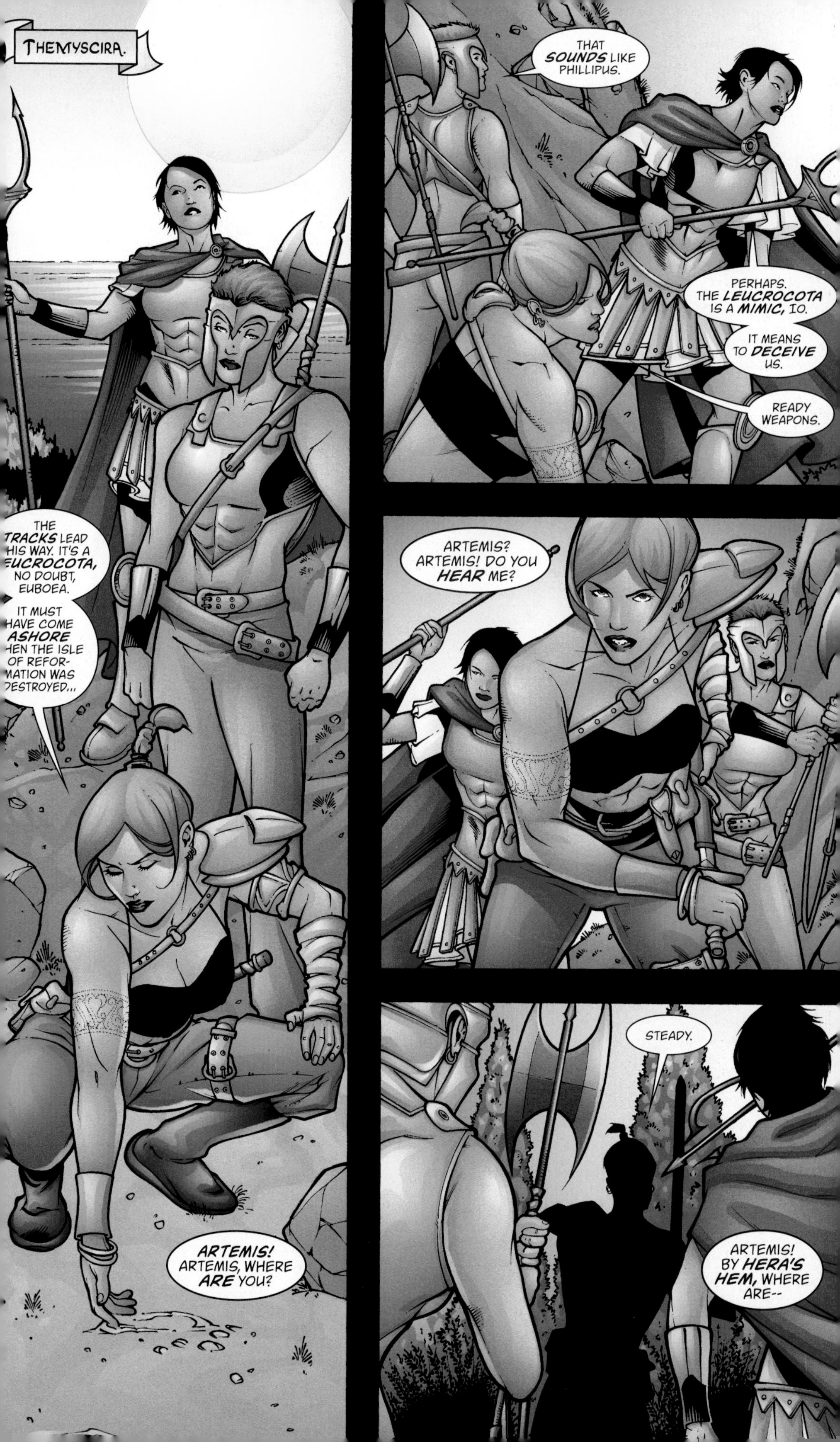
THEMYSCIRA.
THE TRACKS LEAD HIS WAY. IT'S A EUCROCOTA, NO DOUBT, EUBOEA.
IT MUST HAVE COME ASHORE HEN THE ISLE OF REFORMATION WAS DESTROYED...
ARTEMIS! ARTEMIS, WHERE ARE YOU?
THAT SOUNDS LIKE PHILLIPUS.
PERHAPS. THE LEUCROCOTA IS A MIMIC, IO.
IT MEANS TO DECEIVE US.
READY WEAPONS.
ARTEMIS? ARTEMIS! DO YOU HEAR ME?
STEADY.
ARTEMIS! BY HERA'S HEM, WHERE ARE--

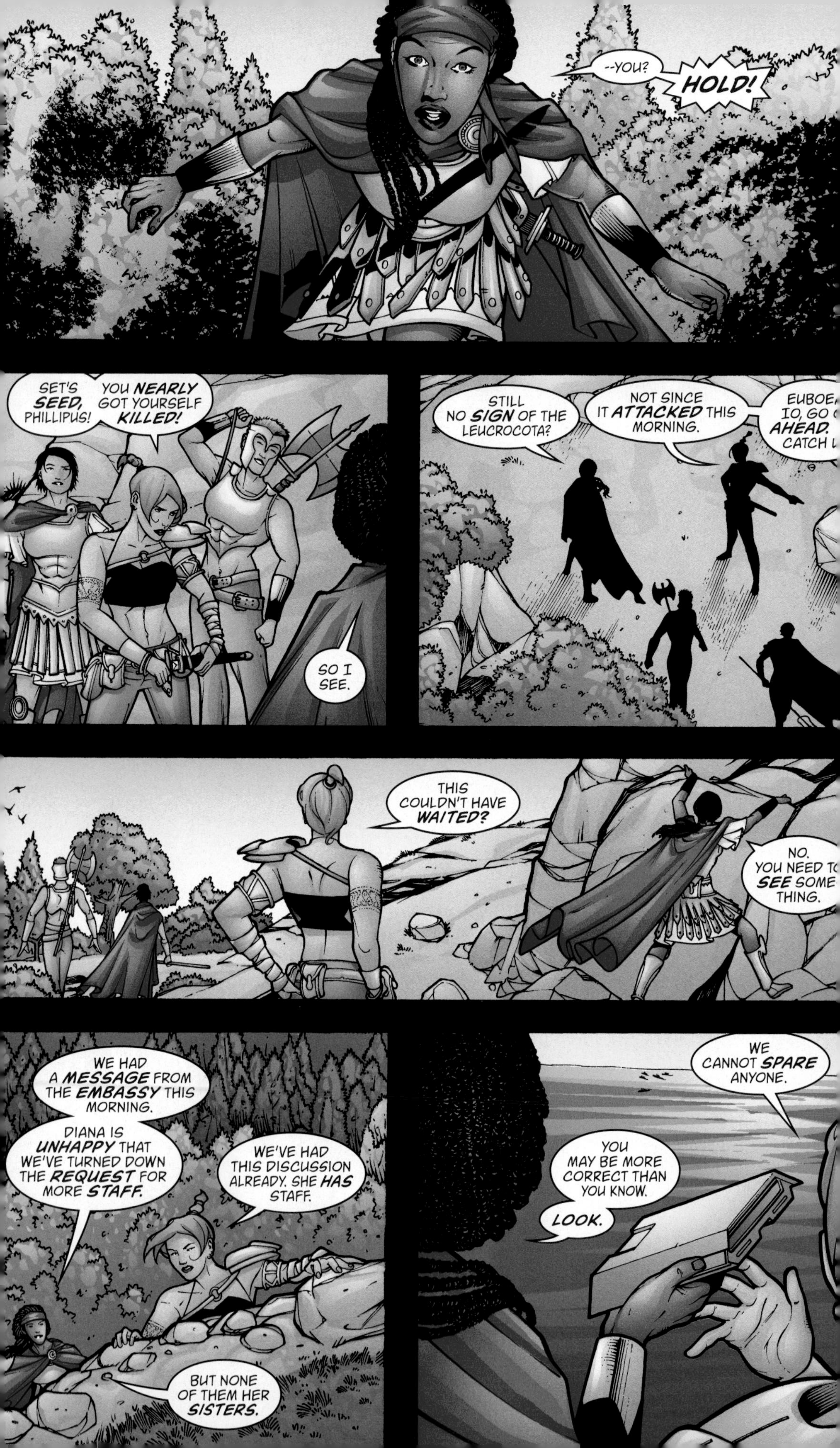
--YOU?
HOLD!
SET'S SEED, PHILLIPUS!
YOU NEARLY GOT YOURSELF KILLED!
SO I SEE.
STILL NO SIGN OF THE LEUCROCOTA?
NOT SINCE IT ATTACKED THIS MORNING.
THIS COULDN'T HAVE WAITED?
NO. YOU NEED TO SEE SOME THING.
WE HAD A MESSAGE FROM THE EMBASSY THIS MORNING.
DIANA IS UNHAPPY THAT WE'VE TURNED DOWN THE REQUEST FOR MORE STAFF.
WE'VE HAD THIS DISCUSSION ALREADY. SHE HAS STAFF.
BUT NONE OF THEM HER SISTERS.
WE CANNOT SPARE ANYONE.
YOU MAY BE MORE CORRECT THAN YOU KNOW.
LOOK.

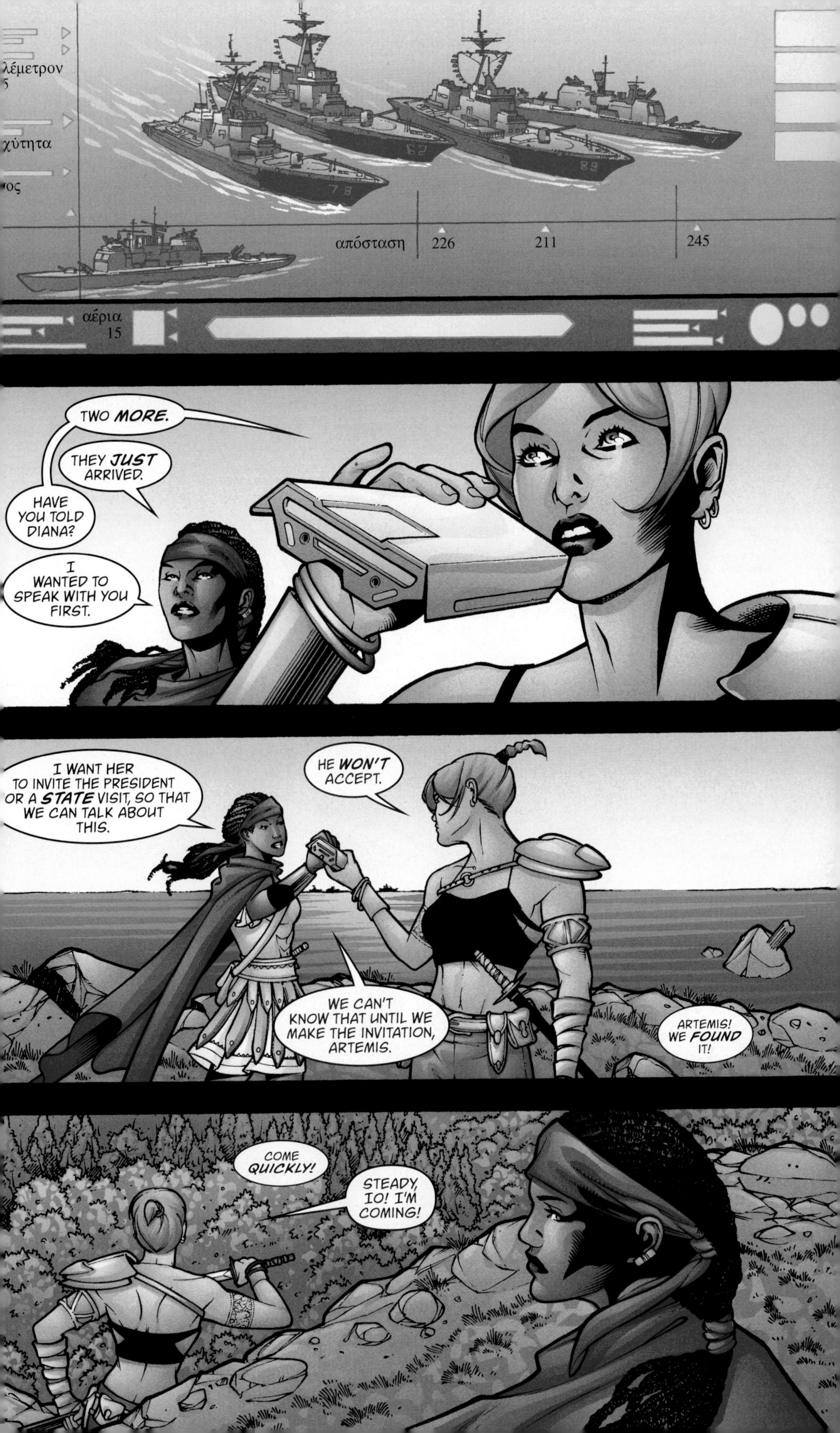
λέμετρον
5
χύτητα
ος
απόσταση
226
211
245
αέρια
15
TWO MORE.
THEY JUST ARRIVED.
HAVE YOU TOLD DIANA?
I WANTED TO SPEAK WITH YOU FIRST.
I WANT HER TO INVITE THE PRESIDENT OR A STATE VISIT, SO THAT WE CAN TALK ABOUT THIS.
HE WON'T ACCEPT.
WE CAN'T KNOW THAT UNTIL WE MAKE THE INVITATION, ARTEMIS.
ARTEMIS! WE FOUND IT!
COME QUICKLY!
STEADY, IO! I'M COMING!

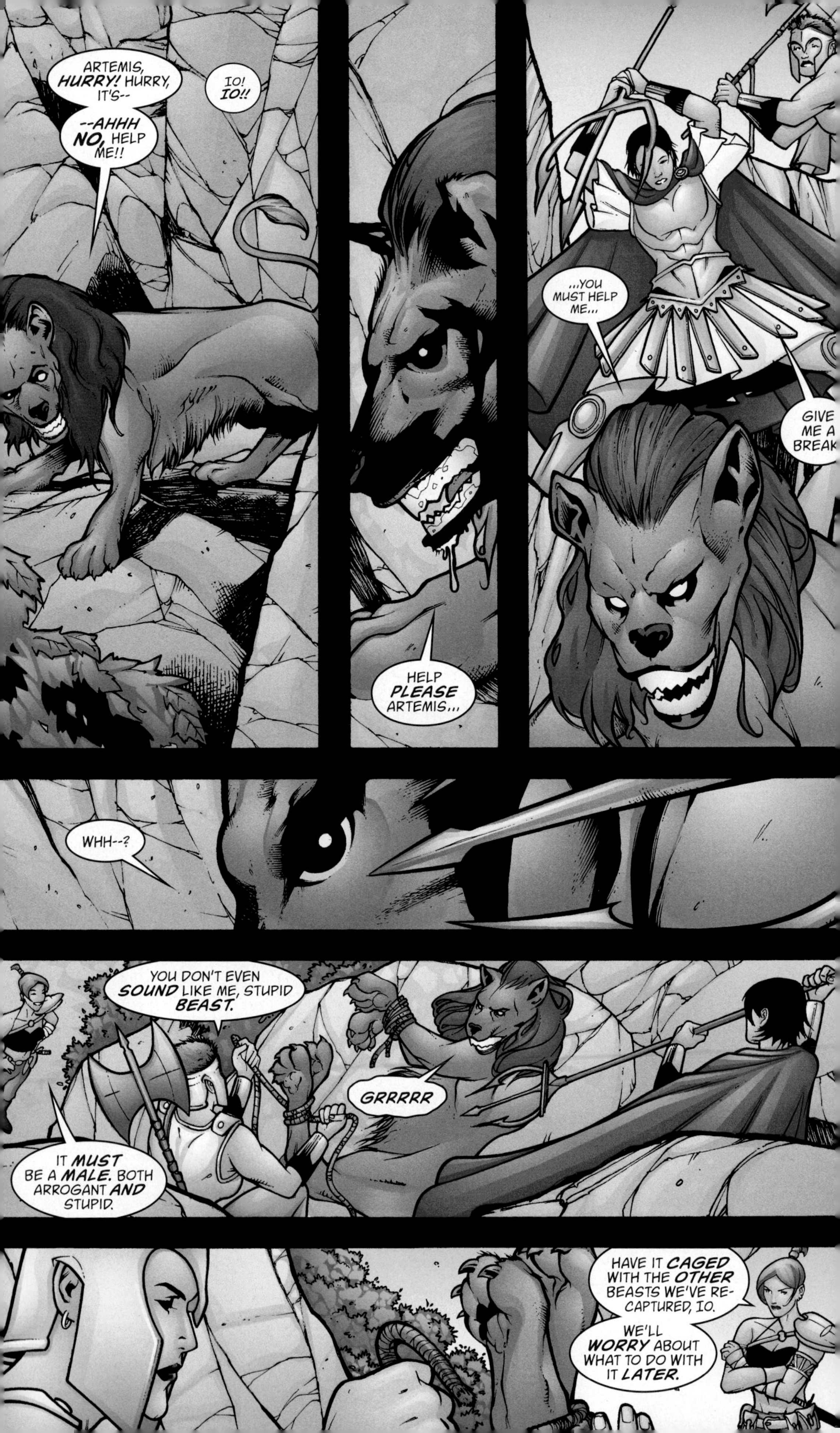

ARTEMIS, HURRY! HURRY, IT'S--
--AHHH NO, HELP ME!!
IO! IO!!
HELP PLEASE ARTEMIS...
...YOU MUST HELP ME...
GIVE ME A BREAK
WHH--?
YOU DON'T EVEN SOUND LIKE ME, STUPID BEAST.
GRRRRR
IT MUST BE A MALE. BOTH ARROGANT AND STUPID.
HAVE IT CAGED WITH THE OTHER BEASTS WE'VE RE-CAPTURED, IO.
WE'LL WORRY ABOUT WHAT TO DO WITH IT LATER.

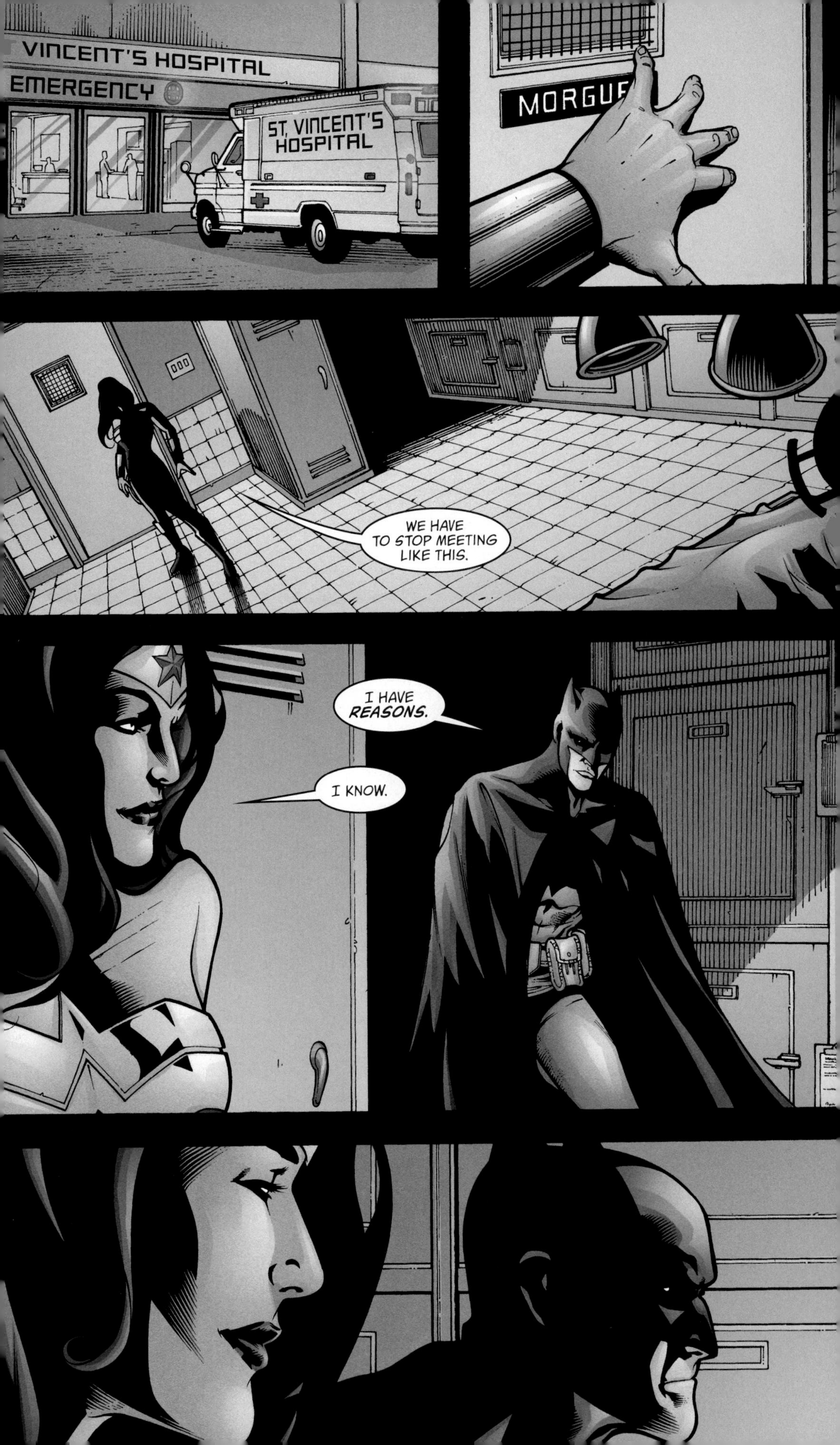
VINCENT'S HOSPITAL
EMERGENCY
ST. VINCENT'S HOSPITAL
MORGUE
WE HAVE TO STOP MEETING LIKE THIS.
I HAVE *REASONS.*
I KNOW.

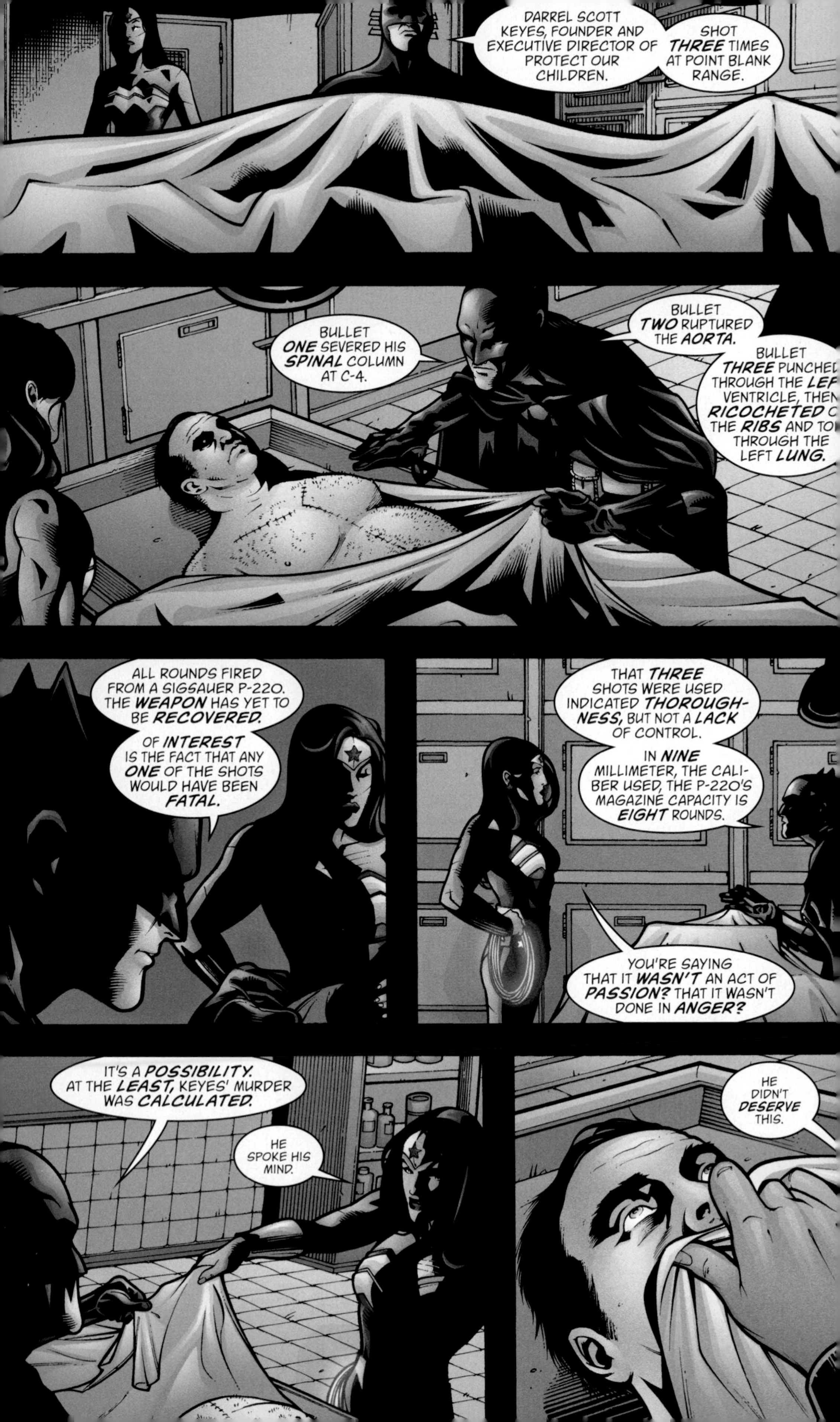

DARREL SCOTT KEYES, FOUNDER AND EXECUTIVE DIRECTOR OF PROTECT OUR CHILDREN.
SHOT THREE TIMES AT POINT BLANK RANGE.
BULLET ONE SEVERED HIS SPINAL COLUMN AT C-4.
BULLET TWO RUPTURED THE AORTA.
BULLET THREE PUNCHED THROUGH THE LEF VENTRICLE, THEN RICOCHETED THE RIBS AND TO THROUGH THE LEFT LUNG.
ALL ROUNDS FIRED FROM A SIGSAUER P-220. THE WEAPON HAS YET TO BE RECOVERED.
OF INTEREST IS THE FACT THAT ANY ONE OF THE SHOTS WOULD HAVE BEEN FATAL.
THAT THREE SHOTS WERE USED INDICATED THOROUGH-NESS, BUT NOT A LACK OF CONTROL.
IN NINE MILLIMETER, THE CALI-BER USED, THE P-220'S MAGAZINE CAPACITY IS EIGHT ROUNDS.
YOU'RE SAYING THAT IT WASN'T AN ACT OF PASSION? THAT IT WASN'T DONE IN ANGER?
IT'S A POSSIBILITY. AT THE LEAST, KEYES' MURDER WAS CALCULATED.
HE SPOKE HIS MIND.
HE DIDN'T DESERVE THIS.

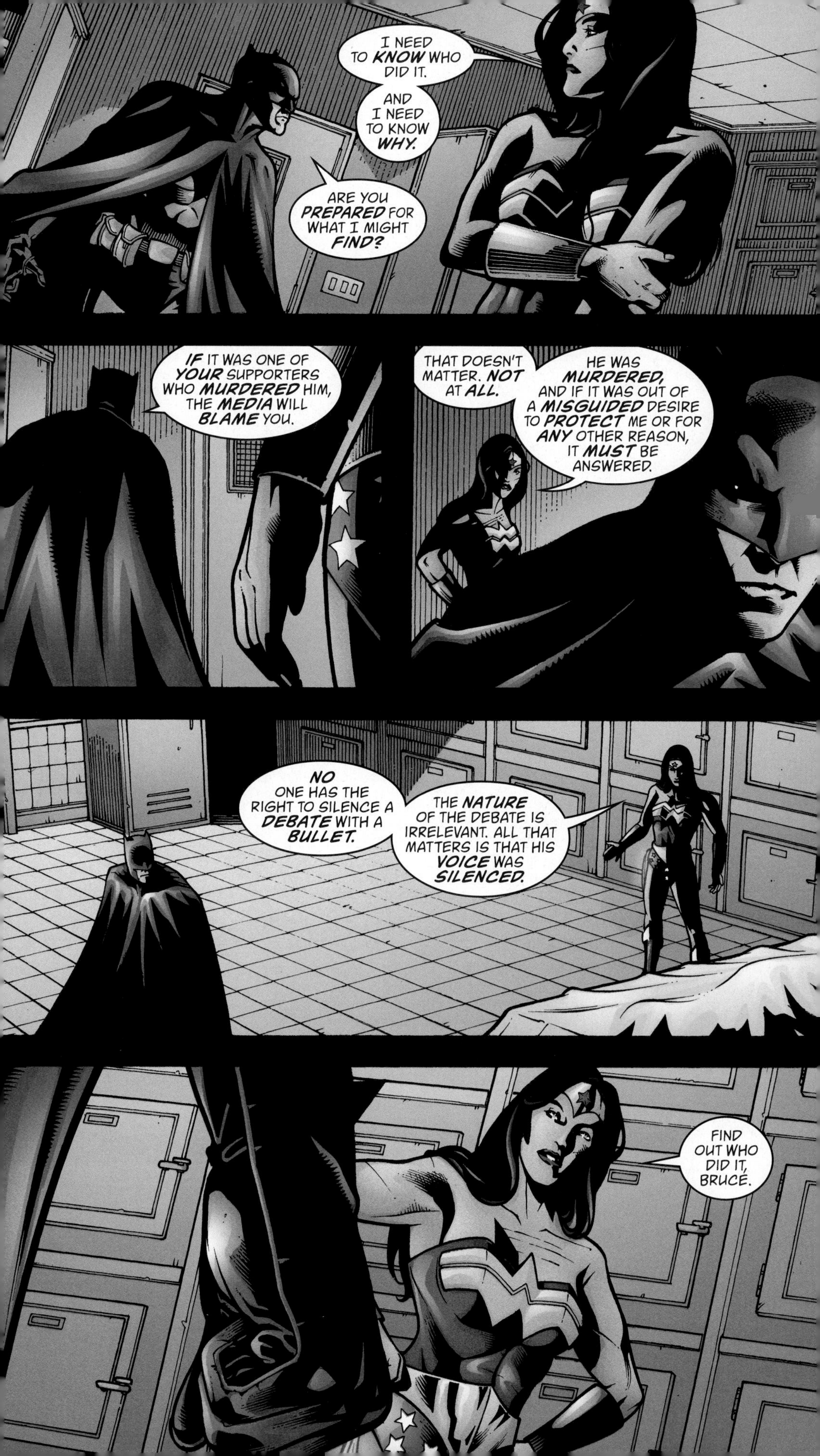

I NEED TO KNOW WHO DID IT.
AND I NEED TO KNOW WHY.
ARE YOU PREPARED FOR WHAT I MIGHT FIND?
IF IT WAS ONE OF YOUR SUPPORTERS WHO MURDERED HIM, THE MEDIA WILL BLAME YOU.
THAT DOESN'T MATTER. NOT AT ALL.
HE WAS MURDERED, AND IF IT WAS OUT OF A MISGUIDED DESIRE TO PROTECT ME OR FOR ANY OTHER REASON, IT MUST BE ANSWERED.
NO ONE HAS THE RIGHT TO SILENCE A DEBATE WITH A BULLET.
THE NATURE OF THE DEBATE IS IRRELEVANT. ALL THAT MATTERS IS THAT HIS VOICE WAS SILENCED.
FIND OUT WHO DID IT, BRUCE.

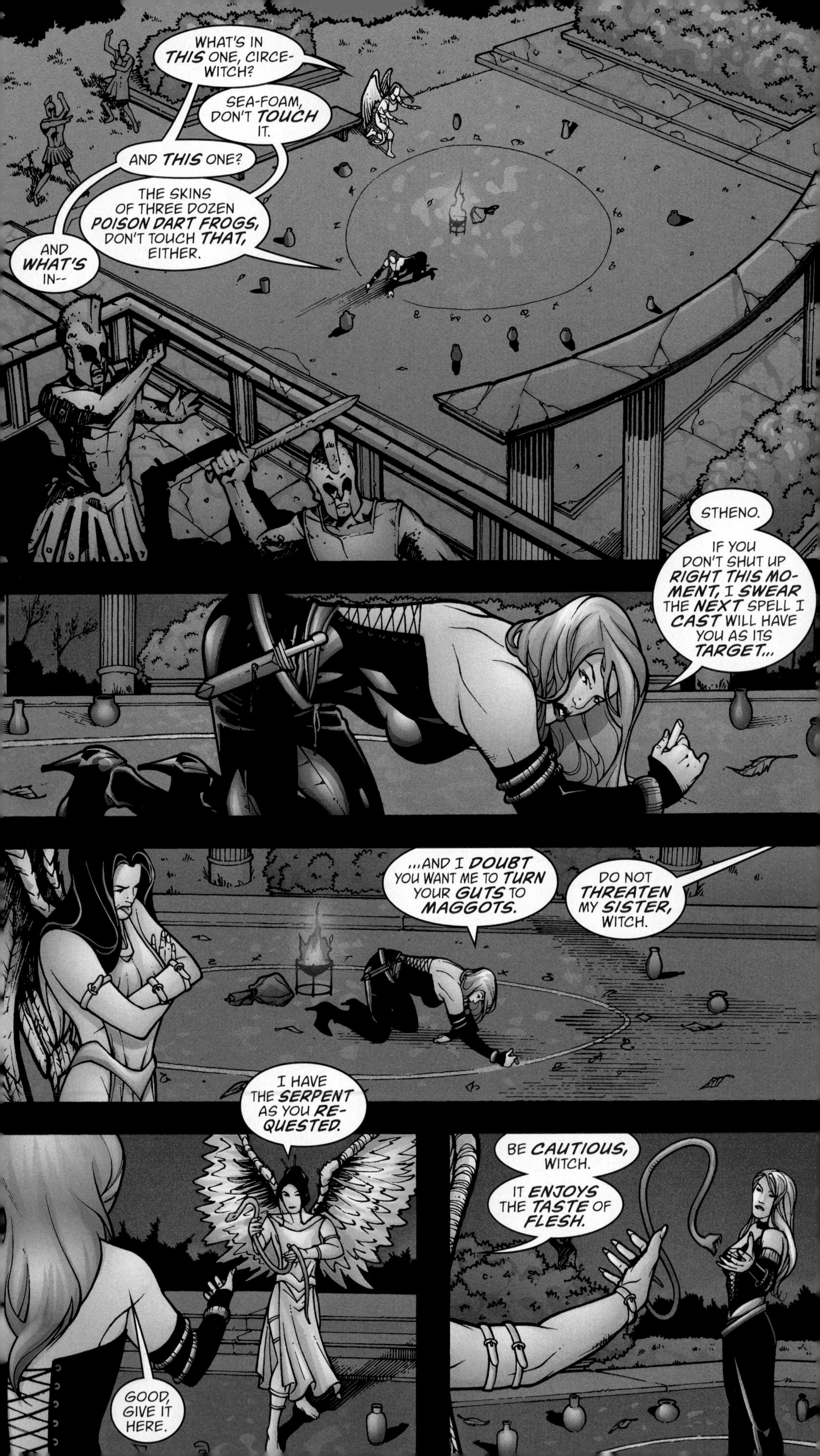
WHAT'S IN THIS ONE, CIRCE-WITCH?
SEA-FOAM, DON'T TOUCH IT.
AND THIS ONE?
THE SKINS OF THREE DOZEN POISON DART FROGS, DON'T TOUCH THAT, EITHER.
AND WHAT'S IN--
STHENO.
IF YOU DON'T SHUT UP RIGHT THIS MO-MENT, I SWEAR THE NEXT SPELL I CAST WILL HAVE YOU AS ITS TARGET...
...AND I DOUBT YOU WANT ME TO TURN YOUR GUTS TO MAGGOTS.
DO NOT THREATEN MY SISTER, WITCH.
I HAVE THE SERPENT AS YOU RE-QUESTED.
GOOD, GIVE IT HERE.
BE CAUTIOUS, WITCH.
IT ENJOYS THE TASTE OF FLESH.

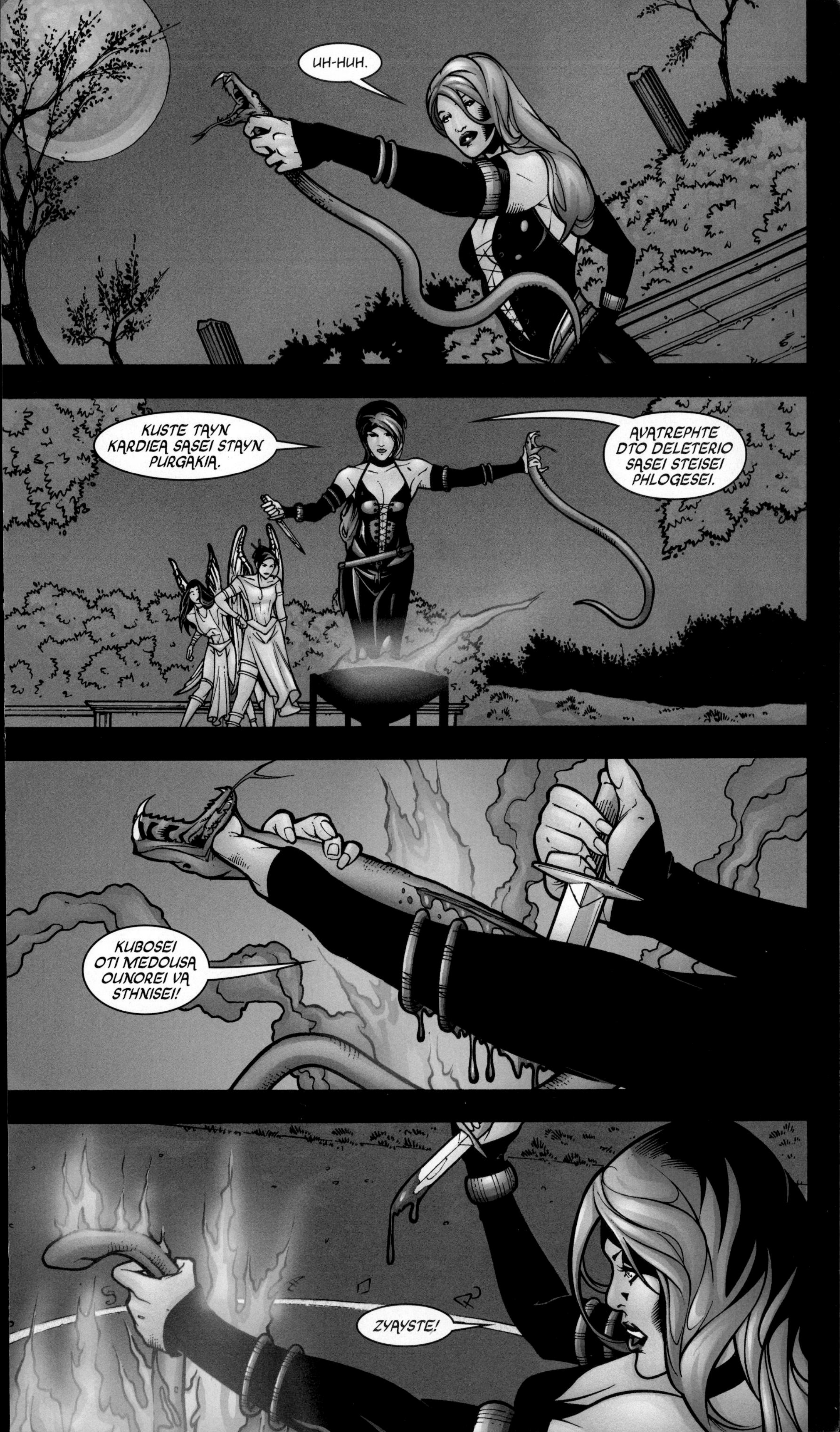
UH-HUH.
KUSTE TAYN KARDIEA SASEI STAYN PURGAKIA.
AVATREPHTE DTO DELETERIO SASEI STEISEI PHLOGESEI.
KUBOSEI OTI MEDOUSA OUNOREI VA STHNISEI!
ZYAYSTE!

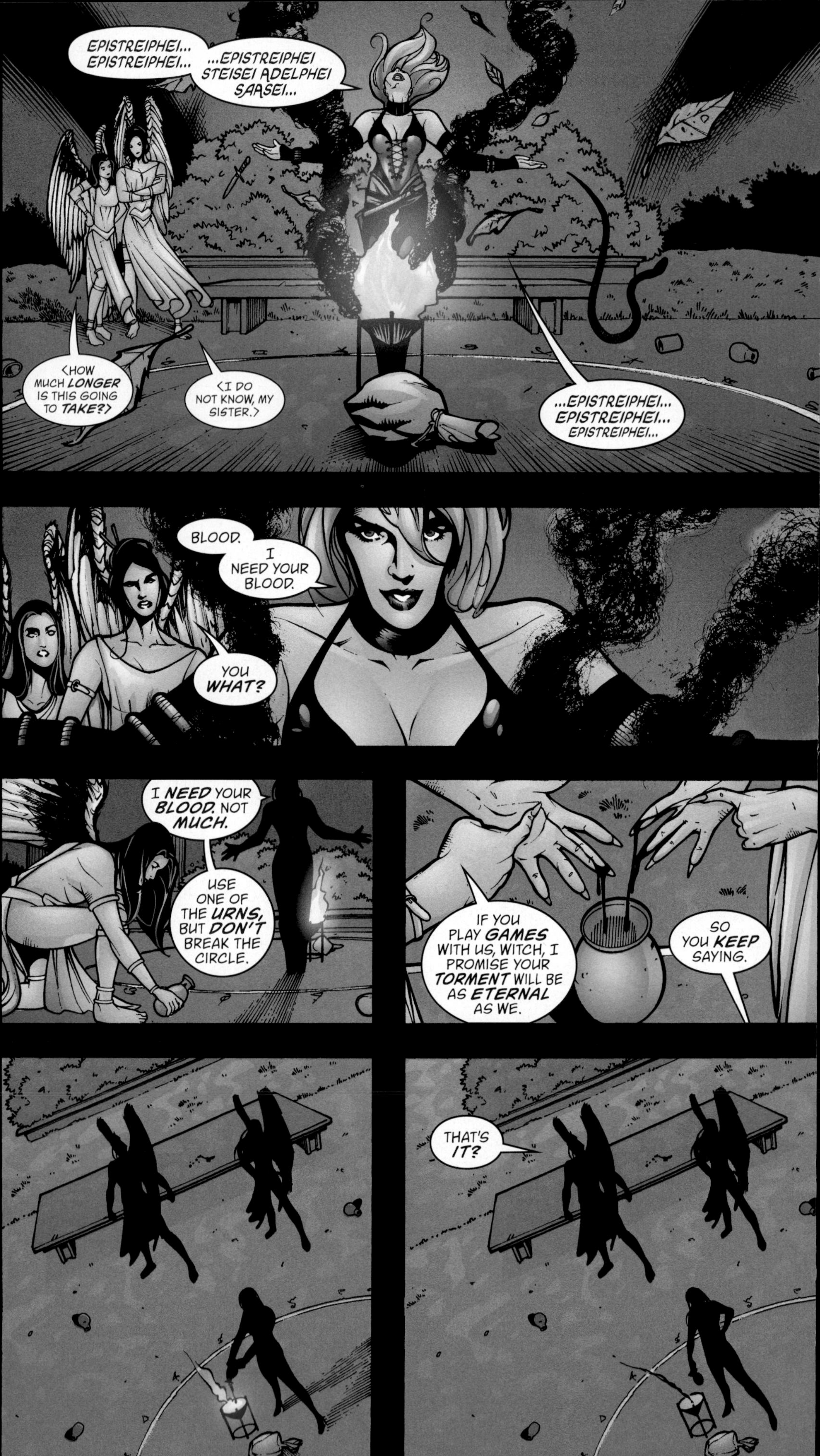
EPISTREIPHEI... EPISTREIPHEI...
...EPISTREIPHEI STEISEI ADELPHEI SAASEI...
<HOW MUCH LONGER IS THIS GOING TO TAKE?>
<I DO NOT KNOW, MY SISTER.>
...EPISTREIPHEI... EPISTREIPHEI... EPISTREIPHEI...
BLOOD. I NEED YOUR BLOOD.
YOU WHAT?
I NEED YOUR BLOOD. NOT MUCH.
USE ONE OF THE URNS, BUT DON'T BREAK THE CIRCLE.
IF YOU PLAY GAMES WITH US, WITCH, I PROMISE YOUR TORMENT WILL BE AS ETERNAL AS WE.
SO YOU KEEP SAYING.
THAT'S IT?

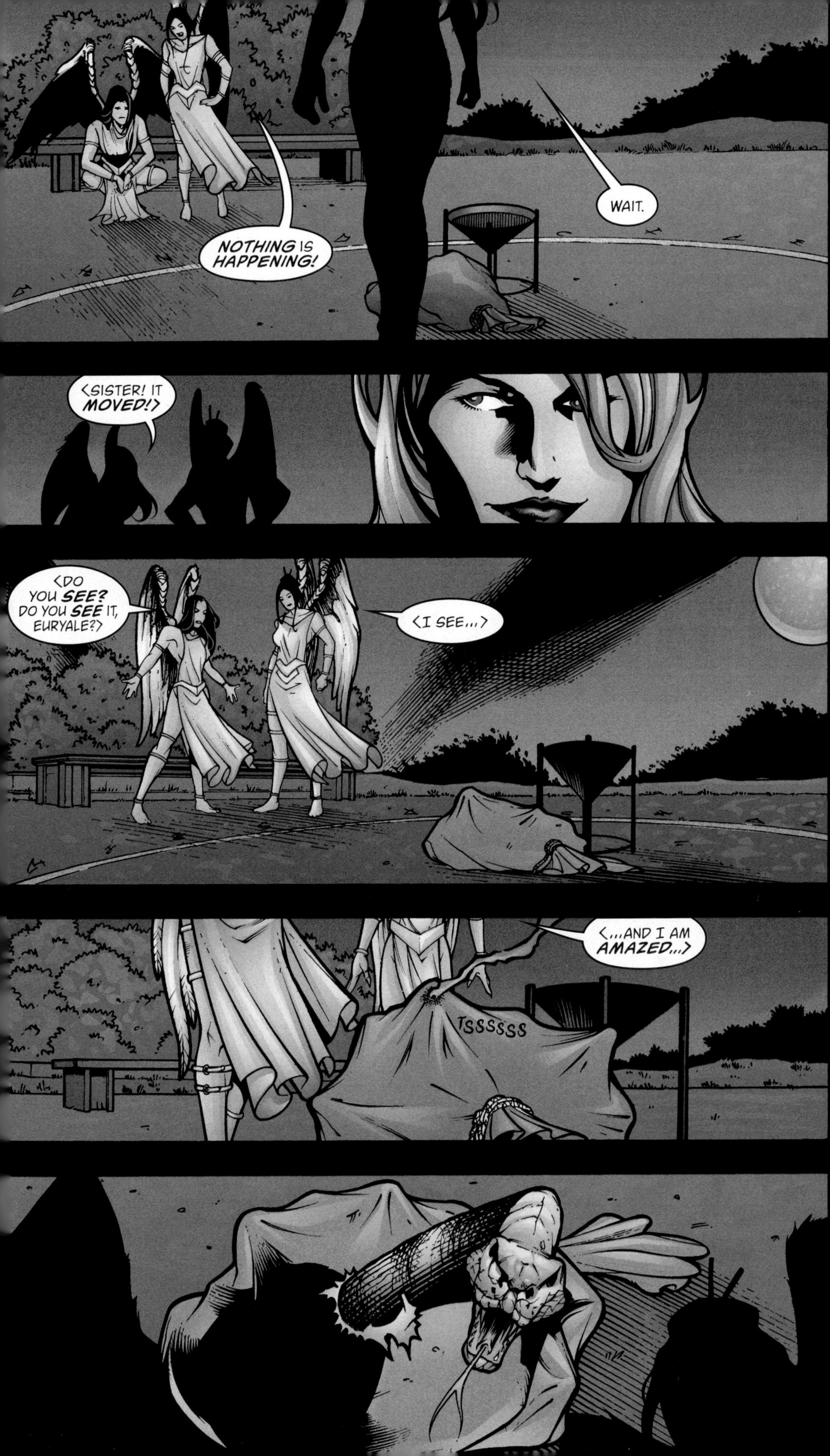
NOTHING IS HAPPENING!
WAIT.
<SISTER! IT MOVED!>
<DO YOU SEE? DO YOU SEE IT, EURYALE?>
<I SEE...>
<...AND I AM AMAZED...>
TSSSSSS

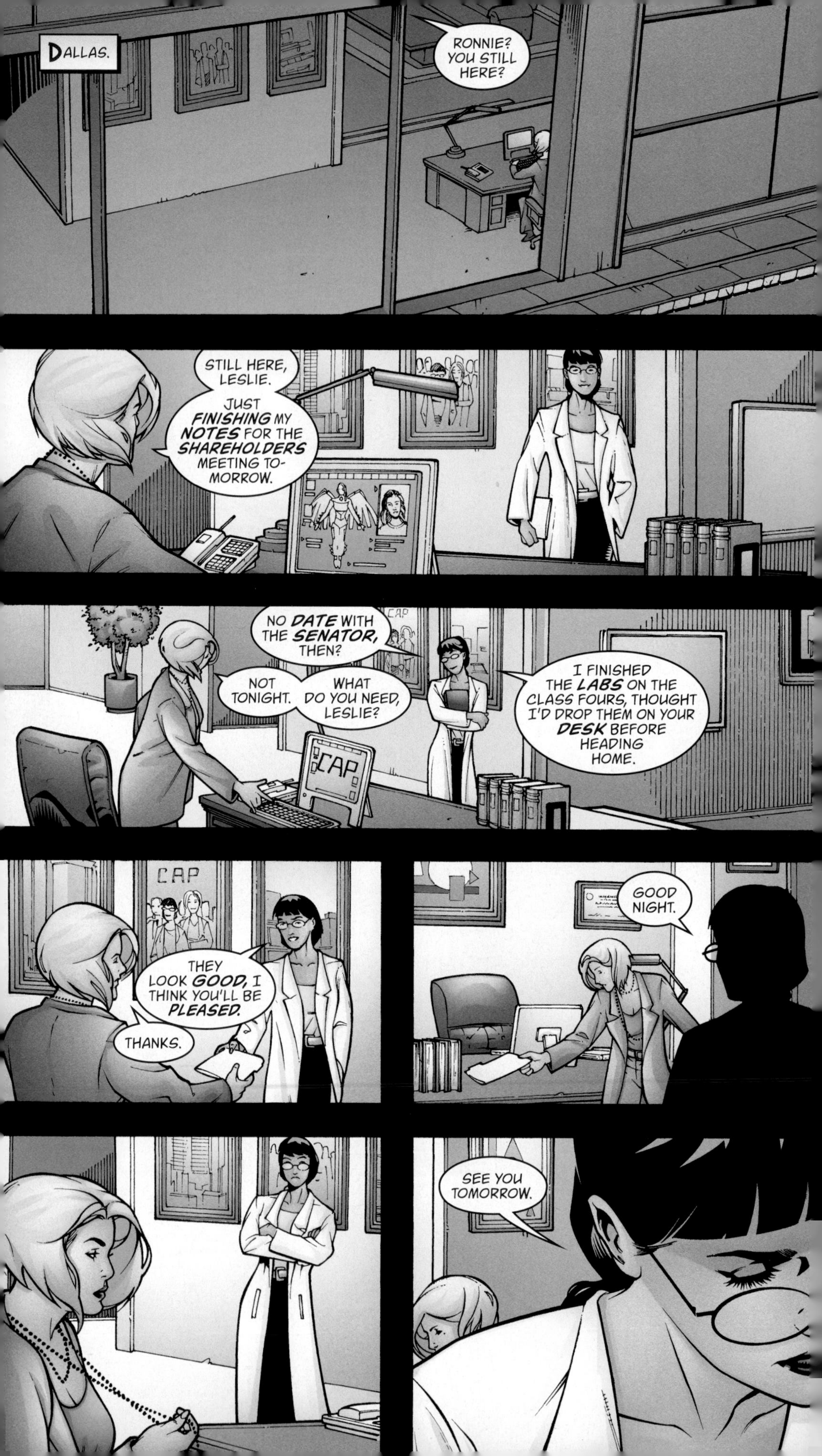
DALLAS.
RONNIE? YOU STILL HERE?
STILL HERE, LESLIE.
JUST FINISHING MY NOTES FOR THE SHAREHOLDERS MEETING TO-MORROW.
NO DATE WITH THE SENATOR, THEN?
NOT TONIGHT.
WHAT DO YOU NEED, LESLIE?
I FINISHED THE LABS ON THE CLASS FOURS, THOUGHT I'D DROP THEM ON YOUR DESK BEFORE HEADING HOME.
CAP
THEY LOOK GOOD, I THINK YOU'LL BE PLEASED.
THANKS.
GOOD NIGHT.
SEE YOU TOMORROW.

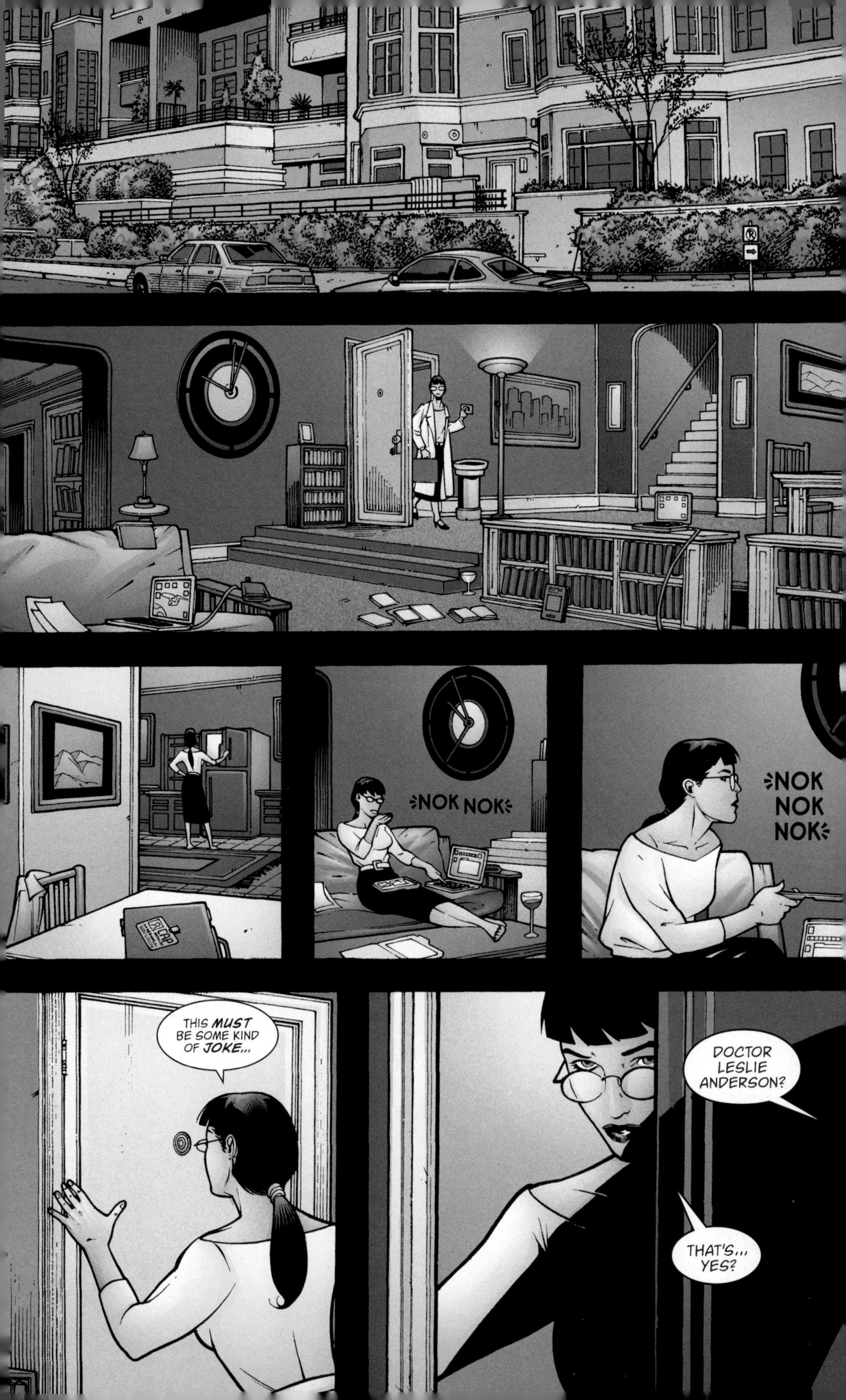
NOK NOK
NOK NOK NOK
THIS MUST BE SOME KIND OF JOKE...
DOCTOR LESLIE ANDERSON?
THAT'S... YES?

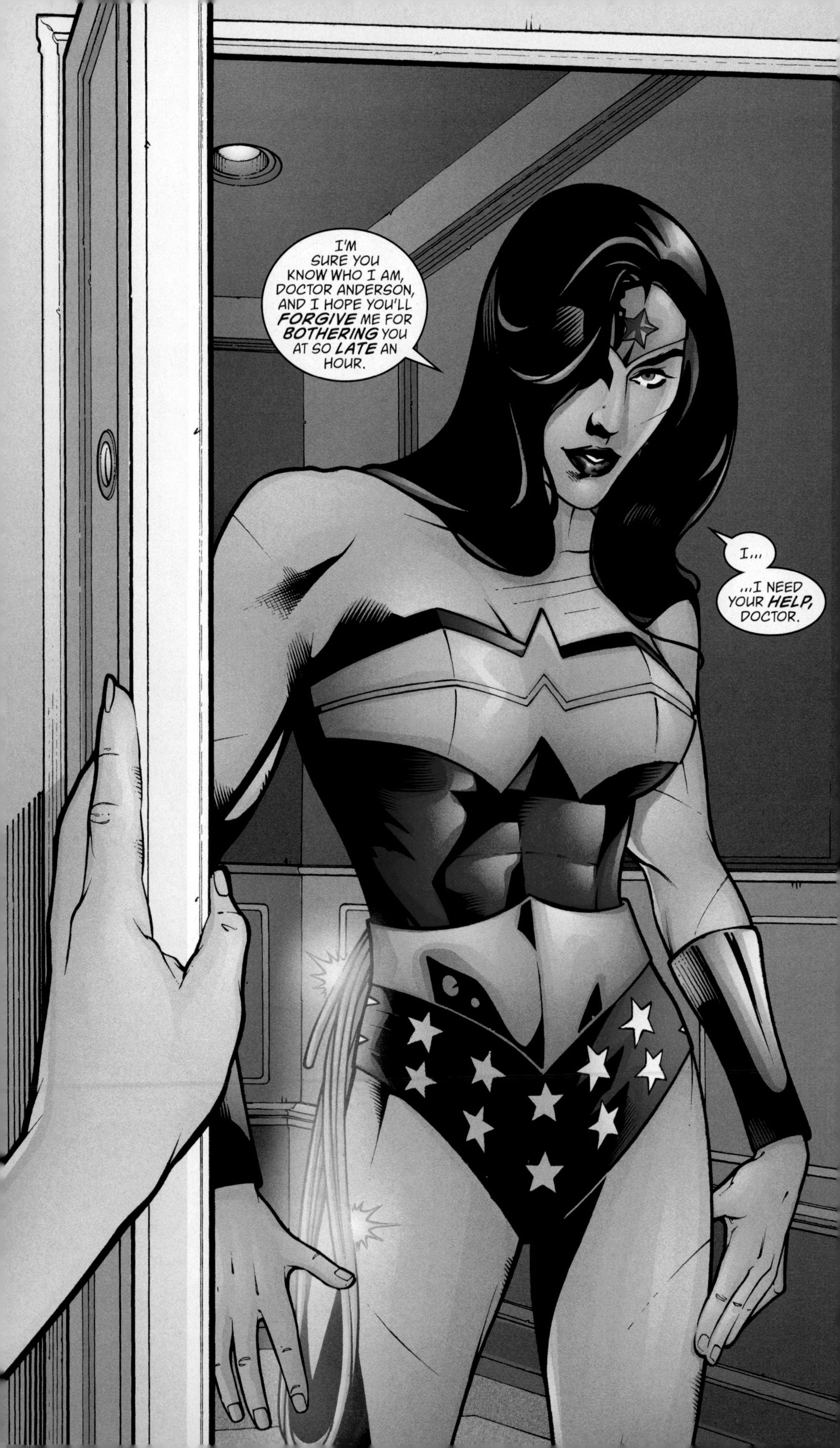
I'M SURE YOU KNOW WHO I AM, DOCTOR ANDERSON, AND I HOPE YOU'LL FORGIVE ME FOR BOTHERING YOU AT SO LATE AN HOUR.
I...
...I NEED YOUR HELP, DOCTOR.

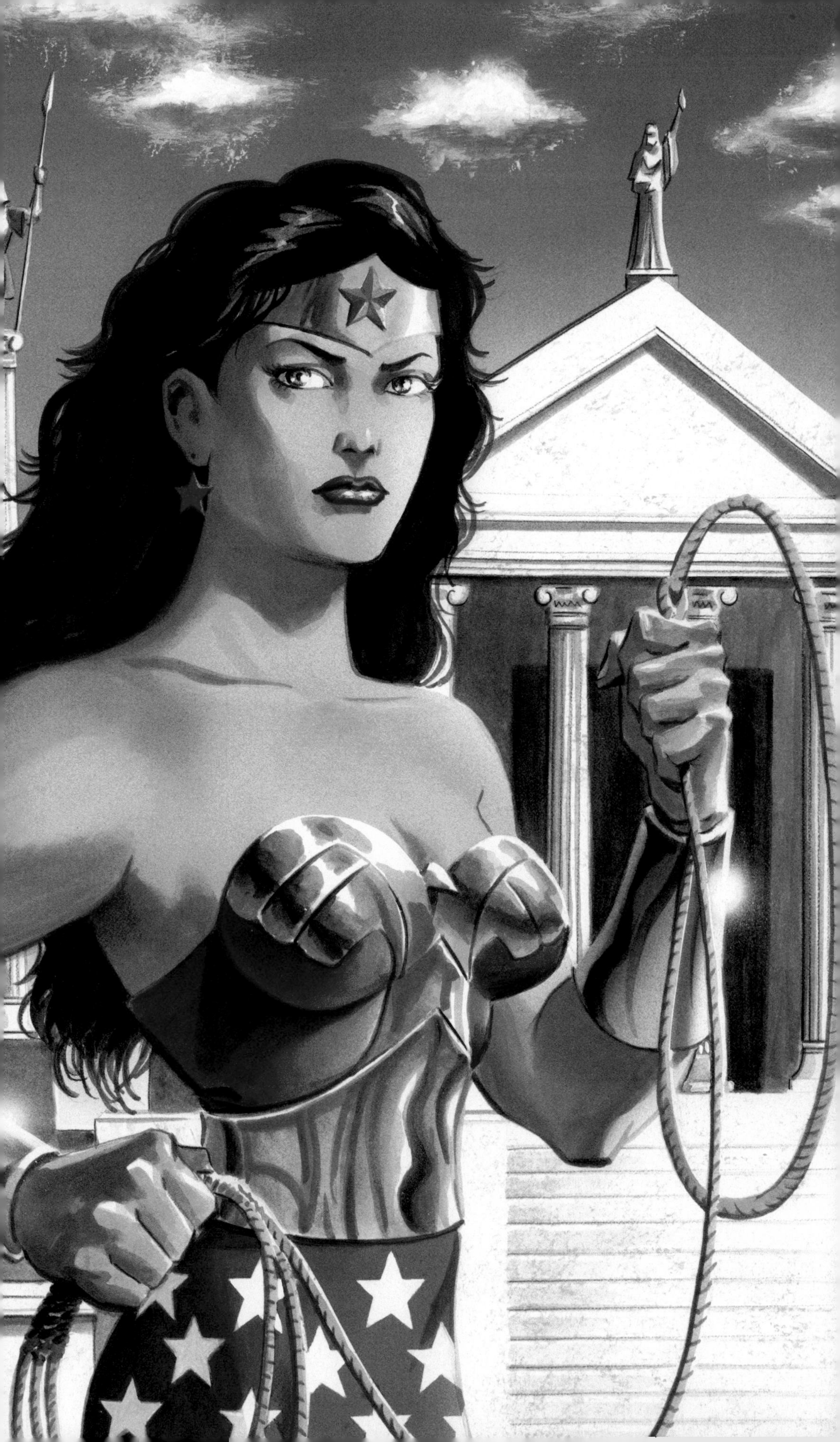

"BITTER PILLS: PART TWO"

Drew Johnson – *pencils*
Ray Snyder – *inks*
Richard Horie, Tanya Horie - *colors*
Matt Wagner – *cover art*

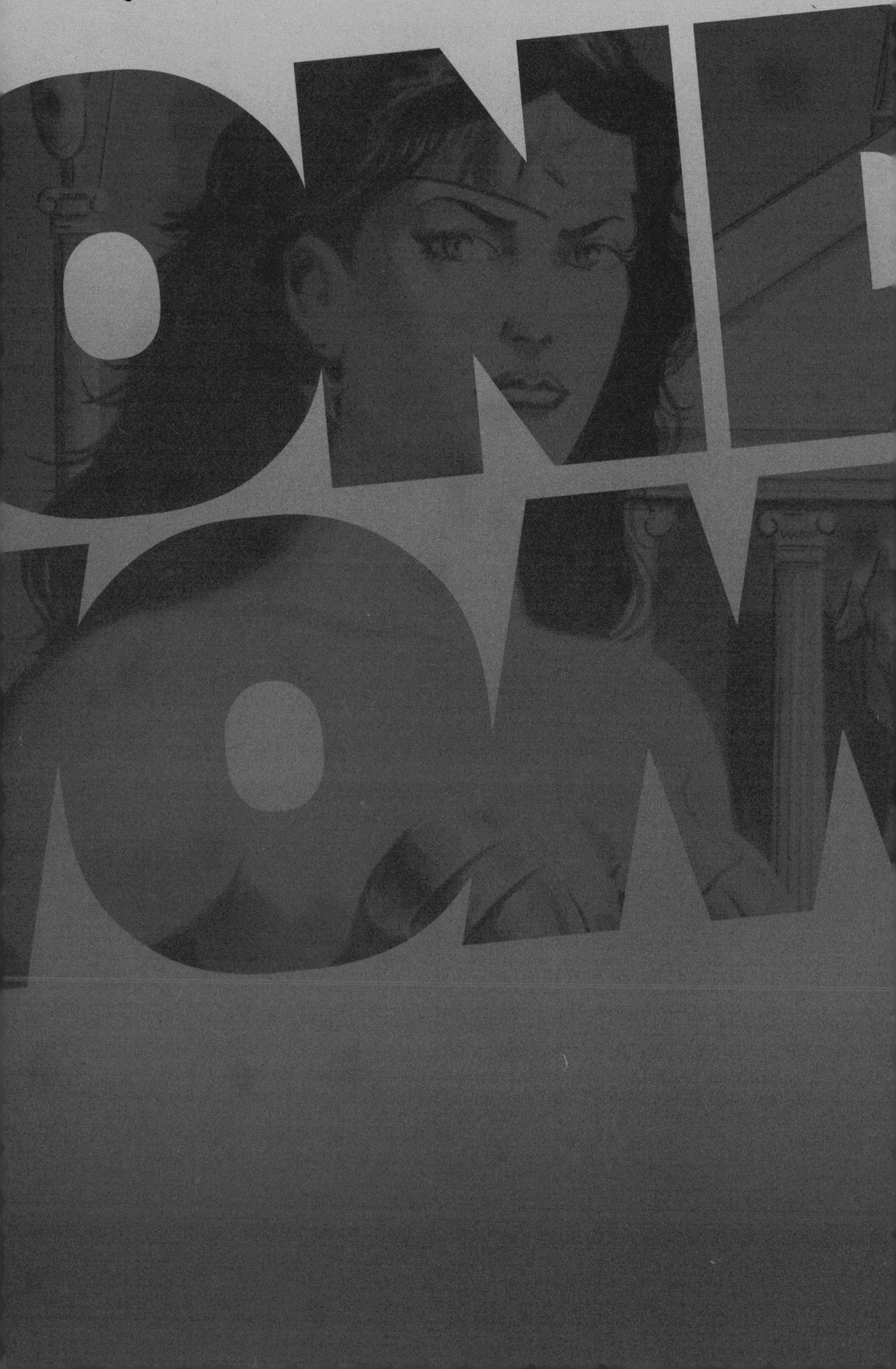

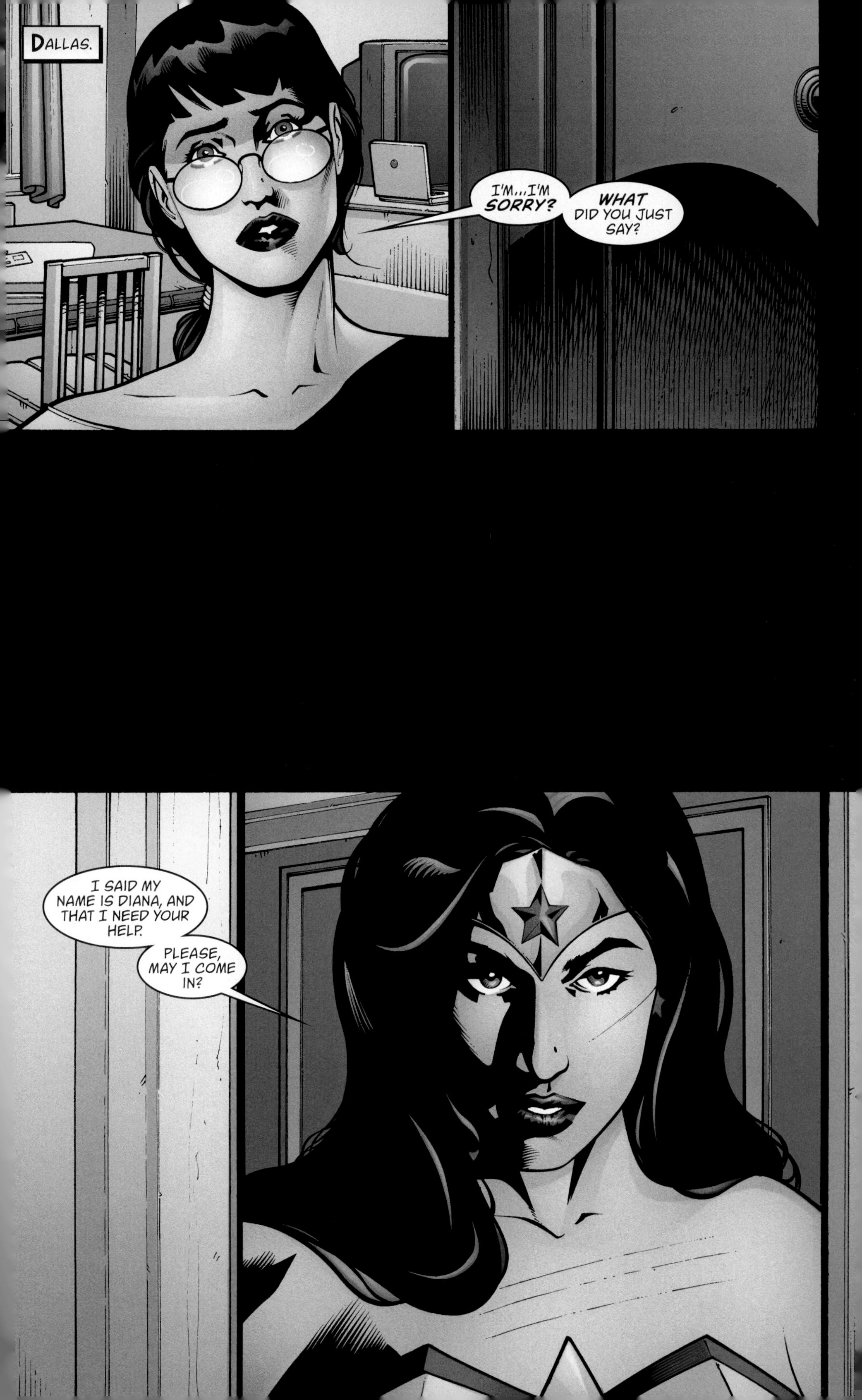
DALLAS.
I'M...I'M SORRY?
WHAT DID YOU JUST SAY?
I SAID MY NAME IS DIANA, AND THAT I NEED YOUR HELP.
PLEASE, MAY I COME IN?

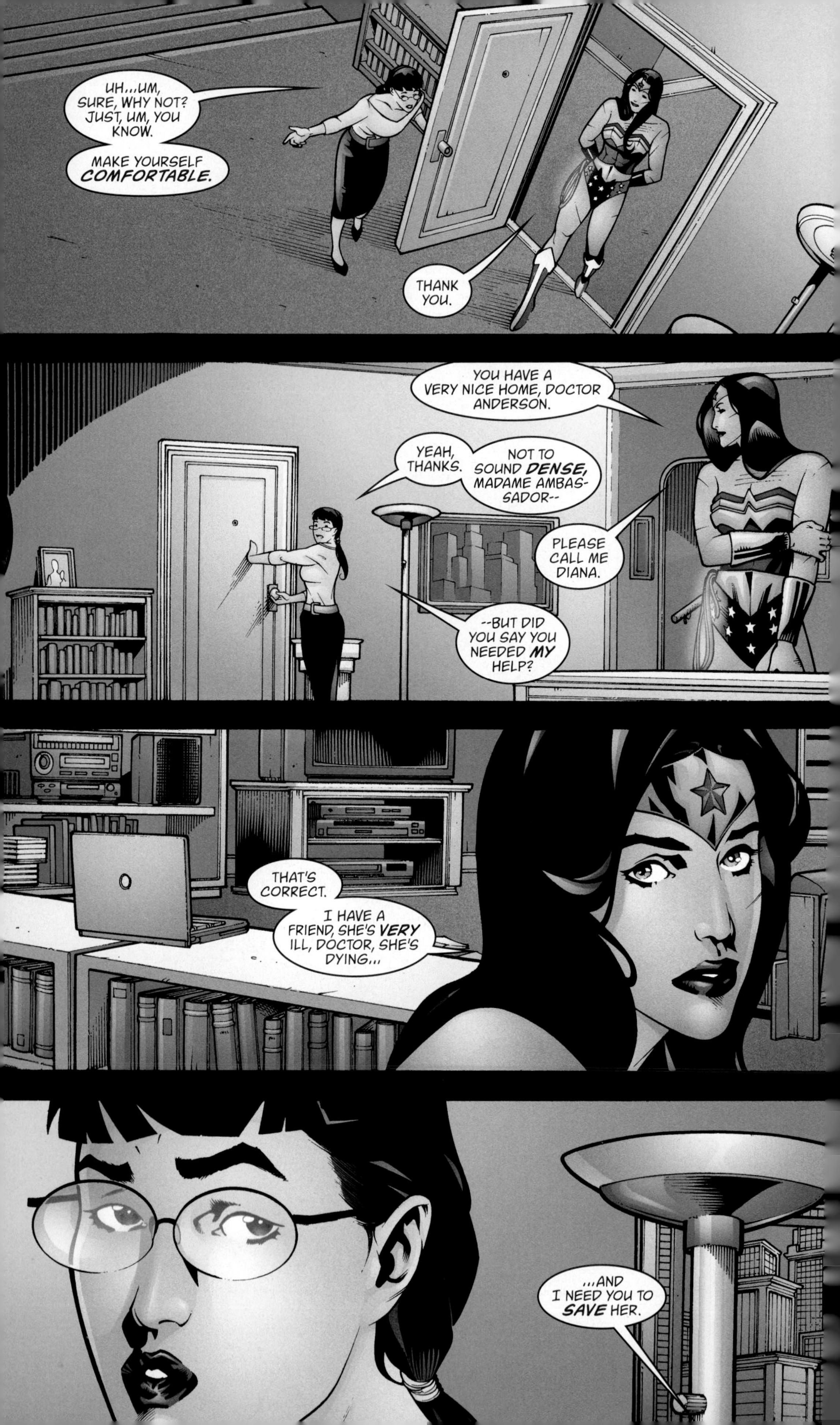
UH...UM, SURE, WHY NOT? JUST, UM, YOU KNOW.
MAKE YOURSELF COMFORTABLE.
THANK YOU.
YOU HAVE A VERY NICE HOME, DOCTOR ANDERSON.
YEAH, THANKS.
NOT TO SOUND DENSE, MADAME AMBASSADOR--
PLEASE CALL ME DIANA.
--BUT DID YOU SAY YOU NEEDED MY HELP?
THAT'S CORRECT.
I HAVE A FRIEND, SHE'S VERY ILL, DOCTOR, SHE'S DYING...
...AND I NEED YOU TO SAVE HER.

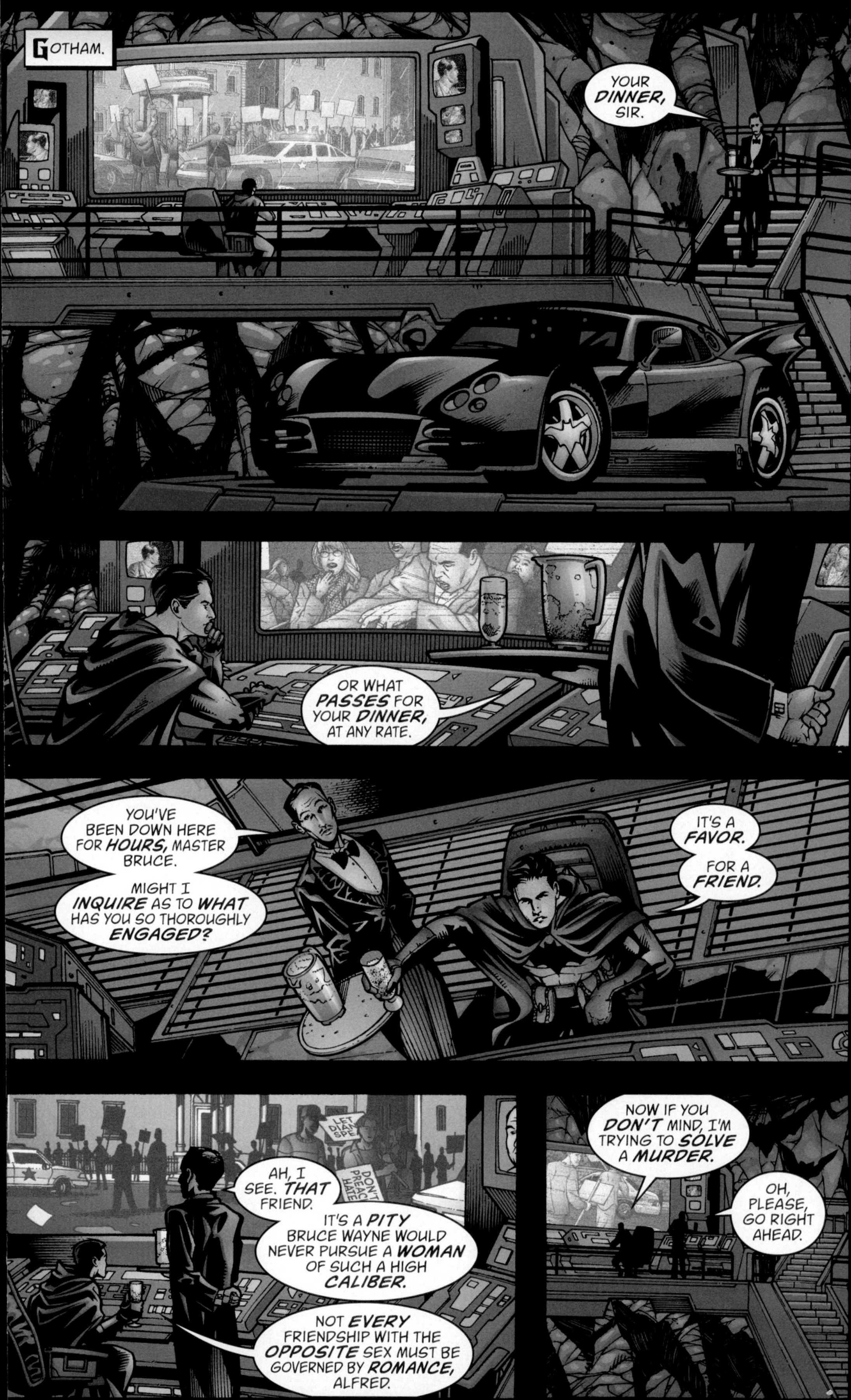
GOTHAM.
YOUR DINNER, SIR.
OR WHAT PASSES FOR YOUR DINNER, AT ANY RATE.
YOU'VE BEEN DOWN HERE FOR HOURS, MASTER BRUCE.
MIGHT I INQUIRE AS TO WHAT HAS YOU SO THOROUGHLY ENGAGED?
IT'S A FAVOR.
FOR A FRIEND.
AH, I SEE. THAT FRIEND.
IT'S A PITY BRUCE WAYNE WOULD NEVER PURSUE A WOMAN OF SUCH A HIGH CALIBER.
NOT EVERY FRIENDSHIP WITH THE OPPOSITE SEX MUST BE GOVERNED BY ROMANCE, ALFRED.
NOW IF YOU DON'T MIND, I'M TRYING TO SOLVE A MURDER.
OH, PLEASE, GO RIGHT AHEAD.

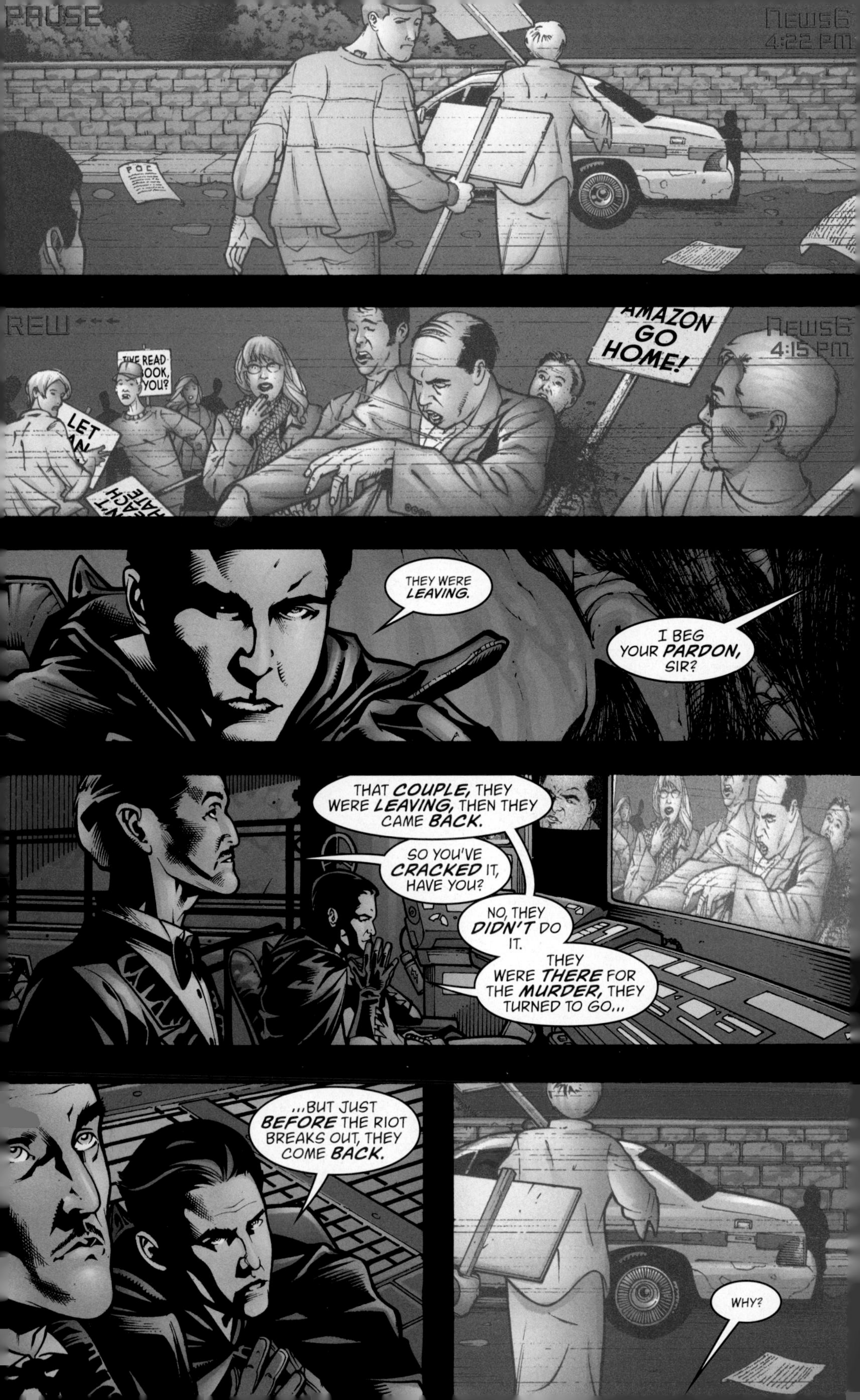
PAUSE
News6
4:22 PM
REW
News6
4:15 PM
AMAZON GO HOME!
THEY WERE *LEAVING.*
I BEG YOUR *PARDON,* SIR?
THAT *COUPLE,* THEY WERE *LEAVING,* THEN THEY CAME *BACK.*
SO YOU'VE *CRACKED* IT, HAVE YOU?
NO, THEY *DIDN'T* DO IT.
THEY WERE *THERE* FOR THE *MURDER,* THEY TURNED TO GO...
...BUT JUST *BEFORE* THE RIOT BREAKS OUT, THEY COME *BACK.*
WHY?

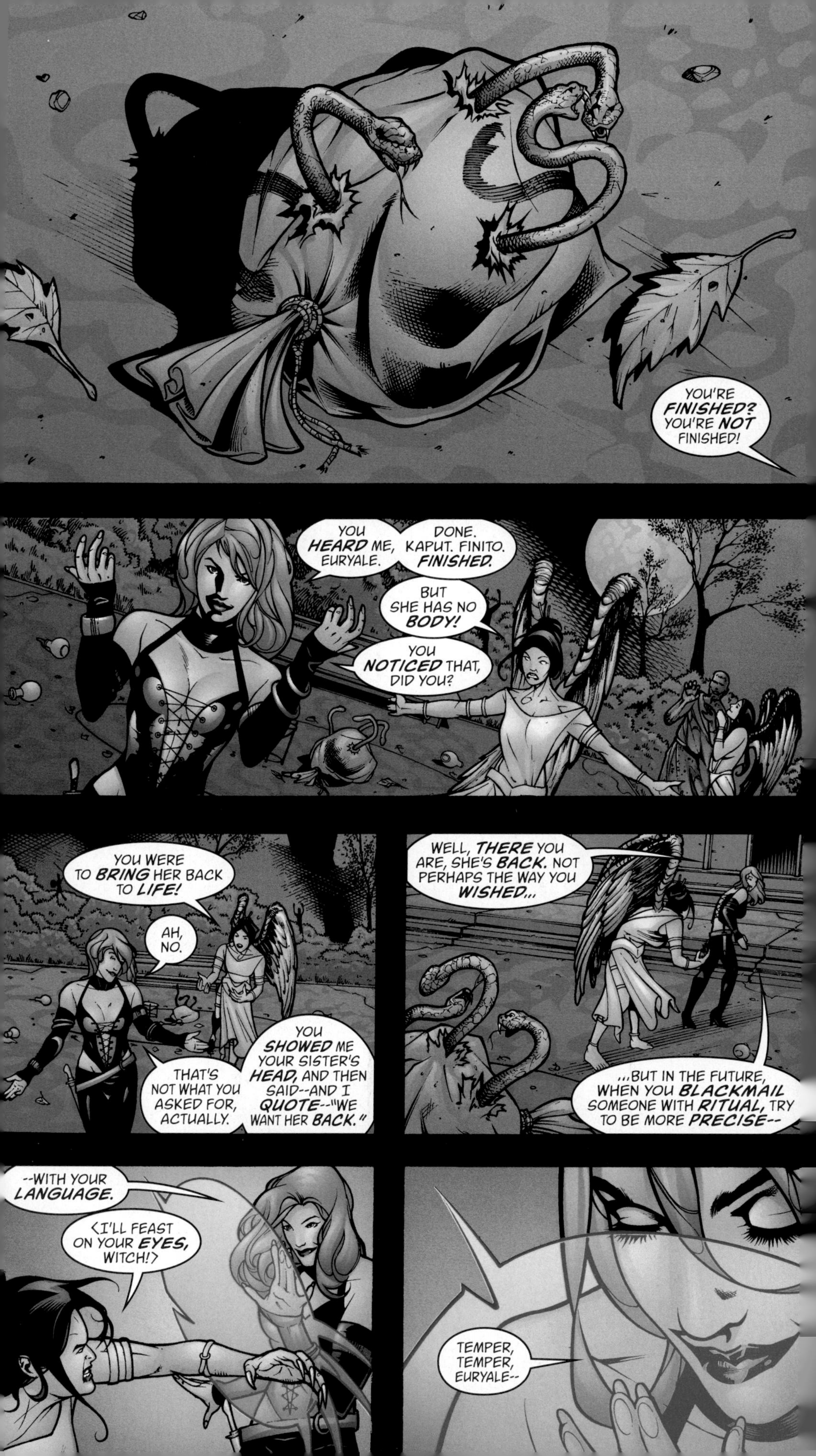

YOU'RE FINISHED? YOU'RE NOT FINISHED!
YOU HEARD ME, EURYALE.
DONE. KAPUT. FINITO. FINISHED.
BUT SHE HAS NO BODY!
YOU NOTICED THAT, DID YOU?
YOU WERE TO BRING HER BACK TO LIFE!
AH, NO.
THAT'S NOT WHAT YOU ASKED FOR, ACTUALLY.
YOU SHOWED ME YOUR SISTER'S HEAD, AND THEN SAID--AND I QUOTE--"WE WANT HER BACK."
WELL, THERE YOU ARE, SHE'S BACK. NOT PERHAPS THE WAY YOU WISHED...
...BUT IN THE FUTURE, WHEN YOU BLACKMAIL SOMEONE WITH RITUAL, TRY TO BE MORE PRECISE--
--WITH YOUR LANGUAGE.
<I'LL FEAST ON YOUR EYES, WITCH!>
TEMPER, TEMPER, EURYALE--

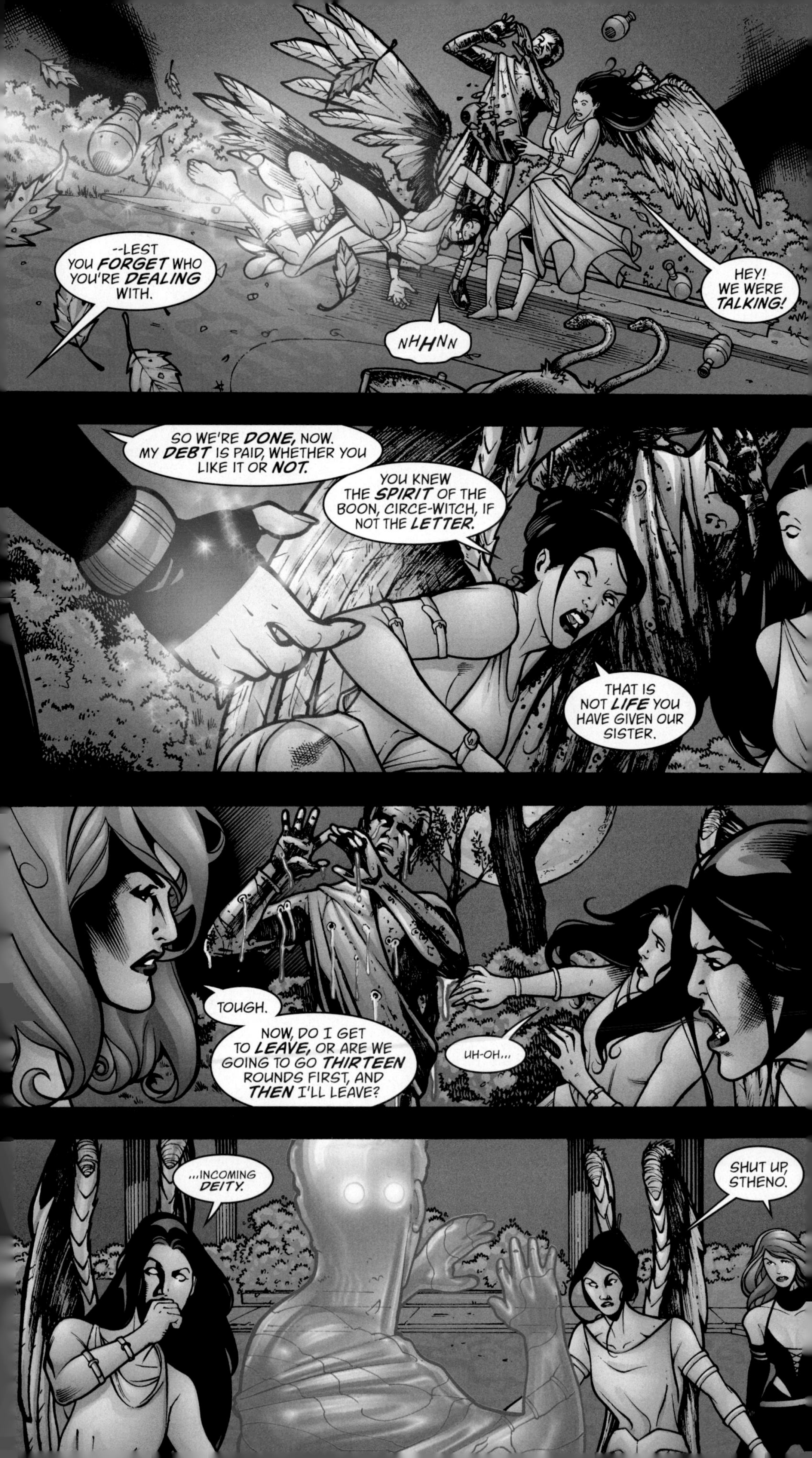
--LEST YOU FORGET WHO YOU'RE DEALING WITH.
NHHNN
HEY! WE WERE TALKING!
SO WE'RE DONE, NOW. MY DEBT IS PAID, WHETHER YOU LIKE IT OR NOT.
YOU KNEW THE SPIRIT OF THE BOON, CIRCE-WITCH, IF NOT THE LETTER.
THAT IS NOT LIFE YOU HAVE GIVEN OUR SISTER.
TOUGH.
NOW, DO I GET TO LEAVE, OR ARE WE GOING TO GO THIRTEEN ROUNDS FIRST, AND THEN I'LL LEAVE?
UH-OH...
...INCOMING DEITY.
SHUT UP, STHENO.

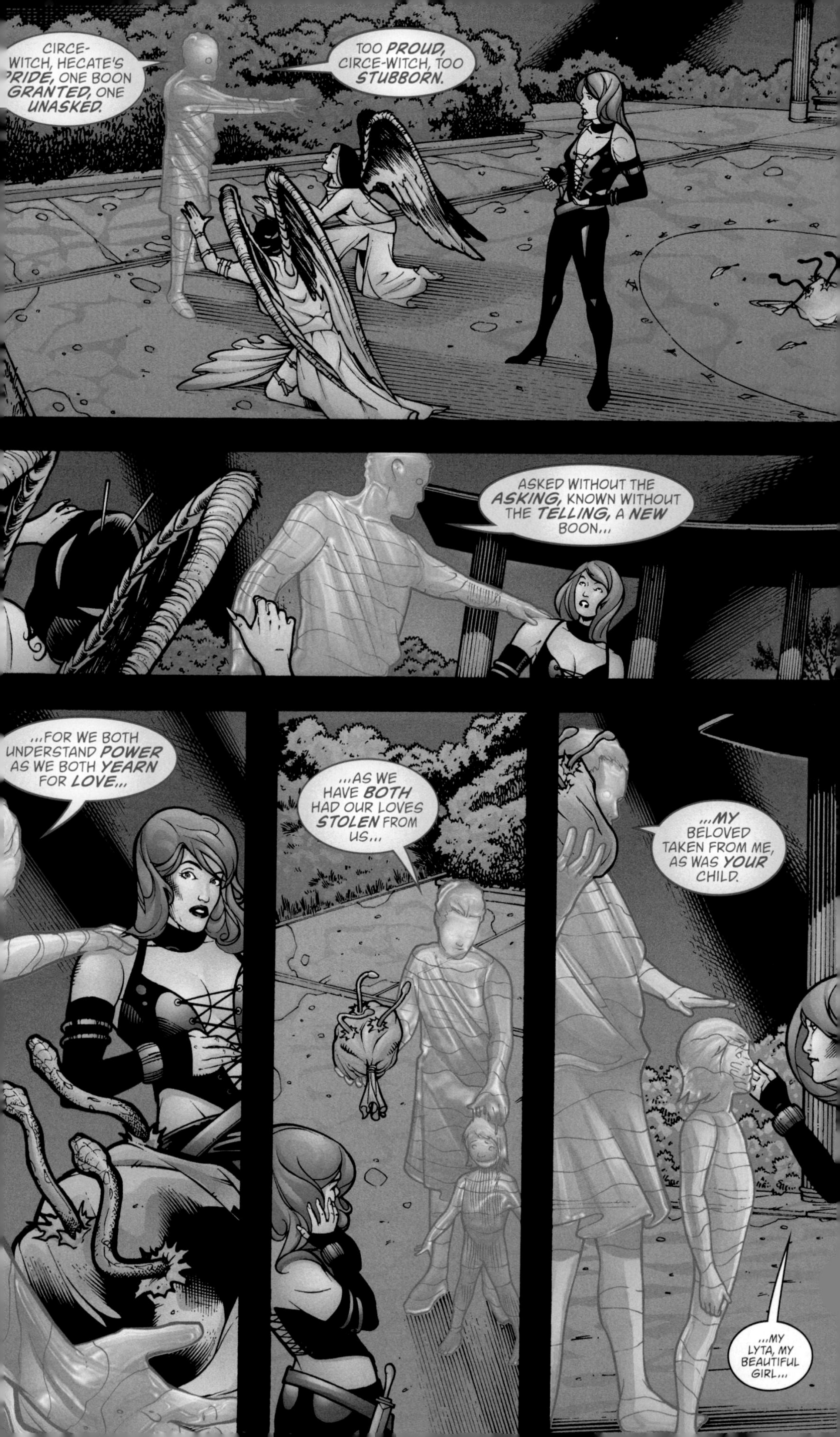
CIRCE-WITCH, HECATE'S PRIDE, ONE BOON GRANTED, ONE UNASKED.
TOO PROUD, CIRCE-WITCH, TOO STUBBORN.
ASKED WITHOUT THE ASKING, KNOWN WITHOUT THE TELLING, A NEW BOON...
...FOR WE BOTH UNDERSTAND POWER AS WE BOTH YEARN FOR LOVE...
...AS WE HAVE BOTH HAD OUR LOVES STOLEN FROM US...
...MY BELOVED TAKEN FROM ME, AS WAS YOUR CHILD.
...MY LYTA, MY BEAUTIFUL GIRL...

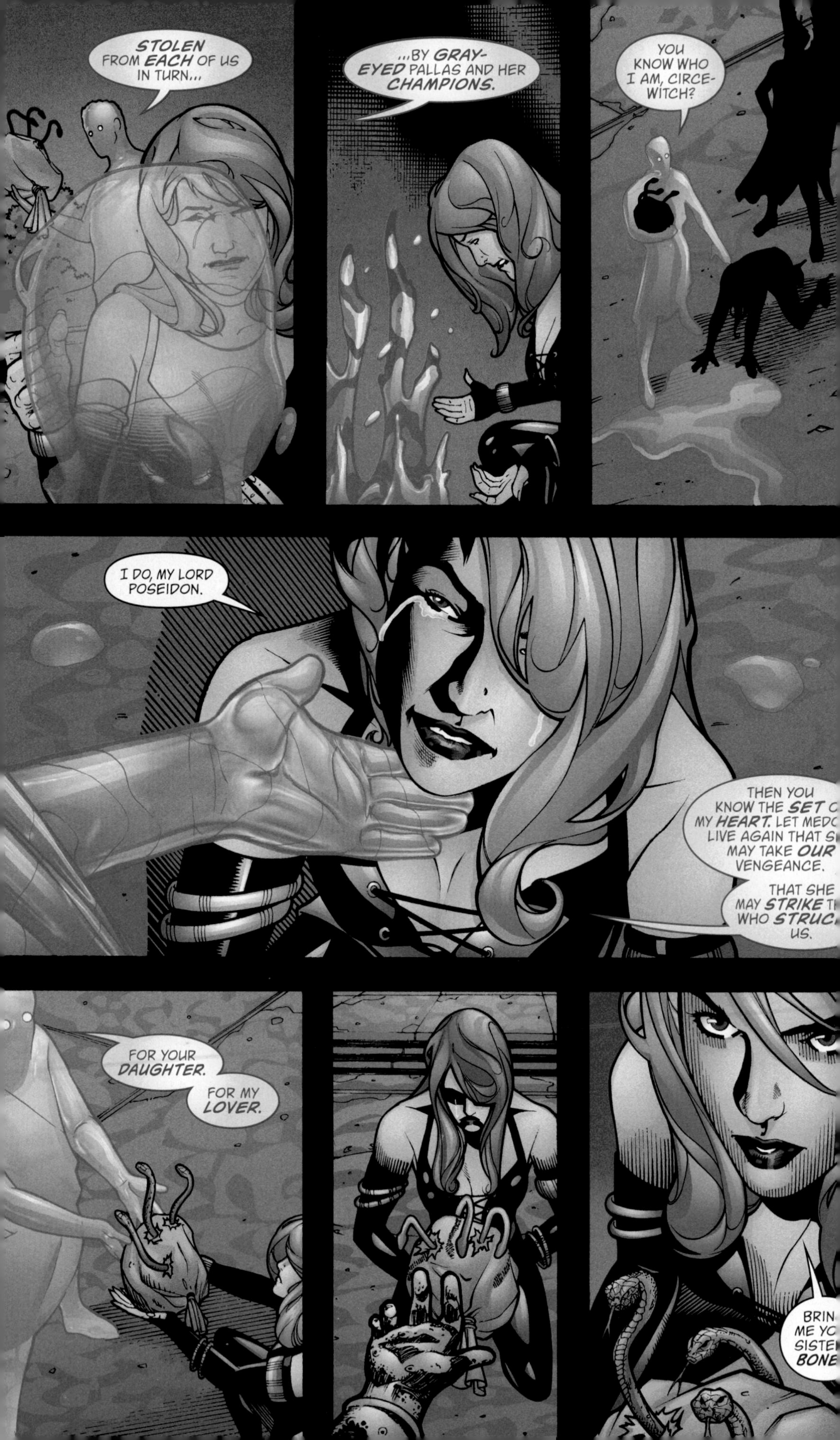
STOLEN FROM EACH OF US IN TURN...
...BY GRAY-EYED PALLAS AND HER CHAMPIONS.
YOU KNOW WHO I AM, CIRCE-WITCH?
I DO, MY LORD POSEIDON.
THEN YOU KNOW THE SET MY HEART. LET MEDO LIVE AGAIN THAT S MAY TAKE OUR VENGEANCE.
THAT SHE MAY STRIKE T WHO STRUC US.
FOR YOUR DAUGHTER.
FOR MY LOVER.
BRIN ME YO SISTE BONE

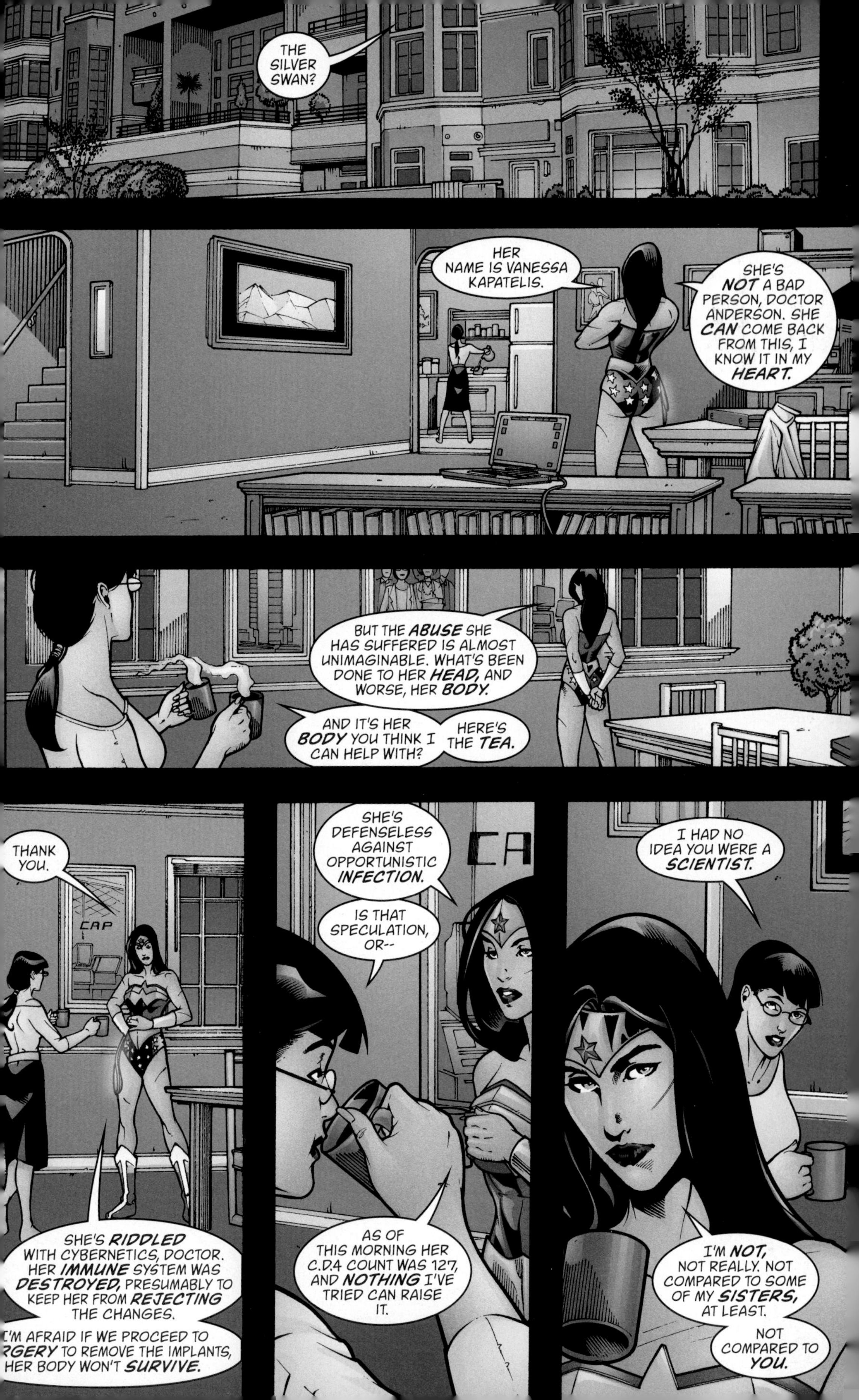
THE SILVER SWAN?
HER NAME IS VANESSA KAPATELIS.
SHE'S NOT A BAD PERSON, DOCTOR ANDERSON. SHE CAN COME BACK FROM THIS, I KNOW IT IN MY HEART.
BUT THE ABUSE SHE HAS SUFFERED IS ALMOST UNIMAGINABLE. WHAT'S BEEN DONE TO HER HEAD, AND WORSE, HER BODY.
AND IT'S HER BODY YOU THINK I CAN HELP WITH?
HERE'S THE TEA.
THANK YOU.
CAP
SHE'S RIDDLED WITH CYBERNETICS, DOCTOR. HER IMMUNE SYSTEM WAS DESTROYED, PRESUMABLY TO KEEP HER FROM REJECTING THE CHANGES.
'M AFRAID IF WE PROCEED TO RGERY TO REMOVE THE IMPLANTS, HER BODY WON'T SURVIVE.
CA
SHE'S DEFENSELESS AGAINST OPPORTUNISTIC INFECTION.
IS THAT SPECULATION, OR--
AS OF THIS MORNING HER C.D.4 COUNT WAS 127, AND NOTHING I'VE TRIED CAN RAISE IT.
I HAD NO IDEA YOU WERE A SCIENTIST.
I'M NOT, NOT REALLY. NOT COMPARED TO SOME OF MY SISTERS, AT LEAST.
NOT COMPARED TO YOU.

UNDERGRADUATE HARVARD, DOCTORATES FROM *M.I.T.*, *U.C.L.A.*, AND JOHNS HOPKINS.

I READ YOUR *A.M.A.* PAPER ON DISCRIMINATORY CHEMOKINE BLOCKERS ON THE PLANE, IT'S *BRILLIANT* WORK.

YOU'RE EVEN A *SURGEON,* WITH RIGHTS AT U.T. SOUTHWESTERN, HERE IN DALLAS, AND SLOAN-KETTERING IN NEW YORK.

CAP

YOU DO YOUR HOMEWORK.

MY P.A. DID, ACTUALLY... ...ODD...

I KNOW, IT'S NOT A VERY FLATTERING *PICTURE* OF ME.

NO, YOU LOOK LOVELY...

...THE WOMAN YOU'RE *WITH* HERE, I'VE SEEN HER *BEFORE.*

THAT'S MY BUSINESS PARTNER, VERONICA CALE.

VERONICA, THAT WAS HER NAME. I SIGNED A *BOOK* FOR HER.

CAP

YOU SIGNED A BOOK FOR RONNIE?

YOU SOUND SURPRISED.

SHE'S NOT REALLY YOUR BIG-GEST FAN.

TO TELL YOU THE *TRUTH,* UNTIL ABOUT AN *HOUR* AGO, I WASN'T, EITHER.

HAVE I *CHANGED* YOUR MIND?

LET'S JUST SAY YOU'RE N— WHO I THOUG— YOU WERE.

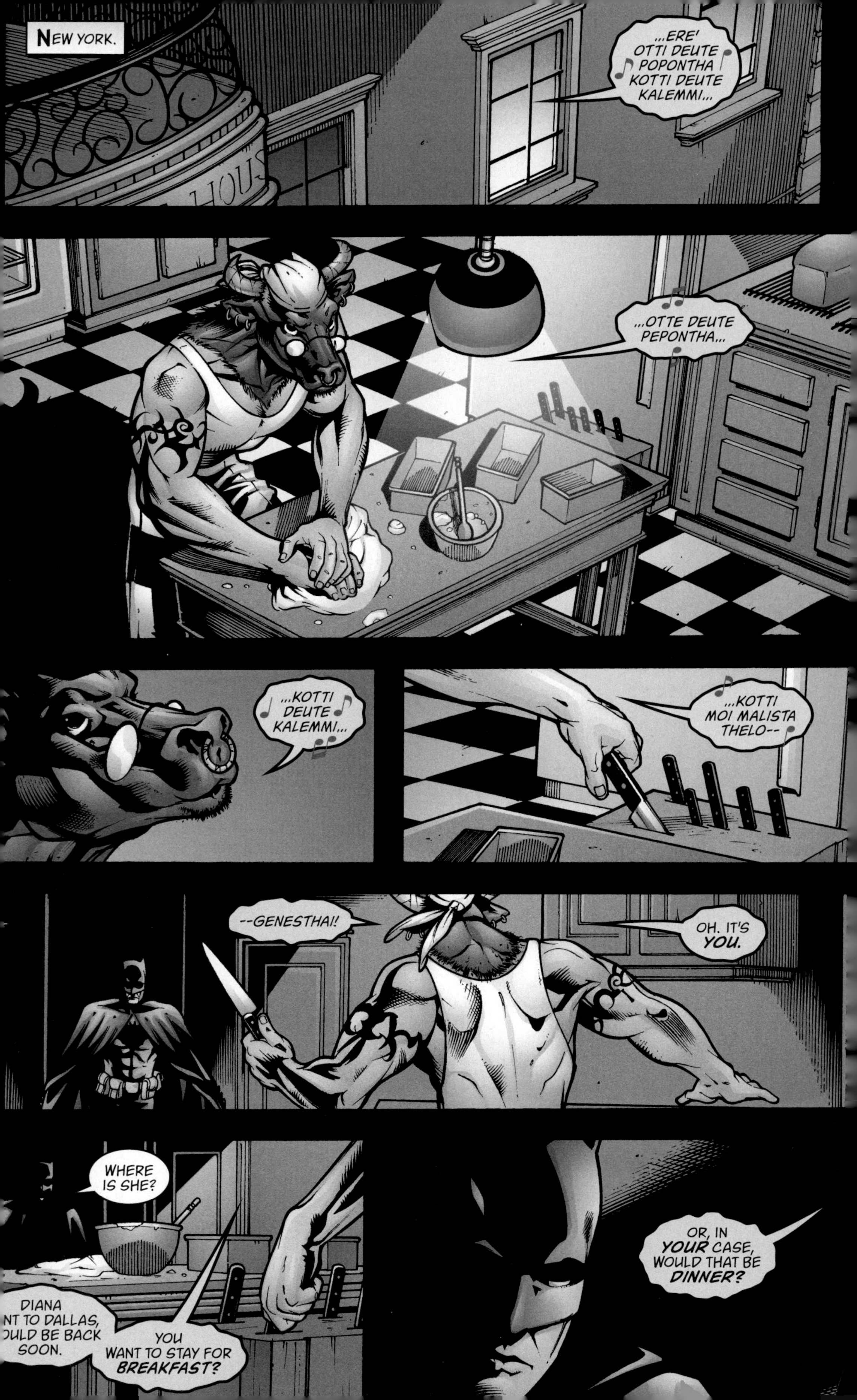
NEW YORK.
...ERE' OTTI DEUTE POPONTHA KOTTI DEUTE KALEMMI...
...OTTE DEUTE PEPONTHA...
...KOTTI DEUTE KALEMMI...
...KOTTI MOI MALISTA THELO--
--GENESTHAI!
OH. IT'S YOU.
WHERE IS SHE?
DIANA
NT TO DALLAS,
OULD BE BACK
SOON.
YOU WANT TO STAY FOR BREAKFAST?
OR, IN YOUR CASE, WOULD THAT BE DINNER?

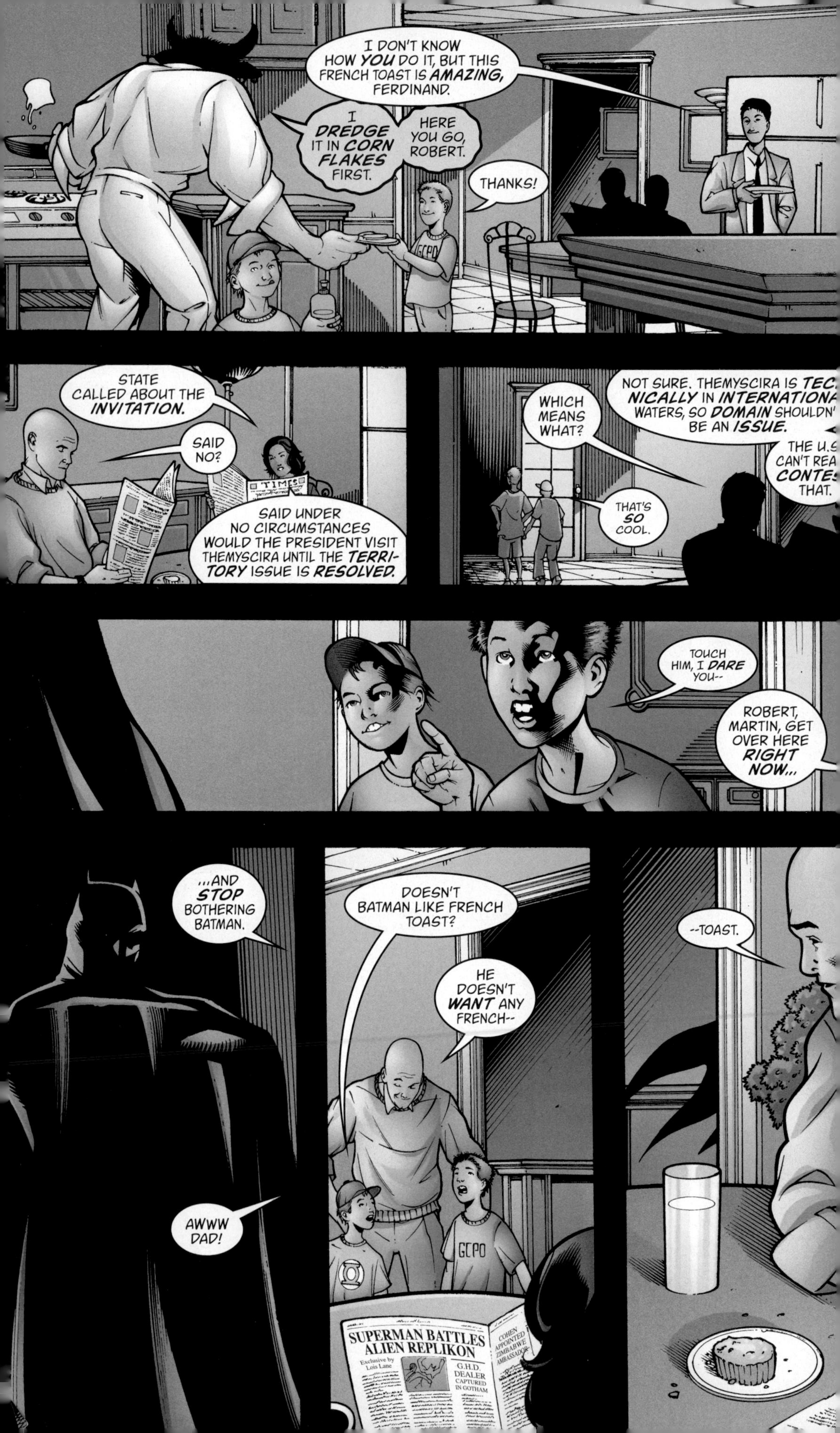
I DON'T KNOW HOW YOU DO IT, BUT THIS FRENCH TOAST IS AMAZING, FERDINAND.
I DREDGE IT IN CORN FLAKES FIRST.
HERE YOU GO, ROBERT.
THANKS!
STATE CALLED ABOUT THE INVITATION.
SAID NO?
SAID UNDER NO CIRCUMSTANCES WOULD THE PRESIDENT VISIT THEMYSCIRA UNTIL THE TERRITORY ISSUE IS RESOLVED.
TIMES
WHICH MEANS WHAT?
NOT SURE. THEMYSCIRA IS TEC NICALLY IN INTERNATIONA WATERS, SO DOMAIN SHOULDN' BE AN ISSUE.
THE U.S CAN'T REA CONTES THAT.
THAT'S SO COOL.
TOUCH HIM, I DARE YOU--
ROBERT, MARTIN, GET OVER HERE RIGHT NOW...
...AND STOP BOTHERING BATMAN.
AWWW DAD!
DOESN'T BATMAN LIKE FRENCH TOAST?
HE DOESN'T WANT ANY FRENCH--
--TOAST.
GCPD
SUPERMAN BATTLES ALIEN REPLIKON
Exclusive by Lois Lane
G.H.D. DEALER CAPTURED IN GOTHAM
COHEN APPOINTED ZIMBABWE AMBASSADOR

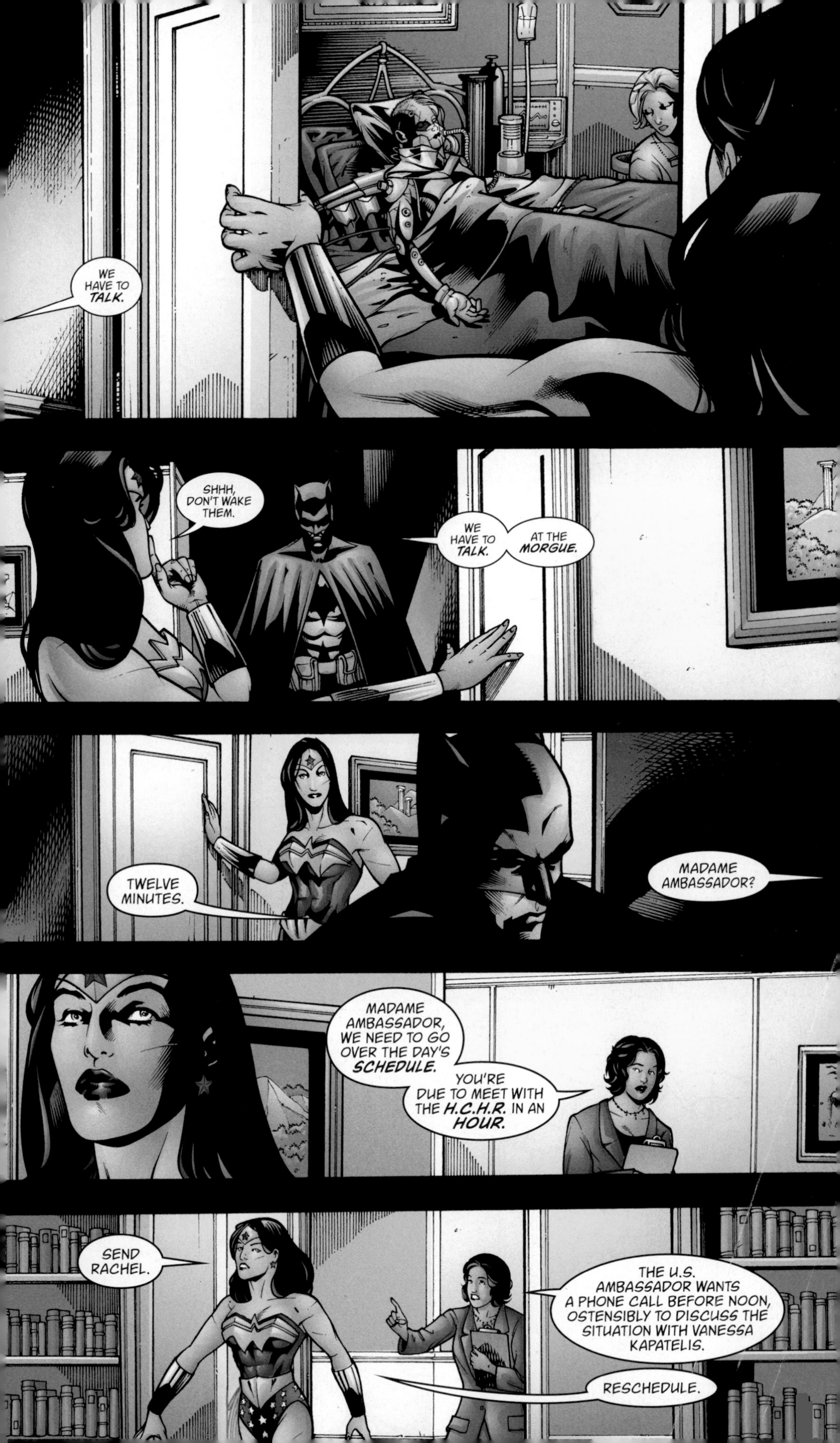
WE HAVE TO TALK.
SHHH, DON'T WAKE THEM.
WE HAVE TO TALK.
AT THE MORGUE.
TWELVE MINUTES.
MADAME AMBASSADOR?
MADAME AMBASSADOR, WE NEED TO GO OVER THE DAY'S SCHEDULE.
YOU'RE DUE TO MEET WITH THE H.C.H.R. IN AN HOUR.
SEND RACHEL.
THE U.S. AMBASSADOR WANTS A PHONE CALL BEFORE NOON, OSTENSIBLY TO DISCUSS THE SITUATION WITH VANESSA KAPATELIS.
RESCHEDULE.

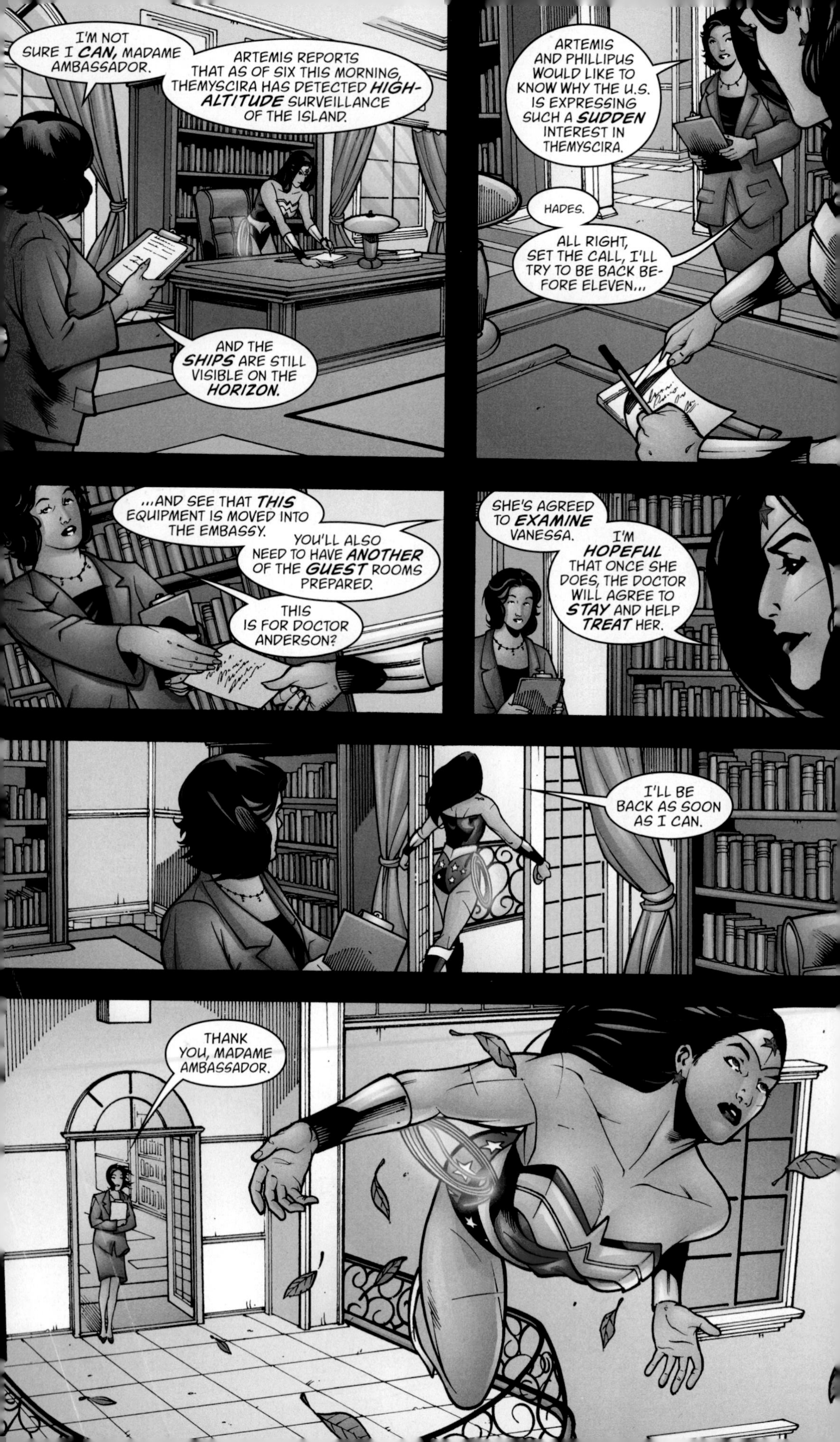

I'M NOT SURE I CAN, MADAME AMBASSADOR.
ARTEMIS REPORTS THAT AS OF SIX THIS MORNING, THEMYSCIRA HAS DETECTED HIGH-ALTITUDE SURVEILLANCE OF THE ISLAND.
AND THE SHIPS ARE STILL VISIBLE ON THE HORIZON.
ARTEMIS AND PHILLIPUS WOULD LIKE TO KNOW WHY THE U.S. IS EXPRESSING SUCH A SUDDEN INTEREST IN THEMYSCIRA.
HADES.
ALL RIGHT, SET THE CALL, I'LL TRY TO BE BACK BEFORE ELEVEN...
...AND SEE THAT THIS EQUIPMENT IS MOVED INTO THE EMBASSY.
YOU'LL ALSO NEED TO HAVE ANOTHER OF THE GUEST ROOMS PREPARED.
THIS IS FOR DOCTOR ANDERSON?
SHE'S AGREED TO EXAMINE VANESSA.
I'M HOPEFUL THAT ONCE SHE DOES, THE DOCTOR WILL AGREE TO STAY AND HELP TREAT HER.
I'LL BE BACK AS SOON AS I CAN.
THANK YOU, MADAME AMBASSADOR.

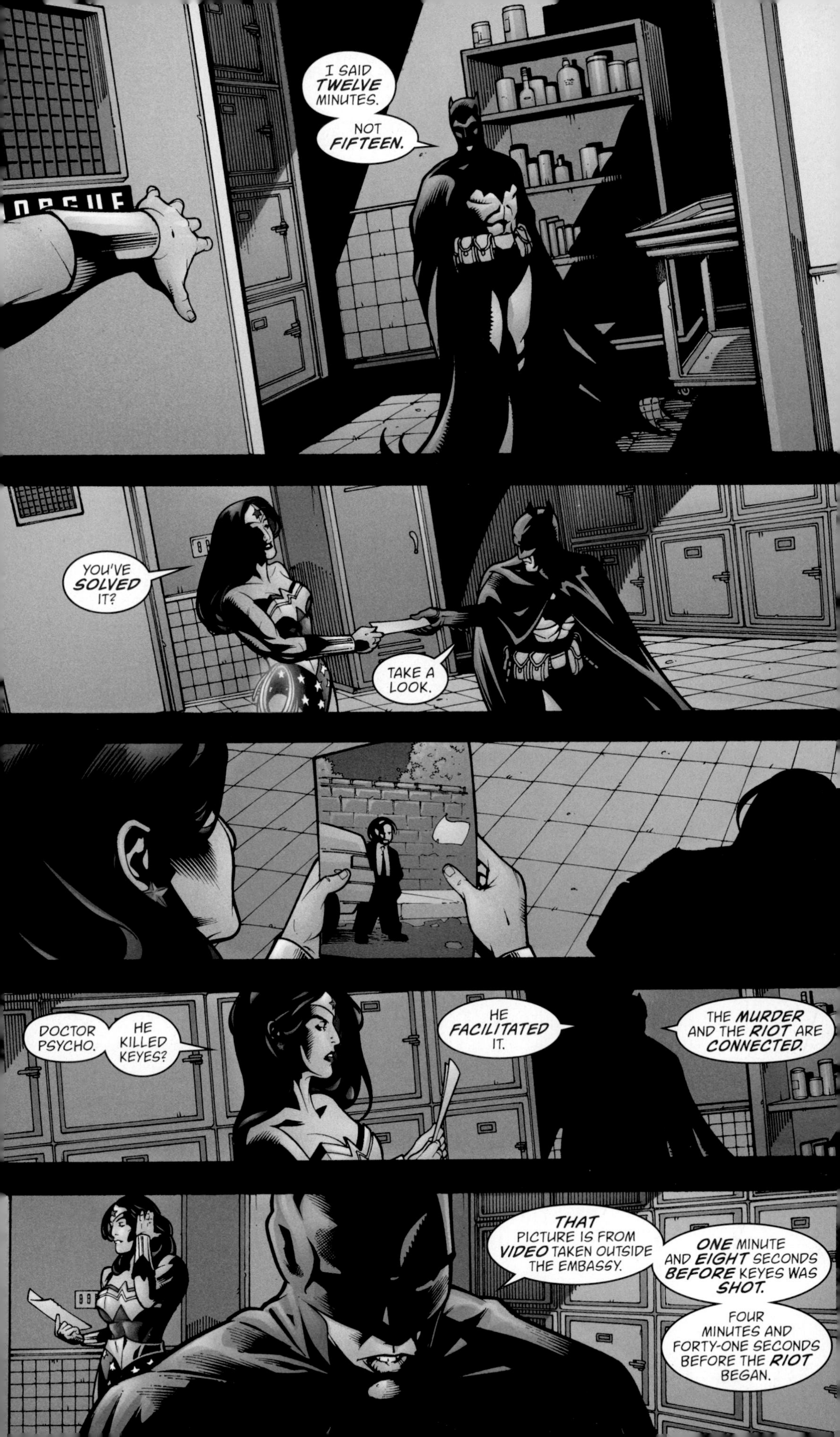
ORGUE
I SAID TWELVE MINUTES.
NOT FIFTEEN.
YOU'VE SOLVED IT?
TAKE A LOOK.
DOCTOR PSYCHO.
HE KILLED KEYES?
HE FACILITATED IT.
THE MURDER AND THE RIOT ARE CONNECTED.
THAT PICTURE IS FROM VIDEO TAKEN OUTSIDE THE EMBASSY.
ONE MINUTE AND EIGHT SECONDS BEFORE KEYES WAS SHOT.
FOUR MINUTES AND FORTY-ONE SECONDS BEFORE THE RIOT BEGAN.

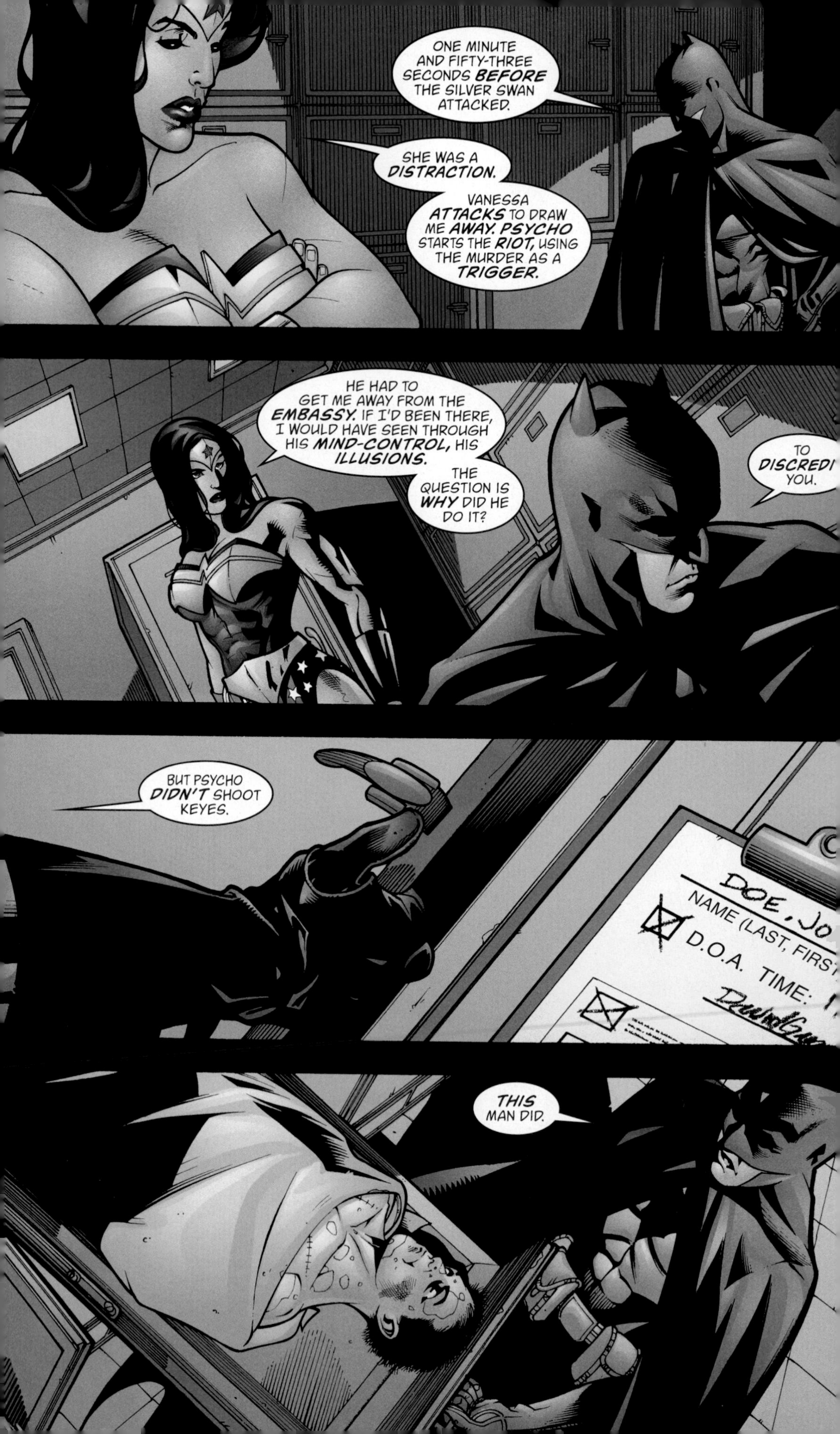
ONE MINUTE AND FIFTY-THREE SECONDS BEFORE THE SILVER SWAN ATTACKED.
SHE WAS A DISTRACTION.
VANESSA ATTACKS TO DRAW ME AWAY. PSYCHO STARTS THE RIOT, USING THE MURDER AS A TRIGGER.
HE HAD TO GET ME AWAY FROM THE EMBASSY. IF I'D BEEN THERE, I WOULD HAVE SEEN THROUGH HIS MIND-CONTROL, HIS ILLUSIONS.
THE QUESTION IS WHY DID HE DO IT?
TO DISCREDI YOU.
BUT PSYCHO DIDN'T SHOOT KEYES.
DOE, JO
NAME (LAST, FIRS
D.O.A. TIME:
THIS MAN DID.

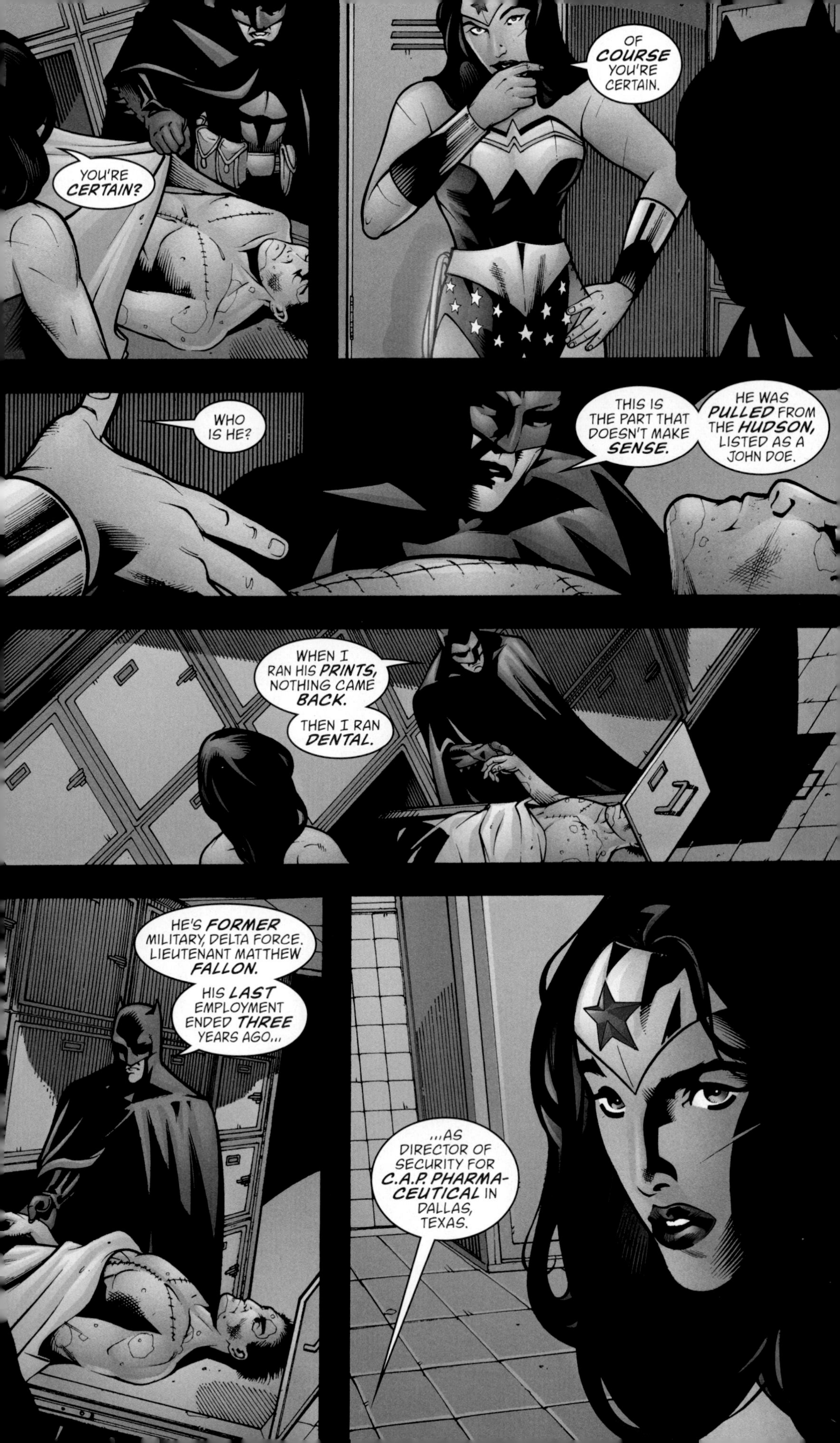
YOU'RE CERTAIN?
OF COURSE YOU'RE CERTAIN.
WHO IS HE?
THIS IS THE PART THAT DOESN'T MAKE SENSE.
HE WAS PULLED FROM THE HUDSON, LISTED AS A JOHN DOE.
WHEN I RAN HIS PRINTS, NOTHING CAME BACK.
THEN I RAN DENTAL.
HE'S FORMER MILITARY, DELTA FORCE. LIEUTENANT MATTHEW FALLON.
HIS LAST EMPLOYMENT ENDED THREE YEARS AGO...
...AS DIRECTOR OF SECURITY FOR C.A.P. PHARMA-CEUTICAL IN DALLAS, TEXAS.

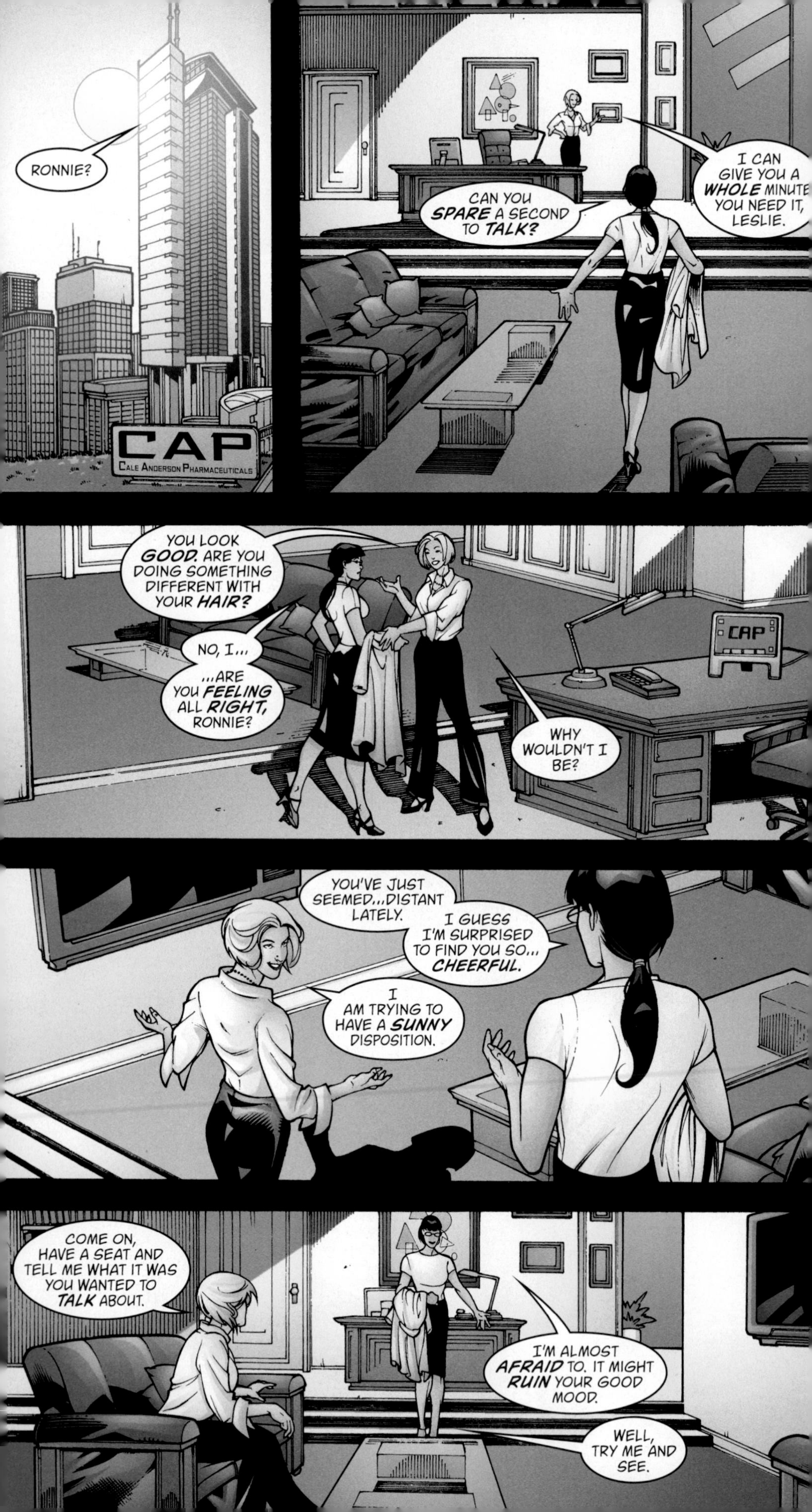
RONNIE?
CAP
CALE ANDERSON PHARMACEUTICALS
CAN YOU SPARE A SECOND TO TALK?
I CAN GIVE YOU A WHOLE MINUTE IF YOU NEED IT, LESLIE.
YOU LOOK GOOD. ARE YOU DOING SOMETHING DIFFERENT WITH YOUR HAIR?
NO, I...
...ARE YOU FEELING ALL RIGHT, RONNIE?
WHY WOULDN'T I BE?
CAP
YOU'VE JUST SEEMED...DISTANT LATELY.
I GUESS I'M SURPRISED TO FIND YOU SO... CHEERFUL.
I AM TRYING TO HAVE A SUNNY DISPOSITION.
COME ON, HAVE A SEAT AND TELL ME WHAT IT WAS YOU WANTED TO TALK ABOUT.
I'M ALMOST AFRAID TO. IT MIGHT RUIN YOUR GOOD MOOD.
WELL, TRY ME AND SEE.

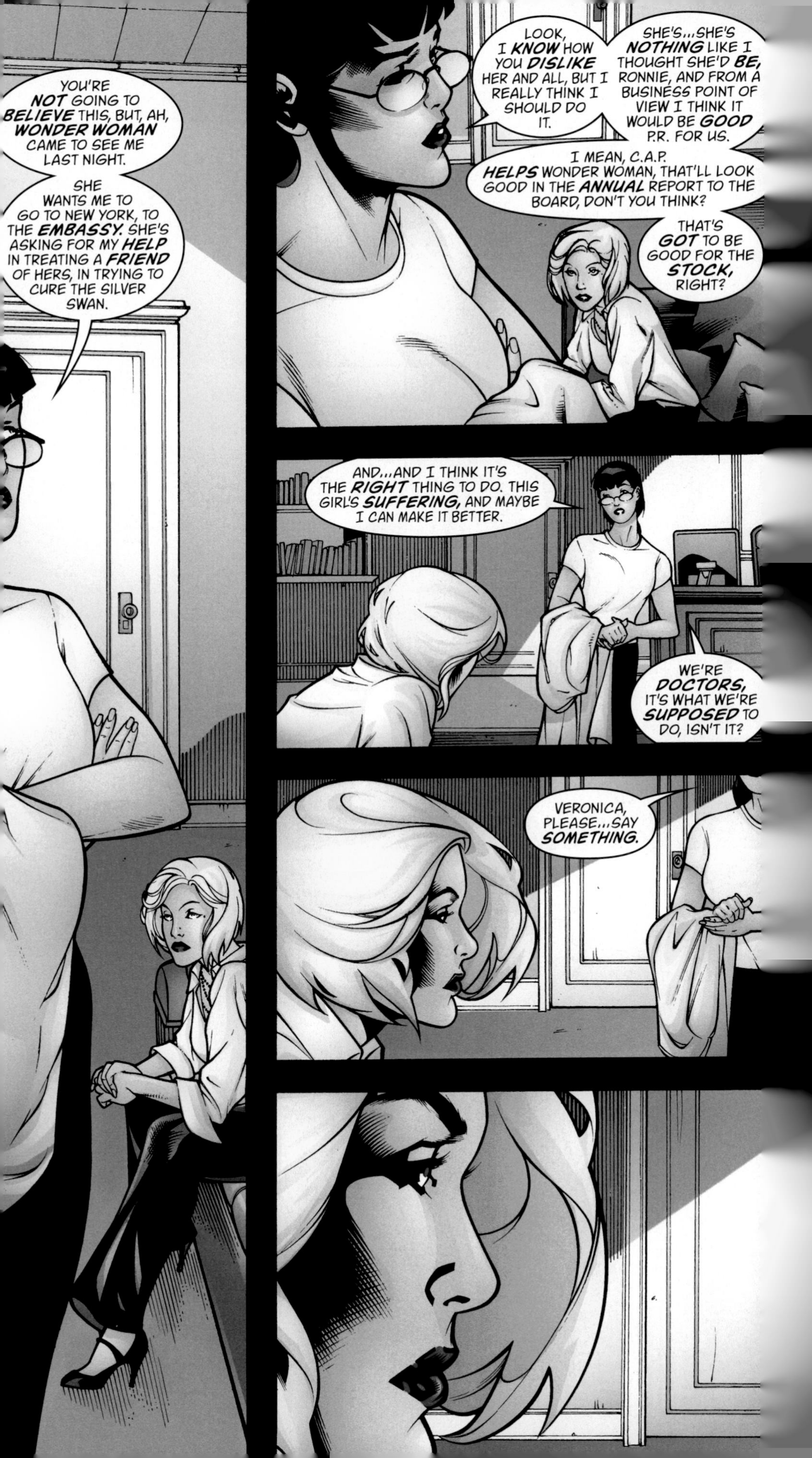
YOU'RE NOT GOING TO BELIEVE THIS, BUT, AH, WONDER WOMAN CAME TO SEE ME LAST NIGHT.
SHE WANTS ME TO GO TO NEW YORK, TO THE EMBASSY. SHE'S ASKING FOR MY HELP IN TREATING A FRIEND OF HERS, IN TRYING TO CURE THE SILVER SWAN.
LOOK, I KNOW HOW YOU DISLIKE HER AND ALL, BUT I REALLY THINK I SHOULD DO IT.
SHE'S...SHE'S NOTHING LIKE I THOUGHT SHE'D BE, RONNIE, AND FROM A BUSINESS POINT OF VIEW I THINK IT WOULD BE GOOD P.R. FOR US.
I MEAN, C.A.P. HELPS WONDER WOMAN, THAT'LL LOOK GOOD IN THE ANNUAL REPORT TO THE BOARD, DON'T YOU THINK?
THAT'S GOT TO BE GOOD FOR THE STOCK, RIGHT?
AND...AND I THINK IT'S THE RIGHT THING TO DO. THIS GIRL'S SUFFERING, AND MAYBE I CAN MAKE IT BETTER.
WE'RE DOCTORS, IT'S WHAT WE'RE SUPPOSED TO DO, ISN'T IT?
VERONICA, PLEASE...SAY SOMETHING.

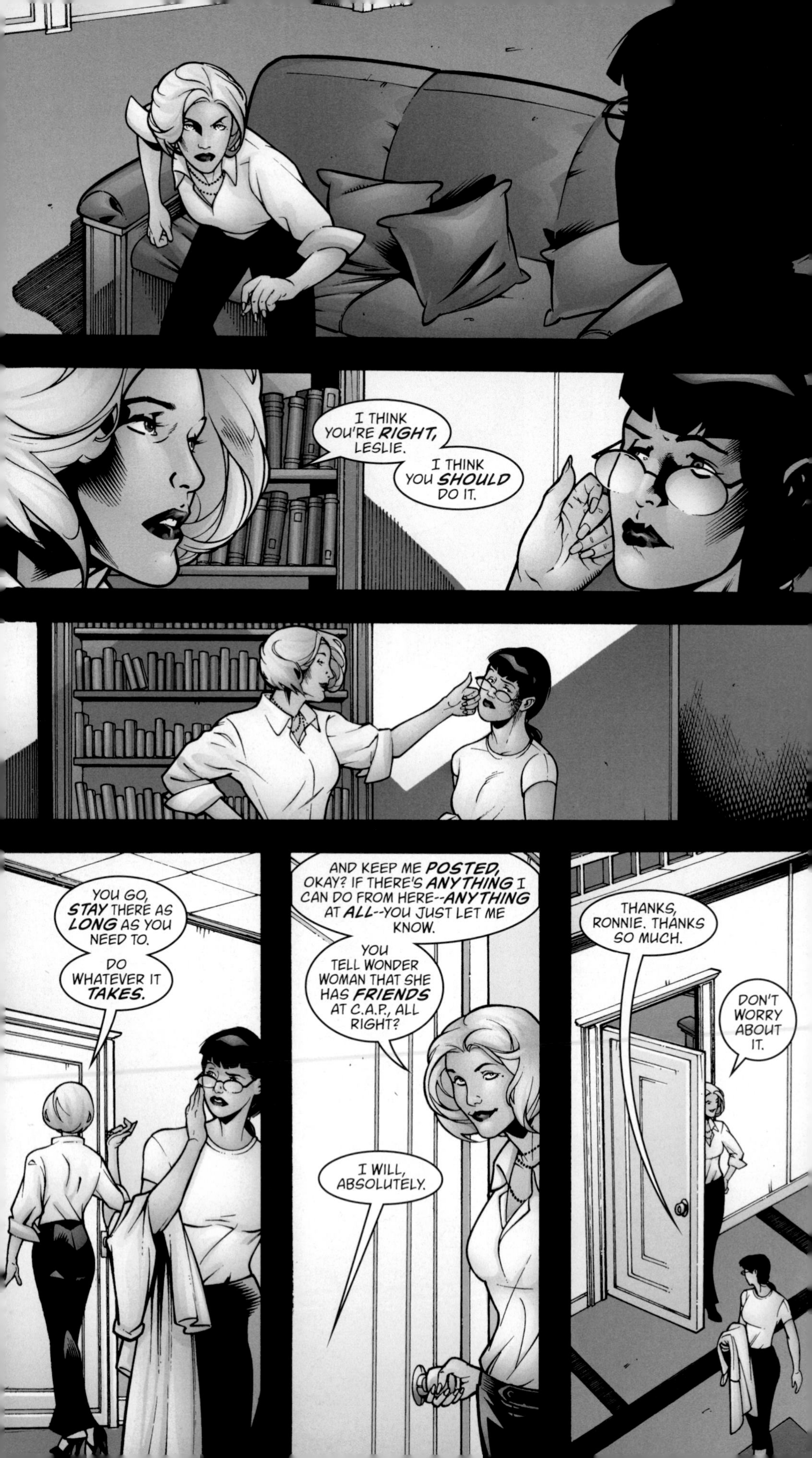
I THINK YOU'RE RIGHT, LESLIE.
I THINK YOU SHOULD DO IT.
YOU GO, STAY THERE AS LONG AS YOU NEED TO.
DO WHATEVER IT TAKES.
AND KEEP ME POSTED, OKAY? IF THERE'S ANYTHING I CAN DO FROM HERE--ANYTHING AT ALL--YOU JUST LET ME KNOW.
YOU TELL WONDER WOMAN THAT SHE HAS FRIENDS AT C.A.P., ALL RIGHT?
I WILL, ABSOLUTELY.
THANKS, RONNIE. THANKS SO MUCH.
DON'T WORRY ABOUT IT.

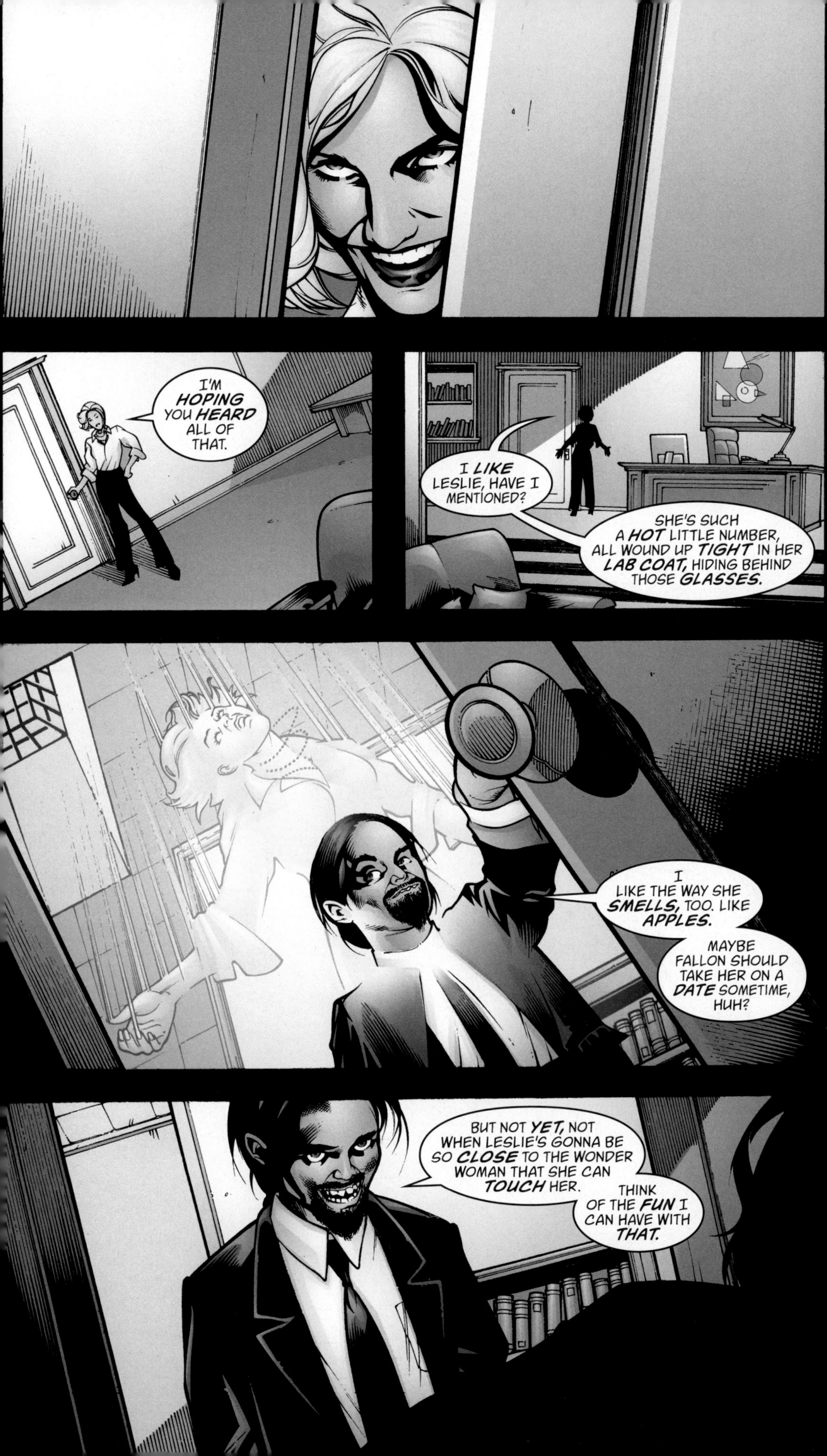
I'M HOPING YOU HEARD ALL OF THAT.
I LIKE LESLIE, HAVE I MENTIONED?
SHE'S SUCH A HOT LITTLE NUMBER, ALL WOUND UP TIGHT IN HER LAB COAT, HIDING BEHIND THOSE GLASSES.
I LIKE THE WAY SHE SMELLS, TOO. LIKE APPLES.
MAYBE FALLON SHOULD TAKE HER ON A DATE SOMETIME, HUH?
BUT NOT YET, NOT WHEN LESLIE'S GONNA BE SO CLOSE TO THE WONDER WOMAN THAT SHE CAN TOUCH HER.
THINK OF THE FUN I CAN HAVE WITH THAT.

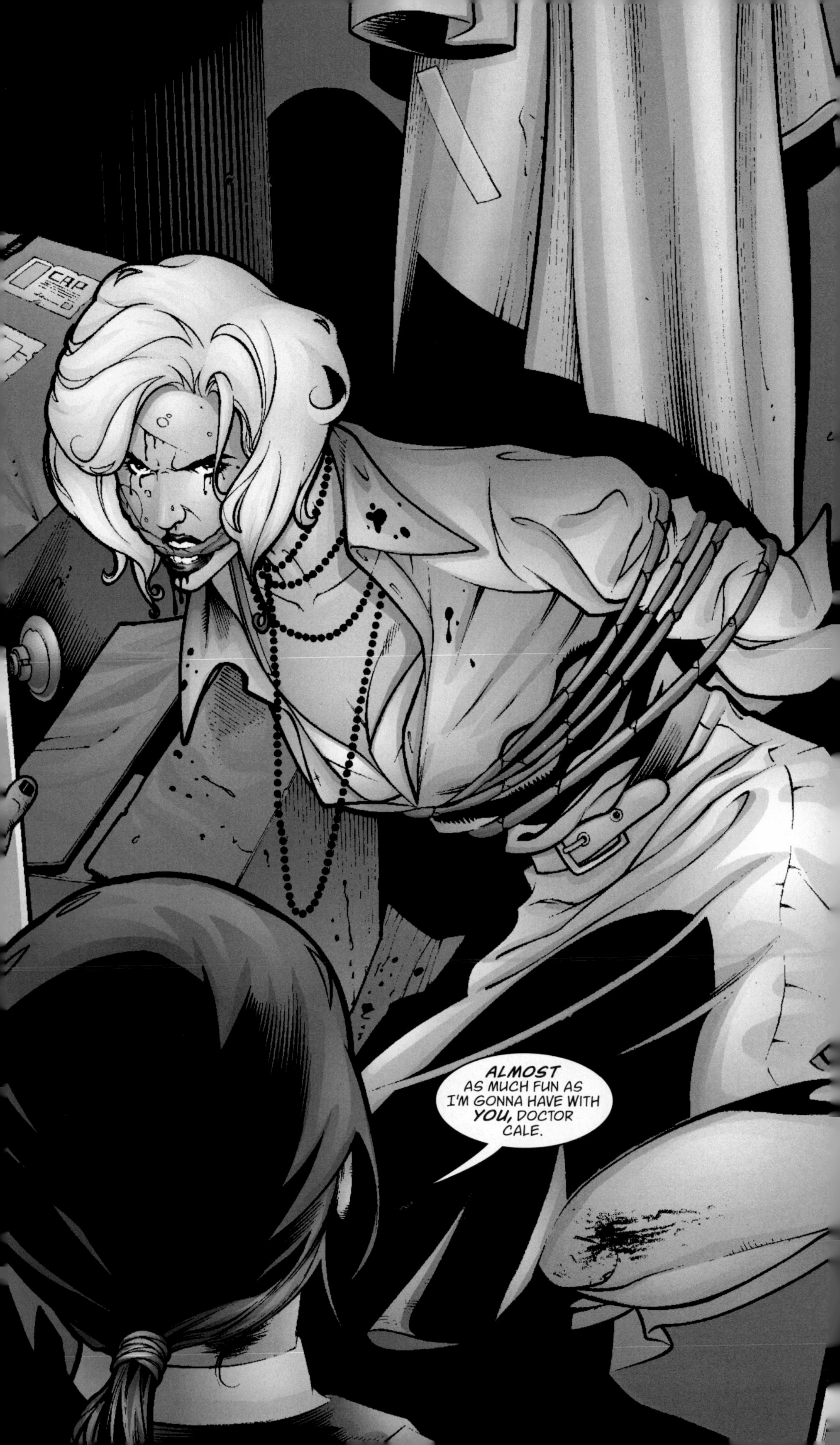
ALMOST AS MUCH FUN AS I'M GONNA HAVE WITH YOU, DOCTOR CALE.

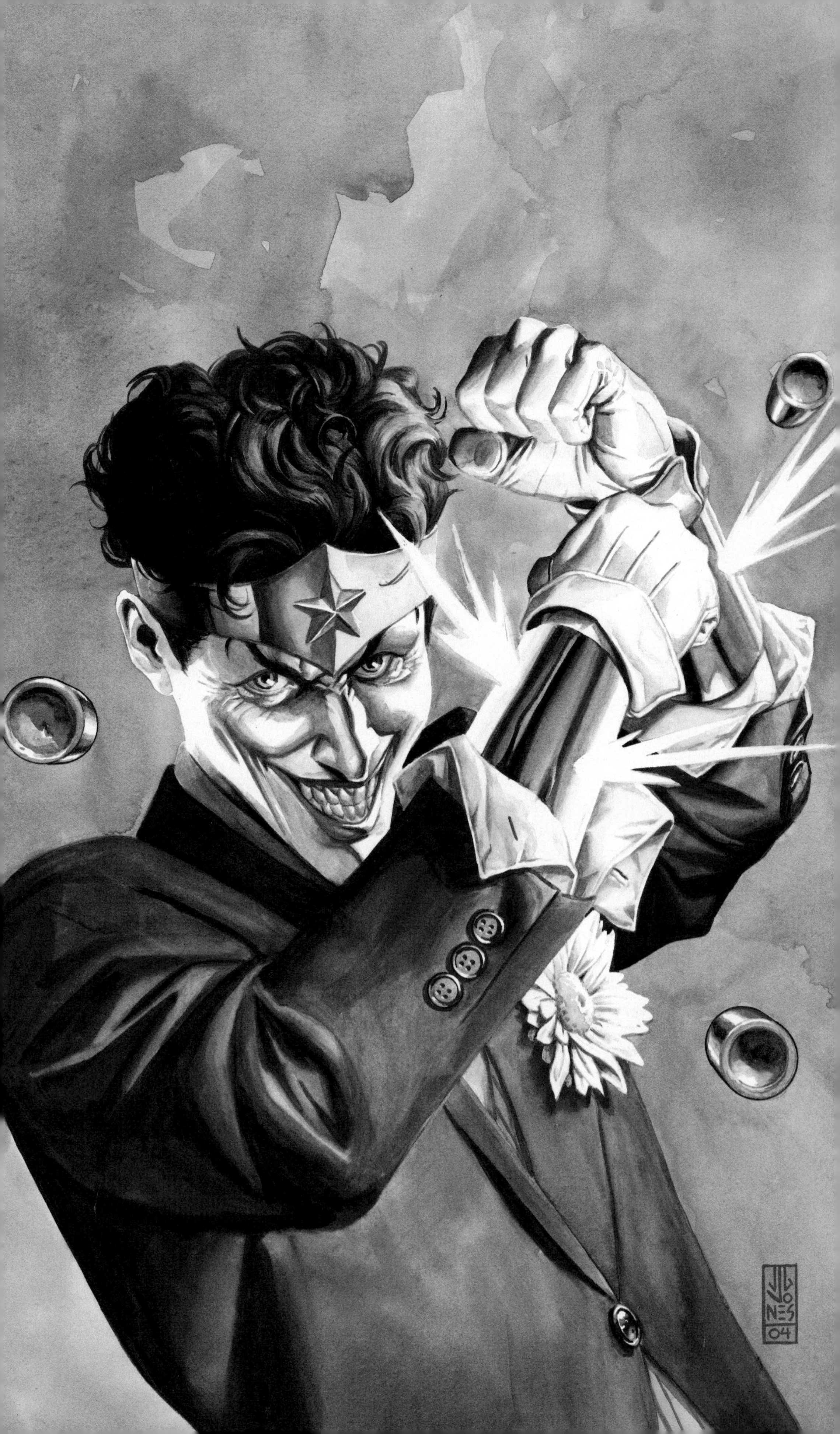
JG JONES 04

“BITTER PILLS: PART THREE”

Drew Johnson – *pencils*
Ray Snyder – *inks*
Richard Horie, Tanya Horie - *colors*
J.G. Jones – *cover art*

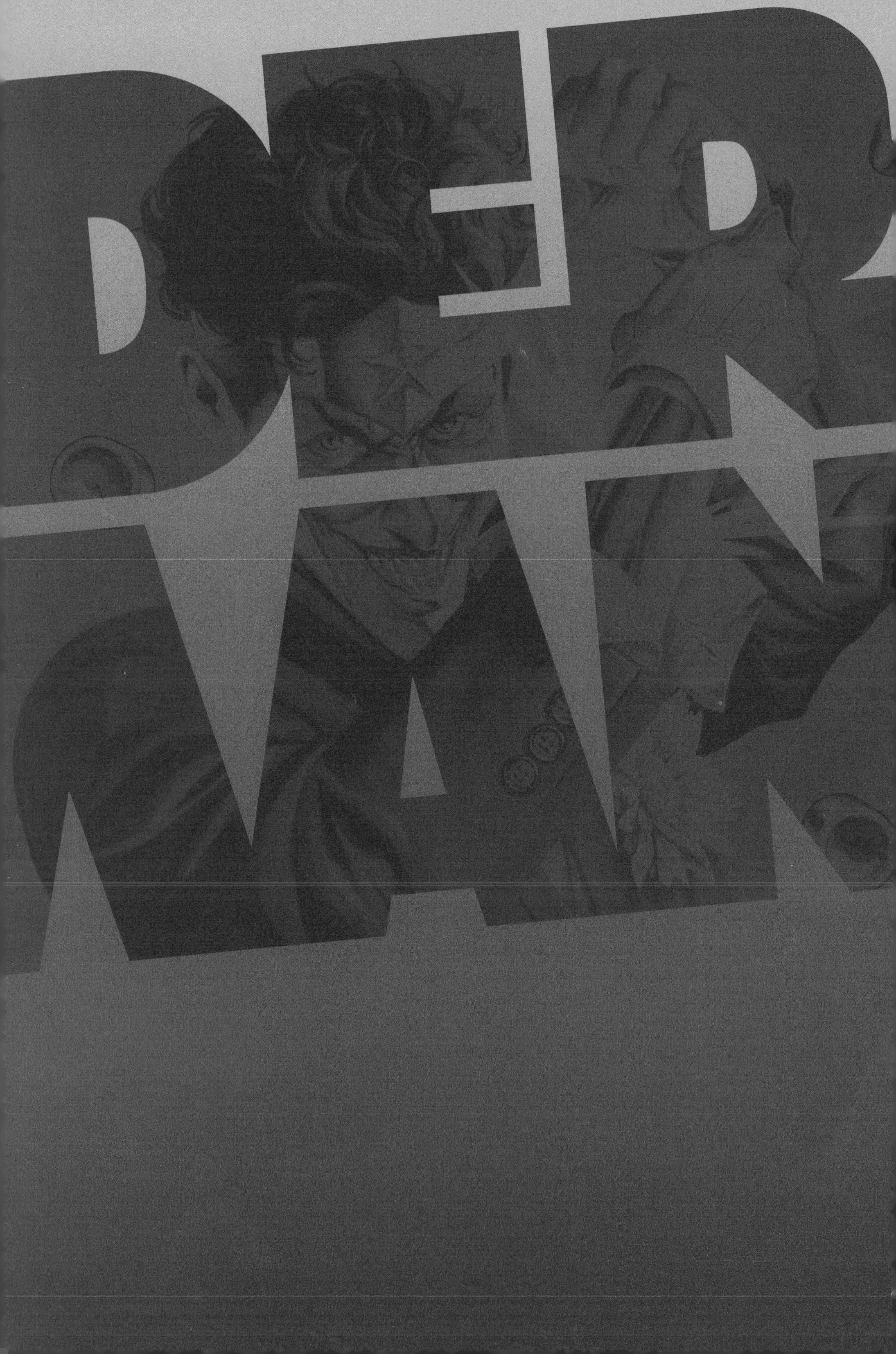

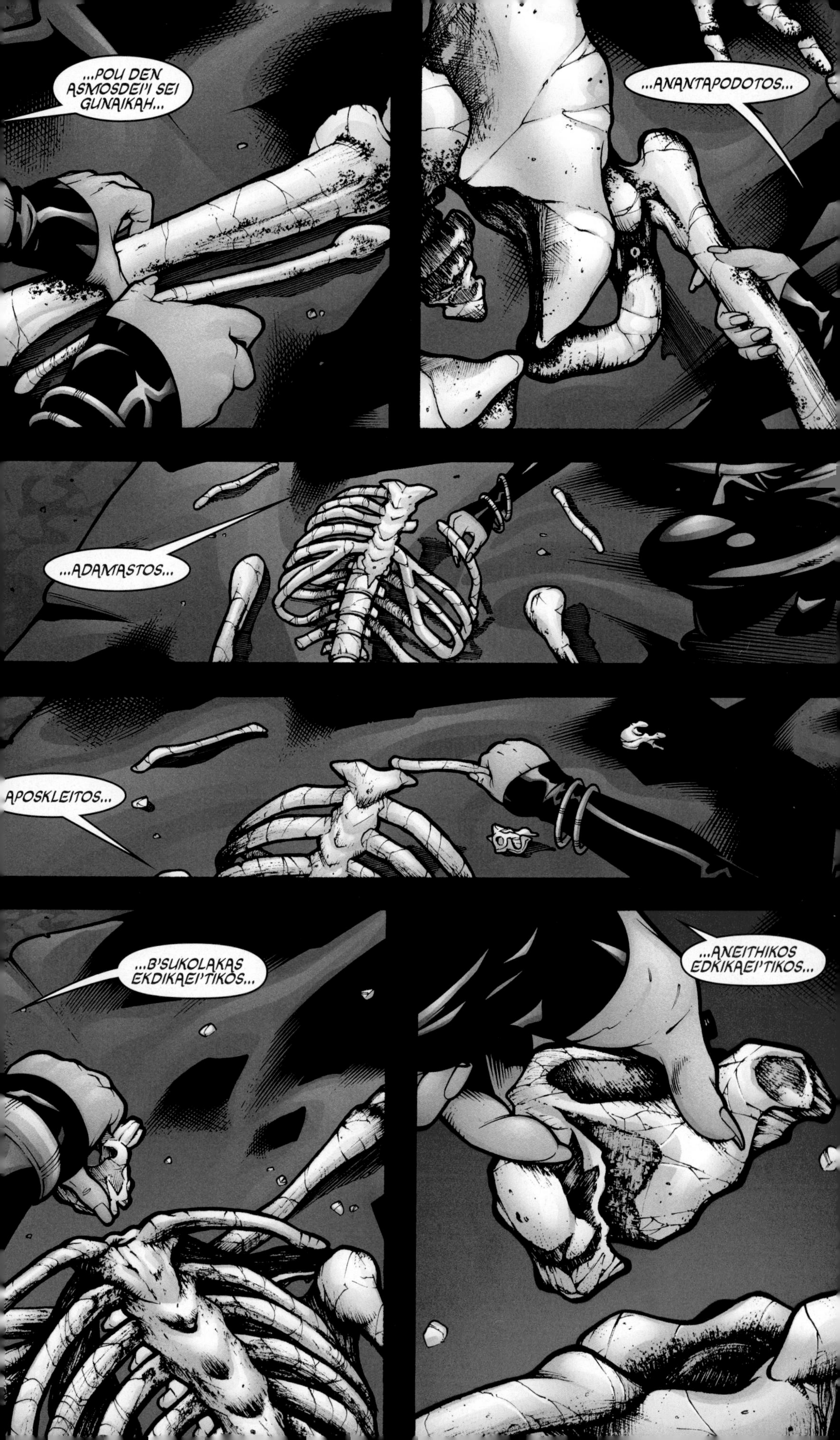
...POU DEN ASMOSDEI'I SEI GUNAIKAH...
...ANANTAPODOTOS...
...ADAMASTOS...
APOSKLEITOS...
...B'SUKOLAKAS EKDIKAEI'TIKOS...
...ANEITHIKOS EDKIKAEI'TIKOS...

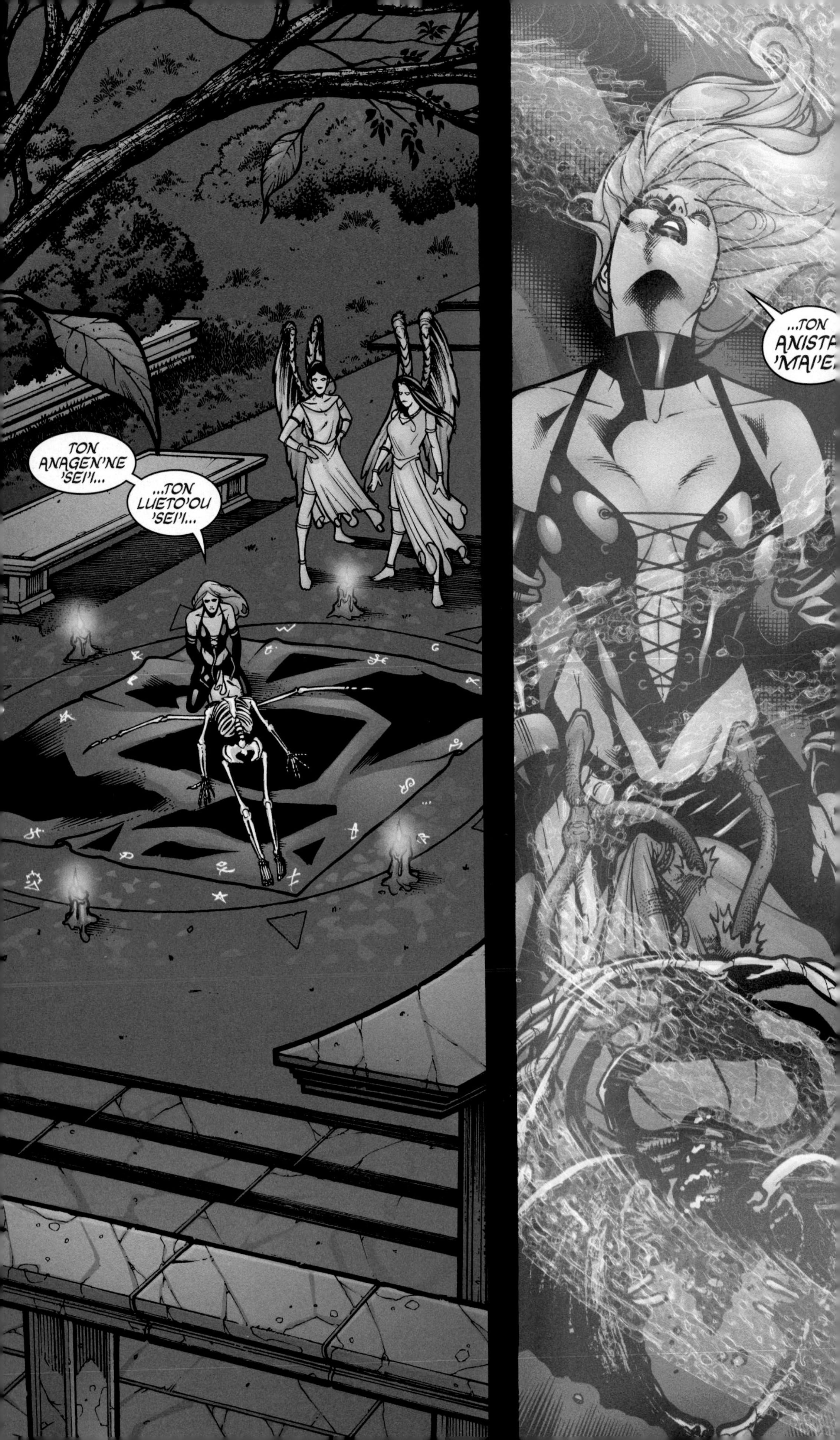
TON ANAGEN'NE 'SEI'I...
...TON LUETO'OU 'SEI'I...
...TON ANIST
'MAI'E

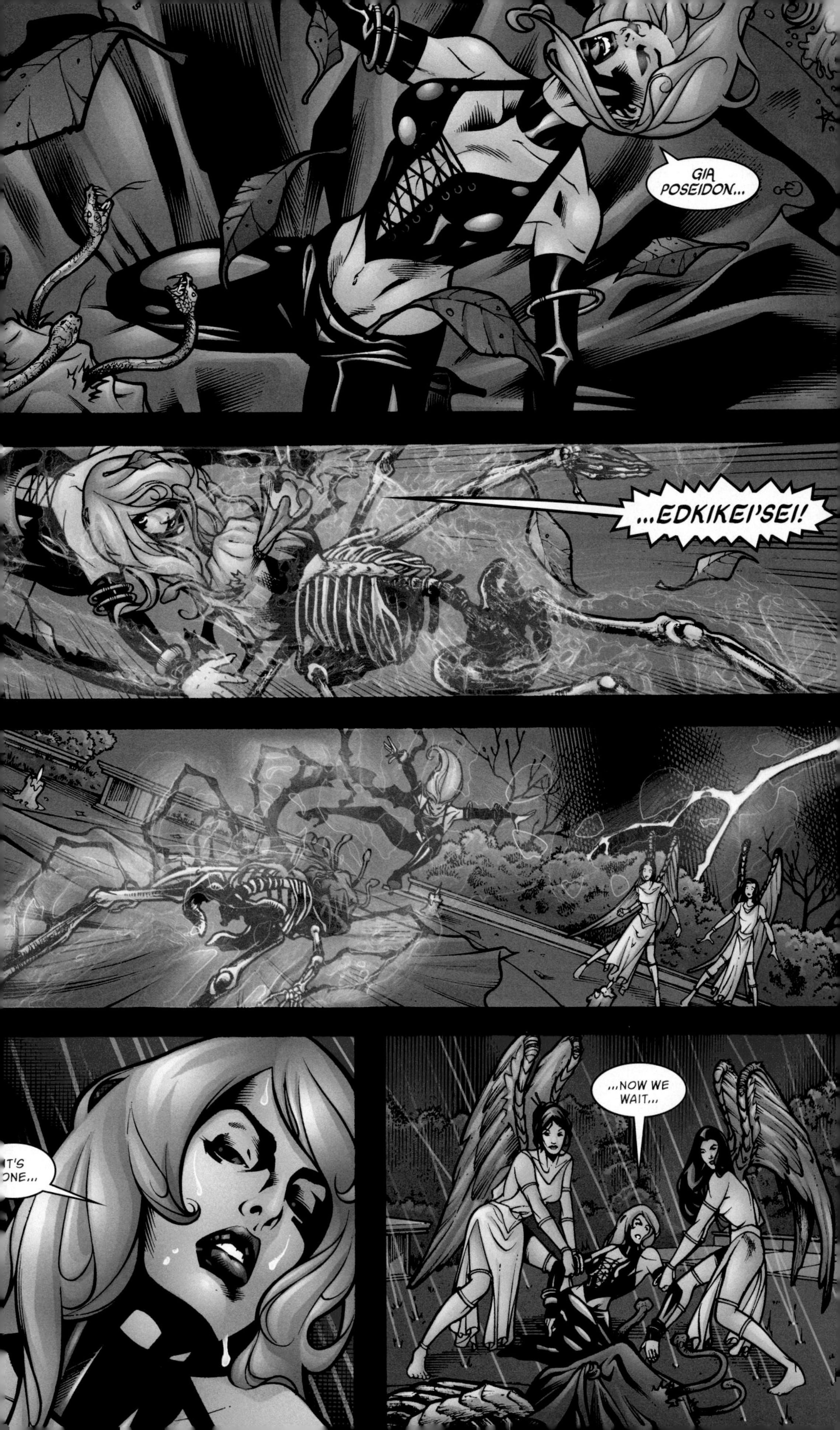
GIA POSEIDON...
...EDKIKEI'SEI!
IT'S ONE...
...NOW WE WAIT...

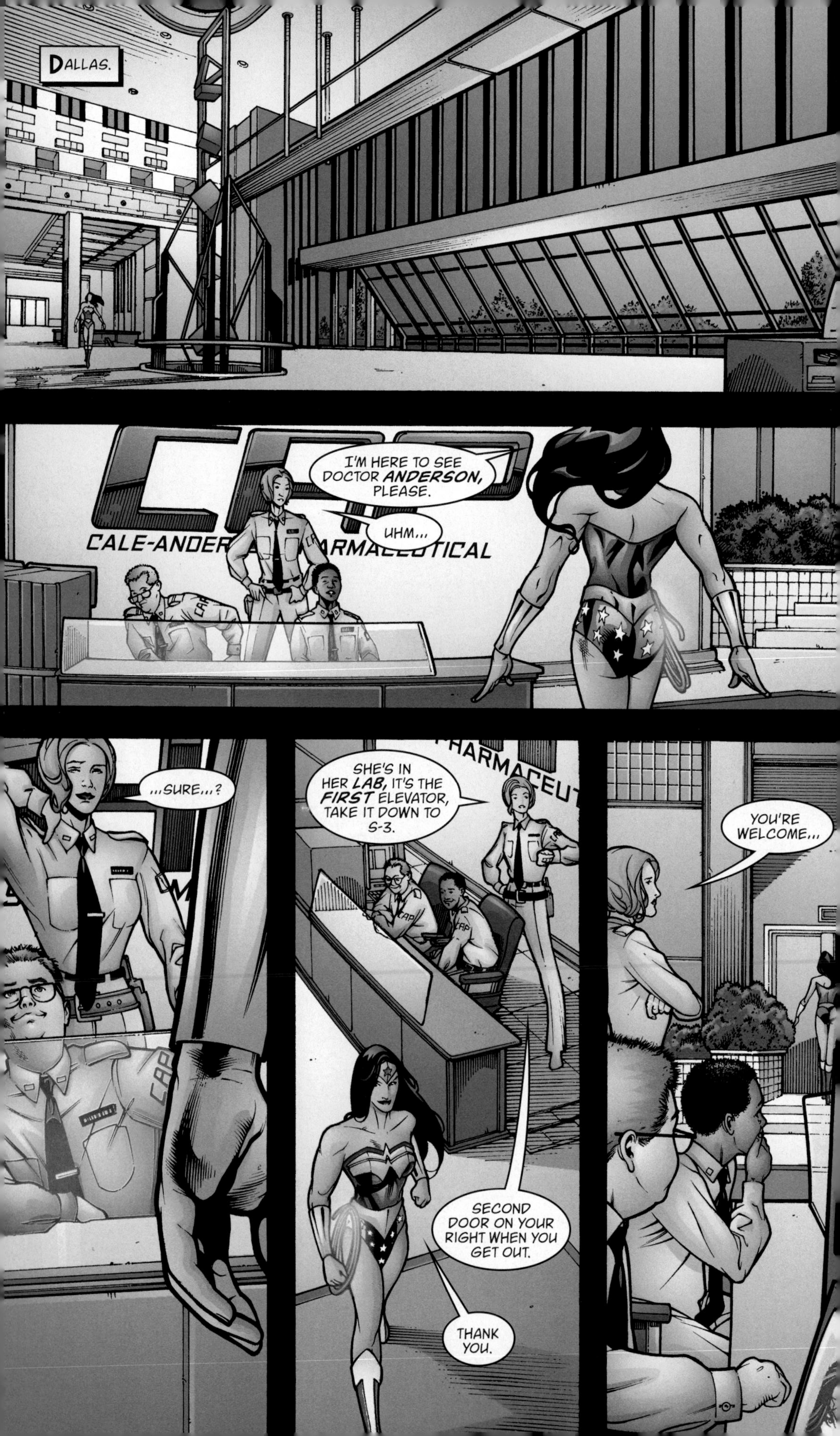
DALLAS.
I'M HERE TO SEE DOCTOR ANDERSON, PLEASE.
UHM...
CALE-ANDER ARMACEUTICAL
...SURE...?
SHE'S IN HER LAB, IT'S THE FIRST ELEVATOR, TAKE IT DOWN TO S-3.
SECOND DOOR ON YOUR RIGHT WHEN YOU GET OUT.
THANK YOU.
YOU'RE WELCOME...

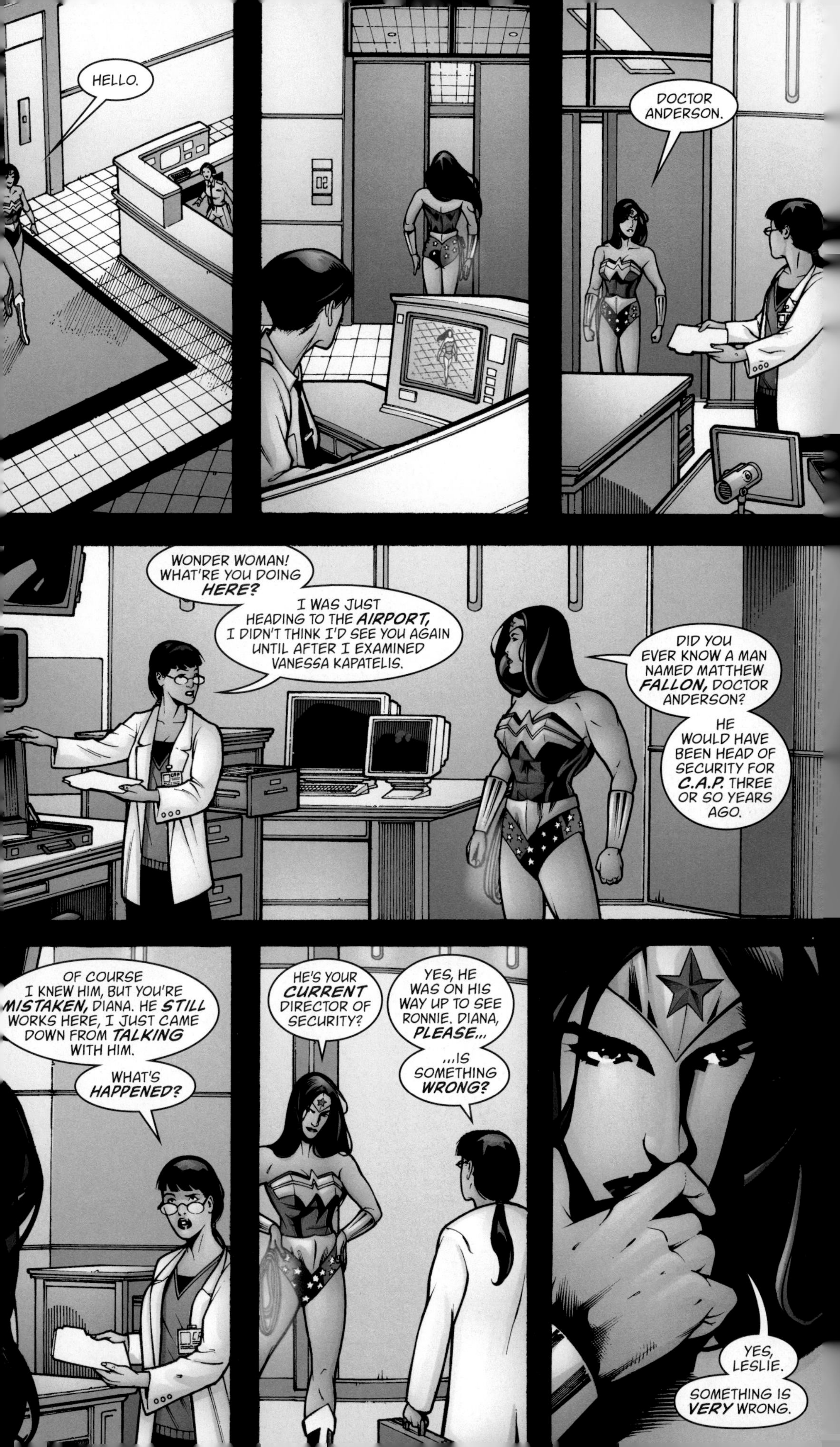
HELLO.
DOCTOR ANDERSON.
WONDER WOMAN! WHAT'RE YOU DOING HERE?
I WAS JUST HEADING TO THE AIRPORT, I DIDN'T THINK I'D SEE YOU AGAIN UNTIL AFTER I EXAMINED VANESSA KAPATELIS.
DID YOU EVER KNOW A MAN NAMED MATTHEW FALLON, DOCTOR ANDERSON?
HE WOULD HAVE BEEN HEAD OF SECURITY FOR C.A.P. THREE OR SO YEARS AGO.
OF COURSE I KNEW HIM, BUT YOU'RE MISTAKEN, DIANA. HE STILL WORKS HERE, I JUST CAME DOWN FROM TALKING WITH HIM.
WHAT'S HAPPENED?
HE'S YOUR CURRENT DIRECTOR OF SECURITY?
YES, HE WAS ON HIS WAY UP TO SEE RONNIE. DIANA, PLEASE...
...IS SOMETHING WRONG?
YES, LESLIE.
SOMETHING IS VERY WRONG.

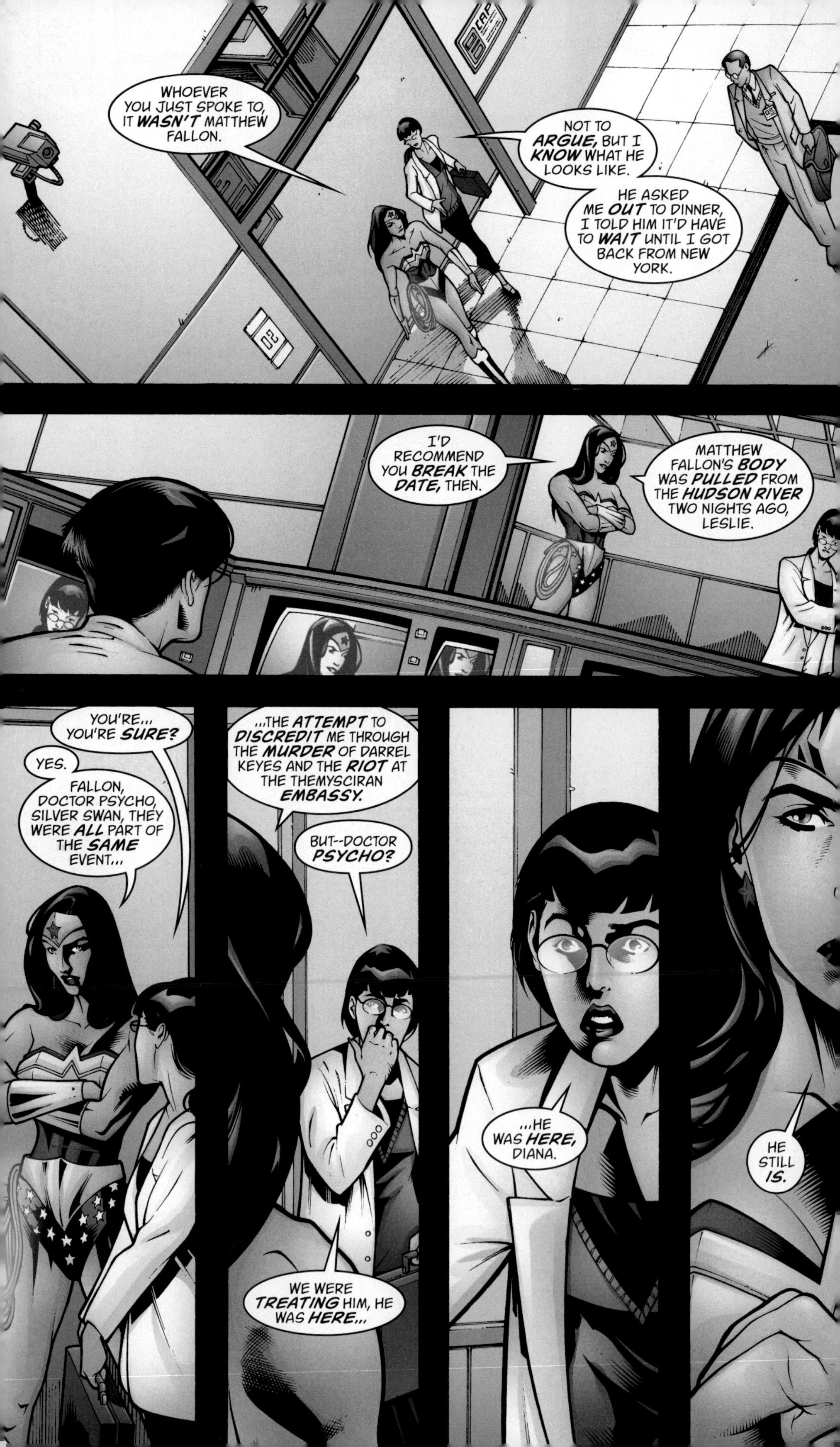
WHOEVER YOU JUST SPOKE TO, IT WASN'T MATTHEW FALLON.
NOT TO ARGUE, BUT I KNOW WHAT HE LOOKS LIKE.
HE ASKED ME OUT TO DINNER, I TOLD HIM IT'D HAVE TO WAIT UNTIL I GOT BACK FROM NEW YORK.
I'D RECOMMEND YOU BREAK THE DATE, THEN.
MATTHEW FALLON'S BODY WAS PULLED FROM THE HUDSON RIVER TWO NIGHTS AGO, LESLIE.
YOU'RE... YOU'RE SURE?
YES.
FALLON, DOCTOR PSYCHO, SILVER SWAN, THEY WERE ALL PART OF THE SAME EVENT...
...THE ATTEMPT TO DISCREDIT ME THROUGH THE MURDER OF DARREL KEYES AND THE RIOT AT THE THEMYSCIRAN EMBASSY.
BUT--DOCTOR PSYCHO?
WE WERE TREATING HIM, HE WAS HERE...
...HE WAS HERE, DIANA.
HE STILL IS.

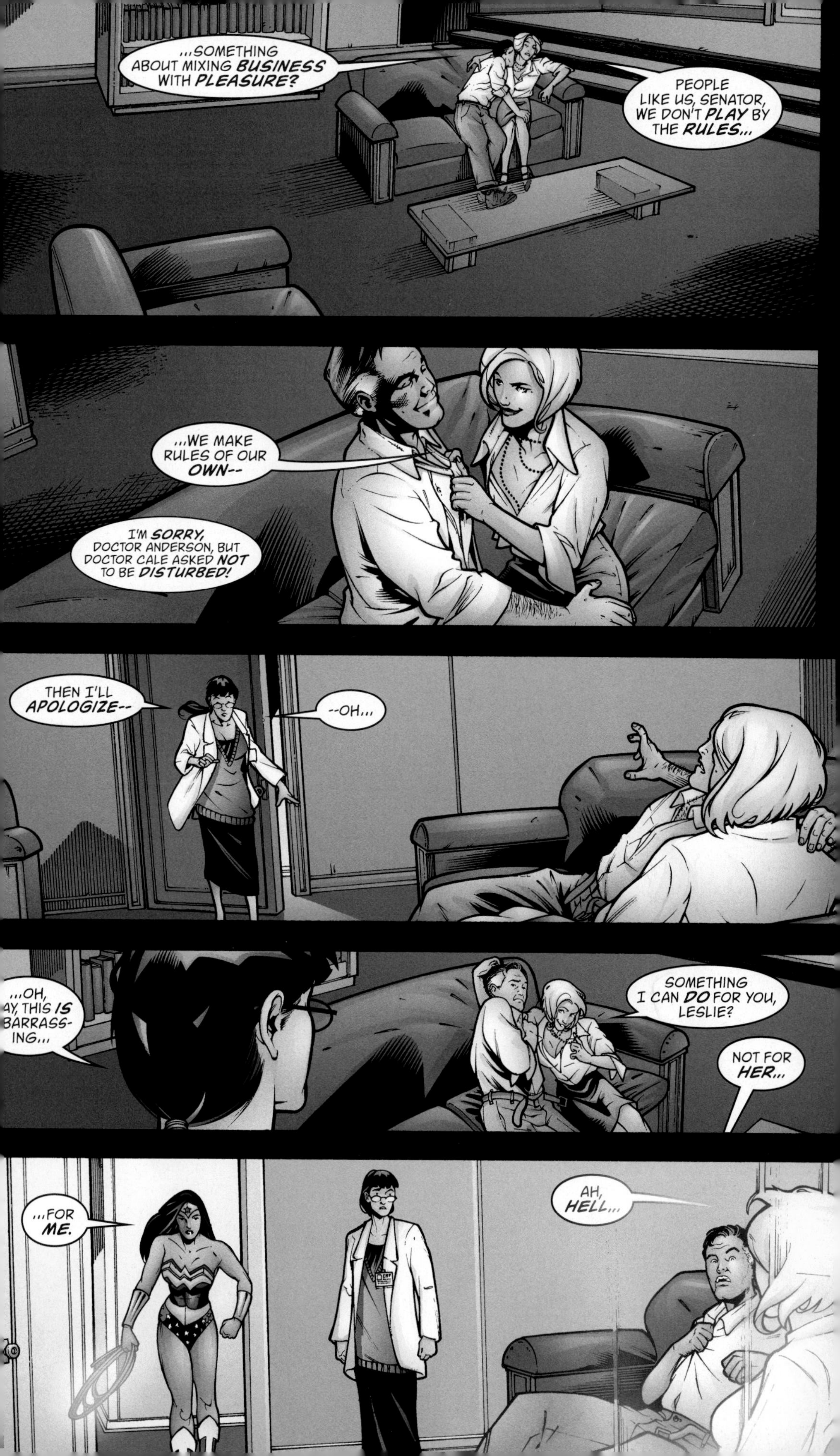

...SOMETHING ABOUT MIXING BUSINESS WITH PLEASURE?
PEOPLE LIKE US, SENATOR, WE DON'T PLAY BY THE RULES...
...WE MAKE RULES OF OUR OWN--
I'M SORRY, DOCTOR ANDERSON, BUT DOCTOR CALE ASKED NOT TO BE DISTURBED!
THEN I'LL APOLOGIZE--
--OH...
...OH, AY, THIS IS BARRASS-ING...
SOMETHING I CAN DO FOR YOU, LESLIE?
NOT FOR HER...
...FOR ME.
AH, HELL...

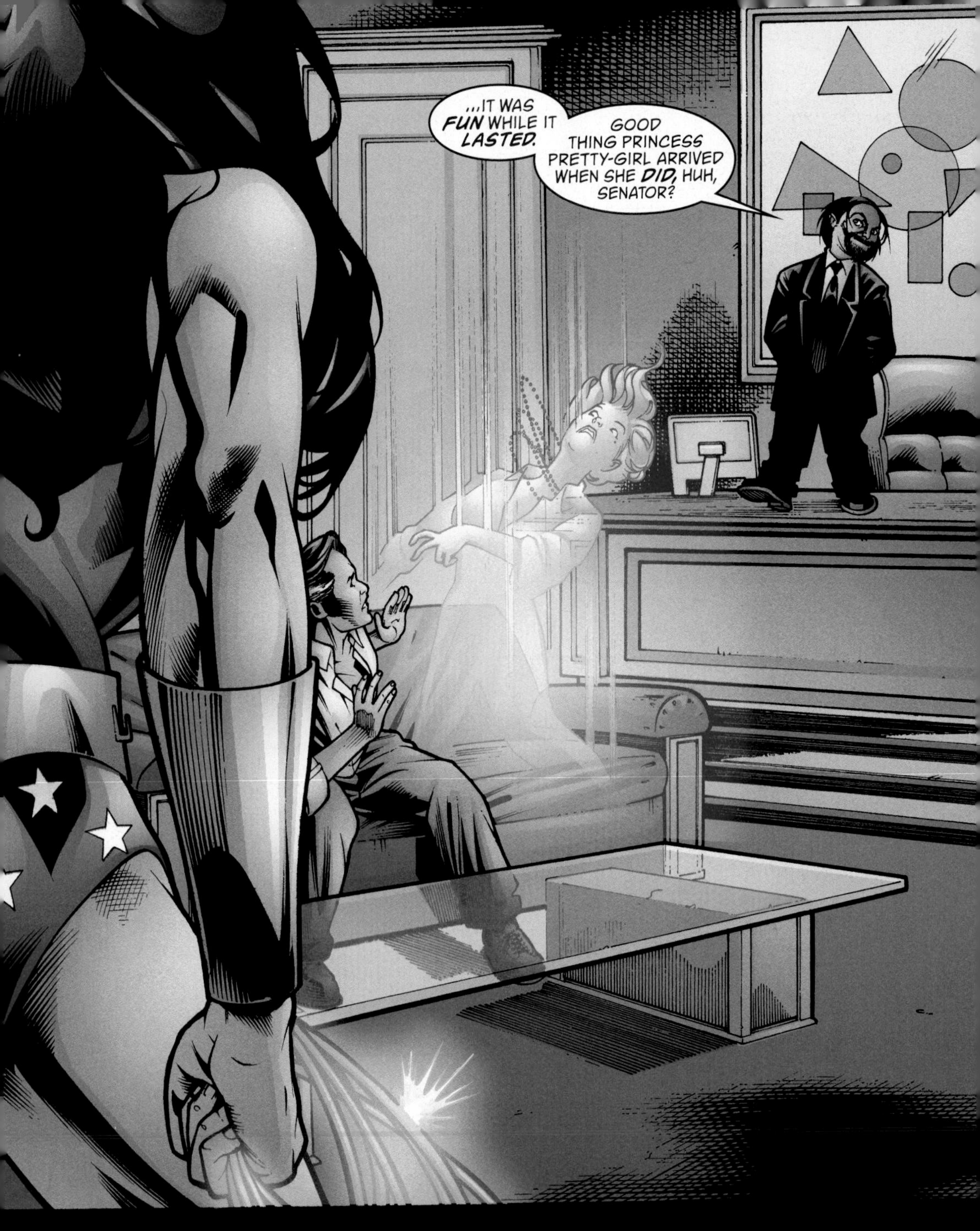
...IT WAS FUN WHILE IT LASTED.
GOOD THING PRINCESS PRETTY-GIRL ARRIVED WHEN SHE DID, HUH, SENATOR?

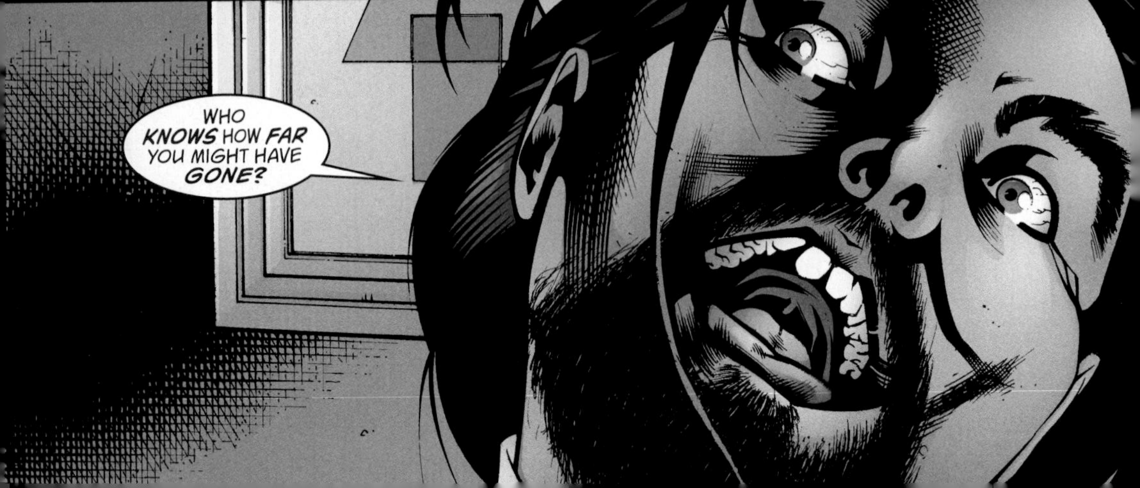
WHO KNOWS HOW FAR YOU MIGHT HAVE GONE?

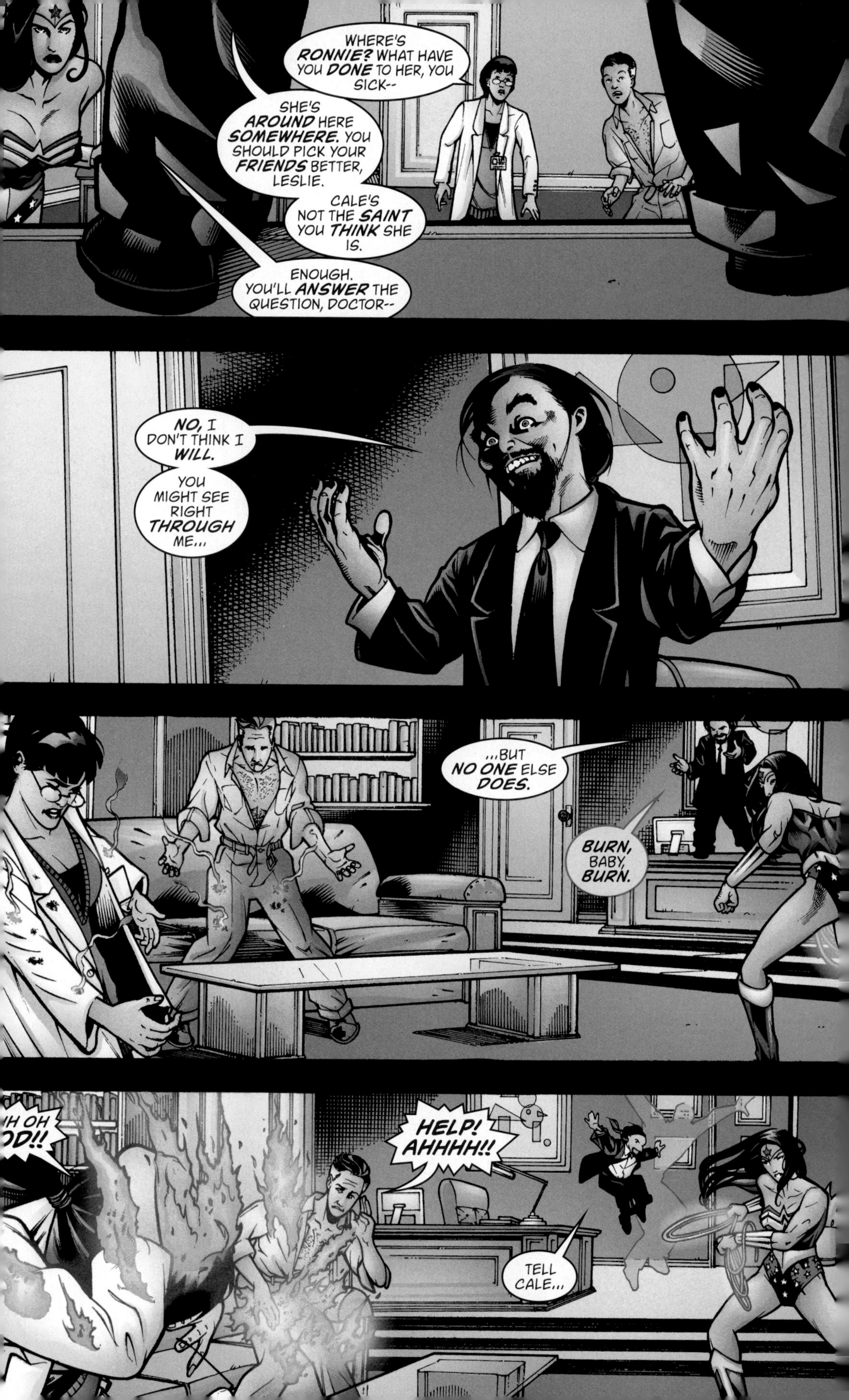
WHERE'S RONNIE? WHAT HAVE YOU DONE TO HER, YOU SICK--
SHE'S AROUND HERE SOMEWHERE. YOU SHOULD PICK YOUR FRIENDS BETTER, LESLIE.
CALE'S NOT THE SAINT YOU THINK SHE IS.
ENOUGH. YOU'LL ANSWER THE QUESTION, DOCTOR--
NO, I DON'T THINK I WILL.
YOU MIGHT SEE RIGHT THROUGH ME...
...BUT NO ONE ELSE DOES.
BURN, BABY, BURN.
HELP! AHHHH!!
TELL CALE...

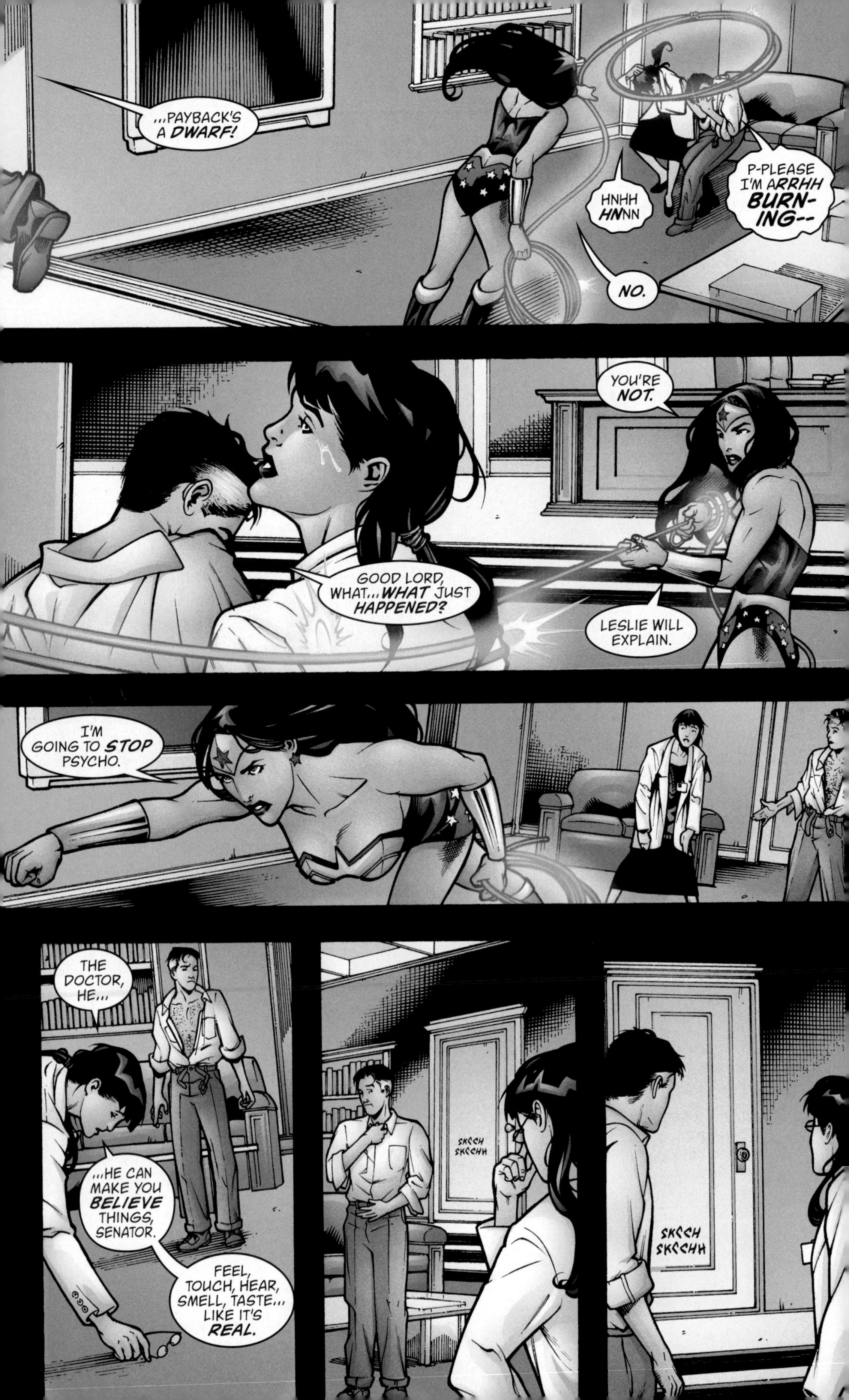
...PAYBACK'S A DWARF!
HNHH HNNN
P-PLEASE I'M ARRHH BURNING--
NO.
YOU'RE NOT.
GOOD LORD, WHAT... WHAT JUST HAPPENED?
LESLIE WILL EXPLAIN.
I'M GOING TO STOP PSYCHO.
THE DOCTOR, HE...
...HE CAN MAKE YOU BELIEVE THINGS, SENATOR.
FEEL, TOUCH, HEAR, SMELL, TASTE... LIKE IT'S REAL.
SKCCH SKCCHH
SKCCH SKCCHH

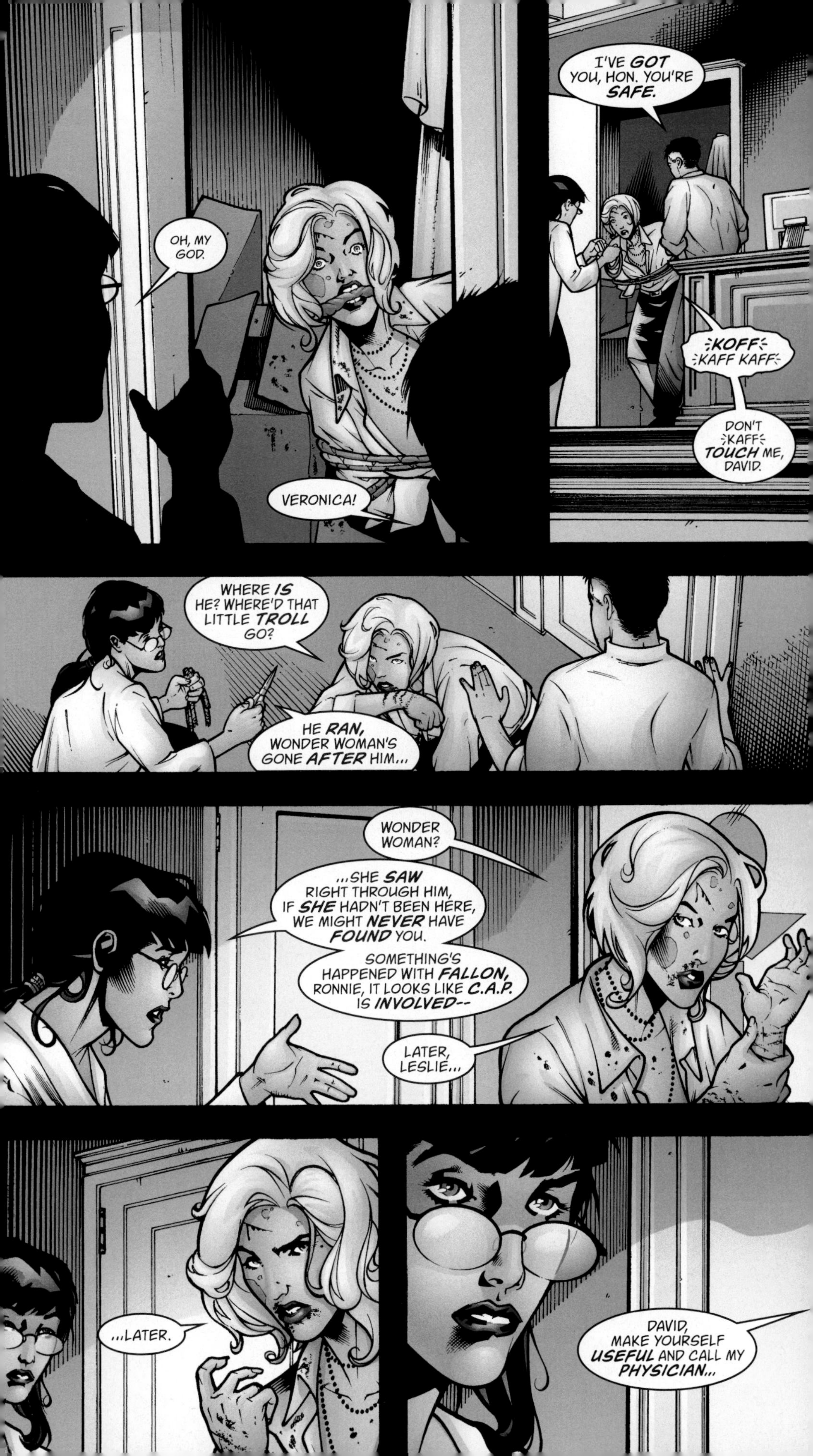
OH, MY GOD.
VERONICA!
I'VE GOT YOU, HON. YOU'RE SAFE.
KOFF KAFF KAFF
DON'T KAFF TOUCH ME, DAVID.
WHERE IS HE? WHERE'D THAT LITTLE TROLL GO?
HE RAN, WONDER WOMAN'S GONE AFTER HIM...
WONDER WOMAN?
...SHE SAW RIGHT THROUGH HIM, IF SHE HADN'T BEEN HERE, WE MIGHT NEVER HAVE FOUND YOU.
SOMETHING'S HAPPENED WITH FALLON, RONNIE, IT LOOKS LIKE C.A.P. IS INVOLVED--
LATER, LESLIE...
...LATER.
DAVID, MAKE YOURSELF USEFUL AND CALL MY PHYSICIAN...

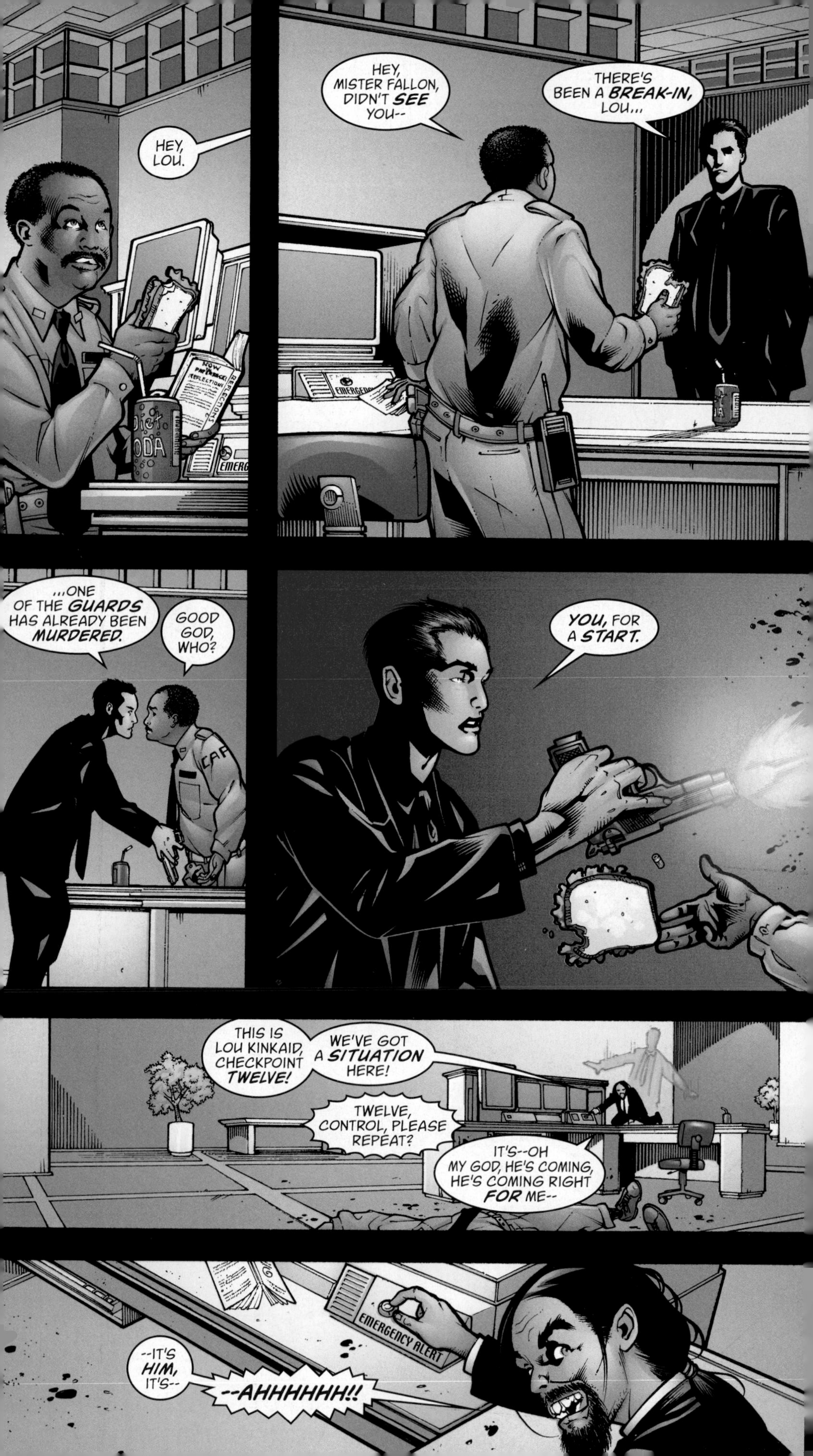
HEY, LOU.
HEY, MISTER FALLON, DIDN'T SEE YOU--
THERE'S BEEN A BREAK-IN, LOU...
EMERGENCY
...ONE OF THE GUARDS HAS ALREADY BEEN MURDERED.
GOOD GOD, WHO?
YOU, FOR A START.
THIS IS LOU KINKAID, CHECKPOINT TWELVE!
WE'VE GOT A SITUATION HERE!
TWELVE, CONTROL, PLEASE REPEAT?
IT'S--OH MY GOD, HE'S COMING, HE'S COMING RIGHT FOR ME--
EMERGENCY ALERT
--IT'S HIM, IT'S--
--AHHHHHH!!

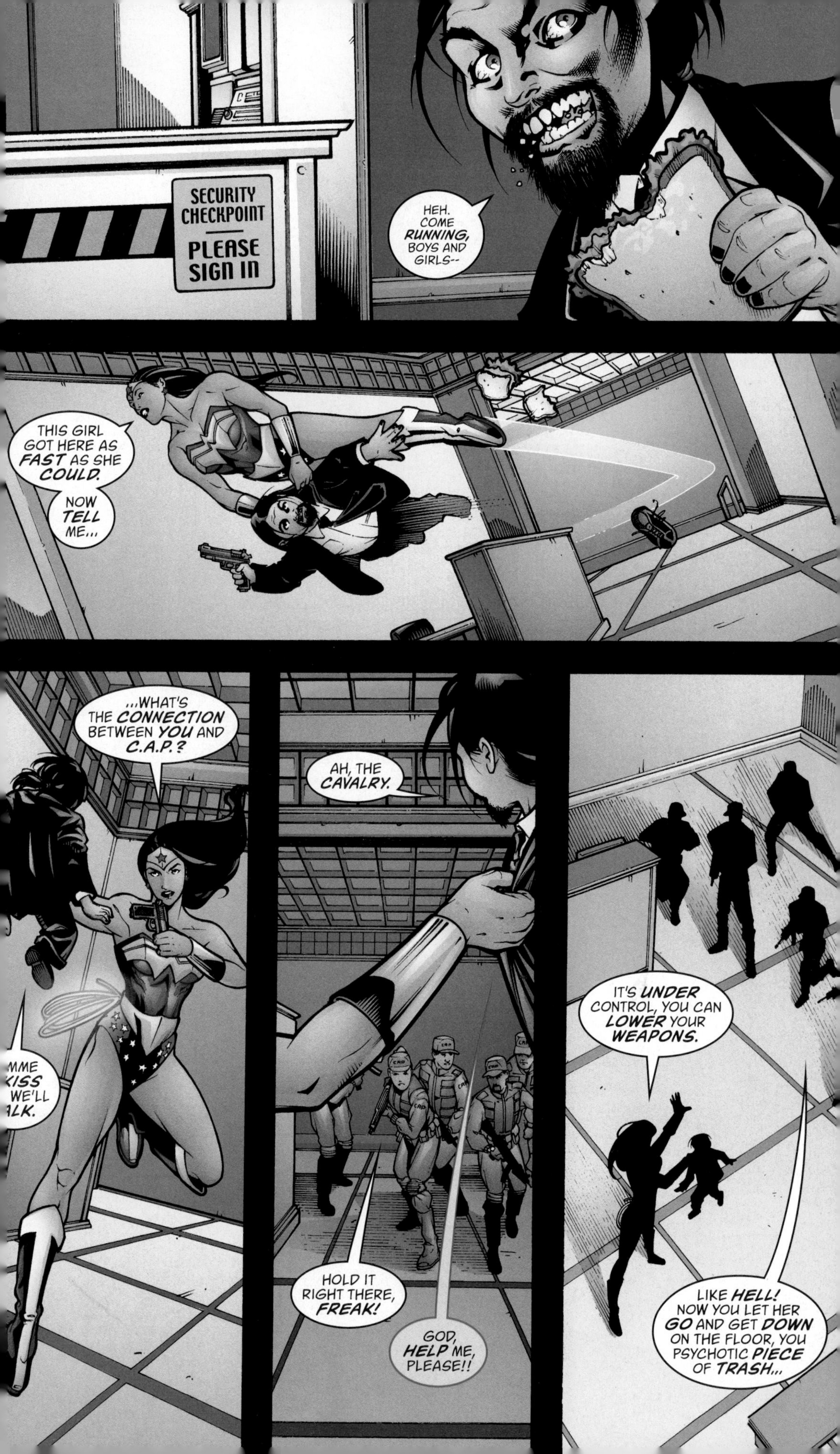
SECURITY CHECKPOINT
PLEASE SIGN IN
HEH. COME RUNNING, BOYS AND GIRLS--
THIS GIRL GOT HERE AS FAST AS SHE COULD.
NOW TELL ME...
...WHAT'S THE CONNECTION BETWEEN YOU AND C.A.P.?
MME KISS WE'LL ALK.
AH, THE CAVALRY.
HOLD IT RIGHT THERE, FREAK!
GOD, HELP ME, PLEASE!!
IT'S UNDER CONTROL, YOU CAN LOWER YOUR WEAPONS.
LIKE HELL! NOW YOU LET HER GO AND GET DOWN ON THE FLOOR, YOU PSYCHOTIC PIECE OF TRASH...

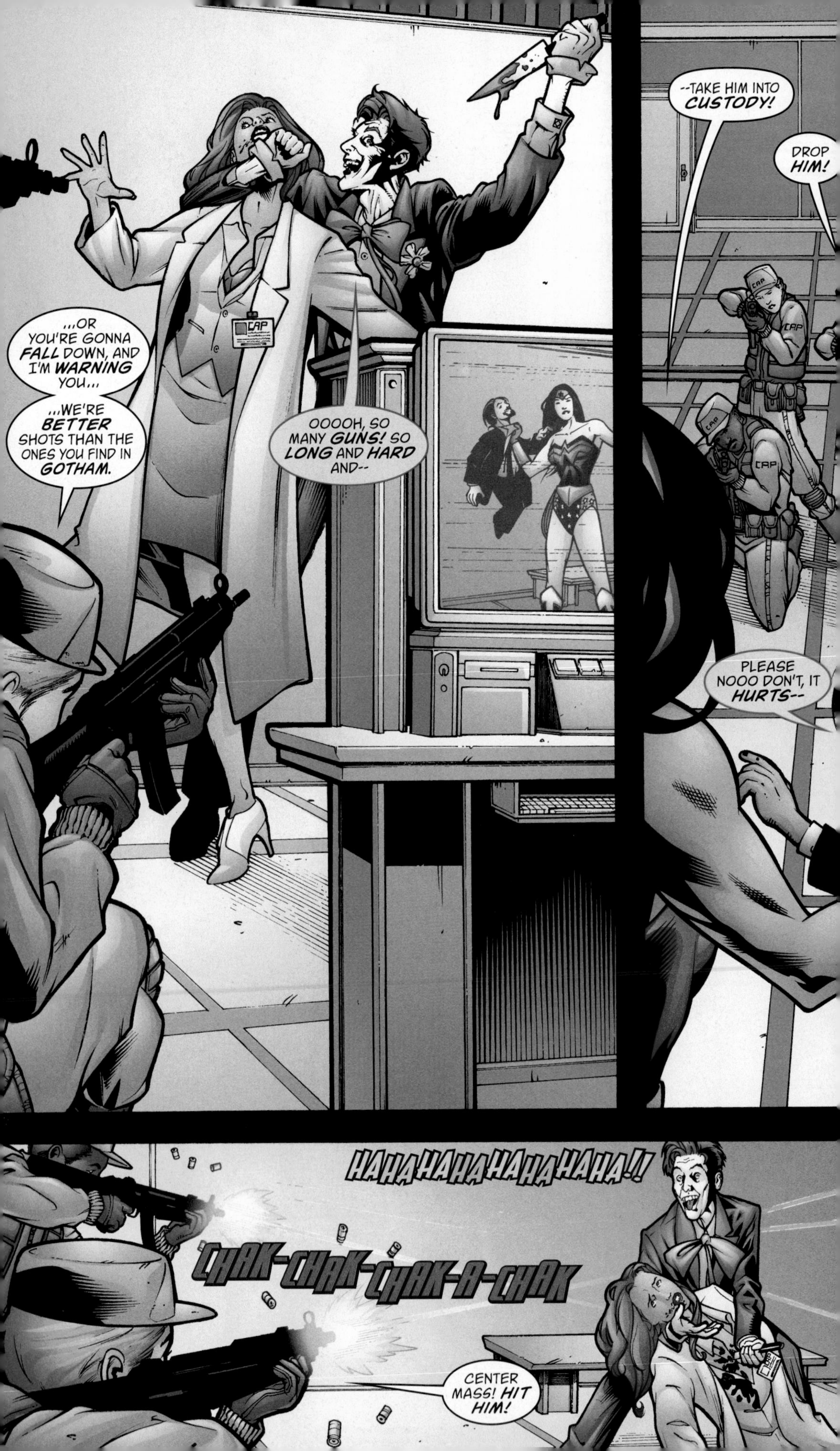
...OR YOU'RE GONNA FALL DOWN, AND I'M WARNING YOU...
...WE'RE BETTER SHOTS THAN THE ONES YOU FIND IN GOTHAM.
OOOOH, SO MANY GUNS! SO LONG AND HARD AND--
--TAKE HIM INTO CUSTODY!
DROP HIM!
PLEASE NOOO DON'T, IT HURTS--
HAHAHAHAHAHAHAHAHAHA!!
CHAK-CHAK-CHAK-A-CHAK
CENTER MASS! HIT HIM!

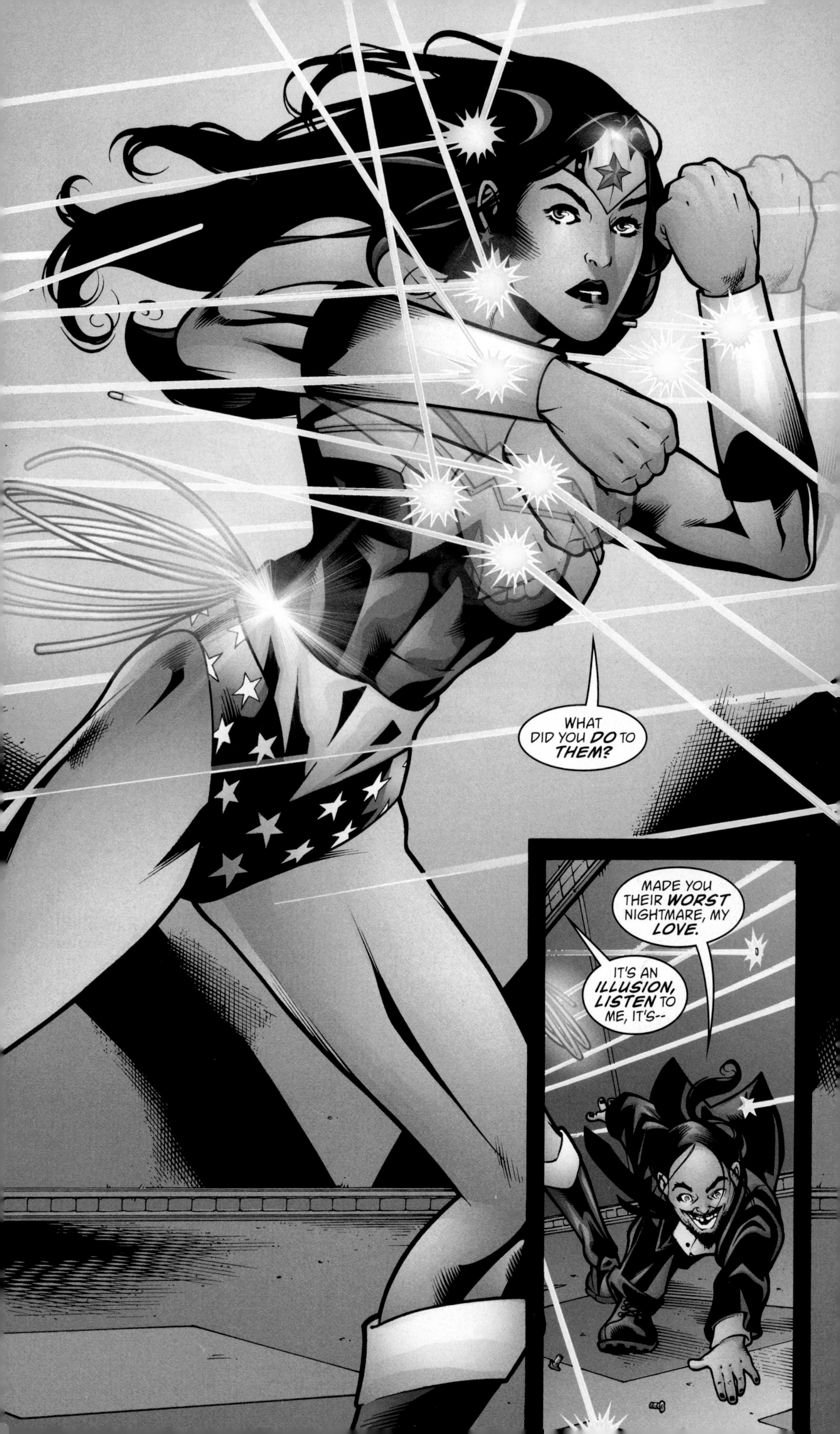
WHAT DID YOU DO TO THEM?
MADE YOU THEIR WORST NIGHTMARE, MY LOVE.
IT'S AN ILLUSION, LISTEN TO ME, IT'S--

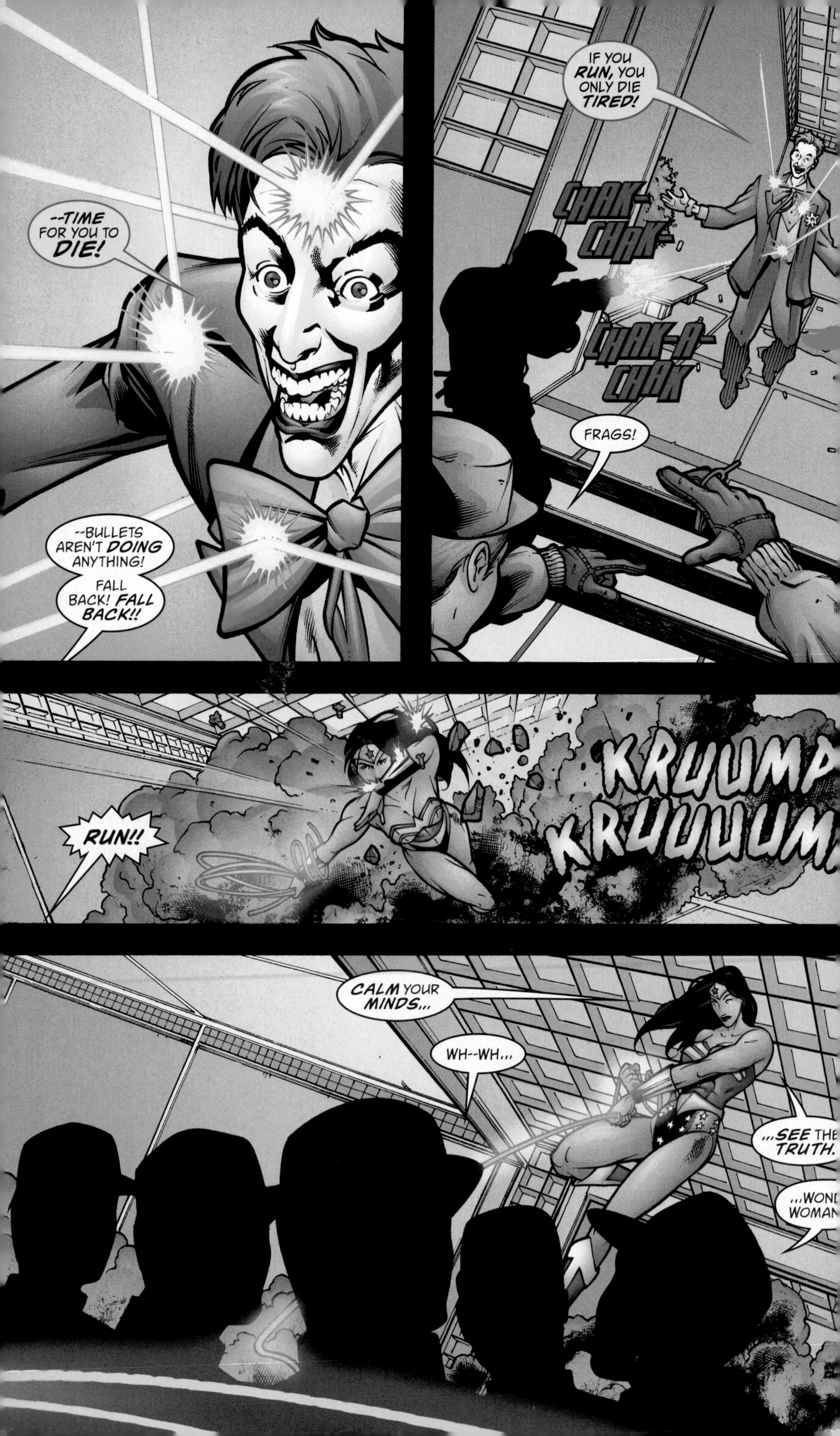
--TIME FOR YOU TO DIE!
--BULLETS AREN'T DOING ANYTHING!
FALL BACK! FALL BACK!!
IF YOU RUN, YOU ONLY DIE TIRED!
CHAK-CHAK
CHAK-A-CHAK
FRAGS!
RUN!!
KRUUMP
KRUUUUUM
CALM YOUR MINDS...
WH--WH...
...SEE THE TRUTH.
...WOND WOMAN

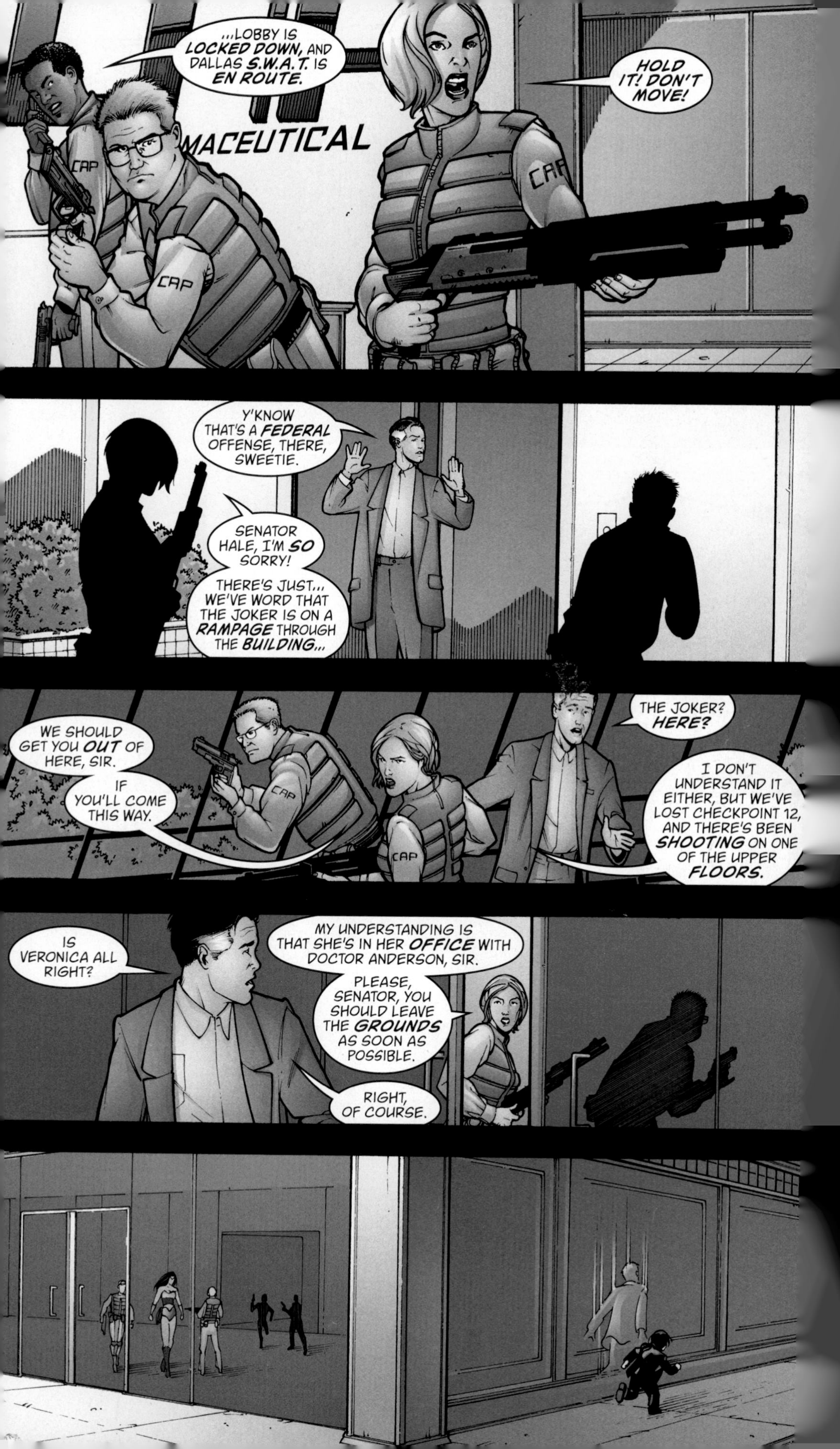
...LOBBY IS LOCKED DOWN, AND DALLAS S.W.A.T. IS EN ROUTE.
HOLD IT! DON'T MOVE!
MACEUTICAL
CAP
CAP
CAP
Y'KNOW THAT'S A FEDERAL OFFENSE, THERE, SWEETIE.
SENATOR HALE, I'M SO SORRY!
THERE'S JUST... WE'VE WORD THAT THE JOKER IS ON A RAMPAGE THROUGH THE BUILDING...
THE JOKER? HERE?
WE SHOULD GET YOU OUT OF HERE, SIR.
IF YOU'LL COME THIS WAY.
I DON'T UNDERSTAND IT EITHER, BUT WE'VE LOST CHECKPOINT 12, AND THERE'S BEEN SHOOTING ON ONE OF THE UPPER FLOORS.
CAP
CAP
IS VERONICA ALL RIGHT?
MY UNDERSTANDING IS THAT SHE'S IN HER OFFICE WITH DOCTOR ANDERSON, SIR.
PLEASE, SENATOR, YOU SHOULD LEAVE THE GROUNDS AS SOON AS POSSIBLE.
RIGHT, OF COURSE.

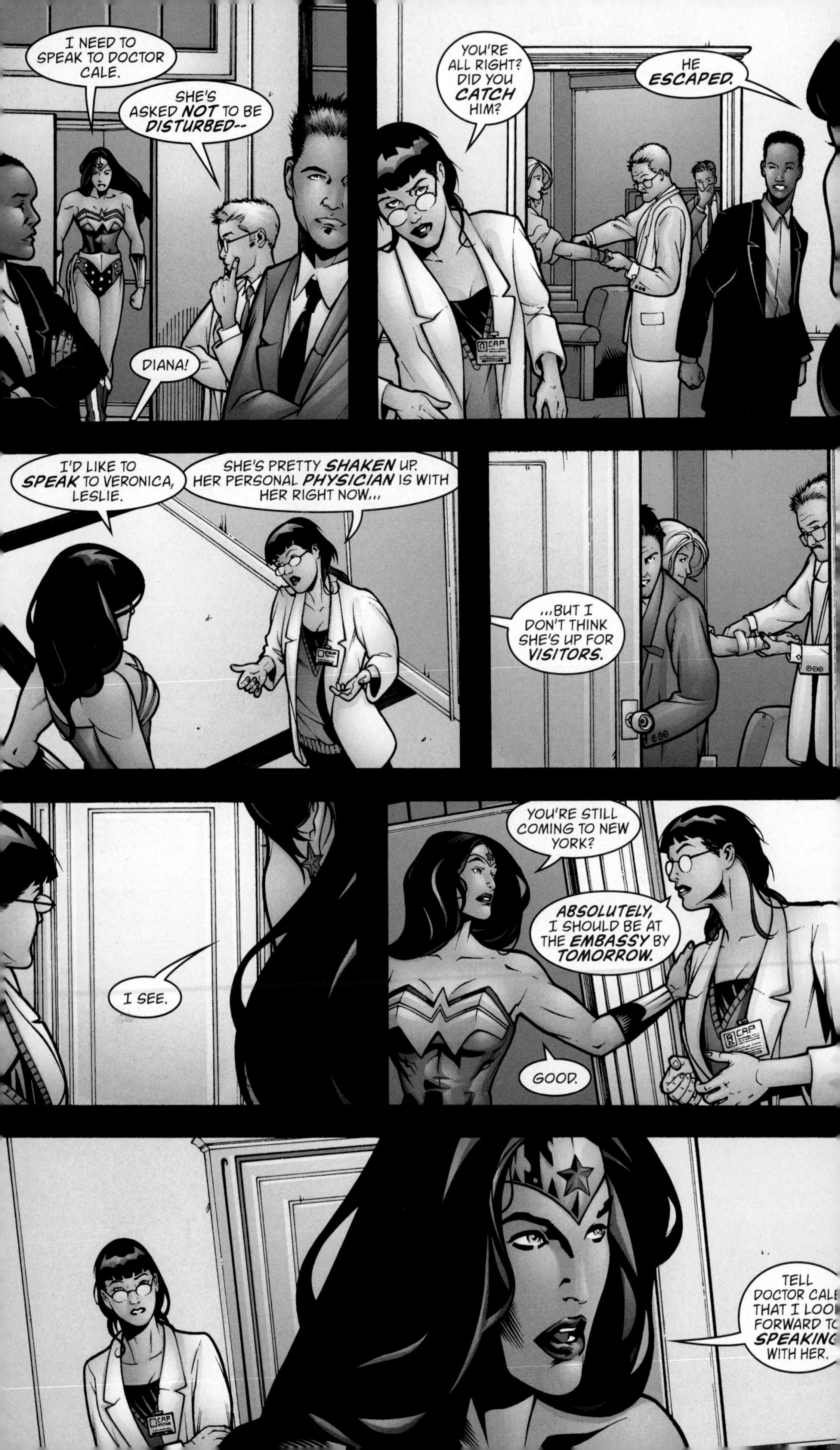
I NEED TO SPEAK TO DOCTOR CALE.
SHE'S ASKED NOT TO BE DISTURBED--
DIANA!
YOU'RE ALL RIGHT? DID YOU CATCH HIM?
HE ESCAPED.
I'D LIKE TO SPEAK TO VERONICA, LESLIE.
SHE'S PRETTY SHAKEN UP. HER PERSONAL PHYSICIAN IS WITH HER RIGHT NOW...
...BUT I DON'T THINK SHE'S UP FOR VISITORS.
I SEE.
YOU'RE STILL COMING TO NEW YORK?
ABSOLUTELY, I SHOULD BE AT THE EMBASSY BY TOMORROW.
GOOD.
TELL DOCTOR CALE THAT I LOOK FORWARD TO SPEAKING WITH HER.

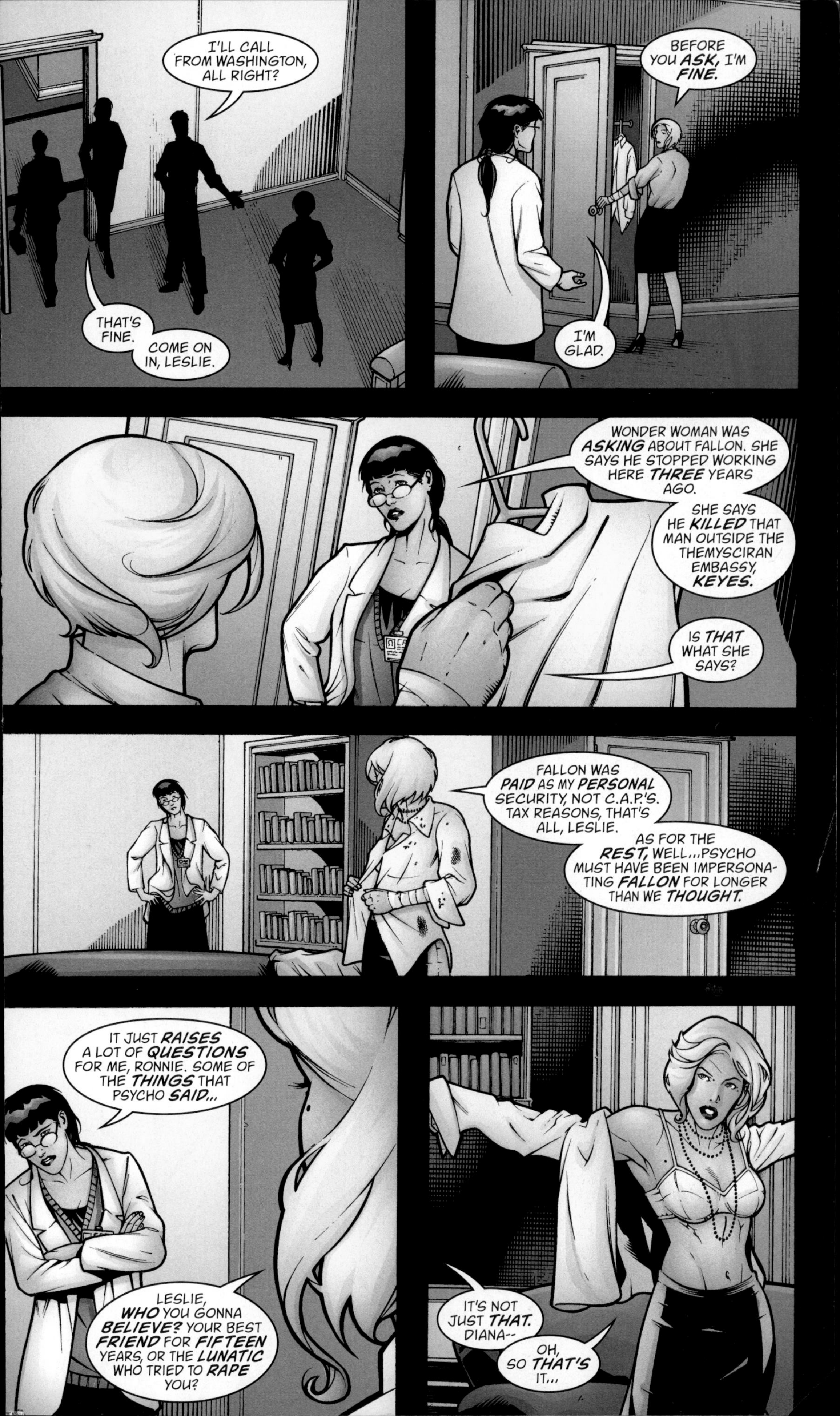
I'LL CALL FROM WASHINGTON, ALL RIGHT?
THAT'S FINE.
COME ON IN, LESLIE.
BEFORE YOU ASK, I'M FINE.
I'M GLAD.
WONDER WOMAN WAS ASKING ABOUT FALLON. SHE SAYS HE STOPPED WORKING HERE THREE YEARS AGO.
SHE SAYS HE KILLED THAT MAN OUTSIDE THE THEMYSCIRAN EMBASSY, KEYES.
IS THAT WHAT SHE SAYS?
FALLON WAS PAID AS MY PERSONAL SECURITY, NOT C.A.P.'S. TAX REASONS, THAT'S ALL, LESLIE.
AS FOR THE REST, WELL...PSYCHO MUST HAVE BEEN IMPERSONATING FALLON FOR LONGER THAN WE THOUGHT.
IT JUST RAISES A LOT OF QUESTIONS FOR ME, RONNIE. SOME OF THE THINGS THAT PSYCHO SAID...
LESLIE, WHO YOU GONNA BELIEVE? YOUR BEST FRIEND FOR FIFTEEN YEARS, OR THE LUNATIC WHO TRIED TO RAPE YOU?
IT'S NOT JUST THAT. DIANA--
OH, SO THAT'S IT...

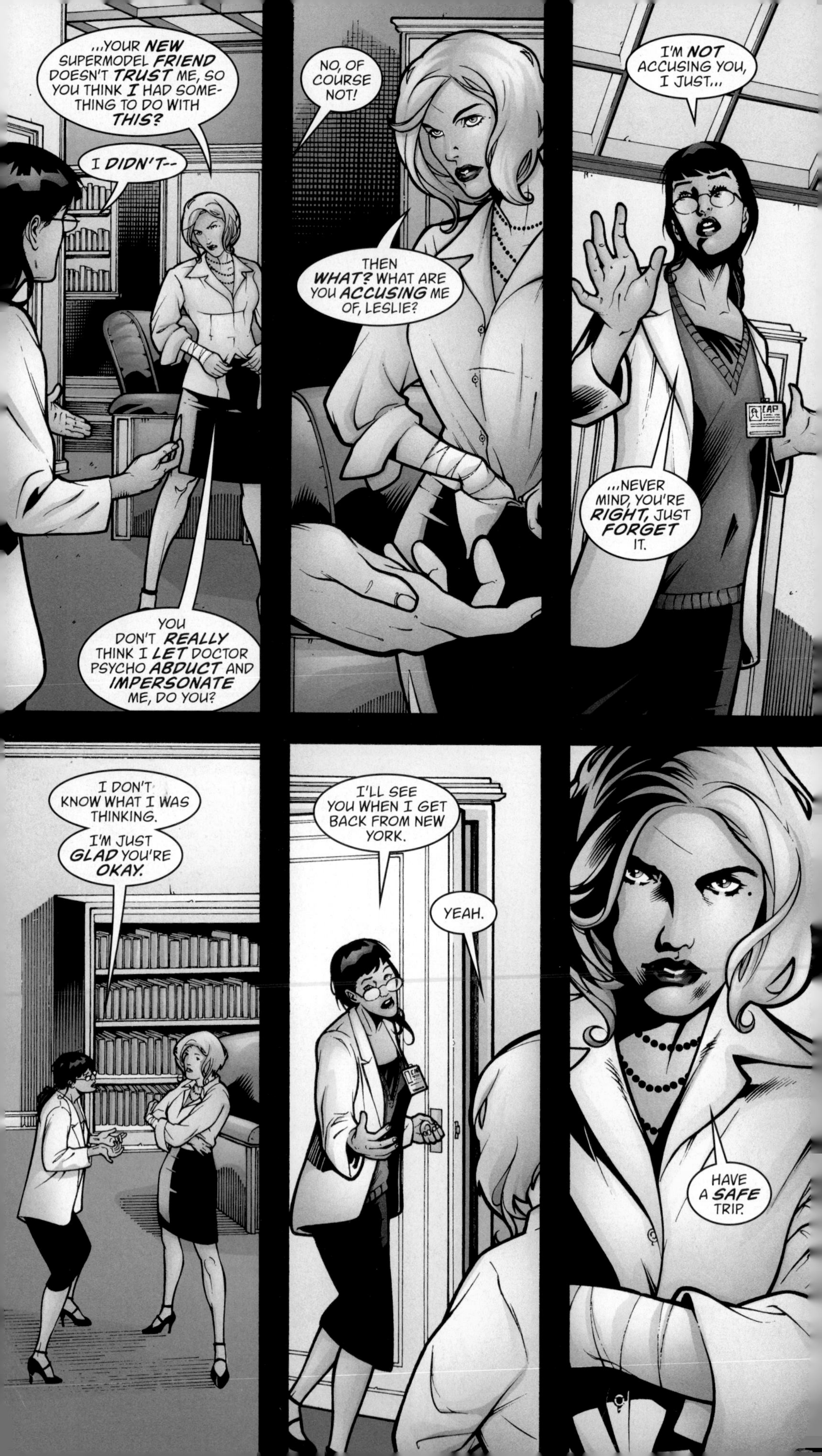
...YOUR NEW SUPERMODEL FRIEND DOESN'T TRUST ME, SO YOU THINK I HAD SOMETHING TO DO WITH THIS?
I DIDN'T--
YOU DON'T REALLY THINK I LET DOCTOR PSYCHO ABDUCT AND IMPERSONATE ME, DO YOU?
NO, OF COURSE NOT!
THEN WHAT? WHAT ARE YOU ACCUSING ME OF, LESLIE?
I'M NOT ACCUSING YOU, I JUST...
...NEVER MIND, YOU'RE RIGHT, JUST FORGET IT.
I DON'T KNOW WHAT I WAS THINKING.
I'M JUST GLAD YOU'RE OKAY.
I'LL SEE YOU WHEN I GET BACK FROM NEW YORK.
YEAH.
HAVE A SAFE TRIP.

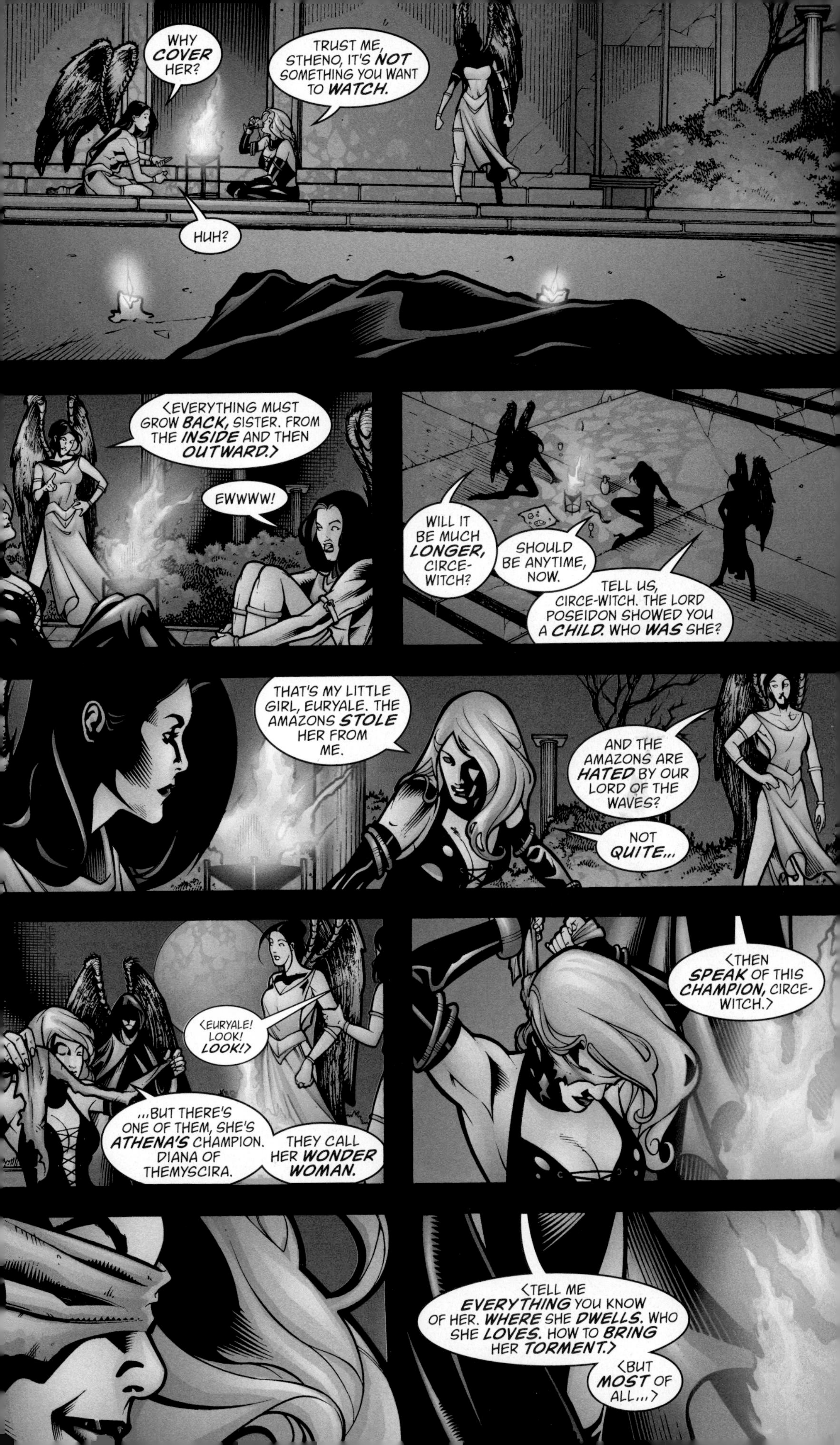
WHY COVER HER?
TRUST ME, STHENO, IT'S NOT SOMETHING YOU WANT TO WATCH.
HUH?
<EVERYTHING MUST GROW BACK, SISTER. FROM THE INSIDE AND THEN OUTWARD.>
EWWWW!
WILL IT BE MUCH LONGER, CIRCE-WITCH?
SHOULD BE ANYTIME, NOW.
TELL US, CIRCE-WITCH. THE LORD POSEIDON SHOWED YOU A CHILD. WHO WAS SHE?
THAT'S MY LITTLE GIRL, EURYALE. THE AMAZONS STOLE HER FROM ME.
AND THE AMAZONS ARE HATED BY OUR LORD OF THE WAVES?
NOT QUITE...
<EURYALE! LOOK! LOOK!>
...BUT THERE'S ONE OF THEM, SHE'S ATHENA'S CHAMPION. DIANA OF THEMYSCIRA.
THEY CALL HER WONDER WOMAN.
<THEN SPEAK OF THIS CHAMPION, CIRCE-WITCH.>
<TELL ME EVERYTHING YOU KNOW OF HER. WHERE SHE DWELLS. WHO SHE LOVES. HOW TO BRING HER TORMENT.>
<BUT MOST OF ALL...>

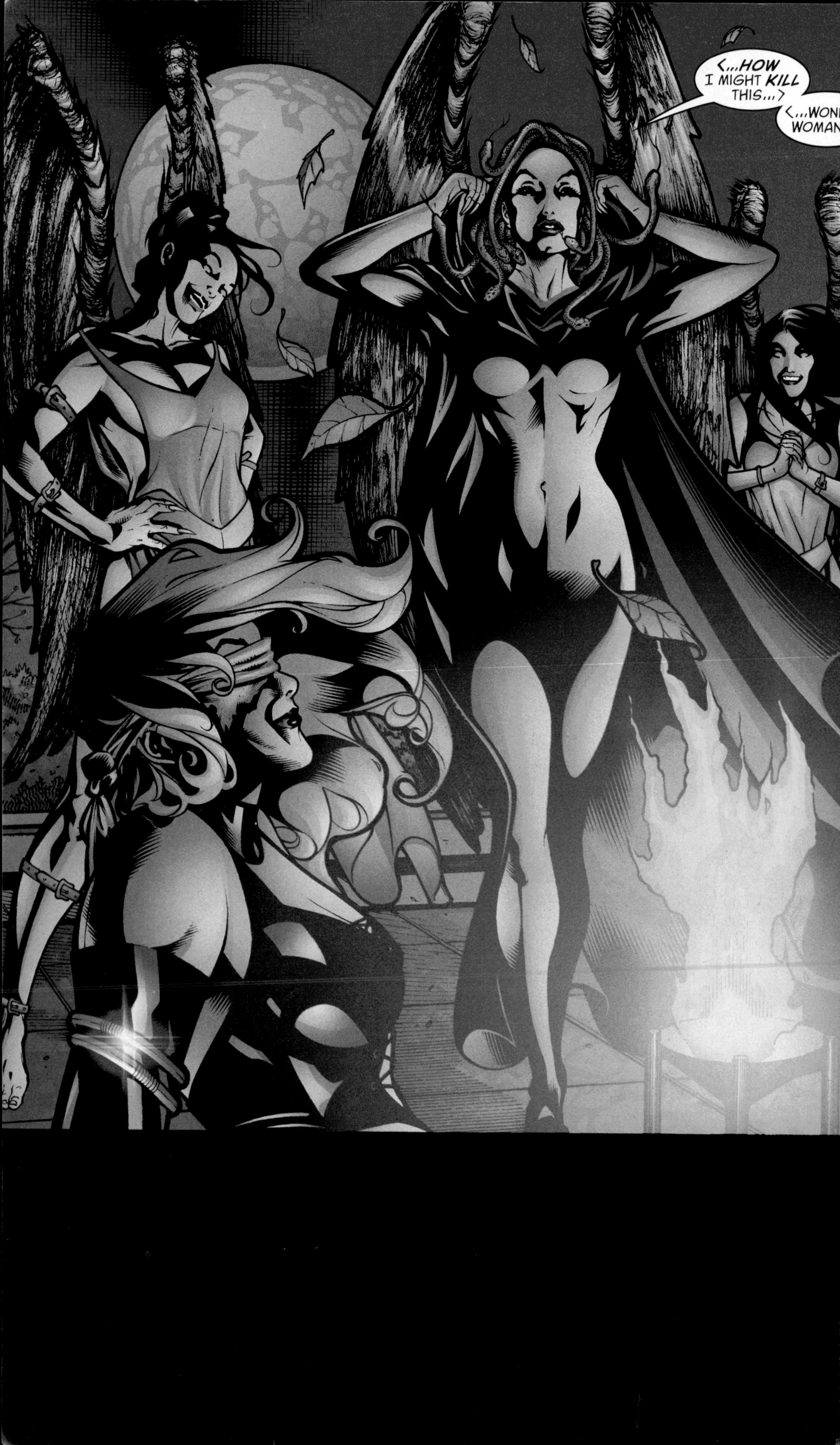
<...HOW I MIGHT KILL THIS...>
<...WON
WOMAN

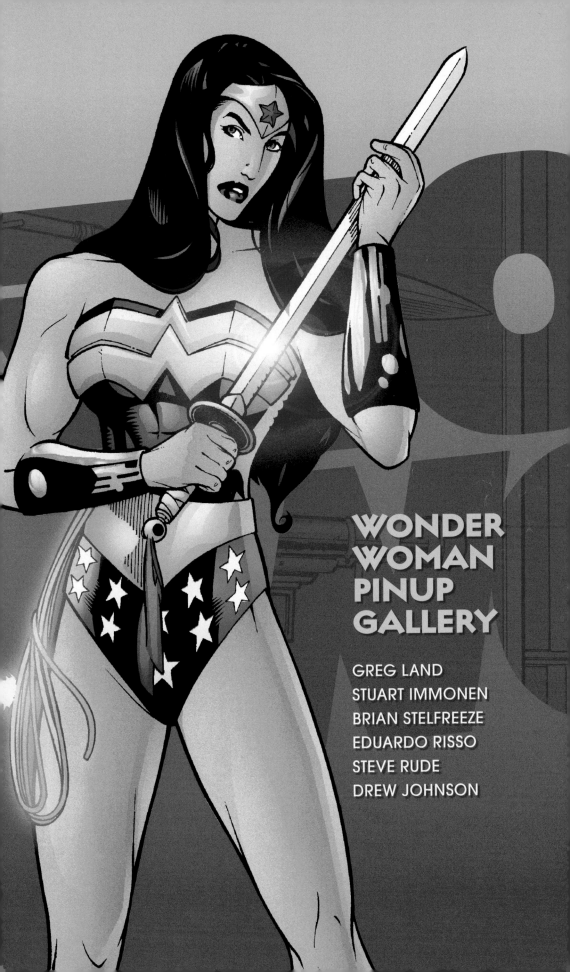

WONDER WOMAN PINUP GALLERY

GREG LAND
STUART IMMONEN
BRIAN STELFREEZE
EDUARDO RISSO
STEVE RUDE
DREW JOHNSON

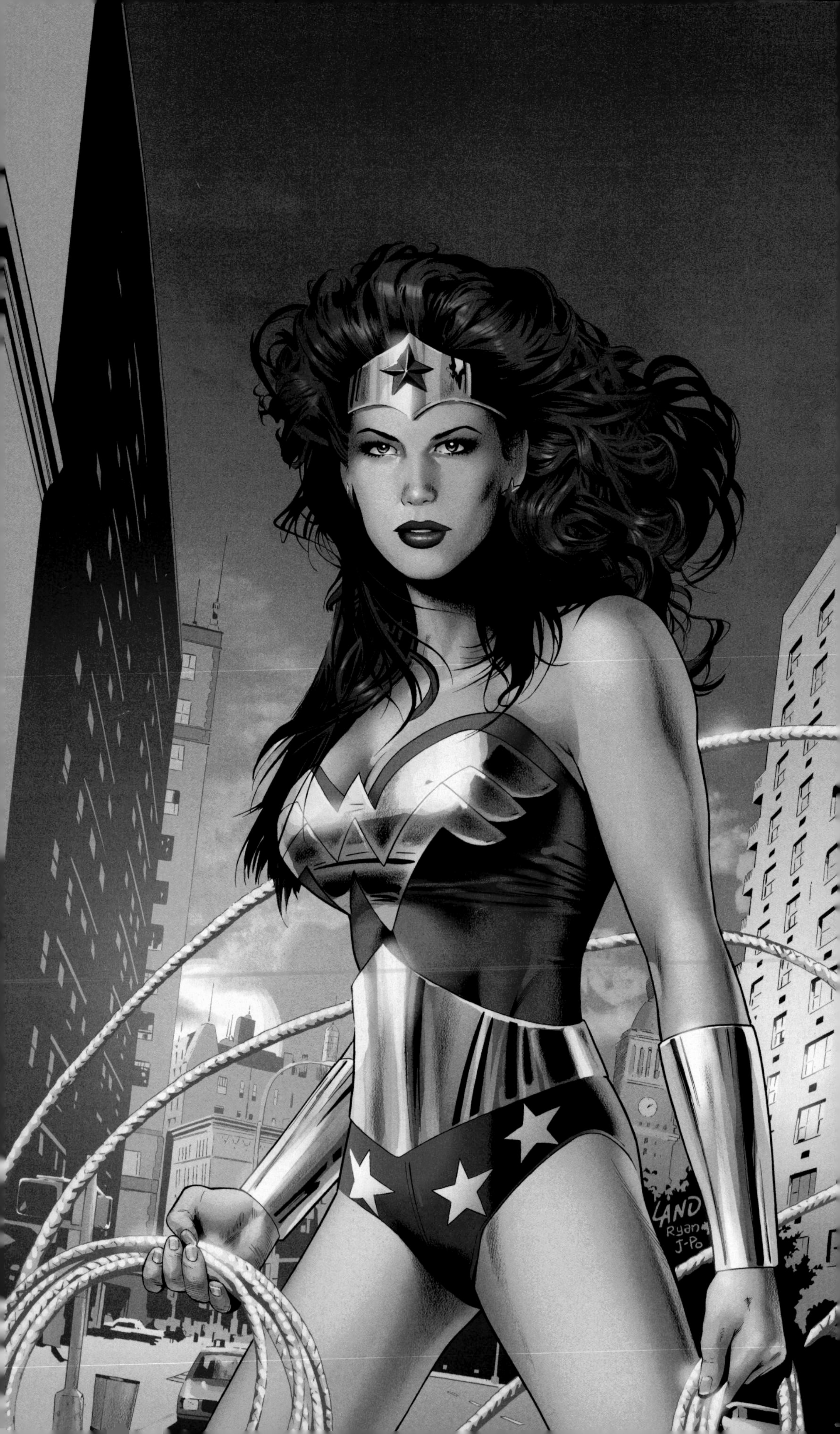
LAND
Ryan
J-Po

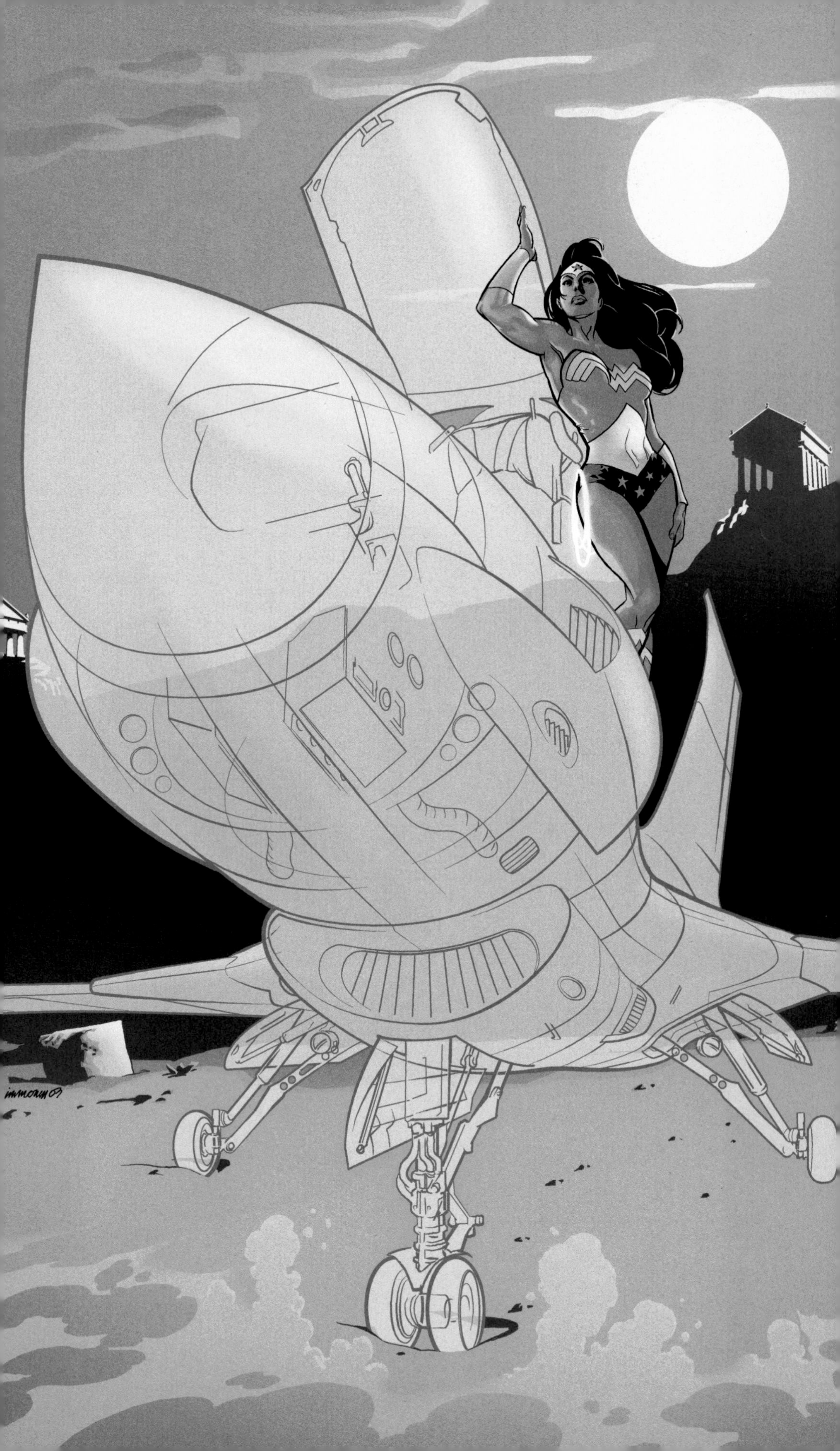

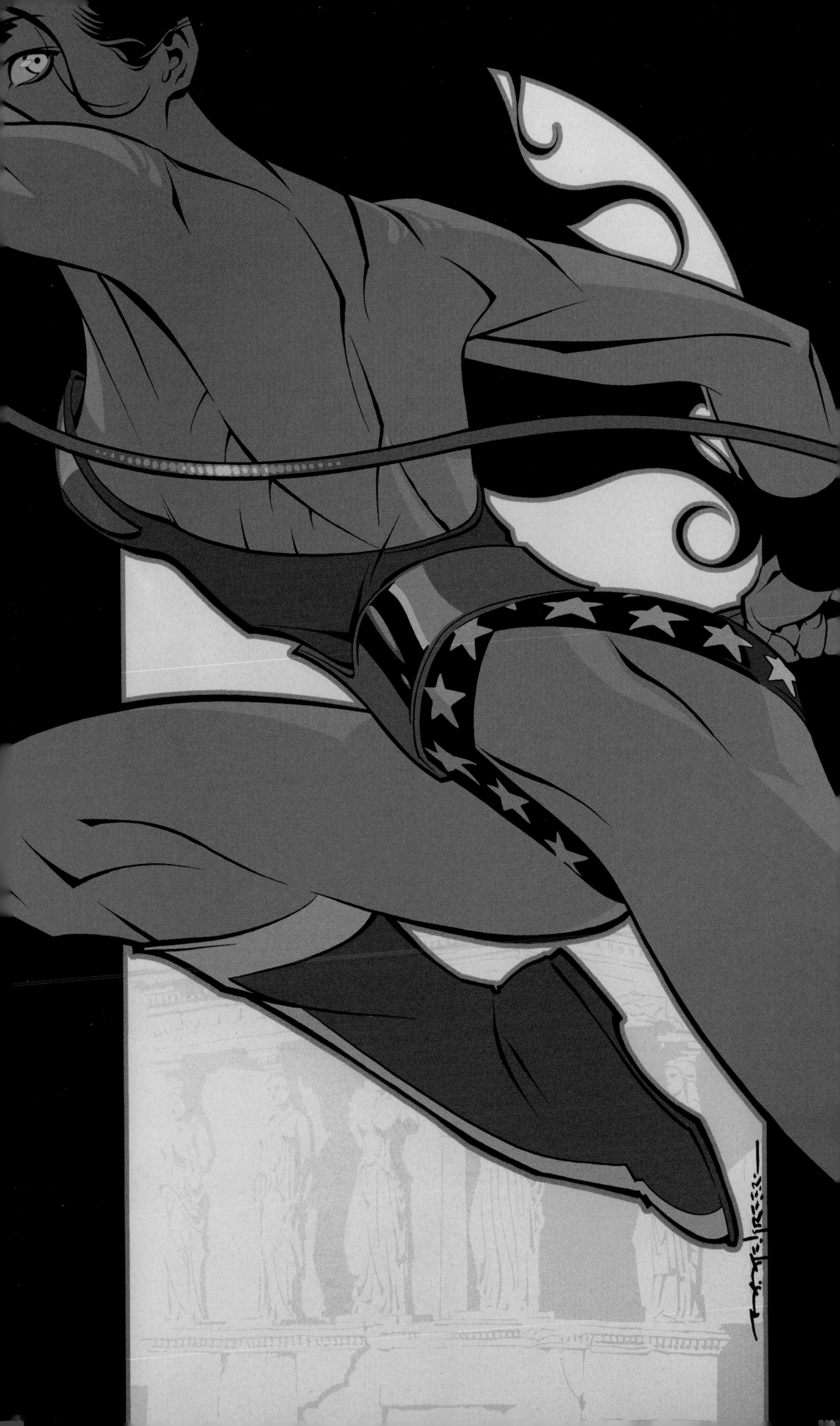

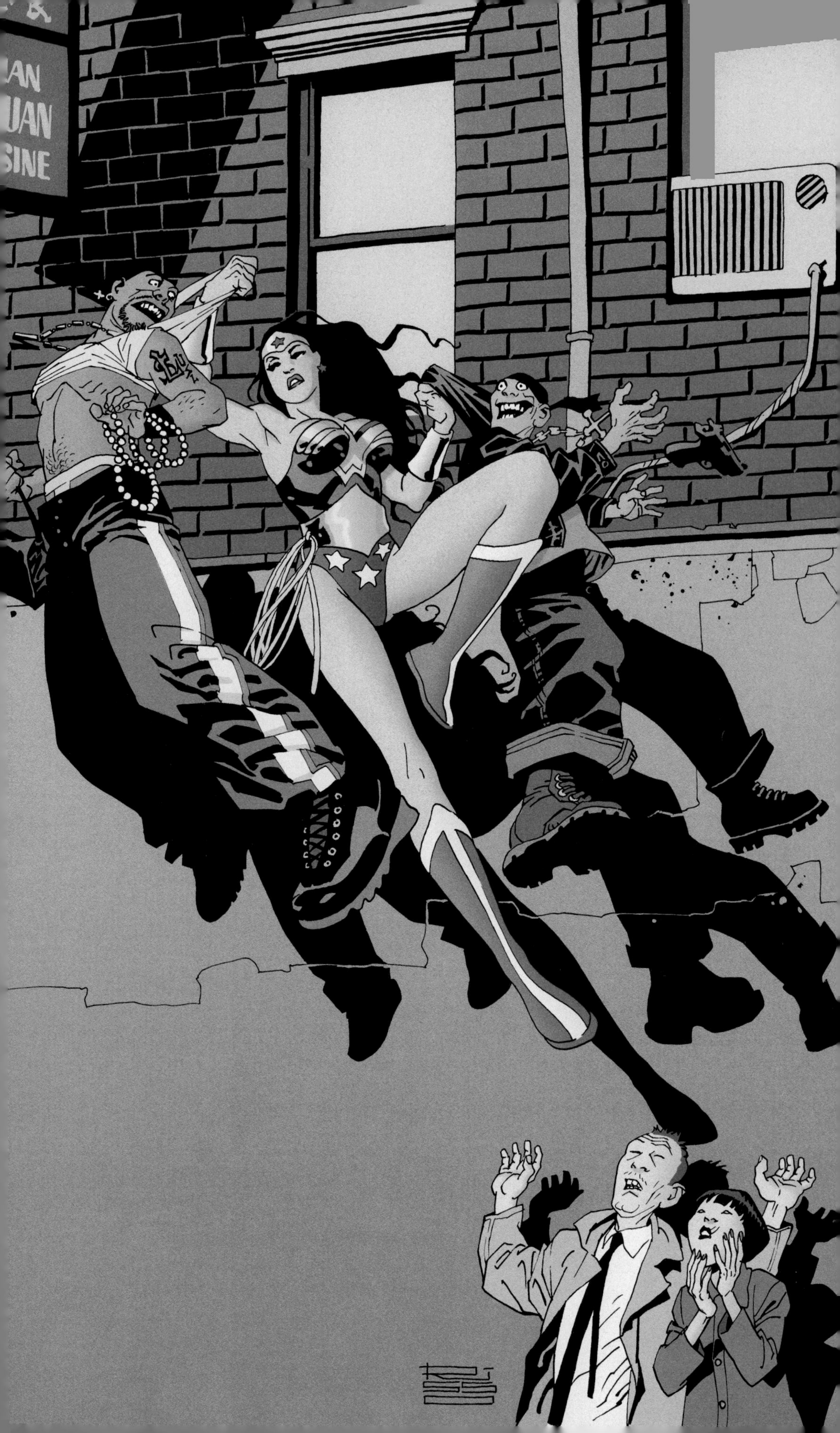
AN
UAN
SINE

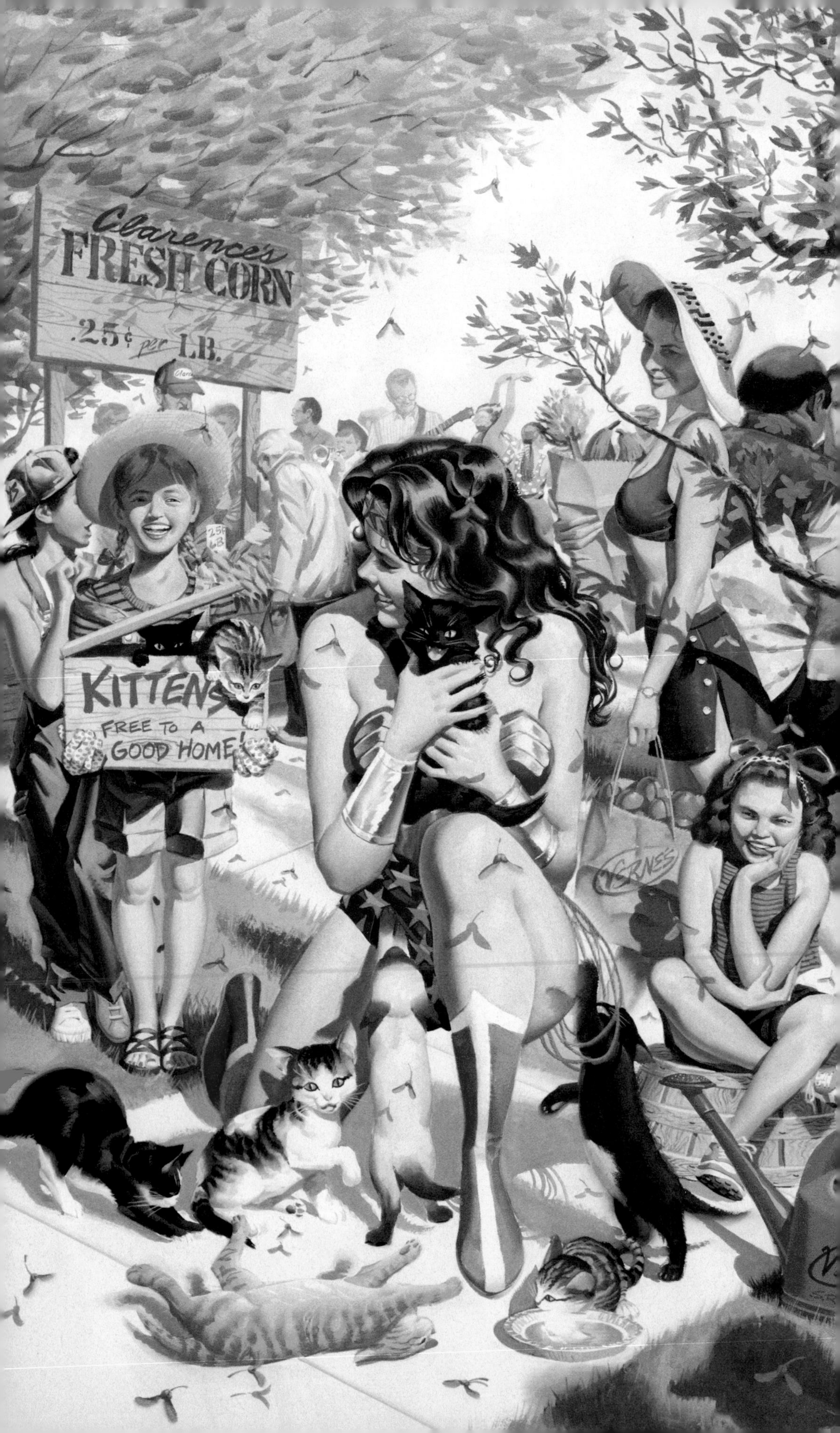

Clarence's
FRESH CORN
.25¢ per LB.
KITTENS
FREE TO A
GOOD HOME!

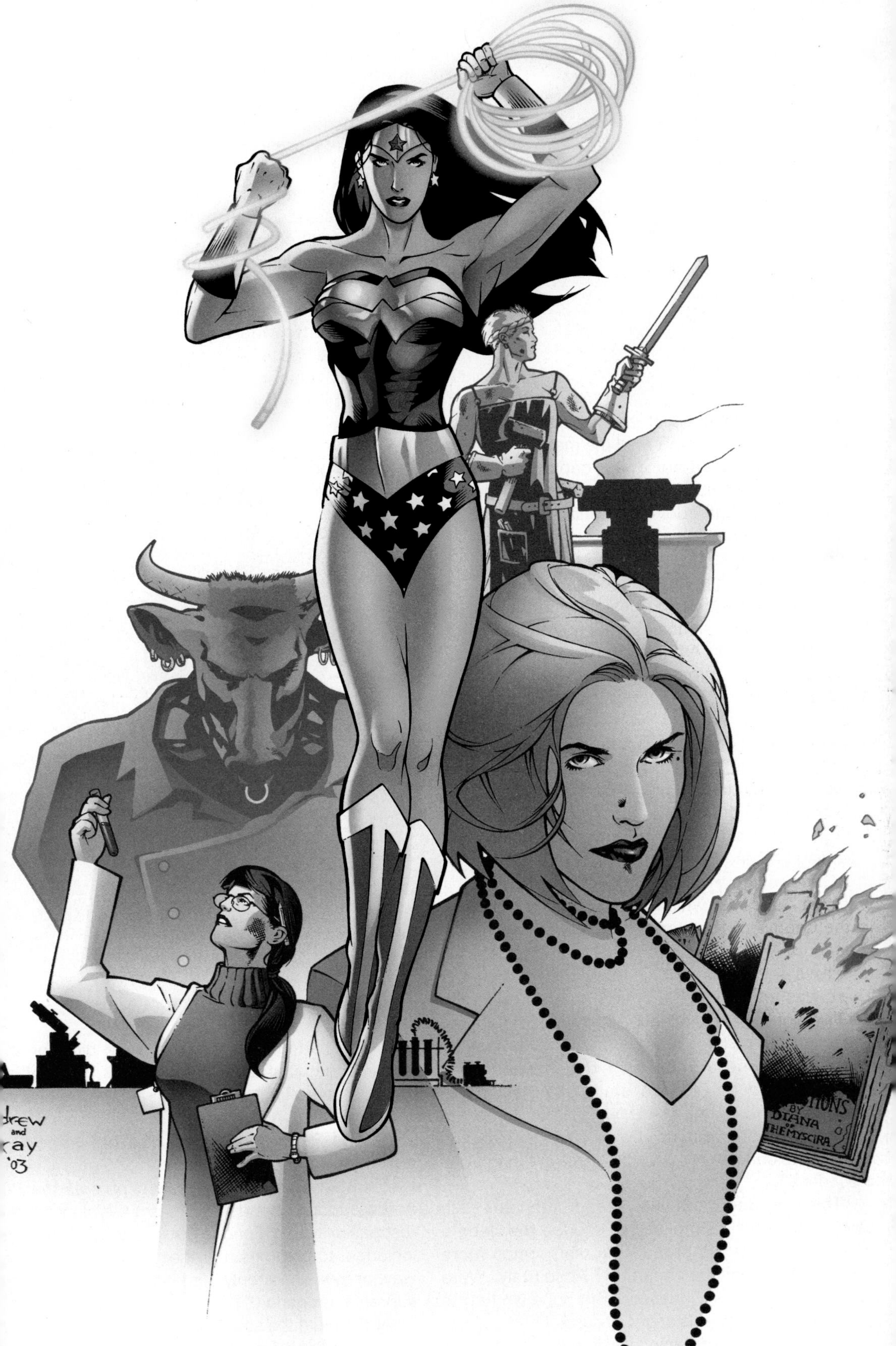
TIONS
BY
DIANA
OF
THEMYSCIRA
drew
and
ay
'03

Calvin —
See attached.
Cale's not going
to be happy.
— Warren

this past week ... ertium
... piendi,
... unt
... egiliu
... t vit,
... ont.
... s in
t... n a
e... s?
P... os
or... n,
qu... e
me...
and
inci
the p
once ... United
Natio... upon Wonder Woman to
resolv... crisis and effect the arrest of General Abaku only further complicated the matter, since she was approached not in her capacity as a member of the Justice League, but rather as the Themysciran Ambassador to the United Nations.

"Clearly this was a unique case, and it required a unique solution," the Secretary-General told Newstime, speaking via telephone. "Of course this would not have been possible with the aid of any other ambassador. But we are speaking of the Themysciran Ambassador to the United Nations, Wonder Woman, a person who has been one of the U.N.'s most visible, and vocal, champions."

But was the decision to call upon Wonder Woman in her dual capacities—as both ambassador and metahuman—justified?

"Absolutely," the Ambassador responds. "The Security Council passed two prior resolutions regarding Itari and General Abaku, both of which the General ignored. The only other option was a military one, which would have resulted in the deaths of thousands—perhaps tens of thousands—of Itari citizens, not to mention countless soldiers on both sides of the conflict. There was an additional concern that an open conflict would have spilled over to neighboring countries, and perhaps drawn Umeci involvement."

Not everyone agrees with this assessment, however, and discussion since the event has continued, both within the U.N. itself, and in other governing bodies. Senator David Hale (R-Texas) is vocal in his concern for what he terms a "dangerous precedent."

"This isn't about the lives saved," Senator Hale says. "It's grossly simplistic to reduce the debate to just that. Was the Wonder Woman option more efficient than a military solution? Absolutely. Were lives spared? Beyond question. But once we turn to metas to solve problems of global conflict and politics, we're skating onto very thin ice. Where does it stop? When we turn to Superman or to Wonder Woman to solve those conflicts that we should be able to solve ourselves, we abdicate our authority, and our responsibility, both as human beings, and, spea personally, for the people we represent."

Perhaps surprisingly, Wonder Woman sh the concern. In her book Reflections: A Collectio Essays and Speeches, she writes, "If there is one I must perform above all others, above my tasks a ambassador of my people, above my responsibilitie an individual of great power, it is to teach... in ac to lead by example; in word, to inspire and energiz

Understandable, then, that many members of international community claimed surprise, and some cases, alarm, at Wonder Woman's involvem in the arrest of Abaku. "No one believes she acte a rogue or irresponsible fashion," says Hale. "Aba crimes shatter the imagination, and there's question he had to be stopped, and brought to jus Wonder Woman clearly acted on behalf of the U But what if she had acted on behalf of Themysc

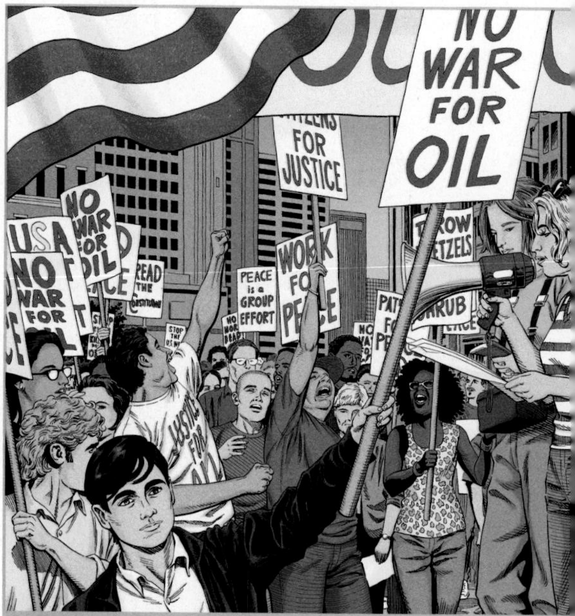
NO WAR FOR OIL
FOR JUSTICE
NO WAR FOR OIL
PEACE is a GROUP EFFORT
WORK FOR PEACE

Ambassador Diana's book, *Reflections,* advocates publi protests, like this one in New York's Times Square fro spring 2003 *(S. Schreck/Airwave Studios)*

What if it hadn't been a Third World dictator sh apprehended, but a duly-elected First World offic The lines are blurring, and I'm afraid they're in dan of being erased."

"If the Security Council had not specific approved my part in the arrest of General Aba I would not have acted, it's as simple as that," Ambassador responds. "We share the planet and responsibility to it. For one person, any person, my included, to presume that their way alone is the c way, or indeed the only best way, would be an ac supreme arrogance."

And should the situation arise again?

"I don't think it will," says Wonder Woman. "I p that it doesn't."

It may be a faint prayer given the recent expuls of U.N. Aid Workers from Umec this past week.

WE SAY: New York Wonder

he's beautiful, talented, and she saves ne world from destruction almost daily. Vhat's next for Wonder Woman? No less an inspiring a generation.

assandra Sandsmark, in torn and faded blue jeans and a gray T-shirt th the words "Property of catraz" stenciled on the front, brushing stray hair out of her es as she looks through the est releases in the CD sec- n. Ten feet away, Wonder oman herself is struggling decide between two boxed s—Mozart or Beethoven. And people are staring, and course they are, because s Wonder Woman stand- g there, the same Wonder oman whose new book is cked in the window displays along the Lexington Avenue le of the store. Wonder oman, wearing jeans and wool sweater with sleeves at don't quite hide the shin- g bracelets at her wrists, and e's standing right there, in e Classical section, and yes, it really is Wonder Girl at the ew Releases.

That's just not something u see every day.

"What about this?" Cassie ks, showing the latest by cNamara Intact to Wonder oman. "Is this any good?"

"It's better than their last um," Wonder Woman says er a pause. "I think he'd obably like it."

When Cassie's asked who she's buying for, she shakes her head, grins, and says, "You'll need a lasso to get an answer out of me."

AMAZING AMAZONS

It's December 17th, almost a week before Christmas, and Diana and Cassie are engaged in a little holiday shopping. Not, perhaps, the most Amazonian of pursuits, but then again, who expects Wonder Woman to have even **heard** of *McNamara Intact*, let alone be able to comment on the relative merits of their latest album? Still, it's so mundane as to be almost unbe- lievable. An Amazon and her protégé shopping? Shouldn't they be out swinging swords or something?

"Right, because Amazons are all about blood, sweat, and tears," says Cassie with a laugh. "After this, we'll go cas- trate some men, don't worry."

"Don't say that," Diana says with a grin. "Someone's sure to take you seriously."

Ridiculous, perhaps, but then again, maybe not. Since the publication of Wonder Woman's book, *Reflections,* touched off a storm of pub- lic debate, the Themysciran Ambassador has been accused of everything from being a visionary to a subversive, and with a few more inflamma- tory stops along the way. It's a debate not without some merit. With chapters on everything from conservation (the Wonder Woman, a vegetarian, has strong views on the environ- ment, and in particular the dam- age that comes from supplying the First World with beef) to the nature of love ("Aphrodite is one of my patrons," Diana is quick to point out. "What was it John Lennon said? *'Love is the flower you've got to let grow.'* Let it grow already, and quit trying to legislate it!"), the book has touched a nerve, and sparked everything from mild debate to public protest. "Which was pre- cisely the point," says Diana. "Where's the purpose in shar- ing my views if people are just going to blindly and blithely accept what I have to say? That's called propaganda, not education."

Debate is one thing, but it hasn't stopped there. "I think it's ridiculous," Cassie says, clearly frustrated. "There's a handful of people who are

WE SAY:

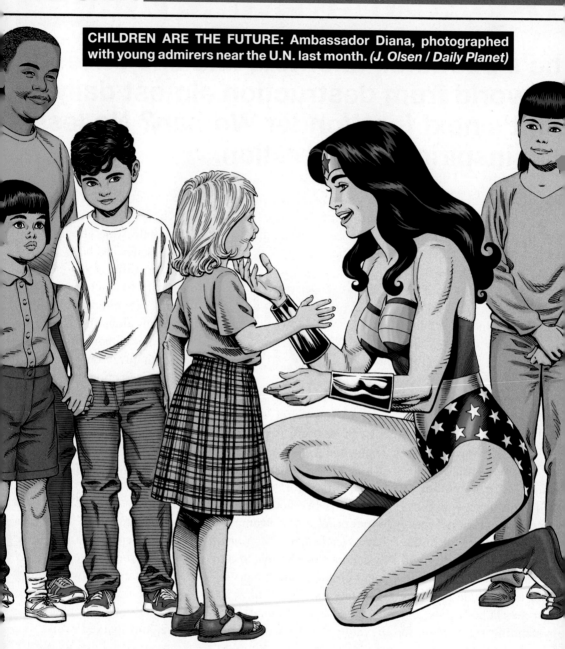

CHILDREN ARE THE FUTURE: Ambassador Diana, photographed with young admirers near the U.N. last month. *(J. Olsen / Daily Planet)*

AMAZONS

accusing Diana of trying to 'pervert' their kids, and that's just… that's just so *backwards.* Themyscira is the most socially and technologically advanced society in the world, they must be doing *something* right. But people hear the word 'Amazon' and the phrase 'island of women' and they suddenly want to hide behind the couch. It's 2004, people, get over it! Stop being afraid of women!"

Diana smiles, listening to Cassie, her piercing blue eyes shining ("It's like looking into the most perfect blue sky," describes one embassy staffer who asked to remain nameless). The fondness the two have for one another is obvious in the way they ban and joke while taking a bre in the store's café—Dia drinks a hibiscus tea, wh Cassie downs a mocha latte their relationship part men and student, part older sist younger sister.

So maybe this is more li it? Maybe **this** is what being Amazon is about?

"Do they have moc

ttes on Themyscira?" asks assie. "No, it's not, but it too… it's the comfort that mes from just, you know, nging out with those who ve you because they see e best in you, and they can rgive the worst. Being an mazon—even an honorary mazon—that's the coolest ing imaginable! To be part that history, and to bring ose ideas, those philosophies d beliefs to the rest of the orld... that's about as cool as ing a Titan."

"About?"

"Well, you guys don't have zza," Cassie says.

Diana laughs. "We're orking on it," she says.

Tea and latte finished, the o gather their purchases and ake for the exit. It's a process at takes twenty-six minutes, each of them is stopped veral times for autographs and

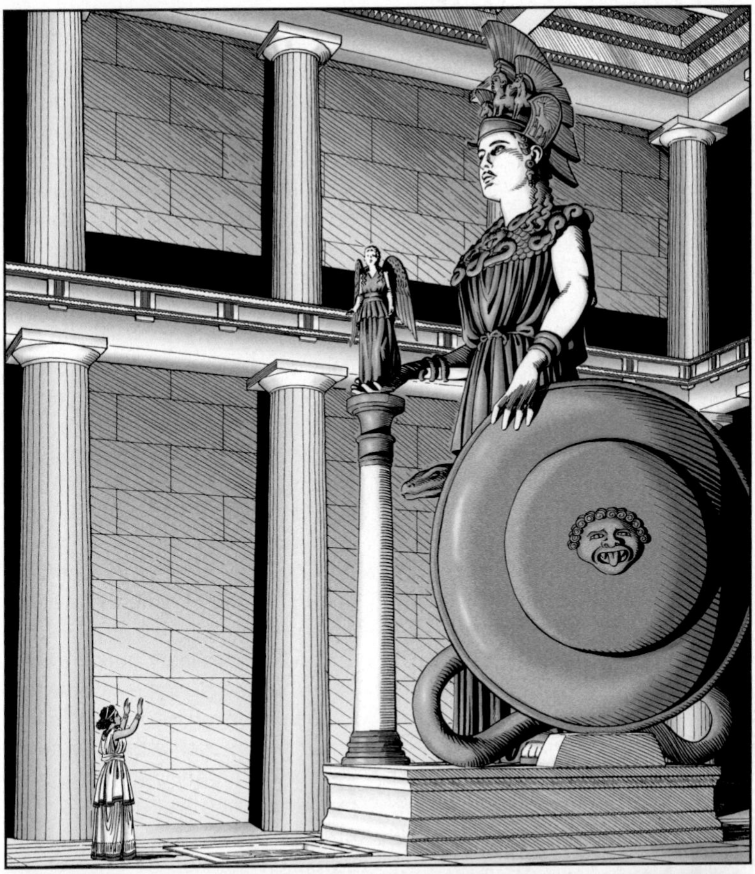

NOT OLD ENOUGH TO BE A CLASSIC:
Worship of Athena, acceptable in *The Odyssey,* provokes debate in modern *Reflections.*

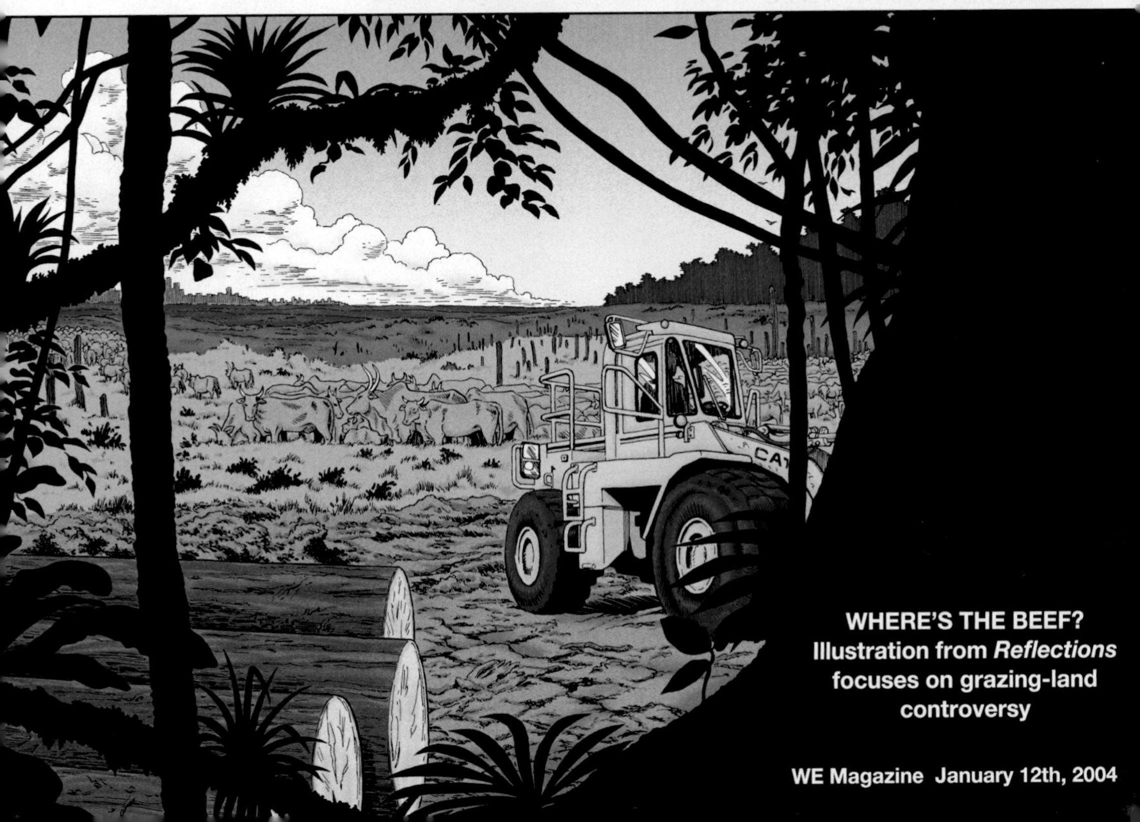
CAT

WHERE'S THE BEEF?
Illustration from *Reflections* focuses on grazing-land controversy

THEMYSCIRA:
MARGINALIZATION IN THE FACE OF MULTILATERALISM

BY RACHEL KEAST

Doctor Rachel Keast is the Legal Attaché at the Themysciran Embassy in New York and advises the Themysciran Ambassador in matters of United Nations proceedings and international law. She is the author of seven books, including the forthcoming Bullets and Bracelets: The Law of Themyscira, Then and Now.

The United States commitment to multilateralism as outlined in the September 2002 release of the National Security Strategy seems to have been swept aside in the recent debate on unilateralism and the efficacy of implementation of the Powell Doctrine. Globalization as such is here to stay, despite national interests to the contrary around the globe. In all this, Themyscira has effectively been reduced to a non-entity, coming lately as it has to the world stage. But examination of the Themysciran principals of diplomacy, sometimes referred to as the Hippolyta Doctrine, may shed new light on future diplomatic proceedings, insofar as multilateralism remains a pressing concern.

Separating those elements that remain well out-of-reach, that are unique to Themyscira, from those practices available to other nations provides a framework of discussion for further advances in diplomatic action and overtures that the United Nations, as well as other sovereign governments, could do well to adopt. With three thousand years of stable, peaceful governance to draw upon prior to its entrée into international global politics, Themyscira offers a unique diplomatic model.

Of course, there is always the issue of Themyscira's military might, which derives not from a strength of numbers, but from a combination of cultural imperatives and technological advantages unique to the nation. Themyscira is, perhaps, the only nation on Earth where not only do all of its citizens serve, but all of them do so willingly, and with pride, and remain at a state of readiness that is the envy of many armies. Presented as such, military action has always existed as a political option for the Amazons.

Yet, recent extraordinary conflicts not withstanding,[1] military force is an option Themyscira is ever loath to use. This is due in part to its self-imposed exile from what the Amazons call the World of the Patriarchy for so many centuries, but more in fact from the fundamental Amazonian understanding of all that a military option entails. As such, the Themysciran military option exists solely for the purpose of defense and is ever exercised only in such times and in such a manner as to insure the safety and continued protection and well-being of her citizens, a right shared by all sovereign nations.

[1] Referring of course to the global defense against Imperiex.

Ironically, perhaps, the presence of this military, backed as it is by the unique science and technology of Themyscira, has committed the nation to a path of peace that as yet stands unshaken. That its technology remains wholly proprietary is certainly of issue; while there are global interests who feel they, too, should have access to all that Themyscira has, it is the responsibility of the island nation's leaders to maintain a guarded stance that would prevent unchecked proliferation. In fact, it would be irresponsible in extremis for Themyscira to do anything else. This, along with many other factors, has further allowed Themyscira to maintain its status as an independent, neutral and peaceful nation participating in global politics.

In fact, Themyscira's main export has been its ideals, in the form of its Ambassador to the United Nations, Diana daughter of Hippolyta, referred to more commonly as the Wonder Woman. These are policy stances that are offered rather than imposed.

Fig 1.1: Connection between "Homeric" Amazons and current Themyscirans a controversy among scholars (Illo by Eric Shanower, used with permission).

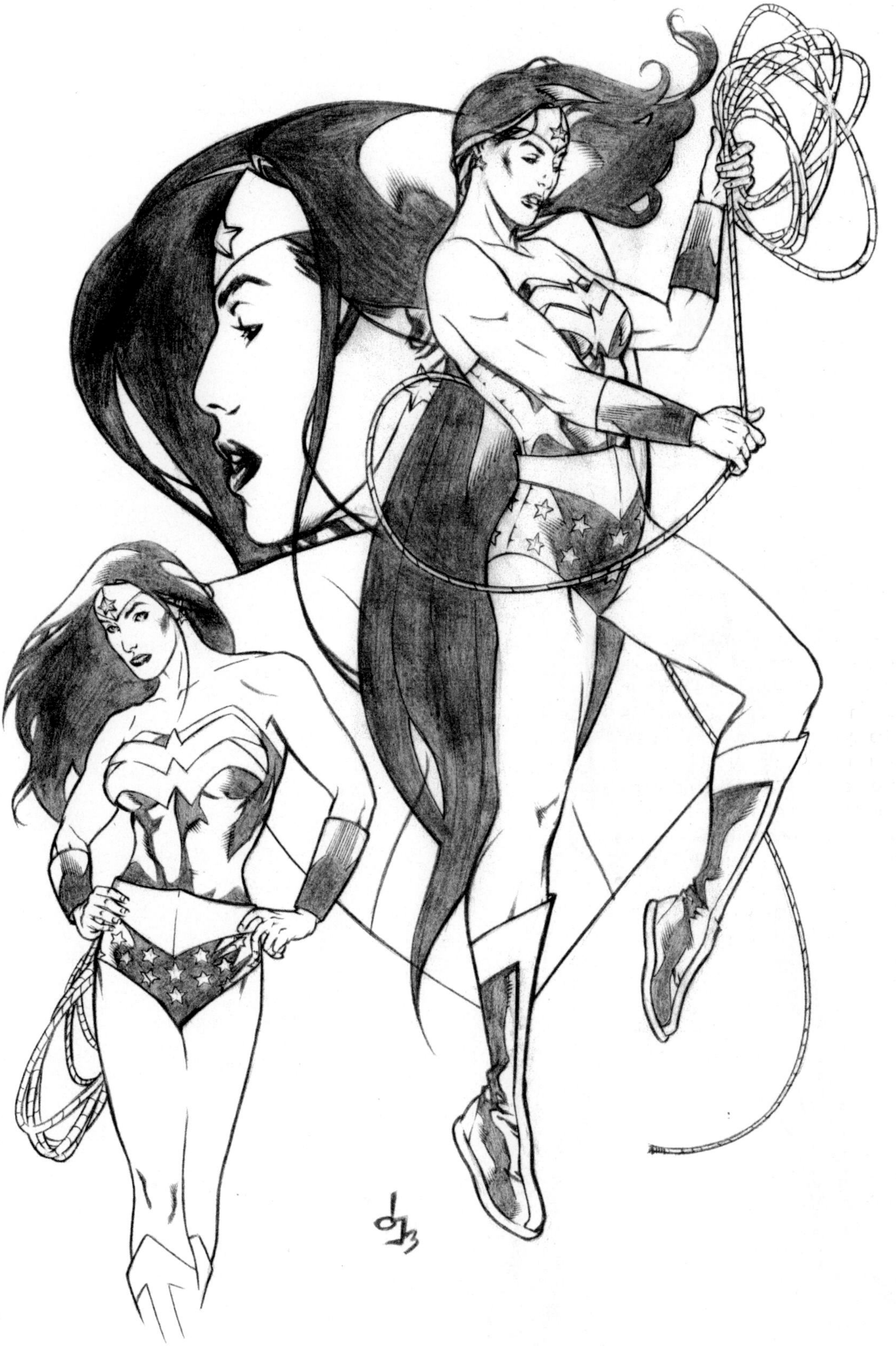

SKETCHES BY DREW JOHNSON

WONDER WOMAN   DESIGN "B"

NOTES + CHANGES —

· STRAIGHTENED CLASSIC
  MANACLE / WRIST BANDS
· CHEST PLATE CLOSER TO
  USUAL DESIGN — JUST
  A TOUCH BROADER ACROSS
  BUST — LET ME KNOW IF
  WE NEED IT STILL SMALLER
· LEATHER ARMORED SKIRT
  STRAIGHTENED + LENGTHENED
  JUST A BIT AS REQUESTED
· ROPE CLIPPED TO BELT

· CLASSIC BOOT DESIGN —
  BUT HEELS ARE FLAT — WHITE
  PART OF BOOT IS RE-ENFORCED

· SAME USUAL OUTFIT UNDER
  SKIRT — IT'S JUST AN
  ADD-ON TO ORIGINAL
  DESIGN.

· LEATHER FLANK PROTECTION
  OVER HIPS AT SIDE OF SKIRT —
  BACK OF SKIRT LOOKS ABOUT
  THE SAME AS FRONT

· THE STRIPS OF THE ARMORED
  SKIRT ARE WEIGHTED BY EACH
  INDIVIDUAL STAR AND WILL
  MOVE AS SHE MOVES — CREATING
  DRAMATIC VISUAL MOVEMENT IN
  ACTION SCENES.

drew 03

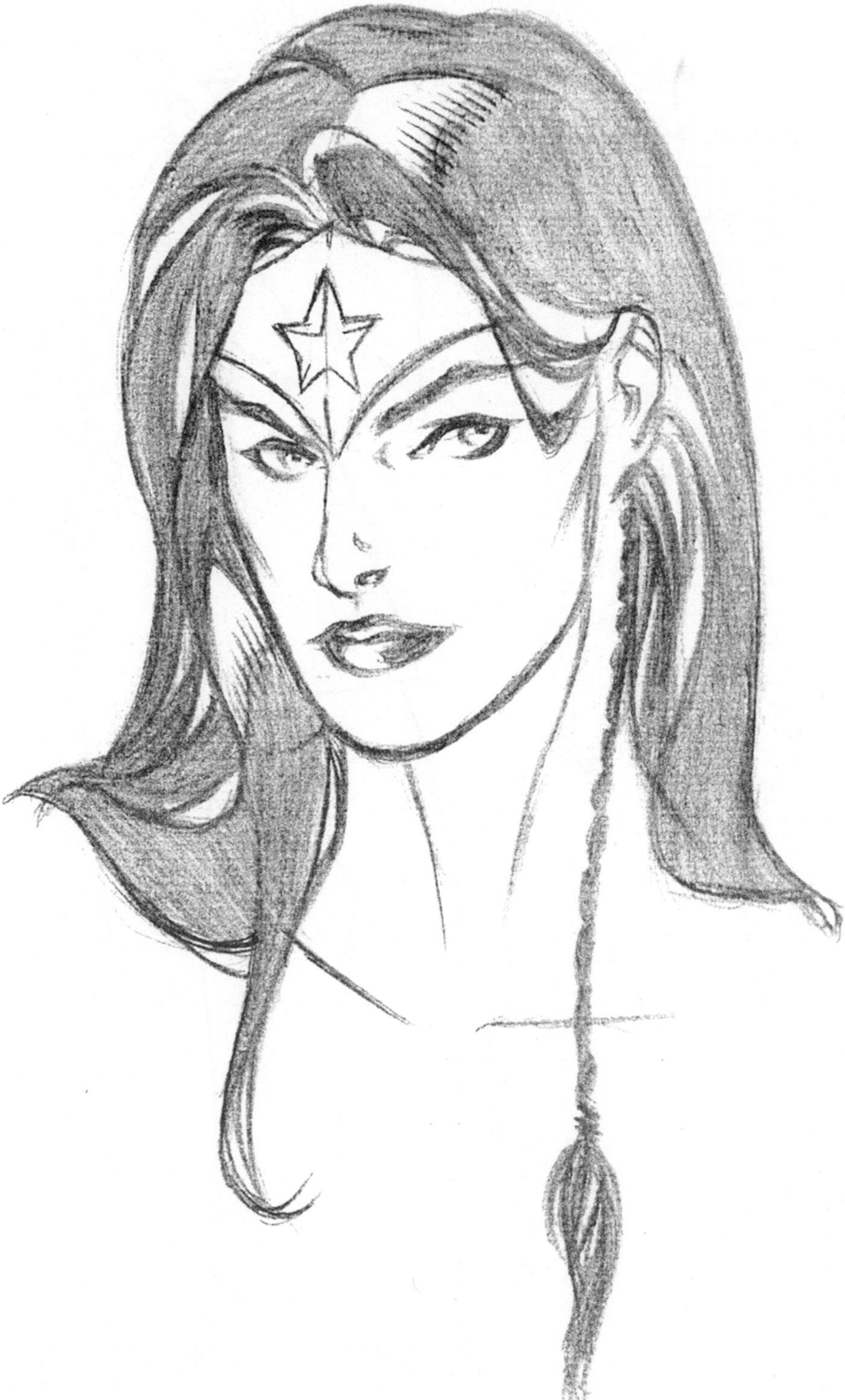

VERONICA CALE

NOTES ON CALE

- BEAUTY MARK BELOW LEFT EYE PROVIDES "VISUAL HOOK"

- COSTUME JEWELRY ROPE OF BLACK PEARLS GIVEN TO HER BY HER MOTHER — SHE <u>ALWAYS</u> WEARS THEM AND THIS PROVIDES ANOTHER "VISUAL HOOK"

ARTEMIS

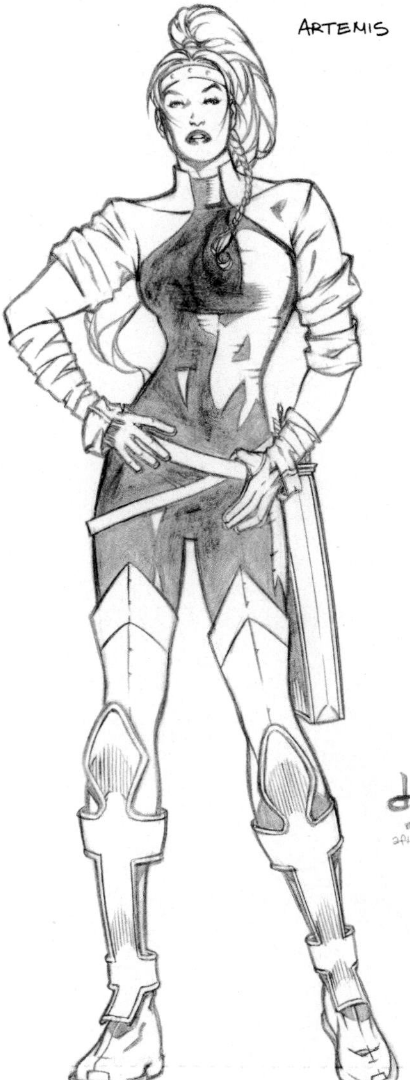

NOTES:

- FOLLOWS MATTHEW CLARKS PREVIOUS DESIGN

dj3
after Clark

10

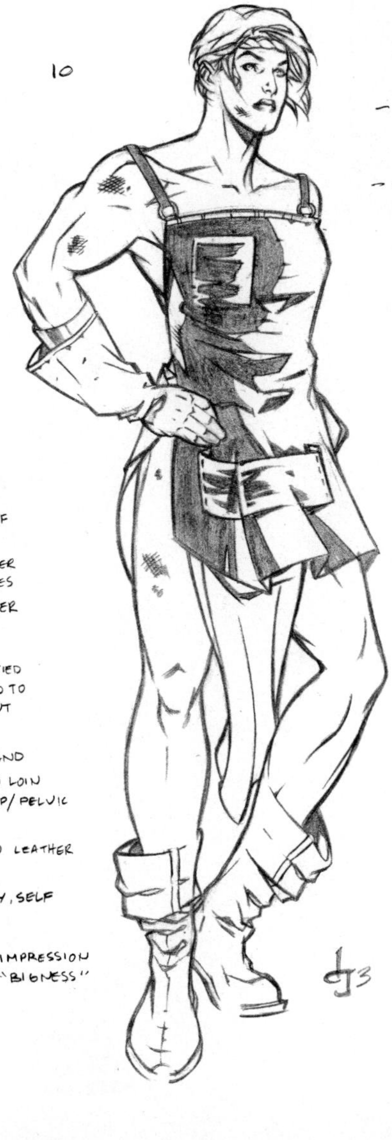
dj3

Keep her simple lookin'

– More ragged hair –

– Check manacles

Linen drape light pants

lengthen apron

mid shin

NOTES:

- SERIOUSLY BUFF ARMS + CHEST
- HEAVY GLOVES OVER AMAZON MANACLES
- HEAVY APRON OVER HER SHIRTLESS TORSO.
- TWISTED RAG TIED 'ROUND HER HEAD TO KEEP SWEAT OUT HER EYES
- WOVEN BELT AND LONG AMAZON LOIN CLOTH OVER HIP/PELVIC REGION
- ROLLED DOWN LEATHER BOOTS
- SHORT, SHAGGY, SELF CUT HAIR
- TALL – GIVES IMPRESSION OF OVERALL "BIGNESS"

LESLIE ANDERSON

NOTES—

• BLACK HAIR w/ BETTY PAGE
  BANGS — PULLED IN PONY TAIL
• BOOKISH GLASSES w/ YELLOW
  TINT
• CONSTANTLY HAS A PEN OR
  2 BEHIND HER EAR
• MODERATE FASHION SENSE
• SINCE SHE'S AT CAP
  SO MUCH — SHE'S OFTEN
  SEEN IN A LAB COAT
• OPPOSITE CALE'S LIGHTER
  HAIR + EYES — ANDERSON
  IS DARKER COMPLECTED
  AND MORE PRONE TO
  LOOKING STERN AND
  SHADOWY

drew
-3-

FERDINAND

NOTES:

  RINGS IN EARS AND NOSE
  CONTRAST "TOUGHNESS"
  AGAINST CHEF'S WHITES

• SLIGHTLY OVERSIZED
  HEAD AND HANDS

• LOOSE-FITTING, COMFORTABLE
  LOOKING CHEF'S WHITES
  WITH BLACK RUBBER-
  SOLED SHOES — STANDARD
  CHEF'S GARB

• BLACK HAIR ON BULL-HEAD
  AND NECK DOWN TO ABOUT
  HIS STERNUM — THEN
  THE REST IS CAUCASIAN-ISH
  FLESH TONE.

• ABOUT 8 FEET TALL AND
  QUITE WIDE BODIED —
  IMPOSING, REALLY.

drew 3

EMBASSY STAFF

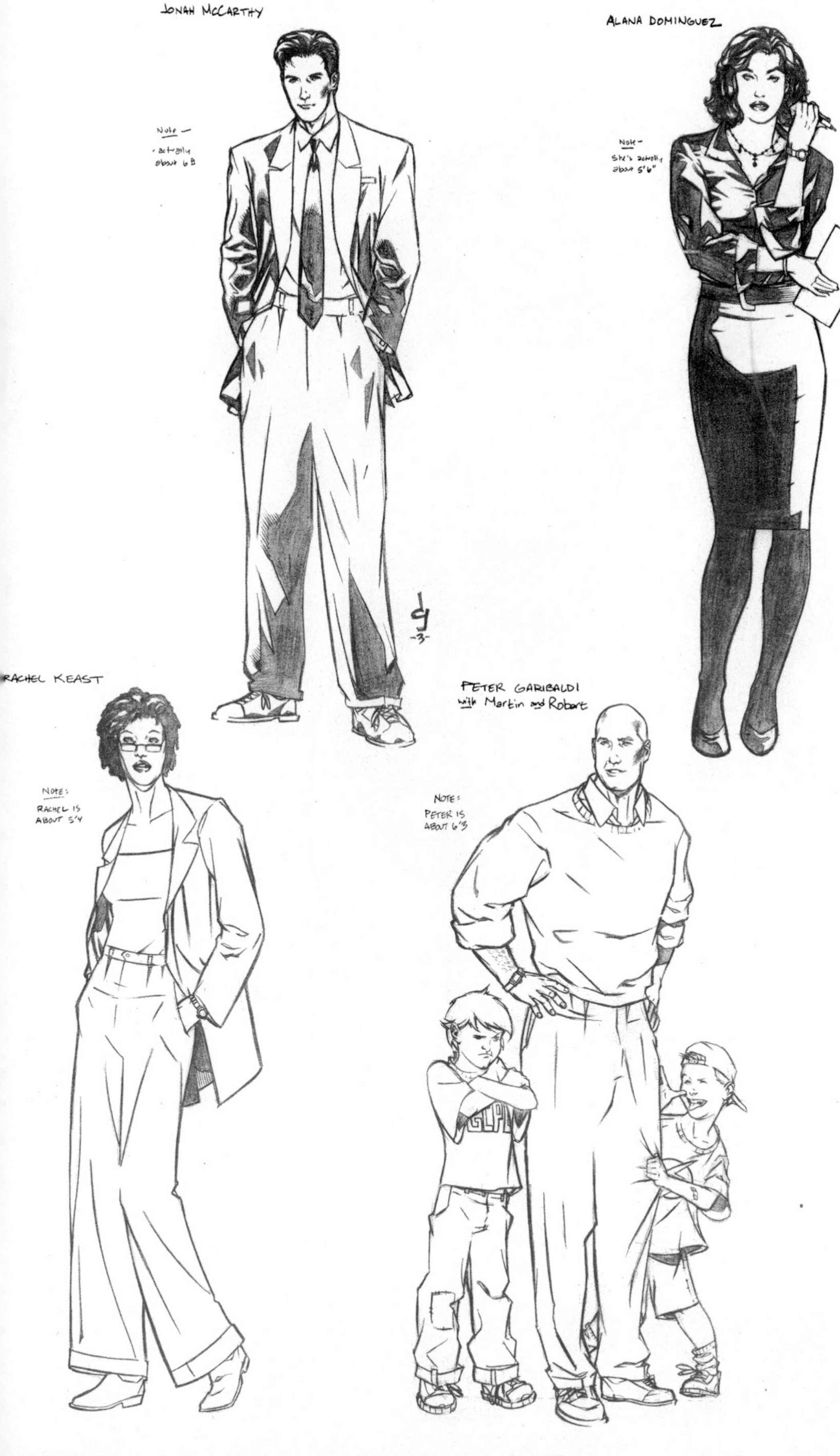
JONAH McCARTHY
Note — actually about 6 ft
ALANA DOMINGUEZ
Note — She's actually about 5'6"
RACHEL KEAST
Note: RACHEL IS ABOUT 5'4
PETER GARIBALDI with Martin and Robert
Note: PETER IS ABOUT 6'3
GLPL

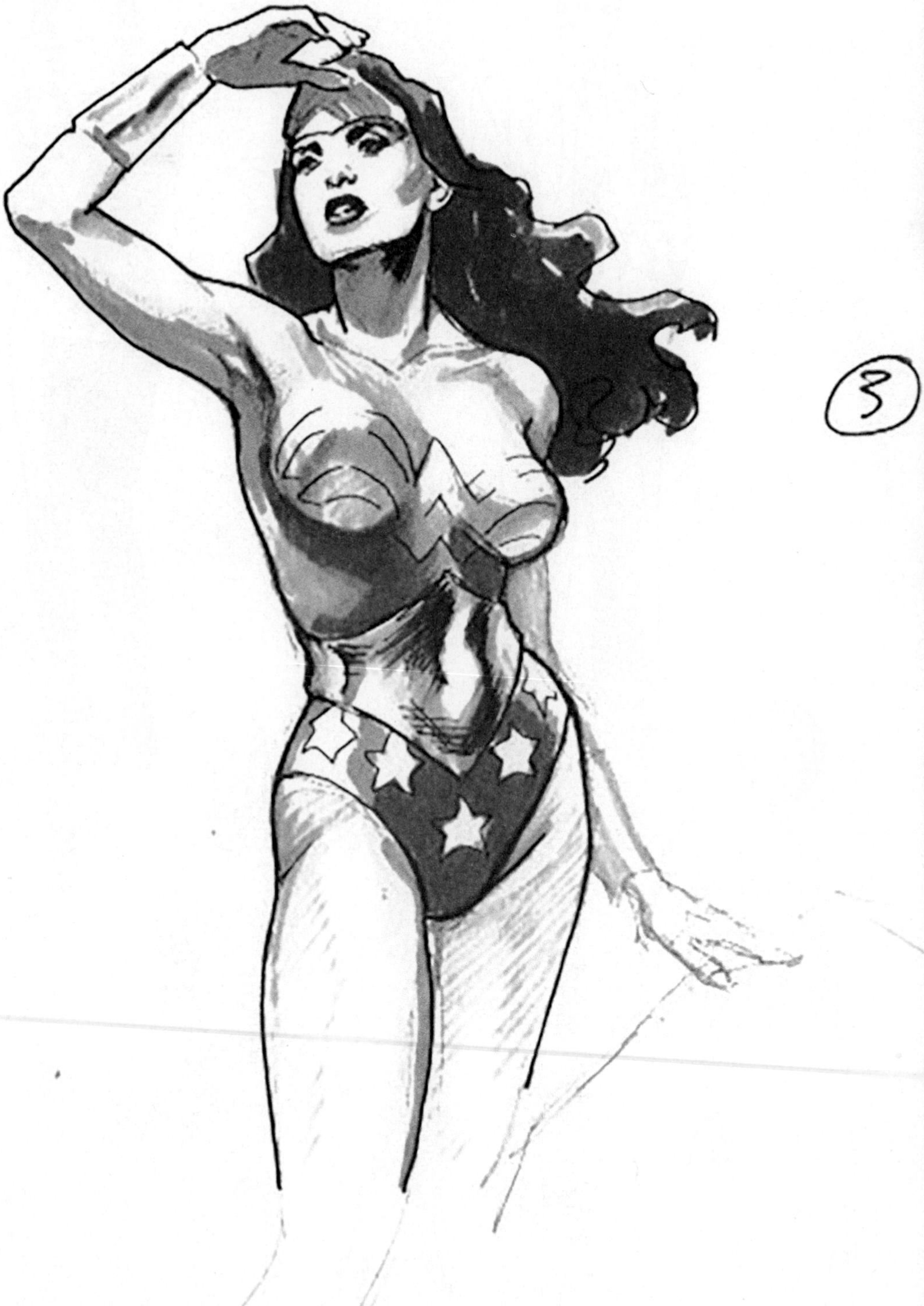
3

SKETCHES
BY **J.G. JONES**

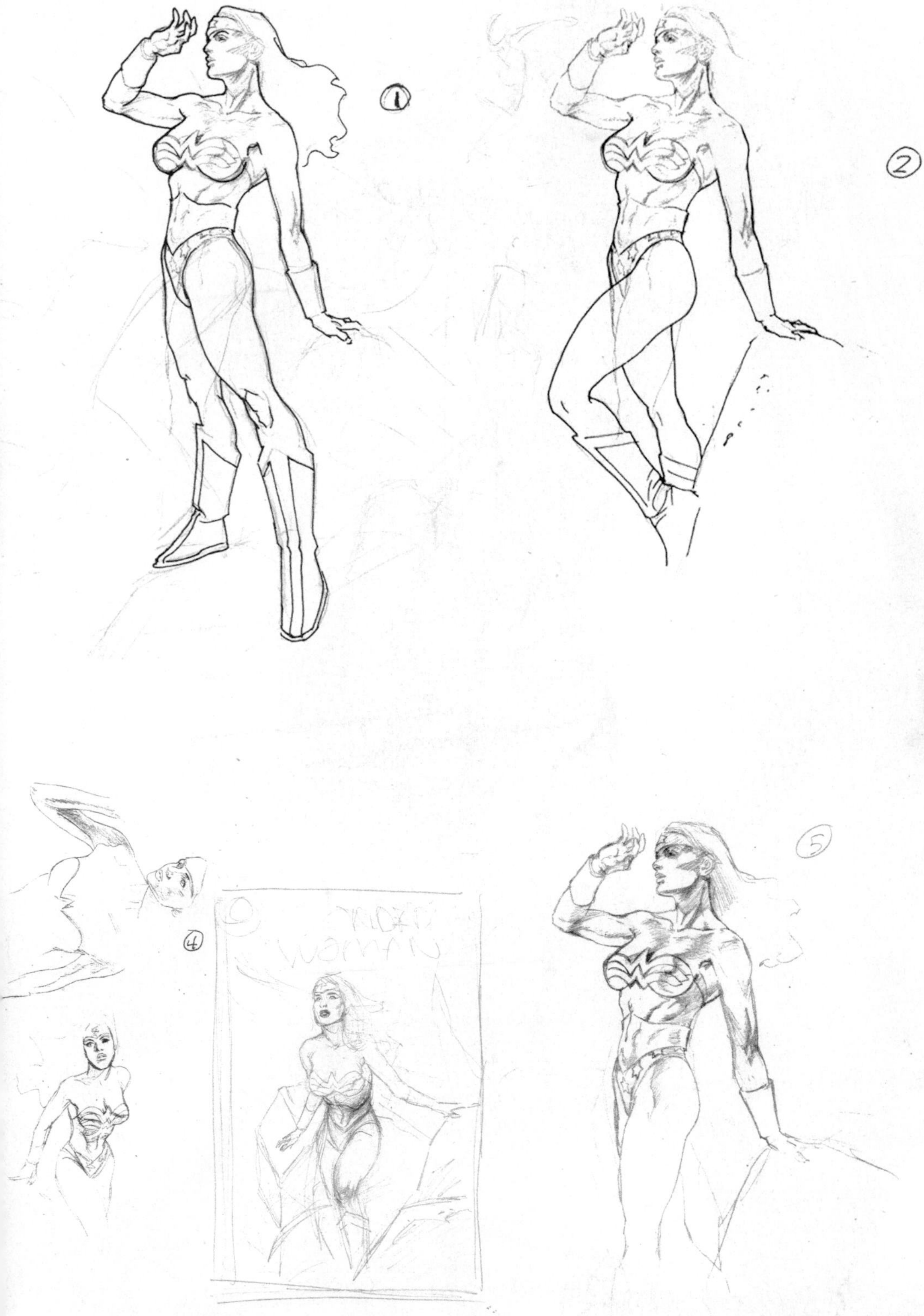
1
2
4
5

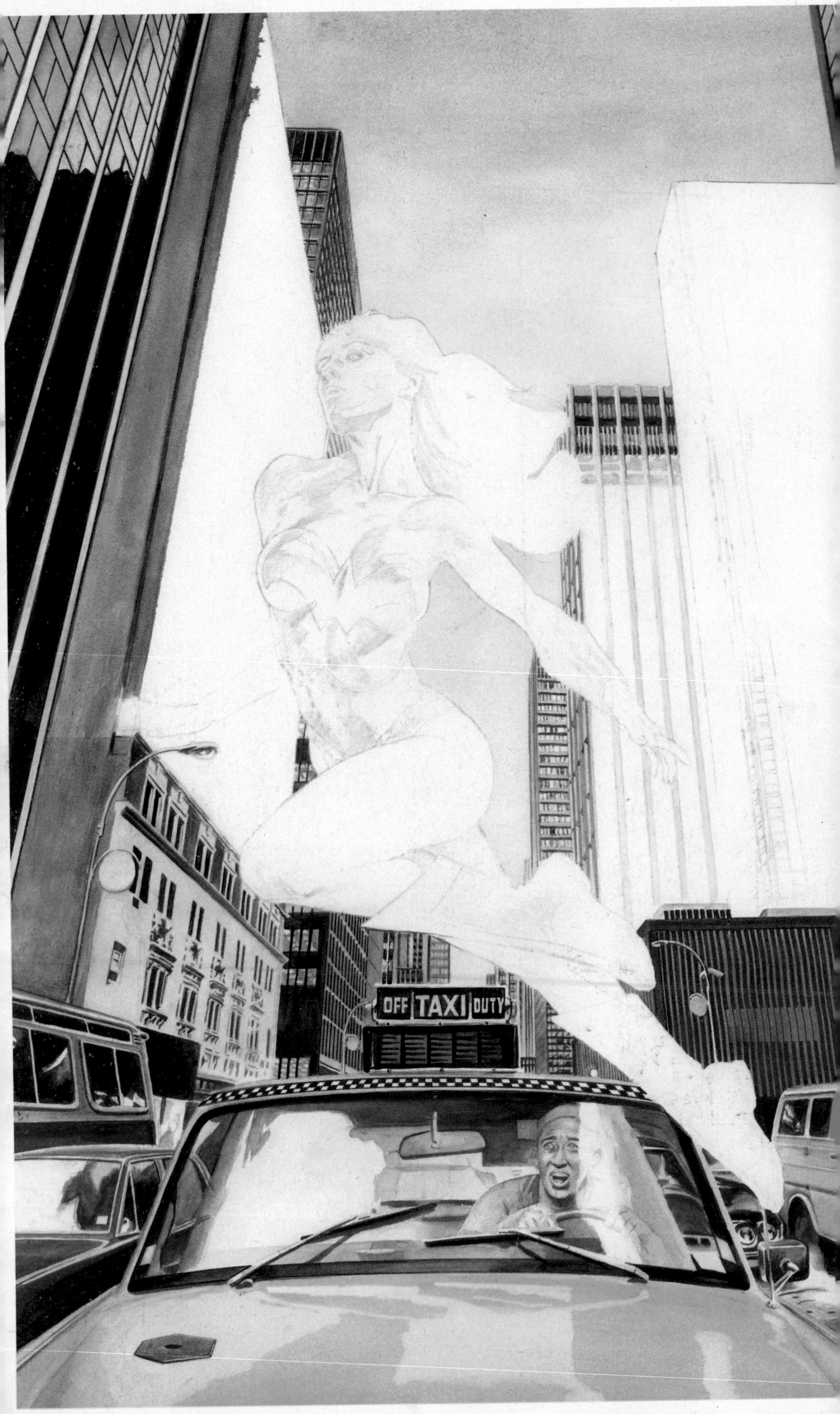

OFF TAXI DUTY